Digital
Photography Bible

Digital
Photography Bible

Ken Milburn

IDG Books Worldwide, Inc.
An International Data Group Company

Foster City, CA ✦ Chicago, IL ✦ Indianapolis, IN ✦ New York, NY

Digital Photography Bible

Published by
IDG Books Worldwide, Inc.
An International Data Group Company
919 E. Hillsdale Blvd., Suite 400
Foster City, CA 94404
www.idgbooks.com (IDG Books Worldwide
Web site)

ISBN: 0-7645-3394-0

Printed in the United States of America

10 9 8 7 6 5 4 3 2

1B/QW/QW/QQ/FC

Distributed in the United States by IDG Books
Worldwide, Inc.

Distributed by CDG Books Canada Inc. for Canada;
by Transworld Publishers Limited in the United
Kingdom; by IDG Norge Books for Norway; by IDG
Sweden Books for Sweden; by IDG Books Australia
Publishing Corporation Pty. Ltd. for Australia and
New Zealand; by TransQuest Publishers Pte Ltd. for
Singapore, Malaysia, Thailand, Indonesia, and Hong
Kong; by Gotop Information Inc. for Taiwan; by ICG
Muse, Inc. for Japan; by Intersoft for South Africa;
by Eyrolles for France; by International Thomson
Publishing for Germany, Austria, and Switzerland;
by Distribuidora Cuspide for Argentina; by LR
International for Brazil; by Galileo Libros for Chile;
by Ediciones ZETA S.C.R. Ltda. for Peru; by WS
Computer Publishing Corporation, Inc., for the
Philippines; by Contemporanea de Ediciones for
Venezuela; by Express Computer Distributors for the
Caribbean and West Indies; by Micronesia Media
Distributor, Inc. for Micronesia; by Chips
Computadoras S.A. de C.V. for Mexico; by Editorial
Norma de Panama S.A. for Panama; by American
Bookshops for Finland.

For general information on IDG Books Worldwide's
books in the U.S., please call our Consumer Customer
Service department at 800-762-2974. For reseller
information, including discounts and premium sales,
please call our Reseller Customer Service
department at 800-434-3422.

For information on where to purchase IDG Books
Worldwide's books outside the U.S., please contact
our International Sales department at 317-596-5530 or
fax 317-572-4002.

For consumer information on foreign language
translations, please contact our Customer Service
department at 800-434-3422, fax 317-572-4002, or
e-mail rights@idgbooks.com.

For information on licensing foreign or domestic
rights, please phone +1-650-653-7098.

For sales inquiries and special prices for bulk
quantities, please contact our Order Services
department at 800-434-3422 or write to the address
above.

For information on using IDG Books Worldwide's
books in the classroom or for ordering examination
copies, please contact our Educational Sales
department at 800-434-2086 or fax 317-572-4005.

For press review copies, author interviews, or other
publicity information, please contact our Public
Relations department at 650-653-7000 or fax
650-653-7500.

For authorization to photocopy items for corporate,
personal, or educational use, please contact
Copyright Clearance Center, 222 Rosewood Drive,
Danvers, MA 01923, or fax 978-750-4470.

Library of Congress Cataloging-in-Publication Data

Milburn, Ken, 1935-
  Digital photography bible / Ken Milburn.
    p. cm.
  ISBN 0-7645-3394-0 (alk. paper)
  1. Photography –Digital techniques. 2. Image
  processing –Digital techniques. I. Title

TR267 .M56 2000
778.3–dc21   00-035001

ABOUT IDG BOOKS WORLDWIDE

Welcome to the world of IDG Books Worldwide.

IDG Books Worldwide, Inc., is a subsidiary of International Data Group, the world's largest publisher of computer-related information and the leading global provider of information services on information technology. IDG was founded more than 30 years ago by Patrick J. McGovern and now employs more than 9,000 people worldwide. IDG publishes more than 290 computer publications in over 75 countries. More than 90 million people read one or more IDG publications each month.

Launched in 1990, IDG Books Worldwide is today the #1 publisher of best-selling computer books in the United States. We are proud to have received eight awards from the Computer Press Association in recognition of editorial excellence and three from Computer Currents' First Annual Readers' Choice Awards. Our best-selling ...For Dummies® series has more than 50 million copies in print with translations in 31 languages. IDG Books Worldwide, through a joint venture with IDG's Hi-Tech Beijing, became the first U.S. publisher to publish a computer book in the People's Republic of China. In record time, IDG Books Worldwide has become the first choice for millions of readers around the world who want to learn how to better manage their businesses.

Our mission is simple. Every one of our books is designed to bring extra value and skill-building instructions to the reader. Our books are written by experts who understand and care about our readers. The knowledge base of our editorial staff comes from years of experience in publishing, education, and journalism — experience we use to produce books to carry us into the new millennium. In short, we care about books, so we attract the best people. We devote special attention to details such as audience, interior design, use of icons, and illustrations. And because we use an efficient process of authoring, editing, and desktop publishing our books electronically, we can spend more time ensuring superior content and less time on the technicalities of making books.

You can count on our commitment to deliver high-quality books at competitive prices on topics you want to read about. At IDG Books Worldwide, we continue in the IDG tradition of delivering quality for more than 30 years. You'll find no better book on a subject than one from IDG Books Worldwide.

John Kilcullen
Chairman and CEO
IDG Books Worldwide, Inc.

Eighth Annual Computer Press Awards ≥1992

Ninth Annual Computer Press Awards ≥1993

Tenth Annual Computer Press Awards ≥1994

Eleventh Annual Computer Press Awards ≥1995

IDG is the world's leading IT media, research and exposition company. Founded in 1964, IDG had 1997 revenues of $2.05 billion and has more than 9,000 employees worldwide. IDG offers the widest range of media options that reach IT buyers in 75 countries representing 95% of worldwide IT spending. IDG's diverse product and services portfolio spans six key areas including print publishing, online publishing, expositions and conferences, market research, education and training, and global marketing services. More than 90 million people read one or more of IDG's 290 magazines and newspapers, including IDG's leading global brands — Computerworld, PC World, Network World, Macworld and the Channel World family of publications. IDG Books Worldwide is one of the fastest-growing computer book publishers in the world, with more than 700 titles in 36 languages. The "...For Dummies®" series alone has more than 50 million copies in print. IDG offers online users the largest network of technology-specific Web sites around the world through IDG.net (http://www.idg.net), which comprises more than 225 targeted Web sites in 55 countries worldwide. International Data Corporation (IDC) is the world's largest provider of information technology data, analysis and consulting, with research centers in over 41 countries and more than 400 research analysts worldwide. IDG World Expo is a leading producer of more than 168 globally branded conferences and expositions in 35 countries including E3 (Electronic Entertainment Expo), Macworld Expo, ComNet, Windows World Expo, ICE (Internet Commerce Expo), Agenda, DEMO, and Spotlight. IDG's training subsidiary, ExecuTrain, is the world's largest computer training company, with more than 230 locations worldwide and 785 training courses. IDG Marketing Services helps industry-leading IT companies build international brand recognition by developing global integrated marketing programs via IDG's print, online and exposition products worldwide. Further information about the company can be found at www.idg.com.   1/26/00

Credits

Acquisitions Editor
Michael Roney

Project Editors
Colleen Dowling
Katharine Dvorak

Technical Editor
Susan Glinert Stevens

Copy Editors
Michael D. Welch
Luann Rouff
Dennis Weaver

Project Coordinators
Linda Marousek
Marcos Vergara

Media Development Specialist
Jake Mason

Permissions Editor
Jessica Montgomery

Media Development Manager
Stephen Noetzel

Graphics and Production Specialists
Robert Bihlmayer
Jude Levinson
Michael Lewis
Victor Pérez-Varela
Dina F Quan
Ramses Ramirez

Illustrators
Mary Jo Richards
Shelley Norr
Brent Savage

Proofreading and Indexing
York Production Services

Cover Illustrator
Joann Vuong

About the Author

Ken Milburn has been a photographer for more than four decades, having worked in advertising, travel, and fashion photography. He has been working with computers since 1981 and has written hundreds of articles, columns, and reviews for such publications as *Publish*, *DV Magazine*, *Computer Graphics World*, *PC World*, *Macworld*, and *Windows Magazine*. He has also published ten other computer books, including *Master Photoshop 5.5 Visually*, Cliff's Notes on *Taking and Printing Digital Photos*, *Photoshop 5.5 Professional Results*, and *Flash 4 Web Animation f/x and Design*. Ken also maintains a practice as a commercial photo-illustrator and has become internationally known for his photo-paintings, which have been featured twice in *Design Graphics Magazine*, in the all-time best-selling poster for the 1988 Sausalito Arts Festival, and in the 1999 American President Lines calendar.

To Nancy, Lane, and Tia — my family

Preface

Digital photography used to be a very small niche market. Then people started realizing that it afforded an almost instantaneous way to share vision and experience on the Web. That realization spurred the sales of digital cameras into the millions over the past couple of years. Lately, those millions of folks have begun realizing that there's much more to digital photography than just using it for casual Web photos. So they've started getting serious about it. This book is for those folks — and for anyone curious about digital photography. That is, it is written especially for the person who wants to make the most of those digital cameras whose prices make them accessible to serious hobbyists, business professionals, and even professional photographers who are not quite ready to spend $25,000 on a digital camera back.

Not that this book doesn't discuss $25,000 camera backs and other professional gear. After all, you should know what is possible and to what level of quality digital photography aspires. It's just that, in the meantime, I'm more concerned with helping you to produce the most professional results possible with what you've got.

The first *Digital Photography Bible*

This is just the beginning of the digital photography industry. When I started this book, a camera with one megapixel of resolution was considered to be hot stuff. As this book goes to press, three times that resolution has become commonplace. At the same time, the software for editing pictures is becoming faster and slicker and new programs are being introduced every day. Dozens of special-purpose programs are also popping out of the woodwork. So there's more and more that you can do with digital photography. This book gives you a good, solid handle on what the possibilities are. However, please realize that I'm already working on gathering materials for the next edition. I'm very eager to hear your suggestions, too. Between now and the time the next edition appears, I'll be posting news and developments on my Web site at the following location:

    www.kenmilburn.com.

How this book is organized

This book covers digital photography basics, tips and tricks, and loads of digital shooting and processing details. You'll find what you need in this book's five parts and the appendixes, outlined as follows.

Part I – Welcome to the World of Digital Photography

Here you get an introduction to the potentials and realities of digital photography and what you can expect to get out of it now and in the near future. Next, you are taught the basics of digitizing conventional photographs so you can manipulate them on the computer. I then show you the basics of making a photo using a digital camera. Then you learn the essentials of setting up an indoor studio for shooting with digital equipment. The next chapter discusses the equipment and software you're most likely to want to add to your computer system. Of course, it also discusses what to look for in the computer system itself. Finally, there's a discussion of the technology that makes digital images work so you have a better understanding of what you're paying for and what the future holds.

Part II – Tips and Tricks for Making Digital Images

This part of the book gets into more detail on converting images from conventional to digital format. There's a chapter on accessories for digital cameras and another on scanners.

Part III – Shooting Digital Images

This part's two chapters take you through more advanced techniques for creating digital images from scratch. The second chapter in this part contains tips and tricks involving accessories that were just becoming available at press time.

Part IV – Choosing the Right Processing Software

This part consists of four chapters, each discussing how to choose a different category of software for processing digital images. Each chapter specializes in a different application: Professional-level image processing, image-processing software for the rest of us, Web processing software, and special-purpose image-processing software.

Part V – Processing Images Digitally

This part of the book consists mostly of a series of hands-on lessons that show you how to set up your computer for digital imaging and then efficiently transfer your images from camera to computer. Next, you learn the basics of Photoshop, the program most widely used for professional-level digital image processing. The next two chapters cover publishing: The first deals with publishing to the Web and the second covers publishing to paper. This part closes with a chapter that introduces the use of specialty processing software that was just coming onto the scene as this book went to press.

Color Gallery

The color gallery is a collection of the author's digital photographs that illustrate some of what digital photography can accomplish as discussed in this book.

Appendixes

This book has three appendixes, each meant to be a reference resource. The first is a listing and chart comparison of the majority of semi-pro to consumer-level digital cameras. The second is a directory of resources for just about everything I could think of that is connected with digital photography. Because this is such a dynamic and fast-changing industry, I'll be continually adding to and updating this appendix online at the following location:

www.kenmilburn.com/Digitalphotographybible

Make this a better book: Talk to the author

I may not be able to answer all the e-mail I get, but I'll certainly read them and your voice will certainly have an influence on future editions. Unfortunately, if I'm up against paying deadlines when you write, it may just not be practical to get back to you right away. Please don't let that discourage you from letting me know what you think — especially if you have constructive suggestions for improving this book. You can reach me at the following address:

ken@kenmilburn.com

Acknowledgments

First and foremost, I would like to thank Mike Roney, senior acquisitions editor at IDG Books, for brainstorming the concepts for this book with me and for sticking by me through a time of major changes in the digital photography industry and a host of other book projects. I'd also like to thank both of my project editors, Katie Dvorak, who started the project and offered infinite patience and a zillion helpful suggestions, and Colleen Dowling, who graciously picked up the pieces after Katie went to *PC World*. I would like to thank Susan Glinert Stevens for her highly knowledgeable technical editing of this book. Technical editors can make or break a book by insuring its accuracy. And a nod, as well, to the book's three copy editors: Michael Welch, Luann Rouff, and Dennis Weaver.

If it weren't for the advice and council of other writers and photographers, life would've been much tougher. For all their help, support, and great hints, I'd like to thank Bob Cowart, Reid Thaler, Roger Mulkey, and Janine Warner.

Several manufacturers of equipment and software provided their products for evaluation — along with their help and patience. I want to thank Karen Thomas Associates and Olympus Camera, Walt & Company and Nikon, Inc., Kodak, Canon USA, Chimera, Lexar Media, Sandisk, and Bogen. These companies all provided equipment, support, and advice. The list of software vendors who helped includes the publishers of all the software mentioned in this book — especially Adobe, MetaCreations, Corel, iGrafx, Extensis, and Ulead.

Contents at a Glance

Contents

Part IV: Choosing the Right Processing Software   273

Chapter 11: Choosing Professional-Level Image-Processing Software 275

Chapter 12: Choosing Small Office/Home Office Image-Processing Software 313

Welcome to the World of Digital Photography

The Digital Photography Advantage

I f digital photography isn't the best thing since sliced bread (and I think it's very close to being that good), it's certainly the best thing since the invention of the Polaroid camera. If you come by your digital photographs the easy way (by taking them with a digital camera), you can see the results much faster than you can process a Polaroid. If you don't like what you see, you just erase it. So by the time you show the proof sheet to a client (or anyone whose opinion you value), there are no embarrassing shots. A digital camera isn't a requirement for digital (or, at least, digitized) photography. You can get higher resolution for the buck by shooting conventionally, and then scanning the film with a slide or drum scanner.

Some foolish folks will tell you that digital photography hasn't quite arrived and that conventional photography can do a better job. Fact is, digital photography can do a much better job in much less time and for a lot less money. That's why you'd be hard put to find a publication of any kind today in which the photographs have not been digitized and, more often than not, digitally manipulated.

Now, it's true that we have a ways to go before digital cameras can produce the image quality we're used to at an equipment cost that we're used to. That's why this book will tell you nearly as much about how to digitize a photograph from film as it will about digital cameras and how to use them. Professional-quality film cameras are three to ten times more affordable than their equally capable digital counterparts.

Furthermore, the process of getting a good picture on film is more comfortably familiar to many photographers. Finally, once the film has been processed, a digitized image can be digitally processed and manipulated in more powerful ways than would likely be the case in a conventional darkroom — even if you leave out the possibilities for surrealism. Other benefits of the digital darkroom include the following:

✦ It is more affordable

✦ No special lighting, space, or plumbing is needed.

✦ You don't have to work in isolation.

✦ The work is immediately ready for exhibit or publication — there's no "drying time."

✦ There is far less environmental pollution because the process uses fewer chemicals.

Having said all that, let me jump back to the subject of digital (filmless) cameras. Even the more affordable ones have a definite place in the professional's camera bag or the businessperson's briefcase. Digital cameras are also magical tools for artists and serious hobbyists. The image quality of the best of today's thousand-dollar digital cameras is good enough to let you make 11 × 14-inch prints that (given a good, affordable, state-of-the-art desktop color printer) can fool most into thinking that they're looking at a well-made Type C color photographic print. And the information and gratification you get from being able to instantly see your photographs will make you a better photographer in much less time. Why? Because you can instantly judge what you did and take the needed steps to correct it. Before long, you'll simply stop taking pictures when it appears that there's a telephone pole growing out of the subject's head. Even if you have to do that because you can't control your shooting position or the subject's, you'll have the postshooting option of easily removing the telephone pole.

The Characteristics of Digital Images

Digital images can be created either from conventional photographic prints, negatives, or slides or from scratch by using a digital camera. This book will cover both processes. It will cover the basic techniques and aesthetics as they apply to either traditional or digital photography. More important, it will cover all the tools and techniques that are specific to digital photography in depth. So, the starting point should be a description of those characteristics that define a digital image. Figure 1-1 depicts a digital camera workflow and a digitized photograph workflow.

Figure 1-1: Digital camera workflow and digitized photograph workflow

Photographs, whether analog or digital, are composed of a mosaic of points of colored light. In digital imaging terms, the color of each of these points of light describes both the color and the intensity of the light that is either reflected from or transmitted through any one of these points of light. The technical differences between analog and digital photography stem from the method of describing the color of a point (various technologies describe these points as a dot or pixel or grain) of light.

In traditional photography, the point is a speck of a light-sensitive physical material that has been chemically processed to change the color of that material. In digital photography, the point is called a pixel (short for picture element). A pixel is one cell in a row-and-column matrix that is one shade of a particular color. That shade is represented in the computer as a piece of hexadecimal code, like this: 009139.

Note that not every digital image is a digital photograph. Digital photographs, by their nature, must always fall into a category of computer graphics generally referred to as a "bitmap." It is also possible (using such graphics software as Adobe Photoshop, Live Picture, and MetaCreation's Painter) to create bitmapped images that are entirely produced by the hand and mind of the artist. In the analog world, we would likely call these works paintings or drawings. Bitmaps are so called because all information is conveyed by assigning a specific color to each individual pixel in the image.

Note The other type of digital image is usually referred to in computerese as a "drawing" rather than a "painting" or "photograph." Computer drawings are so called because most of the information in the image is defined by shape outlines, as they would be in a conventional technical drawing or engineering schematic. Digital drawings are technically categorized as vector images because all of the information in the image is described by geometric formulae (and by other formulae that describe such things as the characteristics of the shapes, such as line weight and color and shaded fills).

In the context of this book, a digital photograph can refer to either an image made with a digital camera or to an image digitized (scanned) from a conventional photograph. Because scanner technology has been with us longer than digital cameras, it has already been covered thoroughly in other publications. So this book will spend more time on digital camera technology than on scanners. Still, you'll find extensive information on the various types of scanners regarding those aspects of their operation that are specific to digitizing photographs. No time will be spent on such office-related scanner operations as document archives, optical character recognition, or faxing.

The Advantages of Digital Photography

Digital imagery is to traditional photography what the Wright brother's first aircraft were to the railroad industry. There will always be photography that uses film and processing because it has a look and some advantages that are unique unto itself. But, for the most part, digital photography has both practical and emotional characteristics that will make it rule. Moreover, it is taking over more quickly than most would have imagined a scant year or so past.

There are numerous reasons why this is so:

- ✦ There are lower barriers against taking a photograph.
- ✦ No film is needed.
- ✦ It provides instant gratification.
- ✦ Instant turnaround is possible.
- ✦ It offers lower ongoing costs.
- ✦ No darkroom or chemicals are needed
- ✦ It offers easy proofing and presentation of images.
- ✦ A digital camera is the perfect artist's sketchbook.
- ✦ Digital images can hold more information about the subject of the photograph.
- ✦ There is no generational degradation when unaltered copies are made of a digital image.
- ✦ Digital photography represents the easiest way to create an image for use on a Web page.

Lower barriers to taking a photograph

Given possession of a digital camera, most of us are much more likely to take a digital photo than to take an analog photo. There are several reasons for this.

✦ **No one ever needs to see your mistakes** because you can erase them instantly (or later). Most digital cameras (and certainly any that I'd recommend) come equipped with an LCD monitor that lets you instantly see your most recent shots. Almost always, you can also review all the images in a session. You can also erase any that you don't like at that time. Finally, when you download the images to your computer, you will have another chance to erase your images.

✦ **A discarded digital photo costs absolutely nothing.** No precious film or processing was expended. The data space that it utilized in the camera's or computer's memory can be retrieved upon erasure. At most, all the image consumed was a fraction of the rechargeable camera battery's power.

✦ **A digital camera can be carried in a purse or shirt pocket.** Even 1.5 megapixel resolution and 3:1 zoom lenses can be made to fit within a tiny profile, as can be seen in Figure 1-2. So, it's easy to fall into the habit of having a camera with you at all times. This means you'll be able to document accidents, thefts, and news events. Even if none of these are your primary reason for buying a digital camera, they may be the reasons that pay for it.

Figure 1-2: Even some semipro high-resolution digital cameras will fit into a shirt pocket.

There is no film to buy or waste

An electronic image sensor formulates digital images and the numerical data is then stored in one of several re-recordable memory devices. While some of these devices are called "digital film," they are no more film than is your computer's RAM, hard drive, or floppy disk. In fact, the only permanent cost of storing a digital image is likely to be a fraction of the space on a write-once CD-ROM disk that you recorded on your own computer. You will find a thorough discussion of various types of devices used for storing digital images and how each fits into the overall plan in Chapter 5.

Instant gratification

In far less time than it takes a Polaroid shot to develop, you can see and show your digital image. I'm surprised the phrase "shoot and show" hasn't caught on yet as a slogan for some consumer-level digicam. By the way, "digicam" has become the buzz name for digital still cameras — particularly those aimed at consumers like the one shown in Figure 1-3.

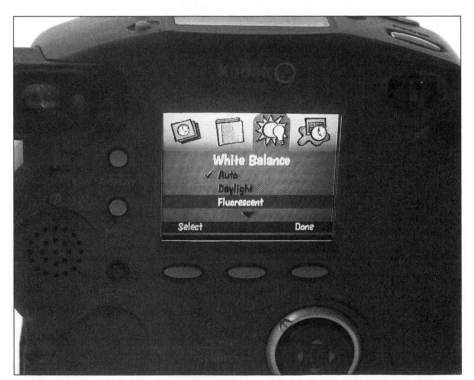

Figure 1-3: The Kodak DC260's LCD screen showing one of the camera's settings menus. Many digital cameras use their LCD screens for this purpose as well as for previewing and reviewing in-camera images.

Anyway, there's actually more to being able to instantly see your images than selfish gratification. If you're shooting images that require the approval of a client or the input of a colleague, you're way ahead. You can get instant client approval and save the cost and disappointment of being asked to reshoot.

Instant delivery

The speed with which you can deliver a digital image to a client is limited only by the speed of your computer and its access to your client. Usually, that means you can deliver the results of an entire news or sports shoot within minutes. Even a 40MB advertising image could be transferred in far less time than if the physical photograph had to travel via express delivery—especially if that delivery had to cross national borders.

Lower costs over time

Although digital cameras are still several times the price of their analog counterparts, the fact that there is no film or processing cost eventually evens the overall cost. Of course, the truth of this statement depends on the extent of your use of the camera. It is also true, as stated above, that you will use the camera more than you would have used its analog counterpart.

Costs are also lower over time because of the "instant client approval and turnaround" factor and because there are seldom shipping charges involved with transmitting these images.

Table 1-1 Cost of Film, Processing, and Prints over Time			
Rolls per Week	*Cost per Roll*	*Cost per Month*	*Cost per Year*
10	$11	$440	$5,200

No darkroom or chemicals needed

Many photographers don't want to give up the control that doing their own darkroom work affords them. Many others bitterly regret that the pressures of time and money make it impractical for them to do their own darkroom work because it means giving up control over the result that will be given to the client or seen by the public.

Digital images are processed, manipulated, and interpreted by computer software such as Adobe Photoshop or Kai's Power Soap.

Easy proofing and presentation of images

All of your pictures can be proofed electronically and instantly. You and your client (if present at the shoot) can even view results immediately after the shutter is pressed.

More important, several software packages will automatically prepare proof-sheet-sized thumbnails of all the images inside a folder (sometimes called a subdirectory). You can then add comments, rotate thumbnails, and either show the results as a slide show onscreen or print proof sheets on a color printer. Figure 1-4 shows just such an electronic proof sheet.

Figure 1-4: A proof sheet prepared in Extensis Portfolio 4.0

Another tool that's useful for instant sharing of your images is a direct-to-print color printer. These generally produce a type of print that looks and feels almost exactly like a Polaroid or a 1-Hour jumbo print. Some of the latest printers of this type will even let you insert the memory card from your camera and then ask how many images you want to print per page—so you can make either proof sheets or any size print up to letter size.

This book will cover what it takes to do instant proofing and what your options are.

A digital camera is the perfect artist's sketchbook

The resolution limitations of "point-and-shoot" digital cameras aren't a factor when you simply use the photograph as the basis for a "painting," as shown in Figure 1-5. You can enlarge the image to any size, and then use the brushes in your image processing program to paint over or smudge the original pixels. The result can look like many styles of traditional painting. You can also use plug-in filters to automate this brush-stroking over selected areas of the image.

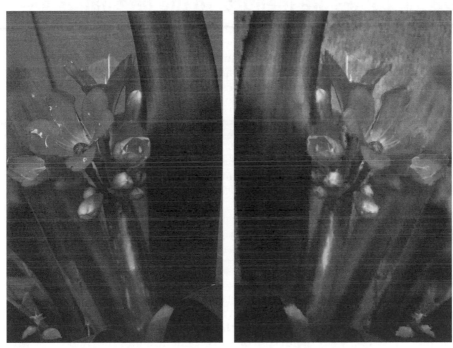

Figure 1-5: Photo before and after being turned into a painting

You can discover how to do this in Chapter 25.

Digital images can hold more information about the subject of the photograph

Since digital images are stored as data, you can store all sorts of other data with them. Some of the newest cameras, such as Kodak's DCS 280, enable you to link to global positioning satellites (GPS) that can automatically annotate each image's time and location. Several cameras let you record voice annotations (and even ambient sound effects) in the camera.

The latest models of some cameras come with downloading software that lets you assign names to image files before you transfer them to your computer (at last, no more filenames like P00022.jpg).

Once you've downloaded digital images to your computer (or scanned them in), you can use image data-management software such as Extensis' Portfolio to categorize images as to type and assign numerous fields of descriptive data.

Digital copies are identical to the original

Because digital images are simply numerical data, one copy of the file is exactly the same as another. As long as the data is kept intact, the image never degrades over time. A print made from a digital image a thousand years from now will look as good or better than a print made from the original. (The reason the image might look better is that printing technologies, papers, and inks are constantly being improved.)

Note

This aspect of digital images concerns many art collectors, who fear that images will lose value when they can be reproduced too easily. The answer is careful registration and numbering of limited print editions Limited edition prints have been in use for some time in photography, lithography and many forms of printmaking. There's no real reason why limited edition digital prints should be any less valuable.

The easiest way to create an image for use on a Web page

Any image you see on a Web page is already digital. Furthermore, it's most likely to be a bitmap. The resolution of Web images is generally lower than that of even the least expensive digital still camera. That's because images larger than 640 × 480 take forever to load and will extend beyond the frame of most user's monitors. So, you can pick up virtually any digital still or video camera, shoot the item you want to put on your Web page, and post it to that Web page within moments. Chapter 8 will tell you more about using video cameras for capturing digital images. Chapter 27 will show you cool techniques for tweaking Web-destined images for peak performance.

The Advantages of Analog Photography

At this point, you may be convinced that it's time to pitch your trusty Nikon F. Actually, you probably know or suspect that we're not entirely ready to eliminate the traditional photographic processes. In fact, we never will. For one thing, the traditional photographic process has a unique and familiar "look and feel," and that will always have a certain value among collectors and connoisseurs. More important, it will be sometime before the cost of buying digital equipment can compete with that for analog equipment.

Other advantages of traditional cameras and photo processing are as follows:

✦ Lower cost of high image quality

✦ Lower cost of cameras

✦ Higher-quality, more accurate optics

✦ No "shutter lag"

✦ Accepted as traditional medium

✦ Easy and affordable to make archival prints

✦ Known function and quality of components and manufacturers

Lower cost of high image quality

The resolution of even the least expensive 35mm film (even if you use it in a ten-dollar "shoot and pitch" camera) is higher than all but the latest and most expensive of digital cameras based on 3mm single-lens reflex (Nikon-type) cameras. Digital SLRs with image resolution approaching that of 35mm film cost approximately $16,000.

Keep in mind, however, that you may not need as much image definition as you get with 35mm film. It is possible to get truly photographic quality 5 × 7-inch prints from digital cameras that currently sell for well under $600 — so long as they advertise "megapixel" resolution. Newer cameras that boast "two megapixel" resolution can produce 8 × 10-inch photo-quality prints and will reproduce as near-full-page magazine photos.

Lower cost of cameras

For the $1,000 you'd spend on a state-of-the-art two-megapixel digicam, you can buy a feature-packed, name-brand 35mm SLR that has all of the features most professionals demand (see Figure 1-6). To look at it another way, the equivalent 35mm pocket camera (auto focus, zoom lens, optical viewfinder) would cost you under $300.

Much more versatility

This is just another way of looking at the lower cost of cameras. Digital cameras that feature interchangeable lenses, through-the-lens viewing, and that can accept the full range of lenses and accessories made for 35mm analog cameras, start at around $6,000.

Figure 1-6: $1,000 worth of semipro digicam versus $1,000 worth of 35mm SLR film camera equipment

Instant response (capture the moment)

A conventional camera captures the intended picture the instant the shutter button is pressed. Digital cameras typically take as much as a full second to register an image after you've clicked. Professional-level digital SLRs have generally licked this problem, but digital studio cameras can take several minutes to record an image.

Accepted as traditional medium

The capabilities and qualities of conventional cameras are a known quantity to virtually any client. So, it may be easier to convince a buyer that you can produce a worthy result if you are using conventional equipment.

Easy and affordable to make archival prints

There are lots of choices, knowledge, experience, and competition when it comes to printing color images from conventional film. Buyers expect the product to have a reasonable life span, so aren't timid about the long-term value of conventional prints. This is an especially important consideration for those of you who are interested in creating collectible or fine art prints. Be assured, however, that it is perfectly possible to make collectible digital art prints. You'll find a full discussion of this topic in Chapters 28 and 29.

Known function and quality of components and manufacturers

People have confidence in the value of their investment when they are contemplating the purchase of a conventional camera made by a long-established and trusted name such as Canon, Hasselblad, Leica, or Nikon.

The winner is . . .

At first glance, it may seem that the advantages of conventional photography make it the obvious choice. Think again. The advantages of digital make it irresistible to many of us — especially casual snapshooters, advertising illustrators, news and sports organizations, documentarians, and Web users.

More important, conventional cameras are often the logical choice for capturing images destined to become digital images. I call that process *hybrid digital photography*.

Hybrid Digital Photography

Hybrid digital photography is just what its name implies: part analog and part digital. Hybrids can either start with analog cameras and film and end up being digitized by some type of scanner (see Figure 1-7), or they can be digital images that are digitally recorded to conventional film and then printed on conventional photographic papers.

Figure 1-7: Analog 35mm camera, film scanner, and computer

There are lots of good reasons for employing hybrid digital photography:

✦ Makes use of equipment you already own

✦ Best of both worlds

✦ Established technology with predictable results

✦ Higher resolution per buck

✦ Ability to digitize existing images

Make use of equipment you already own

You may have already invested a lot of time and money in learning and equipment. None of it need go to waste. If you've made a successful picture, you can certainly digitize it. Just as this book was being prepared, scanner manufacturers were doubling the resolution of desktop slide scanners at the same time that prices were dropping. Desktop flatbed scanners that can scan your prints have become dirt cheap. You can even send it out for drum scanning if you have really demanding imaging requirements.

Best of both worlds

You may not be able to adapt a 400mm telephoto or an 8mm fish-eye lens to your digital camera, but you certainly can if you own a Leica, Cannon, Nikon, or other conventional interchangeable lens single-lens reflex. If your usual subjects and clients require large- or medium-format conventional photography, you can convert the results from those cameras to digital.

Also, if you have requirements for both digital and analog versions of an image (and now that computers and the Web are such a big part of our lives, who doesn't), hybrid digital photography is the shoot-once way to go.

Established technology with predictable results

Hybrid digital photography has been around—especially in the analog-to-scanner version—for much longer than digital cameras. Service bureaus and prepress shops have been using high-end drum scanners for decades, and flatbed scanners have been around for nearly as long. This makes using the digitizing tools more affordable than digital cameras.

Higher resolution per buck

As I said earlier, digital cameras are expensive relative to their analog counterparts, and only the most expensive of these can match the resolution of medium-speed 35mm film. Since you can buy a slide scanner that creates an 18MB image for about the same price as a camera that produces a 3.5MB image, it's easy to see that hybrid digital photography will give you better definition per dollar.

Ability to digitize existing images

No image is too old, too big, too colorful, or too precious to scan (or to photograph and scan). Another way of looking at it is that it's never too late to make an image digital.

The Characteristics of Digital Images

The digital imaging process parrots recording an image on film. You still need a lens to gather and focus the light reflected from the surface of the image. That image is projected onto a light-sensitive surface. If the light-sensitive surface is film, the image needs to be chemically processed. If the result is a negative, the image must again be projected onto a light-sensitive surface and the result chemically processed into a print or transparency.

If the light-sensitive surface is digital, it consists of a chip array that converts the color and intensity of the light into numerical data. That data is then interpreted by computer software (either in or out of the camera) as an image containing a certain number of data points. The number of data points assigned to the picture determines the amount and sharpness of detail that can be discerned by a viewer. That characteristic of a digital image is referred to as its *resolution*. Resolution is expressed in pixels, a computer term that is short for *picture elements*. A pixel in a digital image serves the same function as a single grain of silver or dye in a film slide or negative or of a dot in a screened image printed on an offset press.

Resolving the image

You will hear resolution referred to in several different ways. If an advertiser (or this book, for that matter) wants to give you a general idea of how much detail a camera is capable of recording, it will be referred to as VGA (approximately 640 × 480 pixels) or SuperVGA (approximately 800 × 600 pixels) if the image contains less than a million pixels. Up until the end of 1988, cameras capable of producing truly photographic prints up to 5 × 7 inches were referred to as megapixel cameras and were the highest-resolution cameras available for less than $2,000. Today, that criterion has been moved up to *two megapixels*. There are even several two-megapixel cameras selling for well under $1,000. The difference in price is primarily due to differences in features, user conveniences, and the quality of optics and viewfinders.

The only factors limiting the potential resolution of digital cameras are the cost of high-resolution CCDs and marketing considerations on the part of manufacturers. There are, in fact, some digital cameras for professional studios that exceed the resolution of 4 × 5-inch film. However, these cameras sell for tens of thousands of dollars. Keep in mind that in 1981, a typical desktop computer had 8MB of RAM and sold for around $5,000. Today, you can buy a computer with 32MB of RAM for under $600 and it comes equipped with many more features and peripherals.

A more accurate way to judge the resolution of a camera (or any digital image) is by its pixel dimensions. Width is always stated before height, so you will see figures on a spec sheet (and in our comparison chart in Appendix A) stated this way: 1,542 × 1,024 pixels.

You will also see image resolution referred to in terms of file size. File size is the result of multiplying the total number of pixels by the bit depth of the image, times the number of colors in the image, divided by 8 (because there are 8 bits to 1 byte). So, if we use our 1,524 × 1,024 example and the file is in RGB color (three colors: red, green, and blue), and there are 8 bits of data assigned to each color (as is the case with 24-bit color, aka *true color*), the file will be 4,681,728 bytes (4.7MB). The same file, if we were talking about a four-color CMYK (cyan, magenta, yellow, black) file, would be 7.8MB.

Pixel depth

Another factor that influences the amount of perceived image detail is *pixel depth*. Pixel depth actually defines the number of colors that can be displayed when a file is printed or viewed. (For purposes of clarity, we'll momentarily ignore the characteristics and circumstances of the viewing device or material and the surrounding light.) A pixel depth of 8 bits per color allows us to represent 16.8 million colors in an RGB image. That's actually a few more colors (actually, colors and shades of same) than human eyes can discern. Nevertheless, there are benefits to assigning even more colors per pixel. For one, the additional information can be used for other data, such as additional color channels for masking. More important, you can capture a much wider range of color. So if the scene that's being photographed ranges from very bright (the sun on fresh-fallen snow) to very dark (detail in the moss-covered rocks under the mountain stream), you have much more choice in how to process the digital information in that scene. If you darken the highlights in an image that contains no information for those highlights, you just get muddy gray highlights. Conversely, if there is information in the captured image's highlights, darkening the highlight areas will produce detail in the highlights. The same is true of the ability to lighten shadow areas.

Note It is common that cameras and image processing programs will record or store an image at more than 24 bits, but will only output to 24 bits. You still get a big advantage because you can decide what range (contiguous portion) of the 30 or 36 (or even 48) bits that were captured will be included in the final image.

A bit about maps

Digital photos fall into the category of computer graphics known as *bitmaps*. The other type of computer graphic is called a *vector* or *raster* graphic (see Figure 1-8). Vector graphics have some valuable characteristics, but nearly no application to digital photography, so you won't be bothered with them in the context of this book.

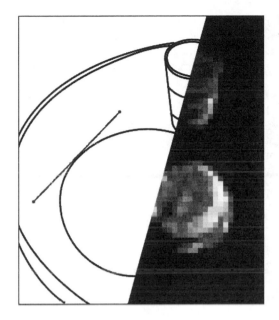

Figure 1-8: Typical vector graphic, typical bitmapped photo

On the other hand, it's a good idea to develop a good understanding of how bitmapped graphics work. Pixels are square (or rectangular) and are arranged in a grid. Depending on the resolution of your camera, image file, or monitor, these pixels are arranged in a grid of rows and columns. Each of the "cells" in this grid is assigned a color (really a shade of a specific color). The changes in color within the grid make up the visual shapes in the image. If the grid cells are small enough, you can see subtle transitions between adjacent colors, resulting in an image that seems to mirror real life.

If the concepts in the above paragraph seem too abstract, think of a mosaic tile tabletop. The artwork on the tabletop is created by placing different colored ceramic tiles in rows and columns. Better yet, take a look at Figure 1-9.

There are two things you need to know about bitmaps:

✦ You can't change the resolution of the image without having some effect on image quality.

✦ The higher the required definition, the higher the required original image resolution and, therefore, the larger the size of the file.

These two facts will determine many of the decisions you make regarding purchasing the components of the digital photography "food chain."

Figure 1-9: The inset at upper right shows the actual pixels, magnified 16 times, inside the small white square in the center of the flower.

If you make the image smaller, some of the colored pixels have to be thrown out, resulting in lost detail. If you make the image larger, some pixels will have to be duplicated. Some programs, such as Adobe Photoshop, make very good guesses as to which pixels should be added or subtracted, but there will still be some loss of sharpness.

Larger files will require more camera memory, faster processing in the camera to decrease the lag time between pictures, faster connection from camera to computer to transfer files, and more storage space on the computer that will do the processing.

Summary

This chapter has been an overview of digital photography as it applies to the meaning of life. It has covered the reasons why it will revolutionize your life as a photographer. Then it went on to cover the essential elements of the various paths to digital technology and when each was most likely to be appropriate to your individual needs. You should leave this chapter with a clear understanding of the difference between pure and hybrid digital photography. I hope I've also made it clear that both have their place in the serious photographer's kit.

The next chapter introduces you to more specific information on the tools and techniques and technology required for hybrid digital photography.

✦   ✦   ✦

The Basics of Making a Photograph Digital

File resolution is often expressed as file size. But the size of the file for a given resolution depends on the depth (number of color shades) of information assigned to each pixel. Learning about *bit depth* is the first step to understanding the process of making a digital photograph.

Dynamic Range and Bit Depth

Pixel depth is usually described in *bits per pixel* because the amount of color information that can be assigned to a pixel depends on the amount of data that can be assigned to that pixel. A 1-bit image can display only black and white (Photoshop calls this a *bitmap*, even though, strictly speaking, all digitized photos are bitmaps regardless of their color depth). An 8-bit image can display 256 colors or shades of gray (that's virtually all the gray shades we can recognize, so 8 bits is enough depth for a photo-quality "black and white" picture). A 16-bit image can display about 64,000 shades of color — a bit depth the industry calls *high color*. A 24-bit image can display 16.8 million colors.

So why do some scanners record image data at 30 bits or 36 bits, or even 48 bits? After all, even 30 bits of color would result in something like *billions* of colors. Why do we need all those colors? Other than the reason I just mentioned, the extra data space can be used to store *alpha channel* information. Alpha channels are 8-bit images that can be used for such things as storing spot colors that will be used for printing a client-specified color, such as the color of type in the corporate logo. Alpha channels are even more commonly used for masking. But most image-editing software adds its own information to the information stored in the basic image file, so you don't need to create an image with more than 24-bit depth in order to make use of alpha channels.

Note

Remember, no device can actually display more colors than there are pixels in the image—even though there may be more information retained in the image file itself, as would be the case in a 32-bit file. So why do we want all that color? Why, so that we'll have it when we need it. It's the same reason lots of photographers (especially digital photographers) always shoot color—even when the immediate need is for black and white. After all, a single command in Photoshop (or whichever image editor you choose) will instantly change the display mode to grayscale. There are even plug-in filters that can imitate the color sensitivity of particular types of black and white film, or that will imitate the effect of a color filter on the black and white image. So why not have it all ways at once? As long as we have the original file, we can always go back to full color.

The real advantage of assigning more than 24 bits per pixel to an image at the capture stage is the amount of information that can be recorded beyond the range of what we can actually print. Think of it as automatic bracketing without having to shoot multiple frames. That's because you've recorded enough data to cover a wide range of f-stops. If you read the chapter on choosing digital cameras, you'll see that some of the high-end cameras claim a dynamic range of 11 (or even 14) f-stops. In photographer's terms, increasing bit depth increases the image's *latitude*. In layman's terms, increasing bit depth increases the amount of detail that is recorded at the extremes of the image's tonal values—that is, in the highlights and shadows.

There's a catch, though. The more latitude you record, the more bit depth is required. The more bit depth you have, the bigger the file gets. In fact, it can get so much bigger that you might find your available RAM and hard-drive space severely cramped. If you're working for a corporation or for ad agencies with big budgets and big demands, you'll just have to buy a faster processor, more RAM, and a bigger hard drive. Come to think of it, if you can afford the typically $20,000 or $30,000 camera that produces those 100MB files, you can easily afford the other hardware to go along with it.

So What's Bracketing?

Wait, if you're not an experienced photographer, maybe you don't know what *bracketing* is. It's the practice of making several shots of the same subject, pose, and composition. Each of the shots is made at a different exposure. In a three-shot bracket, the first shot might be underexposed by one f-stop, the second at the reading suggested by the exposure meter, and the third, one stop over. Some photographers even bracket in quarter-stop increments. This assures them of having recorded the area of most important detail at an exposure that records the most detail. The following figure shows the result of bracketing over a range of three f-stops in half-stop increments.

Bracketed scenic: EV-1.5, EV-1, EV-.5, EV, EV+.5, EV+1, EV+1.5

Bit depth and the Web

There is one instance where bit depths higher than 24-bit true color are a disadvantage: Images destined for display on a Web page or as an attachment to email. Since the Web is a monitor-based medium, the extra depth will only increase file size, thereby slowing transmission time. Furthermore, the most efficient file format for compressing files for the Web is the same file format used by most digital cameras for compressing files as they are photographed. That file format is known as JPEG, for the committee that made the file format specification — the Joint Photographic Experts Group.

Files stored in JPEG format (Windows, DOS, and UNIX) will assign an extension of .jpg to JPEG files. JPEG files can't be stored at bit depths higher than 24 bits.

Note   Most software capable of saving an image to JPEG format will give you a choice of compression ratios. There is a great deal of variance in exactly how much control you are given. This is discussed in much more detail in Chapter 17. For now, just know that Web-destined images should be compressed as much as possible, consistent with the resultant appearance of the image. You can check this out by simply saving your file at several levels of compression and then viewing the result in your Web browser (or even just opening the files in your image editor).

Resolution

Resolution refers to the degree of definition in an image — that is, how much detail one can see in a given amount of space. This is defined by counting the number of individual picture elements. Picture elements are the smallest individually distinguishable component of a bitmapped image. They are nicknamed pixels when referring to digital files and hardware (such as cameras and monitors) and as dots when referring to screened printed materials. Lately, pixels and dots have become more interchangeable terms.

The four different ways of expressing image resolution in pixels (picture elements) are as follows:

✦ As the number of pixels in a given unit of measurement, such as *pixels per inch.* This is a linear measurement, so if the resolution is 2,700 ppi, then a 35mm slide would be 2,700 × 4,050 pixels since the slide image measures approximately 1 by 1½ inches.

✦ As an array, such as 640 × 480 (it is usually understood that we mean pixels when citing such a dimension, unless there are other measurements in the same context that might confuse the issue).

✦ As a total number of pixels. This would be the result of multiplying the pixel (or dot) dimensions of the array. Thus a 640 × 480 image would be 307,200 pixels. A 1,280×960 image would be 1,228,800 pixels — or 1.2 *megapixels.*

✦ As the image's file size. This is the result of multiplying the pixel dimension of the image by the pixel depth of the image and then dividing that by 8 (the number of bits in a byte). Thus, the file size of our 640 × 480 image, were it recorded in 24-bit color, would be (307,000 × 24)/8 = 921,600, or popularly rounded off to 920K.

✦ If we are talking about the amount of definition available within a fixed amount of space, the figures are stated as dots or pixels per inch (dpi or ppi). For instance, the ability of a slide scanner's ability to record detail might be stated as 2,700 dpi.

The issue of resolution is a mightily confusing one to many of us. Mainly, this is because so many of the devices used in digital photography have an inherent resolution of their own that interacts with the resolution of the original digital/digitized file. This includes the resolution of the monitor on which images are (or may be) viewed, printer resolution (which can potentially be many different resolutions for printing the same photo file), onscreen resolution, scanner resolution, camera resolution, and something I'll call audience resolution.

In all these cases, as stated in Chapter 1, reference is being made to either the number of pixels (individual cells of color in a grid-like matrix), dots, or film grain particles in the image. Pixels are defined in the previous chapter, but just so you don't have to flip pages: A pixel is the smallest element in a bitmapped image, which is the type of image for all digital photographs. It is, simply, a square or round pinpoint of light that contains only brightness and color information. Figure 2-1 shows you what a pixel actually looks like at extreme magnification.

Figure 2-1: An image obviously composed of pixels of different shades of gray

Resolution is generally considered to be equivalent to the amount of definition that you will see in an image. While this is generally true, the issue is complicated by the fact that pixels can be any size (witness the exaggerated pixels in the illustration above). They are somewhat equivalent to the dots on a screen-printed page. Smaller pixels, like smaller dots, will produce the illusion of more image definition.

Another factor influencing image definition is viewing distance. The farther you are from an image, the smaller the dots appear to be. As a result, definition seems to be greater.

Note

It is often stated that a camera or image-processing software (such as Adobe Photoshop) can *enhance* or *interpolate* the original resolution of an image. Actually, this is always done by software, even though sometimes that software is embedded in a hardware device such as a camera, scanner, or printer. The software "looks" at the pixels in the image and then decides how to color the pixels that must be duplicated in order to make the picture larger. If the new pixels are shaded to be halfway between the darkness of two neighboring original pixels, the edges defined by those pixels appear to be smoother. This is a process known as *antialiasing*. Interpolating the resolution of an image will certainly make it appear to have higher definition than an image whose original pixels have simply been multiplied. This is because images enlarged by simply multiplying the existing pixels will appear to have jagged edges. See the two visual examples in Figure 2-2.

Figure 2-2: Two versions of the same small portion of an image that has been resized by a factor of 4. Notice the difference in the apparent smoothness of edges, due to antialiasing created by bipolar interpolation.

Camera resolution

Camera resolution is the statistic you see when you read the specification sheet for any of the cameras listed in this bible and on the specification sheets provided by manufacturers. It is usually stated two ways:

✦ The approximate total of the number of pixels the image-capture device (usually the CCD) is capable of capturing. Higher-end point-and-shoot cameras generally round off this figure to the nearest million pixels. A megapixel camera has a resolution of about $1{,}280 \times 960$, though a significantly lower resolution of $1{,}024 \times 768$ comes mighty close (about 900K) to being a megapixel image as well.

✦ The pixel dimensions of the captured image, expressed as n (the width) $\times n$ (the height) with n representing an exact number of pixels (picture elements).

The camera resolution of an image is the most important specification for an image's definition because it dictates the maximum definition that will ever be attainable for that image.

Note   Camera resolution is an accurate measure of picture definition only insofar as all other factors are equal—a fact that's too easily forgotten when we're reading spec sheets. You must also consider the sharpness and contrast of the lens, the ability of the image capture device to make distinctions between subtle differences in color (because, otherwise, subtle differences in color may look the same in some areas, causing a loss in perceived detail), and whether (almost always) the image is compressed when it is saved. See the discussion on compression later in this chapter.

Scanner resolution

Scanner resolution is to a digitized original what camera resolution is to an image that originated digitally. In both instances, you will never get a higher-definition digital image from this specific image file.

However, there is an important difference: The actual quality of a scanned image will depend on the definition inherent in the original. If the original is grainy or screened (composed of printed dots), the definition of the scan will be worse than the original. Of course, the scanning resolution of some types of high-end scanners is so high that it's unlikely that a human could discern the difference in an unmagnified image. (However, scanning at very high resolution will increase file size to an often intolerable degree. More on that later.)

Scanning an image that's been screened or printed with visible photographic grain can result in another definition-defeating visual phenomenon known as a moiré pattern (an example of which can be seen in Figure 2-3). The actual look of individual moiré patterns varies quite a bit, but they result from the fact that it is nearly impossible to keep the pixel grid of the scanner and the dot or grain pattern of the original in register with one another.

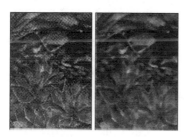

Figure 2-3: Two sections from the same image, one showing a moire pattern, the other not

Note   Most of the software that comes with flatbed scanners (types of scanners are defined and discussed in Chapter 10) have a feature to eliminate moiré patterns. If you must scan screen-printed originals (and aren't violating anyone's copyrights in so doing), the result will certainly make your scan more acceptable looking, which makes this a valuable feature. However, it achieves its effect by intelligent blurring of the scan. The result is a more attractive image with even less detail definition.

When evaluating the resolution of a scanner, always look for the number of dots per inch (expressed as dpi — for instance, 600 dpi). Also, just because you scan at a given resolution doesn't mean that you'll end up with a file of the same resolution. For one thing, many scanners provide an option to scan at a higher horizontal resolution than vertical. However, if the file were imported into your image-processing software at that resolution, it would appear to have been stretched to twice its normal width, so the scanner software has to drop some resolution or double the resolution in one direction before the file is exported. Second, some scanner software will enable you to specify a higher scan resolution than the output file resolution. We'll discuss all the reasons why these things are done in the chapter that covers scanners and their use, Chapter 10.

In the meantime, the most important number to note when comparing the resolution of competing scanners is the highest number that pertains to optical vertical resolution, since horizontal resolution can always be scanned at the same number.

Scanner (and camera) specifications that refer to interpolated resolution are nothing more than useless marketing hype. Photoshop and most worthwhile image-editing software can interpolate the resolution of any image to virtually any degree. Furthermore, Photoshop does the interpolation in a more sophisticated way than most bundled scanner and camera software.

File resolution

File resolution is the resolution of any given computer file. Because this resolution is expressed as either a pixel array or in terms of file size, file resolution may not have a direct correlation to image definition. For instance, you might open the image you shot at 640 × 480 and use software to resize that image by 145 percent to 928 × 696. The image is made larger by placing pixels as much farther apart as the degree of magnification dictates. This is exactly what happens when you project film in an enlarging machine to make a print that's larger than the original negative — except that when this is done digitally, the original pixels don't become physically any larger (see "Printer Resolution"). Instead, the computer software calculates the space between pixels and then uses the color of neighboring pixels to create new pixels that will fill in the in-between spaces.

An especially clever program, if it has been instructed how to do so, can even look at the colors of all the pixels that surround the empty space and then create the new pixel as an average of those colors. The result is a blend between colors in the new pixels that creates the illusion that the image was photographed at the new, higher resolution. The process I've just described is called *interpolation*. Interpolation doesn't increase actual definition, only the illusion of definition. Also, the resultant image will seem to have soft edges.

Regardless how the file came to have its resolution, you will want files that produce the image size you want when printed at 300 dots per inch (generally referred to as dpi) in order to print files of the highest photographic quality. So, a file that is 1,280 × 960 (1.3 megapixels) will produce a photographic-quality print that is approximately 4¼ × 3¼ inches. However, because modern printers print at much higher (600 to 1,440 dpi) resolutions, they can produce a credible image from a lower-resolution file. Most viewers would have a hard time telling the difference if the same size image were printed from a file resolution of only 150 dpi. (Note that the printer is still printing at a much higher number of dots per inch.)

Thus, the camera maker's typical claims (sometimes, I confess, echoed in this book) that a megapixel camera can produce a photographic-quality 5 × 7-inch print. Check out Figure 2-4.

Figure 2-4: Two copies of the same portion of 1,280 × 960 file, one printed at 300 dpi, the other at 150 dpi

Monitor resolution

Monitor resolution doesn't affect the resolution of your image file. It is merely the resolution at which you will preview your images on screen.

Monitor resolution (or projector resolution) can be varied in both Macintosh and Windows operating systems. Exactly how variable will depend on the make and model of the specific monitor (used here to include digital projectors and flat-panel displays such as those on a laptop computer) and on the features of the display card (even if that hardware is built onto the motherboard of your computer).

Most modern monitors (and their associated display cards) on most desktop computers will enable you to display the image at one of three resolutions: 640 × 480, 800 × 600, or 1,024 × 768. Some monitors (usually at least 17-inch) will go to even higher resolutions. Higher display resolutions than those typically used for desktop publishing are more useful in photo editing because you can retain more of the detail in your photo when you're zoomed out far enough to see the whole photo. A higher display resolution also means that you won't have to zoom in so tight in order to be able to view your image at 1:1 resolution (meaning each pixel visible on the display corresponds to the same pixel in the image).

One thing to keep in mind about monitor resolution is that you will get the best compromise between pixels that are large enough to see (so that you can edit them accurately) and small enough to give you the feeling that you are looking at a quality image (not too pixelated or "jaggy") if you display at a resolution that approaches 72 ppi on the size monitor you are using. I say approximately 72 dpi advisedly. Here are the sizes that work best at each resolution, along with the actual dpi of the display at that size:

640 × 480	15-inch or smaller	60 dpi on 14-inch
800 × 600	17-inch	64 dpi
1,024 × 768	19-inch	71 dpi
1,280 × 1,024	21-inch	75 dpi

The figures in the above table are only approximate because the exact size of the picture is adjustable using the hardware controls on each individual monitor. One user might like a black border around the image (which usually gives better edge-to-edge sharpness on low-cost monitors). Others may not want any black border at all, and so may push the image size to slightly larger than the tube itself.

Note   You can display more resolution with fewer colors because the display card requires less onboard display memory (usually called VRAM) to do so. If you have a display card with at least 8MB of RAM, you will be able to display 24-bit true color at 1,024 × 768.

Printer resolution

There are three main methods of obtaining printed output of your digital files:

✦ Desktop printer

✦ Color separations to be used on a printing press

✦ Film recorder

Desktop printer

If you want to maximize the ratio of file size to printer quality when printing color images, the formula in Figure 2-5 is a good rule of thumb.

The reason that this formula works is that the resolution of the printer is made up of dots converted from the three primary colors: red, green, and blue (RGB). Although most desktop color printers print in reflective primary colors, called CMYK (cyan, magenta, yellow, and black), the software that drives them typically makes an automatic conversion of your RGB image. The printer thus takes the RGB information from each of the image's pixels and uses all of its dots to simulate those colors.

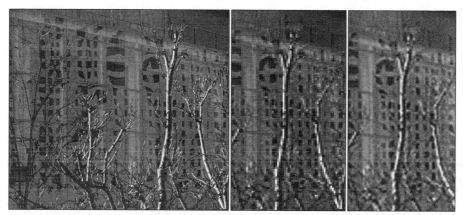

Figure 2-5: Printer resolution / number of primary colors in file = file resolution

Many printers print at twice the definition horizontally as vertically; thus, the printer's resolution is stated as 1,440 × 720 (late model Epson inkjets) or 1,200 × 600 (some Canon, Lexmark, and H-P inkjets). So, if you're printing on an Epson photo printer, does that mean you should make your printer file resolution at 480 dots or 240? Well, in my experience, you don't gain a lot by going to 480 unless your image contains very fine detail. If you are working with high-end lenses and digitizing film with a high-end scanner, and you want to show every hair and pore on the girl's face, set your file resolution at 480 dpi. Otherwise, you probably won't notice the difference at 240 dpi.

Having said all that, a little extra information usually helps. Many will advise you to just set the resolution for all files destined for printing, regardless of the type of output device, at 300 dpi. If you're not the anal type and don't mind reasonable compromises, this is a good one.

The relationship between file resolution and printer resolution

As stated earlier, your image file's resolution (unless you alter it by cropping or resizing) is fixed. If you have a printer that's set to print at 300 dpi and your file is 300 pixels across and 150 pixels high, it will appear on a letter-size (8 ½ × 11 inches) page as being an inch wide and half an inch high. Some printers give you a printing option to "fit to page" (or something similar). If you choose that option, the printer will resize the image to fit the page. Be wary of doing this unless you just want to print a "for position only" proof. The result will be, at best, fuzzy. More likely, you'll just get a very pixelated, jaggy-looking image. A better solution would be to use a more sophisticated interpolation algorithm, such as is employed by Photoshop or Altamira Software's Genuine Fractals, to interpolate the image to a larger size. Don't expect that an interpolated image will give you photographic definition, but at least it will look more acceptable

When to choose lower resolution for printing

Most printers give you a choice of printing resolutions. Most of you will immediately guess that the higher resolutions will give you more definition and a smoother, more photographic-looking transition between color tones. If that was your guess, you just pinned the tail on the donkey. Still, there are drawbacks to picking a higher resolution than you need for your immediate purposes. First, choosing a lower resolution will save you ink. Since color ink isn't cheap, that's an important consideration. Second, uncoated papers look worse when you use inkjet printers at resolutions over 360 dpi because too much ink is absorbed and colors bleed together. The result is uuuugly indeed!

Color separations

If you are having your digital file printed on an offset press, the resolution you will require will depend on the printing process being used. Ask a prepress expert at the print shop that will be printing your file what resolution he or she requires in order to print the best possible reproduction of your image given the specific printing equipment and color separation techniques that will be used.

Film recorder

A film recorder's resolution behaves in the same way as a printer's. Figure that your file's resolution will need to be about one-third that of the film recorder's when the file is dimensioned. Figure 2-6 shows a typical film recorder.

Figure 2-6: A typical film recorder

Making Sure Your File Size Matches Output Resolution

In order to determine the size a file will need to be if you print it at a given resolution, open the Image Size dialog box in your image editor. You'll usually find a way to change the resolution without resizing the image. In Photoshop, you uncheck the box labeled Resample Image. Be sure the Constrain Proportions box is checked (if you're using another image editor, there will probably be a similar command). Now enter the target printing resolution of your file, and the size dimensions of your file will automatically be recalculated.

Audience resolution

If the image is going to be projected, viewed on the Web, or shown in a gallery, the effects of resolution will depend somewhat on the individual viewer and, even more, on the means by which the image is being viewed. It is sufficient to say that the following factors should be considered:

✦ Don't use a file with more resolution than you know the viewer is likely to be able to experience. Doing so will be pointless, and will likely strain the end user's computing resources.

✦ The more distance between the viewer and the image, the higher resolution will appear to be. So, even though the pixels in a projected image may be huge and sparse, the image may appear to have good resolution to an audience that's seated many yards away. Also, gallery prints may look perfectly acceptable at lower resolutions because they are typically viewed from a distance of several feet.

Methods of Digitizing

There are several routes by which an image can become digital. You can make a digital photograph by using a digital camera. Or, you can start with a conventional photograph; either on film as a positive or negative transparency or printed on paper. Then you can use either a scanner, send out to have the image recorded on a Kodak Photo CD, or have a third party (generically called a service bureau) digitize the photo for you by scanning it on their premises. Each of these routes has its place, and most practitioners of digital photography will find reason to use all of them at one time or another.

Digital camera

When you photograph a subject using a digital camera, the image goes straight into the computer—no other digitizing hardware is needed. The advantages of using a digital camera to make digital images are as follows:

✦ **Instant turnaround time:** You can see the pictures on the camera and make decisions as to lighting and composition. You can even use this capability to preview the results you'd get by reshooting the result conventionally.

✦ **Reduced shoot time:** You know if you've got the shot, so there's less need for bracketing, alternate lighting, and shooting extra poses just to "cover your canister."

✦ **Lower operating costs:** There's no film to buy, no processing to pay for. Furthermore, instant turnaround means lower costs for talent, client time on set, and equipment rental.

Types

The characteristics and prices of digital cameras vary as widely as those of their analog counterparts. For the purposes of organizing this book, we have broken these variations down into the following broad price/function categories: pocket, serious prosumer, professional field cameras, and professional studio cameras.

When choosing a camera in any of these categories, pick one with a removable memory feature. Then you can simply swap removable memory units when you've taken as many pictures as one memory module can hold.

Point-and-shoot cameras

These are cameras that fit in a shirt pocket and that typically cost under $500. An example of one of these is shown in Figure 2-7. These cameras tend to be truly point-and-shoot, offering very few options and adjustments. Focus, exposure, and white balance are either fixed or entirely automatic. At the very low end of this range, you might not even get a built-in flash, but this is becoming a rarity. Look for cameras that have a close-up focus setting (macro option). Most have fixed focal-length lenses and an optical viewfinder, and their resolution ranges between 640 × 480 and 1,280 × 960. However, the resolution of these cameras is following the same upward trend as for all digital cameras: resolution (like computer processors) gets twice as good every year to 18 months for a given price level of camera. Megapixel pocket cameras are becoming commonplace.

Many of these cameras use a very small lens that isn't built to accept filters and other lens accessories (such as wide-angle and telephoto converters). It's a bonus if the camera sports a 37mm lens thread (because you can then use lens accessories made for many camcorders). Other bonuses that can be found on many of these cameras are a tripod mount and a burst mode. Look for cameras whose lenses are the equivalent of a 35mm (moderate wide-angle) to 50mm (normal) lens on a 35mm camera. Wide-angle lenses tend to include more of the subject than the job calls for and moving in closer causes distortion.

Figure 2-7: A typical pocket digicam

Pocket cameras are the appropriate tool for the following applications:

✦ Photos intended primarily for display on a Web page, electronic cataloguing (such as kiosk and CD-ROM catalogue) and database management (such as parts and personnel identification).

✦ Event documentation (accidents, crimes, in-field business assignments), and family photos.

✦ I also know several professional photographers who use them to "preview" a shoot instead of using Polaroid film. The digital image gives them a good idea of how to compensate for exposure in a given situation.

It is the cost, small size (always handy), low resolution (low imaging cost and simple digital processing requirements and appropriateness for monitor-based applications) that make these cameras especially appropriate for the applications listed above. Otherwise, most of these functions could be covered as well or better by more costly types of digital cameras—especially their more capable brethren in the next category.

These cameras are not appropriate for situations that call for high image definition, shots that are timing critical (there's usually a lag between the time the shutter is pressed and the time the image is recorded as well as a longer wait between frames), or situations that call for wide-ranging imaging options, such as advertising or editorial photography.

Prosumer cameras

Prosumer is a contraction of professional and consumer. It is a phrase that is often used in the computer press to describe software and gear that has professional capabilities but that is priced within the range of individual consumers. I almost called this category "serious point-and-shoot" because most of these cameras offer lots of automation, yet give photographers a great deal of control over exposure, composition, and focus. The cameras shown in Figure 2-8 are two of the most highly regarded prosumer cameras. This category of cameras overlaps the functionality of many of the low-end professional field cameras. The price range is quite wide: $500 to $3,000. The vast majority fall into the $800 to $1,500 range. They have megapixel or better (two megapixel is becoming commonplace) resolution, 3:1 zoom lenses (typically 35mm to 105mm), options for either automatic or manual control over exposure, larger-than-average LCD displays for viewing through the lens or viewing the images that have been taken, macro focusing capability, and multiple metering and flash operations. Beyond that, the range of features is so broad that you'd best read the use and purpose of all digital camera features that are detailed in Chapter 3.

Figure 2-8: The Olympus D-620-L, a single-lens reflex digicam (pictured with a wide-angle supplementary lens from Tiffen) and the Nikon Coolpix 950, a swivel-lens zoom pocket digicam

Most of the cameras in the point-and-shoot category use either CompactFlash or SmartMedia cards and interface to computers via the serial port. Download times through the serial port can stretch to 30 minutes, but card-reading accessories are available for attaching to a computer through parallel or (better) USB ports. Card-reading attachments download images at a much higher rate of speed.

Serious point-and-shoot cameras often have the image definition and exposure, focus, and white-balance controls equivalent to those found in professional field cameras and are often used by professional photographers. They do not have interchangeable lenses, only occasionally have the ability to synchronize with external flash units (an option well worth looking for), and don't have the ability to share accessories with their analog brethren. Viewfinder accuracy, including the visibility of LCD preview screens, tends to be much higher in LCD cameras.

Serious point-and-shoot cameras can't employ a full range of lenses, especially some of the world's best lenses that are made for 35mm SLR cameras. They don't produce images that are as high in resolution as those you can make from a slide scanner and so their images aren't well suited to print sizes that exceed 5 × 7 inches in most cases — and 8 × 10 inches at best. Many of them enable you to compose and focus through the lens only via the LCD monitor, which has limited usefulness in outdoor lighting.

Applications suitable to serious professional point-and-shoot cameras are many: wedding and event photography, real estate, news coverage (especially if the camera is used by a reporter who lacks photographic experience), illustration, events, and all of the applications suited for pocket cameras (only with better image quality and more control over the variables of image quality).

Professional field cameras

Professional field cameras are built on the chassis of (or, at least built to accept all the accessories for) existing popular models of 35mm single-lens reflex cameras. Their price ranges from $4,000 to $35,000 — depending primarily on resolution and added features. Resolution tends to fall between 1.5 and 6MB. The Kodak DC 315 shown in Figure 2-9 is an entry-level 35mm body professional digital field camera. All are "single-shot" cameras (as are all the categories of cameras above), meaning that the entire image and all the colors are captured instantly. They can use all the lenses available for the camera they are based on, as well as most of the lighting and accessories that are made for that camera. They tend to look like that camera, too, although most appear to have an external motor drive attachment.

The extra space (and weight) is typically used to house PCMCIA cards that contain much more memory than is typically found in Compact Flash and SmartMedia cards typically used in the serious point-and-shoot category. This extra memory is needed because of the higher resolution of the images and because these cameras are intended for on-location use. Thus, it's not often convenient to download to a computer before the next shot is called for. When they do download, the do so at high speed, through either SCSI or FireWire interfaces, rather than the serial interfaces found on lower-priced cameras. Also, their PCMCIA cards can be inserted into most laptop computers or into PCMCIA card readers attached to a computer.

Figure 2-9: The Kodak DC 315, one of the most affordable professional SLRs. This one is based on a Nikon body and accepts all Nikkor AF lenses.

Applications for which these cameras are suited cover nearly the whole gamut, provided resolution is high enough for your purposes. That will depend on the price and model of the camera you choose. Applications that are particularly suited for professional field cameras include medical imaging (easily adaptable to microscopes, special-purpose lenses, and ring lights), photojournalism (instant turnaround, easily adapted to extreme telephoto, can use high shutter speeds, lenses can contain "steady shot" mechanisms), catalog photography (low cost of film and materials, ability to instantly see shot to check for critically important details), and public relations (again, instant turnaround plus ability to synchronize with external portable flash units).

At the high end of the professional field camera range (>$24K), resolution rivals that of single-shot professional studio cameras.

Professional studio cameras

Professional studio cameras include backs that are made to be attachable to medium-format cameras (especially Hassleblad and 6 × 7 format cameras such as those from Fuji) or to 4 × 5 cameras. They are classified (for purposes of this book, at least) as studio cameras because most must be tethered to a computer when taking photos. However, some very well known photographers hook these cameras to battery packs and portable computers and take them out in the field. Figure 2-10 shows a high-resolution digital camera back-mounted on a studio camera while a Macintosh computer acts as its viewfinder.

Figure 2-10: A digital camera back on a 4×5 studio camera

These cameras, like their field counterparts, can make use of almost all accessories and lenses made for their analog studio camera counterparts. The notable exception to this is that multiple-shot and scanning cameras cannot synchronize with strobe units. However, the image-sensing device is almost always smaller than the analog film area, which changes the effective focal length of the lens being used.

I forgot to mention that there are three distinct subcategories of studio cameras (in this context, the word "cameras" includes backs (attachments that turn an analog camera into a digital camera). Some models combine two or three of these functions:

✦ **Single-shot cameras:** Cost between $15,000 and $25,000. Single-shot cameras work in the same way as field cameras, except that they are larger and tend to be backs for medium-format and 4×5 cameras. So, size and weight encourage the use of a tripod, which can impede shooting spontaneity. Resolutions are typically 3,000×2,000 pixels (though many of the imaging devices are square and a few reach higher resolutions). This gives them roughly the same resolution you would get from a midrange desktop slide scanner.

✦ **Multiple-shot cameras:** Can be used only for motionless subjects with a tripod-mounted camera. The camera shoots the same image several times, moving the image sensor exactly 1 pixel between shots, and then superimposes the images on one another to achieve that multiple of the sensor's native resolution. So if three shots are made with a 2,000 pixel square sensor, the result will be 6,000 pixels square. Some of these cameras will let you fire a strobe for each of the multiple shots, but you lose the motion-capture benefit of shooting with strobe.

✦ **Scanning cameras:** These cameras work in a similar manner as a slide scanner, recording strips of the image at very high resolution as the image sensor moves across the image. It is not unusual for these cameras to spend several minutes taking a picture, but the result is astronomically high resolution (and typical file sizes of several hundred megabytes). The benefit is a photograph that contains much more detail and latitude than the best 4×5 film cameras. Scanning cameras are available as both self-contained units and as camera backs. A few models also work as multiple-shot and single-shot cameras. Scanning cameras prices vary over a wide range, but most fall in the $25,000 to $30,000 bracket.

Scanner

Scanners are the instruments most commonly used for digitizing photographs, as well as other types of artwork. If the original is too large to fit your scanner, you could use a camera, but that would be a rare requirement for most. You can also stitch individual scans together.

Scanners come in several incarnations, but only three are significant players in digital photography:

✦ **Flatbed scanners:** Flatbed scanners are the most popular type of scanner for two reasons: they are low in cost and they are capable of serving multiple purposes. They can be used for scanning either flat or transparent artwork, they can be used for optical character recognition, and they can be teamed with software. Flatbed scanners come in a bevy of sizes, have a whole range of feature sets, and vary widely in resolution and color accuracy. You may find flatbed scanners promoted for as little as $50 that seem to offer reasonable resolution and color depth, but be sure to test the unit before buying if quality photo reproduction is your goal. Most of the flatbed scanners that will do a reasonable job of accurately scanning a 4×6-inch snapshot accurately will sport list prices of $200 or better.

Resolutions of 600 dpi and at least 10-bit scans are commonplace and quite adequate for scanning prints and other opaque art. Pay particular attention to the features and power of the scanner plug-in software. You should be able to see a large preview of your scan and to accurately adjust color balance and exposure before making the scan. After all, if you don't have the information in the original, you'll never be able to improve definition (although you'll see later in this book that you can certainly improve the illusion of definition and many other qualities). Many flatbed scanners offer an option for scanning film or slides. Don't expect too much from this option. A transparency adapter is a helpful when it comes to proofing a roll of film, but they lack enough resolution to compete effectively with slide and film scanners (except when it comes to 4 × 5 and larger format transparencies). Figure 2-11 depicts a typical flatbed scanner.

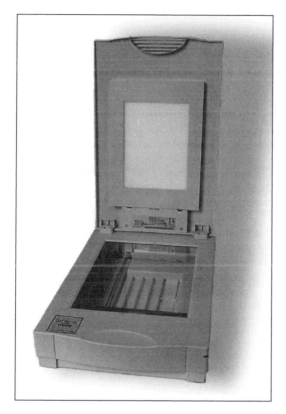

Figure 2-11: The Acerscan 620ST, a typical flatbed scanner with built-in transparency adapter

✦ **Film (slide) scanners:** Are shoebox-sized desktop units built specifically for scanning film and slides. Most are equally adept at scanning either positive or negative images and will automatically save the scan of a negative as a positive. Units made for scanning 35mm film and slides are by far the most popular and cost-effective. Today, most will also scan APS format film as well. Several units will scan at resolutions adequate for making photo-quality 5 × 7-inch prints for around $500. You can cover a wider range of uses with > 2,600-dpi units that sell for between $1,000 and $2,000. Expect to see significantly higher resolutions and wider ranges of features for these prices in the near future. If you shoot mostly with larger format (6×6 cm to 4×5 in) cameras, you will need a multiformat scanner. They are more likely to cost around $4,000, but will do a credible job of scanning any format that your studio or service bureau is likely to encounter.

✦ **Drum scanners:** If you are digitizing a large number of photos destined for high-end print jobs or for prestige clients such as advertising agencies, you will probably want the control, color depth, resolution, and batch scanning capabilities of a drum scanner. Drum scanners can scan either reflective or transparent materials and can generally accommodate larger images — so a single scanner can serve a wide range of purposes. They are ideal in high-end, high-volume applications. These range in price from a low of around $15,000 to tens of thousands.

Photo CD

Photo CD is one of the best ways for both business and professional photographers to digitize analog photos. You take your film to a Photo CD dealer and pick up the CD the next day. It isn't uncommon to find dealers who will scan images for as little as $1 each, so you could scan about 1,000 images before you could pay for a slide scanner capable of recording images of comparable quality. When the CD is returned, a thumbnail sheet that visually identifies all the images on the disk accompanies it. The images are scanned directly from film, whether positive or negative, and then recorded at several resolutions onto a CD-ROM disk that can be read on either a regular computer CD-ROM drive or in other types of CD players that can show the images on a video tube. Such players make it especially easy to show a shoot or portfolio to a group, family, department, or client.

Photo CD comes in two flavors: regular Master Photo CD and Professional Master Photo CD.

The regular Master Photo CD is designed strictly for 35mm. Images are recorded in five different resolutions and the disk can contain up to 100 images. The five resolutions are as follows:

✦ 2,048 × 3,072 pixels

✦ 1,024 × 1,536 pixels

✦ 512 × 768 pixels

✦ 256 × 384 pixels

✦ 128 × 192 pixels

The Master Pro Photo CD adds a sixth resolution option at 4,096 × 6,144 pixels. These disks can store images from all the 2¼-inch wide formats and 4 × 5 film, as well as 35mm. The image capacity of a Pro Photo CD varies from 25 to 100, depending on the range of resolutions you specify and the format of the images.

Note   Kodak has a new CD format available through retail photofinishers called Picture CD. You can find out about Picture CD and more about Photo CD technologies in Chapter 4.

Service bureau

You may need different types of scanners at different times for different purposes. There may also be times when you just don't have the time to do the job yourself. In that case, you can find a whole range of businesses that will scan your images for you. Most specialize in a specific area of expertise, such as prepress work. However, most major cities have at least one service bureau that's capable of making any type of scan or digital studio photo. The service bureau business is highly competitive, so it's also likely that using one will be cost-effective as well. Service bureaus are also excellent sources for good advice as to which brands and models of digital equipment will best suit your requirements. Some even double as dealers (in which case, you may question the objectivity of their buying advice). Service bureaus may also make one or more varieties of large-format digital prints.

Summary

This chapter introduced you to the technical capabilities of the various devices used in digital photography. It discussed the meaning of dynamic range, bit depth, and resolution — including why you should care to know the meaning of these terms and how they fit into the digital photography workflow. Next came a discussion of printing methods and resources and how digital images are likely to be reproduced. Finally, we discussed the difference between pure digital photography (photography that starts with a digital camera) and hybrid digital photography (photography that starts with film and is then digitized by scanning. This section touched on various means of scanning (such as flatbed scanners, slide scanners, Photo CD, and service bureaus) — including introductory advice on when to scan in-house and when to use a service bureau.

The next chapter introduces you to more specific information on the tools and techniques and technology required for hybrid digital photography.

✦   ✦   ✦

Tools for Making a Digital Photograph

Digital cameras have much in common with their analog counterparts. Both have lenses, viewfinders, exposure controls, a shutter-release button, and so forth. This section of the book will explain the basic components of a digital camera, what to look for in each component, and why. The idea is to familiarize you with the technology rather than to make you an expert.

The Anatomy of a Digital Camera

Digital cameras, regardless of job classification or price range, have (or should have) the following basic components:

- ✦ Lens
- ✦ Lens cover
- ✦ Shutter
- ✦ Diaphragm
- ✦ Viewfinder
- ✦ Flash
- ✦ Flat-panel display (LCD)
- ✦ Controls
- ✦ Resolution
- ✦ Image quality settings
- ✦ Digital film
- ✦ Batteries

✦ Computer connections

✦ Tripod thread

Note If you are experienced in serious photography and know your cameras, you may feel that there are features missing from the above list. Rest assured that professional, high-end digital cameras can use almost every accessory and feature of their analog counterparts. In fact, most of them are built into or attach to the back of an established model of a name-brand analog camera.

Lens

The lens is optical plastic or glass that has been shaped and polished to gather light reflected from the subject you are shooting and then focus and project it onto the light-sensitive recording device in the camera. There are ten qualities by which you should judge a lens:

✦ Manufacturer

✦ Material of construction

✦ Coating

✦ Number of elements

✦ Focusing method

✦ Type

✦ Focal length

✦ Maximum aperture

✦ Minimum focusing distance

✦ Exposure control

Manufacturer

If an established and highly regarded manufacturer makes your lens, consider this a definite plus. Manufacturing high-quality optics is an art mastered by few. However, if the camera you're considering is made by a company more famous for its prowess in consumer electronics or computers than for its analog cameras and binoculars, don't expect your pictures to be as sharp or colorful as optics from such companies as Carl Zeiss, Olympus, Canon, Nikon, and others. Even if your camera is made by a company you never heard of, it may feature a name-brand lens. Look at the black ring that surrounds the glass. It is traditional for a lens manufacturer's trade name to appear there (see Figure 3-1).

Focal length

The focal length of the camera's lens determines the angle of view. If the camera is priced under $2,000, it probably uses a lens made exclusively for that camera and the focal length will be expressed as the equivalent of a standard lens for a 35mm film camera. This is a good thing, because the area covered by the camera's imaging chip (light-sensitive device) is typically much smaller than that covered by a frame of 35mm film. So if the real focal length of the lens were given, it would have little functional meaning to the majority of camera users.

Manufacturer's name

Figure 3-1: The manufacturer's name is usually engraved on the face of the lens ring.

On the other hand, professional cameras that are based on conventional camera bodies (or that work as film backs for conventional cameras) use lenses whose focal length is stated as the actual distance between the lens' center of focus and the film plane (or, in this case, the light-sensitive digital image pickup). To get an idea of the field of view for these lenses, you usually have to double the stated focal length, because the actual picture area covered by the pickup chip is usually about half that of the host's film size. However, this is not a hard-and-fast rule. Also, there are a few cameras that build optical compensation into the camera body so that lenses work at their normal focal length. Figure 3-2 shows the angle of view for the three most commonly used lens focal lengths.

On a 35mm camera, a 28mm lens is considered a wide-angle, a 50mm lens is "normal," and a 105mm lens is called a medium telephoto or "portrait" lens.

Maximum aperture

Lens apertures (the size of the opening in the diaphragm) are expressed in something called *f-stops*. The f-stop setting controls a mechanism in the lens called an iris diaphragm. The wider the diaphragm opening, the smaller the f-stop number. Normally, each full f-stop increase enables twice as much light to pass through to the light-sensitive pickup.

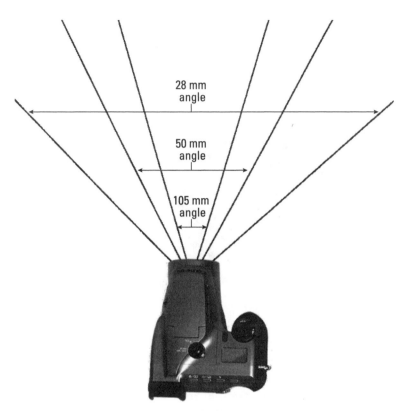

Figure 3-2: Diagram of angle of view for 28mm, 50mm, and 105mm lenses

The lens' maximum aperture is the smallest f-stop number (widest aperture) available for that lens. Maximum aperture determines the camera's ability to perform in low lighting levels. Because the best on-location shots are generally made by available light (because it makes the scene feel more "natural"), maximum aperture may be an important factor in your choice of camera.

Lens apertures (f-stops) also control something called *depth of field*. Depth of field is the distance between the closest and farthest objects that are in reasonably sharp focus. The smaller the aperture (higher the f-stop number), the greater the depth of field. However, because most digital cameras lenses have very short focal lengths, there tends to be more of a problem with too much depth of field. That is because the focal length of the lens is the other factor that controls depth of field: The shorter the focal length of the lens, the greater the depth of field.

Minimum focusing distance

Minimum focusing distance is the specification that indicates how close to the subject you can put the camera. In other words, it controls your ability to make close-ups. If the camera can shoot extreme close-ups (for instance, having something the size of a dime fill the frame to its edges), it is said that the camera has a *macro* capability or mode. Macro capability is required for medical and scientific photography and is nice to have if you want your camera to record documents, evidence, or small details. For instance, is your hobby shooting flowers? The photo in Figure 3-3 could only have been shot in macro mode or with the aid of an auxiliary close-up lens.

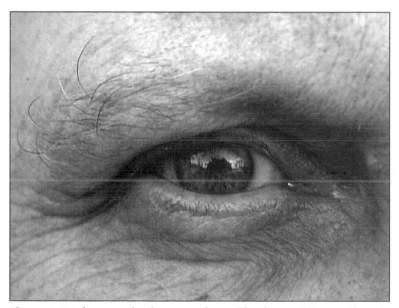

Figure 3-3: Photograph of an eye taken with a lens set in macro mode

Exposure control

Some level of control over exposure is important if you want to be able to control the brightness and contrast of the image in the area of the picture where you want to see the most detail. Exposure can also define the mood of the picture: A high-key, washed-out image may look soft and feminine. You get that effect with overexposure. An underexposed image may look more masculine or more somber.

If you don't want to be bothered with the technicalities of making correct exposures (recording your image at the most flattering level of brightness), look for an automatic exposure feature. If you are a more serious photographer, you will want the option to have more control over exposure so that you can interpret scenes more to your liking. Even if this is the case, you will find automatic exposure control helpful when working in fast action situations that simply don't give you time to use a light meter or to ponder what other settings might be applicable.

Beyond automatic exposure control, digital cameras may give you several ways to manually control exposure:

✦ Lighter/darker

✦ Shutter priority

✦ Aperture priority

✦ Programmed exposure modes

✦ Direct control over shutter speed and f-stop

Lighter/darker

If this is the only exposure control option, you won't be able to specify a particular shutter speed or f-stop. You are enabled to control how much lighter or darker the exposure will be compared to that suggested by the original automatic meter reading. These settings are generally expressed as either f-stops (for example, +1 stop or exposure values, EV). Cameras will vary when it comes to how much choice you have. Some cameras will let you expose in quarter-stop or EV increments, so you could ask for a +1¼ exposure. Usually, you can overexpose or underexpose by at least one stop.

Shutter priority

When in shutter priority mode, exposure is automatic, but you can specify a specific shutter speed. This enables you to specify a high shutter speed if you need to freeze rapid motion. In low-light situations, you can also make sure the shutter is set at high enough speed to overcome the blurring likely to occur when the camera is handheld at slow speeds. You can also force slower shutter speeds if you want to ensure that motion is blurred.

Aperture priority

When in shutter priority mode, exposure is automatic, but you can specify an exact f-stop—the camera adjusts the shutter speed accordingly. This is desirable if you want to be assured of control over depth of field. Control over depth of field is important if several subjects of interest are positioned at varying distances from the lens (think of a meadow full of flowers). Control over the range of image sharpness is equally important if you want to throw foreground and background objects out of focus so that viewer interest will be concentrated on the main subject.

Programmed exposure modes

Programmed exposure modes let you pick a typical situation and then adjust both aperture and shutter speed to settings that are typically best for that situation. For instance, you might have an exposure mode called "backlight." Backlight is the photographer's term for a shooting situation in which the main light source (usually a setting sun) is aimed into the lens. This situation generally causes the meter to underexpose the image, leaving the part of the subject that is facing the camera in darkness. So, a "backlight" programmed exposure mode would compensate for the meter reading by increasing the lens aperture (lowering the f-stop number). Another common programmed mode is "sports." This mode gives preference to the shutter speed setting, making sure that the shutter fires fast enough to freeze motion.

Direct control over shutter speed and f-stop

The most professional cameras, whether or not their price and other features place them in that category, give you the ability to set the shutter at any speed you desire and to set the aperture at any speed you desire. If you use external flash, it is absolutely necessary that you be able to control your f-stop according to the number of lights you use and how much of their light is cast on the subject. Also, you may have reason to use an accessory light meter (more about why you'd want to do that in Chapter 9). If so, you will be able to set your lens and shutter to any of the indicated aperture and shutter settings the meter recommends for the exposure value indicated by the meter's reading.

Material of construction

A lens with glass elements is likely to be of higher optical quality than one made of plastic. However, in these days of high-tech, very high quality images can come from lenses of both types. All other things being equal, though, I'd pick glass.

Coating

Lens coatings cut down on the reflections that can occur on the surfaces of lens elements. When present, such reflections will cause a softening of the image. Some coatings also cut down atmospheric reflections, resulting in more saturated colors — especially skies.

Number of elements

The number of elements in your camera's lens will have an effect on price and quality. A single-element lens is a simple lens, curved on both sides. This is an easy way to focus light on the film plane (image-sensing area) and it works reasonably well. Most low-cost point-and-shoot cameras, whether analog or digital, feature single-element, fixed-focus lenses. This works especially well for shorter focal-length lenses, so a single-element lens on a $200 fixed-focus point-and-shoot camera may be a reasonable compromise.

Lenses that feature multiple elements are, generally speaking, of higher quality. Lenses of longer focal length, those that have variable focal length (zoom lenses), and those meant for extreme close-up work (macro lenses) are much more likely to be of high quality if they have multiple elements.

Focusing method

Almost all digital cameras with noninterchangeable lenses default to being either fixed focus or focus automatically. However, there are wider possibilities and almost all are worth having in one situation or another:

✦ Auto focus

✦ Multiple-zone auto focus

✦ Manual focus

✦ Macro mode

Auto focus

If your camera and lens have auto focus capability, the camera will automatically focus on the subject that is centered in the viewfinder. So the picture will be sharp no matter how dirty the viewfinder or how poor your eyesight. In fact, auto focus is more accurate than our own judgment—most of the time. Pay attention to the word "centered." You may have good reason for wanting to position your main subject away from the center of the frame. Most cameras/lenses that auto focus will enable you to lock focus by partially depressing the shutter button. You can then reframe your picture, and then take the shot by continuing to press the shutter button. As you gain experience as a photographer, you will find this feature more and more important.

Multiple-zone auto focus

The ability to lock focus when auto focusing works well enough when the timing of your shots isn't too critical. However, there are times when there just isn't time to press, move, and shoot: You need to catch the diver just breaking the waves or that beautiful smile just as it peaks. For the "timing is everything" situations, multiple-zone focusing is a bacon-saver. These may work by enabling you to pick one of several squares in the viewfinder or an intersection point in a fixed grid. One scheme even follows the position of your eye's iris as it peers into the viewfinder. The camera assumes that what you're looking at is what you want to focus on. Some models of Canon cameras use this focusing method, but so far it is only found in their professional models (both analog and digital) and in several of their video camcorders.

Fooling Auto Focus

If your camera doesn't enable you to focus manually, you may be able to trick it into focusing at a specific distance. Aim the camera at an object that's the same distance from the lens as the object you want to photograph (but can't because another object is making that camera "think" that it should be the center of attention). Partially depress the shutter release button, and then point the camera at the object of your desire. Press a bit harder to shoot. The camera probably locked focus on the first object. It also probably locked exposure, so try to pick a focus object with midrange tonal values.

Manual focus

There are times when auto focus just doesn't work. The most common instances are when there is glass, a screen, or atmospheric particles between your lens and your subject. The auto focus will probably want to focus on those items, which may be only inches away from the camera. Another situation that's difficult for auto focus is night shots because there may not be enough light to let you focus the camera. Finally, if you're shooting panoramas that will be stitched together, it's a good idea to turn off auto focus so that you don't accidentally change focus from one shot in the series to another (see Chapter 18 for more about shooting panoramas).

You can get around all those situations as long as your camera (or lens) enables you to turn off auto focus so that you can focus manually. If the camera you are using or choosing offers this feature, it's also a good idea to make sure that the lens' focusing ring or dial is easy to grasp and that it is smooth enough to let you make accurate adjustments.

Macro mode

Many lenses and cameras offer something called a macro mode that enables you to focus on objects that are closer to the lens than normal. Just how close a macro mode will let you get varies quite a bit from camera to camera and (in the case of interchangeable lenses) from lens to lens. There's always the chance that you could solve the problem by adding supplementary (screw-on) close-up lenses.

Lens type

Lenses generally fall into one of the following categories:

✦ Integrated

✦ Interchangeable

✦ Single focal length

✦ Zoom

✦ Macro

Integrated

Integrated lenses are part of the camera they came with. They are not meant to be detached from the camera. Almost all digital cameras that sell for less than $3,000 have integrated lenses.

You can, however, add supplementary lenses to most (but not all) integrated lenses. Supplementary lenses generally screw onto the lens barrel thread or slip over it with a friction mount. Supplementary lenses either change the viewing angle of the lens (effective focal length) or enable the lens to focus more closely than even its macro mode will allow.

Interchangeable

These lenses can be detached from the camera, and another lens that uses the same type of lens mount can then replace it. This is one of the most valuable features of professional cameras, because it enables them to utilize many lenses (sometimes even hundreds) that are compatible with a specific type of camera. If you pay for a camera that features interchangeable lenses, pick one that enables you to use auto focus lenses from a major manufacturer of lenses for a similar-format camera — as well as lenses made specifically for that particular camera.

Single focal length

Lenses that have a fixed focal length are common on low-end point-and-shoot cameras because they are economical to manufacture. However, the highest-quality lenses for professional cameras are (all other factors being equal — which is seldom the case) fixed-focus lenses. You'll find the most exacting photographers (generally those who shoot detailed landscapes, food still lifes, or medical images) tend to use fixed focal-length lenses for that reason. However, these photographers are shooting subject matter that tends to stay put until the photographer is good and ready to shoot. This leaves the photographer plenty of time to change lenses. These photographers also tend to be people who are willing to buy professional-level cameras that feature interchangeable lenses.

Zoom

Zoom lenses are those that have variable focal length, which is to say that you can continuously adjust the field of view. This enables you to crop in the camera without having to change the distance between you and the subject. Most point-and-shoot cameras with integrated zoom lenses have you change the focal length of the lens by toggling a switch on the body of the camera. Interchangeable lenses zoom by pushing or pulling a ring on the lens.

If your lens is integrated with your camera and you are at all serious about taking pictures, you need a zoom lens with at least a 3:1 zoom ratio. If your camera's resolution is higher than one megapixel, look for an equivalency rating of 28mm to 85mm. If your camera's resolution is less than that, you will find that cropping imposes a more serious penalty on image quality. That is because the image's resolution doesn't give you enough slack to resize the image to fill the former space without making it obviously pixelated.

Macro

A macro lens is one formulated to maintain maximum edge-to-edge sharpness and contrast when focused on subjects that are very close to the camera. Most macro lenses are made in a single focal length. Usually they have a "normal" field of view, but there are also macro lenses in both wide-angle and moderate telephoto focal lengths.

Thanks to the short focal length of most digital camera lenses, it is fairly easy (and common) for the manufacturers to include a macro focusing capability in the zoom lens. It's a very handy feature. In addition, you may be able to add a supplementary lens that will get you even closer.

Barrel threads

This is a seemingly simple thing—to thread the inside of the lens barrel so that you can screw on filters and supplementary lenses. However, not all cameras (particularly digital ones) have these. For instance, one of my favorite "serious" point-and-shoot digicams, the Kodak DC 260, lacks this feature. The new two-megapixel version of this camera has corrected that oversight, however.

Some digital cameras have lenses that retract into the camera body when powered down. This can mean that a screw-on supplementary lens or filter could interfere with the telescoping mechanism. However, some cameras get around that by letting you use an extension tube. The supplements are screwed onto the tube and the lens is still free to telescope inside the tube.

Lens cover

This seems like too minor an item to even mention, but a scratched lens means the end of optimum image quality for your camera. No lens is easier to scratch or smudge than that on a digital pocket camera. The cameras tend to be so small that it's hard to keep your fingers out of harm's way.

The best lens cover is one that automatically covers the lens when the camera's power is turned off. Then, you never forget to cover the lens before you stick the camera into the pocket that's full of beach sand. Also, check to see that the lens cover is somehow tethered to the camera. If it doesn't come that way, tape a string to the lens cover and tie the other end to the part of the camera where the neck or wrist strap is attached. Then it will be hard to put the camera away without remembering to put the cover back in place. You won't be as likely to lose it, either. Losing the lens cover for a digital camera can be very annoying because the diameter of most of the lenses is so small that you can't easily find a replacement in your local camera store.

If you're shooting with a professional digital camera, you're probably using standard interchangeable lenses that take readily available removable lens caps. If you're shooting on location, put the lens cap into the pocket where you carry your car keys. Then you'll remember to cap the lens before you take off with the camera rattling in the trunk of your car.

Of course, if you can find a source for a spare lens cap, it's a very good idea to get one. You can usually order one from the camera's manufacturer. However, they're rarely in stock, so you may have a long wait. At least they're inexpensive enough that you won't be out a lot of cash in the meantime.

Shutter

If they use one at all, digital cameras use the same two types of shutters as analog cameras: between the lens and focal plane. A between-the-lens shutter has iris-like blades that reside between elements of the lens and open and close to let light in for the specified amount of time. A focal-plane shutter is a slit in a curtain that moves across the image pickup chip's front surface.

Which type of shutter your camera has won't make a whit of difference in most shooting situations. However, leaf shutters open very quickly and stay wide open for their allotted time. This makes it easy to synchronize them with strobe units because their flash duration is usually less than 1/1,000th of a second. Because focal-plane shutters move a slit across the film plane, the chosen shutter speed is only equivalent to how far the slot moves in the allocated time. In other words, it may take 1/100th of a second to make a 1/1,000th of a second exposure because only one-tenth of the photosensitive surface is exposed for that 1/1,000th of a second. As a result, most cameras with a focal-plane shutter have to have the shutter set at 1/60th or even 1/30th of a second in order for the strobe to expose the entire "film plane." Now, that's okay in a studio because the strobe itself will be more than fast enough to freeze any camera shake or subject motion. But it's not so okay if you're shooting outdoors and just want to use the flash to brighten the deep shadows. Why? Because the ambient light is bright enough to make an impression on the film that blurs the image if there is significant camera shade or subject movement.

Note   Most digital camera owners don't need to worry about shutters. That's because their cameras don't have a mechanical shutter. Instead, the length of exposure is determined by the length of time the camera "turns on" the image capture cell. If an actual mechanical shutter exists, it's simply there to protect the image cell from being damaged by light when it's not in use. The biggest drawback to not having a shutter is that there's no "click" when the shutter fires. So, there's no audio cue to tell you when you've captured the exact moment you'd hoped to capture. Some cameras let you turn on an audible beep or click (Kodak's sounds just like a real focal-plane shutter). It's a feature worth having.

Diaphragm

The diaphragm or iris is the mechanism that lets more or less light pass through the lens. When you change the f-stop, the diaphragm opens wider or closes to a smaller diameter. A full f-stop halves or doubles the size of the diaphragm opening, thus allowing half or twice as much light. Each of the following represents a full f-stop: f-3.5, f-5.6, f-8, f-11, f-16, f-22, f-32.

The smallest number is the widest opening, the largest number is the smallest opening. Lens speed (the measure of a lens's ability to gather light) is stated in terms of the largest diaphragm opening of which the lens is capable. So, a really fast lens will have a maximum f-stop of f-2 or even f-1.5.

Very fast lenses cost significantly more than slower ones. If you depend on shooting in low-light situations or your artistic style is distinguished by very shallow depth of field, these lenses are worth their extra cost. Otherwise, they will probably be somewhat less sharp than lenses that have a minimum aperture of f-3.5 or smaller.

Viewfinder

Several types of viewfinders are used on analog cameras. The options are more limited on their digital brethren:

✦ Optical

✦ Reflex

✦ Flat panel (LCD)

Note   If you choose a camera with either an optical or reflex viewfinder and wear glasses or contacts, look for a "diopter adjustment." This is a feature that enables you to focus the image you see to ensure that it is in sharp focus.

Optical

Optical viewfinders are simply lenses in a rectangular housing, offset from the picture-taking lens. Optical viewfinders can be quite accurate at framing the picture, provided the subject is more than 5 feet from the camera. In practice, however, their accuracy varies considerably. It is likely (but not guaranteed) that the more you pay for your optical viewfinder camera, the more accurate its viewfinder is likely to be.

The advantage of optical viewfinders is that they make it easy to frame the subject, even in adverse lighting conditions. Also, cameras with optical viewfinders tend to be quieter than single-lens reflex viewfinders because no mirror or prism has to flip out of the way before the shutter fires. For that reason, photographers who shoot candids, motion picture stills, or in recording studios tend to prefer cameras with optical (or the closely related rangefinder) viewfinders.

Optical viewfinders have noteworthy disadvantages, however. First, because the viewfinder isn't perfectly aligned with the lens, the frame the user sees at close-up distances is offset from the frame viewed by the main camera lens. This phenomenon is called *parallax*. Second, everything in an optical viewfinder, regardless of its distance from the camera, appears to be in sharp focus. This means that there is no preview of depth of field. Finally, you also cannot preview the effect of any filters that are used in front of the lens or see lens flare when it occurs because a bright light is shining directly into the lens. Figure 3-4 is a drawing of the cross-section of an optical viewfinder.

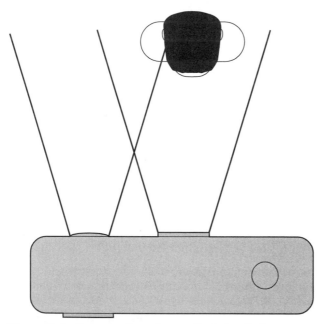

Figure 3-4: Cross-section of an optical viewfinder

Reflex

There are two types of reflex viewfinders: single lens and twin lens. Twin-lens reflexes use two nearly identical camera lenses (and these are rarely interchangeable) — one for previewing the image, the other for taking the picture. The viewing lens projects its image into a separate light-tight section of the camera and onto a mirror, which enables the photographer to see the image upright and reading left to right.

Single-lens reflexes are much more popular and are found in both high-end "serious" (prosumer) point-and-shoot and professional digital cameras. Here, the same lens is used for shooting and viewing. At the instant the shutter is pressed, the mirror flips out of the way so that the light from the lens can pass through to the image pickup area.

The advantage of the single-lens-reflex (SLR — Olympus calls their digital SLRs ZLRs for "zoom lens reflex." It's just sales spin.) is that you see exactly what the film sees. You see exactly the effect of your polarizing filter, exactly your depth of field, and exactly any lens flare that's occurring. The disadvantage is that the cameras are bulkier, noisier, and typically cost about 30 percent more. Figure 3-5 shows the architecture of an SLR.

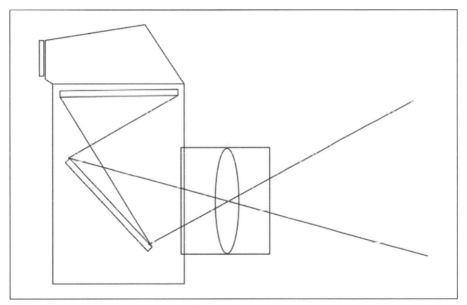

Figure 3-5: Cross-section of a single-lens reflex

Flat panel (LCD)

This type of display is a small version of the type of screen you see on laptop and palmtop computers. Almost all digital cameras these days have one of these, popularly referred to as "LCD (liquid crystal display) panels." Not all of these LCD panels can be used for viewing the image while taking the picture, but it is a feature you should definitely look for if you have a camera with an optical viewfinder — especially if you intend to shoot close-ups. The reason is that these LCDs, like SLRs, see exactly what the lens sees. Unfortunately, the image is too small and too low in resolution to let you accurately check for focus and to let you preview small details.

Also, LCDs tend to wash out when shooting outdoors under any but the most over-cast skies. For that reason, you should look for LCDs that are brighter than normal. Also, before you buy, take a look at the LCD of the camera you want to use while it's in preview mode. Is the refresh rate so slow that any slight camera movement blurs the image beyond recognition? If so, this is not necessarily a fatal flaw. The times you will need to use your LCD as a viewfinder are generally those times when you should mount the camera on a tripod. Most of the time, you should leave the LCD turned off in order to save battery life. Extreme close-ups generally require consis-tent and careful framing. Still, all other things being equal, a faster refresh rate is better.

Flash

Most all point-and-shoot cameras, especially if they're under consideration by seri-ous shooters, have a built-in strobe flash that is powered by the same batteries as the camera. This is a convenient arrangement and keeps down weight and cost. The tradeoff is that batteries get used up quite a bit faster when the strobe is turned on.

Most cameras will present you with several options for controlling the flash. At a minimum, be sure there's a way to turn the flash off. Of course, you could always block it, but if the flash fires when you don't need it to, your battery life will be sig-nificantly shorter. Other desirable options are red-eye elimination, auto (flash fires only when light is insufficient for handheld shooting), and external.

The external option may work in one of two ways: (1) turn off the built-in flash and defer to an external unit; or (2) use the built-in flash to trigger a slave unit in the off-camera flash.

Actually, if you use one of the DigiSlave flash units made by SR Incorporated, as shown in Figure 3-6, you can exercise the second option using any camera that has built-in flash and will let you set the exposure. The reason you need these par-ticular units is because they have built-in sensors that understand the difference between the preflash that many digital cameras use for setting white balance and the brighter flash that occurs at the instant when the shutter fires.

If you want to use professional studio strobes with a semipro digicam, you need to choose a unit that turns off the internal unit and defers to the external unit. All of the cameras that do this will work with standard external strobe units.

All professional cameras synchronize with standard external strobe units, either through a hot-shoe connection, a standard synchronization post, or both.

You can see how external flash is applied to some common shooting situations in Chapter 14.

Figure 3-6: A DigiSlave flash unit. This unit can also be used with conventional cameras and will work with cameras that have hot-shoe or external flash connectors.

Flat-panel display (LCD)

Flat-panel displays are used by almost all 35mm and smaller digicams for reviewing the pictures you've already taken. As noted above, some also use the LCD as the viewfinder or as an alternative viewfinder.

The quality of the preview you see on the LCD panel will determine how accurately you can judge whether to keep a picture you've shot and whether or not you need to reshoot.

Pay attention to the size, resolution, and brightness of the LCD panel. A larger panel not only gives you a bigger preview of your images, but there is more room to display the choices on camera control menus. Higher resolution makes it easier for you to judge sharpness and detail. Brightness is important if you want to be able to see images while working outdoors during the day. A few can even be viewed by either backlight or reflected light. Such panels are a major bonus because backlighting makes them easy to see in dim light. When you're outdoors in bright light, you can see the image just as well or better by placing the panel in reflected mode. Pray for the day when all the LCD panels work this way.

Take a look at Figure 3-7. One very useful digicam feature is an LCD that can be used as a viewfinder and that swivels. This makes it possible to take candids by shooting around a corner, or to shoot over a crowd by holding the camera overhead (see Figure 3-8).

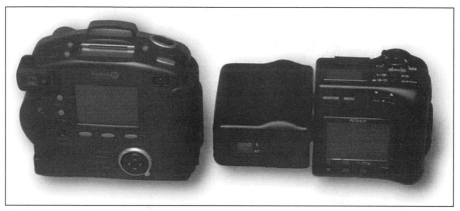

Figure 3-7: The camera on the right has a large, swiveling LCD; the other is a small stationary LCD.

Figure 3-8: Shooting over a crowd with a Nikon 900S

Controls

The way you operate the controls on most under-$3,000 digital cameras is much different than the way you would operate the controls on an analog camera. Of course, if you're working with a professional camera it is probably a modified version of an analog camera, so controls such as the focusing ring, shutter speed dial, and aperture settings will be exactly the same. On a "pure" digital camera, however, many of the controls can be chosen from a menu on an LCD screen. Sometimes this is the main LCD, sometimes it's an auxiliary LCD meant entirely for displaying control menus. Most often, it's a combination of both.

In addition to those controls already mentioned, the following is a list of the controls, options, and features most worth looking for:

- ✦ Lock focus
- ✦ Lock exposure
- ✦ Digital zoom
- ✦ Self-timer
- ✦ Spot meter
- ✦ Center-weighted metering
- ✦ Burst mode
- ✦ Time-lapse mode

- ✦ Voice recording
- ✦ Slide show
- ✦ Album
- ✦ Video out
- ✦ LCD preview
- ✦ External flash
- ✦ Camera-to-camera IRD
- ✦ White balance

Lock focus

We already discussed the convenience of having the ability to freeze focus at the distance of a given target by partially depressing the shutter button. It is also very handy to be able to permanently lock focus so that you can shoot a series of pictures as the camera is rotated. You will then be able to use software to join all the images together into a continuous panorama or QuickTime VR movie for the Web. (If you need to know about QuickTime VR and other digital panoramas, see Chapter 18.)

If you can make focusing entirely manual, focus will stay locked until you manually focus again. Locking focus then becomes a superfluous feature.

Lock exposure

If there is no option to set aperture and shutter speed independent of one another, it is good to be able to lock exposure so that it doesn't change as you rotate the camera for a panorama. You may think that you don't want to shoot panoramas anyway, but once you've tried it, you'll likely change your mind.

Digital zoom

This is a totally useless feature. The camera's firmware simply resamples a small portion of the image to fill the entire frame. You lose the additional detail that you would see if you optically viewed a narrower angle. Adobe Photoshop and most other "digital darkroom" programs will let you crop and enlarge a portion of your image, and you will have achieved the same mushy-looking result. In fact, the Photoshop result will probably look better because its resampling code is "smarter."

Self-timer

This feature delays the firing of the shutter for a specified amount of time after the shutter button is fully depressed. The original idea of a self-timer was to give you time to run in front of the camera to join your friends in a group shot. However, because most digicams (even those of the semipro variety) seldom provide a shutter release cable, a self-timer will ensure that the tripod-mounted camera stays still during a long exposure (because your hands aren't touching the camera body). Without this feature, you won't be able to get steady shots in lighting that requires shutter speeds of 1/30th second or longer.

Spot meter

There are times when you want to be able to measure the light that is reflected from only one small area of the scene to be photographed. For instance, you may want to expose for the flesh tones in a face that is strongly backlit or for the highlights in a snowscape. Some cameras will let you meter only a very small area in the center of the viewfinder. When the camera is in spot metering mode, a small circle will appear in the viewfinder (see Figure 3-9) or on the LCD to indicate the exact size and location of the area being metered.

Figure 3-9: A spot meter circle inside an SLR viewfinder

Burst mode

Some of the most recent models of semipro digicams will enable you to automatically shoot several frames in rapid succession. This enables you to capture a motion sequence like that seen in Figure 3-10. Motion sequences are useful for studying motion, such as a golf swing or a runner's gait. If the camera is placed on a tripod during shooting, a motion sequence can also be used to make an animation for use on a Web page or multimedia presentation. You will find a tutorial on how to do this in Chapter 26.

Figure 3-10: A motion sequence shot in burst mode

Time-lapse mode

A time-lapse mode is one that lets a specified amount of time pass between shots. You place the camera on a tripod (or other rigid mount) and it automatically fires a new frame at the end of each preset interval. It is useful for studying the changes in a subject over an extended period of time (see Figure 3-11). For instance, weather men often use this technique to show changes in cloud cover during the course of a day. It is also often used to show the blossoming of a flower or the metamorphosis of a butterfly.

Voice recording

Some cameras will let you record voice annotations for any of the photos as (or immediately after) they are taken.

Slide show

This enables you to view each photo you've recorded in sequence and at a regular time interval. Most cameras that have this feature will enable you to set the interval. A slide show review feature is especially nice if your camera has a video-out feature as well. Then, you can have the camera automatically "play" the pictures in front of a group audience.

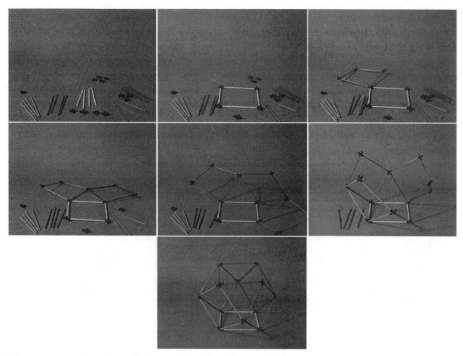

Figure 3-11: A series of photos in a time-lapse sequence

Album

It is very handy to be able to create multiple albums, directories, or folders (the terminology used varies from camera to camera, but the effect is the same) on a single memory card. This ability makes it easy to group photos by subject or by the time they were shot. It also makes it easy to transfer the images on the card to a folder on your computer's hard drive where other files already exist. It's easier because you don't have to rename the files already on the hard drive in order to keep them from being overwritten by new files that may have the same name. You see, most cameras name their files by sequential numbers that start all over again each time you erase the card so that you can record new pictures.

Video out

If your camera can be connected to a TV set, you can show the images to a group of people before deciding which images to keep and which to discard. Or, you can just use the capability for doing instant slide shows. You could also record the slide show onto videotape, which could then be sent to another location. Don't expect great image quality from video. The maximum resolution you're likely to see on a TV set is about 320 × 240 pixels, and resolution and definition both drop on videotape.

Scripting

Some cameras, such as the Kodak DC260, make it possible to program the camera for certain picture-taking situations. For example, a "sports" script might automatically choose a 1/1,000-second shutter speed in order to freeze action and then let the camera automatically choose the correct aperture for the brightness of the ambient light.

White balance

Many shooting conditions tend to affect the overall interpretation of color as your camera sees it — for instance: sunrise, sunset, indoor lighting, and scenes in which significant amounts of the lighting are filtered through or bounced off of colored surfaces.

Most digicams set white balance automatically, but some will let you choose settings for white balance (typically: Daylight, Fluorescent, Tungsten, and Off). The Off setting is particularly valuable if you are shooting a scene that is mostly one color. If the camera is automatically balancing for any of the other settings, it will balance according to the fact that it overwhelmingly sees one color and, therefore, wants to balance accordingly. You will get a color that looks nothing like the original.

If there is no Off setting and you are faced with a scene that is mostly one color that you want to record faithfully, the next best thing is to at least set white balance for the type of lighting that actually exists. In other words, set the camera so that it is forced to balance for tungsten lighting if you are shooting indoors (and don't have daylight fluorescent or halogen bulbs — their light is closer to the color of daylight).

If your camera has settings for fluorescent and halogen or, better yet, lets you pick the color temperature (always expressed in degrees Kelvin) against which you want to balance, and then you're truly lucky.

Of course, new controls are being invented every moment, so consider this just a basic guide. Many of the latest cameras are programmable, making it possible to develop special-purpose settings and special effects even after you have purchased the unit.

Resolution and bit depth

All other things being equal, more resolution is always better. Why? Because you can't put detail into an image that wasn't recorded when you took the picture. If you're shopping for a semipro camera, look for a stated resolution of at least two megapixels. Three-megapixel cameras are becoming commonplace, so if you can find the features you want at that resolution, by all means go for a three-megapixel camera.

However, resolution isn't the only factor influencing image quality. It is also desirable if the camera captures at a bit depth greater than 24 bits, especially if you can save the image at that higher bit depth. It is also a blessing if you have the choice of being able to save the file as uncompressed (see "Image quality settings," next). If the camera does have an "uncompressed" shooting mode, chances are the file is actually compressed in LZW Tiff format, which typically reduces file size by around 50 percent without any compromise in image quality. This is called "lossless compression."

Image quality settings

Any digital camera you'd care to have enables you to save your shots in a compressed JPEG format that also includes a thumbnail. JPEG compresses images by considering that pixels that are "nearly alike" are alike. The more difference you allow between pixels before the compressor considers them alike, the greater the image compression — and the more the quality of your images degrades. Compression engines that cause some degree of image degradation are called "lossy." JPEG compression is lossy.

Most cameras will give you a choice of "quality" settings — in other words, you can choose just how lossy the compression will be. Sometimes you can pick the quality by moving a slider. More often, you're given a multiple choice, such as: Good (which really means crummy), Better (you'll have to look for the difference between it and best, but could really tell the difference between it and an uncompressed image), and Best. Best is often so good that you would swear that you'd never lost a thing.

Never, never, never open a JPEG file and then issue the File ⇨ Save command!!! Every time you do this, the program recompresses the image (it doesn't matter whether you've made any changes since opening) and you lose the same amount of data you lost the first time you compressed it. Do this two or three times and you're guaranteed an image that will make you nauseous. Instead, always either close the file without saving (which works if you're just previewing) or use the Save As command to save it in a lossless format.

The best thing is to be given an option to save without any compression. In truth, most cameras that provide that option (which includes all professional cameras) save the file to TIFF format, using LZW TIFF compression. LZW TIFF (Tagged Image File Format) typically cuts file size in half and is a lossless compressor. Once you've expanded the file, there is no difference between it and the original uncompressed file. Because it is a cross-platform image file format that will retain alpha-channel information (masks), TIFF is also the best format into which you should save JPEG files once you've opened them.

Image capture device

The light-sensitive mechanism in a digital camera is a solid-state device that's manufactured in much the same way as your computer's processor or memory chips.

When it comes to image capture devices, bigger is better for the following reasons:

✦ The chip is closer to the size of conventional film, so there won't be such a disparity between the actual focal length of the lens and its equivalent analog camera focal length.

✦ There's room for more light-sensing units, so resolution is potentially higher.

✦ Light-sensing units are farther apart, so there's less likelihood of *blooming*. Blooming is the bleeding of colors that can occur when adjacent pixels sense and record a color that should have been limited to its neighbor. Blooming is one of the most significant differences one sees in image quality between images recorded by professional and semiprofessional cameras.

There are two types of image capture devices commonly used by digital cameras: CCD (charge coupled device) and CMOS (complementary metal oxide semiconductor). The most common of these is CCD, which has been around for some time — having been invented as an image sensor for video cameras more than a decade ago. CCDs have some advantages. For one thing, they're tiny, so they can be placed in tiny cameras (as explained above, that's also a disadvantage). CCDs tend to be highly sensitive to low light, although sensitivity seems to go down as image quality goes up and still-camera CCDs tend to be far less light sensitive than their video camera cousins (because the result is higher image quality). CDDs also respond smoothly to varying light levels. On the downside, CCDs crowd pixels too closely together, use way too much power, and can't be used to store programming instructions. The one advantage that CCD chips currently offer that can't be outweighed yet is manufacturing quality. Manufacturers have simply had more experience with this type of chip and have become really proficient at making them.

CMOS, the newer technology, has some great potential advantages, and there are some manufacturers who claim that their products have reached the point where quality is at or near its potential. This potential includes a larger light-sensitive area with less pixel crowding, lower cost of manufacture (eventually), and a higher level of integration with other chip functions so that features can be programmed onto the sensor chip. Also, fewer support chips are needed, which could lower the overall cost of making the camera.

If you're faced with choosing between the two technologies, compare the CCD picture with a picture of the same subject (taken with a tripod) taken with a highly respected CMOS-equipped camera of the same resolution. If you don't have the opportunity to do the testing yourself, check out the computer and digital photography magazines that review the latest equipment.

Batteries

Most semipro and pocket cameras use standard AA batteries and/or some variety of rechargeable AA batteries. Not all cameras can take advantage of lithium AA batteries, but those that do have a power source that lasts up to four times longer. Unfortunately, rechargeable lithium batteries had not come to market at the time of this writing. Most digicams use four batteries. A few cameras use two sets of batteries: one for the flash and LCD, the other for the camera. Though it adds a bit of weight, this is an excellent option because you can replace or recharge the flash/LCD batteries separately. Also, when those batteries die, the batteries that take the pictures live on. That gives you the option of still being able to shoot by available light.

Most professional cameras have custom NiCad (nickel cadmium) or NiMH (nickel metal hydride) battery packs that are similar to those used in digital camcorders. It is always a good idea to buy a spare set of batteries (or two, if you're going to be away from your charger for a long time).

Given the choice, use a NiMH rechargeable battery. Unlike NiCads, these batteries can be recharged at any time without shortening their overall lifespan. NiCads "think" that their charging capacity is only as great as the amount of battery power you used before recharging. So you must take the time to discharge them fully before recharging. Unfortunately, not all cameras that can use NiCad rechargeables can use NiMH batteries. Most can, but check with the camera's manufacturer if you want to be sure.

Computer connections

It's very important that you be able to move your pictures from camera to computer in as quick and convenient a manner as possible. The routes by which pictures get from camera to computer can be divided into price ranges or categories of digital cameras because of the types of memory each uses:

✦ Pocket and semipro cameras

✦ Professional field cameras

✦ Professional studio cameras

✦ Video cameras

Pocket and semipro cameras

Pocket and semipro cameras, (with a few exceptions, noted below) use solid-state memory devices such as Compact Flash, SmartMedia, or Sony's new Memory Stick. These devices can all be removed from the camera and placed into a reader that behaves as an external device or into an adapter that fits into an existing standard PCMCIA slot or floppy disk drive.

Virtually all of these cameras will attach to either a Mac or a PC through a standard serial port. It works, if you have patience. However, it typically takes half an hour to download an 8MB memory card. Remember, some of the newest cards are 64- and even 96MB capacities. Imagine how long that takes to download through a serial port!

Adapters are the fastest way to transfer images, and PCMCIA adapters lead that race. Put your Compact Flash memory card into a PCMCIA adapter, slide that into a slot on your laptop, and the CF card is immediately recognized as a standard drive. You can then rename the files if you like, or simply select them and drag them into a folder on your hard drive—time elapsed: somewhere between a few seconds and a couple of minutes. A PCMCIA adapter (shown below) will fit directly into any standard Type 1 slot on either a Mac or Windows laptop computer. You can also purchase PCMCIA adapters that will fit into a floppy drive space or attach to the computer via a USB or parallel port (see "Ports," later in this chapter) and these transfer images every bit as quickly as they transfer to a laptop. If none of these works for you, you can get PCMCIA adapters that attach through the parallel or USB ports. If your camera uses Compact Flash, PCMCIA adapters are also a good choice because PCMCIA cards are used in most 35mm professional field cameras. Figure 3-12 shows a PCMCIA adapter for a Compact Flash card.

Figure 3-12: A PCMCIA adapter for a Compact Flash card

A close second-best alternative for quick downloads is card readers. Card readers look like a mouse with a mouth, the mouth being the slot into which you place the memory card (see Figure 3-13). These cost less than PCMCIA drives for desktop computers (but not less than the adapter card) and there are models from most manufacturers that read both SmartMedia and Compact Flash. These are great if you have a field staff (realtors, insurance adjusters, or people who contribute to your company newsletter, for instance) equipped with cameras from various manufacturers. Figure 3-13 shows several different card reader connections. Also, if you decide later to buy a different make of camera, there's a better chance that you won't also have to buy a different kind of card reader.

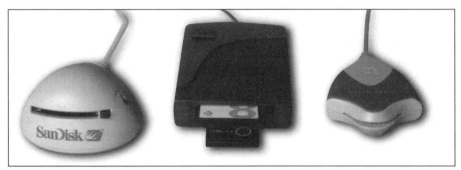

Figure 3-13: Some card readers, each with a different connection

So far, no one offers a "universal" card reader that includes the ability to read Sony's Memory Stick.

If your camera uses SmartMedia cards (see Figure 3-14), you can buy a floppy disk adapter that will fit into almost every computer on the planet (but not with external parallel port drives or with Imation Super Floppy drives). They don't transfer files quite as quickly as a card adapter, but are way faster than through a serial cable. To use them, you simply slip your SmartMedia card into something that looks for all the world like a 3.5-inch floppy. You then insert that into your floppy drive and your operating system recognizes the disk and its contents — just as if it were a real floppy. The difference is that SmartMedia cards can hold up to 32MB of information (at this writing), versus 1.4MB for a double-density floppy.

Figure 3-14: Floppy disk adapter for a SmartMedia card

Ports

There are three types of ports commonly used for connecting semipro digital cameras or adapters to the computer: serial, parallel, and USB (universal serial bus). A fourth type of port is widely used for transferring images and footage from digital video cameras: IEEE 1394 (also known as FireWire or i.LINK) is fast gaining in popularity. SCSI ports are also used for connecting very high resolution professional studio cameras. Each has its advantages and disadvantages:

✦ **Parallel ports** transfer data much faster than a common serial port, can be made to pass data through to a printer, and are found on virtually all Windows laptops and desktop computers. Unfortunately, they are never found on Macs. Furthermore, parallel port connectors and cables are too large to attach to cameras and so are limited to use with card readers. On the downside, there is rarely more than one parallel port on a printer and the max you can have is four. Most parallel port peripherals, however, can be placed inline with a printer without interfering with the operation of either device. You can also attach multiple devices to a switch box, and then connect the switch box to the computer.

✦ **Serial ports** can be found on both Macs and PCs, whether desktop or laptop, and can be used by the same devices. For that reason, serial port connections are provided for almost all semipro and pocket digital cameras. Unfortunately, serial ports transfer data about ten times slower than parallel ports. Most computers are limited to one or two external serial ports and serial devices must each be assigned a specific code, called an IRQ address. For now, all you need to know about IRQ addresses is that it can be a pain to find addresses that don't conflict with one another.

Note
The serial connector for PCs is a different shape than that for Macintosh's, so some serial devices will require an adapter cable for use with a Mac.

✦ **USB ports** have many attractive qualities. First, they can (theoretically) support as many as 64 different devices attached to a single port. Second, the instant you plug in a new device, the computer recognizes and autoconfigures itself for it (provided, of course, that the software driver for that device has been installed on your computer). Third, you can plug in and unplug devices while they are running and while the computer is turned on. Fourth, USB is several times faster than parallel and will also make your scanners into speedier performers. USB cables are lightweight and inexpensive. Camera manufacturers are quickly picking up on the attractive qualities of USB, and you will see more and more USB-equipped cameras as time goes by. USB has just become standard equipment on computers since the introduction of G3-powered Macintoshes and Windows 98/Pentium II-powered PCs. However, all PCI-bus Macs and Wintel desktop computers can be adapted to USB.

✦ **FireWire** is several times faster than even USB. FireWire is the name most commonly used to refer to computer connections that subscribe to the IEEE 1394 interface standard. Sony Corporation calls the same protocol and connectors i.Link, and several Japanese electronics makers have also adapted that name. FireWire has much in common with USB. The connectors are small enough to be incorporated into small cameras and the cables are lightweight and easy to manage. There are no IRQ addresses to worry about, and FireWire devices are instantly recognized by their host computer. If you are transferring video from a digital camcorder, FireWire is the only protocol fast enough to enable you to do that in real time.

✦ **SCSI** (Small Computer Systems Interface) is the only established (read "old-fashioned") port protocol that is fast enough for transferring the 10–100MB files typical of professional studio cameras. In fact, the fastest versions of SCSI are even marginally faster than FireWire (so far). Because SCSI has been around for a while, it is the port generally used for that class of camera. Hopefully, we'll see studio cameras migrating to FireWire, because SCSI cables are bulky, have connectors that follow several form factors, and are highly prone to addressing conflicts.

Tripod thread

If you ever need to run in front of the camera for a self-portrait or want to make sure that it's rock steady while you shoot a close-up, scenic, or night scene, you're going to need a camera that has a tripod thread. Fortunately, most do regardless of price, so you can pass on those that don't. However, make sure those threads are metal and not plastic. If you overtighten the tripod mount, plastic ones are liable to strip out and you may even crack the camera body. Once you have a light leak, you have a dead camera.

Summary

This chapter has discussed the meaning of all the terms and features most commonly encountered when purchasing a digital camera. It can't cover every possible feature, because some features may be available at the time you read this that hadn't been invented when the book was written. However, these basics should stand you in good stead for years to come.

✦   ✦   ✦

The Essentials of the Digital Studio

The first section of this chapter deals with the types of equipment you can use to capture a digital image — or to capture an image that will be converted to digital by scanning. We then move on to the different means of keeping the camera steady, utilizing different types of lighting, and how to best utilize the exposure meters built into a camera to get the correct exposure. We also take a brief look at the advantages of separate, handheld exposure meters.

Cameras

Digital images can be created either from conventional photographs by scanning or by taking the picture with a digital camera or digital camera back. What we're doing here is giving you an overview of cameras that are typically used in particular shooting situations or to solve problems commonly encountered in digital photography. If you already are familiar with a camera and have no immediate need to switch, you may want to skip this section. However, this section will introduce classes of cameras that will be discussed later in the book. It is a good idea to familiarize yourself with these types of cameras so that you truly understand the range of choices that are available to you.

Digital

Digital cameras, by this book's definition, include any device that makes an image that can be directly opened by an image-processing application on a computer. Some of these "cameras," especially at the higher end of the price scale, are really digital backs for conventional cameras.

Note that not all cameras capable of capturing digital stills are still cameras. Both the cameras made for online conferencing and (particularly) digital video cameras can be very useful for shooting stills in certain digital imaging situations.

Digital cameras range in price from under $100 for a conferencing camera that is tethered to a host computer to just under $40,000 for a back (yes, you still have to buy the camera and lenses) that attaches to a studio camera. There is a full range of choices in between, too. So it's a good idea to understand whether the camera you are willing to pay the price for can do the job(s) you want to do.

Conferencing (PC) cameras

Conferencing cameras (see Figure 4-1) are often called PC cameras because they have to be attached directly to a computer in order to do anything at all. Another popular nickname for them is *Webcam*. These cameras usually cost less than $300 (and it's not uncommon these days to find them for under $60). Most have a color image sensor and a lens equivalency of about 50mm (normal) or about the same optical quality as a disposable camera lens. Since there's no need for batteries, an LCD screen, a viewfinder (you use the computer's monitor) or internal memory, Webcams are petite. Because they are on a cable, they can be pointed in almost any direction. Because these cameras are intended to capture motion, they are generally connected to a video capture card. USB is also becoming a popular connection. FireWire would be even better, but FireWire is still a more expensive option for most computers. If your Webcam operates through a video capture card or FireWire connection, you could use the same interface to support a video camera.

Figure 4-1: A conferencing camera

The most common use for conferencing cameras is videoconferencing—either via the Internet or in intracompany applications. If you already use one of these cameras for conferencing, you can put them to use for digital imaging. Applications for which they are particularly well suited are as follows:

✦ Identification portraits

✦ Insurance and inventory recordkeeping

✦ Shooting small objects to be shown on Web pages

✦ Copying flat artwork for use on Web pages

The chief limitations of conferencing cameras are as follows:

✦ Subject and camera must be kept steady for sharp stills

✦ Mediocre optics (typically)

✦ No ability to adjust viewing angle of lens (for example, no zoom capability)

✦ Most are fixed focus

✦ Low resolution (typically 640 × 480 or less)

✦ Dependent on being able to see computer monitor in order to preview the image

Some of the most popular conferencing cameras are as follows:

✦ **Kodak DVC 323:** Eastman Kodak Company, < $170, www.kodak.com

✦ **Connectix QuickCam VC:** Logitech Corp., < $130, www.connectix.com

✦ **Intel Create & Share Camera Pack:** Intel Corp., < $200 www.intel.com

✦ **Panasonic Eggcam:** Panasonic Corp., < $200, www.panasonic.com

✦ **Tekram On Camera:** Tekram, < $225, www.tekram.com

✦ **Vista Imaging ViCam:** Vista Imaging Inc., < $200, www.vistaimaging.com

✦ **Winnov Videum Conference Pro:** Winnov, < $360, www.winnov.com

Point-and-shoot

Point-and-shoot cameras (see Figure 4-2), as categorized in this book, are those cameras whose features are most basic and inexpensive. I often refer to these cameras as pocket cameras because they so easily fit into your pocket (as do at least two or three prosumer cameras). These cameras generally cost less than $600, and more and more are becoming available at under $300. Resolution for cameras in this category once topped out at 640 × 480 pixels, but a decent 1,024 × 768 is becoming more typical and higher resolutions are becoming more commonplace. Viewfinders are of the optical variety. Zoom lenses are rare—most point-and-shoot digicams have a single focal-length lens and some have a digital zoom. (You can crop and enlarge in your image editor and achieve the same or better result, so don't pay extra for this feature.) Other features will vary quite a bit, but you can rest assured that you'll find a wider variety of features on more expensive cameras. You're also likely to find much better optics.

Figure 4-2: A typical point-and-shoot camera

 Caution   If a camera manufacturer doesn't state the camera's *optical* resolution, they're probably trying to put one over on you by giving you the resolution achieved by artificially duplicating pixels. The process is called interpolation and can actually detract from the quality of the image you would have gotten.

Applications for which point-and-shoot digicams are most appropriate are as follows:

✦ Family and vacation snapshots

✦ Panorama-stitched images for use on the Web or in multimedia (see Chapter 18)

✦ Photos for use on Web sites

✦ Insurance recordkeeping

✦ Insurance adjusting

✦ Illustrating a database

- ✦ Personnel and membership records
- ✦ Real estate sales
- ✦ Field reporting (such as location scouting, off-site plant conditions, construction estimates)

The chief limitations of point-and-shoot cameras are as follows:

- ✦ Inability to compensate for special lighting conditions
- ✦ Tend to use wide-angle lenses that cause feature distortions in close-ups (particularly portraits)
- ✦ Not suited to applications that demand pro picture quality
- ✦ Don't get no respect

Some of the best-known examples of point-and-shoot digicams are as follows:

- ✦ **Agfa ePhoto 780:** Agfa, < $399, www.agfahome.com/ephoto
- ✦ **Canon PowerShot 350:** Canon Computer Systems Inc., < $299, www.ccsi.canon.com
- ✦ **Casio QV-200:** Casio Inc., > $300, www.casio.com
- ✦ **Casio QV-700:** Casio Inc., > $400, www.casio.com
- ✦ **Casio QV-770:** Casio Inc., > $400, www.casio.com
- ✦ **Epson PhotoPC 550:** Epson America Inc., < $199, www.epson.com
- ✦ **Fuji DX-7:** Fuji Photo Film U.S.A. Inc., < $499, www.fujifilm.com
- ✦ **HP PhotoSmart C20 Digital Camera:** Hewlett-Packard Co., $400, www.hp.com
- ✦ **Kodak DC120:** Eastman Kodak Co., < $500, www.kodak.com
- ✦ **Kodak DC200:** Eastman Kodak Co., < $400, www.kodak.com
- ✦ **Minolta Dimâge V:** Minolta Corp., < $400, www.minoltausa.com
- ✦ **Olympus D-220L:** Olympus America Inc., > $300, URL: www.olympus.com
- ✦ **Olympus D-320L:** Olympus America Inc., > $400, URL: www.olympus.com
- ✦ **Philips ESP60:** Philips, > $400, www.digitalcamera.philips.com
- ✦ **Ricoh RDC-300Z:** Ricoh Corp., < $400, www.ricohcpg.com
- ✦ **Ricoh RDC-4200:** Ricoh Corp., < $500, www.ricohcpg.com
- ✦ **Toshiba PDR-5:** Toshiba America Inc., < $400, www.toshiba.com/taisisd
- ✦ **Vivitar ViviCam 2700:** Vivitar Corp., < $300, www.vivitar.com

Note   Prices, especially in this category of digital cameras, were falling rapidly as we went to press and will probably be significantly lower by the time you read this.

Prosumer

Prosumer cameras (see Figure 4-3) are the ones that most readers of this book are most likely to find both affordable and useful. I say that because I assume that you spent half a hundred bucks for a big, fat book on digital photography because you were serious about it. So you're likely to want as much of the functionality of a professional camera as you can get. At the same time, the price has to be attainable. I hesitate to say "affordable." Disposable cameras that sell for $7.95 are affordable.

Figure 4-3: A pair of prosumer cameras, the Nikon 950 and the Olympus C-2000

These cameras bridge the very wide gap between point-and-shoot cameras and professional cameras that cost over $6,000. The price range where you're likely to get the most versatility and picture quality for your money is in the range between $800 and $2,000.

Besides price, there are four main areas of difference between prosumer cameras and professional cameras: lens interchangeability, picture quality, complete manual control over focus and exposure, and bulk. Professional cameras are all able to use the full spectrum of lenses made for a similar type or family of film cameras. For instance, many of the Kodak and Nikon professional field cameras are based on Nikon's field cameras and can use most of the lenses made for their 35mm cousins. They can also use almost all of the accessories that their film camera siblings can. For a digital camera to even approach a professional level, it must at least have a variable focal-length (zoom) lens that covers the most popular focal lengths of lenses used on film cameras. The most popular 35mm film camera focal lengths are 28mm, 50mm, and 90mm. Prosumer digital camera optical zooms are more likely to cover a 35–105mm range. The fact that the picture resolution of most prosumer digicams (768–1,300 pixels per inch if enlarged to fill a 35mm frame) is much lower than that of film (2,700–4,000 ppi) means more picture quality must be sacrificed if the picture needs cropping.

It would not be unreasonable to expect a picture resolution in the neighborhood of 1,600 × 1,300 pixels (approximately two megapixels) in a state-of-the-art prosumer camera. That's enough resolution to give you an 11 × 14-inch print that looks pretty reasonable. If the edges and details can be slightly soft, that's plenty of resolution for many professional applications (such as glamour portraiture), but not nearly enough for some others (such as architectural or food photography). On the other hand, if you're shooting for an in-house catalog or newsletter, then your images never need to look truly photographic at sizes larger than 4 × 6 inches. In that case, you could get away with 1,024 × 768 resolution.

Prosumer cameras must give you some means of manually controlling exposure so that you can adapt to special conditions such as night photography, backlighting (the main light — usually the sun — is pointed toward the camera), and superhigh-contrast subjects. You also want to be able to use exposures that will properly interpret subjects that are mostly lighter (a field of white flowers) or darker (a black cat in a coal bin) than normal.

Any means of making the image lighter or darker than normal is useful. The most basic lets you alter the exposure over a range of exposure values (EVs). It's much more useful to be able to do the same while specifying a specific aperture or shutter speed. This will be the case if your camera features aperture priority and shutter priority modes. Specifying aperture priority allows control over depth of focus because you can pick a specific aperture setting while the camera automatically chooses the shutter speed. Shutter priority allows you to stop or blur motion by choosing a specific shutter speed while the camera automatically picks the f-stop.

It is becoming more and more commonplace for prosumer digital cameras (as has been the case for some time for professional film cameras) to offer preprogrammed exposure settings based on lighting that is typical given certain conditions or settings. It works like this: You choose from a list of preprogrammed "modes" — for example: snow, sunset, backlight, or sports. The program then factors the exposure indicated by the camera's meter and adjusts aperture and shutter speed to benefit the situation. You may say that real professional photographers understand how to make these changes instinctively, but even professionals like to save time — especially when shooting conditions may not give them time to make calculations.

Finally, the very best cameras will also give you the option to set any specific shutter speed and aperture combination you choose. Only then will you have complete freedom of expression. You will also then be able to make use of an external exposure meter.

If you are limited to using the built-in exposure meter, some cameras will give you options as to how it is used. At a minimum, you should be able to specify center-weighted metering and be able to lock exposure by partially depressing the shutter button. A spot meter mode is even better. Matrix metering (see Figure 4-4) is even better. Matrix metering allows you to give preference to the image that's in certain (and not necessarily contiguous) portions of the viewfinder. Nikon cameras have a reputation for excellent matrix metering in those cameras (such as the 950S) that offer the feature.

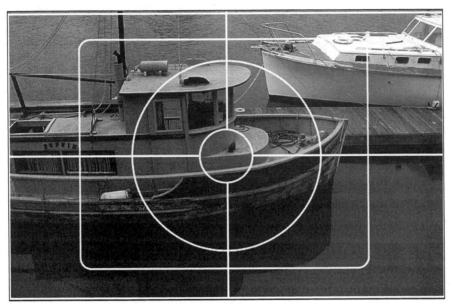

Figure 4-4: A simple matrix metering diagram. Each area is independently metered.

External flash capabilities are found in only a few of these cameras, but it is becoming more popular for very good reason: The lighting that results from on-camera or built-in flash (unless used strictly to fill shadows) is just plain ugly. If you can synch with external flash, you can use bounce lighting, lighting that comes from a more natural direction, and even multiple light sources. More importantly, without external flash, you can't use studio strobe lights — the mainstay of most serious studio photography. Figure 4-5 shows the results of using three flash exposure methods.

Figure 4-5: Direct flash, off-camera flash, bounce flash

Viewfinders in prosumer cameras take one of three forms: Optical, SLR, or LCD. For details on the strengths and weaknesses of various types of viewfinders, see Chapter 3. Here are some of the most popular prosumer cameras:

✦ **Kodak DC260:** Eastman Kodak, > $900

✦ **Kodak DC120:** Eastman Kodak, > $500

✦ **Olympus D-500-L:** Olympus, < $600 if you can find it

✦ **Olympus D-600-L:** Olympus, < $800

✦ **Olympus D-620-L:** Olympus, <$1,200

✦ **Olympus D-400-Z:** Olympus, < $800,

✦ **Olympus D-2500:** Olympus, < $1,500

✦ **Olympus c-2020:** Olympus, < $700

✦ **Olympus C-3030:** Olympus, < $1,000

✦ **Nikon Coolpix 950S:** Nikon USA, Inc., < $1,000

✦ **Fujix FinePix 4700 zoom:** Fujifilm, < $1,000

✦ **Fujix FinePix S1 Pro:** Fujifilm, < $4,000

✦ **Canon PowerShot 70:** Canon USA, Inc., < $1,000

Canon S-20: Canon USA, Inc., < $1,000

✦ **Sony Cyber-shot DSC-F505:** Sony Corp., < $1,000

Applications for which prosumer cameras are well suited are as follows:

✦ Preshoot testing and client approval

✦ Location scouting

✦ Editorial photography

✦ Low-end catalog work

✦ Serious hobby

✦ Basis for digitally manipulated fine art and commercial art

Limitations of prosumer cameras include the following:

✦ Not a replacement for medium- and large-format cameras

✦ Typically not rugged enough for shooting under adverse conditions (wars, bad weather)

✦ Unable to use professional film camera accessories

Professional

Professional digital cameras generally cost more than $4,000, and a few even cost more than $40,000. Professional camera resolution starts where prosumer cameras leave off and moves up to exceed that of even large-format film. However, even where resolution is the same, picture quality can be significantly higher. This is due to several factors: greater pixel depth (30–48 bit), a larger image sensor (which results in less color blooming), better lenses, and little or no lossless image compression. All but a handful of professional cameras are built on or attach to conventional film camera bodies. Professional cameras based on 35mm camera chassis are generally intended for field use, such as magazine and newspaper reportage. Field cameras are as portable as their film camera counterparts — though their bodies tend to be a bit bulkier.

Professional cameras meant primarily for studio use are generally attached in place of the film backs on medium- and large-format film cameras. These fall into three categories, each described in detail in Chapter 2.

Video

It is possible to capture still images from virtually any video source. You will get a better-quality image if you capture the image directly from the camera's output — or at least from the original videotape. Most captured video is of truly crummy quality when compared to the output of even the poorest-quality currently pro-duced digital still cameras. There are, however, certain models of consumer/ prosumer digital video cameras that are exceptions. Although you're still limited to VGA (640 × 480) maximum resolution, some mini-DV format cameras use higher-than-normal shutter speeds and progressive video scanning to produce an image of the quality of 640 × 480-resolution still cameras. Progressive scanning means that the image is recorded from top to bottom in one complete pass, rather than recording the odd lines in one pass and then interlacing the even lines in the next pass (the traditional method for recording video images). Interlaced scanning means that the subject or the camera is likely to move between the odd and even scans, resulting in a fuzzy image. Choosing a model with good optics and accurate and responsive auto focusing is also important. The Canon Optura (see Figure 4-6) pioneered progressive scanning for the mini-DV. The Optura also has external flash synchronization and can capture high shutter speed stop-action stills at a full 30 frames per second.

There are several advantages to using a video camera as your digital camera, especially if you can get by with VGA resolution:

✦ Typically 12× optical zoom.

✦ Extremely light sensitive. Excellent for low-light candids and night shots.

✦ Your investment serves two purposes: stills and video.

✦ Superb image quality and shooting versatility for Web-destined photos.

Figure 4-6: The Canon Optura

Note   Makers of mini-DV camcorders are just beginning to introduce models that can shoot stills at resolutions in the megapixel range. For many, this makes them a more versatile choice than either a still or video camera — particularly if the images are targeted at the Web or in-house types of publications.

Conventional film cameras

Conventional film cameras are often the best sources for digital photographs, especially when the subject and application require the highest-quality image. Few digital cameras can approach the resolution of film or have the versatility afforded by even moderately priced 35mm film cameras. Digital cameras that can meet or beat film resolution are going to cost well over $20,000, will often have to be permanently connected to a computer, and are likely to be bulkier and clumsier than a digital equivalent camera.

Conventional cameras have become well established, and there are whole industries that support accessories for these cameras. Any film camera, to be taken seriously these days, offers both fully automatic and completely manual controls. The 35mm field cameras may also offer a very wide range of programmed exposure settings.

If your conventional camera has a removable back, chances are excellent that it can be converted to a digital camera by simply adding a digital camera back. So, you can start into digital photography with a conventional camera, add the proper scanner to move into digital photography, and graduate to a digital camera back after you've started raking in the clients and the cash.

Film cameras are your best bet if you will be on location for an extended time or if your assignments call for hundreds of exposures. All you have to do to be prepared is to buy enough film to cover the job. There are solutions for digital cameras, too, but they're expensive.

You can certainly make digital photos from "amateur" snapshot and pocket cameras like the one shown in Figure 4-7. Even serious photographers use these from time to time. They tend to be pocketable, so one is likely to have a camera when the need arises unexpectedly. They are less costly, so they are more worth the risk in hazardous situations such as bad weather or high-crime areas. They don't look so "serious," so they may be less intimidating to the indigenous natives. This book won't dwell on these cameras because most of you are likely to be more in need of information about more complex gear. Suffice it to say that a good pocket camera with a zoom lens is a good starting point and makes a good bridge between casual cameras and professional cameras.

Figure 4-7: A typical pocket camera with zoom lens

The more serious film cameras fall into three broad applications categories:

✦ Interchangeable-lens 35mm SLR

✦ Medium format

✦ View camera

The characteristics and applications for each of these are described below. There are so many makes and models that any discussion of specific cameras would fill this book with information that few would care to know. For that reason, the discussion sticks to general guidelines and features worth scouting for.

Interchangeable-lens 35mm SLR

This type of camera uses 35mm film and has a picture area of 1 x 1.5 inches. Viewing is through the lens, via a mirror that flips out of the way just the instant before the shutter fires (so that light can pass through to the film) and a prism that reorients the mirror image to its natural left-to-right state. Lenses can be easily removed and exchanged. You generally have your choice of dozens (even hundreds, in some cases) of lenses that range from extreme wide-angle (viewing angle of 180 degrees or more) to extreme telephoto (viewing angle of 2 to 5 degrees).

Most professionals own this camera type — even if it's not their mainstay camera. The 35mm SLRs are small, quick, versatile, and can produce images of very high quality (virtually all of the Marlboro billboards were shot on 35mm film). So, photographers like to have them available just so they can be prepared to get the shot that otherwise might have gotten away.

The characteristic that endears this camera to most pros is its viewfinder technology. What you see is precisely what you get — except that you always see color, even if shooting black and white. There is no misalignment of viewfinder and lens. You even see any aberrations that might be caused by the lens or light striking its surfaces. You can see the exact effect of a lens accessory (such as a polarizing or softening filter). Finally, you can tell exactly what is in and out of focus.

Finally, you can be assured that you can find film for this camera on any street corner in the world.

If you've decided that this is a format to invest in, you might want to look for the following features. If your budget is unlimited, look for them all. Otherwise, pick the camera that has the features most important to your personality, requirements, and wallet.

✦ **Matrix metering** reads multiple areas of the image and averages the exposure over those areas. Some cameras even enable you to specify which areas you want to favor.

✦ **Spot metering** reads only a tiny portion of the image, usually indicated by a small circle in the center of the viewfinder. This allows you to expose correctly for one small area, such as the highlights in skin tones. You simply point the circle at the area you want to read, partially depress the shutter button to lock in your exposure, move the camera to frame the subject as you wish, and then shoot.

✦ **Optical steady-shot** compensates for camera movement by shifting the position of the image on film so that it stays steady. This feature can be a lifesaver if you're hands are unsteady, if you have to shoot in low light at slow shutter speeds, or if you are using telephoto lenses without a tripod.

✦ **Synch post for external flash** is a standard connection for an external flash. Since the cord that attaches to this type of connection can be of almost any length, this feature is almost a must for cameras that will be used with studio strobes.

✦ **Cable release socket or remote** (either feature) lets you fire the camera without touching (and potentially shaking) the camera. It's a must if you are taking pictures that require exposures longer than 1/60th second and still expect the pictures to be as sharp as your optics and film will allow.

✦ **Predictive auto focus** calculates the speed at which your subject (or the camera) is moving and adjusts the focus as the movement occurs. This seems like a miracle if you shoot sports, birds, or other fast-moving subjects. This feature is most critical with long lenses or close-up subjects.

✦ **Fast auto focus** is important if you're going to use auto focus at all. If you buy a camera with this feature, be sure that you can turn it off because some conditions will fool even the best auto focus programming.

✦ **Preprogrammed exposure modes** are wonderful if you're in too much of a hurry to consider all the variables that are typical in certain situations, such as portraiture, backlighting, sunlit snow, and many others. These modes won't do you much good if you can't understand how to execute them or what their names mean, however. Get your hands on the camera and try taking a look at the menus and controls used to make these things work.

✦ **Removable backs** let you substitute a digital or Polaroid back. This feature is often also used to attach a motor drive. This feature is much more important in medium-format cameras than in 35mm cameras because of the number of accessories available and because there are numerous choices in digital camera backs.

✦ **NiMH or lithium-ion batteries** are rechargeables that don't care how much of their capacity has been used before recharging. They also tend to have longer battery life. If your camera uses AA batteries, you will probably be able to buy NiMH rechargeables, but be sure to check the manufacturer's recommendations.

✦ **Sequence shooting** capabilities are usually indicated by a specification indicating a "burst rate" of so many frames per second (fps). These are useful for automated exposure bracketing and for stop-action sequences. If you shoot sports, war, or other peak-motion action, pick a camera with a burst rate over 5fps. Better yet, buy a camera to which you can add a motor drive.

✦ **Lens availability** is important, and many established camera makers make their lenses so that they fit an entire line of camera models. Nikon AF lenses, for instance, will fit nearly every model of modern Nikon 35mm SLR. As a result, Nikon can afford to offer a huge range of lenses. Furthermore, third-party lens makers are likely to make compatible lenses because they will fit so many models of popular cameras. There are several manufacturers who follow this plan. So should you.

✦ **Shutter speed over 1/1,000th** was unheard of a few years ago. Some of today's 35s can shoot at speeds as high as 1/5,000th of a second — almost fast enough to stop a bullet. Seeing something that you know is moving at the speed of a bullet absolutely frozen can be a beautiful sight.

✦ **Autobracketing** is a feature that requires a modern camera controlled by a computer chip. It enables you to set a range of exposures over and under normal and the f stop (aperture) increments and steps. Then, when you press the shutter button, the camera shoots a sequence of frames, each at a different specified exposure.

✦ **Depth-of-field preview buttons** are a must if you really want to be able to judge actual depth of field. That's because the camera always widens the lens aperture to its maximum to enable you to view and frame the brightest image. However, depth of field increases dramatically as the aperture is made smaller — which is almost always the case when the camera actually takes the picture.

✦ **Multiple exposure capability** doesn't refer to sequence shooting. It is the ability to superimpose an image taken in one instant with an image taken in another instant. In olden days, this happened because you forgot to wind the film or because the film jammed (the latter can still happen). However, there can be good reason for making multiple exposures to achieve a special look or effect.

Medium format

Medium-format cameras (see Figure 4-8) use roll film that is 2.5 inches wide. The film is called 120 (twelve 6 × 6 centimeter frames per roll) or 220 (twelve 6 × 6 centimeter frames per roll). With few exceptions, most cameras will take film of either length. The length of the frames varies. The most popular is 6 × 6 cm (centimeters) or 2¼ inches. Since the film is slightly more than twice as wide as 35mm film, image definition is about four times greater. Photographers originally liked this format because they didn't have to rotate the camera to get a vertical or horizontal shot. Today, most medium-format cameras have rotating backs, so if you choose one of the other frame formats, you can simply rotate the camera back to switch from horizontal to vertical orientation.

Figure 4-8: Several medium-format cameras: Mamiya, Fuji, Bronica, Yashica

More recently a frame ratio of 1:1.2, called "ideal format," has come into vogue. This ratio fits the exact proportions of an 8 × 10-inch print. Since this is the most popular size for a commercial photographic print, shooting at this ratio makes it likely that the photo will minimize cropping (trimming of the original picture area). This results in more consistent picture quality because the print is using a maximum amount of the image definition available given the grain structure of the film used.

The frame sizes of medium-format cameras (see Figure 4-9) and the number of exposures each can place on a roll of 12 film are as follows:

- ◆ 645 (6cm × 4.5cm ideal format)
- ◆ 6 × 6cm (2¼-inch square)
- ◆ 6 × 7 cm (ideal format)
- ◆ 6 × 9 (2¼ × 3¼)

Most medium-format cameras are SLRs, but optical viewfinders are popular with events photographers because these cameras make little sound and framing is quicker and easier when shooting in adverse lighting conditions. Some of these cameras are shaped like a giant 35mm camera, but most look like a small metal box with a lens attached up front. This physical shape makes it more likely that the camera will be cradled in the hands than held up to the cheek or that the camera will be placed on a tripod.

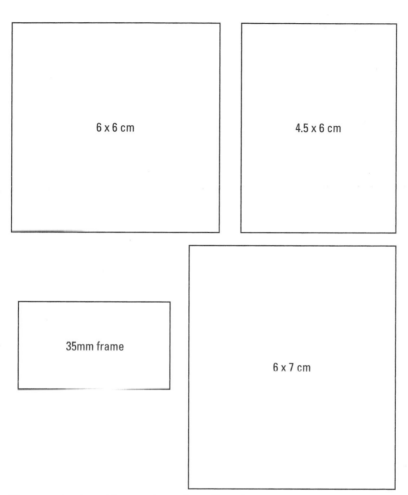

Figure 4-9: Actual frame sizes of medium-format cameras

The higher image definition, combined with the reasonable portability of medium-format cameras, makes them popular for applications when spontaneity and the ability to "capture the moment" are less important than luxurious detail. Almost all studio photographers use medium-format cameras, and they are quite popular as location cameras for such high-end jobs as advertising illustration and annual report covers. Many wedding and event photographers prefer them because they can sell more large prints for higher prices and because the larger images on contact sheets are easier to read and make a more favorable impression.

When it comes to the features you should look for in a medium-format camera, you can consider almost any of the features listed under 35mm SLRs a bonus. The larger format of these cameras means shutters, mirrors, and film movements that are harder to control electronically, and the inclusion of too many options is likely to push your budget beyond your need for them. Besides, these cameras are more likely to be used on a tripod and under conditions in which you have more time to think than when shooting sports or news. Also, it's in the personality of most of the owners of these cameras to want complete control without the hindrance of too much automation. Still, there are features that are important to have:

✦ **Interchangeable backs** let you switch from film to digital to Polaroid. You can also switch from 120 to 220 film for twice as many exposures on a roll. Some medium-format cameras even offer backs that will accept 35mm film. Finally, you can often switch between frame formats. Almost all medium-format SLRs have removable backs.

✦ **Rotating backs** are essential if you're shooting in a format that isn't square. Otherwise, the configuration of these cameras is too awkward for comfortable handling and viewing when you want to compose a vertical shot.

✦ **Interchangeable viewfinders** let you switch between waist-level finders and eye-level prisms (much handier for location shooting of people). Also, it's very handy to be able to place a celluloid on the ground glass so that you can mark the position of an element to be used in a composite photo — or the position of type in the ad headline — or a grid that helps you keep the shots in a panorama aligned with one another.

View camera

View Cameras are large-format cameras. They come in multiple film sizes, but the vast majority use 4 × 5-inch sheet film and have interchangeable backs and lenses. Viewfinding is usually done by removing the film and viewing the image on a ground glass (frosted) screen that takes the place of the film plane. You see exactly what the film sees, so the image is reversed. Cameras that use even larger sizes are popular in applications where the photographer wants to capture every hair and then enlarge the result to fill Grand Central. Okay, I'm exaggerating just a little, but for most of the world's still-life, architectural, and formal portrait photographers, 4 × 5-inch film is more than adequate.

View cameras are also used in the field. In fact, the old Graflex was used for reportage by many newspapers, even through the mid-1960s. Graflex's have been mostly relegated to museums. Today, large-format cameras are used primarily for on-tripod shooting of highly detailed subject matter that doesn't move or whose movement can be controlled. The reasons for this have as much to do with the deliberateness required for control (for instance, you usually have to remove the film from the back before you can frame and focus, and then replace it when you're ready to shoot — a serious barrier to spontaneity) as with the size of the camera. Another big advantage of view cameras is their ability to swing and tilt the lens and film plane (see Figure 4-10). This makes it possible to straighten parallel lines when the camera has to be tilted up to look at a building or to increase depth of field in a still life.

Figure 4-10: A pair of view cameras

Desirable qualities in a view camera are as follows:

✦ **Precision and ruggedness:** It is important that your adjustments don't change as soon as you insert the film holder. It's also important that one adjustment, such as a lens tilt, doesn't change as soon as you make another adjustment. You can test this by making some swings and tilts, focusing carefully, giving the camera a quick shake, and then checking to see if your adjustments have held.

✦ **Easy-to-modify controls:** Can you quickly fold the camera for transportation (more important if your application is landscapes or architecture)? It is easy to reach the controls when you need to focus, swing, and tilt while viewing the image on the ground glass. If you have to keep moving around the camera between adjustments, you'll waste valuable time.

✦ **Digitally adaptable back:** Can you attach a digital back? Large-format photography lends itself particularly well to high-resolution professional digital backs, so don't cripple your investment by cutting yourself out of this option. Check with the makers of digital backs. Leaf, Dicomed, MegaVision, and Phase One are among the most prominent makers. They can tell you which camera models will adapt to their backs. So can most of the camera manufacturers.

✦ **Complete flexibility in swings and tilts:** Be sure that both the lens and back can be swiveled on both the horizontal and vertical axis of the lens and film plane. If you plan to work with wide-angle lenses, look for a camera that has interchangeable bellows. Otherwise, a stiff bellows can interfere with swings and tilts when the bellows is compressed (as it is when used with a short focal-length wide-angle lens).

✦ **Bright ground glass viewfinder:** Try framing and focusing using the camera you plan to buy. Compared to other models, the image should be bright, crisp, and evenly illuminated.

Scanners

Scanners are the mechanisms for digitizing images. There are sheet-fed scanners, flatbed scanners, transparency scanners, and drum scanners. All of these will make a digitized version of any two-dimensional image (even if it's just type or lines). How well it works, however, depends on what you want to scan and which type of scanner you use. Of all these types of scanners, only transparency scanners (those for small-format films are called slide scanners) and drum scanners are really well suited to digital photography. However, the other types of scanners may have some limited use. For that reason, I'll discuss how each type might fit in, the uses for each, and the most desirable features for each type.

When you look for a scanner, regardless of type, look for the fastest connection consistent with your computer. Best of all, look for a USB connection. It's cross-platform, nearly as fast as SCSI, and won't present address conflict problems.

The price of flatbed and slide scanners is plummeting (right along with most of the other pieces in the digital photography puzzle). Many of the low-priced scanners are true bargains, but insist on scanning an image with which you are familiar before you buy. Don't accept a unit that produces muddy, unsharp, or streaked images.

Be careful not to be fooled by claims of superhigh resolution. The only resolution statistic that matters is optical resolution. Interpolated resolution is sheer advertising hype. Your image-editing program can do a better job of interpolating, but that's something you want to do only under the right circumstances. See Chapter 16 for the reasons why.

Sheet-fed scanners

Sheet-fed scanners are inspired by the original Visioneer Paperport. Only about 11 inches wide by 2 or 3 inches deep, they fit quite nicely between a keyboard and monitor. The image is scanned as the paper moves through a slot on one side of the scanner and out a slot on the other side. You can't scan film, stiff papers, thick papers, or three-dimensional objects. Many sheet-fed scanners are limited to monochrome, though later models also scan color. Resolution for this type of scanner generally tops out at about 300 dpi.

Before you buy a sheet-fed scanner that might be used to capture photographic imagery, test it or read the reviews to make sure that the images aren't streaked or banded. Beyond that, the features you most want to find in a sheet-fed scanner are as follows:

✦ **Ability to scan color:** Most who have an interest in digital photography want to work in color at least some of the time. Even if you don't care about color, a color scanner is more likely to produce a higher-resolution, sharper, and smoother scan.

✦ **Bundled software:** Because these scanners take up so little room, they are really handy for scanning documents and converting the text to word processing documents (a process called optical character recognition, OCR). They are wonderful as fax scanners, too. So, you will want to make sure that you get software that is very capable at these two applications. If you're a casual digital photographer, you might also hope for a decent image-processing program. Several of these are discussed in Chapter 16.

Sheet-fed scanners became popular for a while because Visioneer's software made them so easy to use for faxing and OCR, and because their presence on the desktop was so unobtrusive. These are still the best reasons to buy them, but their popularity has faded since the price of more versatile flatbed scanners has dropped to near or below that of most sheet-fed scanners. If you already own a sheet-fed scanner, you can scan the prints of your snapshots and expect to get images that are good enough for practicing image manipulation, placing images in family albums, collecting images for an online database, or for illustrating Web sites and multimedia productions.

Flatbed scanners

Flatbed scanners are boxes with a flat glass scanning area as the topmost surface. This surface is usually large enough to scan a legal-size document, though there are no strict scan size limitations. A flap or lid swings down over the glass area to hold the document being scanned in place. Usually, a fluorescent tube illuminates the surface to be scanned and an image sensor slides from one side of the page to the other, working its way from top to bottom.

The most desirable features are as follows:

✦ **Bit depth greater than 24:** This feature is more important for slide scanners than for flatbed scanners, but will be helpful to anyone using a scanner for photos. A scanning bit depth of more than 24 bits per pixel means that you are capturing more information and that you will have somewhat more control over which parts of that information will be condensed into what will ultimately be a 24-bit true-color RGB file. Some scanners capture 30 or 36 bits but export or save only 24 bits. Try to find a unit that exports the full bit depth to Photoshop if you want to exercise the ultimate level of control.

✦ **Built-in transparency adapter:** One of your primary uses for a flatbed scanner will be to quickly proof your slides and negatives, but you can only do this if you have the ability to scan by transmissive light. You can also use this capability to scan some very small images for use on Web sites and other online content.

✦ **Worthwhile software bundle:** Some scanners come with a full version of Photoshop that's worth more than the cost of the scanner. You should also get a decent OCR and fax package in the bargain. Since you may already have all these things, be sure to also look for software that lets you scan an image that is optimized when it's scanned. Remember, you can't add detail or color depth to an image once it's been digitized.

✦ **Optical resolution of 600 dpi or more:** The higher your scanner's optical resolution, the better your chances of getting the quality you need from photographic prints — especially if you have to scan snapshot-sized prints or small portions of prints. High resolution is especially helpful for scanning small- and medium-format transparencies as well. Ignore interpolated resolution claims altogether. Scanning at higher interpolated resolutions only results in your storing a file that's larger than need be for the actual amount of information it contains.

✦ **Sturdy construction:** Flatbed scanners tend to take more abuse because their size tends to put them in harm's way and because people tend to flop the lids down when they're in a hurry. A flimsy scanner that produced nice images in the beginning will stop doing so if its components get out of alignment or if the case warps.

Transparency scanners

A transparency scanner is about the size of a shoebox, turned so that it fits on its narrow side. At the front of the scanner is usually a slot or drawer into which you insert a slide, strip of film (either positive or negative), an APS film cartridge, or a holder for larger-format film.

It is my opinion that if you're interested in digital photography, the first piece of gear you should buy is a slide scanner dedicated to scanning 35mm slides. Flatbed scanners, even if they have transparency adapters, simply don't scan at high enough resolutions, hold the film flat enough, or eliminate stray light well enough (so scanned transparencies tend to exhibit light flare).

Note   A few flatbed scanners have a separate compartment (usually some sort of drawer arrangement) for scanning film. These compartments usually have film holders for masking the edges of various frame formats, eliminating problems with stray light. Perhaps more importantly, the film isn't in contact with a glass surface, so there's less likelihood of picking up dirt, fingerprints, and Newton rings. However, these scanners still can't scan at as high resolution as dedicated transparency scanners.

Transparency scanners are simply the most affordable means of digitizing photos at resolutions and color depths high enough to be used for professional-quality output. Transparency scanners range in price from about $400 to $4,500 — depending on the manufacturer, the resolution of the scanner, and the maximum size of transparencies that can be scanned. The most popular format is the 35mm slide scanner (most modern ones will also scan APS film). The least expensive of these scan at around 1,800 dpi and at 24 bits per pixel. That's enough resolution for 300 dpi 5 × 7 photos and you can "get away with" making 8 × 10 prints. If you will be reproducing your work as full magazine pages, you will need a scan resolution of at least 2,700 dpi for 35mm scans. This is even enough resolution for even larger finished work because as the finished work becomes larger than page size, the likelihood that people will view the image from a greater distance increases. At greater distances, small flaws aren't as noticeable. Please don't misunderstand me, though. I'm not saying that there aren't situations in which higher scan resolutions aren't desirable. If those are only occasional instances, however, it may make more sense for you to use a slide scanner most of the time. When you do need higher resolution, take the transparency to a service bureau and have them scan the image on a $20,000 drum scanner.

Almost all of today's slide scanners connect through a SCSI port and will work on any computer that has a SCSI connection. Manufacturers tell me they're also very interested in FireWire and USB connections, but are waiting for broader acceptance of the two standards in the professional marketplace.

Meantime, you can expect to see more slide scanners that will produce resolutions up to 4,000 dpi. The Polaroid SprintScan 4000, at about $2,500, is the first of these scanners to appear. However, since the resolution of CCD chips is rising and the price falling . . .

Features that are a bonus in a slide scanner are as follows:

✦ **Fast scanning speeds:** Scanning speeds of over a minute per 35mm slide are simply unacceptable. The fastest I've seen to date is the Nikon Super Coolscan 2000, which scans in less than 20 seconds. If you scan from negatives (which will give you more latitude and, therefore, more picture information to work with), you may need to scan half or two-thirds of the images on the roll. Imagine what happens in a professional shoot, when 40 or 50 rolls may be exposed in a single day.

✦ **Wide dynamic range:** Dynamic range (the amount of information between the lightest and darkest brightness values in the image) is one of the characteristics that distinguishes drum scanners from slide scanners. So, the higher the decimal figure for dynamic range, the richer your scans can be. Forget any transparency scanner whose dynamic range isn't higher than 3.0. The Nikon Super Coolscan 2000 is outstanding in this respect — boasting a dynamic range of 3.6.

✦ **Resolution equal to or greater than 2,700 dpi:** This is the resolution called for to make an 8.5 × 11-inch 300-dpi print. It is also close to the resolution of the "average" film (typically ISO 200 to 400). Of course, there is no such thing as too much resolution — as long as you've got the disk space to store the files.

✦ **Ability to scan multiple frames or slides:** If you have to scan lots of slides (as most serious photographer surely will), you'll find it a big help to be able to scan several slides that were shot at the same time in similar conditions. Meantime, you can make your phone calls or work on processing an image on another computer.

✦ **Scanner software that gives you control over the quality of the scan before the scan is made:** Look for scanners whose control software lets you preview your scan in a window large enough to see how well details are being recorded. You should also be able to choose precise white and black points, make precise color balance adjustments, and correct the histogram of an image on a curve. For a better idea of what this all means, take a look at the exercise that shows you how to scan a slide in Chapter 10.

Applications for which slide scanners are appropriate include a list that would be too long for this chapter. Suffice it to say that slide/transparency scanners are the most cost-effective way to acquire professional-level digital images. Even if their scans are perfect enough for some high-end applications, you will probably benefit from the convenience of having one in-house for somewhat less demanding applications and so that you can do quick tests and comprehensives before sending out for (or spending the time on) a drum scan. On the other hand, if you're not quite ready to spend the $500 to $5,000 that a transparency scanner will set you back, you might consider Photo CD.

Photo CD

Photo CD (see Figure 4-11) is a product of Eastman Kodak, and both the CD and the images are proprietary Kodak formats. You could have your digital photos put on CD-ROM by any service bureau. You can even do it yourself. In neither case will the result be the same as Photo CD.

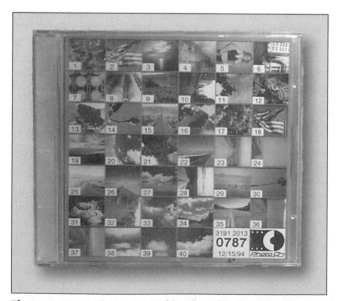

Figure 4-11: A Photo CD and its thumbnail cover

To get a Photo CD, you submit your transparencies or negatives to a service bureau or lab that offers Photo CD scanning. Like all lab work, the color balance and cleanliness of the scans will vary from supplier to supplier. If you're going to have many Photo CDs made, it's a good idea to send the same film to several makers and then compare the results. My own experience has shown me that there isn't always a correlation between price and quality, either — so don't let that be your criteria.

There are three types of Photo CD: Master, Pro Master, and Portfolio. Masters (usually called simply Photo CDs) can hold 100 images and you can add images to a partially filled CD (although this no longer makes much difference in the price because the cost of the CDs has dropped to under $2.00). Each image is recorded at five resolutions between 128×192 and $2,048 \times 3,072$ (approximately 18MB). The highest resolution is roughly equivalent to the 2,700 dpi that is the maximum resolution of most slide scanners. You cannot place images from film formats larger than 35mm onto Master Photo CD (APS film is slightly smaller and can be recorded).

Pro Master Photo CDs can hold only 25 images and the cost for recording is typically $4–$6. However, this format can also take medium- and large-format film, and there is one higher resolution scan of $4,095 \times 6,144$ (approximately 75MB). You may seldom have a need for such as large file, but it's always safer to have too much resolution so you won't have to scan the image again. And, of course, if the client's paying for it, you might as well have the added insurance of knowing that you can use the result in very quality-demanding applications.

Portfolio CDs use only one resolution for recording images and can also contain accompanying sound. This format is useful for the preparation of photographer's and artist's portfolios. It has also been used for multimedia storytelling.

Note

Photo CD images are written in a unique format. In order to read them, your image-processing program will need to know how to recognize the format. There is a Photoshop-compatible plug-in (it comes with Photoshop), so if your image-processing program is compatible with Photoshop plug-ins, you will be able to read these files. You cannot save the file back to Photo CD format without special software, so you should save the file in a well-understood cross-platform format such as TIFF. The CD-ROM format for Photo CD is also unique, but every multisession CD-ROM XA drive can read it.

Here are the reasons you might want to consider Photo CD as the means for digitizing your conventional photos:

✦ **No equipment to buy:** You just drop off your film at any place offering Photo CD service.

✦ **Thumbnails on the CD:** You don't have to guess at which picture goes with which filename. The Photo CD comes back to you with full-color thumbnails and each is labeled with the number that corresponds to the filename.

✦ **Low cost per scan:** Do a little shopping around and you'll find that you can get Master Photo CD scans for as little as $1 each. Even at $3–$5 for Pro Photo CDs, the cost is much lower than the fees charged for custom scanning by service bureaus.

✦ **Multiple resolutions on a single CD:** The advantage in scanning at multiple resolutions is that you get as much detail as is possible at a given resolution. That's because the image isn't resampled in order to change its resolution. Resampling means that the computer has to add or eliminate information according to the "best guess" of a program. So, if an image is made smaller and there's a thin line in the original image, it may either disappear altogether or look much thicker in the reduced image.

✦ **Your original images are permanently archived on a nonerasable medium:** No one is going to accidentally erase the disk. If you want to be really safe, you can even have multiple CDs made from the same roll of film.

Consider Photo CD as the preferred method for digitizing your photos under the following conditions:

✦ **When you can't justify the cost of drum scans:** If you're looking for very high-resolution scans, you have two choices: Pro Master Photo CD or a drum scanner (covered later). Custom drum scans can run between $10 and $50 each and you'll only get one scanning resolution. Pro Master Photo CD will give you six resolutions for each image and you will be able to record several times as many images for the same amount of money.

✦ **When you don't have a multiple-format slide scanner:** If you're shooting medium- or large-format film and can't (yet) justify the cost of a larger-format slide scanner or a drum scanner, Photo CD is the only answer.

✦ **When you don't have a scanner:** If you want to break into digital photography without making a hardware investment (a very good idea for beginners), Photo CD offers you the best chance to get started with high-quality images.

✦ **When you don't want to be bothered with doing scans yourself:** If you're as busy as most people who make a decent living, then you may want to have someone else do all your scanning. After all, a handful of rolls of 35mm film can take hours to scan.

PictureCD

The newest Photo CD (distant) relative is Picture CD, a cooperative effort of Kodak, Adobe, and Intel. PictureCD is related only to the extent that, thanks to Photo CD, Kodak has more experience putting images and multimedia on CD than any other company. Picture CDs can be ordered when you have film processed at a consumer-level minilab, such as the ones at your local drugstores and supermarkets. (See Figure 4-12.)

Figure 4-12: Photo of PictureCD and envelope

Intel's involvement makes Picture CD somewhat more Windows friendly, but
the images are stored in JPEG format at a single resolution of 1,536 × 1,024.
That's roughly equivalent to the resolution of prosumer digital cameras
and the Picture CD costs a lot less than a Photo CD. Anyway, the fact that
the images are stored in a cross-platform format means that you can open
them on the Mac. None of the other features mentioned below work on the
Mac, however.

Picture CD is different from Photo CD in some other important respects, too. First,
you get your images placed on Picture CD when you drop your film at your favorite
film counter. You don't have to go to a photo store or service bureau. Costco, K-
Mart, Walgreen's, Target, and Best Buy were a few of the outlets where Picture CD
was available when this paragraph was written. More are being added all the time.
Second, you get a lot of free software and tips from Kodak. So it's a good idea to try
this for at least one roll of film, just to get the software. Third, the CD costs quite a
bit less than Photo CD.

The CD opens automatically when you insert it into the CD-ROM drive of any
Windows machine that has the CD Auto-Start setting turned on. The graphics
look like a magazine cover that illustrates the monthly change in the CD's
collection of bonus articles and software (see Figure 4-13).

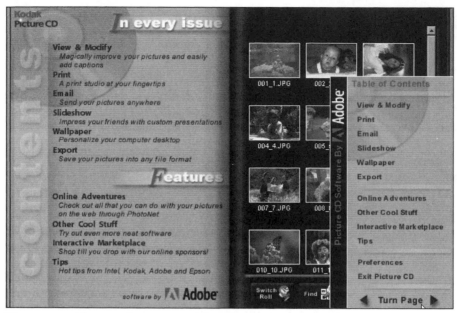

Figure 4-13: The opening screen of the Picture CD

The contents are the interesting part. You get an image-processing program that's even more basic than Adobe PhotoDeluxe. It lets you autocorrect exposure and color balance, crop the image, correct for red-eye (glowing red eyes caused by on-camera flash), rotate, and sharpen. The program is so simple that almost all these commands are executed with the click of a single button. Unfortunately images are recompressed each time a simple change is made because there's no way to save to an uncompressed format before you make the edits. If you want to keep your images in prime shape, save them to .TIF format and then do the editing in another program. If you want to keep costs and the learning curve down, you could choose any of the programs mentioned in Chapter 24.

Other features of the magazine include a fair amount of trial software from various "advertisers" and "tips and tricks" articles on a variety of subjects. For instance, on the first month's issue there was free software from American Greetings for making greeting cards, from MGI Software for making sports trading cards, and from MetaCreations for Kai's PowerGoo — a program for making image distortions. Tips and Tricks articles included "Ten Easy Steps to Taking Better Pictures," "Pictures and the PC," "Software that Makes the Most of Your Photos," and "Get Amazing Prints." Of course, these articles push the sponsor's products, but they're also well designed and highly instructional (especially if you're new to digital photography).

Picture CD also automatically posts your thumbnails to a Web site and links them to the corresponding full-screen resolution image. Once again, you can't use this software to do the same for your other images — only those on the CD. Still, this is a very handy capability. If you like it, you can do the same for all your images with inexpensive programs such as Kai's Photo Soap2.

You can also use the Picture CD to automatically make a picture disk of all the edited images — and you can mix images from several rolls. A Picture Disk is a 3.5-inch floppy that will play an automatic slide show on any Windows computer.

Drum scanners

Drum scanners are the means to getting the highest-quality digital images. They are also very versatile, since they can scan multiple images of different sizes at the same time. They can also scan both reflective (prints) and transmissive (film) images.

So why use anything else? Drum scanners are so costly that they are owned by very few individuals (Okay, I can think of a few very well established professional photographers). They are, however, owned by lots of corporate publications departments, publications, and prepress service bureaus. You usually have to coat the inside of the drum with a special oil that holds the scanned objects flat against the surface of the drum. So there's the danger of picking up dirt in the oil. There's also the necessity of cleaning the oil off the film or print after scanning. Some drum scanners have managed to get away from the use of oil — but the majority still use it. Drum scanners are also physically large — to the extent that, if you work in tight quarters, you might have a tough time finding room to install one.

As you might guess from its name, drum scanners are typically tubular. The images are placed inside the tube. The tube then spins at a high rate of speed while the image sensor travels from one end of the tube to the other. This results in an image that is scanned while the image sensor is precisely equidistant from every part of the image. As you can imagine, the result is perfectly sharp from edge to edge. Also, because the image sensor can focus with absolute precision, there is little to no color bleed from pixel to pixel. This also results in wider dynamic range than can be produced by most other types of scanners.

There are several reasons why drum scanners are worth all the bucks, space, and trouble (provided, of course, that your business has the income to support them):

✦ You can scan both reflective (prints) and transmissive (film).

✦ You can scan multiple images at the same time.

✦ You get higher resolution scans with a greater dynamic range.

✦ They are very fast compared to transparency scanners.

Service bureaus

Service bureaus are businesses that specialize in services that are unaffordable to occasional users, individuals, and smaller businesses. Ironically, they also cater to large corporations that could afford the equipment but that don't want to acquire the expertise required to run the equipment. Large corporations also often don't want to hire specialized staff. Many service bureaus that offer high-quality scans also offer related services, such as making separations for printing, darkroom work for traditional photography, or recording your images onto CD-ROMs (sometimes even in Photo CD format).

Camera Mounts

If you ever want to make photos in dim light or ever want to adjust lights, reflectors, and other accessories while maintaining the position of the camera, you're going to need some kind of a camera mount. The most versatile of these is a tripod, but there are other options that are useful in certain special circumstances.

This isn't meant to be an inventory of all the possible options in camera mounts. The plan is to be able to give you a good enough idea of what some of the options are. If you have requirements that can't be satisfied by one of these, they're probably pretty unusual requirements. Even then, the following options will probably give a better idea of what you need.

The longer the focal length of your lens, the greater the need to hold the camera steady. Unless you've taken lots of yoga classes and can calm your body into relaxed rigidity, you'll need a camera mount any time you shoot with a lens whose 35mm equivalency is more than 200mm at shutter speeds below 1/250th second.

Tripods

The most popular and versatile type of camera mount is the tripod. Tripod legs' lengths telescope to be individually adjustable, and most tripods have a foot that can be either a rubber cup (for carpets, concrete, and hardwood floors) or a spike (to anchor the legs in uneven outdoor terrain).

Whatever tripod you buy should be sturdy enough to keep your camera rock steady indoors or out. Adjustments and locking mechanisms should be quick and easy, too. This is especially true if you'll be using the camera on location, because you'll be in a hurry and because you'll probably want to change positions and locations often.

If you use a tripod on a sandy beach or other terrain where dust and dirt can get inside the screw threads, be sure to clean the areas around where the adjustments are made each time you make a further adjustment. Doing so will greatly extend the life of your tripod.

Tripods for larger cameras need to be sturdier, and photographers often choose those with wooden legs. Wooden legs absorb vibration better and have a more "classic" feel. Their construction is also rock solid.

It almost goes without saying that more portable cameras demand more portable tripods. Still, tripods for smaller cameras come in an even wider variety of sizes and weights. Almost all are made of aluminum, and the best (and most expensive) are made of aluminum alloys or superstrong and lightweight carbon fibers. I'd suggest getting a tripod that's sturdy enough for either a 35mm or medium-format camera, that has quick-release leg adjustments (flip locks are very quick), and that has a uniball head (see the "Tripod heads" section, next). Such a tripod will serve you well both in studio and on location. It will also be able to adapt itself to most of the cameras you're likely to use — even a tiny point-and-shoot.

Tip You'll get maximum versatility from a tripod with interchangeable heads. You may want to switch to a panoramic head for stitched panoramas or to a damped head for use with a video camera.

Tripod heads

Tripod heads are usually interchangeable. Look for those that contain a spirit level or bubble level, so that you can make sure that the horizon is straight. This is especially important for panoramas. Most tripods have interchangeable heads that come in the following major types:

✦ **Conventional:** A conventional tripod head consists of a platform for holding the camera and individual adjustments for vertical and lateral tilt.

✦ **Uniball:** Uniball heads (also called *monoballs* — see Figure 4-14) have a round platform so that it can fit under the camera in any direction. A single lock secures the position of the camera in any vertical, horizontal or in-between tilt angle. Uniballs are the first choice for situations in which you want to quickly shoot many different angles of the same subject or in situations where the subject may move rapidly (such as in fashion, sports, or transportation). Because they are so quick and convenient, many smaller-format photographers pick uniballs as their universal head mount. There are some expensive uniball heads made for large-format cameras. However, uniballs are generally a better choice for medium- to small-format cameras (including consumer and prosumer digital cameras).

✦ **Damped:** The swings and tilts of these heads are damped (cushioned) by viscous fluids (thick, gooey oil). What that means in layman's terms is that you can pan (swing from side to side) and tilt (swing up and down) the camera without its jerking. Damped heads are especially important for use with video cameras, but they are also very handy when you need to shoot action sequences at relatively slow (1/15th to 1/60th second) shutter speeds. This is because the camera stays relatively steady, even if you don't tighten down the pan and tilt controls.

Figure 4-14: A tripod head

✦ **Panoramic:** The best panoramic heads for digital photography are made by
Kaidan. This company specializes in making heads for digital cameras (as well
as for film cameras) that can be used with stitching software. These heads align
the center of the light-sensitive plane (film or digital chip) with both the vertical
and horizontal tilt axis. They also make it possible to quickly swing and tilt with
click stops at exact increments. This makes it much easier and more accurate
for the stitching software to piece together a seamless panorama (see the section in Chapter 18 on panoramic stitching software). There is a very wide range
of panoramic heads and accessories available from this company. You should
check their Web site at www.kaidan.com. The company sells panoramic heads
for as little as $100.

Dollies

Tripod dollies make it much quicker to reposition the tripod when shooting people
or other moving objects. Tripod dollies are sets of wheels that fit on the bottom of
tripod legs. These wheels are usually attached to an adjustable platform so that the
tripod legs won't twist or strain when the camera is rolled. The wheels can be locked
so that the tripod doesn't roll accidentally. Tripod dollies can be big, high-tech, and
expensive. They can also be homemade from a plywood triangle and three locking
wheels—all readily available from your local hardware and lumber yard. Homemade
dollies are fine for use in your studio, but are a pain to transport and are nearly useless on location. You can buy a well-made aluminum tripod dolly for medium-format
and smaller cameras for between $50 and $125. They're available from several tripod
manufacturers. Some will even let you lock at three wheels by pressing a single lever.
Also, try to find a dolly with variable-radius arms. That will allow you to use the tripod with the legs either collapsed or extended.

Lateral arms

A lateral arm fits across the camera platform and allows the camera to ride out to one side of the tripod. This makes it much easier to shoot close-ups over a table, when the tripod might otherwise get in the way. If you use one of these, be sure to weight the tripod so that it won't tip over due to having the weight of the camera so far off center. Lateral arms come in many different lengths. They are almost always sold as accessories, and there are universal ones that will work with most tripods that use a ¼-inch (standard) or ⅜-inch (usually used for heavier cameras) mounting screw.

Mini or tabletop tripods

These are just tiny tripods that you can drop into your backpack or hang on your belt. Then you can set them atop any flat surface, such as a table or car trunk—even on the ground for low-angle shots (see Figure 4-15). Some folks even plant them on their chests. These small tripods come in many price and size ranges, starting at about $15 and a maximum height of about 18 inches.

Figure 4-15: A tabletop tripod in use

Monopods

When the light is too dim for steady handheld shots (exposures longer than 1/60th second) and your mobility is also a premium consideration, monopods are often the solution. Monopods are simply a long stick with a tripod head mounted on the top. By bracing the camera and pushing down, the camera is vertically steady. It is then easier to concentrate on keeping the camera steady from side to side. How steady? You can usually keep the camera still enough to allow you to cut the shutter speed to between one-half and one-quarter the speed required for hand holding. If you can brace the monopod against a table, railing, or other rock-steady object, you can even shoot very long exposures.

You can make a monopod by attaching a tripod head to a broom handle for next to nothing. On the other hand, really good lightweight collapsible ones are available for less than $50.

Camera clamps

Clamps are usually nothing more than an industrial-strength C-clamp with a uniball head soldered to it. They are handy in the field because you can often find a railing or the edge of a table to attach them to. They don't take up much space in your camera bag if you're traveling on a long trip, either. I find them to be a godsend in the studio, too. That's because I can use them clamped on the side of ladders for very high shots. I can also use two ladders alongside a still-life table, clamp a 2 × 4 to the rungs so that it forms a bridge over the table, and then use the camera clamp to align the camera directly over the setup. This works especially well for digital cameras with a video-out connection so that a computer or TV monitor can act as their viewfinder.

Beanbags

Beanbags are simply small cloth (usually nylon) bags filled with metal or polypropylene beads. You can plop one of these on all sorts of uneven but steady surfaces (for example, the hood of a car or a handy boulder), and then nestle the camera into position. You end up with a pretty solid mounting for the camera. You can then use the self-timer or a cable release to fire the camera without jiggling it. Good for exposures up to several seconds long — provided you're not shooting in a strong wind. You can make your own beanbags or buy them for between $15 and $60.

Handheld

There are several types of handheld camera mounts that operate on the theory that the trunks of our bodies are steadier than our hands. These are most useful in situations where the photographer must be light on his or her feet and is using a telephoto or extreme telephoto lens. Gun-stock mounts and chest tripods are but two of the most popular of these. However, a unipod will almost always prove to be a steadier choice. The exception is steadicams.

Steadicams

Steadicam is a trademarked name for a device used mainly in motion picture and video photography. The device moves the camera in the opposite direction of any sudden movement, thus canceling out that movement. However, the term "Steadicam" has come to be applied to virtually any device that accomplishes a similar purpose, and that is how it is used here.

Motion-canceling mounts may work with gyroscopes, mirrors, or movable lens elements. I have mentioned these in reverse order of their bulk and cost. As you might expect, the most effective devices tend to be the most expensive. In-the-lens solutions add little to no bulk to the equipment and only raise the price of lenses slightly. They're probably also the best solution for still cameras and are especially effective for shooting sports and action with long lenses. However, only Canon presently makes a full range of such lenses for still cameras. The use of the Canon lenses is restricted to Canon cameras, unless you can find adapters for your camera.

Lighting

For the most part, the lighting you need for digital photography is the same as the lighting for film photography. The main difference is that it is much easier to change the sensitivity of the image capture (ISO rating) for film than for the typical digital capture device. What that means is that film is more adaptable to a wider range of lighting conditions because you can change to a faster (say, ISO 1000) or slower (ISO 25) film. You can also intentionally keep film in the developer chemicals for more or less than the recommended amount of time. Underdevelopment results in (among other effects) lower effective film sensitivity. Overdevelopment, as you might expect, has the opposite effect. In contrast, most digital cameras are rated at ISO 100. A few digicams, such as the new Nikon 950 and the Olympus C-2020 and C-3030, allow you to double or quadruple the sensitivity rating in trade for a bit more "noise" (image artifacts similar to those that result from too much JPEG compression).

The ability to change film speeds is most important if your shooting style or client requirements demand that you use the lighting provided by nature and circumstance. Photographers call this *available lighting*. In that case, you will need mostly supplemental lighting—either fill-flash or reflectors—to heighten the detail in shadows.

If, on the other hand, you're required to have control over the quality and direction of light, you will need lighting equipment that is bright enough to overwhelm the existing light. Although this type of lighting is often used on location (and even outdoors), it is used so often in formal studio settings that we refer to it here as studio lighting.

There are four basic types of lighting:

- ✦ Available
- ✦ Strobe (flash)
- ✦ Incandescent
- ✦ Reflectors

There are also some important lighting accessories:

✦ Stands

✦ Diffusers

✦ Filters

Available

Available light is just what its name implies — whatever light happens to be shining on your subject when you're ready to take the picture. The sun is the most common source of available light and the most commonly used lighting in photography. Available light that comes from candles, electric signs, and other diverse sources presents some real challenges to the photographer.

Outdoor available

Bright sunlight, especially between 10 a.m. and 3 p.m. (this varies depending on your time zone and geographical location) is typically the least flattering lighting in photography. Skies are often a washed-out solid blue (boring), highlights dramatically overexposed, and hard-edge shadows turn a deep black. Look to reflectors and fill flash to help you out of this. If you're shooting portraits, look for the shade of a tree or a building overhang. If you are shooting close to sunrise or sunset, the color temperature of the light will change dramatically. When you want to show that it's a sunrise, you'll want to disable the automatic white balance of your digital camera. Since the human eye automatically corrects for white balance, you'll want to use automatic white balance when you want the scene to look more natural.

Indoor available

Most digicams aren't sensitive enough to light to allow handheld shooting in any but the brightest of indoor lighting conditions. That's why so many of them come with built-in flash. The use of built-in flash should be avoided except as a special effect. If you must use it, diffuse it (a white handkerchief or tracing paper work well). You might also overpower it by bouncing a slave flash off the walls. Also, take a look at the section on camera mounts for an appropriate way to steady the camera for a long exposure.

You also want to be careful not to let your automatic light meter overexpose available light scenes. Always expose for the highlights in skin tones if you're shooting people and want to capture the atmosphere of the surroundings. If your camera has a spot-metering mode, use it to read the exposure for the most important tones (usually, the skin tones).

There are two other worthwhile suggestions for shooting in dim available light. Use a digital camcorder (or any camcorder, if you don't have a digital one) such as the Optura I used for the shot in Figure 4-16. The resolution will be limited to 640 × 480, but you can stop action in very dim light. It's a great way to shoot a fight in a dark alley or a troupe of flamenco dancers performing in a cave. The best way to shoot in available light is to use a conventional camera loaded with very fast film (say ISO 800). Develop the film at a custom lab that can push (overdevelop) it two stops. The result will be somewhat grainy, but resolution will still be higher than if you were shooting with a video camera.

Figure 4-16: Photograph taken during a party with a camcorder by available light

Strobe (electronic flash)

The most common form of man-made lighting is electronic flash. The photo-hip name for electronic flash is strobe. Strobe flash has completely replaced earlier forms of flash, such as flashbulbs. It has many advantages over the old bulbs, too:

✦ They have the same color temperature as daylight, so you don't need a special type of bulb for fill flash.

✦ They fire at very high speed, so you don't need to concern yourself with motion blur.

✦ The bulb doesn't need to be replaced after every flash. In fact, it lasts a very long time.

There are three basic types of strobe of which you should be aware:

✦ Built-in flash

✦ Portable

✦ Studio strobe

Built-in flash

This is the tiny flash that's usually placed right next to your camera's viewfinder. It's a rare point-and-shoot, prosumer, or 35-mm SLR that doesn't have one of these. Built-in flash is wonderful for shadow fill in harshly sunlit conditions or when a more powerful off-camera strobe is being used. They also make it possible for you to get a picture in dim light when you don't have the time, money, or experience to use another solution. Those are plenty of good reasons to be happy that your camera has one. Still, using on-camera flash as your primary lighting source is probably something you want to avoid. It will usually only light subjects that are within 10–15 feet of the camera. If the subject is close to another object (such as wall), there's usually a harsh background shadow. Most importantly, the light that falls on the subject is too harsh and flat. The result is that people look like deer caught in the headlights, and worse, the light usually reflects off the back of the eyeball — the cause of the phenomenon known as red-eye.

Try to pick a camera that lets you purposely turn off the flash. They're rarer and more expensive, but also try to pick a camera that will synchronize with an external flash. If your camera doesn't offer external flash synchronization, it's still possible to synchronize with an external flash by using a slave unit. A slave unit is a device that fires the external strobe when it senses a sudden flash of light that's brighter than the available light. Of course, that flash would come from your camera's built-in flash. This means that slave units don't need to have a cable between the flash and the camera. There are even external slave units that work with digital cameras that fire the flash twice for each exposed frame: first so that the meter can adjust exposure, again to take the picture. These are available through DigiSlave at www.srelectronics.com.

Portable

Portable strobes are generally about the size of a box of tea bags. Portable strobes can usually be used either on-camera or by attaching a slave to a synch cord. Smaller units are usually less powerful than larger units because they use large bulbs and batteries. However, the real measure of the power is the guide number at ISO 100 (the most common film speed or image sensor rating for light sensitivity). The higher the Guide Number, the brighter the strobe. Nearly all portable strobes are significantly more powerful than built-in strobes. Portable strobes range in price between $20 and $200.

Typical applications for portable strobes include the following:

✦ **On-location bounce flash to simulate natural lighting:** Many of these units are powerful enough to give good overall lighting at moderate apertures when their light is directed at walls, ceilings, or other flat surfaces. The resulting light is soft and natural looking.

✦ **Key lighting:** Because they can be at any distance and angle from the camera, portable strobes can be used at the main lighting source. However, this works best for portraits and other relatively close-range subjects.

✦ **More powerful on-camera lighting:** The light can be attached to the camera or held close to the lens. The effect is simply that of a brighter built-in flash. This is an especially useful technique for outdoor fill flash when shooting subjects that are more than 15 feet away from the camera.

✦ **Highlight or background lighting in conjunction with more powerful studio strobes:** This works best with a slave unit because the studio strobes are generally synchronized with the camera.

✦ **Poor-person's studio strobes:** You can use multiple portable strobes as a low-cost alternative to studio strobes. Of course, they're not as bright, rugged, or controllable as studio strobes. Other drawbacks are that you'll have no modeling light, will need adapters to place them on light stands, and won't be able to maximize depth of field. Multiple portable strobes are best used for portraits and other medium-to-close-up shooting situations.

Features you should look for are as follows:

✦ **Swivel head:** Allows you to bounce flash off the ceiling, rather than directing it at the subject.

✦ **Standard synch post:** For attaching a synch cable to the camera.

✦ **Built-in slave unit:** Eliminates the need for a cable—except when used in very bright lighting conditions (outdoors).

✦ **Wide-angle adjustment:** Spreads the light farther in order to cover the viewing angle of wide-angle lenses.

✦ **Fast recycle time:** Cuts the time you need to wait between exposures and makes the unit more useful for shooting candids and other animated subjects.

✦ **High guide number:** Means you can bounce light more effectively, use smaller apertures, or shoot more distant subjects.

✦ **Adjustable power:** This is an especially desirable feature if you're using a slave unit with a camera that has no capability for controlling aperture independently.

Studio strobe

Studio strobes can be classified as anything that requires a separate floor-standing power pack. That's a pretty broad category. Studio strobes are considerably more powerful than portable strobes. Most will allow you to attach several units to the same power pack, and quite a few power packs will let you adjust the power of each lamp individually.

Note   DigiSlave has recently introduced a slave sensor that can be attached to the synchronization connector of any strobe system and that will give you the option to synch with the second flash of a digital camera.

Studio strobes come in two main configurations: separate power pack and lamp heads, or monolights (see Figure 4-17). Monolights are so called because the power pack is built into the lamp head. The advantage is a more portable and less expensive studio strobe. The tradeoff is ruggedness and brightness. Monolights are more fragile and are top-heavy when perched on a stand. Some monolights allow a second head to be plugged in.

Figure 4-17: The strobe on the left is a monolight; on the right are external power packs that can by attached to individual strobe heads.

Desirable features for Studio Strobes include the following:

✦ Variable energy

✦ Variable energy per lamp head

✦ Auto bracketing

✦ Powerful modeling light

✦ Fast recycle times

✦ Ability to connect to overseas voltages

Some of the applications for studio strobes are as follows:

✦ Stopping action

✦ Controlling the direction and diffusion of light

✦ Balancing light with daylight

Incandescent

Incandescent lights are those that stay illuminated as long as the switch is on. They are the only type of lighting you can use if you're using a medium- or large-format digital camera with a scanning back. They are also a requirement if you are shooting motion video and then capturing your images from that.

The primary advantage of incandescent lights is that you can constantly see and judge the effect they are having on the subject. You'll find this especially important if the surfaces you are photographing are shiny or reflective.

Incandescents come in nearly every size, shape, form factor, and price range. Some of them are even as expensive as studio strobes. You can use high-wattage household light bulbs in aluminum reflectors. How much difference each makes will depend on the following factors:

✦ **How long your exposures can be:** You can use household bulbs in inexpensive hardware store reflectors if you're just copying art or shooting still lifes and have a sturdy tripod. You can even shoot people this way, but asking people to "hold it" kills spontaneity.

✦ **How focused the light needs to be:** If you can bounce the light off a reflector, such as an umbrella or a piece of white foam board, you won't have to worry about spotty lighting. Soft lighting is often best for many types of subjects. This is even more true in digital photography, where you will have more control over contrast in your image processing software. Also, many digital photographs are made in pieces, and then composited into an overall composition. It is easier to eliminate the background when it is evenly lit. It's also usually easier to make realistic matches.

✦ **How even the light needs to be:** If you are photographing flat art or documents, the lighting needs to be perfectly flat (even) over all parts of the subject. This is best accomplished by placing diffused lighting sources at 45-degree angles to the center of the picture and at exactly the same distance from the center of the picture.

✦ **How exacting your color temperature requirements are:** If you are photographing color-critical subject matter (catalog fashion, art works, medical, and scientific photography are all good examples of where this is the case).

Reflectors and diffusers

Nothing has greater influence over the quality of light produced by a light source than the reflector that the light surrounds itself with or the diffuser that is used in combination with that reflector. Portable and built-in strobes have more limited reflector options than do incandescent studio lamps and studio strobes. However, built-in strobes can be covered with tracing paper or fiberglass to diffuse their output and portable strobes can be bounced off ceilings and walls or fired into reflectors such as white- or silver-toned boards, or into umbrella reflectors. For studio lights, both incandescent and strobe, the types of reflectors and diffusers and the advantages of each are as follows:

✦ **Hemispheres:** Bowl-shaped reflectors are the most common type. They generally cast a moderately hard-edged light, though not as hard-edged as that cast by a spotlight. The softness of shadow edges is also influenced by four qualities: the size and curvature of the reflector, the shininess of the reflective surface, and the smoothness of the reflective surface. The larger the reflector, the softer the light. The shallower the bowl, the softer the light (see Figure 4-18). A flat white interior surface will produce softer light than a polished silver surface (also, too highly polished a surface is likely to cause uneven lighting). A textured reflective surface will also produce a softer light. Since highly polished surfaces also produce light that's brighter overall, some silvered surfaces are brushed or pebble-grained so that light will bounce in many directions.

✦ **Umbrellas:** Umbrellas are simply big bowl reflectors that are highly portable because they fold up (like an umbrella — see Figure 4-19). The light is faced into the back of the umbrella (which is covered by white or silver fabric), so it is already somewhat diffused by its own reflector. The result is a very soft light, but you can still control direction.

✦ **Light banks:** I'm not sure why they call them light banks. I think of a "bank" of lights as a column of several lights. Most of today's light banks consist of a single source light inside large nylon rectangular tents. The face of the reflector is generally covered with one or more diffusers. The result is diffuse, but more directional than umbrella reflectors. The effect is most similar to the light from a skylight or window.

Reflective flat surface

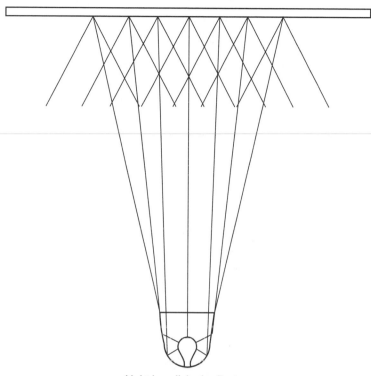

Light in polished reflector

Figure 4-18: Drawing showing how light bounces off a shallow white reflector versus a cone-shaped silvered reflector

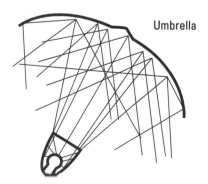

Umbrella

Very diffuse light that can be directed.

Figure 4-19: Drawing showing how light bounces off an umbrella reflector

✦ **Flat surfaces:** One of the best ways to brighten shadows is to use a reflector on the side of the subject opposite the light. This can be anything from a canvas-covered frame to foam-core boards to a roll-up movie screen. One of the least expensive and most effective reflectors for photographing small objects and portraits is a white foam-core board. This can be clamped to a light stand, held in an assistant's hand, or leaned against the side of a still-life table.

✦ **Pattern diffusers:** If you want to create the illusion that light is being filtered through the leaves and branches of a tree or the filigreed pattern of a mosque window, you can cut patterns out of translucent gels or (if you want more opaque patterns) out of black cardboard. These can be placed in front of any of your light sources.

Stands

Anything that will hold your lights at the height and position you want them in will work as a stand. However, you'll have an easier time moving, storing, and adjusting stands that are made for the purpose. Serious light stands will cost you between $40 and $100. Two of the most popular suppliers are Smith-Victor (on the low end) and Bogen (on the professional studio end). If your lights are expensive studio strobes, you'll want sturdy stands with wide-spreading feet. Accessories that are commonly needed are sandbags and waterbags (to ensure that top-heavy setups won't topple) and booms arms for holding lights directly over a still-life table or a foam-core reflector.

Filters (gels)

You can use colored filters in front of lamps to change the color temperature of the lamp. If the gels are being used to project an atmospheric color (say orange and blue on the backdrop to simulate the feeling of a nightclub in a studio shot), you can use inexpensive cellophane from gift wrapping or an art-supply store. Make sure that the gels are far enough in front of the light that they don't catch fire.

Sets and Backgrounds

If you need elaborate settings and don't have a client with a big budget, digital photography can be a lifesaver. Shoot against a blue background and then knock out the background and replace it with a location photo that you shot on location (or an inexpensive stock photo).

Blue and white seamless paper will be indispensable if you're shooting in the studio. Blue is ideal for masking the subject so that you can substitute a background from another file. White is often used because it's clean and simple, and it's easy to set type against it. Of course, many other colors are used as well. You can buy seamless rolls from most serious art-supply and professional photo stores. A 9 × 125 foot seamless costs about $45. A 4-foot wide seamless for portraits and tabletop work costs about $25. You'll also want adjustable stands to hold the paper rolls.

Of course, you can also use all sorts of building materials for a background. Portrait photographers are very fond of using large canvas painter's drop cloths with faux marble and other textured finishes painted on them. The only limit is your imagination.

Light Meters

You need a light meter (often called an exposure meter) in order to know how much (what lens aperture) light you should let strike the light sensor and for how long (shutter speed). Most meters make their calculation based on the proper exposure for an object that is 50-percent gray (that is, exactly half way between pure black and pure white).

Light meters are built in to most 35mm format film and digital cameras and into virtually all prosumer and point-and-shoot digital cameras. They are even built in to a fair number of medium-format cameras. So if your camera has a built-in light meter, you may wonder why you'd consider purchasing one separately. If you're going to take great photographs, you have to be able to measure light accurately and consistently. Following are a few of the reasons a separate meter is a very good idea — or even indispensable:

✦ **To get consistent exposure across several cameras:** Built-in meters vary their interpretation of reflected light from camera to camera and from mode to mode. Furthermore, they all measure light reflected from the subject. So if your subject is a small object against a much lighter or darker background, the reading of overall reflected light can be quite different. Using an external incident light meter will allow you to measure all of the light falling on the subject from a given direction. This is often a much more consistent reading. In any case, if the readings from your two meters differ considerably, you have good grounds to bracket your exposures. For more on measuring exposure, see the section in Chapter 9 called "Using a Light Meter."

✦ **To get a second opinion:** This is closely related to the first reason. If your independent meter gives you an exposure that's markedly different from your built-in meter's reading, you have to think about why. For instance, is there a lot a flare from a reflection in a shiny object? Is your built-in meter way off? One of the cameras I use frequently consistently overexposes by a full f-stop. Since I now know that, I simply make all exposures with that camera at −1EV.

✦ **To measure light falling on the subject rather than that reflected from it:** All built-in meters measure reflected light. The most important types of external meters measure something called "incident light." Incident light is the light falling on the subject itself, whether reflected or coming directly from a light source. The reading from an incident light meter will (or should, if the meter's accurate) suggest a range of correct exposures for an object that's 50-percent gray, regardless what light is reflected by objects in the scene.

✦ **To buy insurance:** Your built-in meter can fail. Having an external meter gives you a backup.

✦ **To be your only means of measuring light:** If you have a camera that lacks a built-in meter but does give you the means to control exposure, you definitely need an external light meter.

✦ **To meter light from external strobes:** If you use external strobes, you'll want a strobe meter. However, strobe meters aren't as necessary for digital cameras because most let you see the image immediately after it's been shot. So if it's overexposed or underexposed, you simply adjust exposure until you get the desired result.

There are quite a few different types of light meters. Each of the following types is described below:

✦ Built-in

✦ Incident light

✦ Handheld

✦ Spot

✦ Multipurpose (strobe meter is dead)

Built-in

Built-in meters measure reflected light, but they vary widely in their methods and options for doing so. They also vary widely in their accuracy and long-term reliability. Many built-in meters will also measure strobe. Some flash-reading internal meters require that the strobe fire twice—once for the reading and again for the exposure.

The best internal meters are the ones that give you all three of the following options: center-weighted metering, matrix metering, and spot metering. Figure 4-20 demonstrates how center-weighting works:

Reflected light

Reflected light meters measure the intensity of light reflected from the subject. Usually, a reflected light meter is used at the position of the camera and aimed at the subject. You can also move in close to the subject to measure the light reflected from a small area or measure the light from the camera's point of view. Most reflected light meters measure light over an angle of approximately 30 degrees.

Figure 4-20: Meter prioritizes the reading from light reflected in the center of the image

The following circumstances provide the best reason for using a standalone reflected light meter:

✦ **Low-cost backup for a built-in meter:** Most reflected light meters retail for well under $100. They provide a good way to check the accuracy and consistency of your camera's meter.

✦ **Can be used to read the light reflected from particular objects in a scene by holding it close to them:** This is the best way to get readings for a zone system calculation.

✦ **Cross-camera portability:** An external meter can be used with all your cameras, so that exposure is consistent from one camera to another.

The most important feature to look for in a reflected light meter is

✦ **Accuracy:** Since you'll probably want this meter to verify the readings from a built-in meter, buy one with a reputation for accuracy. Test it against some other meters that you know to be accurate. Finally, read the reviews in the serious photo magazines.

Incident light

Incident light meters measure the intensity of light falling on a piece of frosted glass or plastic. Most meters come with both flat and half-dome sensor diffusers. Flat diffusers measure the light evenly; dome diffusers will average highlights and shadows. You use these meters by holding them directly in front of the subject and pointing them at the camera.

Applications for incident light meters are as follows:

✦ **When "stray" light** (such as backlighting) or areas of strong reflectance might "fool" a reflected light meter.

✦ **When objects in a scene predominate** but may not be the areas you want to place in the middle of the tonal range.

✦ **When you want to measure several light sources independently,** as in studio lighting.

Qualities to look for in incident light meters are as follows:

✦ **Ability to average readings from several light sources:** This is a big help in studio work when averaging the reading from several individual lights.

✦ **Sensitivity to very low light:** Makes it possible to get accurate readings for midtones when shooting night scenes or subjects that are illuminated by such sources as computer screens or candlelight.

✦ **Ability to freeze reading:** Since you must often place the meter as close as possible to the subject while aiming it at the camera, the readout is often upside-down. You want to be able to turn the meter around without having the meter read the light coming from a different angle.

Spot

Spot meters are reflected light meters that use a lens to narrow the reading to a very small angle. This is typically between 1 and 5 degrees. They accomplish the same thing as when you place a regular reflected light meter within a few inches of a particular area of the subject. The advantage is that you can read almost any small area of any subject without having to waste time and energy running around. You can also meter small areas that might otherwise be inaccessible, such as the highlights in the waterfall on the other side of the canyon.

Worthwhile features include the following:

✦ Variable spot angle from 1–5 degrees

✦ Zoom optical viewfinder

Typical applications include the following:

+ Zone system

+ Measuring distant objects or critically important small areas

+ Highly reflective surfaces

+ Extreme contrast scenes

+ Backlighting situations

Multipurpose

If you are a pro who needs to deal with a wide variety of situations, including strobe, you really only need one meter (see Figure 4-21). For significantly less than the cost of two specialized meters, you can buy one meter that acts as incident, reflective, spot, and flash meters. These are generally digital-readout meters that are accurate to within one-tenth of a stop. For around $200, you can get a model that reads either flash or ambient light. For a bit more, you can get a model that does the same, will also read a combination of flash and ambient light, and will read flash either with or without being connected to a synch cord. For around $350, you can get a meter that does all this and adds a spot meter.

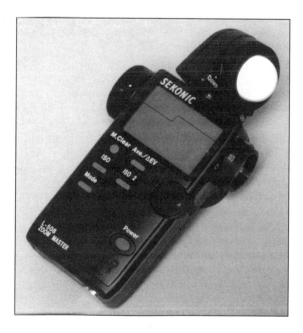

Figure 4-21: This combination meter works as either spot or incident light meter for either ambient light or strobe — even for a combination of the two.

Summary

This chapter has discussed the various types of equipment you are most likely to need for setting up a complete studio for shooting digital photos. It will have been most valuable to readers who are contemplating getting started. Hopefully, it will also serve professionals as a reminder for making a checklist. In the first half of the chapter, the types and application fit of each category of both conventional and digital cameras was discussed. This was followed by the same sort of discussion for all the various studio accessories that are most commonly used — everything from tripods to lighting to seamless backgrounds.

✦   ✦   ✦

The Essentials of the Digital Lab

Aside from an occasional need to overdevelop or underdevelop film to keep the brightness range under control, there's simply no need for chemical processing when doing digital photography. However, you will still need well-chosen equipment in your digital lab if you hope to get the best postshoot results. This chapter will help you understand the necessary (and not so necessary) items for stocking your digital lab.

I'm sure I don't need to tell you that you need a computer for digital photography. The question is, what are the best characteristics of a computer that is to be used for manipulating photographs? The short answer is: lots of everything — lots of memory, lots of performance (speed), lots of color, and lots of monitor real estate. If your interest in digital photography is on the level of commercial work or fine arts, you simply can't have too much memory or too fast a computer. If your interest is solely in on-computer applications for digital photography (such as the Internet or multimedia) or you just want to learn, most any modern (within a couple of generations of the current state-of-the-art) computer with more than 32MB of RAM and a true-color display and monitor will do the trick.

Platform

If you are going to do your own prepress work (converting files to four-color files, color matching, making color separations, placing images into a document layout), you'll find the Macintosh has more followers. Several reasons exist for this, but the main one is that Windows is only just now seriously trying to catch up to the level of color calibration standards that have existed on the Macintosh for some time.

If your sole interest is in acquiring, editing, and manipulating digital images, the choice of platform becomes much less important. One very powerful image-manipulation program, LivePicture 2.6 (and its days may be numbered), runs only on the Macintosh. Some Photoshop plug-in filters run only on the Macintosh (but there are also some that run only under Windows). However, core applications such as Adobe Photoshop, MetaCreations' Painter, and almost all camera and scanner image acquisition software work virtually identically on either Mac or Wintel computers.

Whether Mac or Windows, having USB and FireWire ports on your computer means that you're prepared to connect to the latest developments in digital imaging technology and that you're able to efficiently move images from camera or scanner to computer. The new Apple PowerMac G4 line of computers that feature very fast processors, easy accessibility to expansion slots, built-in USB and serial ports, and a precalibrated color monitor — all for under $3,000.

Speed

Manipulating individual pixels in 24-bit color depth takes lots of computational muscle. While just about any computer can produce results in far less time than it would take to do the same thing in a chemical darkroom, it won't seem that way if all you have to do for an hour is sit and watch the hourglass icon. Get the fastest computer you can afford, as long as it runs all the software you want to run. If you're doing digital photography as a business, the fastest computer you can buy will pay for itself quickly. After all, these days even some of the fastest computers cost less than $3,000 — not including peripherals.

RAM

There's an old adage in the image-processing business: There's no such thing as too much RAM or too much money. Add at least 128MB to the base configuration of the computer you buy. Otherwise, you simply won't be able to get the resolutions you need for commercial or fine arts work — at least not at a speed you'll be willing to tolerate. Another good rule of thumb is that you need at least three times as much RAM as the resolution of the largest image you'll be processing.

It's not all a matter of resolution, either. After all, a typical 35mm scan will only be about 18MB. If we follow our 3:1 rule of thumb, you should only need about 48MB of RAM. However, some operations, especially plug-in filters, require considerable extra memory of their own. You will quickly (if you haven't already) learn the wonders of being able to edit images on multiple layers. Each new layer can require as much memory as is used by the resolution of the base image. So, an 18MB file with four additional layers can easily approach 100MB.

Storage

Having just read the above section on RAM, you may be wondering where you're going to put the hundreds of 18–120MB images that you're going to be producing over the next few months. So you've probably already figured out that, next to RAM, disk storage is of supreme importance. To make a long story short, you should already be thinking about buying a CD-ROM burner. In the meantime, all the other forms of disk storage can make worthwhile contributions to the digital imaging workflow.

Floppies

Floppy disks seem to be on their way out, at least if the rest of the world follows Apple's lead. Meantime, there's at least one excellent use for floppies: artist's portfolios and small electronic catalogs. You can place several dozen true-color, screen-sized (640 × 480 or smaller) JPEG-compressed images on a 50-cent floppy.

Hard drive

The price of hard drives has fallen as precipitously (or more so) as the price of RAM. You will want as large a hard drive as you find affordable, for the following reasons:

✦ You need at least 640MB that you can use for storing files that will be recorded to CD-ROM.

✦ You need at least another free gigabyte of hard drive space to store working digital files. Remember, you're likely to be working on images with multiple layers until they're finished. You may also have several files that are contributing to the finished file. Then there are the facts that you're probably working on more than one project at a time and that many projects involve multiple images.

✦ You need enough hard drive space to store all your program files, plug-in filters, and help files.

✦ The more free disk space you have, the more space is available for virtual memory. Especially for Windows users, this means that there's less likelihood of a crash when you unexpectedly run out of RAM.

You will constantly be loading and saving files that are typically between 18MB and 250MB in size: BIG. So, get the fastest hard drive you can afford. If you're watching your budget, you might consider a smaller superfast drive for your programs and working data and a much bigger but somewhat slower drive for use as a project and CD-ROM content "warehouse." If you plan to do nonlinear digital video editing, be sure to get SCSI or FireWire drives that are very fast and that don't do a thermal recalibration while they're reading data.

What's This About Thermal Recalibration?

This isn't the time to get into an explanation of thermal recalibration. Just know that you should check with the drive literature or the drive maker to see whether the drive does thermal recalibration and whether or not its driver software gives you an option to turn this off. Drives that are labeled AV drives don't do thermal recalibration, but it's also an option on some drives that aren't so labeled. Finally, if you are editing from a digital video source, such as a miniDV camcorder, and have a FireWire connection, you can "get away with" ordinary drives because the software will make sure that the digital data is stored continuously.

Removable media hard drives

Removable media drives (such as those made by Syquest, Iomega, and Imation) are terrific for sending finished files to a service bureau or client. They're also handy for off-loading work in progress and for exchanging files with other computers in your office that aren't hooked to a local area network. Syquest was up for sale at the time of this writing, leaving Iomega as the de facto standard for removable drives. The Imation SuperDisk, which holds slightly more data per disk than a Zip disk and is compatible with floppy drives, may also make some inroads. Still, I'd go with the Iomega, because it's more likely that people with whom you may want to exchange disks have compatible drives.

They're not quite as popular, but much higher capacity (1–2GB) removable drives are available from Syquest and Iomega. Once again, the Iomega Jaz drives have become the de facto standard by default. These drives become nearly indispensable if you want to keep work in progress separated by project or client and want to be able to off-load those catalogs when they're not active. They're also useful for off-loading CD-ROM contents that aren't quite ready to commit to write-once media.

Another type of removable media is read/write optical disks. These seem to have waned in popularity in recent years because the drives mentioned above are cheaper, faster, and use less expensive media.

CD-ROM, CD-RW, and DVD-RAM

If you're going to get serious about digital photography, you're going to want to add a CD recorder to your studio. Then you can archive your files on very cheap media (640MB for well under a dollar if you do a little shopping around) that can't be accidentally erased (unless you use sandpaper or throw the disk on a burning log).

There are actually three kinds of CD-ROM recorders: write-once, read-write, and DVD-RAM. Write-once recorders just make a CD and the data can't be replaced. Read-write recorders record on a special media that enables you to write files to it whenever you want and to erase any that are no longer needed. In other words, it behaves just like a really slow hard drive (well, maybe more like a great big floppy). DVD-RAM can hold about 11 times as much data (about 4.7GB) on *one side* of a disk that's the same size as a CD-ROM. The format was originally invented for distributing motion pictures and high-resolution, fast-action multi-media. It should be especially interesting to you if you also work in digital video. Otherwise, the media and the recorders both cost a bit more, partially negating one of the charms of recording and distributing images on CD-ROM.

Placing images on CD-ROM is also a great way to send files to clients, service bureaus, and publications. If you don't get the CD-ROM back, you won't be out much money. Be sure you make it plain that all images on the CD are copyrighted and (if that's the case) that they're strictly for one-time use.

You can (with software that permits it) write to a single CD several times (this is called a multisession CD-ROM). However, you can only play that CD on the machine that is in the process of recording it. To make that same CD readable by other computers, you must tell the recording software to close out the disk. Once you've done that, you can't record any more sessions to that disk.

Tip

You can write hybrid and PC-format CDs on a Mac, but can't write to Mac-format CDs from a Windows machine. You can, however, write image files into the cross-platform ISO 9660 format on virtually any type of desktop computer. The disks can then be played on virtually any computer.

Display card

You need a display card that interprets in order to be able to send a signal to the computer's monitor that interprets your software and graphics as you expect them to be interpreted.

The computer's display card may, in fact, be either a card plugged into one of your computer's expansion slots or it may be built in to the motherboard. You can get by with the type built in to the motherboard as long as it supports true color (24-bit, 16.8 million colors). You really want it to be able to support true color at a resolution high enough to fill a 21-inch monitor. This is really a matter of assigning more video memory to the display, so if your motherboard's video RAM is expandable, you'll be safe.

The advantages to having the display built on to the motherboard are lower overall cost of the computer and the fact that one expansion slot is available for other purposes. The problem is that it's a bit harder to upgrade the video hardware. Most computers, however, will enable you to turn off the onboard video driver in favor of a plug-in card. If you are running Windows 98 or a Macintosh, you can simply plug in an additional video card and monitor Then you can place all your toolboxes and menus on your old, tiny monitor and use another (probably larger) monitor for editing your pictures.

If you don't have the display built in, it's easy to simply replace one display system with a better one as the technology (inevitably) improves: just remove the old software, pull the old display card from its slot, and follow the instructions for installing a new card and driver software. If you are running a Macintosh or Windows 98, the system will automatically find the new hardware and make all the appropriate changes to the computer's setup instructions.

Your display card will greatly affect the performance of the graphics software you use for processing images. In the best of all worlds, you want a 128-bit display card that uses 8MB or more of RAM and understands the latest graphics and/or multimedia instruction sets for the platform you are working on. If you are running Windows (any flavor), you want to be sure the display card can process all the latest MMX instructions.

Monitor

In the beginning, there was the Sony Trinitron for anyone serious about graphics and prepress applications. Few professionals would consider using anything else. There were lots of other manufacturer's names on those Trinitrons, but they were all made by Sony (see Figure 5-1). Although the technology has since been licensed to other manufacturers, the monitors that use it are still arguably the best. The two primary reasons why this is so are as follows. First, the tube is absolutely flat in the vertical direction (and, in the latest models, in the horizontal direction as well), so there's less glare in the image resulting from the reflection of overhead lighting. There's also less likelihood of barrel and pincushion distortion and greater likelihood of edge-to-edge sharpness. Second, image sharpness and brightness are also above average because these monitors use a single scanning gun to illuminate the monitor's phosphors, rather than one gun for each primary color. The use of a single gun eliminates the chances that the three primary colors will be slightly out of register — particularly as the monitor ages.

Trinitrons have another huge advantage. All the color calibration software understands the monitor's color characteristics — so it is much easier to calibrate these monitors.

If your monitor isn't a Trinitron, don't despair. Other manufacturers have worked so hard at competing with the Trinitron that it's getting harder all the time to find a monitor that's not worthy of image processing. If you see a great buy on another manufacturer's monitor, especially from an established vendor, you're probably getting a decent buy. Here are the things you should look for on the monitor's spec sheets:

✦ **High refresh rate:** A refresh rate of better than 75 MHz at the highest resolution. High refresh rates reduce flicker, which reduces eye strain, which improves your ability to judge picture quality. The higher the refresh rate, the better.

✦ **Name brand:** This is important for more than the obvious reasons. The better-known manufacturers are more likely to be able to supply you with a ColorSync (for Mac, or ICC profile for PC) profile, which will help you greatly to accurately calibrate the monitor.

Figure 5-1: The Radius 19-inch Trinitron monitor sells for as little as $600 on the street. Note the flat vertical edges of the monitor, indicating that it is a true Trinitron.

✦ **High maximum resolution:** You should be able to go to at least 800×600 for a 15-inch monitor, $1,024 \times 768$ for a 17-inch monitor, and $1,280 \times 1,024$ for a 19- or 20-inch monitor. These are higher than the resolutions recommended for what-you-see-is-what-you-get typesetting and page layout. The reason I recommend using a somewhat higher resolution for image editing is that menus get smaller and the image looks tighter and a bit more photographic. Remember, you can always zoom in if you want to examine individual pixels more closely.

✦ **Digital controls:** A complete set of monitor controls let you adjust image height, width, and position, and control three types of distortion: barrel, pincushion, and focus. If you don't get all those controls, proceed with caution. If these controls are digital, they're much easier to readjust should you need to change your screen settings or use the monitor on another computer.

✦ **Degauss button:** You should be able to degauss your monitor before calibrating it.

Digitizing pad

If you're going to do much of the sort of image editing that requires you to retouch small details, carefully make manual selections of objects (you're almost certain to need to do this eventually), or to do any freehand drawing at all, forget trying to use a mouse. It's like trying to make an etching with a bar of soap. What you really want is a digitizing pad (see Figure 5-2).

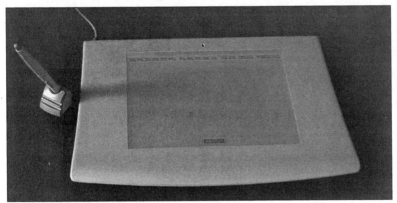

Figure 5-2: The Wacom Intuos 6 × 9-inch digitizing pad

A digitizing pad lets you draw on a flat surface with the pen. The position of the tip of the pen is always precisely related to a corresponding position on the monitor, regardless of whether you picked it up and moved it between strokes. In fact, you can even use a digitizing pen to trace an existing image.

By far the most widely used digitizing pads for digital imaging and fine arts folks are those from Wacom. Wacom pioneered the use of pressure-sensitive pens. Pressure-sensitive pens can change the size of the brush stroke or the transparency of the stroke. Which of these takes effect depends on the setting you make in your image-editing software.

Wacom is also one of the few makers of digitizing pads that uses batteryless pens. Batteries add considerably to the weight of the pen, so you don't get as natural a "feel" from the instrument. Also, when the battery starts to die, unpredictable things start happening to your pen strokes.

Wacom's latest line of digitizing pads takes the feel of natural media even further. For instance, there are new Photoshop plug-ins called Pen Tools and a new "airbrush" pen that lets you control the volume of paint with a wheel, just like a real airbrush. Also, when you tilt the airbrush, the paint area expands and fades with distance from the tip of the brush.

You may be able to find real bargains on other brands of digitizing pads. If so, any digitizing pad is better than a mouse. Other features to look for in a digitizing pad are as follows:

✦ **Wacom-compatible pressure sensitivity:** Many software packages simply don't recognize the pressure-sensitive feature of other manufacturers' pens. Most of them know this and make their pens and pads Wacom-compatible.

✦ **Size:** Size doesn't matter nearly as much as having a pressure-sensitive digitizing pad. Some artists, however, will feel cramped by smaller pads. Big pads can take up lots of desktop, so most feel that a 6 × 9 pad is the best compromise. It feels a little more natural because it's approximately the width of letter-size paper.

✦ **Versatility:** Check to see if there are such extras as plug-ins for pen tools or special painterly effects, and different styles of pens and pucks (such as an airbrush, 4D mouse, or cross-hair puck).

✦ **Resolution:** Anything over 1,000 dpi is workable. Some go as high as 2,500 dpi. More resolution simply means more precise control over the exact placement of the cursor (pen tip). The smaller the tablet in relation to the size of the monitor, the more important the resolution of the pad.

Software

Once you've got the horsepower and accessories you need in the computer platform of your choice, you'll need software to process and manipulate your images. Depending on your requirements, you may be able to get by with the software that came with your digital camera — or you may need to add thousands of dollars worth of software. For that reason, you may want to pay particular attention to software that comes bundled with the hardware you need. For instance, many scanners come with Photoshop. Even if the bundled version of the software is a "light" version that doesn't have all the features of the current version of the product, you will be able to buy the full version at an upgrade cost. Upgrades are usually only one-third the price of full versions. So, if you bought a scanner that came bundled with Photoshop LE, you could upgrade to the full current version of Photoshop for about $400 less than the full version would normally cost you. Some pretty decent flatbed scanners that bundle Photoshop LE can be had for well under $200. It's like getting a $200 discount on Photoshop and a free scanner.

You may need image-processing software in any or all of the following categories:

✦ Office

✦ Professional processing

✦ Compositing

✦ Natural media paint

✦ Batch processing

✦ Internet prep

Office

Individual needs for Internet and e-mail, word processing, spreadsheet, contact management, bookkeeping, and presentation software vary widely and is the subject of hundreds of books. Just be sure that you understand how much of your budget and hard drive space have to be devoted to those applications. Otherwise, you may not have the resources to implement the digital imaging applications that are your goal.

Basic image acquisition and processing

Several kinds of software exist for getting a digital image from camera or scanner converted to data that your computer can manipulate. There are also several categories of software meant strictly for manipulating images, including packages that specialize in preparing images for maximum performance on Web sites.

Professional image processing

The industry standard in this category is Adobe Photoshop (see Figure 5-3). Photoshop has many worthy competitors. Often, people who are serious about digital imaging own several of these programs because some are especially good at masking, mix in some natural-media paint capabilities (covered later), or have some other trait that makes them especially valuable in some particular area. If your interest in digital photography is personal or is restricted to internal company use, programs such as Corel Photo-Paint (Mac and Windows), iGrafx Picture Publisher (Windows only), Deneba Canvas (Mac and Windows), and PaintShop Pro (Windows only) will do the job well. Furthermore, all of these programs can use at least some of the plug-ins that extend Photoshop's already powerful capabilities.

When it comes to image-editing capabilities, Photoshop has lots of worthy competition. The most compelling reason for using Photoshop as your primary image-editing software is its enormous installed base. If you need to share work with another, chances are greatest that they will be using the same program. If you send your work out to be printed, included in a layout, or to a client, the chances are greatest that the program that will be continuing the work on your file will be Photoshop. Of course, almost all other current-version image-editing programs can read a Photoshop file, but you may lose certain Photoshop features. The real value in using the same editor as others who will be continuing work on your files is communications: you will have a common background for discussing the changes that need to be made at the next stage. Another reason for using Photoshop is that virtually all digital cameras and film scanners ship with a Photoshop plug-in. This gives you the ability to acquire images from that device from within your image-editing application, so you don't have to import the files from the device's stand-alone image editor. Finally, if you use Photoshop, you are guaranteed to be able to run any Photoshop-compatible plug-in that strikes your fancy. The reason this is important is that virtually all plug-in manufacturers make their products to be compatible with Photoshop. While most other image-editing programs claim to be Photoshop plug-in compatible, they are often not compatible with all Photoshop plug-ins. This is especially true of acquire modules, Photoshop's native (built-in) plug-ins, and plug-ins designed to be compatible only with the latest version of Photoshop (very rare).

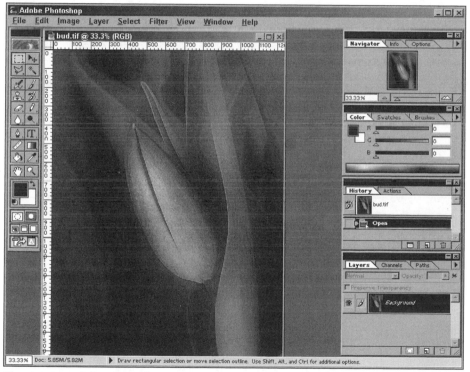

Figure 5-3: Adobe Photoshop 5.0 is the de facto standard in software for processing and manipulating digital images on a professional level.

Compositing

One type of image-editing software is especially capable at making surrealistic special effects images that are actually composed of many individual photographs. They are often used to create the illusion that all of the people and objects in the photograph were captured at the same place and instant. The result can be anything from celebrities in the company of aliens to incredibly beautiful and credible ads showing SUVs perched atop peaks in Monument Valley.

Photoshop is often used for this purpose, but it bogs down when the superhigh-resolution advertising files have to be created from multiple layers. A much better choice—the one used by such pros as John Lund—is Live Picture 2.6 (see Figure 5-4). Live Picture's chief competitor is Macromedia's old product, xRes. Both programs use a technology that makes it possible to work on multilayered, high-resolution files in real time. They can do this even when the host computer is equipped with relatively little memory. This is all made possible by a technology (somewhat different in each case) that stores the files and layers on the hard drive in a variety of resolutions.

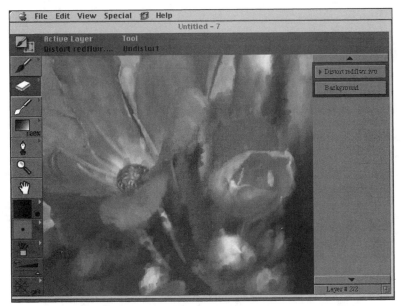

Figure 5-4: LivePicture 2.6 is the most popular Mac program for image compositing.

This type of software is generically term "proxy editing" software. When you are editing an image, the program always uses the lowest-resolution image possible—that is, a "proxy" of the original image. As you work, the computer stores all your actions. When you've completed the job, the computer then repeats the actions you've taken on the full-resolution original files. Any "experimental" steps you took, such as making multiple rotations and transformations to make an object fit the composition, are thrown out. Only those steps necessary to produce the final result are used. This process is called "rendering" the file. Rendering can take anywhere from a few minutes to an hour, but you can be doing other productive things (such as sleeping or eating) in the meantime. Because the rendering process minimizes the number of pixel changes that are made to manipulated objects, the finished product is of much higher visual quality than would be the case if a standard image editor (such as those mentioned in the section above) were used.

Natural media paint

Another type of often-used image-editing program is used to imitate the traditional artist's tools, such as oils, pastels, ink, and watercolors. One program in particular, MetaCreations' Painter (see Figure 5-5), is especially good at this. Painter is priced at around $300, but there's also a version called Painter Classic. Classic is a "light" version of Painter that many Photoshop users find useful for adding special effects to portions of an image — or for turning photos into paintings — while paying plug-in prices. Painter Classic sells for just under $100.

Figure 5-5: MetaCreations' Painter is the leading natural-media paint program.

Many of Photoshop's competitors offer a limited but useful range of brushes that create natural-media-type effects. These aren't nearly as extensive or realistic as those available in either version of Painter, but they may be all you need. Other image editors with some natural-media painting capabilities include Corel Photo Paint 8, Deneba Canvas, Macromedia xRes, and PixelPaintPro3 from Pixel Resources, Inc.

Batch processing

If you do production work for media that requires collecting images from various sources and then giving them all uniform qualities, you need a program that specializes in processing multiple files according to a single set of criteria. For instance, you might want to place travel photos on a Web site that were created at various times on various computers by various photographers. The file sizes range from 40KB to 18MB and are in a variety of file formats (PSD [Photoshop], PICT, TIFF, JPEG, and so on). What you need to do is to convert all of these files to images that will fall within a boundary of 150 × 100 pixels, use the highest level of JPEG compression consistent with acceptable picture quality, and have them all be stored in the same disk directory, consecutively numbered after the filename, and to all have the same file extension and file type. To accomplish all of this in Photoshop, you could spend days.

The only cross-platform (Mac and Windows) program I know of that can accomplish all of the above in one processing run is DeBabelizer. You get an idea of DeBabelizer's Windows interface in Figure 5-6.

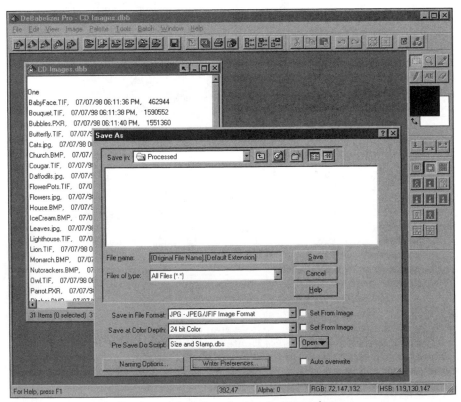

Figure 5-6: DeBabelizer's user interface for batch processing

Internet prep

A new category of image-processing software has arisen over the past couple of years: Internet image preparation software. Web developers often have to process dozens (or even hundreds) of images for a Web site. Small differences in quality and time savings per image can add up to huge savings for the project. Internet Prep software's specialty is making the best compromise between image quality and minimum file size. This category of software also contains other features that make it especially suited to handling the peculiarities of placing bitmapped images on Web sites. These features include making image maps, built-in GIF animation builders, beveled edges and drop shadows (for button making), and very accurate previews for judging image quality before the image is saved and compressed.

Examples of standalone Web image-processing software are Macromedia's Fireworks 2, Adobe's ImageReady (now included with Photoshop, starting with version 5.5 — see Figure 5-7), and ULead's WebRazor. If you already own an older version of Photoshop and want all the capabilities mentioned above, SPG Web Tools works as a Photoshop plug-in. It will also work with some other Photoshop plug-in–compatible applications. You can see ImageReady's user interface in Figure 5-7. Note the large preview window.

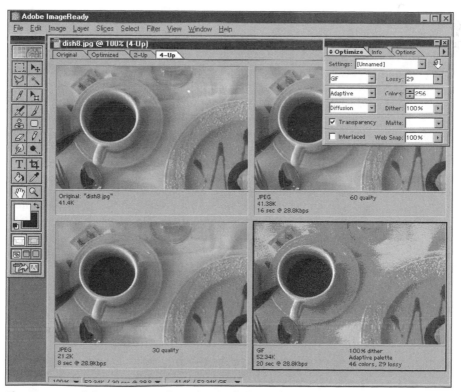

Figure 5-7: Adobe ImageReady at the ready for Web image processing

Asset management software

You will need some program to help you find your graphics files easily — something that lets you see "thumbnails" (contact sheet size images) of your pictures and that lets you rename files from the thumbnails and attach notes to them. If you are a Windows user, you'll be especially in need of one of these programs because Windows doesn't make picture icons of your graphics files as automatically as the Mac does.

The most popular of these programs is Extensis' Portfolio 3.0. It is a cross-platform application and you can freely distribute a portfolio "reader." That means that you can put a Portfolio thumbnail file on all your CDs. Then, anyone who receives the CD can view the images by thumbnail. They can also open them up to 1:1 resolution to inspect them more closely.

Portfolio is by no means your only choice. Canto Cumulus is especially popular with companies that have to manage huge asset inventories (such as news agencies and stock photo vendors). Black Magic Software makes a Mac-only shareware program called Pictodexer that you can download. Windows users can choose from several freeware and shareware programs, such as Irfan Viewer, Thumbs, InView, and AllnView. You can locate all of these utilities online through www.shareware.com.

Other types of graphics software

You have many ways to use the output from illustration and 3D modeling software in your image-editing program. For instance, you might create type and logos in Illustrator or CorelDraw (both vector-based illustration programs) and then export the result to a bitmapped file format that could be used as a layer in a Photoshop file. You could even complete an entire illustration in one of the above programs and then export it to Photoshop or Painter. In Photoshop, you could treat various areas with textures and edge effects. In Painter, you could use the drawing as a sketch for a natural-media painting. You could even combine the two.

3D modeling programs can create realistic-looking sets for cutout photographs. There are also specialized modeling programs that can create content for use in composite digital photographs. MetaCreations makes two of the favorites in this category: Poser 3 and Bryce 3D. Poser creates human figures in a variety of body types, and they can be dressed, lighted, posed, and rendered with a high degree of realism. It's an interesting way to create a crowd, place a figure in the distance to complete a composition, or for use in how-to photos. Bryce 3D creates natural landscapes that can be viewed from any angle and given any sort of cloud cover, weather conditions, and solar angle. You can even have several suns if you want to create science-fiction landscapes. Bryce can make wonderful backgrounds for such subjects as group portraits and car ads.

The programs mentioned above are the major graphics programs that are used in conjunction with photo-editing software such as Photoshop or Picture Publisher. However, virtually all graphics software can create images whose results can be imported into an image editor.

Output

So, what happens once you've captured and digitized your images and processed them in almost any imaginable way using the software mentioned in the previous section? You need to be able to show them to people. In other words, you need to output your images. Of course, you may be sending them to someone else for final output, such as to a service bureau or to your client. There's also the possibility that your images will only be used in electronic form, so there may be no need to print them on paper. Most photographers, however, want to be able to see the image on paper. More importantly, most clients are used to seeing the images on paper — or as slides.

Remember, if you need the output from one of the more expensive printers, you don't have to buy the printer to get it. Contact the manufacturer of the printer whose output you desire. Most maintain a list of companies (service bureaus) that will print your output for you.

What follows is an overview of each type of printer or other output device. Each of these sections will describe the category, explain its general usage and price range, and point you in the direction of the right types of products to look for.

One thing that may be required of any printer you use, especially if you're preparing digital photos for publication, is a PostScript interpreter.

Print Longevity

The conventional wisdom has been that inkjet printers produce prints that fade more rapidly than those made by any other printing technology. This has been true up until recently, because most ink-jet printers used dye-based inks that are very susceptible to atmospheric changes, ultraviolet light, and moisture. Besides, inkjet printer manufacturers have only recently begun to pay attention to the quality of paper. Recently, several manufacturers have been producing pigment-based inks and acid-free, UV-coated papers. Preliminary tests show that prints produced with the right combination of these new inks and papers can outlast just about anything previously known.

PostScript interpreters

A PostScript interpreter, or RIP (raster image processor), translates your images into the language most commonly understood in the printing industry. This makes it essential if you want to make match proofs of images that will be used in printed publications. A PostScript interpreter is also essential for making color-matched color separations that can be sent directly to a print shop.

Many users will use digital photography as part of a prepress workflow. If you fit into that category (most will at some point), you'll want to consider the options that your printer offers for PostScript interpretation. You can add PostScript interpreter software to virtually all popular types of full-color printers. However, generally speaking, you're better off if the interpreter is offered by the manufacturer of your printer. That's because printer features that are specific to your make and model are most likely to be implemented.

Printing is significantly faster for printers that have built-in PostScript interpreters, rather than requiring you to run the interpreter on your computer. However, the cost of the printer is usually significantly higher because the printer must have a built-in computer for interpreting the PostScript code.

If you are planning to run a wide-format printer, you will need a PostScript interpreter before your printer will print much of anything. Always look into which interpreters have been approved and recommended by the manufacturer of your printer.

Office printers

Many of today's office printers, especially laser and inkjet printers, are able to reproduce color photographs well enough to incorporate them into office documents (such as letters or inventory records) or informal in-house publications (such as newsletters). However, it's rare that a printer that can output business documents at a speed high enough to support a small but successful law partnership can also print photographs that look and feel like photographs.

Printers intended primarily for the output of office documents, even those that can do a credible job of printing photographs, have one serious limitation for serious digital photography buffs and professionals: print size. Most are limited to legal-sized (8.5-inch wide) documents. So they won't be able to do you much good if you need to make prints for exhibition, proofs of double-page spreads, or prints for photographer's portfolios.

Office inkjets

Many highly affordable inkjet printers can do a good-to-superb job of printing photographs and a credible job of printing office documents. However, the least expensive of these printers are relatively slow (typically 1–4 text pages per minute), so are best suited to lower-volume personal or entrepreneurial use. However, this situation is changing. A few new, higher-priced (but still under $600) inkjet printers can print text at laser-printer speeds and that use variable-size dots to reproduce continuous tone color. These printers can reproduce digital photographs that it would take an expert to discern from traditional photographic prints. Even some experts might be fooled, as a matter of fact.

Laser printers

Color laser printers simply can't produce color that's good enough for exhibition or for client approval. They can, however, produce very nice-looking photos in office documents and informal publications.

Most laser printers (and all of those that sell for under $1,000) are black and white only. Those that are most useful for reproducing digital photographs print at least 600-dpi resolution and have some version of what Hewlett-Packard calls Ret (Resolution enhancement technology). This technology makes the image resolution of graphics (particularly photos) appear much higher than the printer's 600 dpi by actually varying the size of dots in order to get smoother shades of color.

If you plan to use your office laser for informal publications, you're better off to choose one with a built-in PostScript interpreter. Some models of laser printers will enable you add PostScript as an option. You can also use a software interpreter, but then you diminish one of the major advantages of a laser printer: speed.

Laser printers have another advantage: print longevity. Because the inks used by lasers are pigment-based, their images are far less subject to fading than the output from dye-based inks. This makes them especially suitable for printing materials that will be posted on bulletin boards.

Desktop inkjet printers

Generally speaking, you'll get the most bang for the buck from inkjet printers. All of them, regardless of price, can print a digital photograph on glossy paper that looks and feels like photographic paper and with a quality that could fool any non-critical observer into thinking that they were looking at the real thing. For a few dollars more, there are inkjet printers that either print in six colors, have variable-size dot patterns, or both. Those machines can make prints that will fool all but the most knowledgeable experts and that are certainly of high enough quality for portfolio and exhibition work (see Figure 5-8). There are even desktop inkjet printers that can make prints as wide as 17 inches and that most serious individual professionals and hobbyists can afford (under $2,000).

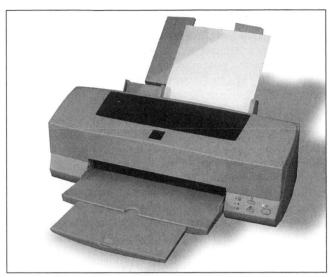

Figure 5-8: The Epson Photo EX prints true photographic quality at sizes up to 11 inches wide.

Don't make the mistake of lumping all inkjet printers together when it comes to print quality. Bubble jets heat the ink until a bubble is formed that forces ink out of the head. The size of the dot can be somewhat unpredictable and the technology is still improving. Piezoelectric technology, so far produced only by Epson, minimizes overspray and splatter. This results in noticeably sharper edges and better-defined dots that result in more vivid and predictable reproduction of the continuous-tone color transitions so essential to the faithful printing of photographs.

Another type of inkjet is used in Iris printers that use variable dot size to produce even more continuous-tone images. These printers are covered under wide-format inkjet printers in one of the following sections. They are mentioned here, however, because the latest development in desktop inkjet printers is variable dot size. Variable dot size was first introduced by Epson in its Stylus 900, a high-speed office inkjet that can also produce incredibly sharp continuous-tone photographs using only four inks.

Another technology pioneered by Epson, and since adopted by other manufacturers, is the use of more than four colors of ink. The Epson Photo series of desktop inkjet printers use six colors. The additional colors are light yellow and light magenta. This allows for the reproduction of subtle changes in light colors without forcing dots to be spaced further apart. The result is the appearance of continuous-tone color, even in such details as highlights and skin tones.

PostScript interpreters are available for many but not all models of desktop inkjet printers. These are all software interpreters. Be sure to check the manufacturer's literature for the inkjet printer you are considering if you feel that a PostScript interpreter will be important to you. You don't need a PostScript interpreter for a desktop inkjet printer if you just want to print personal, portfolio, or exhibition photographs.

Inkjet printers that are suitable for use by photographic professionals for larger than letter-size output fall into the following size and price categories:

✦ **Portfolio inkjets:** These are desktop printers that can make prints up to 11 inches wide. Most will print at any "reasonable" length. These printers work well for creating photographers' and models' portfolios, making exhibition prints, and for printing comprehensive tabloid-size double-page layouts. The Epson 1270, which can make a full-bleed tabloid-size image and can print with long-life inks and papers, is the leading example of this type of printer at the moment.

✦ **Inkjets for proofing and small gallery exhibition:** These should be printers that can print at better than 600 dpi, use archival inks and papers, and can make prints that are at least 16 inches wide. While several 24-inch wide inkjets meet these specifications, they tend to fall outside the price range of all but the most successful photographers. The one notable exception is the Epson 3000, which retails for less than $1,300. You can expect a more competitive situation over the next few months, however.

✦ **Wide-format inkjets:** These printers are generally purchased by service bureaus or corporate art departments. The most highly honored models for printing photos come from Iris, ColorSpan, and Epson (9000 and 4000).

Dye-sublimation printers

The best photographic quality and the most accurate prepress proofs still come from the high-ticket dye-sublimation printers. That is because dye-sublimation printers produce true continuous-tone output. In fact, if anything gives them away as not being traditional photographic prints, it is the fact that there is simply no visible grain structure.

These printers work by heating a plastic ribbon that contains the dye. The heat turns the dye to a gaseous state and these gases are then absorbed by the polyester surface of the paper. As they are absorbed, each point becomes its exact (one of 16 million) color. Because a dye-transfer head typically contains thousands of heat transformers, each of these dots is microscopically tiny. There are no halftone dots (as in lithographic printing) and no color dithering (as in inkjet printing).

So, why doesn't everyone just run out and buy a dye-sub printer? Because they're expensive, slow, and limited to tabloid-size or smaller prints. Proof-quality dye-sub printers start at around $4,000 and graduate up to around $16,000. Some dye-subs cost much less than that, but they don't produce prints that are as sharp and vivid as the best inkjets. The cost of materials per letter-size print is $5 to $8, compared to $2 or less for an inkjet printer. To top it all off, dye-sub printers aren't suitable for printing such office documents as business letters or accounting spreadsheets.

Snapshot printers

One type of dye-sublimation printer generally sells for $300 to $600. These are the small, snapshot-size printers that are used to produce instant prints from prosumer and point-and-shoot digital cameras. These printers are a lot of fun at a party. They also have potential applications in professional assignments when you want to show an instant print to your client before proceeding with the shoot.

On the downside, most of these printers don't produce prints that compare in quality to their more expensive brethren. You pay two to four times as much for a print than if you were to take film to a one-hour film-processing lab. Finally, it will take several minutes to make a print.

Photographic process printers

This is a class of digital printers that, because they use conventional photographic paper (silver-halide technology), have the unmistakable look of real photographic prints. They also have all the archival qualities of the best silver-halide prints. Probably 80 percent of digital photographers would produce all their prints using this technology if it weren't for three considerations: price, size, and chemistry. These printers are very expensive. As a result, most will need to take their work to a service bureau in order to get these prints. Most of these silver-halide printers can print sizes up to 50 inches wide and do not print in CMYK, so no color or gamma loss results from having to convert the original image data. On the downside, they can't print on substrates such as watercolor paper and canvas. As a result, they are best suited to art that is meant to look photographic, rather than "painterly."

✦ **Fujifilm Pictography** machines feature a process that uses lasers on conventional silver-halide photographic paper from a self-contained unit. The result is a continuous-tone print that is indistinguishable from a conventional photograph. Cost of equipment is high, but the materials' cost per print is much lower than dye-sub. This is an excellent choice for minilabs, event photographers, and printing small art and portfolio prints. Pictography printers come in two sizes: the letter-sized model 3000 starts at around $9,000, and the tabloid-size model 4000 starts at around $24,000.

✦ **Durst-Lambda** makes several high-production volume wide-format printers that use silver-halide technology. The top-of-the-line Lambda 130 (around $330,000) and 131 (around $260,000) models produce prints up to 50 inches wide. They print at either 200 or 400 ppi (pixels per inch). The Lambda 76 (approximately $175,000) prints are up to 32 inches wide and the printer maxes out at 200 ppi. Otherwise, the technology and RIPs for these printers are the same. They can print on any standard photographic paper (positive or reversal) or backlit material (which makes them ideal for large-format signage).

✦ **Cymbolic Sciences LightJet** also uses laser technology to print on silver-halide paper. Prints are even crisper than the Durst-Lambda's. However, the pros I've spoken to seem to feel that the LightJet is better suited to large-format prints for the art market because of its slower throughput per image. LightJet printers start at $142,000 for the smallest model. There are three sizes of the printer: LightJet 5300 (max print size, 32 × 50 inches), LightJet 5500 (max print size, 50 × 50), and LightJet 5900 (max print size, 49 × 97). Cymbolic says that print time for a 50-inch square print at 200 ppi is 4.1 minutes.

You can't judge the quality of the prints produced by these machines by their printing resolution — at least not in the same way you would if these were inkjet or laser printers. I've had many prints made on these printers at 200ppi that are razor sharp. At 400 ppi, you can see every minute detail that the sharpest lens can capture. Durst-Lambda also makes the Epsilon 30, a significantly less expensive machine (circa $84,000) that uses fiber-optic LED technology (rather than lasers) to create true-color RGB pixels on silver-halide paper. Maximum paper width for the Epsilon 30 is (you guessed it) 30 inches. Resolution is 254 ppi at 36-bit continuous-tone color depth. Durst considers the market for the Epsilon to be primarily portrait, even, and fine arts studios, as the machine is markedly slower than the Lambda models. Prices are constantly changing as the technology (and the demand for it) evolves, but I have been paying roughly $200 for a 16 × 20-inch print.

Wax thermal printers

Wax thermal printers work much like dye sublimation printers, except that the wax-based color ink never becomes gaseous. Instead, it simply melts onto the surface of the substrate (that's paper, in plain English). The resulting dots of ink are dithered by a method that resembles halftone litho printing — except the dots are typically coarse enough to be easily seen.

The big advantage of wax thermal is that the cost of consumables is far lower. Because the technology is so similar to dye-sub, it's common for manufacturers (Alps, for example) to combine both types of technology into the same printer. Then, you can proof in affordable wax thermal and produce final prints as dye-subs.

Film recorders

Think of film recorders as being reverse slide scanners. Instead of outputting your digital photograph to paper, you record it onto film. The result can be either a positive (slide or transparency) or a negative. You can then treat this output just as you would the conventionally made counterparts. That is, you can record a negative and then print on any conventional paper, make reversal prints from slides and transparencies, or use the transparencies for lightbox presentations and slide shows.

If this gives you the feeling that we have come full circle — right back where we left off when moving from conventional to digital photography — you're absolutely right. The difference is in the power we have over the image's composition, color values, content, and special effects while it's in the digital phase.

The most popular film recorders, partly because of price and partly because of format, are those that record exclusively onto 35mm film. The following are the most popular film recorders today:

✦ **Lasergraphics Personal LFR Plus** (1-800-701-9869) is a high-speed (50 slides/ hour) 35mm scanner. One version can accept a Polaroid proofing back. The LFR Mark II sells for under $10,000, can image up to 700 slides in 8 hours, and also handles 4 × 5 and 6 × 7 camera backs. Resolution is 4,000 dpi — higher than the best 35mm film. Amazingly, this unit can shoot up to seven rolls of 35mm film at one time. It can also handle bulk film. The Mark III has the same features, but resolution drops to 8,000 dpi and the price drops to $14,000. Models DPM II and III are Mark II and III models that have been specially modified for negative film. The DPM models are priced $1,000 higher than the Mark models, but can shoot both negative and positive film. All other specifications are identical.

✦ **Montage Graphics FR2E** is a $7,000 recorder that has 4,000-dpi resolution and will also take film backs from 35mm to 4 × 5. The manufacturer does not recommend it for shooting negatives. A PostScript interpreter is standard for Mac users, but optional for Windows. It works with both Mac and Windows.

✦ **MGI Opal** is a $15,000 4,000-dpi slide recorder that can produce slides from 35mm to 6 × 7 in size. The manufacturer recommends it for producing both positive and negative film from digital files. The unit can be configured for either Mac or PC. PostScript is optional. Another model from the same maker, the Opal Plus, has 8,000-dpi resolution for under $20,000.

✦ **Polaroid 6000** is a 4,000-dpi film recorder designed primarily for 35mm, but it also accommodates a 4 × 5 back or a bulk film back. No 6 × 7 roll film option exists, however. This unit can typically shoot 32 slides an hour in 36-bit color. Critics call it the best for the buck; however, it is not recommended for creating negatives from digital files. Polaroid does make the ProPalette series, which is capable of shooting either positive or negative images. The ProPalette 7000's resolution is 4,000 dpi. This machine is excellent for making color negatives of digital images to be output to conventional prints. However, it's limited to 35mm film. It's also noteworthy for being priced at under $8,000. For about twice the price, the 8000 has backs for 35mm, bulk 35mm, 6 × 7, and 4 × 5 film, captures 8,000-dpi resolution, and shoots both reversal and negative films. The 8000 can produce 50 slides per hour and costs a mere $15,000.

Commercial Film recorders include the Cymbolic Sciences Fire 1000 and the Kodak LVT series. These film recorders are two to three times the price of the units listed above, but can be expected to produce "no excuses" output for professional portfolio presentation or for making final color separations from film. These units will usually be purchased by service bureaus and corporate departments, as they don't fit within the budget of most individuals.

The Cymbolic Sciences Fire 1000 sells for a mere $50,000. It can make transparencies and film up to 8 × 10 inches. A 1,278-dpi 8 × 10 transparency records in 18 minutes.

The Kodak LVT image recorder records on 8 × 10-inch film, but at much higher resolutions and at a much lower cost — around $40,000. Resolution is variable, from 10 to 120 pixels per mm.

A typical price from a service bureau for recording a 35mm slide from a digital image is around $10 for the first image and about half of that for each additional copy from the same file. Of course, this is an average price. You may be able to do considerably better by shopping online, but I find that it pays to be in personal contact. It also pays to submit a print that matches your expectations as to what the finished slide should look like. Never expect service bureaus to be able to read your mind. Otherwise, their individual interpretation can be said to be just as valid as your own.

Summary

This chapter has covered the categories and desirable features of hardware and software you'll be likely to need for processing your digital images. It winds up with a discussion of how to get final output in the form of a photographic-quality print or transparency.

✦   ✦   ✦

The Anatomy of a Digital Image

To more easily relate to the discussion of technical processes and terms in this chapter, it may help to know exactly what happens when you take a digital photograph. The following steps describe what happens from the moment you pull your camera from its bag until the picture is stored on your camera's memory card.

What Happens When You Take a Digital Picture

Some high-end cameras will vary the following routing slightly, but you'll be able to understand the major differences when you read about the different types of image sensors. Meanwhile, here's what happens when you take a digital photo with the typical point-and-shoot digicam:

1. You press or switch the "power on" control, which energizes the computer in the camera. Immediately, an internal processor checks the status of all the current settings and (usually) displays them on one of the camera's LCDs. It should also post a warning if any of the components are not working.

2. You focus on the subject by aiming the camera and gently pushing the shutter button partway down. In the industry, this is called the S1 (short for shutter position #1) position. This activates auto focus and, if you are in "point-and-shoot" mode, also takes a meter reading of the overall light intensity in the frame and sets the camera's exposure controls.

3. You continue to press down on the shutter button, which snaps the picture. Another processor chip tells the image sensor how long it should stay on. The image sensor chip (usually a charge-coupled device, or CCD) is then turned on for the specified fraction of a second. Thus, it is its own shutter. Note that there is usually a delay between the time you press the shutter and the time the CCD activates because the exposure computer needs some time to do its work. These devices are becoming much faster in the latest generations of digital cameras.

4. Each row of pixels recorded by the CCD is sent to another part of the camera's circuitry, where they are checked for white balance, color filtering, aliasing, and blooming (if you have advanced circuitry). The information for each row is then stored in an internal memory buffer.

5. The internal memory buffer and its associated circuitry reassemble the image. The image is then sent to another portion of the camera's circuitry where it is compressed and then sent on to the camera's "digital film" (compact flash card, SmartMemory Card, memory stick, or what have you).

6. Once the picture has been compressed and is ready for downloading to your computer, the camera's processor sends a note to the status LCD readout to reduce the number of available pictures by one. You are now ready to take another picture.

Now you know that the interval for all that must occur between the time you press the shutter button (remember, except in the case of high-end professional cameras, there is no actual shutter) and the time the camera is ready to take another picture can be considerable. This time interval is generally referred to as "click-to-click" time. Another related variable is the interval between the click of the shutter button and the actual capture of the image. Because it's easy to remember, I call this interval "click-to-pic" time.

Click-to-pic time is rarely stated in camera literature, but if you can pick up the camera at a dealer's and take a shot, you can easily judge the delay. Try having the salesperson talk and move when you take his or her picture. Is the subject's expression or position different than when you pressed the button? If so, you should question whether your requirements include the ability to take candid and action photos.

Click-to-click time determines how quickly you will be ready to take the next shot. Note that quicker click-to-click times aren't *necessarily* an indicator of the duration of click-to-pic times.

Image Capture Devices

Although the image storage medium is usually referred to as "digital film," the image capture device is the real digital film — the place where the light reflected from the image is actually captured as a picture.

There are several subtypes of image sensors, but there are only two major technologies, CCD (charge-coupled device) and CMOS (complimentary metal-oxide semiconductor).

CMOS

CMOS may be the wave of the future, but its time had not yet come as this book was going to press. The technology does have some major potential advantages over the currently more prevalent CCD technology, but production techniques and technology have not yet made it cost-effective or brought it up to its potential for image quality. You can see a diagram of a CMOS chip in Figure 6-1.

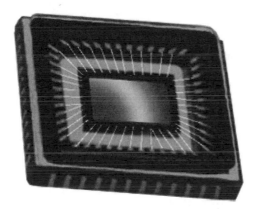

Figure 6-1: A CMOS image sensor

The potential advantages of CMOS are as follows:

✦ **Lower production costs:** This is due to the fact that the production facilities required are the same as for other types of computer chips.

✦ **Ability to combine image capture and processing on the same chip:** This has the potential for both reducing click-to-click time and camera size.

✦ **Programmability:** This enables the chip to incorporate several functions that are currently accomplished by supplementary chipsets in today's CCD cameras.

Although the potential is there, CCD chips are so well entrenched that it will be a while before there is enough demand for CMOS chips to enable them to compete on the basis of both image quality and price. At the moment, most of the CMOS cameras around are low-cost, low-resolution cameras meant for videoconferencing. However, be forewarned that by the time you read this, that may be changing.

CCD

CCD is the prevailing technology for image sensors used in the higher-quality scanners and in virtually all digital still cameras priced at over $300.

Not all CCDs are alike, and it's a good idea to understand the differences between them:

- ✦ Striped arrays
- ✦ Linear arrays
- ✦ Trilinear arrays

Striped arrays

Striped arrays are the type of CCD image sensor you're most likely to encounter. There are two reasons why this is so:

- ✦ The chip can capture all the colors for the entire image in one instant.
- ✦ The subject needn't be stationary during the exposure.

Of course, both of these qualities are essential to any handheld, point-and-shoot camera — especially if it's intended to be used with electronic flash. The individual light sensors (one per pixel of resolution) are arranged in rows and columns. Each of the pixel sensors is coated with a filter to make it sensitive to only one primary color — red, green, or blue (RGB).

Note The new Super CCD recently introduced by Fujifilm is a striped array. However, the pixels are a different shape and are arranged in a slightly different arrangement than is pictured here. The Super CCD uses an octagonally shaped light-sensitive cell, which gives the image the same resolution diagonally as horizontally or vertically. According to Fuji, this results in significantly better image saturation and fewer artifacts.

The filtering pattern used, as shown in Figure 6-2, can be very simple (RGBRGBRGB) or very complex. Which is most effective will depend on many factors — especially the sophistication of the camera's computing circuitry. It is this computing circuitry that figures how to apply the color seen by one sensor to the information seen by all the sensors so that the effective resolution of the image is the total number of sensors in the array. This is a tough concept to grasp, especially if you're used to thinking of how color film works. Color film has three layers of light-sensitive granules stacked atop one another. Each layer sees only its assigned color of light. Because all three layers have approximately the same resolution, image definition needn't be compromised.

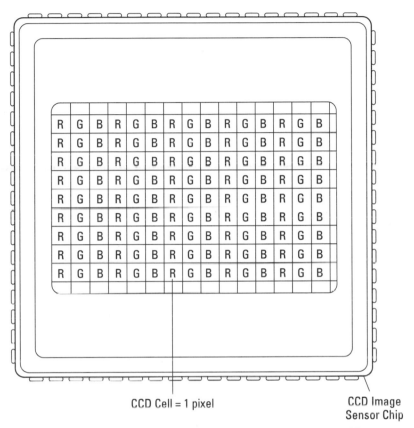

CCD Cell = 1 pixel

CCD Image
Sensor Chip

Figure 6-2: A striped CCD light sensor array showing one possible pattern of RGB filtering

Striped arrays, as I've just said, have all their light sensors on a single plane. Only (approximately, depending on the pattern arrangement) a third of these see light of a given color. However, all see the difference between the brightness of the subject in its area and that in the next. So, a sophisticated formula can be applied that (theoretically, at least) makes it possible for all of the sensors to contribute equally to image definition. If that sounds complicated, that's because it is complicated. The computer scientists who design the chips all try to outsmart one another, so there is a difference between the picture quality you'll see from various manufacturers' images, even though they may have CCDs that use the same resolution. It is also why very high quality professional cameras tend to use one of the other types of CCD arrays.

A variation on striped arrays is the filtered or three-shot array. These are usually large, medium-format arrays. All of the sensors are used for each shot and three shots are made, each filtered for a different primary color. This is much faster than the linear and trilinear arrays described below, but still has a lag of several seconds between each of the three shots. So, you're still limited to motionless subjects and constant light sources. Such camera backs as the Leaf DCB and MegaVisionT2 use three-shot arrays.

A hybrid of the linear array and the three-shot array is the piezo array. This is a linear array that is covered by a grid of piezoelectric filters. During the exposure, the filter layer is moved three times so that each CCD sensor makes a separate exposure for each primary color of light. Most cameras (usually backs for analog cameras) that use this technology also have a single-shot mode in which the filter layer remains stationary and resolution is then interpolated in pretty much the same way as if it were a standard striped array.

Linear arrays

The simplest array is the linear array (see Figure 6-3). A single row of light sensors makes three passes over the image area, each pass filtered for a different primary color. This is the type of array used in most scanners, but it is also widely used in high-end studio cameras.

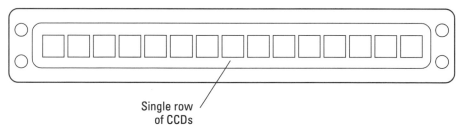

Single row
of CCDs

Figure 6-3: A linear array

Because this array is so simple, it can have a large number of light sensors for a very reasonable price. So, the image can be very high resolution. Image quality is also superior because each sensor records all three colors, so no resolution compromises need to be made by an interpolation algorithm, as is the case with striped arrays.

Because of the amount of time it takes to scan all three colors, most cameras that use linear arrays are limited to photographing static subjects and are restricted to being lit by a steady light source. In other words, flash is out.

Trilinear arrays

Trilinear arrays, as you've probably already guessed, are simply three linear arrays stacked atop one another (see Figure 6-4). Each array is filtered for a single color, so only one scanning pass is required. Very high resolution trilinear arrays still need to be lit by a steady light source, and the subject cannot move. However, there are a few medium-format camera backs that use trilinear arrays that travel fast enough to shoot action and with strobes. These arrays all come on backs that will clip on to standard medium-format analog cameras made by such manufacturers as Hassleblad, Bronica, Pentax, and Fuji. Some of these will also fit the backs of studio view cameras.

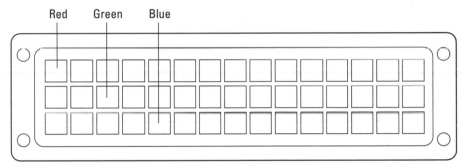

Figure 6-4: A trilinear array

Multiple arrays

This is another CCD arrangement found only in high-end cameras. Three striped arrays are used. Immediately after light passes through the lens, it is split three ways by a prism so that the same image is seen by all three arrays. Each array is filtered for a different primary color. This means that all the sensors can be used to record all the colors. In situations that demand that flash or action-stopping shutter speeds be used, this is the technology capable of producing the highest-quality image. It is also priced accordingly.

Note If your camera has a black and white mode and you intend to print in black and white, use the black and white mode. You will then be using all of the CCDs in the array to record all the image definition.

The Significance of Technical Terms

Regardless of the type of image sensor, there are other technological considerations that go into understanding how your camera makes its images.

Masking

Masking refers to not using all of the image sensors' available pixels in the final image. The most important reason why this is done is to eliminate noise (image trash) that always accumulates at the edge of the CCD array. The other predominant reason is that the manufacturer may want to maintain a height-to-width ratio that's more analogous to the height-to-width-ratios of popular film formats — usually the 3:2 ratio of the 35mm film format.

Interpolation

Interpolation refers to recalculating the elements from one set of data to match the requirements of the elements of another set of data. The term is heard most often when discussing how a higher-resolution image is derived from a lower-resolution image — for instance, digital zoom, image resizing, or the interpolated resolution of a scanning device. Interpolation is also used in digital photography to calculate the definition of an image from pixels that record only one color.

The most important thing to understand about interpolation, when you see the term used on a spec sheet, is that you can do a better job of image resizing in your image-editing software. After all, Photoshop has the full power of your computer at its disposal. If you are impressed by the fact that a camera has a digital zoom or a scanner's 3,000 dpi interpolated resolution, rest assured that the manufacturer has played you for a sucker.

Blooming

Blooming is what happens when the light striking the CCD creates so much energy (because it's so bright or because the CCD is so sensitive to that color of light) that adjacent CCDs read it, too. Typically, the smaller the physical dimensions of the image sensor array, the more likely blooming will occur. It's also more likely in higher-resolution sensors of the same physical dimension because more CCDs are packed toget her in the same amount of space. Some cameras' software is better at sensing when blooming will occur and at compensating for it when the image is processed by the camera. Therefore, not all image sensors of the same type and dimensions will exhibit blooming to the same degree. There are also technologies, called *fixed antiblooming* and *gated antiblooming*, that can help.

Pixel

You probably know the definition of this term by now, but just in case: the word is short for picture element. A pixel is the smallest piece of unique data in a digital picture. It consists of a single rectangle of one specific tone of color out of a possible 16.8 million colors. In a digital photograph, a pixel is equivalent to a single grain of silver in black and white film or to a single printing dot in an offset-printed halftone image.

Gamut

Gamut refers the extent of the range of colors that can be accommodated by a given color model. The more colors, the "wider the gamut."

Color models

Color models (often called "color spaces") are the schemes that are used by various digital and analog devices to interpret color by dividing the colors into mixtures of "primaries." These primaries are usually colors, but they may also be values or qualities (as in the case of the device-independent CIE Lab color model: Lightness, color range A, and color range B).

The color models we are most concerned with in digital photography are those that represent (more or less) the full range of colors visible to the human eye. We call these models "true-color" models.

RGB

Of all the modes that most concern us in digital photography, RGB (red, green, blue) concerns us the most. That's mostly because this is the mode that's native to all digital cameras, digital video cameras, and monitors. It is also because RGB can represent a very wide range of colors (but not quite as wide as Lab).

RGB is called a device-dependent mode because it works when the colors you see are made by light passing through the viewing plane. Thus it is called *transmissive color*. It doesn't matter whether that plane is the tube of a monitor or a film transparency. It works best for these media because adding percentages of the light spectrum's primary colors (red, green, and blue) together derives its colors. Thus, it is called *additive color* because the colors are added to black to get all the colors between black and white.

CMYK

CMYK is the opposite device-dependent color mode to RGB. It's primary colors — cyan, magenta, and yellow are the complementary (opposite) colors of red, green, and blue. CMYK is used for creating color on reflecting surfaces (such as paper and cloth), so it is also known as *reflective color*. Because, if you're going to get photographically true color, you always start with a blank white surface, you have to subtract colors from black in order to get the range of colors between black and white. In other words, the total absence of color is pure white. Thus CMYK is known as subtractive color.

But wait. This mode is called CMYK — not CMY. What does the K stand for? Well, it stands for black. That's because, color theory aside, ink impurities make it nearly impossible to get a solid, neutral black by adding equal amounts (or any amounts) of cyan, magenta, and yellow. So the printing industry has learned to "fake it" by adding carbon black.

Why should digital photographers concern themselves with CMYK if their cameras and monitors are RGB devices? Well, if all your photographs are going to end up on the Web, in slide shows, or on silver-halide conventional prints, you don't. However, the printing press is still the ultimate destination for a large percentage of the work of most digital photographers. So we need to understand how to get from RGB to CMYK (which has a *way* smaller gamut) in the least embarrassing way.

Note   Some solve the problem by working in CMYK from the moment the image is opened in their image-processing program. Then they simply make image adjustments to eliminate any out-of-gamut colors and make sure they don't do anything to introduce new ones. There are two problems with that approach. There is less information in the image than there might have been and there will never be a way to replace it. There may be commands and tools in your image editor that can't be used in any modes other than RBG or Lab.

L*a*b

L*a*b color (often simply spelled Lab or LAB) is *not* device dependent. In other words, its colors will appear the same whether you print on paper or view your image on a monitor. Because the color is described independently of the viewing or printing device, the consistency of the color can be preserved when the file is moved from one device to another.

L*a*b color uses the L channel to contain all the brightness information in the image. If you view this channel by itself, it simply looks like a grayscale photo. The A channel describes the colors that contain any combination of green and red. The B channel describes any colors that combine blue to yellow.

HSB (aka HLS or HSL)

Most image-processing programs don't use this model, but you can find hue, saturation, and brightness controls in your computer system's color picker and they also exist in many image adjustment commands.

Less-than-true-color models

Some so-called color models are really monochrome, black and white, or accommodate only a range of up to 256 specific colors.

Bitmap

We have come to use bitmap as a generic term for an image that is composed of a row-and-column matrix of pixels. That criterion would include all digital photos, regardless of their color model. However, there is a color model called a bitmap that consists of only two colors: absolute white and absolute black. It is used almost exclusively for scanned black and white documents.

A few digital cameras have a bitmap mode that is meant for copying text documents. You can do a better job by shooting in color and then using the Threshold command in your image-editing software. However, you're not likely to find a Threshold command in those programs that are the software equivalent of point-and-shoot cameras.

Grayscale

Grayscale mode contains 256 shades of gray. Some cameras have a "black and white" shooting mode that is really a grayscale, rather than a bitmap mode. This is an advantage because it means that the camera can use all of the CCDs in the image sensor to record all of the detail in the image. So, if you know you are going to shoot black and white, you can expect a more detailed image from a camera that has a black and white shooting mode.

Indexed color

Indexed color is so called because each of its 256 colors has to be linked to a specific place in the color palette that it attached to the file. Because the image is limited to 256 colors and the human eye can see tens or hundreds of thousands (I've never seen any two stats that agree on this — but it's certainly way more than 256), you'll never get a truly photographic color image into indexed color format.

Bit depth

Bit depth refers to how much color data a digital file can record for a single pixel. The more bits per pixel, the more colorful your images can be — up to a point. The most information that's ever used for displaying a file is 24 bits per pixel because the 16.8 million colors that can be displayed at that level are many more colors than any human eye can distinguish between. However, there is an advantage to your camera or scanner being able to record and store more color information in a file. That is, you have a much wider dynamic range. I've yet to see a prosumer or consumer digicam that captures more than 24 bits of information. On the other hand, many of the higher-end linear array cameras capture much more — sometimes as much as 48 bits of information. If you scan from film, 30–bits per pixel is the rule rather than the exception these days.

If you have a camera or scanner that's capable of capturing extended bit depth, you should also find an image-processing program (Photoshop 5+ comes to mind) that will enable you to work in an extended bit-depth mode. Of course, you will eventually have to convert your image to a 24-bit file, but by then you'll at least be able to decide *which* range of 24 bits contains the information you want to keep.

Extended bit depth is also used for CMYK because each color channel of a true-color image needs to contain a full 256 levels of gray. This can't be accomplished at 24 bits per pixel because 4×8 is 32. Although no camera or recorder captures in CMYK, some high-end units immediately (or can be made to immediately) translate the image to CMYK.

Just to make the discussion of bit depth a bit more confusing, extended bit depth can be used for other purposes, such as extra channels of data that can be used to store masks or texture maps. These are called alpha channels. Alpha channels are created by the program that uses them. Each alpha channel is 8 bits deep. So the more alpha channels you add, the deeper the bit depth of the image becomes.

Finally, all images that are less than true color contain fewer than 24 bits per pixel. The fewer the colors, the fewer the bits per pixel. Table 6-1 lists the bit depth and corresponding number of colors

Table 6-1	
Bit Depth and Number of Colors	
Number of Bits Per Pixel	**Number of Colors**
1 bit	2 colors
2 bits	4 colors
3 bits	8 colors
4 bits	16 colors
5 bits	32 colors
6 bits	64 colors
7-bits	128
8-bits	256
16 bits	32,768 (high color)
24 bits	16.8 million (true color)
32 bit	billions

Resolution

Resolution is another of those terms that is used in different ways (or expressed in different terms) when used in reference to different things. It all boils down to this: How many picture elements (whether these be grains of silver, CCD cells, pixels, or printing dots) make up the image? The more pixels per given area, the more detailed your image can be. What follows is, hopefully, a layman's description of resolution as it applies to the various contexts in which the term is used. These descriptions are meant to be accurate in a practical sense, rather than a purely technical one. So if I say, for instance, that each dot on a monitor represents a particular color, that is true only as it relates to the resolution of that monitor as stated by the monitor's literature. In fact, some monitors use three picture guns, one each of which produces a single primary color in varying intensities. Therefore, if you look at the monitor with a magnifier, you will see that three color dots make up each of the dots that make up the resolution of the monitor. I'm assuming here that this level of detail is more about penguins than you care (or need) to know. What matters is that each of the 640 (or whatever) horizontal dots currently being resolved is equivalent to one dot of a single color—even though that one dot is made of three dots.

Interpolation or "digital zoom"

Resolution can be interpolated. In layman's terms, that means that a computer program enlarges or reduces the image and, in the process, calculates its best guess as to how to reinterpret the image so that it won't look too "grainy." If you reduce the size of the image through interpolation, the program has to decide when to throw out information and when to keep it. This is especially chancy if you have fine edge detail, such as hair or a pattern, in the picture. If the program decides to toss all the pixels that make up some of the edges, you will see a noticeable lack of sharpness. A program with a good Unsharp Mask filter can sometimes go a long way toward restoring the illusion of detail.

Because image capture devices tend to record less resolution than we want in the final print, it is much more common to enlarge the image when we are printing for publication or exhibit. This is also true because many of the simpler digicams don't offer any choice of lens other than wide-angle. Some manufacturers try to fool you by giving these cameras a "digital zoom" feature. All this means is that your still camera enlarges the center of your image by some interpolation program that's simple (and simple-minded) enough to store on a portion of a slow and tiny processing chip that will fit inside your itty-bitty camera. I suppose there may be some value in this if you don't digitally process your own images. On the other hand, your image-processing software, no matter how lame, will do a much better job of interpolation. So don't spend extra money for this feature. This feature actually has a place in videotape, because it is very difficult to manually enlarge a small portion of a multiple-frame moving image precisely.

Note   Some interpolation algorithms are so smart that you can make acceptably grainless (or pixel-less if you prefer that metaphor) images that are several times larger than the original. Photoshop has long received high marks in this regard. There are even third-party programs, such as Altamira Group's Genuine Fractals and Lizard Tech's MrSID, that will do an even more sophisticated interpolation that will let you "shoot small and print big."

Megapixel

The resolution that can be produced by a digicam's image sensor is often expressed in "megapixels." Mega means millions, so the term simply implies that there are so many millions of pixels in the image. Last year's top-of-the-line prosumer digicams were the first to achieve resolutions of over one megapixel, and these cameras popularized the term. Today, top-of-the-line digicams are commonly three megapixels.

Too Many Megapixels?

The resolution of "affordable" digital cameras is climbing at about the same rate as the power of other computer chips. In other words, it's been doubling every year. That's a wonderful thing, but it poses a problem: huge files and higher digital film costs. If manufacturers "solve" this problem by defaulting to a higher level of image compression, you will get images that are less detailed because they are "noisier." Thus it will become more important that you have an option to store images with little to no compression. That's a good idea anyway. You'll also need higher-capacity digital film cards and faster connections between camera and computer.

Note   Six megapixels is approximately the resolution of medium-speed 35mm film. Given the speed of development over the last couple of years, I'd say we're about two to three years away from affordable digital cameras that have true film resolution.

EGA

This refers to an 8-bit color depth at 640 × 480 pixels. Some manufacturers state that their cameras have "EGA resolution" and mean that they have 640 × 480 capture resolution (or an option to capture at that depth), but still maintain 24-bit true color. If you see the term "EGA" in a camera spec, be sure to check that this is the case.

Dots per inch

Dots per inch is the measure of resolution for monitors and digital printers. However, when you're talking about color images, there's a big difference. It takes only one dot to show any color on a monitor, whereas it takes three dots (one for each primary color) to do the same thing with a digital printer. That is because each printer dot is a given intensity of a primary color that makes up the shade of color that represents the original dot (pixel) in the image or on the monitor.

This means that if you want to calculate what the resolution of the image must be in order to produce the best resolution at the finished size on paper, you should divide the printed resolution by 3 to get the needed resolution of the image. For instance, the default resolution of most Epson printers is 720 dots per inch. Therefore, you have as much information in your image as your printer can print at around 240 dots per inch. It actually gets a bit more complicated when speaking of Epson printers, because they have an extra high resolution of 1,440 horizontal dots by 720 vertical dots.

Offset printing, on the other hand, states resolution as a matter of lpi (lines per inch). You need approximately two pixels of original image to print one line per inch. So if you're printing a 5 × 7-inch image on paper at 133 lines per inch (fairly standard for a magazine), you need an image that is 1,330 × 1,862 pixels or 266 pixels per inch. That's just a little under 2.5 megapixels, by the way. Because you can easily get away with interpolating up by a factor of 2, most digicam manufacturers will tell you that this is enough resolution to print an 8 × 10-inch photo-quality image. This usually turns out to be subjectively true. In fact, if a little soft focus and low contrast are suited to the subject (think glamour portrait), you can get away with much more.

To play it safe, you should figure on an original image resolution of about 300 pixels per inch. This gives you a little margin in case you need to either print a larger image or print on a higher-resolution device.

What You Should Know About Image Compression

There are many file formats that specialize in making it easier to store image files, which, if you've been reading this chapter, you know will typically be in the range of 5–40MB in their original, uncompressed form. If you are working with high-end professional studio cameras and scanners, file sizes of around 100MB aren't uncommon. So, the idea of image compression becomes rather attractive. After all, how many 100MB files can you store on your hard drive?

If you're shooting digital images in the field, compressing the files in the camera is probably an absolute necessity unless you're Bill Gates and can afford to buy an 8MB memory card for every two or three pictures you shoot in uncompressed mode. Nevertheless, always shoot at the highest level of compression your camera offers. After all, with digital images, you can always delete an image that doesn't deserve the storage space. On the other hand, you'll never be able to correct the flaws that compression introduces, and the more you compress, the more obvious the flaws. Figure 6-5 shows a 200-percent enlargement of a section of an image shot on a digital camera with no compression, super high-quality compression (100 percent), moderate compression (50 percent), and maximum compression (25 percent). At 25 percent, you can hardly tell that those are leaves on the trees.

Original   JPEG 100%   JPEG 50%   JPEG 25%

Figure 6-5: The same image at 200-percent magnification, at four different levels of compression

So you see, you don't really want to compress your images unless it's absolutely necessary. If you stick to the best quality of compression that your camera permits, you're guaranteed to lose as little definition as your camera permits. Just make sure you never resave the image in compressed format — unless you first reduce the size of the image. This is something you will almost always have to do before saving images for the Web, which you will want to compress to reduce file size and thus maximize the speed at which the file loads from the Internet.

Light Sensitivity (ISO Rating)

The light sensitivity of both film and digital image sensors is stated with an ISO rating. ISO ratings generally range between 25 and 1,600, with each doubling of the rating equivalent to one exposure step. An exposure step is one notch on the f-stop or shutter speed dial. Thus, if an exposure of 1/100th second is required at f-5.6 for ISO 100 film, then an exposure of only 1/200th second will be required for ISO 200 film at the same f-stop.

Digital camera sensors have an ISO rating that is meant to be roughly equivalent to that of film with the same rating. Within limits, this makes digital cameras a nice substitute for a Polaroid as a means for previewing the results of the photographer's choice of exposure for a given subject. The difference is that you can expose film for as long as necessary in order to produce the required image brightness. CCDs, on the other hand, become more susceptible to blooming as longer exposures are required. In fact, exposures of several seconds may become totally impractical.

The typical ISO rating for prosumer/consumer digicams is ISO 100 — give or take 25 percent. This means that you can't expect to handhold a shot at dusk or in any but the very brightest of indoor conditions. That's why virtually all digicams have built-in flash. Unfortunately, on-camera flash has the deserved reputation of being the least versatile and least flattering of all light sources. Personally, I try to avoid it like the plague.

A few cameras in the under-$1,500 range will let you change the sensitivity of the image sensor. The Olympus C-3030 and S-2500 and the Nikon 950 and 990 are models that come immediately to mind. It is rare that these cameras let you boost the sensitivity of the sensor higher than ISO 400, but that's high enough to make it entirely practical to shoot (especially if you can handhold at 1/30th of a second) at dusk and in most living room and store interiors. You're still out of luck if you're shooting in a nightclub or on city streets at night.

Some professional news cameras that are built on 35mm frames use much higher-quality image sensors. Even though these are still linear or trilinear arrays, just like a digicam, the quality of their electronics is such that they can stand a much wider range of lighting conditions without undue blooming. You can adjust the ISO rating of some of the cameras all the way up to ISO 1600 with even less noise than a prosumer camera generates at ISO 400.

So how serious a problem is it to shoot at boosted ISO ratings? I'm afraid that a lot depends on your point of view. Let's put it this way: Photographers expect to compromise image quality at higher ISO ratings when they're shooting film. Faster films are grainier, and photographers tend to overdevelop them to push them to even higher ratings — which makes them even grainier. When it is said that an image is "grainy," it is meant that the size of the silver grains that compose the image is large enough that they become visible. This is analogous to the increased image noise you encounter when the digital camera's ISO rating is boosted in a prosumer camera. If you spend enough money for your camera, it's likely to be even less of a problem.

Summary

This chapter discussed some of the more technical aspects of digital imaging. The discussion included how a digital camera goes about recording an image, the types of image capture devices, the significance of technical terms that affect image quality, what you should know about image compressions, and what to make of image sensor light-sensitivity ratings.

✦   ✦   ✦

Tips and Tricks for Making Digital Images

Accessories for Digital Cameras

Often, the success of a photograph is as dependent on knowing which add-ons and accessories to use as it is a matter of choosing the right camera and exposure. Having the right accessories can also do a lot to make life easier for you — starting with choosing the right camera bag and ending with picking a camera-to-computer interface that doesn't waste any more of your time than necessary. After all, you know as well as I do that when the new toy is too much trouble to use, it just gets neglected.

Your Camera Bag

One of the loveliest characteristics of today's digital cameras is that they're small enough to keep with you at all times. Almost all of them are small enough to fit into the pocket of a jacket or a pair of cargo pants. (Ah, cargo pants! Now there's an accessory no photographer — digital or otherwise — should ever be without.) Nevertheless, you'll soon acquire enough accessories to make you want a camera bag.

I actually use two camera bags. One is small enough to carry with me at all times. It is a small (about ten inches square and four inches deep) black nylon bag with a fairly generous front pocket (see Figure 7-1). It is padded (very important — digital cameras can be allergic to hard knocks) and has a Velcro strip inside that enables me to compartmentalize the bag.

Figure 7-1: The "constant companion" camera bag

Here's what I keep inside this bag:

- ✦ Two digital cameras: an Olympus 2020 and a Nikon 950

- ✦ Three CompactFlash and three SmartMedia memory cards

- ✦ A homemade LCD hood (which I sometimes use as a lens hood)

- ✦ My checkbook, a calculator, a cell phone, a Palm Pilot, a portable flash, a tabletop tripod, a pair of accessory lenses (telephoto and wide-angle), the remote control for the Olympus, and a polarizing filter

There's hardly ever a situation where I can't take a picture.

You may be tempted to buy a bigger or a fancier bag. It's a free world, of course. However, consider this: fancier bags tempt thieves — especially if they're made of leather or brushed aluminum. I figure I'm carrying around $3,000 worth of techno stuff in that bag and I sure don't want to lose it. Besides, the TRG palm computer (which is Palm-compatible but uses the same CompactFlash cards for memory as the Nikon 950) has all the valuable notes on it. Bigger bags tend to get left at home.

Actually, I have a much bigger bag. It holds the lamp heads for my strobe units, light stands, a roll-up windshield reflector, and other items I might need on a location shoot. I leave that bag in the trunk of the car until I really need it.

Holding Steady

One of the first accessories you should consider buying is a tripod. Most digital cameras have an ISO rating of around 100. That means that handheld pictures taken in anything but bright lights are going to be blurry. Sure, you can use the on-camera flash — but not if you want the situation you're shooting to look natural or the people you're shooting to look good.

Of course, the idea of toting around a heavy and clumsy tripod doesn't have great sex appeal. There are alternatives that are far less cumbersome. For those occasions (and there are some, as you will see) when you really do need a full-size tripod, take solace in the fact that most digital cameras are lightweights. A lightweight camera (even traditional 35mm and APS film cameras) can do well with a fairly lightweight tripod.

All digital cameras use quarter-inch tripod threads, so be sure that any camera-steadying device you buy uses a quarter-inch mounting screw. Otherwise, you'll be . . . well, you know . . . unscrewed, so to speak.

Tripods aren't just for holding the camera steady, either. They're also the best way to keep the camera in one place while you do something else, like holding an external flash unit high and to one side of the subject. They ensure a consistent point of view when you're shooting pictures in a series. They're also useful in the studio when you're shooting with strobes that are plenty fast enough to freeze both the subject and any possible camera motion. Finally, using a tripod frees you to adjust the lights, stand to one side to direct the model, or step aside and let the client peer through the viewfinder.

Don't jiggle

The first thing you have to consider, even before you think about how you're going to mount the camera, is how you're going to keep it motionless while you press the shutter button. Otherwise, you won't get all the benefit out of having mounted the camera. Of course, one thing you can do is to simply press the shutter button very carefully. Unfortunately, if your hand is the slightest bit unsteady or if you get anxious and press a little too hard, you're still going to jiggle the camera at the moment the shot is taken. The worst of it is that sometimes very slight movement is even more distracting than an obvious motion blur. The picture is just a little less sharp than you wanted it to be.

You have three ways to fire the camera without touching it:

✦ Use the self-timer

✦ Use a cable release

✦ Use a remote control

Use the self-timer

This is likely to be the only method available to you. It is a rare digital camera under $1,500 that features a cable-release thread—a fact that strikes me as brain-dead design. After all, it costs only pennies to add this very useful feature and you can always buy another cable release if your remote control breaks or fails.

Anyway, most digital cameras do have a self-timer feature. This is usually built into the camera's firmware. You push a button or make a menu choice on the camera's LCD. Then, when you push the shutter button, there's a delay of several seconds before the shutter fires. As soon as you push the shutter button, take your hands off the camera. This gives it a chance to steady itself before the shutter fires.

There is one situation in which a self-timer sucks: people. It's one thing to tell the model to freeze at the peak of an expression so that you can make an exposure that lasts a fifteenth of a second. It's quite another to expect the model to "hold it" and still be expected to "look natural" when the shutter fires 10 seconds later. Yes, indeed.

Use a cable release

This brilliant invention (see Figure 7-2) came along long before anyone thought of such high-tech innovations as self-timers and remote controls. It doesn't make you wait one split second longer than the second you want to fire the shutter, and it doesn't jiggle the camera. Best of all, you can buy one at any camera store for a few dollars and it will fit almost any camera—except for most digital cameras (and the most amateurish of 35mm cameras).

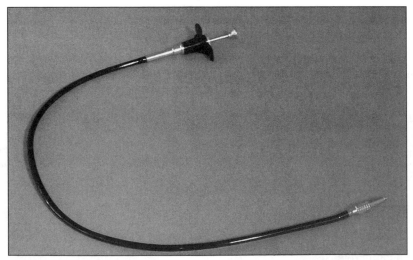

Figure 7-2: A cable release

Cable releases will work on most professional digital cameras. That's because most professional digital cameras are really professional film cameras that have been modified or that use a replaceable digital back.

Use a remote control

You are really lucky if your camera can be used with one of these. Once again, Olympus rules. The C2000, C2020, C3030, and the C2050 all ship with a remote control. Unfortunately, this is still a nearly unique feature at this writing. It's such a good feature that it can't possibly stay that way for long. Olympus' remote (see Figure 7-3) is even smaller than a smart media card and not only fires the shutter but also operates the zoom lens and features a pair of buttons that increase or decrease the exposure by one f-stop. My one complaint is that the unit is so small that it can be easily lost or misplaced.

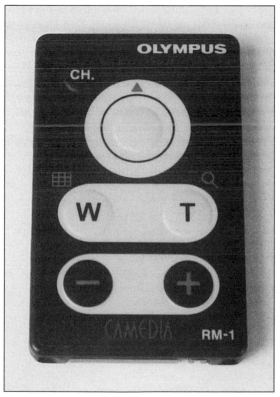

Figure 7-3: The Olympus remote control

Tip If you are working in the studio and your camera has a remote control, you can hook the camera to a TV set to be used as a viewfinder and then zoom the lens and fire the shutter without having to be behind the camera itself. It's an excellent way to communicate with an art director during a commercial shoot or stay comfortable when the camera is mounted at an extremely high or low angle.

Tripods

Tripods are three-legged devices made to keep the camera steady, even on uneven terrain. Full-size tripods have a center post that lets you fine-tune the height of the camera platform. The camera platform (aka tripod head) should have an adjustable tilt from front to back and from side to side. It should also rotate 360 degrees horizontally. If you already own a tripod for your video camera, consider buying a new head for your still camera. Video heads have no side-to-side tilt.

My favorite tripod head is the single control ball-bearing type pictured in Figure 7-4. One twist of the tightening screw and you can move the camera into any position.

Figure 7-4: A ball head lets you adjust the camera with one twist of the screw. The slot in the side makes it possible to take vertically oriented shots.

If you are working in windy conditions or in a crowd, consider rigging a weight under the tripod. My favorite is a small five-pound dumbbell because it's easy to use a small nylon cord to tie it to the apex of the legs. Rig the weight so that it's close to the ground to overcome the top-heaviness caused by placing a camera on a lightweight tripod.

Miniature tripods

I don't always carry a full-height tripod with me, but I always carry a miniature tripod. These little jewels can be lifesavers. As long as there's a tabletop, countertop, or any other solid surface to place it on, you have a steady mount for your camera. The hood and roof of my car have also performed that duty more times than I can count. Miniature or "tabletop" tripods come in a wide range of prices and sizes. The one pictured in Figure 7-5 cost a mere $20 on sale at my local camera store.

Figure 7-5: A miniature (tabletop) tripod

You need to watch out for one thing with miniature tripods. If you set up the bed for a vertical (portrait) shot, there's a good chance that the weight of the camera will tip it over. You can either hold the tripod in place with your hand (not very convenient), get an L-bracket that keeps the camera centered over the head, or get a tripod that has a wide enough leg spread to keep this from happening. The tripod shown in Figure 7-5 is very inexpensive and easy to stow, but I recommend using one with a ball head and three- or four-section legs. These can be nearly as compact and are much more useful.

Full-size tripods

A full-size aluminum tripod should be black. Bright aluminum tripods can cast strange, striped reflections onto your subject. There should be at least three sections in the legs to give you as much flexibility as possible in adjusting individual legs for height or for uneven terrain. You want the maximum extended length to be at least 5 feet so that you can keep the camera steady at eye level.

They are very hard to find, but a boom arm for your tripod will make it possible to aim the camera straight down or to extend it over a tabletop for close-up shots. Bogen makes an excellent accessory "side arm" that fits most tripods and costs less than $50. It is double-headed, so you can attach your pan/tilt head to either end of the arm (see Figure 7-6). You can also hang a counterweight (or your camera bag) on the other end of the arm. You can jury-rig a boom by clamping a pipe or board to your tripod head and then using a clamp (be sure to use a counterweight).

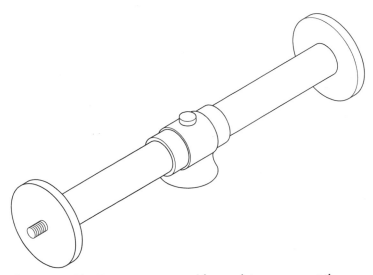

Figure 7-6: The Bogen accessory side arm lets you mount the camera vertically over the floor or a table.

You can make it possible to roll your camera and tripod across smooth floors by adding a dolly (see Figure 7-7). If you're going to do much studio work, a tripod dolly is a most convenient accessory. If you also do video, a dolly is virtually a necessity.

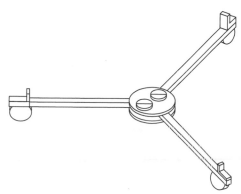

Figure 7-7: A typical tripod dolly

Other means of bracing yourself

Tripods may be the best way of keeping a camera steady, but they're not always around when you need them. There are also situations in which they're just not the best tool for the job.

Monopods

A close relative of the tripod is something called a monopod. Pod means "leg." Mono means "one." You can think of it as a one-legged tripod. Monopods are much easier to carry than tripods. If you're careful, you can shoot at about one-third the shutter speed you can expect for a sharp, unassisted, handheld shot. Get a monopod that can use the same head as your tripod. You may not want to carry a tripod on a hike or into a crowd, but a monopod is far easier to carry. You can even use it as a walking stick. In a crowd, others are far less likely to trip over it. Finally, if you need a rock-steady shot, you can always clamp it to a chair, ladder, or fence. I've even known photographers who piled rocks around the foot of their monopod. If you do that, put a plastic bag over the foot so that you don't get dirt, sand, or water into the working parts.

Neck straps

There are going to be times when you just don't have a tripod handy. If you're smart, you have already found some means to attach a professional neck strap to your camera. This won't always be easy, because a lot of the designers of digital cameras haven't been thoughtful enough to place neck strap loops on either side of the camera. Most (but not all) have at least one place where you can attach a strap. Get one of those wire key-ring loops and thread it through that retainer. You can then attach the neckstrap clips (see Figure 7-8) to the key ring.

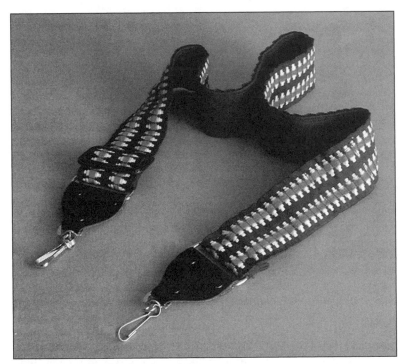

Figure 7-8: A professional neck strap

A good neck strap is the first investment you should make to protect the investment in your digital camera. It makes it possible to always keep the camera on you and at the ready. It makes it difficult for a thief to quietly pocket your small camera when you're not looking. Plus, you won't drop your camera on the concrete when you're pushed or startled. Best of all, using the neck strap provides a way to steady your camera.

Here's how: Sling the neck strap so that it passes your neck on one side and under your arm on the other. Keep spreading out the strap until it's so tight that there's pressure pulling the camera toward you. Hold the camera on both sides with your hands and push out (see Figure 7-9). Start breathing in very slowly as you press the shutter button. I don't claim to have a very steady hand, but with practice I've been able to get acceptably steady shots at 1/5th of a second.

Finally, there are also a variety of pistol and rifle grips (these usually require a cable-release socket), as well as chest braces.

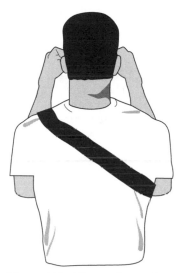

Figure 7-9: The neckstrap brace

Accessories for panoramas and object movies

Most, if not all, of the Olympus digital cameras ship with a program that enables you to seamlessly join a series of images from side to side so that you can shoot a 360-degree panorama. This "stitching" software is getting better and better at finding the areas in adjoining images that should match one another, even if they're a little out of alignment. So, if you have the right software these days (see Chapter 21), you can shoot a pretty decent handheld panorama.

Tip   Some of the Olympus cameras come with panorama software that places a grid on the LCD to help you keep the horizon aligned and to give you a guideline for overlapping the edges. If shooting panoramas is something you're likely to want to do often, you might want to keep your eyes out for such a feature.

On the other hand, no matter how "clever" your stitching program, you will do a better job if your camera is kept absolutely level as it rotates, takes pictures at regular intervals of rotation, and is rotated about the optical axis. This last requirement is the hard part. Most professional and semiprofessional film cameras have a mark that indicates the location of the camera's optical axis. It would be nice if more digicams bore this mark. Then, you can adjust your panoramic tripod head so that this mark is centered over the tripod's mounting screw. (You may need a special mounting device in order to center this mark.)

At the very least, you will want to use a level on your tripod head. Some tripods come with levels built in to their heads. You can also buy tilt and pan heads that have a built-in level.

If your tripod doesn't have a level, there's another answer. Take a small, flat piece of sheet metal and drill a hole that makes it easy to place it over your tripod screw. Then you'll have a platform that protrudes out the back of your camera. You can place a small carpenter's level on the metal. The whole rig (see Figure 7-10) should cost you less than $5.

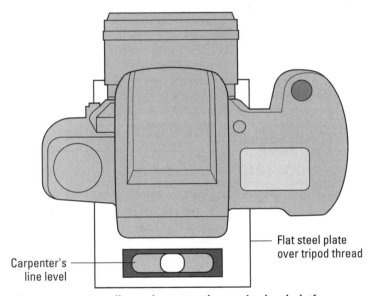

Flat steel plate
over tripod thread

Carpenter's
line level

Figure 7-10: A small metal scrap makes a nice level platform — especially useful on ball-bearing heads.

There is one company, Kaidan, that specializes in making accessories for making panoramic and object sequences. You can find them at http:www.kaidan.com. You will discover that there are quite a few of these accessories in quite a large price range.

Buying External Flash Units

The capability to use a flash unit that can be fired at some distance from the camera will only be found in upper-echelon prosumer cameras and in most all professional cameras. This is equally true of both film and digital cameras. There are two basic types of external flash units. Although each of these categories can be used in many different situations, I break them down this way:

✦ Event

✦ Studio

Event strobes

Event strobes integrate the battery pack and the flash head and are small enough to be dropped into a camera bag. They vary in size from a pack of cigarettes to a ball peen hammer. They also vary in power. Generally speaking, the more power the better. However, depending on your budget and your requirements, you'll want to pick the best compromise between versatility and price.

Try to find a unit that will give you a guide rating of around 120 at ISO 100 (the typical speed rating for a digital camera). This means that you can shoot at an f-stop of about f-11 if your subject is about 10 feet away. In fact, you'll want to shoot with the flash to one side of the camera and at least a couple of feet above it. The rules for lighting with portable flash are no different than for any other type of lighting (see Chapter 4), except that you're generally in circumstances that don't permit heavy equipment and light stands. If you don't have an assistant, you may have to bounce the flash off the ceiling (or a nearby wall) in order to get a natural effect.

You'll also want to try to find a single unit that can be used in as many ways as possible. Otherwise, you'll eventually end up having to buy several different strobe units. Get one with a flash head that tilts. Another very useful feature is a built-in slave sensor (see "Other Strobe Accessories," later in this chapter) so that you can trigger the unit from your camera's built-in flash.

Some cameras, such as the Nikon Coolpix 950, are meant to be used only with proprietary external flash units. These are generally automatic and respond to information that the camera collects on how much light is striking the subject during a flash and then automatically adjust the duration of the flash for the proper exposure. There are also automatic flash units that work independently of the camera's electronics. These have a built-in light sensor that internally adjusts the flash for the proper duration. Automatic flash units are helpful when you're just getting used to flash, have to do a lot of bounce lighting, or if you don't have the experience to quickly "guestimate" the proper settings. They're also extremely helpful if your camera doesn't give you direct control over the f-stop.

If your camera does give you control over the f-stop, you can save money by buying a nonautomatic unit. You'll also get a unit that does what you ask it to do, rather than what it insists on doing. Personally, I'd rather save the money to invest in a handheld combination strobe meter (see "Choosing Light Meters," later in this chapter).

Event flash units have three types of connectors:

✦ Proprietary

✦ A pc cord

✦ Hot-shoe units

Proprietary connectors are designed to force you to buy your flash from the manufacturer of your camera. Incidentally, they may also make it possible to use some automated flash exposure features. Most importantly, they will prevent you from being able to use a unit that offers just the features you want at the price you want to pay for them. Personally, I avoid proprietary connections like the plague.

The pc cord connector is the most universally useful choice. You can buy all sorts of extension chords for them, they work well with studio flash, and you can always buy a replacement cord when you wear out the one that came with the unit.

Hot-shoe units work off the hot-shoe synch connection featured on some cameras.

Note A hot-shoe connection is actually an excellent way to go. You can easily buy a small connector that lets you connect a standard synch chord, yet you still have the option of mounting a hot-shoe flash on the camera itself.

Studio strobes

Studio strobes are often taken on location for advertising and interior photography — but it takes a crew. These are big units, often powerful enough to light an entire room (or SUV). All of them work off of standard pc cords. If your camera doesn't have a digital delay, you can also use them with slave units — so you may be able to fire them without a synch cord.

Studio strobes come in two basic types:

✦ Monolights

✦ Powerpacks

Monolights

Monolights have the powerpack built into the lamp head. Most will only fire one light, but most all of these units have a built-in slave sensor. The built-in slaves and powerpacks make them very easy to take on location because you can pack three to six of them in a single case that's easily transported in the trunk of a car. They're also nice on location because they're not tethered together at the powerpack, so it's a little less likely that the public will be tripping over the cords. I say a little less likely because most of these units are not battery-powered, so they still need to be plugged in to a wall socket.

Of course, there's no reason you can't use monolights in the studio. Their portability simply makes them more versatile. Also, because the lights are independent of a central powerpack, you can add lights as your budget swells and the need arises.

Powerpacks

Powerpack units are divided into those designed for use on location and those designed strictly for studio use. The location units generally contain a battery pack. This means that they can be used in areas where there's no electricity. On the other hand, virtually all battery packs are meant to power more than one flash head. Look for a unit that will let you adjust the power to different levels for different heads. It's a fairly common feature.

Other strobe accessories

As soon as you think about using off-camera flash, you'd better start thinking about the accessories that make them work, from flash connectors to light stands.

Slave units

Slave units are used for firing flash heads that are some distance away from the camera without the need for daisy-chained synch cords.

There are three types of slave units. In order of cost, they are as follows:

✦ Photoelectric

✦ Infrared

✦ Radio-controlled

Photoelectric slaves are very inexpensive. They make it possible to use an external flash with any camera that has a built-in flash — and that includes most all digicams. They're often built in to external portable and monolight units. In fact, you should shop for units that come so equipped because you'll find them to be much more versatile. You can also buy individual units that have either a hot-shoe connector or a pc-cord synch post, so that they can be connected to either studio or portable strobe units. This is an item that you should always have in your kit. The downside to photo-electric slaves is that they're useless at press events and parties. That's because everyone who has a throwaway camera will set off your slaves every time they take a shot. Also, you can't use most of them outdoors, so they're no good for fill flash.

Infrared slaves are the next step up. Unauthorized flashes don't set them off and you can use them at events. Their limitations are that they have to be used in the line of sight and their range is limited (compared to radio-controlled remotes).

The best thing since sliced bread is radio remotes. You can place auxiliary units behind walls (so that they can light a distant area without being seen), use them at events, and use them outdoors on location. Their cost, at around $100 per transmitter/receiver, can get a little scary when you're equipping multiple units. On the other hand, if you have an important event to cover or a major on-location commercial shoot, you'll cover their cost in one sitting.

Light stands

If you're going to use off-camera strobe at anything more than arm's length from the camera and you don't have an assistant, you'll need one or more light stands. You can find single-leg light stands that have a heavy weight at the bottom. They're sturdy and take up little space. They're also excellent for holding up backdrop rolls. However, moving them around is nasty work.

Most light stands have a tripod base and several telescoping sections (see Figure 7-11). Look for a unit that has adjustable leg spread and buy 10- or 12-foot-tall units.

You may need diameter adapters (small sleeves with a hole in the center) to make the lamp heads attach securely to the light stands. Generally, these are supplied with or can be ordered from the manufacturer of your lamp head at a very reasonable price.

Another accessory that I find very handy is a hot-shoe light-stand adapter (see Figure 7-12). These make it possible to mount a hot-shoe-type portable flash atop a light stand. Because light stands weigh little and assistants can be expensive, this is an excellent way to light event portraits and on-location scenes.

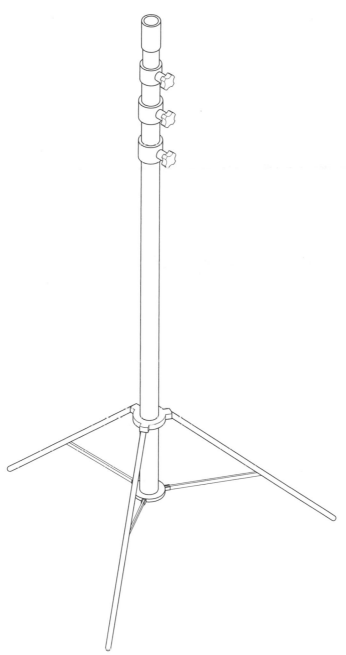

Figure 7-11: A typical lightweight 10-foot light stand

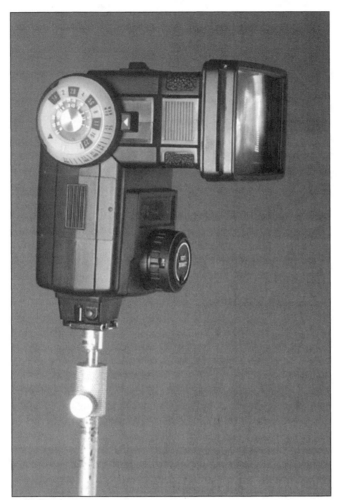

Figure 7-12: A hot-shoe adapter for a light stand holds this Digi-Slave flash unit in place.

Reflectors

Reflectors are the most portable and lowest-cost means for lightening the shadows in an image, regardless of the type of light source used. The ones I find most useful for both studio and location work are foam-core sheets. You can buy these at your local office supply that are black on one side and white on the other. You can also buy them that are white on one side and silver on the other. You can buy one of each for less than $10. The advantage of foam core is that it's lightweight, so you can easily clamp it to a light stand (see Figure 7-13) or a ladder and position it where you want it. The white side is the one you'll use the most. It provides a soft neutral fill with no hotspots. Silver is better when the reflector has to be some distance from the subject because it reflects brighter and more focused light. Black is useful for occasions when you want to set a strong mood by deepening the shadows, rather than filling them. A large piece of black felt (which can also double as a background) is also useful for absorbing light on the shadow side of the subject when you have a larger subject.

Figure 7-13: A sheet of white foam core attached to a light stand with a spring clamp

Windshield sunscreens also come in versions that are silver on one side and white on the other. They, too, work well with clamps and light stands. However, I usually use them handheld when shooting close-ups outdoors. The silver side is especially useful on cloudy days to lend a little contrast to the scene and to brighten up the shadows under your subject's eyes.

Flats, covered with insulation foam core, are terrific studio reflectors for large subjects. I make a frame of 1 × 2-inch fir and staple the foam core to either or both sides. You can paint one side flat black to use as a light absorber. I also use these flats during open studios for hanging fine-art prints of my work.

Umbrellas make wonderful semidirectional reflectors for imitating the light from an open window. These look just like the umbrellas you carry out in the rain, except that their stalks are straight so that they will line up directly with the lamp head (see Figure 7-14). By the way, when you buy your lamp heads, you'll want to make sure that they can accommodate an umbrella reflector.

Figure 7-14: An umbrella reflector attached to a studio strobe

Lightboxes, like umbrellas, project a soft light, but it is noticeably more focused than the light from an umbrella. Lightboxes are extremely useful in product shots when you want directed, but soft-edged light.

A lightbox (see Figure 7-15) envelopes the lamp head in black nylon, lined with either a white or silver lining. They come in a whole variety of sizes. The bigger the lightbox (often called a *light bank* for reasons that entirely escape me), the softer the light and the more appropriate for lighting large subjects. Lightboxes are the favorite primary light in Richard Avedon–type glamour portraits. They are also widely used in product shots.

Figure 7-15: A top-of-the-line Chimera lightbox

The cost of strobes and their accessories

I could have given the rough prices of each of these items in context, but it's easier to judge what you'll have to spend if you have all the costs grouped in a table. Keep in mind, however, that prices change overnight and that there can be a great disparity between manufacturers' suggested retail prices (which I try to use here in Table 7-1) and the prices you can find on the Internet or in *Shutterbug* magazine.

Table 7-1
Prices of Strobes and Accessories

Type	Typical Features/Power	Low	High
Portable	Hot shoe (GN 100)	$50	$70
Bracket portable	Professional press (GN 150)	$200	$600
Monolight	250 to 1,500 watt seconds	$350	$2,000
Powerpack	240 ws to 2,400 ws	$290	$2,000
Light head	Up to 1,000 ws	$175	$400
Light stand	8–12 feet, lightweight to heavy duty	$25	$200
Umbrella reflector	24–48 inch diameter	$30	$100
Photoelectric slave		$25	$50
Radio slave		$100	$400
Lightbox	12 × 6 inches to 54 × 72 inches	$90	$500
Flash meters	Simple Novatron to combo unit with built-in spot meter	$100	$450

Choosing Light Meters

Three types of light meters may be useful to you:

✦ The meter built into your camera

✦ Ambient light meters

✦ Ambient/strobe meters

Built-in meters

Built-in meters vary considerably in their options and in their accuracy. All of them will get you a daylight exposure that will produce a readable image — provided you have access to decent image-editing software. As you get closer to the $1,000 price range for digicams, you can expect both accuracy and versatility. The meter will likely be sensitive to much lower light levels and will give you a choice of one of three types of metering:

✦ Center-weighted

✦ Matrix

✦ Spot

Incident Light Reading from Built-in Meters?

All built-in meters read reflected light (see "Ambient light meters," later in this chapter). However, if you want to get an incident light reading without buying a separate meter, there are a couple of tricks you can try: 18-percent gray cards and ping-pong balls. You'll have to get the gray card from a camera store. If you take your reading from an 18-percent gray card, you will get the reading for the brightness of the light falling on the subject at that angle. You can read either the highlights or the shadows, depending on which way you face the card. A better idea is to cut a ping-pong ball in half and place it directly in front of your meter's lens (which may or may not be the camera's lens—read your manual). Because you are reading a half-dome, you will get a reading for both highlights and shadows. You may have to adjust exposure to compensate for the density of the ping-pong ball, so it's best to shoot a few test photos before you depend on this technique for critical exposures.

Center-weighted metering

Center-weighted metering gives more weight to the brightness values in the center of the image than to that at the edges. The idea is to avoid too much influence from the shading in overly dark or light (such as the sky) backgrounds. Unfortunately, photos are usually compositionally stronger when the subject is not dead center. Most digicams will let you aim at the subject to focus and get a meter reading, freeze those settings when you depress the shutter slightly, and then enable you to move the camera before completing the shot by fully depressing the shutter button.

Matrix metering

Matrix metering is a specialty of late-model Nikon cameras, though its popularity has caused it to spread to others. Matrix metering divides the picture area and then averages the meter reading, depending on the location of the various metering segments. More weight is given to segments in the center of the screen than to those at the sides, and more weight is given to segments at the bottom of the screen than at the top.

Unfortunately, the sophisticated level of matrix metering found in professional and semiprofessional film SLRs is not yet available in under-$5,000 digicams. The film cameras with the best matrix metering let you assign your own importance to each segment of the matrix. Of course, this almost requires an SLR because you need to be able to see the matrix overlaid on the exact view of the picture being photographed. Of course, you could do this on the LCD, but in bright sunlight you'd be unable to see much of anything.

Ambient light meters

Ambient light meters are external meters meant to read existing continuous light. They don't read the light from strobes, which makes them fine if you don't own or plan to own strobes. They're also about half the price of meters that also read strobe.

Ambient light meters come in models that can read incident or reflected light, or both. There are even models that have a spot metering mode. The brands that seem to generally get the highest praise are Sekonic and Gossen. Both companies make a wide variety of meters. I've been using meters from both companies throughout the production of this book and have found them both to be extremely accurate. However, I should qualify this by saying that I have not tested every single model in both lines.

Ambient/strobe meters

Personally, I'm a big fan of combination meters that do "everything." Of course, how much of everything varies from model to model. My favorite meter is the Gossen Luna Pro Digital F (see Figure 7-16), which is entirely battery-powered and doesn't need to be connected to a strobe unit in order to get a reading. It reads both incident and reflected light. You switch modes by simply sliding the dome from one side to another. For ambient light, I like to use the meter in both modes, and then make a subjective judgment on how I'd like to compromise the readings. To take a strobe reading, you just set the meter for strobe, press a button, fire the strobe, and take a look at the resultant reading. Using this meter well requires a minimum of study. The uses for the controls are obvious enough to be discovered by experimentation. I also like this meter for its compact size—it easily fits into my digital camera bag. Best of all, if you shop around you can buy one for under $200—a pittance for a device that can keep you looking like a pro.

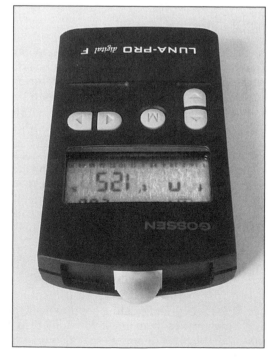

Figure 7-16: The Gossen Lunasix Pro combination ambient/strobe meter

My "other" meter is a Sekonic L508 Zoom Master that does all of the above and then adds a very precise spot meter (see Figure 7-17). Spot meters are indispensable when a small area in the frame contains the most visually important subject matter. They are also great for calculating the exact range of data that you'll want to capture. Some digital cameras, such as the Nikon Coolpix 950, will let you adjust the contrast of the image. So, if the spot meter tells you that you've got an unusually wide range of brightness to cover, you can adjust the camera to record lower contrast. Lowering the captured contrast will help you to capture as much of the existing tonal values as possible. Doing so will give you much more freedom in Photoshop to adjust the final values to your liking.

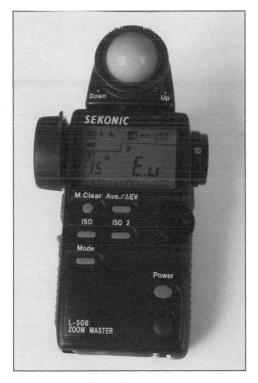

Figure 7-17: The Sekonic L508 ambient/strobe meter that measures reflected, incident, and spot areas

What About Lens Accessories?

One of the big drawbacks of digital cameras under $2,000 is the lack of interchangeable lenses. However, if your camera has a screw-thread ring inside the front of the lens barrel, you will probably be able to add supplementary lenses. There will also be times when you'll need filters and lens hoods.

Note Some cameras cannot use lens accessories. This is usually because they have lens barrels that retract into the camera when the lens is not in use. The Olympus C2000, C2020, and C3030 have such a barrel, but Olympus makes a special adapter that fits outside the lens. Check with the manufacturer of your camera.

Adapter rings

On the front of the lens barrel you will see a (*nn*mm, where the *nn* represents the diameter of the screw thread. If this is a diameter in which filters and auxiliary lenses are commonly available, you may not need adapter rings. On the other hand, you may want to use filters or lens hoods that you've already purchased for your film camera. In that case, you'll want a step-up ring (see Figure 7-18).

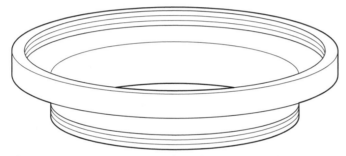

Figure 7-18: A step-up ring adapts larger standard-size accessories to a smaller mount.

Common filter diameters

The following sizes of filters are readily available through Tiffen. If your camera's thread diameter doesn't match one of these, you will need a step-up ring made by your camera's manufacturer.

37mm	40.5mm	43mm	46mm	49mm
52mm	55mm	58mm	62mm	67mm
72mm	77mm	82mm	86mm	

Filters

Photographic filters are optically treated and coated glass meant to either correct the color of light or to lend a special effect to the scene. Here are the most important categories of filters, along with a description of why you might want to use them:

✦ UV (ultraviolet)

✦ Polarizing

✦ Light balancing

✦ Special effects

✦ Color correction

✦ Color enhancing

✦ Black and white

UV

If you want to protect your investment in a precious digital camera, the first accessory you will purchase is a UV (ultraviolet) filter. UV filters' primary purpose is protecting the front surface of your lens. They also remove ultraviolet haze, which tends to lighten skies and distant objects. UV filters have little effect when not shooting skies or distant landscapes, so you might as well leave them in place at all times — except, of course, when you need to mount a different filter. A UV filter costs about $15.

Polarizing

Polarizing filters remove glare caused by reflected light. They also tend to improve color saturation. They also darken blue skies much more dramatically than UV filters and tend to make colors look more saturated. A polarizing filter costs about $30.

Light balancing

Light-balancing filters are of two varieties: neutral density and color temperature converters.

Neutral density (gray) filters reduce the light coming through the lens so that you can use a wider aperture to get less depth of field when shooting in brightly lit circumstances. These filters come in one-stop increments.

Color temperature converters change the color of light to balance the type of film being used. They are not necessary for digital cameras because you can do the same thing faster by using your camera's white balance. Some cameras, however, won't let you manually dictate the lighting type. For those cameras, you may want to use a color temperature converter to force a specific mood effect. Still, you could do a better job of that by just changing the color balance in your image-editing software.

Special effects

Special effects filters are most often used to soften all or part of the image. Sometimes they are also slightly tinted to warm the image at the same time it is softened. Softening filters may also be slightly scored so that light spreads along the score lines to create effects ranging from misty landscapes to star highlights. Of course, these are all effects that you can create after the fact in most image-editing programs. Andromeda software (www.andromeda.com) makes a whole series of plug-in filters that imitate special effects filters.

Color correction

These are filters that are meant to take an overall color cast out of the image. If you're working with digital images, you can usually do a better job of this in your image editor.

Color enhancing

There are two types of color-enhancing filters that are widely used: warming and saturation-boosting. Once again, you can easily do both of these jobs to a more controllable degree in your image-editing software.

Black and white

If your camera has a black and white mode, you might be interested in some of the filters commonly used to create effects in black and white photography:

✦ #8 yellow

✦ #15 deep yellow (often called orange)

✦ #11 green

✦ #25 red

Yellow filters are generally used for outdoor photography with black and white film because they darken skies and make them more dramatic. You could use a polarizing filter to achieve virtually the same effect. Green filters tend to lighten Caucasian skin tones and to make them contrast more strongly with their surroundings. They are often used in black and white fashion and portrait photography. Red filters create very dark skies and bright clouds. When they're used with infrared film, foliage turns white and shadow detail is increased immensely.

Lens hoods

Lens hoods prevent stray light from striking the lens, creating lens flare when it is not wanted. They are also great protection against scratching your lens by bumping into something when the camera is hanging around your neck.

Lens hoods for professional digital cameras can be bought anywhere, because professional digital cameras use the same lenses as film cameras. Lens hoods that will fit the small diameter of most prosumer digital cameras' lenses can be hard to find.

Tip

If you have a hard time finding lens accessories or a step-up ring small enough to fit your digital camera's lens, try places that sell video cameras. Most home video cameras have lenses that are comparable in diameter to those found on most digicams.

Focal length and macro lens adapters

If your camera is able to take screw-on lens adapters, chances are good that you can use an optical adapter that effectively changes the focal length of your lens at its widest aperture to a multiple of its usual focal length. There are also adapters that make it possible to work at closer focusing distances. Figure 7-19 shows the Tiffen 1.8× telephoto adapter mounted in front of the Olympus D620L's lens. This adapter can only be used when the lens is zoomed all the way out.

Figure 7-19: The Tiffen 1.8× telephoto adapter and a 52mm step-up ring

These lenses work best with SLR-type digital cameras because you can see what you're getting while you're shooting and because the cameras focus automatically through the lens. However, you may be able to use these accessories by viewing your shot on the LCD of the camera.

Adapters can be purchased that increase or decrease the focal length of the lens by 1.4 to 2 times. Macro adapters are available that enable you to focus 2×, 4×, and

5 × closer than normal. Rough costs for these accessories can be seen in the following table:

Step-up ring	$15
2 × or 4 × Macro	$100
Wide-angle adapter	$75–$150
Telephoto adapter	$75–$150

Some adapters can be reversed to provide either 2 × or 4 × closer focusing in a single adapter. The same is true of telephoto and wide-angle adapters for film cameras, which you may be able to adapt for use with your digital camera.

Digital Film

As soon as the image sensor reads a digital image, it is stored on memory media — anything from floppy disks to miniature disk drives. For professional studio cameras, the storage media is generally a computer's memory, as the camera is tethered directly to a computer. For professional SLR-format cameras, the storage media is generally a PCMCIA card (often simply called a pc card) of the same type as used by your laptop. Lately, small hard drives such as the 350MB drive made by IBM have become popular.

Prosumer- and consumer-level digicams generally use either SmartMedia or CompactFlash cards (see Figure 7-20). The Canon A70 will use two CompactFlash cards and the Olympus C2500 can simultaneously use one CompactFlash card and one SmartMedia card.

Figure 7-20: *Left:* A CompactFlash (CF) card; *Right:* A SmartMedia card

Each of these memory formats has unique advantages, but both have something in common: widespread standard use. CompactFlash is slightly more popular than SmartMedia, but choosing a camera that uses either format will assure you of being able to move up to a wider choice of cameras once you've collected several of these cards. It also means that you're more likely to be able to find extra cards when you're in a foreign country on a location shoot.

Both formats come in a wide variety of capacities, and the maximum capacity of both formats keeps going up. At this writing, it is possible to buy a card in either format that holds 128MB worth of images. This would enable you to store about 250 "superhigh-quality" digital images on a single card.

CompactFlash card's advantages are programmability and ruggedness. The circuitry isn't exposed, as it is with SmartMedia, so there's less chance of ruining the card by scratching or fingerprinting it.

The cost per megabyte of digital film tends to decrease with the capacity of the memory card, although very high capacity cards may sell for a premium for the near future.

It is always a good idea to have more than one memory card. Otherwise, you'll find yourself away from your computer and "out of film." Of course, you can always erase some images. However, you don't want to rely on that because you will come to the point where you'll have to erase images that you'd rather keep.

The following list gives you a rough idea of the costs of digital film:

2MB	$30
4MB	$50
8MB	$40
16MB	$60
32MB	$100

If you purchase several SmartMedia cards, you might want to purchase Olympus' SmartMedia Wallet to give yourself an organized way to carry and protect the extra cards. These are available through B&H Photo at www.bhphoto.com.

Batteries

Digital cameras eat AA batteries to the point where they will cost you more than film unless you buy rechargeables. These come in two varieties: NiCad (nickel-cadmium) and NiMH (nickel metal-hydride).

The batteries you want are the NiMH batteries. They will last two to three times longer when used in a digital camera than NiCads and they don't have to be fully discharged before recharging. Of course, NiMH batteries cost two to three times as much as NiCads and they're a little harder to find. However, you can buy them online for about $30 for a set of four Quest batteries with a Maha charger.

Note   I mention the Quest batteries because they're getting all the buzz on the digital camera list servers as being the longest lasting and least expensive.

Card Readers

If you're new to digital photography, it won't be long before you'll want a card reader of some kind. Card readers will cut the time is takes to transfer images from your camera to a computer to a fraction of the time it takes to transfer them directly from the camera. This is even true (to a lesser degree, of course) if your camera has a USB port (as many of the newer Kodak models do).

Lexar, Olympus, Simple Technologies, and Microtech all make card readers (though that's not an exclusive list). Some models will even read multiple card formats.

Card readers are available for all of the standard interfaces: serial, parallel, SCSI (though not very popular), and USB. The best of these choices is USB, for the following reasons:

✦ The data transfer rate is much faster than any but the latest SCSI or FireWire standards. Olympus states that their USB readers download 80 times faster than a serial connection — about one image per second at the super high quality compression setting.

✦ The connections and the interface are exactly the same regardless of computer platform (Windows users will have to have Windows 98 or 2000).

✦ You can plug the device into any computer with a USB port — though you'll need to install the driver for the card reader first. This makes it much more likely that you'll be able to find a computer you can download to when you're in the field.

✦ The readers will easily fit into a small camera bag because the cable and connector are very small and no power supply is required (USB card readers can take their power from the computer).

Most card readers sell for around $80, though I have seen a few bundled with cameras and have occasionally found them on "special" for as little as $50. Card readers that can read multiple formats will cost more, but it certainly beats having to buy more than one if your business has to support users of different brands of digital cameras.

If you own a laptop computer, you might also consider a PCMCIA adapter as your card reader. In fact, if your laptop doesn't have a USB port, this is your best choice. Furthermore, PCMCIA cards are even faster at transferring images than USB readers — but then you'll probably want to transfer the images from your laptop to your desktop computer. In either case, a PCMCIA card is the fastest and most portable way to download your images.

Note   It is possible to buy a PCMCIA card with a USB connection. This isn't as fast as using a PCMCIA card reader, but it may make it easier for you to use the same card reader on your desktop machine as you use on your laptop.

Odds and Ends That Count

When it comes to accessories, the list of possibilities is endless. You can always think of one thing more. A couple that fall outside the easy categories are LCD hoods and exposure targets.

LCD hoods are an absolute necessity for anyone serious about shooting with a digital camera. That's because (even though they're getting a lot better — and some are a lot better than others) it's tough to see the image clearly if you're shooting in light that's bright enough to enable a handheld exposure at ISO 100. You can easily make your own LCD hood from a piece of lintless matte-black cardboard, available at any art supply house. See the diagram in Figure 7-21.

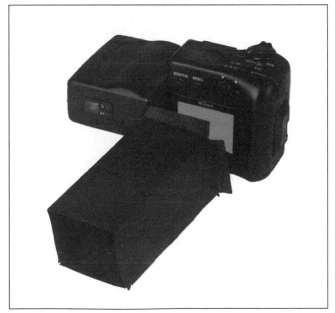

Figure 7-21: A homemade LCD hood

Another way to keep the LCD shaded is simply to throw a dark cloth over your head. Your local fabric store will have something appropriate. A yard-square piece of tightly woven black nylon, seamed around the edges, will do quite nicely.

Now, if you want something much more professional and sexy-looking (and you don't mind spending $20, the Hoodman nylon LCD hood fits 2–4-inch LCDs. You can order it through the Web site at www.hoodmanusa.com. The one I really like is from Photosolve. It's a rigid plastic with a magnifier that fits over the LCD screen. This makes it somewhat easier to use the LCD screen for focusing, as well as shielding it from light. You can check out this item at www.photosolve.com.

Gray cards are very useful for setting your built-in meter to a neutral brightness level. A pair of Kodak R-27 18-percent gray cards can be purchased from B&H Photo for $14.95. No-name gray cards are available from the same source for about half that price.

Summary

This chapter has told you all about the real cost of working with digital cameras, especially of the prosumer variety. To put it another way, it's been a compendium of the accessories you're most likely to need in order to get specific types of jobs done.

✦   ✦   ✦

Scanner Tips

It may be true that ultimately a digital image doesn't care how it originated. Nevertheless, it's a good idea to understand the pros and cons of starting with a digital camera versus digitizing the product of a conventional camera. Then, if you decide that you need to scan (and there will certainly be times when you will), you should know whether and when to buy a slide scanner or a flatbed or to take your images to a service bureau for drum scanning. Next, you need to know what features to look for and how much you should expect to spend for those features. Finally, you want to know how to calibrate your scanner so that what you scan produces a file that contains as much data from the original as possible.

The Advantages of Scanning over Digital Shooting

Not all digital photos start out that way. In fact, it's fair to say that the vast majority of digitized photos started out on film. Then someone took a digital picture of the analog picture by using a device called a scanner. A scanner is simply a device in which the image sensor (usually a linear CCD array, just like in a digital camera) is moved across the analog print or negative. The image is then converted to digital format (see Chapter 6). There are several important advantages to scanning over shooting a digital original, especially if you're on a budget:

- ✦ You can use the camera you've become used to and all the accessories that are available for it.

- ✦ You can capture greater color depth and dynamic range.

- ✦ You can capture higher resolution.

- ✦ It's the only way to digitize images that have already been captured on film.

Having pointed out these advantages, it's time to issue some warnings as to what they mean. First, not all scanners are the same. For instance, in order to get better resolution from a flatbed scanner, you'll probably have to scan an enlarged print—even if you have a transparency adapter. Also, some scanners (they get scarcer as time goes by) just aren't well suited to capturing photographic color because they implant too much noise in the image or because their scanning motors cause streaking and banding. If you're thinking about buying a really cheap scanner, be sure to look up reviews for it on the Web or in the leading computer magazines. Come to think of it, that's sound advice for scanners, cameras, and just about any other digital device.

Although you should certainly consider any characteristics in a scanner that make it more able to work in a wider variety of useful tasks, such as faxing and document interpretation, we're going to concentrate on those qualities in a scanner that make it a good bet for digitizing photos.

The Different Types of Scanners

There are three basic types of scanners that are capable of digitizing images well enough to be considered of photographic quality:

- ✦ Flatbed
- ✦ Slide
- ✦ Drum

Flatbed

Flatbed scanners are the type most widely used for office work and will give you the most versatility. They are designed primarily for scanning documents and photographic prints—that is, reflective positive images on paper. Almost all can be used to optically recognize and store the content of documents and even come with OCR (optical character recognition) software for this purpose. Many also come with software that enables you to use the scanner as a fax machine.

Cross-Reference

For a more comprehensive look at these and other types of scanners (and scanner accessories) check out Chapter 4.

The price range for flatbed scanners is enormous—from about $70 to tens of thousands. Many come with or can be accessorized with a transparency adapter that consists of a lightbox above the glass bed of the scanner. This makes it possible to scan film by transmitted light as well as prints. However, resolution and other factors limit the scanning of transparencies to proofing and FPO (for position only) purposes. Acer makes a scanner in this category, the 620 ST, that gives you a transparency adapter and a flatbed scanner at $140.

There are flatbed scanners with a film drawer that do a much better job of scanning film because the film doesn't have to be in contact with the glass flatbed and because the film is placed in holders that mask it from the light. These models are designed primarily for the graphic arts community and range in price from around $600 to around $2,000. When it comes to scanning film, these scanners are still not even close to a match with a slide scanner, but are more than adequate for onscreen, Web, FPO, and proof purposes. Agfa and Microtek are two companies that make such scanners. If you're unfamiliar with flatbed scanners, you can get an idea of where all the functional areas of various types and options are by taking a look at Figure 8-1.

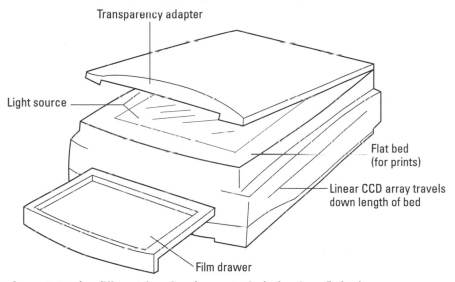

Figure 8-1: The different functional areas typical of various flatbed scanners

Flatbed scanners typically scan images at a maximum optical resolution of 600 dots per inch, although it is not uncommon to find mid- to high-end models that will scan at twice that. For instance, the Umax PowerLook 3000 scans at an optical resolution of $1,220 \times 3,048$ for reflective art and $3,048 \times 3,048$ for film. That's higher resolution for film than the majority of slide scanners and the cost is lower than that f or many film scanners intended for large-format film.

Slide

If your primary goal in purchasing a scanner is to digitize images or if you are willing to spend more for a machine that's specifically designed for the job, a film scanner is the way to go. They will scan either positive or negative film. Virtually all of these that sell for under $2,000 are made for scanning 35mm and APS film. At around $500 (give or take a hundred), you can expect about three megapixels of resolution (just a little less than 2,000 dpi). At around $1,000, you can expect resolution of just under 3,000 dpi—or six megapixels. This is approximately the same resolution as medium-speed 35mm color film. At $2,000 there is the Polaroid SprintScan 4000 (which stands for the scanner's optical resolution). The result is a higher Dmax rating (3.4) than most slide scanners and enough resolution to provide extra image sharpness for all film and to match that of the finest-grained color slide films.

 Tip   The best buy in a slide scanner as this went to press was the Nikon Coolscan III, which had just dropped to a suggested retail price of $799. It gives you the new digital ICE technology, 30-bit scanning depth, and 2,700 dpi resolution.

There are a couple of medium-format film scanners that can scan medium-format film that are under $5,000, but to get the most out of large-format film, you should plan on sending your film to a service bureau that uses a high-end drum scanner. An option for 4 × 5 film (and smaller formats as well) is the Nikon LS 4500. This is a desktop film scanner that retails for around $12,000. It uses dual lenses to scan 35mm at 3,000 dpi and 4 × 5 film at 1,000 dpi. Leaf and Polaroid also make 4 × 5 film scanners in roughly the same price range. Figure 8-2 shows a pair of typical film scanners.

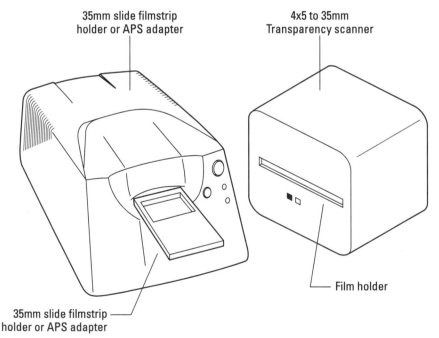

35mm slide filmstrip holder or APS adapter

4x5 to 35mm Transparency scanner

35mm slide filmstrip holder or APS adapter

Film holder

Figure 8-2: A typical slide scanner and multiformat desktop film scanner

Drum

Drum scanners are very high end professional prepress digitizers. They have resolutions that typically range from 4,000 to 10,000 dpi for *any* type of original and can scan anything from 35mm film to (depending on model and price) poster-size prints. Several prepress professionals I spoke to feel that high-end flatbeds can do as good or better a job as the lowest-priced drum scanners, so the real apparent value is in drum scanners that sell in the range above $20,000 ($30,000 being considered fairly typical). Figure 8-3 shows a typical drum scanner.

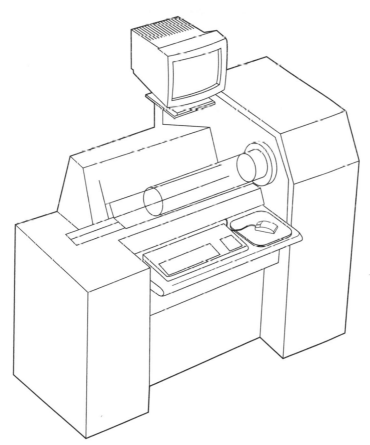

Figure 8-3: A typical drum scanner

Desirable Features in a Scanner

Before you rush out to buy a scanner, it's a good idea to get a clue as to what you should be looking for. That's not always as obvious as one might think. Explanations follow, but first, here's the list of the areas into which you should inquire:

✦ Value

✦ Transparency adapter or drawer (for flatbeds)

✦ Speed

✦ Resolution

✦ Bit depth and dynamic range

✦ Signal-to-noise ratio

✦ Simplicity of operations

✦ Total control over image quality

✦ Control software

✦ Bundled software

✦ Versatility

✦ Connections

Value

These days, all midrange to low-end flatbed scanners are relatively good values. That is to say that prices have dropped dramatically for all types of scanners (though professional prepress drum scanners have tended to stay in the stratosphere). Quality has improved, too. So today, you can expect to get 600-dpi optical resolution, a density rating of 3.0 or better, and a bit depth of at least 10 bits per channel (30-bit RGB true color) for well under $200.

The difference will come in the individual scanner's ruggedness, the comparative quality of components (such as stepper motors and image sensor circuitry), the bundled software, and the functions that can be accomplished within the same unit.

To determine value, decide what you want to do and make sure you're not paying for features that are of little or no significance to your way of working. Also, make some judgment based on how long you plan to keep this scanner. It may make sense to buy a cheaper unit that will go out of adjustment in a couple of years if you know that you're going to want to move up to a more capable unit once you can afford it.

Scanners, particularly at the low end, tend to vary in performance from one unit to the next. So first pick the features and price you have in mind, and then make sure you walk into a dealer's store where you can test the scanner you want to buy. If you want to buy via catalog or the Internet, make sure the vendor has a 30-day money-back guarantee so that you can test the unit when you receive it.

Finally, check the unit's specifications for all of the following categories and pick the unit that gives you the most for your buck. This can be important even if you don't plan to keep the scanner. A unit with better specifications and more features is likely to command a higher resale price.

Transparency adapter or drawer

If your reason for buying a flatbed scanner is primarily for digitizing photographs, you'll want a unit that gives you the option of adding a transparency adapter. A transparency adapter places a light source above the scanning bed so that light can be transmitted through negatives and slides.

The price of transparency adapters used to run close to $1,000, but today they seldom run more than an extra $100 and there are several models in the under-$200 category. Transparency adapters are nearly indispensable for making digital contact sheets from film, an example of which is shown in Figure 8-4. They are also handy for quickly digitizing images to be used for position only (FPO) when putting together design concepts. Finally, if you shoot medium- to large-format film and have a scanner with better than 1,000-dpi optical resolution, they are also a far more affordable alternative to desktop film scanners. However, don't expect a professional level of quality from under $2,000 flatbeds. Figure 8-4 shows an example of a contact proof sheet of 35mm film made with a transparency adapter at 600 dpi.

Figure 8-4: A contact sheet made on a flatbed scanner with a transparency adapter

A much better alternative to a transparency adapter is a film drawer. This is a unit that slides into the scanner between the flatbed's light source and the image sensor and (usually) eliminates the need to have glass between the film and the sensor. This eliminates the possibility of Newton rings and dirty glass. Drawers also generally mask the edges of film. The result is a much sharper and cleaner film scan than can be expected from a transparency adapter. Figure 8-5 shows the drawer in Microtek's Scanmaker 5.

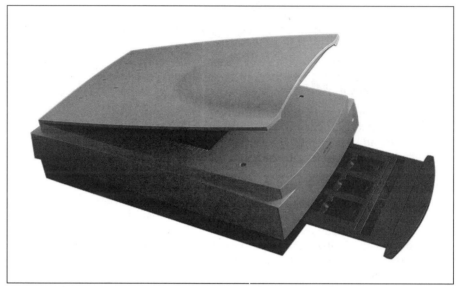

Figure 8-5: The Microtek Scanmaker 5 showing the transparency drawer

Speed

Time is money. Scanners get faster as technology gets better and cheaper. If you're buying a state-of-the-art desktop unit, you should be able to scan a full page of three-channel 30-bit color in just about one minute. A slide scanner should be able to scan a slide in about the same amount of time, although some of the best will do the job in under 30 seconds.

I find that speed in a slide scanner is even more important than in a flatbed because I tend to want to scan most of the images in a 36-exposure roll. However, remember that scanning speed isn't the whole story with a slide scanner. A unit that will sequentially scan six frames in the same film holder will be at least three times as fast as a unit that forces you to load, position, and scan one frame at a time.

Resolution

It must be obvious by now that the more resolution you can capture, the better. After all, you can always reduce the size of an image at less of a penalty than you pay for resizing to a larger size.

If you are capturing images that will be used at a much smaller size than the maximum resolution permits, you will want to make a separate scan for that purpose if you want to ensure the best possible quality. It is rare that the image reduction commands in an image editor will do as good a job of recording as much original image detail as if you had scanned at or close to the target resolution in the first place.

Having said all that, you can get pretty much all the resolution in a scanner that you're willing to pay for. Drum scanners in the stratospheric price ranges can capture 8,000 dots per inch — even from prints.

More realistically, you should expect at least the following resolution at the following price points in Table 8-1.

Table 8-1 Price versus Resolution		
Price Range	**Scanner Type**	**Minimum Acceptable Optical Resolution**
Under $200	Flatbed	600 dpi
Approximately $500	Flatbed Film	600×1,200 dpi 1,600 dpi
Approximately $1,000	Flatbed Film	600×1,200 dpi (but some will be higher) 2,700 dpi
$2,000–$2,500	Flatbed	1,600 dpi

Interpolated resolution

Almost all flatbed scanners emphasize their maximum *interpolated* resolution, rather than their actual optical resolution. This is almost as big a scam for scanners as it is for digital cameras, because your image-processing program will do at least as good a job of interpolating up as an on-chip program built in to your scanner. However, there is one advantage to higher interpolated resolution: being able to scale up the image at the same time you're scanning may save you some time. That's because you won't have to perform a separate operation in Photoshop (or whatever your image editor) just to do the scaling.

Downsampling

Downsampling is the opposite of interpolation. The image is reduced in size by throwing out a number of pixels. There actually is an advantage to doing this at scan time. Because fewer dot samples are taken in the first place, the resulting compressed matrix of pixels is likely to be more faithful to the original image than if the program simply discards pixels. However, you should be aware that the extent to which this is true will depend on the formula used to determine the downsampling and on the other factors that determine the quality of the scanner's image. Try it several ways with different types of subject matter until you get a good feel for what works best.

Bit depth, dynamic range, and density

A true-color RGB image assigns 8 bits per pixel per color channel to recording the image. This produces approximately 16.8 million colors, which is actually more colors than most of us can distinguish. Yet most of today's scanners (in fact, any that you should consider worthwhile) will acquire 10, 12, or even 14 bits per pixel per channel. This means that some can record several times as many colors as we can see. So what's the point?

Well, theoretically, the point is that the more colors a scanner can capture, the wider the range of colors we can use in the image we want to keep. The bummer is that most scanners won't export all the color they can capture, dropping all but 24 bits of that color. If the scanner is wise enough to keep the best range of colors (or gives you the controls to choose the best range), then there's still an advantage. Otherwise, more bit depth is just advertising hype.

Note One reason that so few scanners let you save all the data you capture is that it's only been since the release of Photoshop 5.0 that most image editors would enable you to import more than 8 bits per channel. Several competitors have since followed suit. At last it is becoming fairly common for graphic-arts-oriented flatbeds to enable the export of their full bit depth.

Another advantage of using a scanner that can capture higher bit depths is that it's also likely to be able to capture a wider dynamic range. Dynamic range is the difference between the brightest and darkest pixels in the image. Although bit depth determines exactly how many variations of color (hue, saturation, and brightness) can be captured, dynamic range describes the number of colors that can be clearly distinguished from one another.

If you combine bit depth and dynamic range, you come to a quantifier known as density, or D. Density is determined by subtracting the values of the darkest (D_{min}) and lightest (D_{max}) values. Typical densities for various photographic media are as follows:

Prints	D 2.0
Negatives	D 3.0
Slides	D 4.0

Signal-to-noise ratio

Noise is the interpretation of circuit-generated electrical fluctuations as image data. Manufacturers try to isolate the electrical fluctuations that are the result of exposure to light from those that are caused by cross talk between CCD elements and the like. As you might expect, more expensive and sophisticated units do a better job of this than inexpensive ones.

Signal-to-noise ratio is simply the average strength of noise signals compared to the average strength of the image data.

The greater the signal-to-noise ratio, the lower the likelihood that you will see random color patterns in the highlights and shadows of the image.

Simplicity of operations

Slide scanners are typically easier to operate than flatbed scanners because they're dedicated to a single task: getting the most faithful possible reproduction of the image on film. Figure 8-6 shows you the scanner software for the Nikon LS-1000.

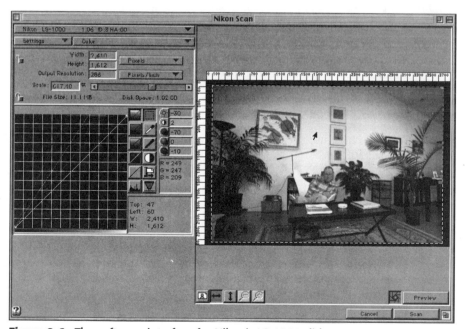

Figure 8-6: The software interface for Nikon's LS-1000 slide scanner

Flatbed scanners are another matter. They can be used for many different types of tasks, so the ease with which you can get your scanner to perform the desired task at the optimal settings for that task becomes important. Most flatbeds can be used to scan a photograph, scan a typed page to be sent as an e-mail, scan a page of type to be translated into text in a word-processing document, scan the grayscale image of a page to be sent as a fax, and so forth. The current trend is to place a miniature keypad on the front of the scanner. To scan an image, you press the proper color or shape button. The computer then automatically loads the image-processing software, prescans the image so that you can see a preview and lets you click OK if you like the way the prescan looks.

If you're doing critical image scanning, you'll probably want to do considerable fine-tuning in the image scanning software, but a one-touch feature can still save you time. If you also send faxes or e-mails, and do optical character recognition, these one-touch features make life even less stressful.

Total control over image quality

The scanning software that comes with a scanner can make or break your ability to use the scanner wisely. Here are the questions you should ask yourself when examining this software:

✦ Can I scan both positives and negatives (not a consideration if your scanner can't accept some sort of transparency adapter)?

✦ Is the image preview window large enough to make an accurate judgment as to the validity of image controls?

✦ How familiar looking are the image-adjustment controls? Will I have to be able to pat my head and rub my tummy in order to be able to use them properly, or will my Photoshop training stand me in good stead?

✦ Can you adjust images for both the composite channel and all individual channels using both levels (histogram sliders) and curves (variable brightness curves) controls?

✦ Is there a descreening control, and can I turn it on and off?

✦ Can I use it as a plug-in so that I can work from inside my image editor?

Bundled application software

These days, buying a scanner can be a great way to get free software — often of greater value than the price of the scanner. An image-processing program often ships with the scanner, though it's not often Photoshop. Still, you can find plenty of image-processing power (and some features Photoshop doesn't even have) in such programs as Jasc's Paint Shop Pro, Corel Photo-Paint 8 or 9, and Micrografx Picture Publisher. If you're really careful at shopping, you might even end up with a copy of MetaCreation's Painter. Although many of these programs come with the scanner in a "light" version, you can generally upgrade to a full and current versions at a very reasonable price.

If you are buying a flatbed scanner in the under-$200 price category, the image-processing software you're most likely to get is Adobe PhotoDeLuxe. PhotoDeluxe does many basic things quite well. It even does fairly complex things automatically. Best of all, it is fully Photoshop compatible and, in fact, uses the same image-processing engine. However, if you really want control over the results of scanning, you're still going to need Photoshop, Picture Publisher, Photo-Paint, Ulead's PhotoImpact, or Paint Shop Pro. That's because PhotoDeluxe doesn't have unsharp masking, halftone control, or levels/curve image adjustment controls. Notwithstanding those shortcomings, if you are just getting started and want the simplest way to get a reasonably good job done with the lowest learning curve, PhotoDeluxe is an excellent way to go.

Note If you're just starting out, but expect to get serious about your digital darkroom work, look for a scanner that bundles Photoshop LE. You'll get the interface and most of the main functions of Photoshop at a price that practically includes a free scanner.

Many of the readers of this book will already own the image-processing software of their dreams. If you're buying a flatbed scanner, chances are good that those folks will be more interested in the OCR and fax software that's offered. The best OCR packages I've tried are (in no particular order) Caere's OmniPage, Xerox's TextBridge Classic, and Visioneer's PaperPort software. These also happen to be the three OCR applications that I most often see bundled with flatbed scanners — even those at the lower end of the price range scale.

What You Can Expect for What You Pay

In order to choose a scanner, it may help to have a bit of guidance as to which features you can expect to get for a given amount of money. Out of necessity, these are rough guidelines. How much you actually pay is probably going to be less by the time you read this, and you will probably get more features. Besides, there will be tradeoffs. For instance, some units will give you better software or a transparency adapter in exchange for lower resolution. Table 8-2 lists the features and prices for flatbed scanners, and Table 8-3 lists the same for slide scanners.

Table 8-2
Flatbed Scanner Features and Prices

Feature	Under $200	Under $600	Around $2,000
Transparency adapter	Becoming commonplace, but some models don't even have the option	May have transparency drawer	Should have transparency drawer
Optical resolution	600×1,200	600×1,200	1,000+ dpi
Bit depth	30 bit	36 bit	36–48 bit
Signal-to-noise ratio	Mostly acceptable, but be careful	Professional	Superb
Density rating	Less than 3.0	Less than 3.0 for reflective, slightly better for transparencies	3.2–3.6
Application software	PhotoDeluxe, OCR, Fax	Photoshop LE, Photo-Paint, OCR, fax	Photoshop 4+, OCR, fax
Pushbutton or "one-touch" operation	Common	Sometimes	Seldom
Connection	USB, parallel	USB, parallel, SCSI	SCSI

Table 8-3
Slide Scanner Features and Prices

Feature	Around $500	About $1,000	Around $2,000
Optical resolution	1,600–2,400	2,700 dpi	2,700–4,000 dpi
Bit depth	30 bit	36 bit	36 bit with 36-bit output
Signal-to-noise ratio	Good	Professional	Superb
Density rating	Around 3.0	3.2–3.6	3.2–3.6
Application software	PhotoDeluxe or equivalent	Photoshop LE, Photo-Paint, Picture Publisher, Digital Ice*, Genuine Fractals*	Digital Ice*, Genuine Fractals*
Connection	SCSI	SCSI	SCSI
Film holder			Automatic advance for multiple slides, negatives

* See the following sections for more information on Digital Ice and Genuine Fractals.

Digital Ice

Digital Ice is a feature on the Nikon Coolscan III and SuperCoolscan 2000. It is software that scans the top, nonimage layer of the film and subtracts the signal from any part of the image that isn't perfectly clear from the image. I have tested this software in using the SuperScan 2000. It is undoubtedly superior to software such as PhotoDeluxe or Xaos Tools' FlashBox that removes scratches. Such software tends to give more overall softening to the image (see the "Using the Scanner Software Properly" section later in this chapter).

Altamira Genuine Fractals

This, too, is software distributed with the Nikon film scanners. This is a new category of software for making extreme image compressions without the visually noticeable lossiness that occurs with JPEG-compressed files. You can read more about this software later in this chapter.

Unlike Digital Ice, Genuine Fractals can be purchased separately for about $160 (or $250 for the PrintPro version). Genuine Fractals is able to compress images to a quarter of their original size and enlarge them to more than ten times their original size with no sign of pixelization or "jaggies." You might also want to consider Lizard Tech's Mr. Sid. Mr. Sid promises to compress to even higher degrees with no visible loss in quality or detail.

Proper Preparations for Scanning

Before you start scanning, you should make sure that you're ready to do the best job you can. Of course, you can always rescan if you discover later that you could've done a better job. Unfortunately, the chances are excellent that you won't because you will have already put too much time into improving and editing the image you scanned the first time.

Choosing the best film for scanning

Your choice of film may be dictated by considerations other than which film will give you the best scanning quality. For instance, your client may prefer a particular film, so you take the path of least resistance. In that case, you'll simply want to get the best scan you can from the film you've got. Such considerations aside, the first step you'll want to take is to choose a film that will give you as wide a range of colors as possible and one that exhibits the finest grain and sharpness. Of course, you'll also have to use a film that will enable you to work within the range of aperture and shutter speed appropriate to the subject. So, if you're working in dim light or with fast-moving subjects, you need to use a faster (and, therefore, grainier) film than if you can put your camera on a tripod or are working in a studio with strobes.

Having said all that, I tend to use negative film in most situations because the film, being less contrasty, is able to capture a much wider range of tonal values and doesn't tend to block up in the highlights. On the other hand, if I want to get the most detail and contrast out of a subject photographed in very flat lighting, slide film is likely to be a better choice due to its greater contrast and (typically) more saturated colors.

Keep it clean

Be sure to keep your film clean. One of the lovely things about working digitally is that its much easier to retouch a digital image than to retouch a negative or print. Nevertheless, it still takes time.

There are a few accessories you don't want to be without:

✦ A camel's hair brush (preferably with an air bulb)

✦ A piezoelectric antistatic gun

✦ Optician's cleaners

✦ Canned air or air compressor

Camel's hair brush

The camel's hair brush is for keeping the dirt out of small crevices, such as you'll find in film holders, in the hinges of flatbed scanners, and around the slot in the front of your slide scanner. I don't recommend using brushes to clean film, glass surfaces, and lenses. First, the brush can create static electricity on those surfaces and that actually *attracts* dust. Second, brushes can pick up finger and facial oils and transfer them to the surface of lenses and film. That can do more harm than good.

Antistatic gun

This is a piezoelectric pistol-like device that zaps film and scanner glass with a negative electrical charge that actually repels dust, hair, and lint. These guys are so hard to find I don't even know what they cost, but they're worth their weight in gold. The big photo stores in metropolitan areas that cater to professional photographers are the place to start looking.

Optician's cleaners

Don't use paper towels and household glass cleaner. Paper towels are made of wood pulp and can actually make minute scratches on lenses and film. Sometimes these scratches are so fine that you can hardly see them, but they will diffuse light and cause the image to lose sharpness and contrast.

Instead, buy the cleaners and tissues or cloths that are made for cleaning glasses and lenses from your optician or camera store.

Canned compressed air

This stuff is indispensable. It gives a good blast of air to blow dust away from film, lenses, even the parts of a film scanner that you can't reach. I buy it in six-packs at my local warehouse store for just a little over a buck a can.

Turn it on and keep it warm

Make sure your scanner has been warmed up for half an hour or so before doing any actual scanning. If you're in a shop that makes scans several times a day, turn the scanner on when you open shop and leave it on until quitting time. Otherwise, you may find that colors will shift. That could throw off your calibration.

Properly orient the original

Make sure your negative or print is perfectly squared away. If you have to rotate your images in your image editor, you will sacrifice some sharpness and detail. Some scanner software gives you an option to automatically square up the image. Don't rely on such a feature unless your end use for the scan simply isn't critical.

Calibrate and experiment

When you first start using your scanner, carefully pick four to six successful images that are markedly different from one another in terms of principal color, dynamic range, and detail. Make sure that a couple of these are portraits. People tend to be more critical of skin tones than any other subject matter when it comes to proper color balance. Make adjustments in the controls until the same adjustments work well for the whole group. Better yet, go through the calibration process described next.

Calibrating a Scanner

When you calibrate your scanner, what you really want to do is calibrate your system. You can do this in one of two ways: guesswork or scientific precision. Because scientific precision costs extra, we'll start with the guesswork method. In either case, you start by calibrating your monitor. Those processes are described in detail in Chapter 17.

Calibrating by estimating

If you don't have a calibrator or calibration software — or even Adobe Gamma, set your monitor as follows:

✦ Reduce the Brightness to about 38 percent

✦ Turn the contrast all the way up

✦ Reduce the color temperature to either 6,500K or 5,000K (better)

The resultant display will be duller and warmer — which is as it should be because you are trying to imitate reflective color on paper.

Most folks have some software that, at least, helps you to make more educated guesses. Mac users can use the Monitors and Sound Control Panel in the Mac OS. If you have Photoshop, you can use the Adobe Gamma application that ships as a part of Photoshop, regardless of whether you're a Mac or Windows user. Windows users who are using versions older than Windows 98 should upgrade.

You can also take a step up and use the software-only monitor calibration products from such companies as Color Blind (Prove-It), Monaco Systems (EZ Color), and Praxisoft WiziWYG. All three of these applications sell for less than $80 in their software-only versions and give you a bit more to go on than Adobe Gamma. All three also offer versions that will work with a Colorimeter at under $500 (see the section entitled "Precision Calibration" later in this chapter).

After calibrating your monitor, make a scanner target (see Figure 8-7). Open an image that you're familiar with. It should contain a portrait of a Caucasian person (because these are the skin tones of which we're most critical) and a fair amount of color. At the bottom of the image, make a grayscale chart and a color chart. You can make the chart by choosing the gray shades and primary colors from the Swatches palette in Photoshop.

Figure 8-7: A homemade scanner target

Print the chart on your color printer, making adjustments until the printed output closely matches what you see on your calibrated monitor. When you're satisfied that you've come as close as possible to printing what you see on your monitor, make at least two identical copies. If you're using an inkjet printer to print your target, be sure to reprint your target periodically. Most inkjet prints fade over time.

Now you can calibrate your scanner(s). Put the printed target on your flatbed scanner and make adjustments until the preview window looks as much as possible like the target. It's a good idea, when possible, to have the target image file open in your image editor at the same time as you are scanning the printed target. That way, you get a side-by-side comparison (see Figure 8-8).

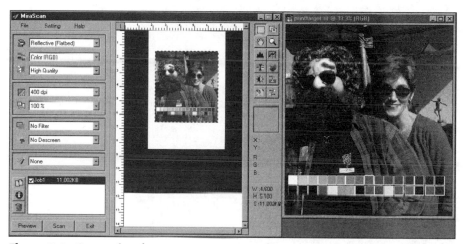

Figure 8-8: Comparing the target on screen to the scanner control's preview window

If you are calibrating a slide scanner, it's not quite so easy. You'll have to photograph your target. This gets complicated because you'll have to test film and exposure until you get a reasonable representation of the target on film. Then you can hope to match your scan to the original image on your monitor.

Premade scanner and camera targets

Although a homemade target is better than no target, the most successful calibration results from having a target that is absolutely consistent, no matter where you find it. Several manufacturers make such targets for a variety of purposes.

Camera targets are useful for coordinating the color interpretation of a digital camera or film with the corrections that will be necessary to make it match the other components in your system. One particularly popular camera target is the Jobo Color Card, which sells for about $20. It has primary and secondary color patches as well as six gray patches. The 11.4 × 16.9cm card is large enough to be held or propped up for shooting at the beginning of each roll of film or memory card. This gives you a known comparison for balancing the white point of the film or camera. The card folds to 4.5 × 6.6 inches and is made of plastic so that it can be cleaned with a damp cloth.

Another favorite camera target is the Macbeth Color checker (see Figure 8-9). This is a 9×13-inch card with 24 color squares — including those meant to represent skin, foliage, and sky. A Macbeth card sells for around $50.

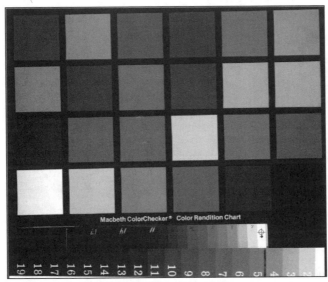

Figure 8-9: The Macbeth Color Checker is meant to be a camera target, but can be used as a scanner target as well.

An excellent target for either flatbed scanners or transparency adapters is the one provided by Monaco Systems with their EZ Color calibration and profiling software, shown in Figure 8-10. Unfortunately, you have to buy the whole package to get the profiling card. At least this gives you an idea of what such a card looks like.

Finally, for calibrating film scanners, Kodak makes the IT8 target as a slide in several formats. The 35mm version is $40, and the 4×5 version is $100. You can order these targets from Monaco Systems at www.monacosys.com.

Precision calibration

In order to calibrate your monitor to represent what you'll print out as closely as possible, you'll need to purchase a software system with a colorimeter. A colorimeter is a device that works by attaching suction cups to the surface of a monitor, and then reading changes in light and color as software adjusts the monitor. The monitor is then brought directly into line with how the output will look on paper.

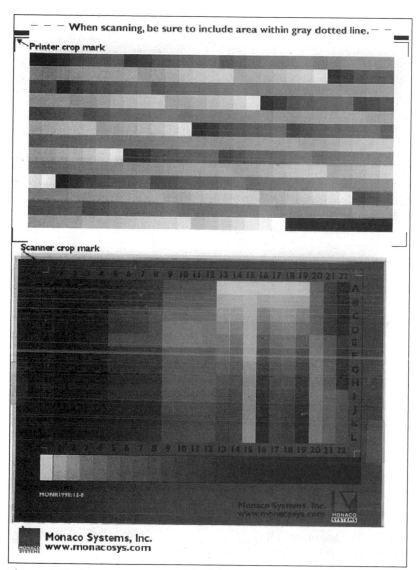

Figure 8-10: Monaco target used for both profiling and calibration

The lovely thing about working with a colorimeter is that it's so easy. You follow a few instructions on the screen and, presto, your monitor is calibrated. The bad thing about colorimeters is that they've been expensive, up until very recently. Now you can get one with any of the software-only calibrators I mentioned above, and the prices hover around $500. WyziWIG Deluxe is $600, EZ Color is $500, and ProveIt! is a mere $300.

Proving that you don't always get what you pay for, ProveIt! does both profiling and calibration and can be used for profiling LCDs and networked systems. The entire interface for calibration is "wizard" driven. You just follow the prompts onscreen. Anytime you're puzzled about what you're supposed to do next, you can just click a button and that phase of the operation is well explained in plain English.

Using and Creating ICC Profiles

ICC profiles make it much easier to translate the interpretation of color generated by one device (camera, scanner, monitor, printer) into the interpretation of another device. In Photoshop 5+, you can even embed a profile in the image file so that another computer with Photoshop 5+ installed can properly translate it. Other image-editing programs are already starting to follow suit.

If you have a fairly recent Mac, you have Color Sync. Color Sync is a system utility (small program) that coordinates the profiles of devices that talk to one another. Windows 98 and 2000 use ICM color management.

There are two ways to get profiles: from a vendor (such as Cone Editions or the manufacturer of your device) or by using software to profile the device. Software is the best solution for monitors and scanners because their color characteristics change over time. For digital cameras, you'd best get the profile from the manufacturer of your camera.

Tip   You can make your own scanner profiles if you're willing to invest in Monaco EZ Color, which costs $299 for the software-only version and $499 with a monitor calibration instrument. It's not an insignificant investment, but it is the lowest-cost means of creating your own scanner profiles I've yet come across.

Profiles for printers are a mixed bag. Those that come with the printer are just fine as long as you stick with the manufacturer's own paper and ink. Even "compatible" papers and inks made for nonarchival use will come reasonably close to meeting your expectations — though there are definitely exceptions. Kodak photo-quality glossy papers and Epson inks, for instance, are not a very good match. The inks tend to pool and colors have a decided cast.

The problem with using the manufacturer's printer profiles comes when you start using paper and ink combinations that are off the beaten path. Archival inks and papers used in printing fine arts produce results that need considerable correction. To make matters worse, the possible combination of nonstandard inks and nonstandard papers makes the number of possible profiles almost mind-boggling. There is an easy answer, however. Cone Editions and its subsidiary, InkJet Mall, sell profiles for a wide variety of combinations of the most popular archival inks and papers. Each of these profiles sells for $40 and makes it quite easy to set up Photoshop 5+ for printing on Epson printers with the most widely used combinations of archival inks and papers. You can find these profiles at www.inkjetmall.com.

Using the Scanner Software Properly

Once everything has been properly profiled and calibrated, you can start scanning. Scanner software is different for nearly every scanner. Nevertheless, virtually all scanner software presents some similar choices:

✦ Positive or negative

✦ Type of image: color, grayscale, or line art (bitmap)

✦ Scanning resolution

✦ Exposure adjustment

✦ Color balance adjustment

✦ Elimination of screen patterns

If you have a transparency adapter, film tray, or a film scanner, you should have a means of specifying whether you want to scan positive or negative transparencies. Look for scanner software that lets you specify the type of negative film. There can be quite a difference in the way different major negative films appear once the orange mask is removed from the image.

Almost all scanners let you choose from a wide variety of scanning resolutions. If you are scanning to create an archival file that will have enough detail for most fine art and publication purposes, aim for a file size of between 25 and 40MB. Unless you are working with larger film formats, this will be enough resolution to capture all the detail in the film. On the other hand, if you know you are going to use the file for a particular purpose, make another scan that is just the right resolution for that purpose and you will get a sharper, cleaner scan. If you are scanning for publication, the resolution should be approximately twice the lines per inch (screen frequency). If you're outputting to a printer, it should be one-third the printer's resolution (the number of dots per inch divided by three primary colors).

Use your scanner's controls to bring exposure, contrast, and color balance as close to your desired goals as possible. Doing so will ensure that you have as much information in your data as possible. That's why you don't want to rely entirely on using your image-editing software for making such corrections. In Figure 8-11, you can see the interface for the Microtek Scanmaker 5.

If you're not scanning from printed materials, be sure to turn off the feature that removes screens. It's usually labeled something like "screen removal." If this feature is left on, you'll get a slightly unfocused scan. That's because a Gaussian blur is part of the technique for removing the original screen dot pattern. If you are scanning from printed materials, it's likely that you will see a pattern that resembles an oil slick. This *moiré pattern* results from the pattern of the printing dots being out of register with the pixel matrix of the scanning resolution.

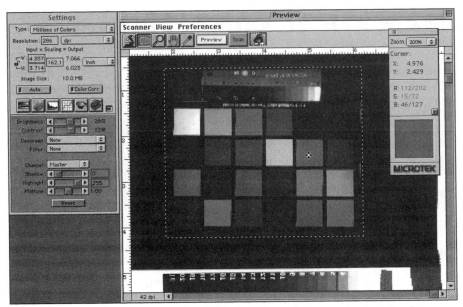

Figure 8-11: The interface for controlling the Microtek Scanmaker 5 flatbed scanner

By the same token, if you're scanning from film, be sure to turn off the scratch removal feature if your film doesn't have any scratches to remove. Also, turn it off if your scanner's scratch removal doesn't use Digital Ice or another method of reading only the protective film layer. Other methods remove scratches by blurring edges.

Summary

This chapter hasn't tried to substitute for your scanner's manuals, but to give you some good advice on what to watch for and what to avoid. I've also tried to give you some related tips as to how to deal with color workflow issues.

✦   ✦   ✦

Shooting Digital Images

Guidelines for Making Successful Photos

This chapter is all about the things you should think of before you take a digital picture — especially those things that are peculiar to the taking of a digital photograph. I start out with the general considerations. Toward the end of the chapter, we start looking into the special circumstances that surround shooting portraits, real estate, small catalog items, and flat art work and documents.

Considerations Unique to Digital Photography

If you are planning to take your digital photographs with a digital camera (rather than digitizing them from analog photos), you should be aware of some of the characteristics unique to digital cameras.

Unlimited film

Any professional photographer will tell you that one of the secrets to success is to take lots of pictures. This is especially true if timing is a critical factor. Even when it's not, it's much easier to choose exactly the right point of view, exposure, composition, and quality of light when you can carefully and deliberately choose between a variety of images.

Even though we know this, film photographers aren't likely to take as many pictures as possible unless we're on a really tall budget. The digital camera removes the excuse not to shoot because "film" is free — especially if there's a computer handy that you can download to. Even if that isn't the case, you can always review the first dozen or so pictures, and then throw out all but the best three or four. Then you have room on the same memory card to shoot another eight or ten shots, keep the best two or three, and so forth.

Of course, you can greatly extend this flexibility if you have access to a laptop, so that you can download images in the field. Also, keep in mind that the capacity of memory cards for digital cameras keeps going up and the price per megabyte keeps going down.

Shutter lag

If your pictures depend on timing, be sure you are using a professional or prosumer-level camera with two-megapixel resolution or higher. This is not an absolute require-ment, but most less-expensive and earlier-generation digicams exhibit a marked delay between the time the shutter trigger is fully depressed and the time the exposure is actually made.

If you have such a camera, there is something you can do about it: practice, practice, practice. What you need to practice doing is anticipating the peak of a motion or expression. Let's say you're shooting a baseball game and you need to capture the instant before the ball actually strikes the first baseman's glove. You will have to learn to shoot an instant after the ball leaves the second baseman's hand. Furthermore, you'll have to get good at picking just the right instant.

If you frequently shoot similar situations, such as a model breaking into a smile, try videotaping such moments. Then play back the repeat moment over and over while you practice firing your camera. You'll get a good sense of when you have to shoot to anticipate that peak of action or expression. In fact, you'll be amazed at how much your timing will improve as a result of such practice — even when you don't have to worry about shutter lag.

Tip

When you are faced with anticipating shutter lag in order to get the peak of the action, start counting aloud at the instant you press the shutter button. After a while you'll get a good idea of how many of these "beats" have to pass before the shutter fires. A bit more practice and you'll figure out how far ahead of time you need to press the shutter in order to have the shutter "click" at the desired moment.

By the way, since most digital cameras don't have actual shutters (the image sensor just activates for the required fraction of a second), there's no shutter click. Look for a camera that gives you some audio clue as to when the picture-taking instant occurs. Many digital cameras will give you a little beep. Several Kodak models actually simulate a shutter click — a great idea. Unless all your digital photos will be of static subjects while your camera is mounted on a tripod, don't even think about buying a camera that doesn't give you some sort of audio signal at the firing of the "shutter."

Exposing for highlights

Digital cameras, especially those priced under $2,000, tend to overexpose highlights and bright reds. The result is that there is no detail or texture in those areas. If there are important bright areas in your subject, reduce your exposure by one stop (–1 EV). Most of the time, you can do this even when the camera doesn't offer any exposure control. You point the center of the image at the very lightest part of the subject and press the shutter button slightly. This locks the exposure reading so that you can move the camera to frame your subject as you'd desired. Press the shutter button all the way down to actually take the picture.

Of course, you have much more control over this situation if your camera provides some means of manual exposure control. Most of the over-$500 cameras (and even some lower-priced ones) will let you change the exposure value (EV). To expose for the highlights, set the camera at EV –1. If you have a professional camera (or one of the very best prosumer cameras, such as the Olympus 2500), you can actually set the shutter speed and aperture (f-stop) independently. Usually, such cameras will display the currently chosen settings. So, you just reduce the meter reading by one f-stop to make the shutter speed twice as fast. F-stops are smaller when the number is higher, just as shutter speeds are faster when the number is higher (because they represent a fraction of a second).

Blooming

Blooming is what happens when adjacent image sensor cells pick up the light that is actually focused on a neighbor. This tends to occur to a much greater degree as the price of your camera goes down. It especially tends to be a problem in the range of colors from red to purple. Light-colored fabrics and the petals of flowers in that range can lose much of the detail that gives them texture and depth due to blooming.

If you own a professional camera, you probably won't have much of a problem with blooming. If your camera cost less than $500, it's almost guaranteed to be a noticeable problem. Cameras that are priced in between vary in quality. Read the knowledgeable reviewers. However, just because a camera exhibits some blooming when faced with very bright highlights or pinks and fuchsias shouldn't entirely disqualify it. The camera may do very well in many other respects.

There is something you can do about blooming: Cut your exposure slightly. If you have lots of reds, especially very bright and light shades, drop your exposure by about one half stop (EV-.5). Your picture may seem too dark on preview, but you'll be able to fix most of that in your image-editing program. Digital image sensors seem to be much better at capturing detail at lower light levels (up to a point) than at very bright light levels.

White balance

Different ambient light sources have different colors (or, more scientifically, color temperatures). That's why slide film comes in daylight (outdoor) and tungsten (indoor) flavors. The overall color tint imposed by the color of the ambient light can be corrected during the printmaking process, so negative film comes balanced only for daylight. The problem comes when the main light sources are mixed or when you want to maintain the color of atmospheric lighting.

Most digital cameras automatically compensate for the color temperature of the ambient light, though they vary considerably in their ability to "guess." Some cameras measure the actual light coming through the lens or, better yet, will let you take a white balance reading through a milky white plastic lens cap. This is a feature that is especially common on video cameras.

For creative purposes, it helps to have a camera that will let you deliberately set the white balance to match the color temperature of a specific type of prevailing light. If this is the case, you will be able to make the camera intentionally record a daylight scene that is "too warm" by setting the color balance for tungsten light or too green by setting the color balance for fluorescent light. Daylight and flash are essentially the same color temperature, though flash is often slightly bluer.

Shooting a picture at the wrong color balance isn't nearly the problem for digital images as for film. That's because it's very easy to compensate for color balance in your image-processing program. However, you will lose some image definition (data) in the process. This is only noticeable in extreme cases or when you also do considerable exposure compensation. Still, remember the garbage in/garbage out rule. The cleaner the image you start with, the cleaner the image you end up with.

Long exposures

Film doesn't much care how long you have to leave the shutter open in order to collect enough light to get visible detail in your image. If you have to shoot that black cat in a coal bin at midnight, no problem. Just dose the cat with sleeping pills so it won't move for an hour or so and put the camera on a good, solid tripod.

Try that with a digital camera, especially one costing less than several thousand bucks, and you'll likely end up with nothing but Jackson Pollock–like specks of color against a brownish-black field. Digital engineers would call this pure noise.

What we're saying here is that digital image sensors don't like making exposures much longer than half a second. If getting the picture is more important than getting the picture quality, you can get away with a few seconds. That should get you a pretty decent shot of Las Vegas Boulevard at night. After that, it's all downhill. Fall back on your film camera.

Too much depth of field

Depth of field is the range between the nearest and farthest subjects that appear to be in sharp focus.

Digital cameras almost always give you too much depth of field — a characteristic that they share with video cameras. That is because the CCD chips used in these cameras are typically one-fourth to two-thirds the size of a 35mm still frame. So, a digital camera lens that is the *equivalent* of a given 35mm camera's focal length has to actually be one-fourth to two-thirds that of the real focal length of the equivalent lens. In other words, a 50mm "normal" lens on a 35mm camera would be only a 25mm lens on a prosumer-level digital camera.

Now, here's the problem: The shorter the actual focal length of a lens, the greater the depth of field. Sometimes, especially when shooting extreme close-ups, the relatively extreme depth of field offered by a digital camera is an advantage.

More often, extreme depth of field is a drag. All of the distracting elements such as phone wires and flowered wallpaper are just sharp enough to make the viewer's eyes wander away from the main subject. Figure 9-1 illustrates the fist that Bob Cowart shot with the Olympus C-2000. In the photo on the left, you can see that nearly everything is in sharp focus. The same photo, on the right, has been manipulated in Photoshop 5.5 to blur the parts of the picture that would have been closer and more distant.

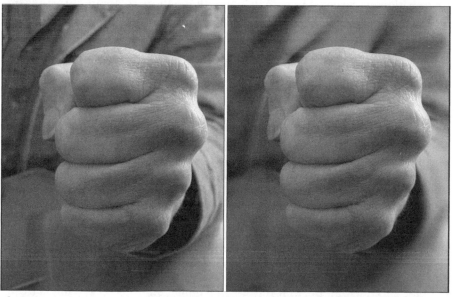

Figure 9-1: It is hard to control depth of field for most handheld digicams. The background in the figure on the right was blurred in an image-editing program.

What can you do about the too-much-depth-of-field problem? Well, if worst comes to worst, you can always select your main subject and blur everything else in your image editor. This isn't quite as easy as it sounds. In order to keep the out-of-focus areas looking natural, you'll have to blur closer objects first and less. Then, select the areas that are farther away and blur them more. Feather your selections so that the differing degrees of blurring (out-of-focusness) blend together.

Here's what you can do to avoid having to resort to your image editor:

✦ Shoot from an angle that places your subject against a plain (or at least, simpler) background.

✦ Use a slow shutter speed and have your subject move parallel to the lens while you pan. The subject will stay sharp while the background streaks.

✦ Shoot in strong backlight and expose for the shaded side of the subject.

The Rules of Good Composition

So much for the special properties of digital cameras. Beyond that, any digital photographer can benefit from an awareness of the guidelines for making good photographs. Awareness of the rules that tend to lead to good composition is a good place to start because they pertain regardless of the location or conditions in which the photograph is shot.

Composition, in case you're not familiar with the term, refers to the arrangement of the various objects in the picture in relationship to one another. Even when these objects are immobile, you can affect their arrangement by changing your point of view. Also, the highlight and shadow areas of the picture, especially if they are prominent, can contribute as much to the composition as the positioning of objects themselves.

These rules are made to be broken

The first rule of good composition is that there really are no rules. That is because following certain rules too closely can result in visual clichés that may cause a viewer to lose interest. Cliché composition tends to make viewers feel that they've "been there and done that." This is especially true if a particular composition of a particular subject has become an icon. We will greatly admire Ansel Adams' classic study of Yosemite's Half Dome. Take another picture of Half Dome from the same POV and the viewer's likely first thought is, "Not as good as Ansel Adams' shot." It probably doesn't even matter that the vegetation, weather, and mood are entirely different.

To put it another way, the first rule of good composition is: Try to find a fresh point of view.

Now that we've drummed that into your head, you can start to appreciate the other rules with some perspective.

The two-thirds rule

The two-thirds rule is one of the oldest and most tried-and-true compositional guidelines. It's also called the rule of thirds. The idea is to draw an imaginary 3×3 grid across your picture. Any point where the grid lines intersect is a point where the eye naturally tends to find a center of interest. The intersections that are two-thirds from one edge of the picture are the points of greatest interest — thus the two-thirds appellation. Figure 9-2 shows this grid at its points of primary interest.

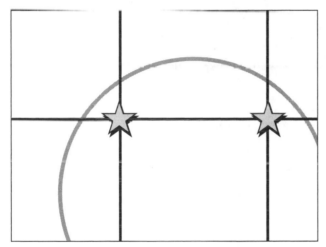

Figure 9-2: The stars represent the main points of interest.

In the real world, you'll find it nearly impossible to strictly place the center of interest at one of these points. Fortunately, "somewhere in the vicinity" is close enough. Also, virtually any placement of the center of interest that is closer to one of the two-thirds lines is more desirable than placing it too close to the center or too close to one of the edges. Placing the center of interest too close to the center of the picture just tends to make it a boring composition. Placing the center of interest too close to the edge tends to lead our eyes completely out of the picture, rather than drawing them in.

Of course, there's an exception to this rule. When you're trying to picture power and intractability, placing the subject dead center makes us feel that there's no way around it. Figure 9-3 is a perfect example.

Figure 9-3: The composition is the message in this image where the center of interest is at the center of the image.

The shapes of a composition

Maybe you didn't even know that compositions had shapes. Strictly speaking, maybe not. But compositions in which the eye is led in a circle, along an S-curve, about the perimeter of a triangle, up or down a C-curve, or down a V all tend to work in particular ways:

- ✦ **The S-curve:** S-curves gently lead our eye into the picture. S-curve compositions are generally soothing and pass multiple points of interest. S-curves also have a way of denoting femininity.

- ✦ **The Triangle:** A triangle is the strongest geometric shape. Use triangular compositions to denote strength.

- ✦ **The C-curve:** A C-curve is useful for framing the subject or gently leading our eye into the picture.

- ✦ **The V:** A V-shape tends to emphasize perspective and to pull you from one of the edges of the picture to its center of interest.

Seldom is there only one center of interest in a photograph. Different points of interest can form the path of a compositional shape. This helps to ensure that the viewer's eye will travel from one point of interest to another. Shapes also tend to carry emotional messages.

The circle

A circle shape imprisons our eye and forces our eye toward the center of the circle. Circles are also liberating, in that they can take us away from the rectangular boundary common to almost all photographs.

The most common use of circular composition is the vignette. A vignette is made by fading the image out from the center until it is framed in a circle of lightness or darkness. Usually, the vignette fades to complete white or black, but it can be much more subtle and still be effective. Figure 9-4 shows a traditional vignette surrounding a traditional portrait.

Figure 9-4: A vignette forms a circle to hold the focus of attention on this portrait.

Framing the Subject

The main thing that distinguishes a color photograph from real life is that it is seen in a square frame, rather than as a panorama with no definitely defined edges. Along with composition, what we put into that frame makes the difference between a picture and a great picture. Here are some things to think about when framing the subject.

Don't include anything unimportant

The short words for this are "move in close." Force the viewer to concentrate on the thing you want to show. This advice goes for panoramic landscapes as well as for macro photographs of bugs. In other words, it may be that what you want the viewer to see includes a lot of territory. Nevertheless, you want to be sure that the frame doesn't include so much that your audience misses the point.

Keep the background simple

Unless clutter is the point of the picture (a portrait of your great aunt's attic), avoid clutter. Clutter, by my definition, is anything that distracts from the subject. Unless ugliness is the point of the picture, clutter is anything unattractive: telephone lines, litter, and so forth.

The three best techniques for keeping the background simple are as follows:

✦ Place your subject against an area of relatively unadorned space, such as a wall or a distant (and preferably out of focus) landscape.

✦ Throw the background out of focus. If you're shooting with a prosumer or consumer-level digital camera, you may have to resort to blurring the background in your image editor.

✦ Blur the background with motion. To do that, pick a background that's in motion or put your subject in motion and use a long enough exposure that the background is truly blurred. It will take some practice to get this technique down. Fortunately, with digital film, all you lose is time.

The exceptions to this rule are those times when the background itself is a strong contributor to the picture's message. Maybe it is all the "stuff" that enriches the subject of the portrait. Maybe it's just the texture of the atmosphere. If the background is important, you want to do everything possible to keep it razor sharp. Use a tripod and a small aperture if at all possible.

Use lighting contrasts to strengthen composition

You'll see in the section below on lighting that strong lighting contrast is often undesirable. However, in those instances where it is desirable, you capitalize on that fact by using it to strengthen your composition and the compositional shapes. Don't be afraid to use light to lead the eye.

Leave space in front of motion

If you are shooting action, especially if speed (as opposed to climax) is the point, leave lead space in front of the subject. Remembering the rule of two-thirds, keep the fast-moving subject headed into the empty two-thirds of the frame.

Use perspective

Place your main subject between objects that are large and close to the camera and others that are small and far away. Alternatively, find converging lines that give the viewer a feeling of space and depth. This gives the viewer the feeling of being there, of being surrounded by real space.

The Rules of Good Lighting

Photography is nothing without light. In fact, strictly speaking, it is nothing more than the recording of the way the ambient light is reflected from the surfaces framed by the camera's viewfinder. The sooner you learn what to expect from the way light behaves and how to make the best of it, the better photographer you become.

Expose for highlights

We've already covered this ground. Digital image sensors tend to "block up" or bloom in the highlight areas. If there's important detail in the highlights, or if the highlights occupy more than a small percentage of the image area, you'd be wise to underexpose by half an EV. Even underexposing by a full EV is preferable to burned-out highlights — especially since your image-editing software can recover a great deal of detail in the shadow areas.

Tip Something important that I didn't mention earlier: It is especially important when you're exposing for the highlights to shoot at the highest-quality compression setting that your camera allows. When you use your image-editing software to compensate for underexposed shadows, there is a tendency to exaggerate the noise (random flecks of bright colors) that tends to collect in the shadows. The more highly compressed the image, the more objectionable the noise in the shadows is likely to be.

Use natural lighting whenever possible

Granted, there are plenty of times when using the prevailing natural light isn't possible. However, all other things being equal, it's almost always preferable to artificial lighting. Why? Well, because it looks believable. We're used to seeing things that way. You can shoot in natural light, crop the subject so closely that you can barely identify the surroundings, and still make a pretty good guess as to the subject's general surroundings. You know instinctively whether the photo was taken in direct sunlight at midday, outdoors in the shade, indoors by lamplight, or in a neon-lit nightclub.

The worst kind of unnatural lighting you can use is the built-in flash unit. Does t his mean you should never use the built-in flash? Certainly not, if it means missing an important picture. If your camera won't let you shoot a long enough exposure, operate at a wide enough lens aperture, or boost the ISO rating of the image sensor — why you're probably not going to be able to shoot candids indoors or at night. Motionless subjects (even if you just ask them to be motionless) usually won't pose a problem even then — as long as your camera is advanced enough to let you make long exposures and as long as you have a tripod or some other means of keeping the camera steady while you shoot.

If you're going to shoot candids in dim available light, it's a really good idea to use an external incident light meter (see Chapter 8). That's because you'll almost always be shooting in contrasty lighting conditions in which only the light falling directly on your subject is important. An external incident light meter will give you the ability to measure the brightness of the actual prevailing (ambient) light and to see exactly what your shutter speed and aperture combination should be. If you don't have access to an external light meter, the next best thing is a camera with spot metering. Then you can read from the area of greatest importance to you (such as the highlights on faces).

Use reflectors and fill flash in bright sun

If you have to shoot close-ups in bright sunlight, you may want to consider balancing the harsh lighting contrast by supplementing the light directed into the shadows. Nearly all digital cameras with built-in flash let you choose a fill-flash mode, which is an easy way to solve the problem (see Figure 9-5). However, not all cameras are equal in their ability to balance the fill flash with the brighter light. Some (usually less expensive) cameras just fire the flash without adjusting its duration. This may work out if the sunlight is really bright or if you're more than 6 feet away from your subject. Otherwise, the fill light is likely to be brighter than the sunlight. It's likely that the only way you'll find out is by testing or reading reviews of the particular camera you're using. Also, most digicams priced over $500 will actually adjust the duration of the flash in relationship to the brightness of the prevailing light. If your tests indicate that the flash tends to be too bright in relationship to the sunlight, tape a few layers of facial tissue or tracing paper over the flash. This has the additional benefit of diffusing the flash so that it doesn't create harsh countershadows, as shown in Figure 9-6. It's also a good technique for extreme close-ups because the amount of light from the flash is reduced.

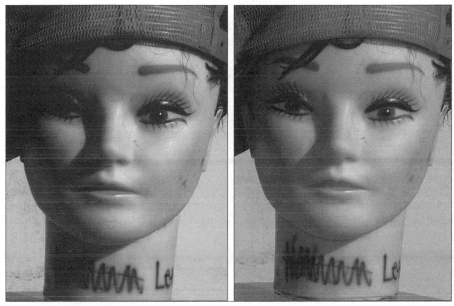

Figure 9-5: The mannequin on the left was shot in direct sunlight; on the right is the same shot with the Olympus C-2000's flash fill.

Figure 9-6: Taping tissue over the built-in flash diffuses the light and also reduces the amount of light used for fill or close-up flash.

Use the shade or a cloudy day

One way you may be able to control overly contrasty lighting is to simply move your subject out of the glare of a direct main light, such as the sun. If you want detail in your shadow areas, take your pictures when it's overcast or hazy. If it's a smaller, moveable subject or people that you're shooting and you can control the location (such as not shooting candids or reportage) use a shaded area — preferably one in which light is reflected off a nearby building so that you're not overpowered by toplight.

Some Guidelines for Frequently Encountered Situations

What follows are some brief guidelines to consider whenever your assignment calls for shooting one of the following frequently encountered situations. These types of assignments are particularly common in small business and corporate photography:

✦ Portraits

✦ Candids and action

✦ Scenics

✦ Real estate

✦ Evidence

✦ Small items

✦ Flat artwork and documents

Shooting portraits

All too often, when we say the word portrait, we think of something very stiff and formal. However, even the most formal portraits are best when they capture their subject in a relaxed and real moment. It's really no different from a candid portrait except for the attire of the subject, and the fact that the picture is usually taken with controlled lighting in studio conditions. But even an informal portrait like the one in Figure 9-7 follows the guidelines for successful portraiture.

Light to set the desired mood: beauty versus the beast

Be aware of the lighting. Generally, the most flattering light comes from above and to one side of the camera so that the cast shadows give modeling and dimension to the subject. Soft light keeps the detail in the shadows and minimizes aging and skin problems as well as imparting a feeling of softness that is particularly appropriate to women. On the other hand, harsher lighting can make men look more rugged.

Figure 9-7: A quiet moment of thought adds character to the beauty.

High-fashion glamour lighting is often more contrasty, with the light closer to the camera. This gives a somewhat more dramatic feel while cutting shadows under the eyes and in wrinkles.

Keep depth of field shallow

Doing so will keep interest focused on the face you are portraying. The exception to this rule is the portrait that reveals the character of the subject by the surroundings. In that case, you want to keep the details of the surroundings in sharp focus so that the viewer won't tend to dismiss their importance. Figure 9-8 is a good example of such a portrait.

Figure 9-8: You get it pretty quickly that Mary is a painter and musician.

Use a medium telephoto lens (except for drama)

Some car advertisements tell us that wider is better. Well, with portraits, closer is better. We get the feeling of being more intimate with our subjects. The problem with this is that most snapshot cameras have wide-angle lenses that make people's noses look as though they lie a lot (remember Pinocchio?). The fact that their eyes recede into being beady little things doesn't help with the feeling of trust, either.

So the trick is to stay a little farther away when you're moving in close. You can do that by zooming all the way out if you have a zoom lens. If not, make sure your camera has a threaded lens mount and will accept supplementary lenses. Users of professional cameras should switch to a medium telephoto (85mm to 110mm 35mm camera equivalent).

Caricature portraits are best with wide-angle lens

If you want to exaggerate expressions, you might actually try using a wide-angle lens (or zoom to your camera's widest-angle position).

Shooting candids and action

Taking successful pictures that involve catching the spur of the moment takes more practice than any other aspect of photography. You have to learn to "lead the bird." That is, you have to press the trigger a very short time before the action actually happens. This is so that the fraction of a second delay between that instant and the instant when the exposure is actually being made coincide.

Use a camera that has no shutter lag

With lower-cost digital cameras, it takes even more practice because there's a definite lag between the press of the shutter button and the instant of the actual exposure (see "Shutter lag," above). If you're serious about shooting action, plan to spend enough to buy a camera that has no noticeable shutter lag. Look for a recently introduced camera that costs more than, oh, $700.

Use a camera that lets you use shutter priority

If either you or the camera or the subject is likely to be moving quickly at the moment the picture is taken, you want to be sure you're shooting at a high enough shutter speed to capture the action. Generally, the lower limit of that speed is around 1/250th of a second. Cameras that rely entirely on automatic exposure will rarely set the shutter speed that high. So, you want a camera that gives you shutter priority so that you can dictate the shutter speed and let the autoexposure mechanism pick the aperture.

Absolute manual control is also an advantage, but much more so for an experienced photographer who can make quick accurate guesses as to what exposure should be while his or her subject moves rapidly between shade, direct light, and backlighting.

Use a camera that lets you choose the ISO rating

If you can boost your ISO rating, the chances are much better that you'll be able to choose a fast enough shutter speed to freeze the action. There's hardly ever a time when you won't want to be able to shoot at the fastest possible shutter speed.

If you're into serious journalistic action, such as war and sports, don't even think about anything less than one of the professional 35mm SLR cameras. The Nikon D1 has shutter speeds up to 1/8,000 of a second and will enable you to boost the ISO rating to around 2,000.

Get your camera turned on and set up in advance

If you know you're going into a situation where timing is everything, you have to be ready to shoot at an instant's notice. Turn on your camera the minute you hit the street. You'll use up batteries at a ridiculous rate, so be sure to keep your eye on the battery-use LCD. Carry lots of spare rechargeable batteries. I also buy a large box of disposable alkaline batteries at my local discount warehouse, just so I've got something to use in a real emergency.

Note It may be a good idea to carry some alkalines for insurance against suddenly dead batteries. Remember, however, that they may die after shooting only a few frames. They are a good alternative only when there is no other.

Use a zoom lens

You won't have time to change lenses. You may also not be able to get very close to the action. Stadiums won't let you on the field, and getting too close to a street fight can be dangerous. So, the best possible scenario involves using a camera with interchangeable lenses and using a zoom lens with a medium telephoto to extreme telephoto range.

By the way, any time you have to use long lenses, it becomes even more important that you stay steady. The very slightest camera movement becomes highly exaggerated when applied to distant subjects. You probably won't want to be anchored to a tripod, but chest braces and neck straps can be a big help.

Learn to follow your subject

One way to get a great feeling of action is to swing the camera so that you keep up exactly with the motion of the subject. This makes the subject appear to the camera to be relatively still while the background moves rapidly. I've already proposed this technique for simplifying backgrounds, but it contributes even more to action photography. It gives us the feeling that the subject is moving very rapidly. It also helps you to freeze the action of the subject itself.

One last thing about shooting candids. If they're intended to catch people while they're unaware they're being photographed, it's a great help to have a camera that has a rotating LCD viewer. This makes it possible to shoot over crowds and still be able to frame what's going on. You can also face in an entirely different direction than the camera — which can fool people into thinking that you're not interested in them.

Shooting scenics

Almost everyone shoots scenics of some sort, even though few of us are in Ansel Adams' or Loren Soderberg's league. Although blurry and shocking shots of scenery can be effective, most of this is due to shock value. Most scenics are taken to remember or to promote the beauty of the vista before the camera. Use a camera that will give you all the sharpness and image detail you can get.

If you hope to get your digital scenics hung in galleries or used in Sierra Club calendars, count on spending $10,000 or more on a professional digital back for a medium- or large-format camera. These cameras are ideal for scenics (except for all the stuff you might have to haul around in the wilderness — including a computer) because they can capture far more detail than even film. If you can't afford that, film may be your only option.

For the rest of us, thank heavens we can share scenic shots among our friends, use them on our Web sites, or have them decorate the text in articles and catalogs without demanding the ultimate in technological virtuosity.

Regardless of which camp you fall into, there are a few things you should keep in mind when preparing to shoot scenery.

Never shoot at midday

Boring light is almost always a guarantee of a boring photograph. Get up and out at the crack of dawn, and make absolutely sure to be there at sunset. Buy some plastic bags and raingear, and don't be afraid of lousy weather — it can often be amazingly dramatic.

In any case, you'll nearly never want to shoot when the sun is straight overhead. That's when the skies are most likely to be blank, the lighting contrast harshest, and the modeling of the landscape the least dimensional.

Take along a tripod

Whatever you do, use a tripod. The landscape isn't going to jump up and run away. You can let go of the camera and meditate on the landscape. You can wait for slight changes in the light and in the clouds. The longer you stay in one area, the greater your chances of catching all the elements at their most dramatic. Finally, it would be a total waste to lose any detail due to even the slightest camera movement. Speaking of which, if it's a windy day, do something to add extra weight to your tripod so that the wind doesn't cause it to shake or sway.

Stop down for extreme depth of field

Use the smallest aperture your camera will allow. That will give you the greatest depth of field. It's an odd thing, but it's almost never attractive to see any part of a scenic even slightly out of focus. Once again, you can see good reason to choose a camera that at least gives you control over shutter or aperture priority. If you stop down to the smallest f-stop, you will automatically get a slow shutter speed.

Of course, inexpensive digital cameras may not give you a choice of more than one or two apertures. As long as you don't have anything *really* close to the lens, that won't be a problem. Focus at any distance greater than ten feet and everything from about five feet to infinity will be in sharp focus.

Make sure you capture a full range of tones

Once again, you need to make particularly sure that highlights aren't overexposed. If your scene is really still, make two exposures with a tripod-mounted camera: one for the highlights and one for the shadows. Later, you'll be able to place one of these photos immediately atop the other on layers in your image-processing program. Then you can erase away portions of layers you don't want to keep.

If you don't want to take the time to make two exposures with an absolutely stationary camera, your next best bet is to use a camera that lets you lower contrast. This is the digital equivalent of the old landscape photographer's trick of exposing for the shadows and developing for the highlights. The picture may seem a little lifeless when you first open it in your image editor, but at least all the detail is there. Then it's a relatively easy matter to individually select areas in which you wish to alter brightness and contrast. One camera that lets you alter contrast is the Nikon Coolpix 950.

Shooting real estate

A great many businesses and business people need to shoot buildings, and not always because they are in the real estate business. Architects, journalists, and insurance adjusters are just a few of those who come to mind. The first thing you should do when shooting the exteriors of buildings is to keep all the rules for shooting scenics in mind.

Keep vertical lines parallel

When shooting buildings, you want to avoid the thing called *keystone distortion* Keystoning is perspective distortion that makes one or two edges of the building seem much closer than their opposites. At the same time, the walls seem to be leaning into one another, and sometimes the roof seems to be caving in or the building seems to be sliding downhill.

If you are using a handheld camera (or anything other than a digital back on a view camera), there won't be much you can do to correct this distortion. First, avoid shooting from an extremely low or high angle (unless you're trying to make a dramatic statement). Ideally, you want to keep the camera back parallel to the face of the building. Of course, there will be times when that would mean cutting the building off, so you'll have to compromise. Second, leave some space around the area that you definitely want to include in the photograph. Then you'll have room to use the distortion and perspective-correction transformation tools in your image-editing program to correct the problem.

Make use of walkways and driveways

Or any other path that leads your eye to the building and makes you want to enter. Such paths also help to give scale to the building. It can also be a good idea to show some of the building's inhabitants or contents that give us a clue as to what the interior is like. Proceed with caution when it comes to such props, however. You don't want the landscape to seem cluttered, and you (probably) don't want to detract attention from the building.

Shooting for the record

One of the most useful jobs for any kind of digital camera is documentation of the facts. This can include as wide a variety of subject matter as skin lesions for medical records, household items for inventory purposes, and the details of an accident scene for insurance or medical purposes.

Show scale, time, date

It's often a good idea to place something of a known size in the frame with the object being documented — especially when it is the size of the object that is being documented. The best way to show time and date is using a camera that gives you the option to time and date stamp the image.

Show shadow detail

Most of the time, we're not trying for pretty here. We just want the facts. If texture is important to showing the relevant details (as in footprints or skin lesions) be sure there's enough cross lighting to bring it out. Otherwise, don't be bashful about using on-camera flash. Outdoors, it will bring out the shadow detail. In low light, it will ensure that you get a sharp, evenly lit picture.

Shoot close-up details

If you're documenting an occurrence, as you would be if you were gathering legal evidence, be sure to shoot close-up details as well as the overall scenes. You should do this in such as way that you can still see what the relationship of the details is to the overall scene.

Shooting small items

You may need to photograph small items such as pottery, jewelry, catalog merchandise, and the like. These shots are a little different from the documentation of small items mentioned above. The difference is that these are "beauty" shots. The criteria is impact, not accuracy — though accuracy in color is extremely important in catalog and art photography.

Use a tripod and arrange things carefully

Shooting small items is another instance where a tripod is a near imperative. Because small items are so small, you want to carefully study your shooting angle and the lighting, and you want to be able to move items in relationship to one another without changing the position of the camera. Moving the camera might force you to start arranging all over again.

Use diffusers and fill reflectors

You don't want the perfectly even lighting required for flat artwork, but you do need to be careful of harsh lighting and glare (unless, of course, it's for a rare and deliberate effect). All sorts of light sources, including spotlights, can be appropriate from time to time. In general, however, a pair of large lightboxes is your best insurance. Also, get lots of small white and black foam-core boards to use as light reflectors and absorbers.

One particularly sticky problem is glassware, which includes perfume and wine bottles. You want to backlight these items so that you can see through the glass and the liquid. However, that tends to darken the light falling on labels. Since you're working digitally, make two exposures, one for the backlighting and the other for labels and other foreground details. Using your image editor, place both photos on separate layers in the same document and erase away the parts of each layer that you don't want to show. Be sure to use a soft-edged eraser so that you can seamlessly blend the layers together.

Treat surfaces when necessary

Glare can be a big problem when photographing small objects. If the glare isn't too strong, you may be able to cure it by applying some sort of "dulling potion" to the surface of the objects you're shooting. Ladies' facial powder is a good one because it wipes away easily, but be careful to choose a neutral color — not the stuff that puts a blush on her face. Also, you can get special dulling spray in most professional photo stores. Be sure that this is dulling spray for shooting, not for turning the glossy surface of a photo into a matte surface. Sprays for print surfaces are made to last forever and never come off. Using it on a client's artwork could put you in line for a serious lawsuit.

Consider using a light table

One way to make sure that light penetrates translucent objects and that surface shadows aren't a problem is to light the objects from below. The easiest way to build a structure for doing this is to use a large sheet of thick, white milky plastic and a pair of folding sawhorses. Rest the plastic on the sawhorses, place a light source beneath the plastic, and then light the rest of your still life as required.

Shooting flat art work

Everything I say here about shooting flat artwork applies to making copies of any kind — even documents. The only real difference in copying text documents is that you may want to shoot in line art or text mode if your camera has such a feature. If not, expose for a gray card and use your image editor to reduce the image to black and white. In Photoshop, this is best done with the Threshold command. However, not all image editors have such a command.

Tip   Also, consider using a scanner instead. Scanners are excellent for copying flat artwork — as long is the artwork is small enough to fit on the scanner bed.

Stay parallel and centered

A copy stand can be a big help, but if you don't have one, you can use levels and a string or plumb line. A copy stand places the camera on a pedestal or dolly so that it can be moved closer or farther from the artwork without tilting or swiveling either the camera or the artwork. Also, make sure that the exact center of the artwork is centered on your lens.

You can build a good copy stand with a wooden box, a tabletop tripod or tripod head, a folding conference table, some wood, and some C-clamps. Mount the tripod head on the leading edge of the box. Use a tripod head that has a built-in level (or buy a small level) and make sure that it's absolutely level once it's mounted on the box. You will also need a bracket that will let you turn the camera sideways for shooting vertical paintings. You will be able to use this same bracket for shooting panoramas. Set up the table and place the box atop it. Measure to make sure that the box is centered on the table. Place the wood railings on either side of the box and clamp the end of each to the table so that it won't move. Now you can keep the box and camera centered as you move in and out by pushing the box between the two rails. Place this entire rig so that it's perpendicular to a wall covered with black felt. Make a mark (or place a sticker) that's directly in line with the center of your lens.

Now, when you hang the artwork, you will make sure that it's centered over the centering spot you made on the black felt. Figure 9-9 shows a diagram of this whole arrangement.

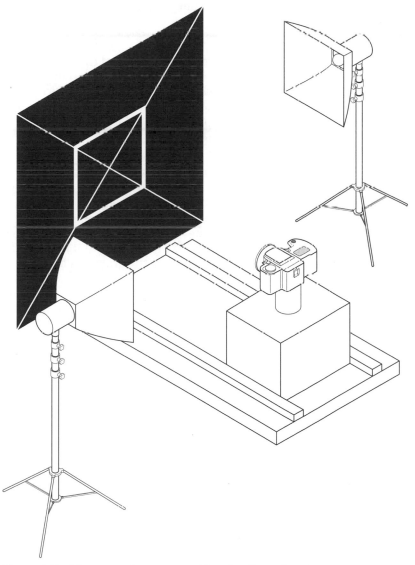

Figure 9-9: A homemade copy stand for shooting artwork

Use soft, even, flat lighting

You can use either tungsten or strobe lighting, since your subject isn't going to move. If you use strobe, make sure that your white balance control is set to either strobe or flash. Otherwise, since you're probably shooting indoors, you will automatically be balanced for flash.

For lighting, you should use soft lights of equal brightness on either side of the camera. They should be precisely equidistant from the artwork and at about a 45-degree angle from the artwork's center point.

Use a polarizing filter

You will need to make sure there is no glare on the surface of the painting or print. First, make sure that the glass has been removed from the frame (unless that's just totally impossible). Next, make sure you have a polarizing filter. By turning the polarizing filter as you're viewing the image on the LCD (or other through-the-lens viewfinder such as the ground glass on a view camera or the viewfinder of an SLR), you will see even the most subtle glare disappear.

Use an external meter

When you're copying artwork, you want to copy the brightness values that are actually in the picture — definitely not those that the camera "guesses" are the correct balance between highlights and shadows. Use an external incident light meter (see Chapter 8) if your camera allows completely manual exposure settings. Cameras that don't should be outlawed, but since that's sadly not the case, at least buy yourself a gray card. Take the light reading from the gray card by placing it in the center of the artwork, slightly depressing the shutter button, removing the gray card, and then pressing harder to fire the shutter. Pressing the shutter button partway will (on almost all automatic cameras, but read your instruction manual to be sure) lock the exposure and focus until you finish depressing the shutter button.

Summary

In this chapter I've given you a number of abbreviated formulae for success as regards the special circumstances surrounding digital photography and the special circumstances involved in shooting particular types of subjects. The chapter concluded with sections on shooting action and candids, portraits, buildings, small items, documentary details, and flat artwork.

✦   ✦   ✦

Tips, Tricks, and Gadgets

Now that you have a general idea of how to make basic preparations for typically encountered shooting situations, we can move on to those things that can be added on or taken advantage of in order to further increase your chances of success. This is a hodge-podge of tips and tricks, so there's no particular organizational thread.

Take Your Best Shot

The latest in Nikon's prosumer digital camera series (the 950, 990, and 800) features an automatic means of ensuring that you preserve the most jitter-free of a series of shots. What the feature does is make ten exposures in succession, 1.5 seconds apart. The camera's internal programming then determines which photo has the least motion blur and automatically discards the other nine photos. It's a great option that I'm hoping to see more and more other camera makers imitate.

Nikon calls this mode Best Shot Selector. It is especially useful at the zoom's longest focal length. It's even more useful if you're going to use supplementary lenses to get even more of a telephoto effect. You should, however, be aware that there are times when a best-shot mode is most appropriate:

✦ **The subject should be static.** Landscapes and still lifes are the best candidates. If the impact of the picture depends on "catching the moment," you'll risk losing it. After all, you have no way of knowing in advance which of the ten shots the camera will keep. Furthermore, the sequence takes 15 seconds to shoot. Any single thing that was moving will have long since entered and left the frame in that time.

✦ **Use it when in telephoto mode.** The narrower your lens' field of view, the more exaggerated the effects of even the slightest camera motion. If you're using a lens of 150mm or higher 35mm lens equivalent focal length and you're shooting a static subject, use best-shot mode. If there's any wind or ground vibration (often the case when shooting from a bridge or mountain top), there may be slight camera vibration even when you're using a tripod.

✦ **Use it when you're handholding the shot.** Even with a wide-angle lens, if you're shooting a static subject and crispness and detail are important to the concept of the shot, use best-shot mode (if your camera has such a thing).

Okay, it's a great feature, but what if your camera doesn't have a best-shot mode? Simple. See if your camera has a mode for sequence shots (often called burst mode). It's not nearly as convenient, because your camera probably won't shoot as many shots to pick from. Furthermore, all those that it does shoot get stored on the camera's memory card. Nevertheless, you will have greatly increased your chances of being a sharpshooter. Of course, you will have to use your own brain's jitter-detection software when you compare the captured images. To save space, it's wise to preview the shots on the camera's LCD and then delete any that are obviously unacceptable while you're still on location. However, you don't want to make the final decision until you can compare the best frames on your computer screen. Your camera's LCD just isn't of high enough resolution.

One last thing. Maybe your camera has neither a best-shot nor a burst mode. Well, it's just a little more trouble to take a few extra "insurance" shots when you're shooting. Any professional photographer will tell you that that's good advice in any shooting situation.

Get the Power to Last

If you're traveling or shooting lots of pictures on a commercial assignment, or are in a situation where you need to use your camera's LCD most of the time, you're in danger of running out of battery power at just the moment when you need it most.

There are lots of ways to help solve this problem. The most obvious of these is to keep your camera's AC adapter, spare batteries, and a battery charger with you at all times. Then, at least you can swap batteries and start recharging the old ones.

However, that's not a good enough solution if you're on the run while you're shooting. You can't plug into AC, and you will have left your charging batteries far behind. You can buy a gazillion batteries and charge them all up, but be sure you're using NiMH batteries that can be recharged at any time without shortening their life. Still, that's not the best solution, either. First of all, it's Milburn's Law that the only time you need to change batteries is the exact moment at which you could have captured a great shot. Second, if you're truly on the run, you may not be able to stop for a reload without losing your subject.

External battery packs to the rescue. SR, Inc., the company that makes the DigiSlave flash units, also makes an external battery pack that's built in to an L-bracket that features a hot shoe for holding an external strobe flash. You get about three times the battery life, along with a grip that helps you to hold the camera more firmly. That's enough power to get you through most daylong assignments. Some other manufacturers also make external battery packs that are small enough to drop into a shirt pocket or clip onto a belt loop — so they're hardly in the way at all. You'll find the sources for several of these packs in the Resources Directory at the back of the book.

Freezing the Action

Some of the newest cameras coming out this year have shutter speeds of 1/1,000 of a second and even higher. It is worth looking for one of those cameras if you are planning to shoot sports, shoot from moving vehicles, do motion studies, or have to do a majority of your work with a handheld camera. Ultrahigh shutter speeds have also been available for some time in 35mm professional digital cameras — but especially in the new Fuji S1 and the fairly new Nikon D1.

If you aren't lucky enough to be in possession of a digicam with superhigh shutter speeds, at least use the fastest shutter speed you've got in those situations. There are a few other tricks that will help:

✦ **Learn to catch action at its peak.** Most sports and other fast-moving subjects have spots in their movement where there is a momentary pause. Some good examples are the moment at which a trampoline artist reaches the top of the bounce or a football player pauses to make a catch. It takes a lot of practice, but you can learn to anticipate when those pauses are going to occur.

✦ **Shoot the action from head-on.** There's not nearly as much blur when an object is moving toward you as when it's moving across the film plane.

✦ **Pan with the subject.** If you swing the camera as the subject moves across the film plane, you will get a more motionless subject and a blurred background. Not only will the subject be sharper and more recognizable, the blurred background will increase the feeling of motion.

Use a Test Target in Your First Shot

A test target is a card made to exact color specifications specifically for the purpose of calibrating photographic devices. They are mentioned elsewhere in this book in conjunction with calibrating monitors, printers, and scanners.

The most popular targets are the Kodak 18-percent gray card and the Macbeth color card. Both are shown in Figure 10-1.

Figure 10-1: The Kodak 18-percent gray card and the Macbeth color checker

You can most easily get an accurate white balance, as well as balancing contrast, by including one of these cards in the first photo you plan to shoot in a series. If you're shooting pictures of people, have one of them hold the card for the first shot. (Of course, if you're shooting candids, put the camera on its self-timer and shoot the first shot of yourself holding the card.) If you're shooting outdoors, shoot a new color card image any time you get cloud cover or point the camera in a different direction, or move closer to a wall whose color might influence the direction and color of light. If you're shooting in the studio, you only need to shoot a new color card shot if you change the background color (because some of its color always bounces off the walls) or when you move the lights.

Once the film is downloaded (or processed and scanned), you can use the image adjustment commands in your image editor to balance the photo for the values in the card.

Here's how to adjust the image to match the card if you're using Photoshop 4.0 or later. If you're using another image editor that doesn't have adjustment layers (or another command that translates to the same thing), you'll just have to record your settings as a macro and then run the macro on all the other shots that you made under the same conditions (camera positioning and angle, time of day, and so on). If your image editor has neither adjustment layers nor a macro capability, you'll just have to write down all your settings, open the images one at a time, and repeat the same settings before resaving each file.

Okay, so here's the Photoshop method:

1. Open the lead image that contains the gray card.

2. Choose Layer ⇨ New ⇨ Adjustment Layer. The Adjustment layer dialog box will appear (see Figure 10-2). Choose Levels from the Type pull-down menu. Leave the other settings at their defaults and click OK. The standard Levels dialog box will appear.

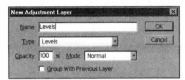

Figure 10-2: The Adjustment layer dialog box

3. Choose the black eyedropper (it's under the Auto button) and click the square in the lower-right corner of the Macbeth target. This area of the image should become completely black.

4. Choose the White Eyedropper and click the white square on the Macbeth chart. Now your gamma should be pretty well balanced from black to white, but you may still have a color cast.

5. Choose the Gray Eyedropper and click either the 18-percent gray card (if you used one) or on the 50-percent (18-percent reflectance) gray square on the Macbeth card. It's immediately to the left of the black square. This will automatically color balance your image so that the square is a neutral gray (see Figure 10-3).

   Now your image-editing program's assessment of the values in this image are correct. If you want a different interpretation (you often will, for subjective reasons), you can continue to adjust the Levels commands, add new adjustment layers for color balance, curves, or what have you.

6. Once you've added the necessary adjustment layers, open the next image in the series. Don't close the window for the test shot. Click to activate the window for the test shot.

7. Choose Window ⇨ Show Layers to make sure the Layers palette is showing. Drag each of the adjustment layers to the open window of the new file. This will automatically adjust the image in the new file.

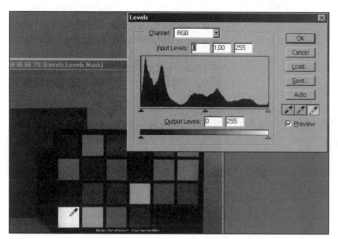

Figure 10-3: Using the eyedroppers in the Levels dialog box

8. Save the new file and close it, but don't close the window for the original test shot. Open the file for the next shot in the series and then drag the layers from the Layers palette for the test shot into the image window for the new shot. Save the file, close it, and open the next shot in the series. Just keep repeating this process as long as you have photos in the same series.

Bingo! Each of the photos in the series has values that are consistent with the other photos in the series.

Turning Your Rangefinder Camera into an SLR

The acronym SLR stands for single lens reflex, meaning a type of camera that uses a mirror and prism to redirect exactly the same image as the film sees to the camera's viewfinder. Because framing is always 100-percent accurate, this is the type of camera most often used by professionals.

Unfortunately, very few affordable digital cameras are SLRs (Olympus, Sony, and a few others make some notable exceptions). This is because the SLR optics raise the cost of the camera.

Having an SLR may seem less important to digital camera owners. Most digital cameras will let you use their LCD screens as a viewfinder, so you can see pretty much what the imaging element sees (though the actual image is often about 10-percent larger). It's certainly a handy enough feature that you wouldn't want to do without it, but it's not a complete substitute for an SLR. If you're shooting a close-up or using a supplementary lens that blocks the field of view of the viewfinder, you simply can't do without this feature. In the case of a supplementary lens blocking the viewfinder, that's not even the whole problem. The other problem is that the optical viewfinder can't see the same angle of view as the supplementary lens — so you're forced to use the LCD if you want accurate framing. When shooting extreme close-ups, the subject will be off-center in the image if it's properly framed in the optical viewfinder.

Now comes the bummer: What you see on the LCD viewfinder is typically undecipherable for one, the other, or a combination of the two following reasons:

✦ There's too much glare from extraneous light, so that you can't clearly make out what's showing on the LCD screen — never mind whether the colors and exposure values are what you want them to be.

✦ The image is too small, so you can't tell whether close-ups are clearly in focus — especially if you wear glasses.

Well, for a mere $16 you can buy a solution for both of these problems. Phil Williams makes a whole series of useful gadgets for extending digital photography. He makes these things in his garage and sells them for very reasonable prices through his Web site, called Photosolve. One of his gadgets is a hood called Extend-a-View that attaches to the back of most digital cameras with a small strip of Velcro, so that it can be removed whenever it might get in the way of working with the optical viewfinder. Figure 10-4 is a picture of the Extend-a-View.

Figure 10-4: The Extend-a-View attachment for LCD viewing screens

There are several wonderful things about the Extend-a-View:

✦ It incorporates a 2 × magnifying lens, so you can see the image at twice its size. This makes focusing on macro subjects very easy.

✦ No stray light gets through to the LCD, so the picture is bright and clear — even in the glare of noonday sun.

✦ It is a solid piece of rugged but lightweight plastic. It doesn't get beat up as quickly as less flexible LCD hoods.

The Extend-a-View only costs $16, and what a bargain. The mounting flanges are located at its top and sides, so they don't cover up controls that are often found directly below an LCD screen. You can contact Photosolve on the Web at www. photosolve.com.

Another company, called Hoodman (see the Resources Directory) sells an LCD hood that folds up. It's only a couple of bucks more than Extend-a-View. Although it doesn't have a magnifier, it's very handy when you want to use one of the cameras with a twist LCD to shoot from an otherwise unreachable angle. In those situations, the Extend-a-View would be useless because the magnifier would get in the way of your view of the screen if you were having to hold the camera at arms length.

Two-Shot Lighting

There are times when you just can't get the balance of lighting that you need in a photo. A common occurrence is liquid (such as liquor, soap, or a soft drink) in a glass and a bottle. To show off the liquid best, you want to underlight it so that the liquid glows. To show off the bottle and the label, you want more direct lighting that will highlight the edges and the shape of the bottle. Figure 10-5 shows just such a circumstance. The photographs were shot by my neighbor, Roger Mulkey. At left is the exposure for the bottle. In the middle is the exposure for the liquid. At right is the effect of combining the two photos. You can see what a dramatic improvement has been made.

Figure 10-5: The two shots at left have been combined to give the result shown at right.

Imagine shooting a lit birthday cake. The candle flames are so bright that you have to underexpose dramatically in order to see anything other than a blow-out flare. At the same time, you want to get the chocolate cake, which is rather dark, to look rich, textured, and scrumptious.

Digital photography is ideally suited to solving this problem. You simply make a photograph that's exactly right for each of the conflicting areas, place them on perfectly registered layers in an image-editing program, and erase away those portions of each layer that aren't needed. The following step-by-step instructions will give you a clearer idea of how this is done.

1. Place your camera on a tripod so that it doesn't move between exposures.

2. Set your camera as though it were photographing a very bright subject. A spot meter (or a spot-metering feature in your camera) helps. Meter just the candle flame. If you can't do that, just set your camera in manual mode and choose a high shutter speed and f-stop, and then bracket over a three-stop range. Bracketing means making exposures in half-stop increments, with your best estimate being the exposure in the middle. If your camera can't do either of the above, see if it has the ability to underexpose and set it at minus (-) whatever the highest allowable number is.

3. Turn off all the lights and take your photo(s) of just the candle flame(s), according to the instructions in Step 2.

4. Make sure that the camera isn't moved AT ALL. If it moves, you'll have to start from Step 1. Now, set your lighting for the cake and take the photograph(s). If it is a chocolate cake, you may want to make at least one "overexposure" to compensate for the darkness of the chocolate.

5. Transfer your images to the computer and open them all in your image editor (it will have to be able to accommodate layers). Keep the best shots of the flame and the cake.

6. In the flame photo, issue a Select All command followed by a Cut or Copy command. Activate the window of the cake photo and issue a Paste command. Since both images are digital photos, and since the camera didn't move between shots, all the details in both images will be in perfect register. Also, each will be on its own layer.

7. Activate the layer with image that contains the most keepable subject matter. In this example, that would be the chocolate cake. Move the selected layer to the bottom of the stack.

8. Turn off all but the bottom layer and make any image adjustments necessary to make it look as good as possible.

9. Select the layer that was exposed for the highlights and adjust it so that the highlights show the desired detail and color balance.

10. Choose your Eraser tool, set its opacity at a fairly low percentage, and erase away as much of the top layer as interferes with being able to see the bottom layer. You may want to start erasing by making the top layer temporarily transparent, so that you can see the underlying layer. However, be sure to make the top layer totally opaque before you finish so that you can see any "seams" between the erased areas and the underlying layer. If you see them, use a more feathered eraser at a lower opacity or pressure setting to blend away the seams.

That's all there is to it. Of course, you could make this procedure very complex for certain types of assignments by combining a number of different photos on different layers.

Printing Digital Images Online

You can get real, conventional snapshot prints on conventional paper without ever having to buy a color printer or having to go down to your local photo store. Well, actually, many local photo stores also offer a similar service. It's just more convenient—especially if you have a wide-band Internet connection such as DSL or a cable modem—to simply send in your pictures over the wire. You will get the prints back, in sizes up to 8 × 10 inches, within a few days.

There are quite a few such online services. More are being added almost daily as the popularity of digital cameras rises. Here are a few handy URLs:

✦ **Kodak QuickPrints:** www.kodak.com/go/quickprints

✦ **AOL You've Got Pictures:** AOL keyword: Pictures

✦ **Mystic Color Lab:** www.mysticcolorlab.com

✦ **EZprints:** www.ezprints.com

✦ **Pix.com:** www.pix.com (hundreds of gift items)

✦ **Club Photo:** www.clubphoto.com (here, you share as well as print)

You'll find that pricing, delivery, and the range of services vary from company to company. Most of these companies charge around fifty cents for a typical 4 × 6 glossy print that looks just like the ones you get from your local photo store or drug store. You can usually order prints in other sizes (usually up to 8 × 10 inches), on coffee mugs, mouse pads, aprons, t-shirts, sweatshirts, jigsaw puzzles, and calendars.

The colors in the images you get back will vary from those you saw on your monitor. This is more or less inevitable. You can minimize surprises by ordering some test prints of a color chart you've photographed. When you get the print back, use your image-editing program to make the original image look as much like the print as possible. Make careful notations as to what those settings are. From then on, make the same adjustments on all the images you plan to send in for prints. Be sure you do this on duplicates of the original image, so that you don't lose your original data. Better yet, create a macro that will repeat these settings for any image you plan to send in.

Preparing your photos for printing online

Preparing your photos for printing online is a relatively easy task, especially if you have a photo editor such as Photoshop that will automate the processing of a series of photos. If you're going to have your digital photos printed on conventional photo paper, be sure you use the highest-quality 24-bit color file your digital camera can produce as a starter. Don't use any of the greater compression levels unless you don't mind seeing artifacts in your prints. Traditional print film is more likely to make compression artifacts visible.

There are four basic things that you want to do before sending your images in:

1. Crop your image so its proportions match the size print you want made.
2. Match your image resolution to the size print you want made.
3. Compress your image so that you can submit it in a minimum of online time without making a noticeable sacrifice in image quality.
4. Make sure your file is in the right format and uses an acceptable filename.

Getting the proportions right

Different print sizes have different height-to-width proportions. If you don't crop your images to match those proportions, you're likely to have uneven borders on the prints that are returned to you.

The following are the cropping proportions to use for each print size:

Print Size	Proportion
4 × 6	1:1.5
5 × 7	1:1.4
8 × 10	1:1.25

If you use Photoshop as your image editor, getting the right proportions is easy. If you're using another image editor, look for a similar feature. Here's how to do it in Photoshop:

1. Open the image you intend to have printed.

2. Choose the Rectangular Selection tool. Click Window ➪ Show Options if this palette isn't already open.

3. In the Options palette, choose Constrained Aspect Ratio from the Style pull-down menu.

4. Enter the ratio into the Width and Height fields. Keep in mind whether your image is vertical (portrait) or horizontal (landscape).

5. Drag the selection marquee to enclose as much of the photo as you want to print. The aspect ratio will stay correct at all times. You can move the marquee by dragging inside the marquee while the tool is still active (chosen).

6. When the marquee encloses exactly the desired area, choose Image ➪ Crop.

You can also use the Crop tool. Set the Width, Height, and Resolution in the Options palette after you have clicked the Fixed Target Size checkbox.

Caution   Be sure you don't crop your digital camera images to the point where they contain less resolution than needed for the size print you're planning to order.

Matching the image resolution to the print size

Generally speaking, when you're making a photographic print, the more resolution you have in the original, the better. However, since you want to transmit these images over the Web, you want to choose a resolution low enough that you won't see a serious difference in the image quality. This will cut the time it takes you to transmit your file to the printing service.

Choosing the right compression compromise

Try to use only the higher levels of compression that are available to your camera. If you're going to manipulate the image before sending it in for printing, convert your digital file to a lossless format such as TIFF before starting. Save your file to the lossless format while making your manipulations. Then save it back to JPEG format only when you're preparing to send the file in for printing. When you save to JPEG, your image manipulation program will generally ask for the quality level. Choose Best, Maximum, or whatever the least lossy level is called.

You might want to try some test prints before you place a large order, just to see how much compression loss you can stand. If so, save the same image at different levels of compression. Use the text tool in your image-editing program to type the level of compression on each saved image. Then, when you get the prints back, you can examine them to see how much compression you're willing to put up with. This will vary from person to person—depending on whether image quality or simply having a record of the moment is more important.

Acceptable file formats

Though you'll probably want to use JPEG to save transmission time, quite a few file formats are acceptable. If quality is more important to you than turnaround time, you can always put your files on removable media and mail or express them to the printmaking service. The following file formats are acceptable to Kodak: JPG, JPEG, BMP, TIFF, GIF, PBM, PPM, and PGM.

Make sure the filename you use doesn't contain spaces and isn't over 35 characters long—including the file extension (the three letters after the dot). If you create your images on a Mac, it can be a good idea to add an extension to the filename so that image editors on other platforms will make the file compatible with that platform's image-editing programs.

Advanced Image Stitching

Image stitching is what happens when you join images that have been shot by rotating the camera between shots into a seamless panorama. Lots of software will do that—but imagine having one software application that could do all of the following:

- ✦ Make a very high resolution image from several low-res digital camera images
- ✦ Make a vertical panorama
- ✦ Seamlessly join scans of documents that are too big to fit on your scanner
- ✦ Correct barrel distortion caused by your digital camera's wide-angle lens
- ✦ Stitch together images from a wide variety of cameras and lenses
- ✦ Stitch together images with no limitation on the resolution of the individual images (or of the finished product)

The only product I know of that can do all this is Enroute PowerStitch. It was just being released in the last few days before this book went to press. Unlike Enroute's other panoramic stitching software, this package is meant for pros.

Like some of the less expensive stitching products, PowerStitch will make some attempt at seamlessly joining images that were shot by guessing at the amount of rotation between shots. It also gives you considerable control over how the image is placed.

The user interface consists of two windows: The PowerStitch Workspace and the Image List. You can stitch images from a variety of formats. When you choose File ⇨ Open, you choose the file(s) you want to open. They appear in the workspace, which is the inside of a globe. The names of the open files also appear in the Image List. You can see this interface in Figure 10-6.

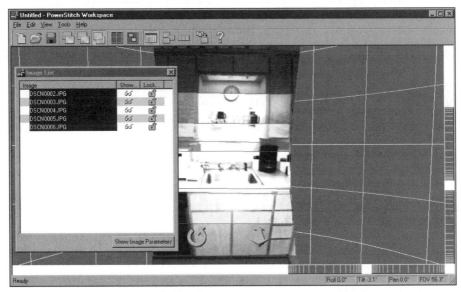

Figure 10-6: The PowerStitch interface

To arrange the pictures in the arrangement that will compose the composite picture, you drag them around in the PowerStitch Workspace until they're more or less in the correct position. The final positioning of each image is accomplished by a variety of means. You can enter adjustments for roll, tilt, pan, field of view, and barrel distortion (bowing of straight lines at the edges of some wide-angle lenses) directly into the Image List (see Figure 10-7). You can also control all of these things with controls in the PowerStitch Workspace. All of this control adds up to an ability to create very high fidelity stitched images. It also adds up to a fairly long learning curve.

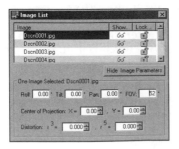

Figure 10-7: The Image List with the image parameters showing

PowerStitch's tutorial tells you that if you want perfectly seamless stitching, you need to know the exact angle of view of your camera's lens. Enroute gives you several ways of calculating that — including taking a picture and measuring from the center out. They also give you a very nice chart showing the 35mm equivalent field of view for all focal lengths of lenses. If you use a zoom lens, you should zoom all the way in or out so that you know exactly what the focal length of the lens is. Otherwise, with the camera on a tripod, you'll have to take a picture of a wall. Have a friend mark the wall at the very edges of the picture's width. Place a pushpin at each mark, and then pull a string from the pushpins to the camera's approximate film plane (the location of the surface of the image sensor) and then back to the other pushpin. Then, with a protractor, you can measure the angle.

You should also shoot from a tripod-mounted camera with a leveled head. If you have a panoramic tripod head, such as one of those made by Kaidan (see the Resource Directory), so much the better. A Kaidan head keeps the camera level and centered on the pan head even when rotated for a vertical shot. Kaidan heads also give you a preset for the exact degree of rotation and keep the camera over its optical center in respect to the center of the pan head.

If the object is to stitch together images so that you end up with one higher-resolution image, you need to keep the camera parallel to the subject as you frame each section of what will become the finished image. Also, you want to move the camera along a path parallel to the subject, as diagrammed in Figure 10-8.

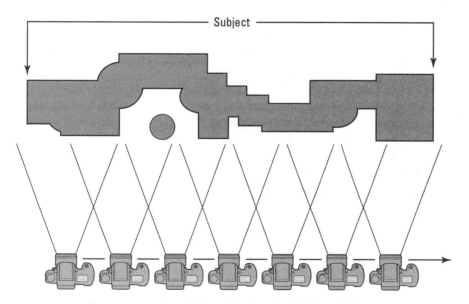

Camera moved parallel to subject for straight-line stitching

Figure 10-8: Move the camera parallel to the subject for a higher-resolution 2D composite.

If you want a QuickTime VR panorama—or one that has a fish-eye effect, you'll want to place the camera on a tripod, level the head, and then move an exact amount from side to side (or top to bottom).

So far, in order to save space, I've shown you shots that were stitched together side by side. PowerStitch lets you stitch together images from top to bottom as well. That's how you would put together an image of higher resolution than any single frame could produce. You could also make your camera simulate a fish eye by placing the camera on a tripod, and then making several sets of pans: One series across the horizontal center, others across higher and lower horizontal axis. Figure 10-9 shows a vertical panorama of a kitchen.

Figure 10-9: The shots in this panorama were taken by swiveling the lens of a Nikon 950. The original stitched image is a 26MB file.

Correcting barrel distortion with PowerStitch

One of the most prevalent problems with the zoom lenses on digital cameras is that some show a marked degree of barrel distortion when the lens is zoomed to its widest angle (shortest focal length). PowerStitch makes it very easy to correct this distortion. You just load an image into the program, zoom in so that it fills the window, and then select it in the Image List. Then, you click the scrolling arrows at the right of the Distortion fields and watch the image's edges expand and contract. When the edges are neutral, you render the image and save the file. Figure 10-10 shows the accuracy and ease with which you can correct barrel distortion.

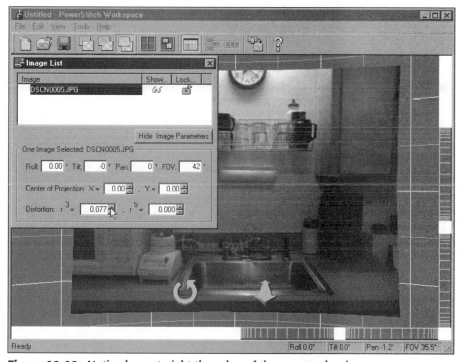

Figure 10-10: Notice how straight the edge of the counter has become.

Summary

This chapter has been a potpourri of advanced tips and an introduction to some very worthwhile gadgets. Hopefully, it has provided (or will provide) some solutions to problems you've found especially troublesome.

✦　　✦　　✦

Choosing the Right Processing Software

◆ ◆ ◆ ◆

◆ ◆ ◆ ◆

Choosing Professional-Level Image-Processing Software

CHAPTER

11

For most professionals, choosing an image-processing program is easy. You simply choose what most of the rest of the industry is using: Adobe Photoshop 5.5. Those of us who want an image-processing program that doesn't limit what we can produce as an end product face much tougher choices. In order to gain market share, most of Photoshop's competitors (those that haven't fallen by the wayside) have dropped their prices to less than half of Photoshop's price. They also strive to add a variety of features that Photoshop doesn't have. One program in this category, Live Picture, has become the leading specialist at integrating separate photographs into a seamless whole — a process the industry calls *photocompositing*. This chapter highlights the most attractive choices in no-holds-barred image-processing programs. You may find that, thanks to the affordability of the competition and the fight to add special features, you want to own several of these programs.

Aside from sorting through the features and price wars, two other problems are associated with choosing a pro-level image-processing program:

✦ How to know which image-processing programs fit in this category

✦ Understanding what the other image-processing categories are (and when to choose them)

Identifying Professional-Level Image-Processing Programs

Before I even get into this, I should warn you that categorizing products is a dangerous game. Software publishers compete by trying hard to offer more features than "the other guy" at a lower price. One of the methods for doing that is to borrow features from programs that would otherwise cause you to spend more money.

Keeping that in mind, understand that although there are many differences between professional image-processing programs, they tend to have certain characteristics in common:

✦ They cost more than $50.

✦ They don't come bundled with digital cameras that cost less than $800 (at least not currently).

✦ They offer a full range of professional features for image correction, editing, manipulation, retouching, compositing, and special effects.

✦ Layered editing (sometimes called objects) is supported.

✦ They support a comprehensive range of file formats and input devices (cameras and scanners) and output devices (printers, video, and film recorders).

✦ They are compatible with most Photoshop plug-ins.

✦ They produce professional-quality output, including PostScript, four-color separation, calibration bars, undercolor removal, dot gain, and all that graphic-geeky stuff. Most also offer support for Pantone and other spot color palettes. (Of course, all of these things are useless if you can't produce a good print.)

Price

Image-processing programs with professional features start at $99.50 retail, though street prices may dip below that. One of the reasons for that dip seems to be a marketing decision based on the idea that the public's perception of programs that sell in the same price range as PhotoDeluxe and Photoshop 2 are meant for a less serious audience.

Buying it bundled

You won't find professional-level photo editors bundled with the more affordable digital cameras. This isn't because the camera manufacturers can't afford the license fees, but because they assume that the majority of these buyers want things made as easy for them as possible. Rather than having control over every aspect of an image, some users would rather have a program that takes care of correcting common problems at the push of a button. As a result, the image-processing programs that are included in the price of these cameras fall into the category I call *SOHO* (*Small Office Home Office*) image processors. You will find more on SOHO image-processing software in Chapter 16.

Professional-level image-processing programs are often bundled with scanners, particularly those in the price range over $300. That doesn't mean, however, that all scanners come with a professional image editor. When they do include one, it is likely to be a "light" version of the program, or something other than Photoshop. Before you buy, check how current the version of the software is and which (if any) of the program's features have been eliminated. The good news is that when a bundled program's features have been limited, you usually have the opportunity to upgrade to the full version of the program at a very reasonable price.

Automating frequently used command sequences

If you are working in a production environment, you will definitely need a program that enables you to link a series of frequently used commands to a particular menu choice or keystroke combination. For instance, with one click you could apply all the needed commands to fit an image within a particular size and color palette and then save it to GIF format for publication on the Web.

Image-processing features

A professional-level image-processing program will enable you to alter all or part of an image in virtually any way imaginable. It will provide the tools needed for altering exposure, contrast, tonal values, and color balance. It will also provide a full range of painting and retouching tools; including an airbrush, paintbrush, clone tool, and blending tools. You will also have numerous ways to isolate portions of the image so that they are protected from subsequent commands. In other words, you'll have a full set of selection and masking tools — including some that help automate the masking process.

Layer (object) editing

Layer editing is one characteristic of pro digital darkrooms that really sets them apart from their "click 'n fix" brethren. You can isolate as many images as you like within a separate file. These images appear to be stacked directly atop one another and any transparent portion of the image reveals the image below it. You can control how each of the layers affect underlying layers, meaning that their pixels are added, subtracted, multiplied, and so forth. You can also control the transparency of the entire layer.

File and device support

Most professional image editors will let you open all commonly used bitmap file types (including the17 separate file types in Photoshop 5). Photoshop 5 and some other programs will also open and then rasterize (turn into bitmaps) some vector file types.

Photoshop plug-in compatibility

Photoshop pioneered the use of plug-in extensions to the program. These make 0it possible to import new types of files or to interface with such devices as new digital cameras and scanners. They also make it possible to create many special effects, such as simulating paint brush strokes in various artistic styles, making motion blurs, or distorting selections. With so many powerful plug-ins available now, using a program that doesn't support them means giving up considerable image-processing power.

Key Features and What They Mean

In addition to accessory programs and plug-ins, I use three core programs: Photoshop, Painter, and LivePicture. There are considerable overlapping functions between these programs, but I typically use them for the following features:

✦ **Photoshop:** Correcting, manipulating, and retouching the image

✦ **Painter:** Natural-media paint tools and lighting effects

✦ **LivePicture:** Distortions, transformations, and compositing

If the program you choose doesn't have a feature you want, chances are good it's available through a Photoshop-compatible plug-in or a special-purpose program.

When looking for a professional image-editing program, you should look for strong and flexible features in the following categories:

- ✦ Installed base
- ✦ Interface familiarity
- ✦ Painting and retouching
- ✦ Image editing
- ✦ Special effects processing
- ✦ Wacom tablet compatibility
- ✦ Calibration and prepress preparation
- ✦ Image compositing

Installed base

It will behoove you to use a program that is also used by your client, service bureau, or publisher. This way, you can be assured that the other party's program can read your files. Often you'll want to share the work on a project, and it's easier when both parties speak the same image manipulation language.

Interface familiarity

When you drive another person's car, you likely already know the location and use of the brake pedal and steering wheel. It's also easier to "drive" a new program if you understand the layout of the controls. You want to find a program that feels familiar. It doesn't matter if you're brand new to graphics programs, because the program that you buy will turn out to be a good training ground for other graphics programs.

Painting and retouching

Painting and retouching tools and features should be as rich as possible. At a minimum, the toolbox should include the following tools: a paintbrush, an airbrush, a pencil (for drawing hard-edged lines), a line tool (for drawing straight lines), and a cloning tool.

Check for flexibility in the program's ability to do gradient fills. Can it do multiple shapes of gradients? Can you use more than two colors? Can you use an unlimited number of colors? Can one of the "colors" be transparent?

Photoshop and a few other programs also include the ability to create vector paths, just like those used in illustration programs. Depending on the program, these paths can be stroked with any of the brushes or automatically converted to a selection or mask.

One professional image editor, MetaCreation's Painter, lets you paint brush strokes that imitate traditional artist's tools, materials, and even painting styles. Some other programs offer some natural-media brush strokes, but none offer as many choices or as much flexibility as Painter. Nevertheless, any natural-media capabilities can be considered a bonus, unless you want to keep all your work looking strictly photographic.

Image editing

Image editing is the term usually applied to programs that perform as digital darkrooms, because it is a good catchall term. We also use the term because those functions that control the qualities of the image are among the most important. You should be able to control not only brightness and contrast, but also where the whitest and blackest tones in the image fall and where the midtones lie. A good image-editing program should also give you control over color balance and saturation, as well as the ability to substitute one color for another (which is very useful in catalog work).

Image files can be quite large, so it's a good idea to choose a program that enables you to edit a section of a file without having to load the entire file. If the program has this capability, it will also be able to seamlessly reintegrate the edited section with the entire image file. Another highly desirable feature is the ability to let you edit a low-resolution version of the image in memory, and then automatically apply those edits to the overall file after all the editing has been done. Applying the edits is called *rendering* the image. The advantage is that your edits can take place in real time. The technology for this was pioneered by Live Picture and still exists in that product. Similar technology was used in Macromedia xRes, which was a cross-platform product that has since faded from the scene. A new product from Satori is just now emerging. You'll find more details on Satori FilmFX later in this chapter.

You should also have darkroom tools for editing small areas of the image, including burn (darken), dodge (lighten), desaturate (remove color), blur, sharpen, and smudge. You should be able to rotate the image to any degree — preferably either by typing an exact number or by dragging a corner of the image or current selection.

Another useful effect that I've yet to encounter integrated into anything but Live Picture is the ability to shrink or exaggerate portions of the image by stroking them with a brush. The result is very smooth transitions between rescaled portions of an object and the originals. This enables you to do such things as make caricatures that look like photographs of something real (but as yet unseen by human eyes).

You won't be able to effectively edit portions of an image unless you can quickly and accurately select the portion you want to edit. Your selection tools should include the following: Rectangle, Oval, Row, Column, Lasso, Polygon, Magic Lasso, and Magic Wand.

Special-effects processing

This is the area in which professional image-processing programs seem to vary the most. However, most are compatible with Photoshop plug-ins, so you can add an awesome variety of special effects if you're willing to pay the extra cost of the plug-ins.

Wacom tablet compatibility

You will have a much easier time working in image editing programs if you use a pressure-sensitive digitizing tablet and pen. This is especially true regarding making selections, retouching, and using the tools that affect brush-sized areas of the image. These devices take a little getting used to if your usual control device is a mouse, but the productivity payoff is enormous. Most tablets, regardless of who makes them, are compatible with the Wacom drivers. For that reason, these drivers are the ones most commonly supported by graphics software of all types (not just image editors).

Prepress preparation

If you are going to send all your images to prepress specialists before publication, this capability will be less important to you than if you plan to do the work yourself. Of course, these features become very significant if you *are* the prepress specialist. If that is the case, you already know what to look for in the program. Just make sure the program has what you need.

If you don't have a great need for accurate color calibration, make sure that you can use an ICC profile for your display, scanner, and printer. You will then be able to do a reasonable job of calibration by using inexpensive color calibration software such as EZ Color. Some image-processing programs also are able to take advantage of Apple ColorSync and Microsoft ICM (Windows 98 only) and their compatibility with ICC (International Color Consortium) profiles.

Color calibration and prepress considerations are complex topics. You'll find a helpful and comprehensive discussion of them in Chapter 15.

Image compositing

All of the features mentioned above will help you make smoothly composited images from multiple image files. However, you will be more successful at making realistic images with consistent tonal values and image sharpness if you use a program that renders the composited image from the original files *after* you've done all the necessary masking, cutting, pasting, resizing, and rotating. If a program has to rearrange the image's pixels after each of these steps is accomplished, you simply can't avoid losing a lot of pixel information. Some programs, such as Photoshop 5, will let you make a number of transformations before rendering the result (to transform means to scale, stretch, rotate, or distort). However, only programs that let you work with a lower-resolution representation of the original file until rendering time will be able to do this as smoothly as possible. Such a capability is often referred to as *proxy editing* because the file you are performing the work on is a temporary, low-resolution (how low depends on your current zoom level) version of the original. Live Picture, Satori, and (if you can still find a copy) Macromedia's xRes are all capable of working this way.

Choosing Products

The following sections describe the marketing position and features of each of the major professional image-editing programs. All of these programs can easily share files with one another, even if the programs are running on different operating systems. Some people I know own all of them, just so they can use a feature that is unique or particularly useful in each of them. The undisputed market leader is Adobe Photoshop, with a market share better than 80 percent (higher on the Mac, a bit lower for Windows). Some of the others' functionality is at or near parity with Photoshop's: Corel Photo-Paint, iGrafx Picture Publisher, and Paint Shop Pro. Others, such as Painter (natural media), Live Picture, Satori (compositing, and proxy editing), and Canvas (image editing combined with a full complement of vector illustration and publishing tools) have such unique characteristics that they are often purchased as an enhancement to Photoshop. All except Painter 5 cost less than a third of Photoshop's price, and some of them dip well below that — so owning several of these programs may not be as financially foolhardy as it sounds. There is even a version of Painter, called Painter Classic, that retails for less than $100 and comes bundled with some digitizing pads.

Photoshop 5

As well as owning the bulk of the market, Photoshop 5 has all but a few of the significant features for image editing, as described in the first half of this chapter.

Furthermore, these features can usually be implemented in a variety of ways that make the product easy to tailor to your own needs and personality. The as-yet-unimplemented features are proxy editing, natural media, and the ability to combine raster and vector images within the same file. The map of Photoshop's interface, shown in Figure 11-1, provides a quick overview of the program's user interface and functionality. Almost all other image-editing programs, particularly those in this chapter, take their interface cues from Photoshop.

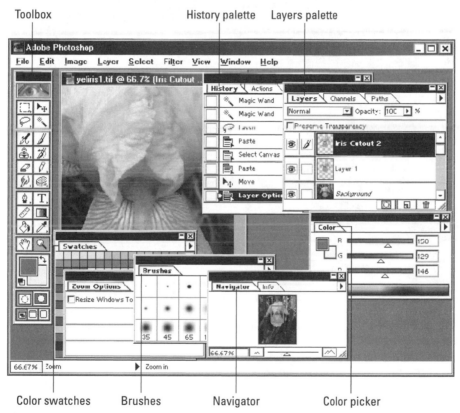

Figure 11-1: The components of the Photoshop interface

Automation

Photoshop introduced the Actions palette in version 4.0, and new versions continue to polish this macro recording capability. Like many of Photoshop's most powerful features, Actions are structured around a palette (see Figure 11-2). Action is simply a trademarked name for macro recording. You start a new Action by selecting it from the menu, clicking the Record icon, and choosing those commands that you want to execute automatically. When you've finished recording, you click the Stop icon and Photoshop saves the Action so that it can be repeated. You can choose your own names for Actions, edit and add to them after they've been recorded, and turn individual commands on or off before executing the Action.

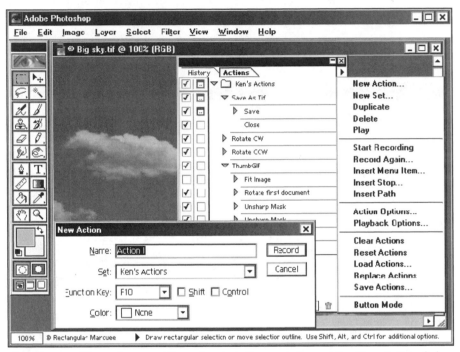

Figure 11-2: Shown here are Photoshop's Actions palette and the New Action dialog box. The palette is shown with the menu extended so that you can see the range of commands that can be applied to an Action. The New Actions dialog box enables you to name the action, designate a folder for it, assign function and modifier keys that will execute it when pressed, and color the Action's name bar in the Actions palette.

Painting and retouching

Photoshop is entirely compatible with Wacom digitizing pads, including the new Intuos features, which means that the painting and retouching tools can be applied in a familiar and accurate way. The painting and retouching tools are shown in Table 11-1. The brush shapes, the stroke made with the brush, and options for each type of brush are shown alongside the brush's toolbox icon.

Table 11-1
Photoshop Tools, Shapes, and Options

Tool	Icon	Default Shapes	Brush Options
Brush		Although the default shapes are perfect circles, you can adjust the angle, roundness, edge sharpness, spacing, and diameter.	Brush behavior is controlled through an Options dialog box that lets you change the Apply mode, stroke opacity, number of steps to fade, whether edges will be wet (darker), and whether to fade to transparent or the background color.
Airbrush		Note that the default brushes are exactly the same as the default brushes for the paintbrush. So are the brush options.	Same as paintbrush, except the default pressure (same as transparency) is 50 percent and there is no wet edges option.
Pencil		Notice that all the brush shapes are sharp-edged. Brush options offer no way to soften them (though they appear to). Other options match those for other brushes.	Unique option to Auto Erase lets you automatically paint the background color.
Line		Notice that all the brush shapes are sharp-edged. Brush options offer no way to soften them (though they appear to). Other options match those for other brushes.	Weight sets the width of the line in pixels. Check to indicate an arrowhead at the start or end. The Shape button chooses the length, width, and curvature of the arrowhead. Lines can be smooth-edged (antialiased), unlike pencil.
Clone		Although the default shapes are perfect circles, you can adjust the angle, roundness, edge sharpness, spacing, and diameter.	Check Aligned to copy all of another part of the image relative to where new strokes are placed. Check Use All Layers to clone all of an image that is made of several layers.

Continued

Table 11-1 *(continued)*

Tool	Icon	Default Shapes	Brush Options
Eraser		Eraser brushes are the same as the brush type chosen in the Eraser Options dialog box: Paintbrush, Airbrush, or Pencil. The Block mode is a fixed-size block that erases a specific number of pixels based on the current zoom level.	The eraser paints with the background color or to transparency on named layers if the Preserve Transparency box in the Layers Palette is *unchecked*. Erase to history. Will "paint" the history state into the area that you erase at the eraser's currently specified opacity.
History Brush		History brushes are the same as the brush type chosen in the Eraser Options dialog box: Paintbrush, Airbrush, or Pencil.	Checking Impressionist causes the snapshot pixels to be smudged when stroked.
Blur		The Blur brushes are the same as the paintbrush brushes.	Default pressure is 50 percent. Pressure controls the amount of blurring. You can choose to blur all visible objects, regardless of layer.
Sharpen		The Sharpen brushes are the same as the paintbrush brushes.	Default pressure is 50 percent. Pressure controls the amount of blurring. You can choose to blur all visible objects, regardless of layer.
Smudge		The Smudge brushes are the same as the paintbrush brushes.	Default pressure is 50 percent. Pressure controls the amount of blurring. You can choose to blur all visible objects, regardless of layer.
Fill		None	In addition to the options already mentioned under the Fill tool, you can set Opacity level. Check Preserve Transparency if you want to affect only visible pixels within a transparent background.

Tool	Icon	Default Shapes	Brush Options
Gradient		Gradients can be linear, radial, angled (conical), reflective (cylindrical), or diamond-shaped.	In addition to the usual transparency and add mode options, you can choose from a list of premade gradients (including multicolor and transparent). Three checkboxes activate layer transparency, dithering to smooth blends, and reversing the order of colors in the gradient.

Tip You can also make custom brush shapes from any rectangular selection in an image. If you want silhouetted object shapes, just draw or scan the object and fill it with black against a white background, and then place a marquee around it and choose the command Define Brush.

Painting with Filters

Photoshop doesn't let you assign special effects to your brushes, but there's a workaround that makes Photoshop considerably more powerful than the competition:

1. Copy the layer of the image onto which you want to paint the special effect.

2. Filter the copied layer with the desired special effect.

3. Use the History Brush palette to make a snapshot.

4. Delete the special effect layer (optional, but saves memory).

5. Click the History Brush box in the History Brush palette (to activate the History brush).

6. Choose the History Brush tool. Set the brush options as desired.

7. Paint in the special effect.

8. Delete the Special Effect snapshot to save memory, and continue.

Image editing

Photoshop's image-editing capabilities are far too numerous for complete coverage here. However, the following sections highlight some of the most powerful aspects of Photoshop's image-editing commands.

Layers

Image editing can be done on multiple layers (think of these as overlays). Layers can have transparent areas or you can attach masks to overlays that hide portions of the image. You can change the way these overlays interact with the layers beneath them by using preset image calculations (see Figure 11-3).

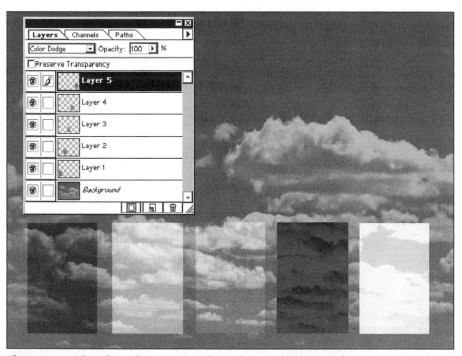

Figure 11-3: The Photoshop Layers palette shows a background image and five layers. Dragging the position of the layer bars changes the stacking order. A checkerboard indicates transparent areas of layers. At the top left of the Layers palette is a drop-down menu that lets you change the way the active (highlighted) layer works with the visible portions of any underlying layers (Blending mode). Each layer has been blended as follows (left to right): Multiply, Screen, Overlay, Exclusion, Color Dodge. There are a total of 17 Blending modes for layers.

It is possible to merge, flatten, flip, copy, and clip together Photoshop's layers in any combination. You can also use layer effects to automatically add drop shadows, bevels, or glows to any shape residing on the target layer. Finally, there are commands for automatically distributing and aligning multiple layers.

Tonal control

You can control the tonal values in an image in many ways. Just as you can in some of the SOHO image editors, you can choose to make an automatic tonal correction with one click. If you're unsure of how to operate the controls, the Variations command will open a screenfull of thumbnails, each with a color or gamma variation. Click the one that looks best to you and your image is automatically adjusted to match.

When you want absolute tonal control over specific areas of the image, you have many methods available to you (flexibility is one of the hallmarks of professional-level programs). You can apply all of these controls to any selected portion of an image on any active (chosen) layer, either to one color channel or to the composite color channel. Most of these controls will even let you target your changes to shadows, midtones, or highlights. Two of the most useful and powerful tonal control commands are Levels and Curves (see Figures 11-4 and 11-5).

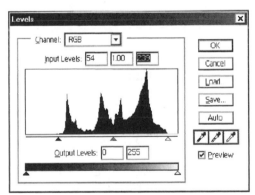

Figure 11-4: The Levels dialog box shows a histogram that indicates the number of pixels assigned to a given level of brightness in the image. You can adjust the shadow and midtone, and highlight areas by dragging the three pointers under the histogram. This changes the values smoothly and, unlike the Curves command, doesn't alter the overall color balance of the image. You can also lower image contrast by lowering the output value of highlights (making them darker), shadows (making them brighter) or both. Choosing one of the droppers and clicking in the image places that portion of the image at black, 50 percent gray, or white.

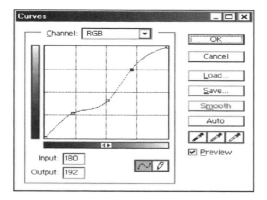

Figure 11-5: Clicking anywhere on the curve anchors a control point that can be dragged to change the curve. If the Preview box is checked, you automatically see the result of your adjustment in the image.

The Curves dialog box provides the ability to control the intensity of the image at as many as fourteen points along the gamma curve. This is much more precise control than is afforded by the Levels command. You can also use the command to create bizarre and surrealistic tonal shifts.

Photoshop 4 and later also have Adjustment layers. Using an Adjustment layer causes the adjustment to affect all underlying layers, rather than just the current layer. Image adjustment commands you can apply to Adjustment layers include Levels, Curves, Brightness/Contrast, Color Balance, Hue/Saturation, Selective Color, Channel Mixer, Invert, Threshold, and Posterize.

Finally, Photoshop has a complete set of tools for controlling tonal values by stroking in specific areas of the image. These include burn (darken), dodge (lighten), and sponge (desaturate color).

Color controls

Photoshop is also very rich in commands for controlling the color in an image. This includes both overall color balance and the control of specific colors within the image. A simple listing of the related commands gives you a pretty good idea of the degree of this flexibility: Color Balance, Hue/Saturation, Desaturate, Replace Color, Selective Color, Channel Mixer, and Posterize.

The Replace Color command lets you replace all the colors within a chosen range of pixels with any other color in the rainbow. All the brightness values for the original color are maintained in the adjusted image. This means that if you are doing special effects photography, you can change the color of the sky. If you are doing catalog photography, you can shoot an item in one color, and then change it to match all the colors being offered.

Selective color lets you change the values actually assigned to any of the primary or complementary colors.

Darkroom brushes

Photoshop has three brushes (tools) that are used to alter brush-sized (1 to 1,000 pixel radius) portions of the image by hand: Burn (to darken), Dodge (to lighten), and Sponge (to change color saturation). Repeated stroking with any of these brushes increases the degree of change made by the tool. You can also adjust the intensity of the effect (1–100 percent) for each of these tools. The Burn and Dodge tools can be made to affect only midtones, shadows, or highlights. The Sponge tool can be used to either saturate or desaturate. Figure 11-6 shows the effect of each of these tools on the same image.

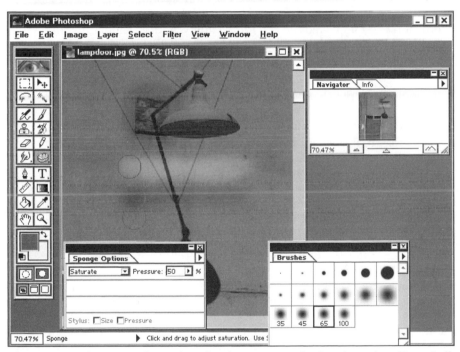

Figure 11-6: The image shown here has been composited to show the effect of all three darkroom tools. From top to bottom: Dodge, Burn, and Sponge.

Special-effects processing

Photoshop is nearly unique in providing users with the means to interactively create their own filters as well as to control the mathematics for interlayer blending. Although these capabilities were once a major feature of Photoshop, Photoshop 5's preprogrammed special effects are so extensive that few still take advantage of being able to create their own filters or control the mathematics for inter-layer blending.

Photoshop also comes with a truly impressive array of built-in filters and blending effects. There are 98 built-in filters, including the ability to use paper textures and lighting effects.

Calibration and prepress preparation

Photoshop 5 offers complete support for ICC color profiles. ICC stands for International Color Consortium — an industry trade group that sets standards for profiling the color characteristics of digital devices such as monitors, scanners, and cameras. This makes cross-device color calibration much easier and more accurate.

Photoshop 5 has improved the calibration utility, Adobe Gamma, and has added support for it and spot color channels. With spot color channels, you can specify an exact swatch color for any of the leading spot color books, such as Pantone. This makes it possible to exactly match colors used in company logos or the colors of apparel in catalogs.

Ease of navigation

It is very easy to find your way around in large files when working in Photoshop. This is important because your image may be many times larger than your screen when viewed at actual pixel size. In addition to the standard scrolling and panning bars, you can activate handscrolling simply by pressing the spacebar. You can also choose to open a Navigator window. The Navigator window indicates the limits of the current view of the image with a rectangle. You can change the view in a workspace by dragging the white rectangle in the Navigator window (see Figure 11-7).

Image compositing

Image compositing is the art of making a picture that consists of what were originally several images, each photographed separately. Compositing by digital means can be as simple as dropping portions of images atop one another to simulate the traditional artist's collage, or as complex as making it appear that a purely imaginary situation occurred in reality. Although Photoshop has some very strong compositing tools, it is not nearly as well suited to photorealistic montage (compositing to achieve the illusion of a new reality) as programs such as Live Picture and xRes.

Selection tools

Photoshop's collection of selection tools include the expected Rectangular, Oval, Freehand, and "Magic Wand" (automatic selection of a contiguous area of pixels that fall within a user-specified range of tonal values). Version 5 added tools for automatically tracing the edges in an image with either a selection marquee or a Bezier-curve (vector) path. These are called the Magnetic Lasso and the Magnetic Pen (see Figure 11-8).

Figure 11-7: Photoshop's Navigator makes it easy to move instantly to any portion of the image. You can zoom directly to any magnification by dragging the slider at the bottom of the Navigator panel.

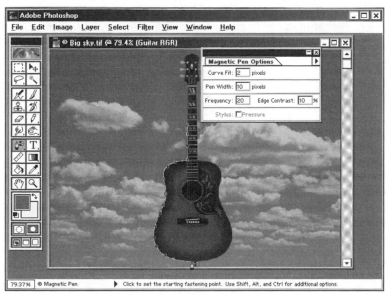

Figure 11-8: The Magnetic Pen automatically snaps a curve to any edge formed by contrasting pixels. You can specify how closely the curve fits, the distance between control points, the width of the pixel matrix that an edge must fall within, and the level of contrast that must exist before a pixel will be considered an edge.

The Magnetic Lasso has the same controls and works in the same way as the Magnetic Pen, except that it creates a selection, rather than a vector path. However, you can always convert paths to selections or export them to an illustration program. Selection tools also include a Color range command that creates masks on any range of colors that you select in an image. Finally, Photoshop's QuickMask mode lets you use any of the brushes to paint a selection mask directly on the image—or to modify one that already exists.

In addition to the normal channels used for primary colors, Photoshop lets you have as many as 24 alpha channels. These can be used for storing and retrieving selections, activating them only when needed.

Layer controls

Layers are even more powerful for compositing purposes than for darkroom manipulation. For instance, you can erase portions of the image on a layer by either using an eraser brush or deleting the contents of selections. In either case, the erased portion of the image can have any level of transparency. This isn't the only way to float an image. You can also use a layer mask to hide portions of a layer without destroying the data on that layer. Moreover, the same characteristics of Photoshop's layers that make them so powerful for image editing also contribute to the program's compositing capabilities.

Photoshop's weakness, when it comes to compositing, is that as of version 5 there was still no proxy-editing capability. The result is that one must be careful not to reshape and resize the components of the composited image too much or too often. Otherwise, elements in the image will become downright dirty or mushy.

Wacom compatibility

Photoshop is thoroughly compatible with Wacom tablets for both pressure-sensitivity and eraser functions. Some of the new Intuos tools have to be implemented through special drivers (for the time being), but that is currently the case for all of Photoshop's competitors as well.

Painter 5

Painter's forte is its ability to create bitmapped images that can look as though they were created with traditional artist's tools. It is equally adept at creating surface textures and effects that may be anything but traditional. The two images in Figure 11-9 show a digital photograph and a "painterly" interpretation made in Painter.

Figure 11-9: The flower on the left is the original digital photograph from an Olympus d-620-L camera. The same image is shown on the right as handbrushed in Painter.

Installed base

Painter and Painter Classic (the "light" version of Painter) have almost cornered the entire market for natural-media paint programs. Other programs have some natural-media painting capabilities, but none are as rich as Painter Classic—and Painter 6 is even richer.

Interface familiarity

The Painter programs are often used in tandem with a more traditional image-editing program, such as Photoshop. This is true despite the fact that Painter has very powerful image-editing capabilities of its own—and it is partly because the Photoshop interface is more familiar to more professionals. The Painter interface is pretty much unique. This is not to say that the interface isn't brilliant. However, if you're going to spend lots of time in Painter, I suggest you use a two-monitor setup so that you can put the toolboxes and dialog boxes on a monitor separate from the working image. Otherwise, you'll find that the user interface takes up lots of your screen real estate. Of course, you can always turn off the dialog boxes and recall them only when you need them.

You'll get a better idea of Painter's interface by taking a look at Figure 11-10.

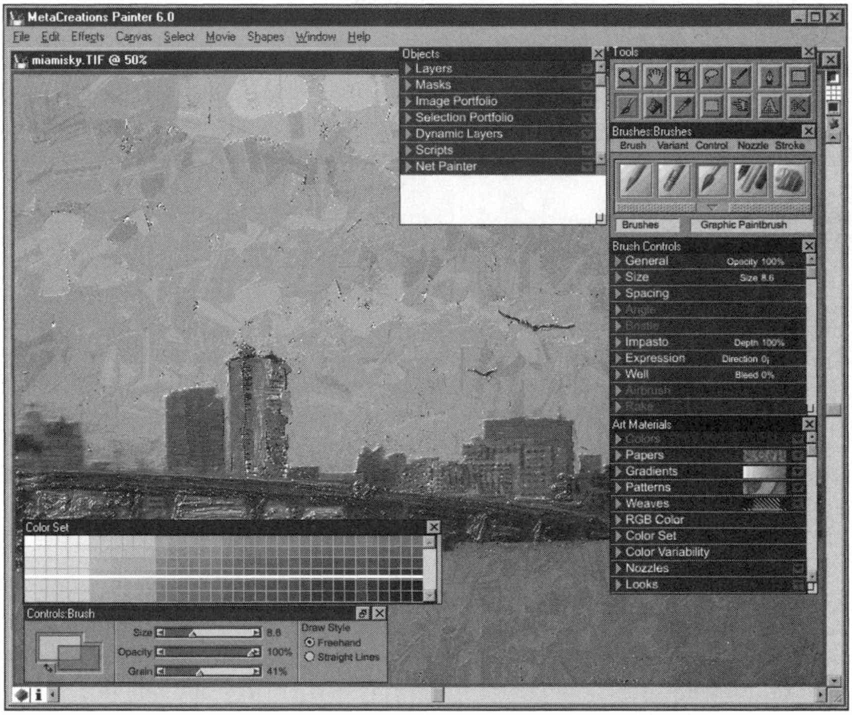

Figure 11-10: The Painter Interface, with the default palettes showing

Painting and retouching

As the name implies, Painter excels at painting. You can get nearly every imaginable brush effect and can even make adjustments to create your own. However, painting solid colors is marginally slower than in many other programs because every time you resize the brush it has to recalculate the effect it will produce at that size — even if the effect is flat color. Also, there is no way to see the exact size of the brush as you paint. You can, however, see the brush's diameter as you are dragging the resizing slider.

Painter 5 has an even more powerful cloning capability than does Photoshop. You can create a new layer and have any of the brushes clone from the base image to the new layer. You can also clone from one area of the same layer to another.

You get a hint of the variety of Painter's brushes in Figure 11-11, which shows the Brushes palette.

Painter can also paint with masked objects, such as leaves or clouds (see "Image Compositing," later in this chapter).

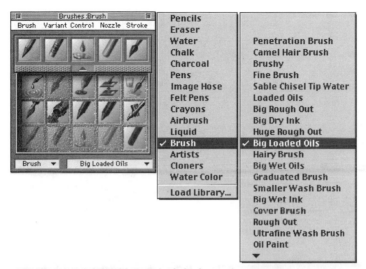

Figure 11-11: This is Painter's default Brushes palette. You can load other palettes from disk. The menu in the center lists all the default brushes. The menu on the right lists preset variations for the paintbrush.

Image editing

Painter 5 has professional-level image-editing capabilities. However, these aren't quite as flexible or sophisticated as those in the latest version of Photoshop. Still, if you need to adjust image qualities with a curve, you can drag the curve or you can draw it freehand—much as you can in Photoshop. Painter has no Levels command.

Painter does have layers, but they're called *image floaters*. Floaters differ from Photoshop layers in that floaters are automatically trimmed to a rectangular size just large enough to contain all visible pixels. Layers imported from Photoshop are automatically trimmed, and their opacity is converted. You can't count on being able to directly convert layer modes between Photoshop and Painter in version 5, though this may be changed in version 6.

Special-effects processing

An especially valuable aspect of Painter is its ability to distort images selectively. You can do this by creating a special layer called a *Liquid Lens.* A Liquid Lens layer lets you play with distorting the image on the underlying layer without permanently distorting the underlying layer. There's also an Eraser tool that lets you reverse the distortion gradually, so you can add and subtract until you get exactly the degree and type of distortion you are looking for. This tool has both artistic and photographic uses. Artistically, you can turn real objects into surrealistic forms. Photographically, you can use the tool to reshape part of an object so that it fits seamlessly together with another object in a composited image. You can even move the Liquid Lens layer around on the image to see the distortion occur in different places. You get an idea of the power of this tool in Figure 11-12.

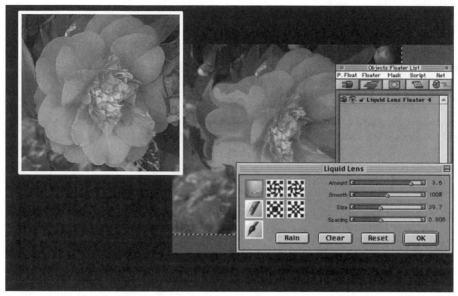

Figure 11-12: Painter's Liquid Lens layer can be used to distort all or any part of an image in a variety of ways. Several of the tools have been used to create the distortions in the flower shown on the right.

Note   Painter is compatible with Photoshop plug-in filters.

Calibration and pre-press preparation

Painter 6 uses the Kodak Color Management System, which integrates with your computer's operating system for system-wide color management. You can incorporate the ICC profiles for your monitor, printer, and scanner into the KCMS for system-wide color matching. You do, however, have the option of not installing KCMS if you prefer working in some other way.

Ease of navigation

Navigating about a large image is conventional: There are scrollbars and a Hand tool for interactive panning and scrolling. As in Photoshop, you press the spacebar to activate the Hand tool while using other tools. Double-clicking the Hand tool sizes the image to fit the portion of the screen that isn't occupied by dialog boxes. Double-clicking the Magnifier tool zooms the image to actual pixels (100 percent).

Image compositing

Painter has a special brush called the Image Hose. The Image Hose can paint with masked photos (called *nozzles*). It is quite easy to make your own nozzles. You can make adjustments to the size, direction, number, and placement of different images and many other factors. Figure 11-13 shows an example of images painted with the Image Hose.

Figure 11-13: Everything in this image, except the solid color background, was painted with the Image Hose.

Painter 6 has Photoshop-compatible layers. You can mathematically combine layers, just as with Photoshop's Blend modes. Painter calls these *composite methods,* and many of them parallel Photoshop's. You can change the size of floaters, add drop shadows, and create the equivalent of layer effects (but in a much more powerful way that includes several special effects not found in Photoshop).

Painter can do very limited proxy editing. You can use a low-resolution image as a special type of layer called a *Reference layer.* Reference layers can be treated just as regular layers when it comes to transforming (stretching and resizing) and positioning (moving and rotating), but all the changes actually take place only when you convert the Reference layer to a Standard layer. Also, only when you convert the Reference layer to a Standard layer can you actually make any changes to the image itself, such as painting or burning and dodging.

Wacom compatibility

Painter is such a great showcase for pressure-sensitive tablets that it's no surprise that it is totally Wacom-compatible. Painter 6 has added built-in Intuos compatibility, including full use of the airbrush pen.

Live Picture 2.6

Live Picture was the first major program to use proxy editing, and it was adopted by quite a few professional illustrators when it first arrived on the scene. At the time, the several hundred megabytes of memory required for compositing images at the resolutions required by ad agencies cost thousands of dollars to accomplish in Photoshop. Because Live Picture works with a low-resolution proxy of the original image, it could composite many layers in a file of several hundred megabytes, even when there was as little as 64MB of RAM in the computer. Computers were a great deal slower then, too. Live Picture's proxy editing made it practical to do all manner of image manipulation and distortion in real time, making it doubly attractive. Professional photographic illustrators of the caliber of John Lund and Gerald Bybee paid over two thousand dollars for the program. Today the program is much more capable, more Photoshop-compatible, and costs less than $300. The annoying hardware protection device is gone, too.

Installed base

Live Picture is still used mostly by professional photodigital illustrators. Therefore, its installed base is relatively small, although it has pretty much managed to keep the professional image-compositing and distortion-effects markets all to itself.

Interface familiarity

The program's interface was designed by Kai Krause, who is famous for playful and highly visual interfaces that bear the unique stamp of his personality (and, usually, the KPT logo). Once you get used to Live Picture's interface, you'll find it highly useful — especially for the purpose for which it's intended. However, if you're used to Photoshop-derived interfaces, you have a learning curve ahead. One look at Figure 11-14 will give you a good idea of what I mean.

Painting and retouching

This isn't the program for detailed painting and retouching. That's not to say that Live Picture can't do it. You'll certainly want to smooth some edges in Live Picture. You'll want to add colors or change the coloring of some objects, too. It's just easier to retouch small details in pixel-oriented programs such as Photoshop, and then complete the big picture in Live Picture.

Live Picture has a limited range of brush sizes, and brush shapes are limited to circles. This isn't as limiting as it sounds, however, because the circumference of the brush stays the same regardless of the magnification of the image. Therefore, if you want to work on details, you just zoom way in. However, this does represent a new workflow that takes some getting used to.

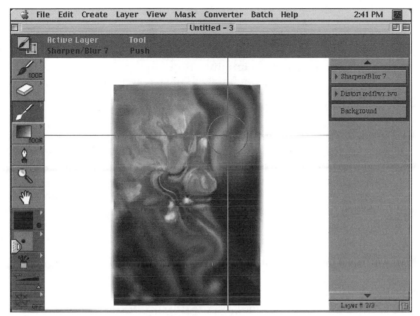

Figure 11-14: Live Picture has two interfaces: one for positioning layers, the other for making creative manipulations. This is the Creation workspace. Note the layers in the palette on the right.

Image editing

Image editing is a mixed bag. You don't get the "50 ways to skin a cat" sort of flexibility that Photoshop offers when it comes to adjusting image values. On the other hand, the fact that you are working in layers for each operation makes it easy to go back to a particular adjustment and change it. Remember, you're always working on a proxy, so no matter how many changes you've made to the image, nothing is ever modified until the image is rendered. At that time, Live Picture modifies the original image structure only exactly as much as is needed in order to produce the result.

Special-effects processing

Live Picture 2.6 is compatible with Photoshop 3 filters — meaning that some of the newer filters may not be compatible. You even have a choice of having the filter affect the composite image or only the active layer.

Live Picture is also capable of adjusting the transparency of layer images, and uses its brushes to enable you to control transparency in specific areas as well.

Calibration and pre-press preparation

Live Picture 2.6 is pre-Photoshop 5 state-of-calibration. In other words, you cannot embed ICC profiles in the file. However, in all other respects it is compliant with all calibration standards.

Ease of navigation

Live Picture's navigation is through *views*. Each view is a different proxy image. You can create different effects and edits in each view, and in the end everything will be integrated with the whole. It's not as intuitive as getting around in Photoshop's Navigator, but it works well enough and makes sense given the proxy technology that makes Live Picture tick.

Image compositing

This is Live Picture's forte. So far, nothing I've seen beats it. This is because proxy editing lets you work huge files in real time. All the layers remain active until render time, so you can make any change the art director wants — even long after you thought you were done (as long as you kept a copy of the prerendered file). The masking and edge-blending tools make it easy to create object edges that blend perfectly smoothly with surrounding objects — leaving no hint that yours is a "cut-and-paste" production. Most important, the pixels from the original are actually rearranged once. The result is minimal loss of detail and quality.

Wacom compatibility

Live Picture is Wacom-compatible, but pressure doesn't change the size of the brush. It only changes the intensity of the effect.

Corel Photo-Paint 9

Corel Photo-Paint has been included in the very popular CorelDraw suite for several versions now. Amazingly, this program is being enhanced and nurtured almost to the same degree as CorelDraw itself. Now that these programs are shipping for both Macintosh and Windows platforms, Adobe has a fierce competitor on two fronts.

Installed base

CorelDraw became the de facto standard illustration program for the Windows environment while Adobe took its time porting Illustrator and Photoshop to Windows. Corel's pricing and the strength of the capabilities offered by a bundle that can supply all the needs of a corporate graphics department keep it highly popular.

Interface familiarity

Photo-Paint's interface has become increasingly integrated with the CorelDraw interface, making it unique. Still, you're not likely to have much trouble recognizing the function of the tool icons. Learning the command menus will take a bit longer. You can see the Corel Photo-Paint 8 interface in Figure 11-15.

Figure 11-15: Two of the Photo-Paint palettes are shown: The Brush Tool Settings and the Objects options.

Painting and retouching

Photo-Paint offers a decent collection of (very basic) natural-media brushes: brush, pencil, crayon, charcoal, chalk, spray can, calligraphic pen, highlighter, marker, and felt-tip pen. Choose any of these and you can find numerous variations on a drop-down menu in the Brush Tools palette.

The clone brush can be either aligned or not. You can also clone from a saved file, so you can imitate the effect you get when you clone to a new layer in Painter.

Image editing

Photo-Paint has a companion feature to Photoshop's Adjustment layers. The Photo-Paint version is called *lenses*. Photo-Paint has more types of lenses than Photoshop has Adjustment layer types. Many of the additional types let you create filter effects, such as impressionist brush strokes or noise. Image adjustments are even a bit more powerful than in Photoshop. You can also run plug-ins from inside the image adjustment dialog boxes, so you can filter and make the adjustment at the same time.

Special-effects processing

Photo-Paint 9 is not compatible with Photoshop plug-ins, but its native effects are more versatile and more powerful than most of those in Photoshop — particularly with respect to artistic filters and 3D filters. There are also some amazing special effects. For instance, you can make it rain or snow and even fill the sky with stars. Almost all of Photo-Paint's special-effects filters let you see a preview of the image before you have to commit. Furthermore, almost all present you with a wide range of adjustments, so you have powerful control over such things as noise patterns, line thickness, and just about anything else you can think of.

 Tip   If you're a professional illustrator or need to do a variety of special effects, you may well find it worth your while to purchase Photo-Paint 9 for its special effects filters alone. At $99, this program costs less than most sets of Photoshop filters.

Calibration and pre-press preparation

There is no monitor calibration utility similar to Adobe Gamma included with Photo-Paint 9, so you're best advised to use a system-wide monitor and printer calibration program such as ColorBlind ProveIt!

Ease of navigation

The spacebar works to get you a Hand tool, but only when it's not being co-opted by something else, such as switching between palettes. There's a navigation bar at the top of the screen that will take you to any degree of magnification. You can also zoom directly to active objects.

You can't press Tab (or do anything else) to toggle the palettes on and off all at once. It would be much easier if you could do so.

Automation

You can assign keyboard shortcuts to any Photo-Paint tool or command. You can also customize palettes and toolbars. Photo-Paint also has a rich macro recording language. You can save macros and play them back on any file. The Macintosh version of Photo-Paint uses AppleScript as its scripting language.

Image compositing

In Photo-Paint, layers are called *objects*. As in Painter, the layers are trimmed to include only the visible pixels (unless you force the program to do otherwise).

There is a Pen tool for drawing and saving vector shapes. These shapes can be automatically converted to selections. Photo-Paint's Noise lens is the best tool I've found for interactively creating grain patterns that will match another area of the image. Finally, there's a History brush and an object nozzle.

Web image preparation

Photo-Paint can convert any image to any of the three Web image file formats: GIF, JPEG, or PNG. You are given a fair degree of control over the appearance of optimally compressed files. You can even preview your image while changing settings so that you can see the result you would get before you save the file. This is one of the great advantages of standalone programs such as Adobe ImageReady and Macromedia Fireworks (see Chapter 13).

You can also make image maps in Photo-Paint. The method's a bit strange: You assign links to the objects (layers) in an image. If you want to cut different areas of a photograph into an image map, you simply place each image on a different object level, click a tab, and assign an URL. The program also provides the means to publish your image maps as either client-side, server-side, or both.

Photo-Paint also lets you create movies. You can use an image as a background, and layer objects as the moving "actors." You can then designate a number of frames and place the objects in the proper location in each frame to give the illusion that the objects are in motion when the movie is played back. Movies can be saved in either Corel's movie format or as animated GIFs.

Wacom compatibility

Photo-Paint 8 is compatible with pressure-sensitive pads. The pressure sensitivity can be made to affect either brush size, color transparency, or both.

iGrafx Picture Publisher 8

Picture Publisher is a Web-repurposed powerhouse image-editing package. The program is limited to Windows computers, but it has just about any feature you could want, cranks out the work, and sells for peanuts. iGrafx throws in a collection of stock photos.

Note   By the time you read this, iGrafx has plans to roll Picture Publisher into a multi-purpose tool for creating both vector and bitmapped images. The announced name for this new product is iGrafx Designer. At that time, you may find that the program has some new capabilities.

Installed base

I never have understood why this program has had such a tough time gaining a foothold. Sadly, the company never delivered a promised Mac version. That may be at least part of the reason, as Mac addicts get a lot of respect when it comes to imaging. This is due, no doubt, to the fact that the majority of the well-known digital artists are Mac users (though this seems to be very slowly changing). Regardless, you have plenty of reasons to choose Picture Publisher if you're a Windows user.

Not only will you have a tough time getting a better balance of price and performance, you'll also get a top-notch Web graphics tool, some natural-media paint tools, and the ability to work in proxy-editing mode. You'll also get a free library of 10,000 stock photos.

Interface familiarity

Picture Publisher's interface is no Photoshop copycat, but you'll recognize the meaning of most of the icons. There are also some features whose names won't instantly identify their purpose, because people have tended to accept Photoshop's terms for that feature as generic. For instance, there's the use of *objects* as the term for *layers;* and selections are automatically called *masks,* even if they haven't yet been saved to a channel. You won't notice these minor distractions as you become more familiar with the product. Of course, if you haven't already been trained in Photoshop and don't have to trade info with Photoshop users, it won't be a problem anyway. For a look at Picture Publisher's interface, see Figure 11-16.

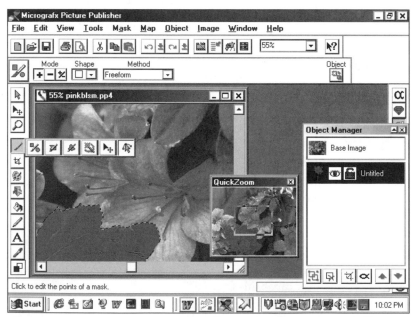

Figure 11-16: This is the Picture Publisher interface. Almost all the tools have multiple fly-out options. All the tool setting options are shown in the horizontal icon bar just above the image-editing window, making it very easy to change settings as you work.

Painting and retouching

No problem here. There's a full range of standard brushes and a selection of natural-media brushes whose power falls somewhere in between Photo-Paint's and Paint Shop Pro's. There's also a very capable Clone tool.

There is a built-in macro for automatically removing red-eye, so you don't have to step down to a SOHO editor to get that capability.

Image editing

Picture Publisher has outstanding image-editing capabilities. It provides even more ways to adjust the colors and values in an image than does Photoshop. It even has visual modes for both color balance and brightness/contrast. Because the thumbnails for each of these operations are separate, the images present a larger preview.

Picture Publisher's version of the History brush is superior as well. You can delete any command without deleting any that follow it. The image is then reprocessed as though that particular command had never been issued.

Special-effects processing

Picture Publisher claims to be 100 percent compatible with Photoshop plug-ins. I didn't test them all, but those I did test worked well. Picture Publisher also sports quite a few filters of its own. Most imitate some of Photoshop's built-in filters.

Calibration and pre-press preparation

Picture Publisher has a very easy-to-use monitor gamma utility, similar to Photoshop's. The program can also make use of the Kodak Color Management System and ICC device profiles. There is no way, however, to embed ICC profiles in the image files.

Ease of navigation

There's a QuickZoom window that is similar to Photoshop's Navigator. You can instantly move to any part of the image by dragging a zoom rectangle around the part of the image you want to view. Also, you can press the spacebar and drag any existing zoom rectangle to a new location. QuickZoom is shown in Figure 11-17.

Figure 11-17: With the QuickZoom you can instantly move anywhere in the image at exactly the zoom level you desire — just drag a new rectangle.

Image compositing

One very nice feature is that you can automatically feather the edges of objects to blend them with their surroundings. There's no need to make a selection, invert it, and then erase—as you would have to do in order to get the same effect in Photoshop. The list of blend modes is quite a bit shorter than Photoshop's, but the ones you're most likely to use are all there.

Automation

Picture Publisher has recordable macros, and can batch-process file conversions.

Web image preparation

This is the area that iGrafx is focusing on of late. If this product weren't such a capable professional image-editing program, you'd be reading about it in Chapter 25. The program has a built-in animated GIF builder, has incorporated one of the very best JPEG compression utilities (from Digital Frontiers), and provides excellent previews when saving to Web file formats (see Figure 11-18).

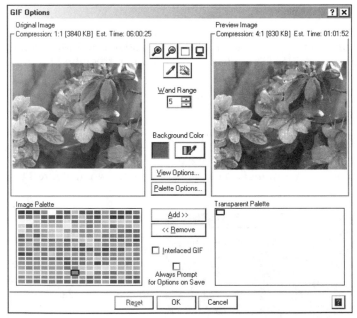

Figure 11-18: The Picture Publisher GIF Options dialog box lets you preview cutouts against any color background. From the existing background, you can select colors that will become transparent on export. Click the Monitor icon and the result of your settings is shown full-screen.

Wacom compatibility

Picture Publisher is compatible with pressure-sensitive digitizing pads. You can set the pen to be sensitive to size, transparency, or both. There are no tilt or eraser settings, however.

Paint Shop Pro 5

Paint Shop Pro started life as shareware. Because it has always been a solid product with above-average image-editing capabilities and "feels" like Photoshop, the program became very popular. Even now, it's a rare bargain at under $100. It has even inspired a few books. Now in version 5, it has added layers and can import layered files from Photoshop. The program is now almost fully compatible with Wacom tablets — save the Intuos features that came after the latest Paint Shop Pro revisions.

Installed base

Paint Shop Pro has a large installed base, but there is no Macintosh version. It has won a soft spot in the hearts of serious amateurs and students whose budgets can't yet accommodate Photoshop.

Interface familiarity

Though not quite an imitation of Photoshop's interface, it could be fairly said that Paint Shop Pro is an excellent Photoshop training camp (see Figure 11-19).

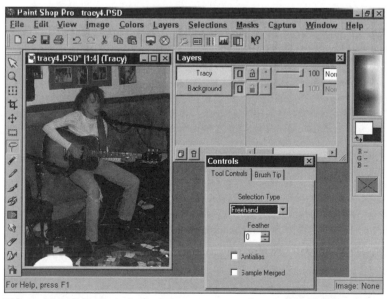

Figure 11-19: No pale imitation, you can see instantly that this program has most of the functionality of Photoshop. Note the layer menu and the Tool Controls.

Painting and retouching

In addition to having nearly all of Photoshop's painting and retouching capabilities, Paint Shop Pro offers an equivalent to Painter's Image Hose and a few natural-media effects for brushes: crayon, chalk, charcoal, pen, marker, and pencil. You can also add a paper texture to strokes. The natural-media effects don't rival Painter's, but they're useful all the same.

Paint Shop Pro 5 also has unlimited undos and a History Brush feature. Darkroom tools are even more comprehensive than Photoshop's.

Image editing

Paint Shop Pro gives you considerable latitude over adjusting the qualities of the image, but doesn't do it with quite the finesse and polish of Photoshop 5.5. You can control where the blacks, whites, and midtones fall in a dialog box that also lets you use droppers to pick the white, mid, and black points in the image. You can also control gamma with a Curve dialog box, but you can't control where each point on the curve falls, as in Photoshop. Color balance controls are excellent. You can also colorize objects, and can posterize (change the number bit-per-pixel, another way of changing the number of colors).

Special-effects processing

Paint Shop Pro is completely compatible with Photoshop import/export plug-ins and filters.

Calibration and pre-press preparation

Paint Shop Pro supports the preparation of CMYK color separations. There's also a fundamental monitor calibration utility for adjusting Gamma that's quite similar to Photoshop's.

Ease of navigation

Navigation around large images is perfectly standard: scrollbars and magnifiers. There is no Hand tool for panning and scrolling, and nothing equivalent to views or a navigation window.

Image compositing

While Paint Shop Pro doesn't have nearly the power to squish and deform portions of an image as LivePicture, it does have a freeform deformation brush and a push brush that accomplish a similar purpose.

Layers lack image adjustment capabilities, but otherwise are on a par with the power of Photoshop's layers.

Web image preparation

You can save files to Web formats, including GIF, JPEG, and PNG. However, you have no control over the degree of color reduction, the compression method, palettes, or other factors that can be critically important when optimizing graphics for the Web. For that, you'll still want a program such as Macromedia Fireworks or Adobe ImageReady.

On a more positive note, Paint Shop Pro does come with a program that does GIF animations.

Wacom compatibility

Paint Shop Pro is fully Wacom-compatible.

Summary

This chapter has reviewed the leading professional image-editing software. Although there isn't room to cover every worthy program here, several others — despite not being as well known — certainly bear looking into. Among these are Wright Design and Deneba Canvas. In the next chapter, we'll look at the incredible values you can get in image-editing software, for those of you whose needs are more basic and who have a more limited budget for software. I think you'll be surprised to discover just how much power you can get for a fraction of the price of Photoshop, Painter, or LivePicture.

✦　　✦　　✦

Choosing Small Office/Home Office Image-Processing Software

Here's a quick and dirty definition of SOHO image-processing software: *Software that lets you make your photographs look professional in a few button clicks.* It must have a user interface that even the computer-phobic can warm up to. It is software that has to be so affordable that you're willing to take a chance on working with it even if you don't understand its function (think of it as "point-and-click" software for people who use "point-and-click" cameras).

What Is SOHO Image-Processing Software?

The acronym SOHO sounds cool, but its meaning would be clearer if it were called *SBHO,* for *small business/home office.* After all, few of us think of image-processing software as business software. Nonetheless, thousand of entrepreneurs, consultants, and small businesses (which I define as businesses in which many employees perform in multiple job categories) make use of images. More and more of these businesses are using their computers and software to process and publish those images internally. Very few of these businesses are in the photography, advertising, illustration, or printing industries. Those industries will use the software covered in Chapter 15.

The rest of us will prefer more affordable, easier-to-use software that covers applications for photography that go beyond the processing and basic retouching of the photo. Such extra capabilities might include the ability to place photos in business publications and promotional documents, make family photo albums, and manage image libraries. Some might even automate the process of placing your photos on the family or company Web site or stitch your pictures into a panoramic view.

Is SOHO image-processing software good enough for your needs?

I know professional photographers who adamantly insist that we shouldn't do more to a photograph digitally than can be done in a conventional darkroom. If you're one of those, a SOHO program is probably all you'll ever need.

Caution   If you're a professional (or *prosumer* — a serious amateur) intending to use SOHO image-processing software, make sure the program has no limitation on file size and that you're using a computer that's fast enough to process large images.

I also know professional photographers who use SOHO software to prep their images for client approval. They want something that they can have their receptionist or assistant use to quickly process the dozens of images taken in a day's shoot so that each is blemish-free and has the correct exposure and color balance. It's a step that costs little, saves time later, and makes them look like even better photographers.

If your business, family, or fraternity uses a lot of photos and you want a product that will make you look much more accomplished as a photographer, you'll find SOHO image-processing software a perfect fit — at least until you get into it so deeply that you want to go further. When that happens, what the heck, you only spent $50 or so.

Key Features of SOHO Image-Processing Software

Before you even begin to look at SOHO software at your local retailers, you should understand the primary functions of this type of software. You also need to know what features are most desirable to a given type of user and why.

User interface

Look for a program that is uncluttered by crowded toolboxes, space-hogging palettes, and telephone-directory–length menus. *KISS* (short for, *Keep It Simple, Stupid*) is definitely the principle that should have been applied to the interface design. Figure 12-1 compares the Photoshop 5 interface and the PhotoDeluxe interface.

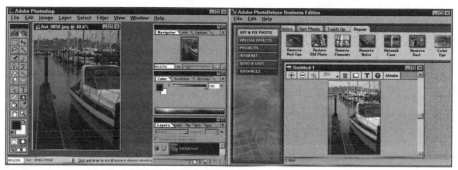

Figure 12-1: Compare the default Photoshop interface (left) to the interface for a typical operation in Adobe PhotoDeluxe 3.0.

Most of these programs prompt you through the steps needed in order to accomplish one of the basic tasks. Be wary of programs that overdo the hand-holding. You want help, but you don't want constant, unnecessary help.

Image input

All of the SOHO image-editing programs mentioned in this chapter will interface directly with TWAIN devices. Most will also interface with Photoshop plug-ins, so you can directly acquire images from a scanner or Photo CD. Sooner or later, you're likely to want to make use of Photo CD (or its close relative, Picture CD).

All image-processing programs give you access to the majority of established bitmapped image file formats. It's a bonus if they keep up with the latest developments and give you direct access to PNG, Photo CD, and LivePix formats.

Make sure that the program you choose doesn't place a limit on image size. You want to have the freedom to store your images at the highest resolution at which you can acquire them—then you'll always be able to use them for any purpose.

Note   Remember that you can never make a digital picture contain more information than the original.

Image processing

The program you choose should do a good job of correcting brightness, contrast, and gamma (the intensity curve between light and dark) in a mouse click or two. You won't know if this is really the case unless you do a little testing with a variety of familiar images. Of course, that may be difficult to do if you want to buy the program off the Internet or from a mass merchandiser. The next best thing is to read the online publications that cater to digital photographers. You'll find a list of these in Appendix B at the back of this book. Also, you want an option to use a manual brightness/contrast control. There will be times when you'll find it advantageous to interpret an image as brighter (ephemeral beauty, burning deserts) or darker (night scenes, mysterious or evil characters) than would otherwise be "correct" exposure.

Color balance is a little tougher. If you pick a program that forces you to balance color automatically, there will be times when you're going to get some pretty bizarre results. For instance, if you shoot late in the evening and want to retain the orange-ish mood of the light, being forced to rely on automatic color balancing might make a picture look as if it were shot at noon, rather than at sunset.

Look for some special-effects processing. Most of these programs are compatible with Photoshop plug-in filters, but you'll want built-in effects for blurring, sharpening, motion blurs, and drop shadows. Then you'll at least be able to achieve the most frequently needed effects without having to pay more for the effect than you paid for your processing software.

Image editing

Making precise enough selections when you combine the selected object with a new background takes training and talent — or very smart software. Otherwise, the subject you want placed on a plain background or in a fantasy scene will show a ragged seam around its silhouette. The problem is, the person who is most likely to be in the market for SOHO processing software is least likely to practice enough to be perfect. So you need very smart selection software. Two tools are especially valuable: an *automatic lasso* and a *magic wand* with a feature that clears holes from inside a selection.

An automatic lasso snaps the selection between obviously contrasting pixels as you drag the cursor around the perimeter of the object you want to select. Magic wands select all the contiguous pixels that fall within a specified range of the same colors. This makes it easy to select shapes that contrast strongly with their surroundings. Unfortunately, those shapes usually have spots of contrasting or darker colors that fall within their selection boundaries. So once they select the shape, there are holes in the selection. Luckily, there's a button you can click to zap the holes, saving you lots of time and anguish.

Automatic cleanup

It's nearly impossible to keep dust and scratches away from film and off the glass on your scanner. Too often, you'll even get Photo CD and CD-ROM scans from your service bureau that show these defects. Another very common problem is that older photographs may have become cracked and spotted from lack of careful handling and storage.

Fixing tiny scratches and spots can be painstaking and time-consuming. Most SOHO programs have a tool that automatically corrects these problems. You simply drag a marquee around the affected area and click the "fixit" tool.

 Caution Automatic cleanup (scratch and dust removal) works brilliantly most of the time. However, there will be times when automatically repaired areas will simply become too soft, or grainless. That's because most of these tools achieve their results by intermingling pixels where there is a stark contrast between the pixels. If you have a lot of texture in that area (think of a herringbone jacket or a field of carpet grass), it is suddenly lost.

You can work around the occasional "auto-fix" problem if you also have a Clone tool. If you didn't read the previous chapter, a Clone tool is a brush that lets you pick up pixels from one area of the image and replicate them wherever the brush touches down. In other words, you can take the texture from one area and paint with it in another area.

Image management

Any SOHO processor worth its salt provides you with some way to visually recognize your images. The best ones will automatically show thumbnails of the images in any directory you choose during a File ⇨ Open command (although it may be called something like "Get the Picture"). Others may have to open the image beforehand to create the thumbnail, so it's only useful for pictures that you've already worked on with that particular processing software.

It is also very helpful if the program lets you rename images and rotate their thumbnails without having to first open the image. This is a good thing for two reasons. First, it saves you time and may preserve the quality of your images. The second reason needs a little explanation. Most digital cameras save their images in JPEG format in order to conserve space on their digital memory cards (or digital film, as it's often called). Every time an image is stored in JPEG format, it is recompressed. JPEG compression is *lossy*—that is, it achieves a high ratio between the image size and the file size by considering some dissimilar pixels to be similar. So the more you have to open and resave a JPEG file, the worse its image quality becomes.

Automatic framing

Automatic framing may at first seem like nothing more than a cute gimmick. However, you can often greatly enhance the appearance of pictures if they are framed in the context of a Web page, presentation slide, or promotional flyer. Of course, they look nice in family albums or on postcards, too. Figure 12-2 shows the framing interface for PhotoDeluxe.

Figure 12-2: PhotoDeluxe forces you to scale an image to fit its frames.

The best programs give you a choice of picture frames that can be automatically placed around your active photo. Some programs even enable you to go to the framing interface and simply load any image on any drive into the selected frame. And some programs automatically size the frame to fit the image, while others force you to scale the image to fit the frame. I prefer the first approach because it means that I can crop my image for the exact composition I want. The frame will then match the composition.

If you need to use framing a lot, look for a program that has framing styles that you like. I find most of them too frilly or ornamental, and would prefer at least a choice of more modern and subtle styles.

Caution Use automatic frames sparingly on Web sites. Attractive as they are, they can add considerable bulk to the size of the file. Remember that there are more pixels (bits of data) around the edges of an image than at the center.

Document publishing

All the SOHO image-processors come with a variety of templates for documents into which you can drop your images. You can then print them out on your laser printer or color inkjet. You can create all sorts of useful short-run documents in this fashion. Examples are business cards, greeting cards, flyers and bulletins, letter-heads, and many others.

The question is not whether the package you choose will do this — most will. The question is whether the style and type of templates that you want are available with the package you choose. Another good question is whether more templates are available for download elsewhere. One of the best ways to check this out is to visit the software publisher's Web site. In fact, that's a good way to check for most of the details listed in this chapter. The promotional blurbs on the packaging may just not tell you enough. You will find a directory of manufacturer's and publisher's Web sites in Appendix B at the back of this book.

Web publishing

If you maintain your own Web site for showing your digital photography (or the results of incorporating it into your work), you may want to buy a SOHO package for the sole purpose of publishing images to your Web pages. There seems to be a trend afoot to add more and better Web publishing features to these programs. Some of them enable you to assign links to all the thumbnails in a directory and then automatically publish them to a thumbnails page on your site, as well as publishing the pages to which the individual pictures are linked. It's a great way to keep your site dynamic without spending much time on site maintenance.

These programs vary quite a bit in the way they do Web publishing; especially as regards the amount of tweaking you can do to maximize compression of the images and how automated the publishing routine is.

Choosing SOHO Image-Processing Software

There are many SOHO image-processing software products, far too many to cover them all in this book. I've chosen those products that seem to strike the best balance between being easy to use, having the capability to turn out professional-looking photos, and solving commonly encountered business problems. The programs covered in this chapter are as follows:

✦ Adobe Systems *PhotoDeluxe 3.0* (Macintosh and Windows. Home Edition, $49.95; Business Edition, $79)

✦ ScanSoft's *Kai's Photo Soap 2* (Macintosh and Windows, $29.95)

✦ Microsoft *Picture It! 99* (Windows only, $54.95)

✦ Xaos Tool's *Flashbox* (Windows only, $49)

Some of these products have capabilities that are covered in greater depth in other chapters of this book. Those capabilities are special-effects filters, Web image preparation, and panoramic stitching. You may want to read those sections before deciding whether one of the following programs is worth the puny $50 investment.

PhotoDeluxe 3.0

Adobe wastes no time letting you know that PhotoDeluxe is based on the same image-processing engine as Photoshop. That in itself is a pretty high recommendation. I feel some sense of security in knowing that if I pre-process images in PhotoDeluxe for quick client approval, I can open the result in Photoshop and proceed from there without any rude surprises. In other words, the picture will look the same in Photoshop as it did in PhotoDeluxe.

Cross-Reference

Because both programs are from the same publisher, there are many similarities between PhotoDeluxe and Photoshop; you may want to flip to Chapter 11, which covers professional image-processing software.

Image input

PhotoDeluxe features a command called Photo Direct Access that can eliminate the need for using digital camera software. Whenever the right drive has been present, I've found this a blessing in testing cameras for this book. I don't have to load the software for each camera. Furthermore, the software that acquires the image is consistent across cameras. That makes it possible to get a better idea of whether a problem such as soft images is caused by poor optics or by software interpretation of the compressed file. It would be nice if Photo Direct Access were smart enough to recognize any camera that happened to be attached to the serial port, a USB port, or a FireWire port. No such luck—at least not in this version. So far, the software recognizes only a few of the lower-end cameras from Kodak, Nikon, Olympus, and Epson (see Figure 12-3). As time goes by, it is reasonable to expect that you will find more and more drivers posted on the Adobe site.

Figure 12-3: The Photo Direct Access feature, showing the camera drivers that originally shipped with PhotoDeluxe Business Edition

PhotoDeluxe gives you direct access (no plug-in needed) to a very long list of bitmapped file formats. Most important, Adobe has kept up with the latest developments and will directly import PNG, LivePix, and Photo CD formats. It will also open and automatically rasterize (convert to bitmap) EPS vector files that have a TIFF preview attached.

Image processing (exposure and color balance)

PhotoDeluxe makes image processing a snap—or I should say a click. It has Extensis' Intellihance feature built in. Click its icon and the "most likely" tonal and color corrections are made automatically. About 80 percent of the time, these corrections are done better than an inexperienced operator could do on his or her own. For those times when you don't get the result you want, PhotoDeluxe uses a simplified version of Photoshop's Variations palette, which shows the image with several variations in color balance. You can click any of these multiple times to change the result seen in the Current Pick thumbnail (see Figure 12-4). When you like the image you see in the Current Pick, just click OK. If the cumulative result of your clicking gets too bizarre, just click Cancel and start over.

Figure 12-4: The Variations palette lets you visually pick the color balance you like by clicking its thumbnail.

If all the easy routes fail, you still have the basic brightness/contrast and RGB color balance sliders. They're as complex as you can make image-processing in PhotoDeluxe.

Special-effects processing includes many of the most frequently used Photoshop filters: Colored Pencil, Bas Relief, Note Paper, Crackle, Solarize, Accented Edges, Emboss, Pinch, Ripple, Shear, Sphere, Twirl, Pond Ripple, Negative, Soften, Noise, Circular, Wind, Page Curl, Chalk & Charcoal, Cloud Texture, Chrome, Neon Glow, Patchwork, and Funnel.

You can also fill selections with a solid color or gradient, create drop shadows from text or objects, feather the selection, or change the image to black and white (actually grayscale).

Image selection and compositing

PhotoDeluxe has two "modes" of operation: Easy, the default mode, lets beginners do the basics without having to practice or learn much. Advanced mode lets you operate the program from a considerably extended menu bar. If you're going to do any pixel-specific selecting and compositing, you'll quickly find yourself operating in Advanced mode. That's because Easy mode only offers two selection tools: a rectangle and a magic wand. Advanced mode adds freehand (trace) and polygon lassos. There is also an automatic lasso that snaps to the edge of contrasting areas of pixels; and an oval selection tool in addition to the rectangle.

PhotoDeluxe also has layers, so you can select objects and stack them atop one another to create a composite image. There's no Layers palette on any of the menus or buttons, but if you click the right mouse button, you get a Layers palette. It looks and acts very much like Photoshop's. If you want to change the stacking order, you just select the item you want to move and then drag it up or down. Just as in Photoshop, you can click the Eye icon to hide or reveal a layer. As you might expect, there are many fewer blend modes. In order to access them, change a layer, or name a layer, you have to double-click the layer name bar in the Layers palette. Figure 12-5 shows the Layers palette and the Layer Options dialog box.

Figure 12-5: The PhotoDeluxe Layers palette is a simplified version of Photoshop's.

Automated cleanup (scratches and dust)

PhotoDeluxe lets you automatically clean three of the problems that commonly occur with low-end digital cameras and digitized images: scratches and dust, Moiré patterns, and JPEG artifacts. It seems to accomplish all three with a minimum of unnecessary blurring of the image. The code seems to take into account that the more highly contrasting edges of shapes should be left alone while the image is corrected in areas where pixels are more similar to one another (see Figure 12-6).

Image management

PhotoDeluxe creates a thumbnail only after you've opened and saved an image. It also creates thumbnails after downloading images directly from a camera. From that time on, any time you open a directory containing files that have been processed in PhotoDeluxe, the thumbnails will show up in the Easy Photo browser (see Figure 12-7).

Figure 12-6: You can see in the preview window that graininess has been reduced, while the edges of the apple and stem are razor-sharp.

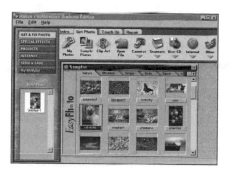

Figure 12-7: Subfolders in a directory are indicated by the tabs at the top of the thumbnails browser. Thumbnails are large enough to be easily recognized. Double-click a thumbnail and the file opens automatically.

Automatic framing

There are a mere thirteen frame styles to choose from, each in a horizontal and vertical version, for a total of 26 frames. Frames can't be sized to fit the image, but they come in three sizes: 3 × 5, 4 × 6, and 5 × 7. When you place a photo in the frame (by dragging it in from the Hold Photo window), it is easy to drag handles in order to scale the image to fit the frame. Of course, this may cause some loss of image data. It's not usually too serious, as you're not making a large change in the number of pixels.

Document publishing

This is where the business edition of PhotoDeluxe really shines. There are thousands of templates to choose from and more are available through the Business Week Business Guided Activities Web site. Most of the templates are small-office–oriented. You can choose from calendars, holiday cards, business cards, invitations, albums, event tickets, Web banners, Web background images, buttons, titles, framed and drop-shadowed photos, labels (for floppies, CD-ROMs, video and audio tapes in several styles), letterhead, envelopes, report covers, compliment slips, flyers, coupons, direct mail cards, retail displays, and T-shirt transfers.

Web publishing

PhotoDeluxe can send your image to a Web page if you have Adobe PageMill installed. First it sends the image to the application. You then use PageMill to publish your page to the Net.

The Send to Web Page button will also save your images to GIF or JPEG format. If you want to save to PNG, you have to use the ordinary File ➪ Save routine. However, there's no optimization on the level of Adobe Image Ready or Macromedia Fireworks that helps you compress and preview your images for maximum Web efficiency.

Kai's Photo Soap 2

As you might guess from the fact that it's called Kai's Photo Soap, this is the SOHO image processor with the interface you want to hug. It's just downright pretty to look at. Photo Soap is also the program to use if you have a Web site for images. Because the interface actually uses QuickTime movies to animate some of its icons, you'll need to install QuickTime 3.0 on your system. Don't panic — it's free and available on the Soap CD-ROM.

Image input

Photo Soap 2's image input is Photoshop-standard. You can open most of the common graphics file formats, including LivePix, but not PNG. You can also use any of the Photoshop plug-ins and open any TWAIN-compliant device. So if your digital camera comes with a Photoshop plug-in, you'll be able to read the files directly from your camera.

Image processing (exposure and color balance)

Soap always works on a duplicate of the original photo. So no matter what you do, you haven't ruined the original until you consciously opt to write over it or throw it out. You can also make multiple changes to an image before they are rendered because nothing actually happens to the working image until you click an Apply button. This is especially nice if you're working with a low-resolution digital camera (or low-resolution digitized video images) because you have so few pixels to spare before the image becomes garbage. On top of that, Soap 2 has multiple levels of undo, so you can back up several steps if you make a mistake.

Image editing

Soap 2 has only one selection tool (a magic wand color-range selector), yet you can do compositing quite well. The program does have layers. You can apply transparency to layers and can apply a half-dozen or so of the most popular *blend modes* (mathematical calculations between layers that create visual effects). You can also change the size of layers, crop them, and rotate them. So how do you cut out objects to combine them into a new scene (composite photo)? You erase away the part of the image that you don't need using Soap's Eraser tool.

You can adjust contrast or run effects over the entire image in a single step. You can also brush on the same controls. Because you can adjust the transparency, size, fade rate, and spacing for all the brushes, you have considerable control over how burning, dodging, contrast control, and even the Find Edges filters are applied. An eraser tool can also be used to erase part of the area that a brush covered.

Automatic cleanup (scratches and dust)

Soap's brushes can be used for cleanup and repair. One of the cleanup tasks is cloning, and you can clone with any of the brushes. You can also brush on red-eye elimination. You can use brushes to auto-remove dust and scratches in specific areas, thus avoiding softening the entire photo. You can also throw specific areas of the image out of focus by apply a blur effect with a brush (see Figure 12-8). Cleanup effects include sharpen, blur, smooth, heal, red-eye, clone, and plug-ins. This means that you can brush on any plug-in effect.

Figure 12-8: Here you see the large brush after applying the blur effect to the area behind the artist's head. You can switch from Brush mode to Overall Image mode by clicking the Brush icon in the upper-right corner of the Effects palette.

Image management

One of Photo Soap 2's neatest tricks is its ability to quickly create thumbnails of any folder you open (see Figure 12-9).

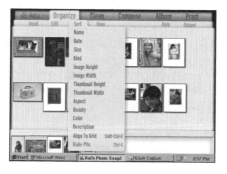

Figure 12-9: The group of images in the top section of the screen have been placed there simply by opening a folder from the Input menu. You place the images you want to work with in the tray below by dragging them. They are then available for any of Soap's other operations.

When files are opened, they are placed on Soap's (not your operating system's) desktop. If you drag images into piles, they're automatically grouped together when you double-click the top item in the stack. Then any command you can issue from the desktop, such as Delete or Sort, will be applied to all the images in that stack. In Figure 12-9, you'll notice that the desktop images can be sorted by many different criteria.

You can save a set of thumbnails so that you'll have the same group to work with the next time you need to return to the same or a similar project. You can switch the view of a set to a contact sheet or Lightbox view. Contact sheets automatically show the notes you've made on files. Lightbox view shows the images as a set of slides. Placing the cursor over the button in the lower right corner of the slide causes the data for that slide to appear. You can see both views in the composite screenshot shown in Figure 12-10.

You can rotate and rename files in any of these views without disturbing the original file. As I've pointed out earlier, this is important when organizing files downloaded from digital cameras.

If you want to work on one or more images in any of Soap's other command groups, you have to place them in the program's workspace.

Figure 12-10: This is a composite of two screens, each a different view of Soap's thumbnails. On the left is the Lightbox view; on the right is the Contact Sheet view.

Automatic framing

Well, Soap doesn't have any frames as such. It is hoped that you'll be able to download some from the Web site (www.scansoft.com/products/soap/). At the time of this writing, ScanSoft had just purchased the program from MetaCreations and had not yet posted the extra styles to their site. There are 24 album styles built into the program. Most of the album styles have several page layouts that you can pick and almost all of them require that you place more than one image on a page. If you're a photographer or an artist trying to show your work to maximum benefit, you want to show it at a size that fills the screen in most people's browsers. That means you want to show it at approximately 270 pixels high and no more than 575 pixels wide if it's to fit inside the borders of Internet Explorer running on a 13-inch monitor at 640×480 pixels. That is currently the case for about 80 percent of viewers.

The album styles are professionally designed. Most of the styles are of the "homey" variety (carved leather, weathered wood, wedding lace, and so on) but there are a few more business-like styles.

To create an album, you just choose a style and a page layout. Then you drag an image from the image tray into any of the page's picture frames. If the picture is larger than the frame, the picture will automatically downsize itself to fit. If it's smaller than the frame, the frame will automatically size and proportion itself to fit the picture. This is just the way it should be to ensure maximum picture quality. You can get a good idea of how this interface works by looking at Figure 12-11.

Figure 12-11: To place a photo in an album, drag the picture from the image tray to the picture frame. The frame automatically sizes itself to fit the picture.

Document publishing

Soap doesn't come with any templates for publishing business documents. It has another very useful trick, however. You can print any mixture of multiple photos on a single sheet of paper. You can also print your contact sheets and albums.

Web publishing

Soap includes tools for direct publishing of thumbnails and albums to the Web. You can create an album from images that are all in a given folder (subdirectory). An entire page of thumbnails is created from the files in the folder. These files are automatically linked to pages in any album you create. Viewers browsing the resulting Web site can click a thumbnail and find themselves on the page of the album where the large version of the thumbnail resides. Viewers can then flip back and forth through the album pages, jump back to the thumbnails page, or switch to a different album. For photographers, artists, realtors, and catalog stores, this has to be the coolest thing ever.

FlashBox

FlashBox is very family-oriented. Its motto should be "fun with fotos." There are props and hairdos that you can add to photos of your friends to do "total makeovers." You can do plastic surgery, distort into caricatures, and add tattoos.

The FlashBox interface puts access to all the operational modes right in front of you. There's never any need to move the picture from one workflow space to another, as there is in Kai's Photo Soap. Figure 12-12 shows the FlashBox interface.

The emphasis, when it came to designing the tools for this program, was to make the operations quick and fun — not picky and precise.

Figure 12-12: The FlashBox interface

Image input

FlashBox lets you input directly from some Kodak cameras. Others could be added, but hadn't been as of this writing. You can also input from any TWAIN device, which gives you direct access to most scanners and even some digital cameras. You can open files from JPEG, BMP, PNG, Targa, or SGI. Unfortunately, there's no input from or output to PSD (layered Photoshop files), TIFF, PICT, Photo CD, or FlashPix.

Image processing

Image processing is much more automatic than is the case with either PhotoDeluxe or Kai's Photo Soap 2. All the controls can be either automatically applied to the entire image or brushed on with either a small, medium, or large brush. Brushes are the same size on the screen, regardless of zoom level. So if you want to work on a very small area, you zoom way in and then work with the small brush.

Image editing (selection and compositing)

You can work in multiple layers and control the transparency of layers. However, there's no Layers palette. If you want to select a hidden layer, you have to use a tool to bring it to the top of the stack, and then click it.

Note   FlashBox has no selection tools. However, you can erase parts of an image with a brush so that you can see underlying layers in a composite.

There are also built-in images that you can use for compositing. There are numerous props that are cutout images from the Clement Mok PhotoDisc Objects collection. These can be placed and scaled so that you can put popcorn, bowling pins, or anything else you'd like into your picture. There are also collections of props and tools called Xubes that are grouped according to effects for creating particular categories of pictures, such as Garden (hoses, flowers, butterflies) or Body (tattoos, clothing). Each of the theme boxes contains tools that let you spray on small cutout images.

Automated cleanup

There are cleanup tools for both scratches and red-eye. You can apply these to either the entire image or you can brush the effect into specific areas. There's a healthy range of darkroom tools that let you recolor, burn, dodge, and auto-correct

Image management

FlashBox has an equivalent to the image tray in Soap called a *Shoebox*. Shoeboxes show strips of small thumbnails so that you can pick working images visually. You can make your own Shoebox, and several come with the program.

Automatic framing

This is one of FlashBox's strengths. There are dozens of frames. The frames can be resized to fit the image by dragging their corners. Most of the frames, however, are too cute and homey to be practical for use in business applications. You can get an idea of the frames, tools, and props available for the Garden Flowers Xube in Figure 12-13.

Figure 12-13: Choose an Xube and all the Projects, Backgrounds, Frames, Lettering, Props, Tools, and Special Effects bars extend across the screen. Clicking the down arrow on any of these bars reveals more of the options for that bar. To use any item, just click or drag it into your picture.

Document publishing

As you must have guessed by now, FlashBox doesn't present you with many templates for business documents. There are, however, many options for such projects as bookmarks, greeting cards, calendars, banners, and signs.

Web publishing

FlashBox has no special Web publishing capability. You just take the finished images and process them using the tools and instructions in Chapter 13.

Picture It! 99

The worst thing you can say about Microsoft's Picture It! 99 is that the best "image processing for dummies" software isn't (yet, at least) available for the Macintosh. Maybe Microsoft thinks that most dummies buy a PC? (I know; it's a bad joke, but I just couldn't resist.)

Three qualities really make Picture It! 99 stand out:

✦ **It has the most easily understood interface.** This is because the designers didn't feel that you had to get entirely away from the look and feel of a computer. So if you've used a computer, you'll still know how to open and save a file without having to crack the manual to find out which magical combination of buttons to click.

✦ **It offers fairly decent performance.** It's not nearly as quick as Photoshop, but you won't find yourself impatiently drumming your fingers nearly as often as you would with Soap, FlashBox, or PhotoDeluxe.

✦ **It has the best combination of home and business features.** For instance, there are templates for business cards, flyers, and certificates.

Image input

There's nothing magical or secret about how you open image files in Picture It! 99. You use the File ➪ Open command on the menu bar. As soon as you do, you're presented with a wizard-type interface that lets you open files from any type of a drive attached to your computer. All the latest trends in file formats are covered: Photo CD, TIFF, GIF, JPEG, PNG, and Macintosh PICT. You can also open and automatically rasterize several vector file formats: AutoCAD DXF, generic EPS (PostScript), CorelDraw, and enhanced metafiles. You can see the Picture It! file-opening interface in Figure 12-14.

Figure 12-14: As soon as you choose File ➪ Open, Picture It! presents this wizard to help you choose the right file. Once you've chosen a folder, the thumbnails are created automatically. You can open a file by dragging it onto the filmstrip at the bottom of the screen.

There's direct input from cameras that have a Photoshop plug-in module installed and from scanners with TWAIN interfaces.

Image processing

You can do all image processing either automatically, by adjusting sliders while previewing the results in the workspace; or by brushing the adjustments into specific areas. Image processing controls exist for brightness/contrast, color balance, and transparency. You don't have to turn previewing off and on — it's always working.

Image editing (selection and compositing)

This is a two-disk set, so there is room for hundreds of photographs, including skies and backgrounds. The program also uses layers, and you can see thumbnails of each layer as you work. You can drag layers to re-order the stack and can switch from working on one layer to working on another by clicking the target layer's thumbnail.

Picture It! 99 also has an edge-finding lasso that should be imitated by everyone. It drags a marquee to show the width of the pixels it uses to search for an edge. It's a visual aid that is a big help when it comes to selecting exactly the edge pixels you want. Of course, no automatic tool is perfect.

Automatic cleanup

This feature automatically removes dust spots, scratches, red-eye, and wrinkles. Picture It! 99 also has a Clone tool, so you can remove unsightly trash and telephone lines from your pictures. As is the case with FlashBox, brush sizes are the same regardless of zoom level. That means you have to zoom way out to make very large strokes, or way in to make very small ones.

Image management

Picture It! 99 doesn't create any permanent thumbnail files or contact sheets. You do see thumbnails of any compatible graphics files as soon as you open a folder that contains them. I wish Microsoft would make this a permanent feature of Windows.

Automatic framing

Framing is a piece of cake. You choose the frame from a visual catalog, and then drag the image from the filmstrip to the frame. The image is automatically placed behind the frame. All you have to do is scale the image to fit by dragging handles that appear automatically. Unfortunately, the frame doesn't rescale to fit the photo. If the image is too small, you'll have to stretch it to fit — losing detail in the process.

Document publishing

There aren't nearly as many business document templates as in the PhotoDeluxe Business Edition, but there are quite a few that are useful for business. These include business cards, several types of business announcements and greeting cards, a selection of flyers, and some certificates. You can see the interface for choosing a document template in Figure 12-15.

Publishing documents, like everything else in Picture It! 99, is a wizard-led procedure.

Web publishing

Picture It! 99 doesn't publish thumbnails or images directly to Web pages. Currently, that is the exclusive domain of Kai's Photo Soap 2. However, you can automatically send and e-mail greeting cards. You can also place any number of the images on the filmstrip into a slide show and then e-mail the slide show.

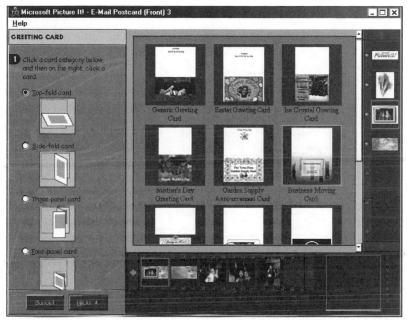

Figure 12-15: To choose a document template, just choose the style you like, drag the picture you want to include into the picture space, edit any of the text layers, and then click a button to print the file.

Summary

This chapter has covered the purpose and desirable features of low-cost digital photo processing software meant for use in the home and in small businesses. It started with a guide to the features you should hope to find in these programs. It also discussed why you should hope to find those features. The last third of the chapter covered the specific attributes and attractions of four of the most popular programs in this category: Adobe Systems' *PhotoDeluxe 3.0*, ScanSoft's *Kai's Photo Soap 2*, Microsoft's *Picture It! 99*, and Xaos Tool's *FlashBox*.

The next chapter takes a similar approach, introducing you to software whose core function is to produce performance-optimized images for publication on the Internet.

✦ ✦ ✦

Choosing Web Image-Processing Software

You can certainly use any of the image-processing software mentioned in the two previous chapters to prepare images for the Web. Simply converting an RGB file to indexed color and then saving it as a GIF file isn't tricky at all. It's even easier to save a file to JPEG format. So what's so special about software that specializes in preparing graphics for the Web? For one thing, images are used on the Web to call attention to the functionality of a site. That makes them important, but not if you don't see them until many seconds after their page loads. So the actual success of your Web graphics depends on your being able to strike the best balance between the best-looking picture and the fastest-loading picture.

As you will see later in this chapter, about half a dozen factors influence that compromise. If you use a standard image processing program, you may not be able to control all those factors. Even if you can do all the possible tweaks, you'll have to do them all by trial and error. At the very least, Web image-processing software will let you preview your changes and compare them with the original before you commit to saving the file. If you multiply the ten minutes to half an hour per image that it takes to do the same job in Photoshop times the number of images in a typical Web site, you'll quickly see how investing a couple of hundred bucks in Web-processing software can pay off.

Some Web processing software can do much more than tweak GIFs, JPEG, and PNG files. It's worth looking into those extra features (they're all covered in the next section) because if you shop carefully, you won't have to pay a penny more to get them.

Cross-Reference This chapter covers choosing software for preparing images for publication on the Web. The processes and considerations for Web image preparation are the subject of Chapter 18.

Key Features and What They Mean

When evaluating a Web image-processing program, you should look for and understand features in the following categories:

✦ Web optimization of images

✦ Reduction to the Web-safe palette

✦ Sophistication of the dithering algorithm

✦ Interlacing

✦ Live preview

✦ Making animated GIFs

✦ Tiled backgrounds

✦ Image maps

✦ Button-making capabilities

✦ Previewing in a browser

✦ Batch processing

✦ Image editing

The importance of each of these features and why you should look for them are explained in the following sections. Note that there are many other useful features in some Web image-processing programs. However, these features can usually be found in other programs or plug-ins as well. Such features include automatic drop-shadow and edge-generation for buttons and text, bitmap stroking of vector curves (pen tool), and automatic creation of seamless background tiles from a selected portion of the image.

Web optimization of images

The primary job of Web image-processing software is to maximize the performance of your Web page photos and other graphics. What it takes to maximize graphics and photos will depend first on which Web format (GIF, JPEG, or PNG) you choose for your images. The most important of these formats for most photographs is JPEG because JPEG files can contain millions of colors and still provide a choice of compression ratios and other performance-enhancing factors. However, there will be times when you will want to reduce the number of colors in a photograph for a more graphic, harder-edged look. Such images are generally best saved to a GIF file in order to avoid the blurry edges and surprise chunks of color that can appear in a JPEG image that has been overcompressed in order to achieve an equivalent file size. Also, GIF files can be assigned a transparent color (usually white or 50 percent gray).

PNG (Portable Network Graphics) files can be either indexed or true-color and can also have transparency. However, only Internet Explorer and Netscape version 4 or later can read PNG files without a separately installed plug-in. So it's not as likely that you'll want to use them because you risk losing viewers unless you are designing for a corporate Internet (called an *intranet*). Then it may be possible for the corporation to dictate the type and version of browser to be used.

Exactly how a program optimizes Web graphics will vary considerably — at least in terms of interface nomenclature — from program to program. The best way to judge a program's ability to optimize Web graphics is to choose a set of images that can be used as a benchmark. Choose three to five images that are all the same size. One or two of these should be flat-colored, hard-edged graphics with text (such as logos, signs, or buttons). The rest should be photographs that differ in tonal and color range. You should have the following: (1) a low-key, high-contrast image, (2) a high-key low-contrast image, and (3) a full-range and very colorful image. Save each of these images to both GIF and JPEG formats using your regular image-processing software and write down the numbers.

Tip

When testing Web image-processing software, save these same images in the same format and compare the file sizes with the originals. Are the file sizes significantly smaller and do the new images look as good or better than the uncompressed originals? If so, you've found worthy Web image-processing software. If not, the value of anything else the program does is somewhat diminished because you'll undoubtedly have to invest in another program or plug-in that can make your Web graphics perform as needed.

Reduction to the Web-safe palette

This is something that almost all image-processing software that's been published since 1997 provides a means of doing. If you haven't yet become familiar with the term "Web-safe palette," it refers to the 216 colors that are shared by both Macintosh and Windows platforms when viewing files on the Web. This is not to say that viewers can't see other colors on your Web pages — only that *how* they see them will vary according to the browser they are using and the display system (video card and monitor) being used by their computer. So you may want to make sure that certain colors, such as those in headlines, buttons, and other informational graphics, are consistent from computer to computer. It is easier to do that if the Web image-processing software you are using makes it easy to convert an image to Web-safe colors without completely reinterpreting the colors in the original.

Sophistication of the dithering algorithm

When you reduce color photographs to GIF format, it is necessary to remove all but 256 of the 16.8 million colors that were possible in the original. The colors in your photograph may or may not (depending on the subject) be close to those in the indexed color palette. If your image contains mostly one color (for example, a photo of a pile of oranges, or a beach at sunset), you can simply create a palette of 256 shades of that color and end up with something that looks pretty close to the original. However, if your image uses most of the colors in the rainbow, you will see lots of posterization (a flattening of many shades of a color into one solid color) in the indexed color image. To make matters worse, you usually want to use significantly fewer colors than 256. So how do you keep any semblance of natural colors and gradations? The answer is *dithering*. Dithering is a means of simulating colors that aren't actually in the palette. This is done by interspersing colors that are in the palette in such a way that, when you view them from a distance, they simulate another color. In other words, our eyes mix the colors. I can't show you this on a black-and-white page, but if you look at Figure 13-1, you'll see the banding that occurs without dithering and you can see the checkerboard pattern of dithered colors in the more natural-looking image at the right.

Figure 13-1: The flower on the left has been reduced to Web-safe colors; the one on the right has been dithered using the same palette, creating a more photographic illusion.

As you can see, dithering can be a big help if you must save a photographic image in GIF format, especially if you also have to use Web-safe colors. How much help it can be will depend on how well the program "guesses" at how to make up the dithering pattern.

Interlacing

Both GIF and JPEG files can be saved in a format that transmits images to a browser in stages—first at lower resolution, ultimately at full resolution. This helps to minimize the appearance of blank image boxes on a Web page because the low-resolution version of the file transmits very quickly. The trade-off is that when the file is saved at multiple resolutions, the size of the file is actually larger. It is proportionately larger for small files, so you don't want to save to a dual-resolution format unless the image is bigger than thumbnail size. Therefore, the program you choose should give you a choice of saving at dual resolutions or not. Dual-resolution GIF files are called *interlaced*. Dual-resolution JPEG files are called *progressive*.

Previewing results

The ability to preview the results of your choices in compression options, color reductions, and the other factors that increase performance (but decrease image quality) is a major reason for buying a program dedicated to processing images for the Web. You must be able to see a comparison between your original and the *optimized* (also know as *compromised*) image that results from your choice of settings. Moreover, the preview window should be large enough to let you carefully examine details in post-processed images. Figure 13-2 shows the Fireworks export preview window, simultaneously showing four versions of the same file, each using a different set of settings.

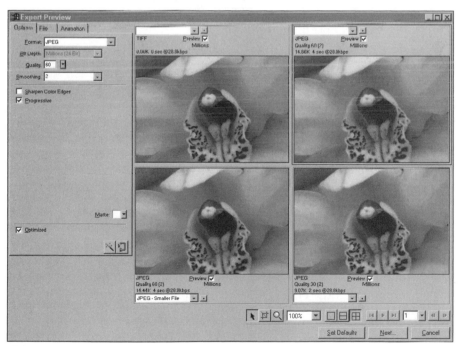

Figure 13-2: Fireworks' outstanding preview feature lets you see up to four different sets of settings side-by-side. You can then choose to save the version that makes the best compromise between upload performance (file size) and image quality.

Making animated GIFs

An animated GIF is the most universally viewable type of Web animation. It is nothing more than a recent version of the GIF file specification that enables multiple images to be stored in the same file. Called GIF 89a, the specification enables the frames to be exchanged at a user-specified rate. If the program you choose enables you to build animated GIFs by *tweening* (automatically creating the frames in be*tween* a start and stop frame), you will be able to save a lot of time animating objects as they move across the screen, changing their scale, or changing their profile. Also, look for an animation capability that enables you to control the duration of a frame, the place-ment of a frame, and the *frame disposal method* (what happens to one frame as another replaces it). Disposal methods should include the following:

✦ **None.** This option creates the smallest file, but frames simply stack atop one another. It can be useful when you want to show things piling up.

✦ **Unspecified.** This lets the browser decide how to dispose of frames. It results in smaller files, but reduces control over the disposal method.

✦ **Restore to Previous.** This option restores the previous frame when the cur-rent frame's time is up. It is useful for animating transparent GIF objects across a larger background image.

✦ **Restore to Background.** This will restore to the Web page's background color, thus making animated objects with transparent backgrounds seem to float over the page.

Onion-skinning, temporarily reducing the opacity of frames so that you can see the position of objects in relation to one another, is another important feature for animation.

Note   If your image-editing program doesn't have a built-in capability for creating ani-mated GIFs, there are a number of such programs available from online libraries as either freeware or shareware. There are many resources for such software, but two of the best are www.cnet.com/downloads and www.zdnet.com.

Tiled backgrounds

One frequent use for photos on the Web is as texture tiles for backgrounds. Using a single photograph for the entire background requires using too large a file. The page takes forever to load. You can create a realistic texture (such as a lawn or concrete wall) by selecting a small area of a photograph and turning that into a seamless tile (see Chapter 25). The small tile file is then loaded only once and automatically repeated in rows and columns by the browser. The trick is in making the tile seam-less. Some Web image prep packages make this process quick and painless. Some also make their tiles more "seamless" than others.

Image maps

Image maps make it possible to assign Internet links to selected areas within an image. You can designate circular, rectangular, or irregular (polygonal) shapes in the image as *hot spots* (areas with links to other URLs). A hot spot can be linked to anything (text, graphic, photo, animation, movie, and sound) on the same page, on another page on the same site, or to any page on any other site on the Web.

> **Note**
>
> Image maps can be client-side or server-side. In client-side image maps, the viewer's browser activates the links. In server-side image maps, there must be code on the server instructing the server how to link to the hot spots on image maps. Some image-processing programs, such as Adobe Image Ready, will create only client-side image maps.

It is possible to achieve a similar result with sliced images. However, the main advantage of sliced images is apparent in images that occupy more than a third of the screen, because slicing makes images appear to load faster (each slice is a much smaller image than the overall image). The advantage of image slices is that you can attach rollover actions to them (see "Button-making capabilities," next).

Button-making capabilities

Sometimes it's hard to remember that buttons can be any sort of graphic that has a link attached. One of the most effective types of buttons are small photographs of something that represents where you want the user to go or what you want the user to do. Examples might be a gardening site that has a flower as a button to link to the flower seeds page, and a carrot as a button for navigating to the vegetable seeds page. You can always place such photographs on a Web page in your Web-authoring program and then turn them into buttons by assigning a link to them. However, some Web image-preparation programs let you establish the link before you export the graphic. This is a help because you can use the same link for any number of Web pages or sites, simply by exporting to them.

Another useful feature is the ability to create edge effects around text and shapes. There are many ways you can use such things as rounded or beveled edges or drop shadows. For instance, they give depth to a photo or make it more obvious that a shape is meant to be a button (see Figure 13-3).

The most useful button capability of all is the ability to slice images so that each section loads as an independent graphic. There are two advantages to this: (1) A large image can be made to load much faster, and more important (2) each section can be linked so that different areas of the picture navigate to different parts of the Web page, site, or other sites.

Figure 13-3: Notice how the photograph of the banana with a drop shadow gives more depth to the page and how much more the banana button on the right looks like it should be clicked than the one on the left.

Another desirable capability is JavaScript generation for *roll-over events*. Roll-over events refer to the possible states of the mouse as the cursor passes over a specific area of the image. Rollover events go by the following (or similar) names:

✦ **Up:** The appearance of the target when the mouse isn't in any other specific state. The cursor isn't hovering over any area to which a behavior has been assigned.

✦ **Over:** The appearance of the target area when the cursor is over it.

✦ **Click (or Over Down):** The appearance of the target area when the cursor is over it and the mouse button is clicked.

✦ **Down:** What happens after the cursor is clicked when it is over the target.

Previewing in a browser

If the Web image-processing program can build animations or can create JavaScript roll-over events, you'll want to know what the results will look like in a browser. It will speed your workflow if you can preview the file in a browser before you have to leave the program. Then you can make sure everything is working before you incorporate the results into a site and post the changes to the Web.

Batch processing

Batch processing is the ability to change specific characteristics of multiple image files at the same time. Suppose you want to convert 200 thumbnails to dithered GIFs that are no wider than 60 pixels and no higher than 100 pixels. Furthermore, suppose those files might originate in a variety of file formats. It could take you all day (maybe even a couple of days) to make all the conversions. Batch processing would take care of the job for you. The king of the batch-processing world is a program called DeBabelizer, which you can read much more about in Chapters 18 and 24.

Image editing

Oddly enough, image editing and processing are almost entirely left out of the two leading Web image-editing programs. You might be able to brighten or darken an image, but image processing is most often left to the programs covered in Chapters 15 and 16. Curiously, some of the less-expensive programs covered in Chapter 16 include quite a few of the Web image-preparation capabilities mentioned in this chapter.

Choosing Products (A Comparative Review)

Three products lead the pack in Web image-preparation: Adobe's ImageReady, Macromedia's Fireworks 2, and ULead's PhotoImpact . PhotoImpact also has enough image-processing capabilities to make it qualify for Chapter 11, "Professional Image Processing Software." I just don't want to waste your valuable time making you read about it in two different places.

Adobe ImageReady (Mac, Windows $199)

Photoshop users will feel right at home the moment they open ImageReady. The icons and terminology used by the two programs are identical when it comes to those features that are shared (or semi-shared) by both. Not that the tool or command shared by both programs always does exactly the same thing; the ImageReady version is usually operationally simplified or has been automated. The program sells for the exact same $199 as Macromedia Fireworks 2, so you'll want to study the personalities of both programs carefully before you buy one.

ImageReady is cross-platform. That is, it runs on all the current-generation versions of Windows, Windows NT, and Macintosh OS operating systems.

Web optimization of images

Palette optimization is one facet of optimizing GIF and 8-bit PNG images for the Web. That is because there are only 256 possible colors. An image that is being converted from 16 million colors will look best if those 256 colors are closest to those that predominate in the original. Optimized palettes are made automatically to use one or more "schemes" for creating the needed new palettes. In ImageReady, there are three choices for palette optimization: *Adaptive* (equivalent to Photoshop 5's default method), *Perceptual* (which weights colors for human sensitivity, usually improving the results), and the new *Selective* (a faster variant of Perceptual, which produces different results). There are also four other palette options: Custom lets you create your own color or import the palette from any saved palette file and then change it at will. There's also a Web-safe palette and system palettes for both Mac and Windows system colors. Both system palettes are available regardless of which platform you're running the program on.

When saving GIF or PNG files that have a transparent color assigned, you can use a matte command that recolors edge pixels that don't match the target background. This eliminates the ugly halo effect (UHE) that occurs when edge pixels are close to the transparent color but do not match the background color.

ImageReady lets you choose the number of colors you want to use in 8-bit images. It will automatically generate a palette of as few colors as you can get away with, but there is nothing to stop you from entering the number color you prefer. You can also preview the optimized colors and delete specific colors if you like.

ImageReady optimizes files for saving in GIF, JPEG, and PNG formats (both 8-bit and 24-bit).

Sophistication of the dithering algorithm

ImageReady dithers so well that it requires a bit of peering in order to tell that the image has been dithered. I should qualify this statement to refer to those cases when the Dither slider is set to its maximum. The more highly dithered an image, the larger its file size will be (because the compression software can't repeat the same information for as large a space). ImageReady lets you set exactly the desired amount of dithering by dragging a slider from 0 to 100 percent. Figure 13-4 shows images that have been reduced to 64 colors and dithered at 50 percent and 100 percent, respectively.

Figure 13-4: The image on the left has been dithered 50 percent in ImageReady; the image on the right has been dithered 100 percent.

Interlacing

Progressive, or interlaced, settings are available for all applicable Web file types. In all instances, the selection is made by checking a checkbox.

Live preview

ImageReady has a much different previewing style than arch-competitor Fireworks. Rather than a divided screen, tabs appear at the top of the workspace window from the moment you open a file. The program is constantly generating an optimized version of the image every time you make a change. You can change optimized file types and settings at any time by making changes in the Optimize palette (see Figure 13-5). You can switch from a view of the current settings to a view of the original by clicking the tab. You can also copy the workspace window by dragging the tab to a blank space. Then you can see the original and the optimized file at the same time. You can also create a duplicate of the optimized window that retains the optimization settings that prevailed when the duplicate was made. Then you can compare any optimization changes with those that were made when you created the duplicate.

If you prefer the settings in the duplicate, you just save it instead of the original.

Figure 13-5: The Optimize palette is seen at the upper right. You switch settings and file types mostly through the use of pull down menus. Here, a duplicate has been made of the workspace so that you can see both the original and the optimized image at the same time.

Making animated GIFs

ImageReady automatically creates animations from layers. To *onion-skin*, all you have to do is change the transparency between layers so that you can see how the changes in layers register with one another.

ImageReady also lets you tween layer position and/or transparency. All you have to do is duplicate a frame to a new frame, change the position or transparency in the new frame, and then execute a tween command. When its dialog box pops up, you check position or transparency or both. Click OK and the in-between frames are automatically added. You can get a better idea of the simplicity of the animation process by checking out Figure 13-6.

Figure 13-6: You make animations by selecting layers in the Layers palette (upper right), which automatically appear as frames in the Animation palette. You can place any number of layers in order and they can reappear as many times as you like.

Tiled backgrounds

You can make "seamless" tiled backgrounds in ImageReady with a single command. However, the tiles are made seamless by blending the pixels along the edges of the selected rectangle. You can also hand-make a more realistic seamless tile by using the Photoshop Overlap command. There are instructions on how to do this in Photoshop in Chapter 25. You could use ImageReady for creating a tile using the same technique.

Image maps

You make image maps by selecting areas of the photo and then copying and pasting the selected area to a new layer. Links are then assigned to the layers in the Layer Options dialog box (see Figure 13-7), and the entire image is exported as an image map using the File ⇨ Export ⇨ Save HTML command.

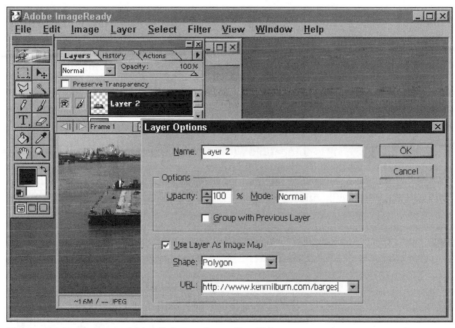

Figure 13-7: If you assign a link to a layer, it will become an image map when you save the optimized file.

Button-making capabilities

ImageReady can be used to slice images into smaller files. You can also assign roll-over behaviors to the slices, and you can animate one or more of the slices. However, the code for doing this must be written separately. If you're not a JavaScript programmer, you could do these things in Fireworks 2 and the program will write the code for you.

Previewing in a browser

Not only can you preview animations and image maps in a browser, you can set up as many browsers as you like using the Preferences dialog box.

Batch processing

You can save any optimization settings as a script (ImageReady calls it a *droplet*) that can be applied during batch file processing to any number of files. Droplets are applications that will run all the commands in an Action as soon as you drag an image, file, or folder icon to the Droplet icon and drop it. You can put droplets on your computer's desktop and they will launch ImageReady and automatically process the file as per the Action(s) contained in the droplet. You can even place droplets in an Action, and can place multiple Actions in droplets. As if all that weren't powerful enough, any optimization setting you've made for an image can be saved as a droplet. A droplet provides a very convenient way to employ consistent optimization to a whole series of files; for instance, to all the files in your Web gallery.

ImageReady sports an Actions palette, just like Photoshop 5's. ImageReady also has unlimited undo, with each step you've made recorded in a History palette. At any time, you can turn your past commands into a batch command by selecting the desired steps from the History palette and simply dragging them into the Actions palette. Photoshop Actions, however, can't be transferred to Image Ready.

Image editing

ImageReady has much more extensive image-editing and adjustment capabilities than Fireworks. ImageReady is compatible with Photoshop layers and layer effects. You can do simplified versions of Photoshop's Brightness and Contrast and Hue/Saturation/Lightness functions. There's also a simplified version of the Variations command that lets you pick image adjustments from representational thumbnails; and there are Automatic Contrast and Automatic Color Balance commands that make adjustments with a single mouse click or keystroke combination. You can get a pretty good idea of ImageReady's image adjustments in Figure 13-8.

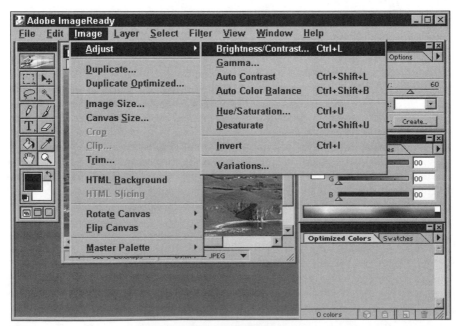

Figure 13-8: The ImageReady Image ⇨ Adjust menu

If you own Photoshop or have another favorite image editor, ImageReady will let you "jump to" that program and edit the image you are currently working on without having to load it again. You can jump back to ImageReady any time you want to do more Web-specific operations, such as making an image map—a very cool feature.

ImageReady is compatible with most Photoshop-compatible plug-ins, except for the following: Extensis PhotoText, Extensis MaskPro, XAOS Tools Paint Alchemy 2.0.1, MetaTools KPT3 Interform Save Movie feature, 3D Texture Painter, Photoshop 3D Transform, HSL&HSB, Amiga HAM file format (Macintosh only), and MacPaint file format.

Macromedia fireworks

Until ImageReady 2.0 became available only as part of Photoshop, it competed directly in price with Macromedia's Fireworks. However, Fireworks' interface isn't particularly reminiscent of Photoshop's. Folks who are more familiar with Freehand or Flash will feel a bit more at home. What the two programs have in common is a nearly equal capability for letting you experiment with the optimization of Web files while interactively previewing the results. Fireworks makes such sophisticated operations as image slicing, JavaScripted roll-over behaviors, and animations both powerful and easy. You can see Fireworks' "look and feel" in Figure 13-9.

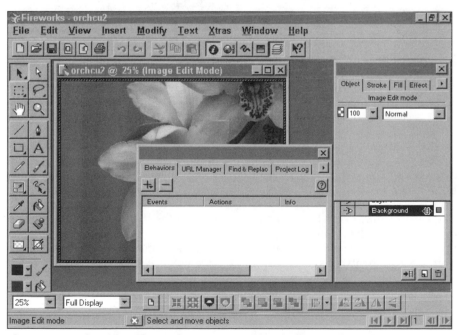

Figure 13-9: The Fireworks workspace as you'd typically experience it

Web optimization of images

Fireworks doesn't show you a preview of optimized files until you're ready to save the file. You have to choose File ➪ Export to open the Export Preview dialog box, and then you see a preview window that looks like the one shown in Figure 13-10.

Figure 13-10: Fireworks' GIF export optimization interface

Fireworks offers more options for optimizing images than does ImageReady. For JPEGs, you choose the level of quality by moving a slider or by typing in a per centage. You can elect to have pixel smoothing, which tends to soften the image but creates smaller files. Conversely, you can elect to sharpen edges.

The GIF optimization feature includes more palettes than ImageReady, but no perceptual color adaptations. You can use the current image's palette, a Web-safe palette, an adaptive palette that uses only Web-safe colors, system palettes for both operating systems, and custom palettes you create.

Regardless of the file format you export to, you can see the optimized file size and the download time (by default, over a 28.8 modem).

Sophistication of the dithering algorithm

Fireworks' dithering is also variable between 0 and 100 percent and looks every bit as good as ImageReady's.

Interlacing

Interlaced is an option for GIFs, and Progressive is an option for JPEG and PNG files.

Live preview

When it comes to previewing capabilities, ImageReady 2.0 and Fireworks 3 are quite similar. Fireworks lets you simultaneously see as many as three different sets of settings, plus the original, at the same time.

Making animated GIFs

The process of making animated GIFs is much different in Fireworks than in Image Ready. Both programs can do automatic tweening of movement, transformations, and scaling. Fireworks uses symbols and instances of symbols for tweening, and layers are not used in animation at all.

Image maps

Fireworks creates image maps in a fashion that is similar to ImageReady. You first select the portion of the image you want to link, and then insert the selection as a symbol. You can then select the symbol object and instruct that it be used as a "hot spot." Then you simply type the appropriate link into the appropriate dialog box.

Fireworks can generate HTML that is styled specifically for either Macromedia DreamWeaver 3 or for Microsoft FrontPage. Fireworks will also generate "generic" HTML code.

Button-making capabilities

Just as in ImageReady, Fireworks 3 lets you slice images by dragging a rectangle to cover any portion of the image, and then create JavaScript roll-over events for any slice or attach "behaviors" to any slice. Of course, events and behaviors can be attached to button objects as well.

Fireworks also has the ability to create automatic edge and drop-shadow effects for any symbol. You can even create multiple effects for the same symbol.

Previewing in a browser

You can instantly preview any active file in any browser that's installed on your system. You simply use the Preferences command to designate the location of each browser application you want to use. Then, when you execute the Preview in Browser command, you are asked which browser you'd like to use. This makes it very easy to check the results of your work — especially where animations, events, and behaviors have been used — in all of the most popular browsers.

Batch processing

Fireworks 3 now has a History palette, and you can create a script that can be run by a batch command by simply highlighting the steps you've taken to process your file and clicking a button at the bottom of the palette. This saves the chosen steps as a single command file. You can then have the Batch command execute that same command on any number of chosen files.

Image editing

Fireworks 3 includes a fair amount of image-editing capabilities. You can change brightness and contrast as well as work with more sophisticated adjustments; Levels and Curves dialog boxes, for instance. Other image adjustments include the ability to adjust hue and saturation.

There are also painting and retouching tools; and you have the ability to stroke along paths. Brushes even include such natural-media effects as charcoal, calligraphy, felt tip, and watercolor. However, Fireworks emphasizes the addition of graphics, text, button effects, roll-over events, and behaviors to existing bitmapped graphics over the processing of the image. There is also a Path tool that automatically strokes with the currently chosen brush and becomes a bitmapped floating object. You can specify line width, softness (feathering), transparency, and texture for any of the brush tools. If you want to change these characteristics later, you just select the stroke (remember, it's an individual object) and change the settings.

Fireworks is compatible with Photoshop's built-in plug-ins and with most Photoshop-compatible third-party plug-ins.

PhotoImpact

PhotoImpact is a very reasonably priced (under $80) semi-professional image editor fully integrated with an image manager, screen capture program, and highly competitive Web graphics editor. There are also extensive libraries of prepackaged graphic elements for Web page design, such as buttons, frames, and navigation icons. The user interface for this program is friendly, entertaining, and unintimidating, without insulting your intelligence. All sorts of effects and tasks can be accomplished by simply choosing the effect in a gallery and then watching it applied to a chosen object. The text effects alone blow away those I've seen in any other image-editing program, as do the automatic button makers.

Note   PhotoImpact is the only one of the three major Web image-preparation programs discussed in this chapter that is for Windows only.

The image editor even includes such sophisticated tools as natural-media brushes, brush-on particle effects (such as fire, rain, clouds, smoke), and a useful range of filters. There are also layers, channels, and masks.

Web capabilities include the automatic generation of seamless tiles for backgrounds, a GIF animation capability, image maps, image slicing, JavaScript roll-overs, and image optimization.

You can get an idea of PhotoImpact's interface in Figure 13-11, but you can find out considerably more by taking a look at the trial version of the program that's on this book's CD-ROM. If you already own and are happy with an image-editing program, you might also consider ULead's Web Razor Pro. Web Razor provides all the Web capabilities without the overhead or expense of such a powerful image editor and at a more reasonable price.

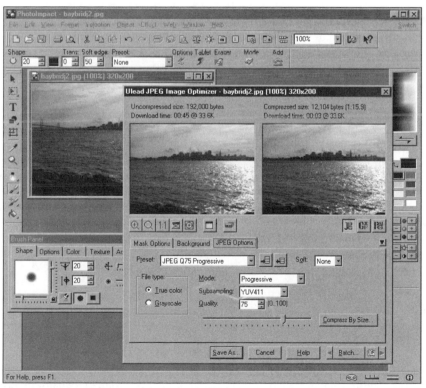

Figure 13-11: PhotoImpact's image-editing interface, brush controls panel, and JPEG Optimizer.

Photoshop Plug-Ins

If your main concern in preparing graphics for the Web is optimizing GIFs and JPEGs and you have a Photoshop plug-in–compatible image processor, you might prefer to just keep working in that context. You can purchase plug-ins that do an outstanding job of optimizing GIFs and JPEGs. There are many of these programs, some of them shareware. The leading contenders are from former partners Digital Frontiers (HVS ColorGIF, HVS ColorJPEG) and Boxtop Software (ImageVice, PhotoGIF, and Photo JPEG). These two companies also make other software for Web image-preparation and animation, but because this book deals with issues involving digital photographs, they're not covered here.

Another advantage of using plug-ins is that you can use Photoshop's Actions to batch-process Web file optimization. The standalone programs covered in the beginning of this chapter will do batch processing, but many of you will already be familiar with Photoshop's Actions. Using a plug-in might cut your learning curve time.

Perhaps the most important advantage to using plug-ins is that they may offer you even more options for controlling the degree and method of optimization. The result may be a smaller file, a better-looking image, or both.

BoxTop Software's ImageVice 2.0

ImageVice is different from other 8-bit image optimization programs in that it isn't meant specifically for saving to any particular file format. It does all its data-reducing tricks as a filter working on the RGB image. As a result, it's equally adapt at making the smallest possible file at the best possible quality to be saved to any 8-bit format: GIF, PNG, PICT, or BMP. That fact should make this product uniquely interesting to those who are interested in high-performance graphics for multimedia as well as for the Web.

ImageVice also provides more ways to tweak an image than any of the products that directly export a GIF. You can see all of these controls in the ImageVice dialog box, shown in Figure 13-12.

Because the effect of the controls is dependent of the qualities of the individual image, using sliders makes the necessary experimentation feel more interactive. Also, previewing reoccurs each time you make a change.

Because ImageVice works on RGB files and works like an effects filter, you can perform its functions within specific selections or on specific layers. This means that you can tweak one part of the image differently than another. It's a good idea to work on layers by making selections and then copying their contents to a new layer. If you don't like the results in a given area, you can delete the affected layer and repeat the process using different settings. When you have exactly what you want, just flatten the layers, convert to indexed color, and export to GIF.

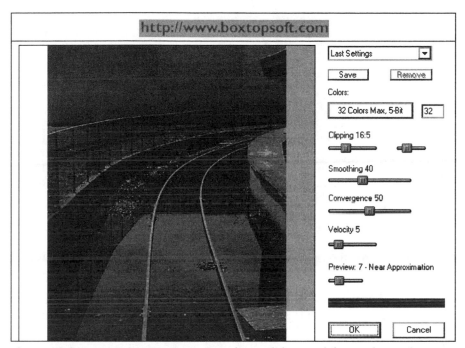

Figure 13-12: Most of ImageVice's controls are sliders, and the results can be previewed instantly.

Because understanding the purpose of ImageVice's controls is a good education in effective color reduction, here's a list of the controls and an explanation of what each does:

✦ **Colors:** This lets you choose the number of colors to be used. You can either pick the number of colors from a pull-down depth menu or you can type in an odd number of colors if you know that you need a number of colors that are in-between the number of colors available at set bit depths. Although bit depth is the main determinant of ultimate file size, the exact number of colors can have an influence. That's because the more times a color is repeated in a row of pixels, the more highly compressed is the resulting image.

✦ **Clipping:** This lets you cut off the number of colors that will be devoted to the deepest shadows and the brightest highlights. In other words, shadows below the chosen level of darkness are turned into one common color — black. Highlights above the chosen level of brightness are all turned to the same near-white shade. (You may want to reserve absolute white for transparency.)

✦ **Smoothing:** This determines the point of variance at which colors are merged to become a single color. The effect of this slider is so subtle it is hard to notice in most images.

✦ **Convergence and Velocity:** These interact with each other to make very subtle changes in adjacent pixels, which can make a big difference in compressibility.

✦ **Preview:** This controls the balance between the speed and the accuracy of the preview.

Digital Frontier's HVS Color

HVS Color is really two plug-ins in a single package: HVS ColorGIF and HVS ColorJPEG. Both are packaged as both filters and export plug-ins. The filters will work with any image-processing or graphics program that supports Photoshop-compatible plug-ins. The export filters work in Photoshop, but not all other programs that are compatible with Photoshop plug-ins.

The HVS filter plug-ins work with RGB files but enable you to export to 8-bit GIF (HVS ColorGIF) or 24-bit JPEG directly from the RGB file without disturbing the original file in the workspace. This makes it easy to save several versions of the file with different settings without compromising the original. This is especially important when saving JPEGs because the lossiness of that compression technique is cumulative. In other words, each time you save, there is further loss of information. Even if you save at a high-quality setting, resaving several times will eventually result in downright unacceptable image quality.

Also, as is the case with ImageVice, the filter plug-ins let you use different settings for different layers or selections when reducing colors to GIF format.

HVS ColorGIF

HVS ColorGIF 2.0 has a smaller preview window than ImageVice's but still shows the image at 100 percent. Scrollbars make it possible to move around the image so that you can examine it closely for subtle changes as the result of altering settings. Most of the controls available in ImageVice are also available in ColorGIF. However, the interface is quite a bit more crowded because the commands related to specifying the characteristics of the GIF export are also included. You'll get a very good idea of what HVS ColorGIF can do by just looking over the interface, as shown in Figure 13-13.

You can also create an alpha channel (mask channel or saved selection) for an image. The masked area will then appear as a transparent area. There are clever ways in which the program deals with reducing the number of colors to as few as actually exist in the image. First, the Exact palette option appears only if you've started with a limited number of colors; for instance, if you're working on a Text and Shape button that only contains five flat colors — or you've already reduced colors to a specific number by using ImageVice. The Optimize checkbox, as is the case with many competitors, automatically reduces the number of colors to those actually existing in the image. However, the checkbox is automatically grayed out unless there are fewer colors in the image than result from whatever other settings

Party Babe: You can even take digital picture in near darkness. I shot this one with a Canon Optura digital video camera and transferred it to computer via FireWire. I used Auto Contrast to snap up the image, and then boosted Saturation about 15 percent. Next, I put KPT Equalizer to work to soup up the color even more and to exaggerate the noise into very visible grain.

Coffee Girl: This shot made use of the Olympus C2000 camera's built-in flash in automatic fill mode. Though it did a great job of balancing the light from the window and the ambient light in the room, it left an unnatural shadow outlining the girl. The clone brush took care of the shadow. I made a selection around the book and the food on the table, feathered it a great deal, and then used the brightness control to darken it.

Student: This student in a Berkeley coffee house was complimented by the light coming through the window and the warm tones in the walls. I boosted the ISO sensitivity of the Olympus C2000 to ISO 400 and used no flash. I stretched one side of the image to straighten the window sill, and feathered a freehand selection to about 60 pixels. I increased the image contrast to emphasize the student of film noir. The selection was inverted, expanded, and the image darkened around the edges.

Stools: Lovely composition, but lifeless, I thought. Also, the cropped object in the upper-right corner bothered me, so I cloned it out. Then I extracted the duck from where it was sitting on a piling in a Mill Valley pond and put it on the stone stool. I heightened image contrast and color, and then used the Photoshop Poster Edges filter to better define the edges and to hide the noise in the digital photo. The camera was the Olympus 620L.

Miami Sky 1: It got cold and windy on this day, but it sure pumped up the drama in the sky. I cloned out the small objects in the water. I wanted even more drama in the sky, so I created a new layer and knocked out the sky so I could see the original sky beneath it. Then I used the Photoshop Levels control and the Hue, Saturation, Lightness control to pump up the contrast and colors in the sky. Finally, I intentionally oversharpened the foreground to bring out the texture and lines in the buildings. I used a Nikon 950 camera.

Art Car: For those of you who were there in the late '60s, the old Berkeley still lives into the new millennium. I made this shot with a fixed-lens digicam and "faked" a wide-angle lens by stitching two photos together in PowerStitch. The results are awesome: the two students walking by are barely blurred. Other small improvements were a darkening of the corners to keep the viewer's interest on the car and a little street-cleaning with the clone tool.

Beach Neon: Amazing how much detail you can get in the shadows in a digital image. On the other hand, highlights block up at the slightest provocation. Most of the work on this photo involved darkening the lady's T-shirt, the beach towels, and one of the neon signs. This is a Nikon 950 photo.

Reflections: I picked this title because that's what the art made me think of. Actually, these are reflections in the window of a studio in a Miami artist's cooperative showroom on Lincoln Road. I took the picture with the Olympus C2000 boosted to an ISO of 400, handheld with no tripod. A little exposure compensation using the Photoshop Levels command and some burning in on the right side were all the processing needed.

Maria: This is one of JavaRama's superstar baristas, her tip jar, and a mannequin she made up to look just like her while begging for tips. As you can see, Maria is an artist's canvas from head to toe. I shot this with an Olympus C2000 completely by available light. I spot metered in automatic exposure mode with the ISO boosted to 400. The only adjustment was a slight variation in color balance.

Creek Bridge: I liked the composition of this photo of the jogging trail along Miller Creek, but the colors, contrast, and sky seemed rather bland. I copied the image onto three separate layers, and then used Photoshop's Extract command to knock out the sky in one layer and the creek in another. I then treated the background layer with the Sky Effects in KPT 6 and made the sky a deeper blue. Then I filled the creek with the same color using a blend mode that made the fill color the image. Finally, the scenery was color-saturated and adjusted with the Levels (histogram) command.

Beach News: Very little needed doing here, but a few small touches can make a big difference such as cloning the electrical conduit out of the palm trunk. I burned in the highlights on the lady reading the paper to tone them down somewhat, and I cropped a little off the left side to get rid of some unneeded and distracting elements there. Finally, I adjusted the color balance and exposure slightly.

Miami Moderne: It was the funky overcast weather that day on Lincoln Road that made this shot possible. Direct sunlight would have caused unbearable glare on the shiny metal. A slight improvement in contrast and exposure bring focus to the image. The clone brush rid us of the intruding furniture at the top of the frame.

Beachin': Once again, I replaced the sky. After all, doesn't the sun always shine on Miami Beach? So little contrast existed between the horizon line and the sky that it was tough to get a clean extraction. Also, I needed to do a little exposure correction on the foreground.

Beachfront: Look at the difference just a little cropping and a slight adjustment in contrast and brightness can make. I did some burning-in of the main beach umbrella. This photo came from the Nikon Coolpix 950.

Miami Beach: I took this "aerial" shot of Miami Beach with the Olympus Camedia C2000 from the window of an office building on Lincoln Road. A blue sunscreen laminated to the window gave a heavy blue tint to the image. To correct it, I used the white eyedropper in the Photoshop Levels dialog box to get the correct white balance. I then moved the midtones lever slightly to provide the widest range of tones.

Deco Tower: This building has got to be South Beach's ultimate art deco statement. I shot it on the run, and then fixed it up in Photoshop 5.5. I straightened the building and centered it in the frame, and then cropped out the bottom of the picture. Those palms were just too organic. I erased the sky and then used a small portion of the sunset sky from a photograph taken at Alameda beach in Northern California. Who says this isn't one world? A Nikon Coolpix 950 is at work here.

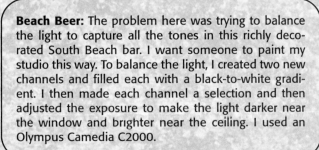

Beach Beer: The problem here was trying to balance the light to capture all the tones in this richly decorated South Beach bar. I want someone to paint my studio this way. To balance the light, I created two new channels and filled each with a black-to-white gradient. I then made each channel a selection and then adjusted the exposure to make the light darker near the window and brighter near the ceiling. I used an Olympus Camedia C2000.

Lifeguard Shacks: One of the beauties of working digitally is the ability to print multiple images on the same sheet of paper. I brought these three into Photoshop on separate layers, and then cropped, sized, and arranged them on the common canvas. This is also a useful layout or storyboarding technique.

Gull and Masts: With this photo, shot on a gray and rainy day, I wanted the viewer to feel the strength and texture of the masts, contrasted with the bird's delicacy and freedom. I used the red channel as the texture map for the Lighting Effects filter in Photoshop and did a little fiddling with brightness and contrast. I captured the original image using the Canon PowerShot 70 camera.

Janine: I often use various filters to make photographs resemble paintings — usually in some very complex combination and finished off with hand-applied individual brushstrokes in such programs as Painter, Deep Paint, or Studio Artist. But sometimes, simpler is better. This portrait of Janine Warner was put through one of Photoshop's Artistic filters. Then I made the halo effect by making a freehand selection around Janine, inverting it, feathering the edges to an extreme, and then darkening the edges with the Brightness controls.

Miller Creek 2: This painting-like interpretation of the Kodak DC260 photo of Miller Creek resulted from a fair amount of trial and error. I used the Magic Wand to select the sky and then the selection was saved and reused several times, first to darken and saturate the sky, and then to contain the KPT 6 Sky Effects. Once I applied the sky effects, I made them partly transparent and then used the Overlay blend mode. Then I inverted the selection and added considerable contrast and color saturation to the creek and the river. Finally, Xaos Tools' Paint Alchemy was applied and then faded.

I've Got Mail: My old mailbox in Mill Valley. I rotated and stretched the image to make the principle lines in the building run parallel to the frame of the photo. Then I cropped the image and made a basic exposure adjustment. I selected and darkened the center mailbox. Then the lower half of the image was burned in using a gradient channel as a selection. Finally, I used KPT Equalizer to dramatically emphasize the edges (okay — overemphasize).

Bay Sunset: Digital cameras have to choose their white balance from the prevailing reflected colors, rather than from the prevailing color of the ambient light. Photoshop's Auto Levels command boosted contrast and found the proper white balance in one click. Once again, a gradient channel mask helped to balance the overall values between the sky and the bayscape.

Sonita's Tree: It's hard to improve on this woman. Nevertheless, a little retouching to smooth some sun wrinkles was called for. I cropped the edges to add more focus to the tree's geometry. The Lighting filter helped me vignette the edges and corners.

Taco Dog: One of the problems with popular digicams is their lack of control over depth of field. Here, I made the most of Photoshop's Magnetic Lasso to select the foreground figure. I inverted the selection and darkened and blurred the background. Then I used the burn-in tool to darken the dog, the upper arm, and the tattoo.

Yerba Night: This night shot was actually made in late evening using an Olympus Camedia C2000. This is one of those happy accidents. Nothing whatsoever needed to be done to improve the shot — not even an exposure adjustment. Even more amazing is that this shot was handheld, using a balcony railing as a brace. The Olympus Camedia C2000 was in automatic mode. In the early evening, there was just enough light in the sky to provide some detail in the shadows. I spot-metered, focusing on the round light in the San Francisco Museum of Modern Art tower.

Vedge-o-Matic: I used a Kodak DC260 to shoot this photo of neighborhood art in Oakland's Jingletown. The Lighting filter helped me emphasize the truck after cropping the image. I also used the KPT 6 Equalizer to define the edges in the image.

Street Art: One of the things that drives me nuts is the default assumption that the onboard flash should fire any time the camera senses that there is too little light for a handheld shot. Here, I cloned out the flash shadow, as well as the shadow of some photographer's head.

Sausalito Evening: The first two images are obviously handheld shots made from a resaurant balcony on Sausalito's waterfront as the winter sun set and the fog rolled in. Although made only minutes apart, you can see the difference in light quality. I made the finished image by placing each original on a separate layer in Photoshop, and then moving them with the Move tool until they were in perfect register. Adjustment layers and Blend modes were responsible for the final balance in lighting.

Bike Shop: This image is actually a composite of two photos. The original background didn't contain the motorcycle, so I used the Extract command to separate the bike from its background. Then I pasted its layer onto the street in front of the bikeshop. I created a new layer between the bike and the shop and used semitransparent black, soft-edged brush strokes to create the shadows under the wheels. Adding the right shadows is often the trick that makes the "pasted" item look as though it belongs in the scene rather than floating atop it.

Boat Clouds: Here I used the image editor, Photoshop, to dramatize an already luscious sunset over San Francisco Bay. I boosted both the color saturation and the image contrast. I did some cropping to make the layout fit, and also used a filter to create the illusion that the picture was shot on very grainy film.

Bud: Sometimes a little retouching can save the day. On those days, the most valuable tool in your image editor is the clone tool. This tool picks up the color and pattern from one section of the image and uses that information as you paint over another part of the image. In this image I also boosted the color saturation and used the blur tool to soften specific regions.

you've used. This saves you from having to count colors in the palette. The number of colors assigned and the number actually used are reported in the status box at the bottom right of the filter's window. You can also automatically convert the output gamma from Mac, Windows, or that of your monitor to that of the Web.

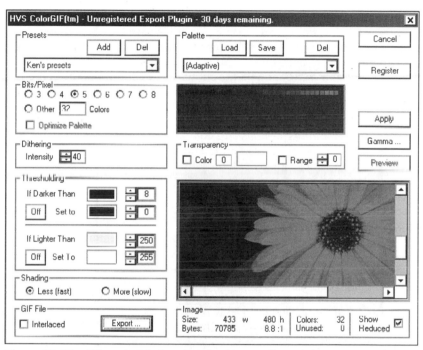

Figure 13-13: Although this interface looks complicated the program gives you the ability to optimize your files.

ColorGIF can assign a single palette to a whole series of images. The colors in the common palette are derived from the colors most commonly found across the whole group of images to which the palette will be assigned.

You can use ColorGIF to apply the settings to the current RGB image without converting it to indexed color, so it can be used to similar effect as ImageVice. To do so, you simply click the Apply button. Then you could save the resulting color-reduced image to formats other than GIF. Unlike ImageVice, you have the alternative of clicking the Export button to save the image directly to GIF format.

HVS ColorJPEG

ColorJPEG is Digital Frontiers' filter for exporting images to JPEG. For photographic images that don't have text or other flat-color, sharp-edged areas as part of the competition, JPEG is a much better looking and more efficient choice of compression types. It's also easier to convert an image to JPEG because there are fewer tweaking options. However, you can make a noticeable difference in both appearance and performance. Filters such as ColorJPEG can be a big help because they offer more powerful tweaks than are built in to image-processing program's Save As JPEG commands.

The image preview window is even smaller than ColorGIF's, but you still have the same scrollbars for navigation and the image is still shown at 100 percent. You don't have to click a Preview button to see the results of the current settings. The program is so quick that there's no need for one: You preview instantly as you change settings. The download times for a 28.8 modem are shown at the bottom of the screen and change dynamically as you change the settings.

Because the filter works as output only, your original file is never altered. So you can save the image at various settings and compare them later for image quality by opening them all simultaneously in Photoshop. Of course, this is a bit more time-consuming than seeing side-by-side variations, as you can in ImageReady or Fireworks. The trade-off is that you save some time by not having to exit your primary image-editing application.

JPEG images are compressed according to rules contained in a table called a Q (quality)-table. HVS ColorJPEG actually gives you the ability to use more than one Q-table. This makes it possible to have Q-tables that have been tweaked to give the best image quality at varying compression (quality) levels based on the type of information contained in the image. If you look at Figure 13-14, you will notice four icons for Q-table presets. You can also use sliders that adjust the sharpness and intensity of edges. Sharp and contrasting edges in an image often display artifacts called *rings* that make it look as though barnacles have attached themselves to the line. You can reduce the chances of this happening by softening the edges. Of course, you always have to make a subjective compromise between how soft the edges can be in order to preserve image detail and how small you can make your file. Once you've made that decision, you can save the settings as a custom Q-table that you can apply to other similar images.

If you are using Photoshop, you can also use HVS ColorJPEG (or ColorGIF) to batch process image files. Place all the files you want to batch process into the same folder. Just process one file when recording an Action. Save the Action to a meaningful name. Then execute the File ⇨ Automate ⇨ Batch command.

Note   On a Macintosh, when you are trying to judge the file size of a compressed image, don't judge by the file size given in the Finder. That figure includes both the data fork (actual amount of image data) and the resource fork. The resource fork has no influence on the performance of the file. If you have a program that shows the size of the file in the preview window, you will get a much more accurate assessment of file size as regards Web performance.

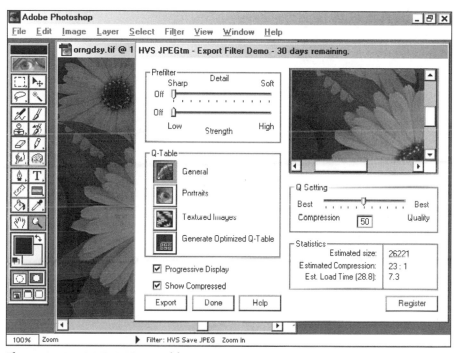

Figure 13-14: HVS JPEGs Q-table presets

Summary

This chapter discussed how to choose software for processing Web images. The discussion included key features and their purpose. It also differentiated between standalone and plug-in Web image-processing programs.

✦   ✦   ✦

Accessory Image-Processing Software

Accessory software, in the context of this book, is software that can enhance your digital imaging capabilities in some way. This excludes programs that process your digital photographs, but can include programs that create images on their own that you might add to your digital photographs.

You can bet that by the time this book hits the shelves, there will be at least a few new marvels in accessory software. You can even bet that there are a few programs we just didn't have room for. As for those that are mentioned here, you should at least be aware of why they are important to a large number of digital photographers. Then you'll have a reasonable idea of when and whether they might solve a problem for you.

The categories of accessory software discussed in this chapter include the following:

✦ Batch image processing

✦ Image database managers (portfolio)

✦ Panoramic stitching

✦ Natural-media painting

✦ Drawing programs (for creating complex paths that can be brushed)

✦ Vector tracing

✦ 3D programs

✦ Novelty programs

Batch Image Processing

Batch image-processing programs take the dreariness out of monotonous jobs. Their job is to perform repetitive image-processing chores automatically on large numbers of files. In cost and complexity, they vary from the simple to the sublime — with prices to match.

The most common job required of batch processing software is converting files from one file type to another. Ordinarily, you'd have to open the file in your image processor, make any needed changes to the orientation and color model, and then save each image to a single common file format. Now imagine how much easier it would be to perform one operation that does all that for a hundred files than it is to do all that a hundred times.

Equilibrium DeBabelizer

DeBabelizer is easily the most professional and powerful batch image processor. It comes in versions for both Macintosh and Windows, though the interface and feature set differ somewhat from platform to platform. Macintosh users who don't need all the features of the full version (and there are far too many for some of us) can buy a much less costly LE version.

DeBabelizer can be set up to translate one set of image originals (the set can be any size) into many — versions that can be used for multiple purposes. You can, for instance, create a set of thumbnails in GIF format all scaled to fit within one size, a set of full-frame Web page images, a series of images for printing on a large format printer, a set of images for use in a print catalog, and a set of images to be printed for a photo album. Once you've set all that up, one press of a key processes all the images in the variety of ways you need them. They can even be sent to different directories, stored in different filename sequences, and so forth. Heck, you can even go nuts and set up several different and unrelated batch operations and then have the program run them in sequence while you take a nap.

DeBabelizer does an excellent job of optimizing a palette that can be used for a whole group of graphics. This is especially important if you are placing files into an animated GIF or into some presentation managers. This is because those applications use the first palette encountered for all graphics. Because colors are indexed to a particular location in the palette, the colors in any given image will shift according to what colors are assigned to what location in the common palette.

Some of the features found in the latest version include the following:

✦ DeBabelizer can now automatically process layered Photoshop files into flattened formats.

✦ It can now recompress animated GIFs to eliminate data that doesn't change between frames. Equilibrium claims that this can make the file as much as 75 percent smaller.

DeBabelizer can automatically acquire, process, and optimize images from any digital camera. If you are wise enough to save your images to disk in a non-lossy format, DeBabelizer can automatically convert the images as they are acquired. It can also convert and batch-process images from Photo CDs. Among the zillions of bitmapped file formats that DeBabelizer supports are FlashPix and MegaPixel.

You may have stayed away from DeBabelizer because of its reputation for complexity. Of course, nothing this flexible is likely to be dead simple. On the other hand, the more recent versions of the program (both Windows and Macintosh) have been made far more intuitive than their predecessors. All of the program's power can be accessed by making menu and dialog box selections (see Figure 14-1).

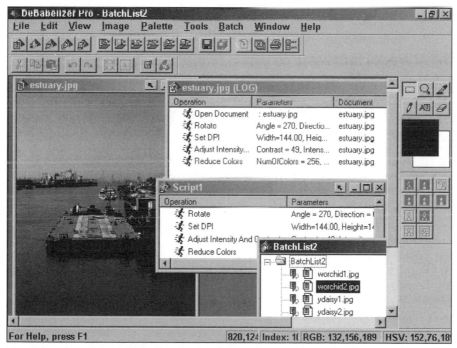

Figure 14-1: Using DeBabelizer is simple: Load a test file, make your menu selections for modifications, open the log file to which your commands were automatically added, and then drag any you'd like to keep into the script window. Next, open a batch list window and drag filenames from a browser into the batch list. Now you can just right-click to run the script on the entire list of files.

DeBabelizer can also do a considerable amount of batch image-processing. This can be especially valuable in commercial shoots when a lab misunderstands a processing instruction. It can also be invaluable if your internal light meter suddenly becomes inaccurate by a stop or two (something that actually happened to one of the cameras being tested for this book). The image processing it does falls into categories that can be applied wholesale to groups of images:

✦ Adjust frame (canvas) size without changing the size of the image.

✦ Resize images according to the following criteria: absolute, common, specific, relative, and percentage. All let you specify the placement of the image in the frame.

✦ Scale to specific size, half size, or double size.

✦ PC to Mac and Mac to PC aspect ratio adjustment.

✦ Flip, rotate, or trim the image (by a specific amount across all images).

✦ Change the number of dots-per-inch assigned to an image for printing. If you want a whole series of images to be printed in one publication, for example, you can automatically convert all of them to the correct printing resolution.

✦ Color and exposure controls include the following: intensity, contrast, gamma, hue, saturation, and brightness. You can make these settings interactively, using a sample image with full preview.

✦ Channel control enables quick viewing of RGB and alpha channels.

✦ Swap and shift channels from one location to another.

One thing that makes DeBabelizer much easier to use is that one expert can set up a frequently repeated routine and then save all the settings under a name describing the appropriate job application. At any later time, anyone could run that set of settings on any set of objects. Of course, this is handy for saving time even if you don't have assistants.

Image database managers

You won't be dealing with digital photography for very long before you start wondering where to find all the images you've shot, scanned, and processed in different ways. Very quickly, textual names become meaningless. Macintosh owners have a big advantage because at least their file icons bear some resemblance to the graphics files they represent.

 Note   Although Windows 98 can be set up to use thumbnails as file icons, that's not the way most users configure it. Part of the reason is because most Windows users don't take the time to learn to do it. Even if you do show files as icons, the icons are too small to enable you to distinguish between subtle differences in similar images.

Even so, what we all really need is a program that's tailored to the job of managing images. Its first job should be making the equivalent of a photographer's contact sheet: rows and columns of thumbnail images that are large enough to give you a good idea of which of the thirty frames of Sally had that incredibly captivating smile. Also, at a minimum, each of those thumbnails needs to have the name of the file attached to it. You should also be able to store these contact sheets as files that can be transferred into the folders containing the related images. If you can do that, you can also put a contact sheet on each of the Zip disks and CD-ROMs where you will ultimately store or ship a group of images. Next, it's a big help if you can publish the contact sheets directly to a Web page, with each of the thumbnails linked to a larger representation of that image.

Using your image-processing program

There are now many ways to do all this. Some image-editing programs, such as Picture Publisher, Corel PhotoPaint 9, and ULead PhotoImpact 5, already do automatic, filename–associated, thumbnail-making. Even Photoshop can make thumbnails with a built-in action, but you have to type all the filenames yourself (see Figure 14-2). A fair number of shareware programs can also do that, in case your image-processing program doesn't have the capability built-in. One of the most popular of these is Thumbs Plus, which is now available for both the PC and Mac.

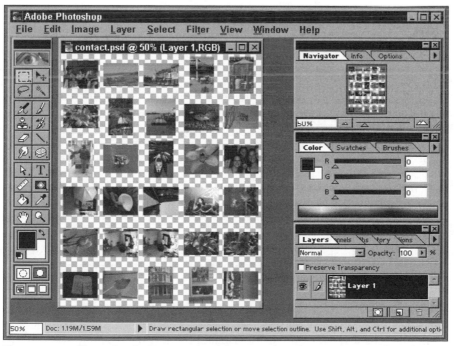

Figure 14-2: Photoshop's Contact Sheet feature takes time and extra effort, but in version 5.5 you have the option of automatically adding the filenames as captions. At least you can rotate a thumbnail without overwriting the original JPEG file.

Renaming and Rotating Your Camera's Images

You may think that it would be simple enough to open all the files in your image editor and then save each one with a new name. Bad idea. As soon as you save a JPEG file twice, you've increased the number of artifacts (compression trash) by about four times. Camedia lets you rename the files without ever opening them, yet you can see the thumbnails. Therefore, you know you're giving your files the name you intended to give them.

The job these programs do varies so much in detail that you should read the rest of this chapter to see if you're satisfied with what you've got or want to add a more powerful program for image management.

Software that comes with your camera

If your images are created by a digital camera (rather than scanned), you may get thumbnail cataloging in the bargain. One of the best camera utilities I've seen is Olympus' Camedia. I use it for downloading images from almost all the digital cameras featured in this book. You can just copy your images from the camera into a directory (especially easy if you have a card reader or PCMCIA adapter). As soon as you open the folder you copied the files to, you open Camedia and browse to that folder. Camedia makes a set of thumbnails of all the JPEG files in that folder — usually in less than thirty seconds. Click a thumbnail to select it, press F2, and you can type a new name for that file. This is something you almost always want to do because digital cameras typically "name" their files with sequential numbers. After your second shoot, you won't have a clue which filename belongs to which image in the first shoot unless you make a separate list by hand and then associate the names.

Caution

Most image editors won't let you rotate the thumbnails without rotating the image itself (which means opening and resampling (even worse!) and then resaving the JPEG. Don't do it. If you must, make copies of the files whose thumbnails you want to rotate. Then rotate the copies.

PhotoImpact's Album utility will let you rotate thumbnails without resampling the original. This image editor can also download directly from digital cameras — in case you don't have Camedia.

You can add comments to the thumbnails that Camedia makes, but you can't really sort and search data by keywords and that sort of thing. You can print out sheets of the thumbnails, too. However, if you transfer the file folder to another computer, you won't be able to see the thumbnails unless you've transferred Camedia there, too. You can get a more touchy-feely sense of Camedia by checking out Figure 14-3.

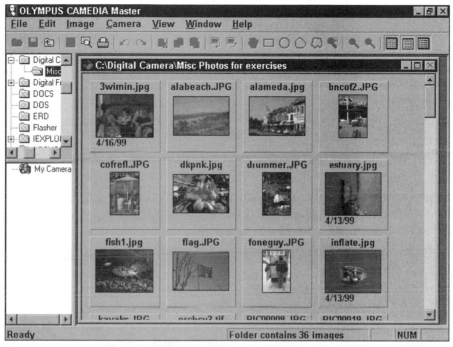

Figure 14-3: Camedia gives you a quick thumbnail preview of the images in your digital camera or in any folder on your hard drive. It's also very handy for renaming JPEGs.

Dedicated image-management programs

Ultimately, however, you want a serious image-management program. The market leader is Extensis' Portfolio 5. Another strong contender is Cerious Software's Thumbs Plus. Portfolio is a better choice for corporate image management. It's also more likely to be installed on the computers of your clients and colleagues. Perhaps most important of all, you can freely distribute a Portfolio player on any of your discs that need to be sent to a publisher, service bureau, or client.

Thumbs Plus is shareware; and when you do buy the license, it's about one-third the price of Portfolio. A closer look at both of these programs will give you a firmer foundation when you're finally looking for whatever program in this category is considered to be state-of-the-art and you're ready to fork over your hard-earned money.

Both of these programs actually belong in a somewhat more elevated category than the programs covered earlier in this section. These guys are full-blown multimedia resource managers. Both now run on either Macs or PCs. You can manage virtually every kind of image file, video file, or (in the case of Portfolio) sound file. These programs recognize several dozen file types.

You can attach all sorts of descriptive data to your files and then search by any of those fields. For example, you could find all the yellow flowers, all the roses, all the roses shot on July 4, 1997, and so forth (provided, of course, that you are conscientious enough to put all that data into the appropriate fields).

These programs also let you post sheets of thumbnails directly to a Web page. This is a major advantage for artists, photographers, and stock media agencies that must constantly post new images to their sites.

You can also play a slide show from the images in any thumbnail album produced by either of these programs.

Cerious Software's Thumbs Plus

Thumbs Plus is easy to download, install, and use. The program does its primary job of making thumbnails and making it easy for you to rename your files almost automatically. You open the program, use the browser window (see Figure 14-4) to find the folder where the files you want to see reside, and the thumbnails instantly start generating themselves. You can set options for showing file dimensions, resolution, and time and date, and these things all appear at the same instant as the thumbnail.

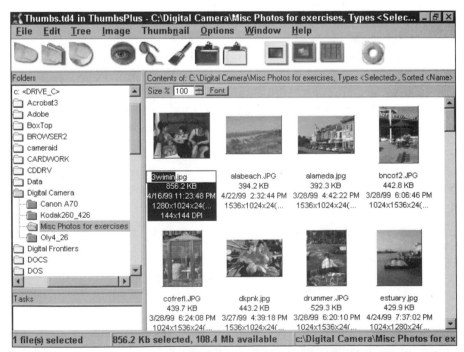

Figure 14-4: With Thumbs Plus, renaming a file and a thumbnail simultaneously is as easy as double-clicking the filename. Notice that only the name is selected, so you don't disturb the extension when you rename.

Note Because Thumbs Plus is for Windows only, you won't be able to send your catalogue sheets to a Mac-based client or colleague.

Thumbs Plus is also capable of changing the exposure, gamma, and color balance of images. There are some very useful filters for sharpening, softening, antialiasing, and special effects — some of which I haven't seen in any other program. This is no substitute for Photoshop, but it's great for making the sort of overall corrections that may be obviously needed as soon as you see the thumbnail of an image. If you make these corrections, be sure to save the file to a non-lossy format (that is not JPEG). It can convert files between dozens of file formats and even perform conversions on multiple files.

Building Web pages full of thumbnails is easy. A wizard walks you through the process (see Figure 14-5) and the thumbnails are all automatically linked to the images that created them. You can specify the number of rows and columns for the thumbnails and they are automatically linked to the original file. Thumbs Plus even creates a directory where are the files and HTML pages are placed so that the links are maintained when you publish to the Web. You can see one of the pages from the wizard in Figure 14-5, and the resultant thumbnail Web page in Figure 14-6.

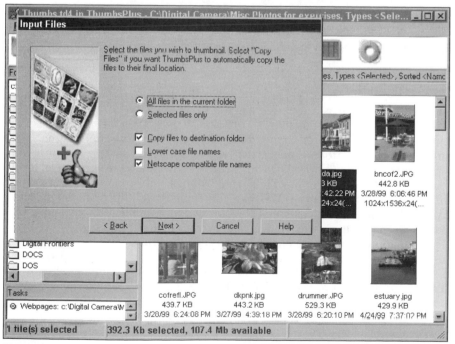

Figure 14-5: To build a thumbnail page, you just click to answer multiple-choice questions in this wizard. If you're more expert, you can work outside of the wizard.

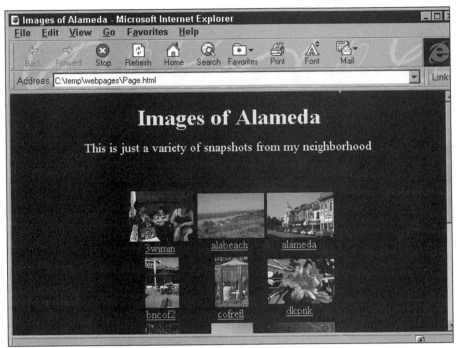

Figure 14-6: Building this thumbnail page took me less than three minutes.

Extensis' Portfolio

Portfolio started life as Adobe Fetch and it's now available as a server-based corporate multimedia-resource manager. Portfolio 5.0 makes it possible to coordinate and share multimedia resource catalogs over networks and across platforms. One feature that makes Portfolio especially attractive is that the catalog file format is cross-platform (Mac and Windows). Once you create the catalog, you can read it on any computer. Catalogs can contain imported database information. You can also export catalogs or specified items as Web pages. Freely distributable catalog players make it possible to place catalogs onto CD-ROMs and other distributable media. Don't plan to distribute the player on floppies, even though the catalogs themselves can fit nicely on floppies (as they consist only of JPEG thumbnails). The player is nearly as large as the application, at about 7MB. However, distributing catalogs on floppies is entirely practical in situations in which you know that the recipient already has Portfolio or the free browser installed. This makes it easy for a client or service bureau to read your contact sheets before ordering or creating prints.

A given catalog can contain any number of items (thumbnails and icons). Each catalog item can contain any number of searchable keywords, up to 32,000 characters of descriptive text, and any number of custom data fields. Data fields for specialized types of information such at Date and Time and URLs are also included. Also, you can search and replace data by specific fields.

If you know how to use Applescript (Macintosh) or Visual Basic (Windows), you can automate repetitive tasks.

Although Portfolio isn't quite as familiar-feeling as Thumbs Plus, you can learn the basics in a few minutes. Thumbnails are larger, which makes it easier to see details, such as facial expressions, without having to enlarge the image. If you do want to enlarge the image, you can double-click to get a full-size or fit-to-screen preview. You can get a clear idea of Portfolio's interface and the look of its image thumbnails in Figure 14-7.

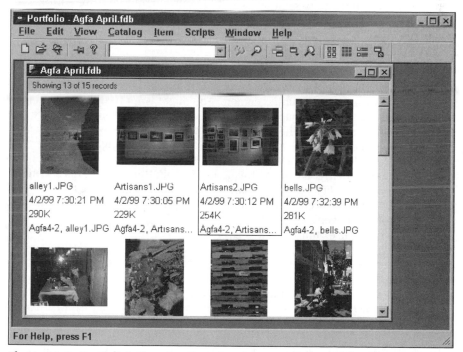

Figure 14-7: Portfolio's thumbnail captions can contain any of the file properties, descriptions, or keywords you designate.

You can rotate thumbnails without disturbing the originals. You can rename the originals, but there's no function key assigned. Instead, you have to press a three-key combination or choose the command from the menu. You can create border images in your image editor and Portfolio can place the border behind each of the gallery's thumbnails.

Portfolio can also publish thumbnails as Web pages and can link them. You size and customize your thumbnail gallery as you would like it to appear on the Web page. Then you select those images that you want to appear. Any you don't select (such as multiple shots of the same subject or thumbnails of sound or video files) are simply left out. Unfortunately, you can't export any borders you might have created. On export, Portfolio automatically creates a folder for the HTML pages, and a subfolder for the images. All links are relative, so you can directly publish the files to your Web site.

Portfolio isn't an image editor, not even on the most primary level. You can, however, click a thumbnail to select it, press a key combination, and have any designated image editor open automatically in that application. You lose the free editor that comes with Thumbs Plus, but gain the advantage of never having to switch image managers in order to be able to edit in your current favorite editor.

Panoramic stitching

Many, perhaps most, of the current crop of digicams come with panoramic stitching software. This category of software knows how to piece together images that were taken by rotating a tripod-mounted camera. You might want to piece together three or four frames for a banner-shaped wide-angle view of a scene, such as a city skyline. You might want to piece together a 360-degree view of a scene, put it into a QuickTime VR movie, and let a viewer use a mouse to pan and zoom through the scene. Some of this software also lets you encircle an object with a camera, and then it stitches the frames together so that you can use the mouse to spin the object. This second method is known as *object stitching*. It's impossible to show you, in the static black-and-white pages of a book, just how effective QuickTime VR (and some competitive technologies) can be. If you haven't experienced it, you should. Go to www.quicktime.com and play with some of the examples.

Note Some digital cameras have a panoramic shooting mode. It places a grid or positioning diagram on the LCD screen so you can keep the center of the picture aligned as you rotate, and the point of overlap is at a consistent distance from the edges of each frame that will make up the panorama. If you plan to shoot many panoramas, look for this feature. It's extremely helpful.

Although QuickTime VR movies are the most common use of stitching software, it can also be useful for piecing together vistas that your camera simply can't shoot with the lenses you own. Most stitching programs will (and should) let you stitch together less-than-360-degree panoramas from a left-to-right sequence of shots. You should then be able to save the results to a standard file type (preferably a non-lossy format), open it in your favorite image processor, and crop and retouch it. Most of today's color printers print to any length, so you can make large panoramas with your inexpensive desktop inkjet. Some stitching programs, such as LivePicture's PhotoVista, will create panoramas that can be run as Java applets on the Web or that can be played in Real Audio's RealSpace format.

Other stitching programs will let you stitch from top to bottom as well as from side to side. This enables you to produce startlingly wide-angle photos with lenses of normal focal length. Enroute Imaging's QuickStitch is such a program. Because it's unique, I'll start with QuickStitch, and then cover more conventional QTVR stitching products.

Before we continue, you should familiarize yourself with some special techniques that are either needed or helpful (depending on the stitching program and the subject) when shooting images for stitching. You'll find these detailed in Chapter 9 in the section on shooting a panorama.

Enroute Imaging's QuickStitch Suite

QuickStitch Suite is actually two Enroute products that can be bought separately, bundled together for fewer than ninety dollars. The two products are QuickStitch and QuickStitch 360. Despite the similarity in their names, the two products serve different purposes. QuickStitch stitches together images in rows and columns, rather than as an end-to-end panorama. QuickStitch is used either to greatly increase the resolution of your digicam or to enable it to take shots that simulate the use of an extreme wide-angle lens (up to 180 degrees of coverage). QuickStitch 360 is a direct competitor to the other two products covered in this section of the chapter, Live Picture's PhotoVista and PictureWork's Spin Panorama. Even more powerful (but at a premium price) is Enroute's newest program, PowerStitch. PowerStitch is covered in Chapter 20, which describes new developments in accessory software.

QuickStitch

What makes QuickStitch unique is that it can do bi-directional stitching. In other words, you can stitch together rows and columns of images. You can stitch images together with or without warping (the fish-eye effect that's natural to an extreme wide-angle lens), enabling you to make the images look like a very wide angle lens shot or you can use a longer lens and move the camera parallel to the subject, and then stitch together a very high resolution image.

Another thing that sets QuickStitch apart is that it is designed specifically for handheld shots. The pictures don't even have to be very well aligned, as long as there's plenty of overlap. The program automatically figures out what to keep and what to throw away from each frame. It also does its job very quickly. It's easier to visualize what this all means if you take a look at Figure 14-8.

Figure 14-8: The nine separately exposed snapshots on the left were automatically stitched together to produce a higher-resolution and wider-angle photo (on the right) than the originating camera and lens would have permitted.

You can save the stitched files to any of several popular formats, including TIFF (others are BMP, JPG, PICT, and SFW). So you can save to a format that is lossless and cross-platform, and then manipulate the results in your image editor.

QuickStitch is the easiest to use of all the stitching programs I've tried. You open a directory, click an image to see a preview (so you can be sure it's the right one for the sequence), and then drag it into the appropriate matrix location. The matrix can be any size up to six megapixels. The next thing you do is click a "stitch" button. There is no need to tell the program what lens you used or where you think the pictures should meet, and no need to use a tripod and level to ensure correct registration (although you may have your own reasons for wanting to do so). Instead, you just wait a few seconds to see a perfectly joined image. All that's left to do is crop the edges. All of this takes place in the workspace shown in Figure 14-9.

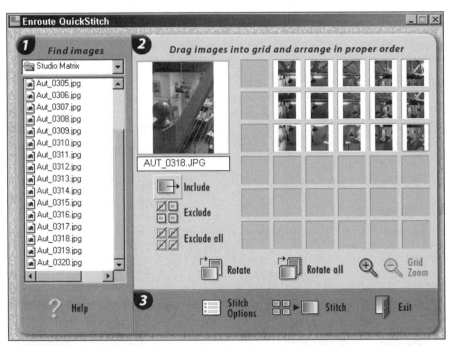

Figure 14-9: Putting together a matrix of images is pretty much a matter of drag and drop in QuickStitch.

QuickStitch 360

QuickStitch 360 shares a lot of the same ease-of-use brilliance, but is oriented to the production of full 360-degree QuickTimeVR panoramas. However, you can create panoramas in high resolution and save them as TIFF, JPG, .BMP, or PICT in addition to QTVR.

The program automates such technical details as having to specify camera lens focal length, where to join image (though you can choose to be specific), having to match exposure from frame to frame, ghost elimination, and automatic cropping. On the other hand, you can always exert manual control over any of the aforementioned features. There are numerous options for output resolution, you have a choice of three levels of VR compression, and you can choose the size of the viewer window.

Note

QuickStitch comes bundled with Olympus, Nikon, and Ricoh cameras. It's also downloadable from the Web by going to www.enroute.com. If you want to buy it by itself, it's less than $50. The current list price for QuickStitch 360 is $69.95. You can also buy a package that includes both versions for $99.95.

Live Picture PhotoVista 1.3

PhotoVista 1.3 is actually a total rewrite of one of the first and foremost panoramic stitching programs. It's just as easy to use as QuickStitch 360, though it doesn't save to TIFF format so you can edit the stiched panorama in your image-editing program(s). All of PhotoVista's commands are represented by icons. To load the frames, you use a browser-like dialog box to choose files and add them to the list. Then you drag them to sort their order. When you click OK, the pictures appear in order in the workspace (see Figure 14-10).

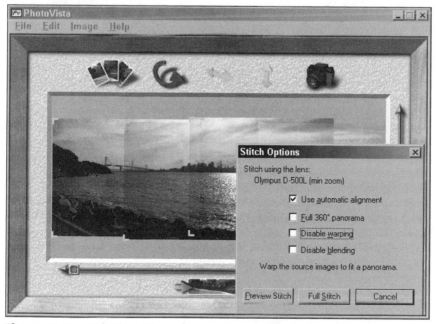

Figure 14-10: With PhotoVista, choose a few options in the dialog box, click the Full Stitch icon at bottom center, and your work is done.

Tip   Cameras that have a "panorama mode" generally lock the exposure of all the frames in the panorama to match the exposure chosen for the first frame. This prevents the camera from automatically changing exposure when the camera is rotated to face the sun (or a dark wall).

This version of the software does an excellent job of exposure correction and seamless stitching, even if the camera isn't on a tripod and the spacing between shots isn't exactly regular. You just try to leave about a 20 percent overlap. One of the biggest problems in shooting panoramas with point-and-shoot cameras is that they can set very different exposures for different frames. The result can be very obvious seams between frames. I shot the frames for Figure 14-11 especially to point out this problem. Nothing could be more likely to cause a problem than shooting directly into late afternoon sun. The panorama shown in Figure 14-11 was entirely automatically stitched by PhotoVista. One could swear it was shot with a dedicated panoramic camera.

Figure 14-11: Four separate shots comprise this view of San Francisco from Treasure Island. PhotoVista automatically compensated for extreme differences in exposure.

Note   Live Picture recently sold all its assets to MGI Software, which continues to sell all the Live Picture applications. One of these, which should also be of interest to digital photographers, is a more expensive QuickTime VR program that makes "object movies." Called Reality Studio, the program lets you photograph an object from all sides. Once all the images have been processed by the program, you can place the image on a Web site. Viewers can then drag the object to view it from as many sides as it was photographed from. Reality Studio also does panoramas. The price is $129.95.

Natural-Media Painting

Natural-media painting simply means making brush strokes that look like those made by traditional artists' brushes, pens, and other media. Several image-processing programs (see Chapter 17) come with a few natural-media tools. You can also create brushes from texture patterns in Photoshop that will somewhat simulate the look of pastels. You can also use artistic or brush-stroke plug-in filters in combination with such "natural media." The best examples of these are Xaos Tools' Paint Alchemy 2. You can find an exercise that turns a photograph of a flower into a painting in Chapter 22. Figure 14-12 shows a photograph of a flower that is being turned into a digital oil painting.

Figure 14-12: On the left you can see the original, untouched photograph. The right half has been reworked with natural-media brushes in Painter Classic.

Two programs capable of a wide range of truly natural natural-media effects are MetaCreation's Painter 6 and Painter Classic.

MetaCreation's Painter and Painter Classic

Both Painter and Painter Classic are based on the same software engine; and the brush, surface texture (for example, canvas, watercolor paper, linen), and lighting tools are nearly identical. The two program's interfaces are nearly identical as well, though Classic's is somewhat simpler.

Painter Classic

Painter Classic actually has more brushes than Painter 6 (the extras will likely be included in the next version of Painter) and costs less than $100. This makes it ideal as an accessory to your image-processing program. What you give up for $200 are, in Photoshop terms, layers and Adjustment layers, Web processing/publishing capabilities, and a few of Painter's more esoteric commands. What you gain is relative simplicity.

Both programs share a "look and feel" that is pictured in Figure 14-13.

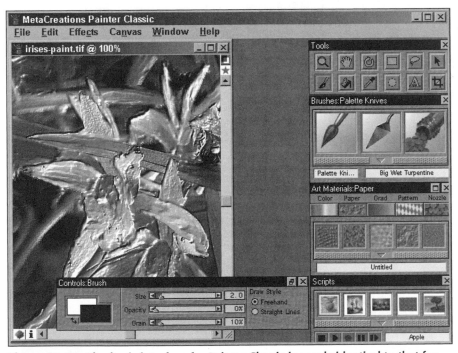

Figure 14-13: The basic interface for Painter Classic is nearly identical to that for Painter 5.5, though somewhat less cluttered.

In addition to literally hundreds of very realistic natural-media brushes and paper textures, you can make the brush strokes take on a three-dimensional appearance, as though you'd layered on thick paint.

I said that Painter Classic doesn't have layers, but it does have a type of layer called *Tracing Paper*. The Tracing Paper feature is shared by both Painter versions. It enables you to use any of the natural-media brushes to paint in only what you brush over. You can even use different photographs as clone sources for elements that appear in the same painting. In Figure 14-14, elements from the photo on the left have been cloned onto Tracing Paper on the right.

Figure 14-14: Shown on the left is the original photo. On the right are elements that have been cloned onto tracing paper with pastels.

Painter 6

Painter 6 can import layered Photoshop 5 files and Adobe Illustrator files. Like Classic, it is also compatible with Photoshop plug-in filters. Its native layers are called *floaters,* and unlike Photoshop's layers, they are only as large as the area that uses colored pixels. Painter 6 also has something called *dynamic floaters,* which are roughly equivalent to Photoshop's Adjustment layers. The difference is that you can apply special effects to them, such as molten metal. You can then change the effects without destroying the actual data on underlying layers. Of course, you can also use dynamic floaters to adjust color characteristics, much as you can in Photoshop. Layers also give Painter 6 the ability to contain more powerful text features. Text can be edited after it has been entered. You can also tilt, rotate, stretch, and scale text. Text can be created with instantly appearing drop shadows, and you can configure the distance, angle, and feathering of those drop shadows.

These are only the major differences between Painter 6 and Painter Classic. There are also dozens of more subtle differences, too numerous to describe here.

Note   A pair of new programs that feature powerful natural-media painting capabilities have created quite a buzz since this chapter was written. These programs, Deep Paint (Windows only) and Studio Artist (Mac only), are reviewed in Chapter 20.

Drawing programs

Drawing programs, like most image-processing programs, are used to create pictures and graphics. However, the graphics created by drawing programs tend to have a cleaner, harder-edged look. That's because their shapes are created by geometrical formulae, rather than by freeform pixel mosaics. At first, you might think that these two types of graphics were so different from each other as to be as incompatible as oil and water. However, Photoshop and most other image-processing programs can read vector images and translate (render) them to a pixel image. You can then place that pixel image (also called a *rasterized* image) onto a layer and use the power of the image-processing tools and filters to enhance it and to make it look more photographic. You might, for instance, use the shape from the drawing program as a mask so that you could put a photograph inside it. In fact, drawing programs are excellent for making all manner of mask shapes that can be used in your image-processing program.

You might also combine a drawing and a photograph in order to abstract or dramatize the subject. Most important, you might draw something that was inconvenient or impossible to photograph, bring it into a photographic composition, and then use photographic tools and effects to make it look as though it had been part of the original composition. This technique is often used in courtroom presentations to show how something might have happened. It is also used extensively in advertising to combine logotypes or prototype products with a live scene. Figures 14-15 and 14-16 show an example of how the Star tool in Adobe Illustrator can quickly create a shape that's difficult to draw by hand, and how the result can be quickly manipulated by Photoshop to look more photographic. The resultant star could then become one of thousands in a night sky, the twinkle in a diamond, or highlights radiating from the water's surface.

Many drawing programs compete vigorously. Most of them have die-hard fans and all have features that the others don't. By far, the most used by professional designers is Adobe Illustrator. Other drawing programs that "have the power" are Macromedia FreeHand, CorelDraw, and Deneba Canvas (which also includes bitmap editing capabilities).

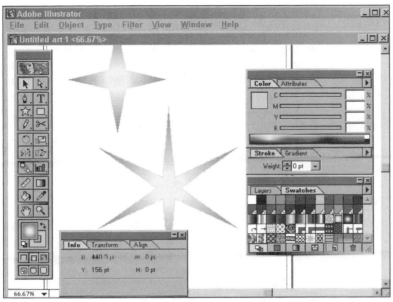

Figure 14-15: A Star or Polygon tool was used to automatically make the star shape, and the star was filled with a circular gradient so that it is brighter in the center.

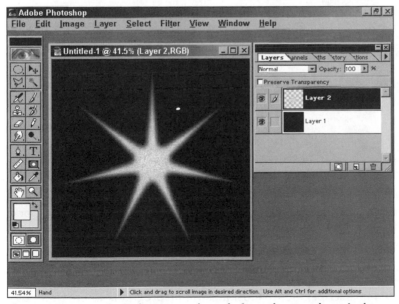

Figure 14-16: In Photoshop, a mask made from the star shape is then contracted and feathered to soften the edges of the star, and then inverted and the contents deleted so that the edges of the star blend with its surroundings. A noise filter adds film grain and the Dodge tool is used to make the center of the star even brighter.

Vector Tracing

Not only can you use drawing tools to create shapes that you can export and turn into "photographs," you can use drawing tools to turn photographs into drawings. Among those familiar with graphics software, the best-known example of this is the drawing of Hedy Lamar on the cover of CorelDraw 8.

All of the programs mentioned above can be used to place a photograph on one layer. One can then trace over the photograph using that program's Bézier-curve (vector) drawing tools (see Figure 14-17). If you aren't a great sketcher, here's a way to look like one. It's also a very good way to represent a photographed product as a technical drawing or to make it part of a hand-drawn poster.

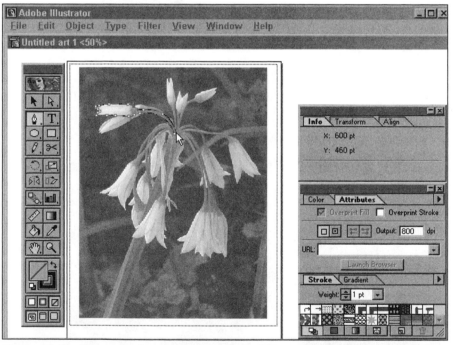

Figure 14-17: This photo has been placed on a layer and scaled to the size of the drawing. Then the layer is dimmed to make the drawing stand out. The layer is locked and a new layer is created for the drawing. Lines are then hand-traced over the original.

You can also use the path tools in Photoshop and many other image-processing programs to create drawings that can be exported as Adobe Illustrator or EPS (Encapsulated Postscript) files to most illustration programs where they could be greatly enhanced.

Auto-tracing

Hand-tracing can produce some beautiful results, but it takes time and practice to get results like the Corel signature Hedy Lamar drawing. An alternative is to use *automatic tracing*, or *auto-tracing*. The most sophisticated automatic tracing I've found is in a standalone program called Adobe Streamline. However, if you already own an illustration program, chances are excellent that it will do a decent job of auto-tracing.

When auto-tracing photographs, it is a good idea to reduce the levels of color in the image. The extent to which you want to do this will depend on the final effect you want to achieve. Also, if you don't want background objects, mask them out before doing the auto-tracing. Both these procedures will greatly speed auto-tracing and will also make it much easier to edit the end result. Figure 14-18 shows the same image I started to hand-trace in Illustrator after having been masked, color-reduced, and auto-traced in Adobe Streamline. Streamline has a full set of curve-editing tools, so you can easily zoom in and hand-edit the auto-traced result, and then use the line drawing in an illustration or presentation program.

Figure 14-18: The result of auto-tracing in Adobe Streamline. The background was masked and then filled with a solid color. The flowers were posterized to four colors.

3D Programs

If you have or can get your hands on a 3D modeling program that does ray-traced rendering, you can create photo-realistic product prototypes that you can composite into a photographic background. There's an immense advantage in working with a digital model, rather than the real thing, because you can alter the camera's distance, point-of-view (POV), and lens focal length; and the angle and quality of light falling on the subject. This makes it much more likely that you'll be able to match the position of the item to the host photograph. The scene shown in Figure 14-19 is composed of a digital camera snapshot, a 3D model of an alien that was "lit" to match the on-camera flash used in the snapshot, 3D lettering created in another 3D program, and a 3D landscape used as a background and foreground. All these components were pieced together in Photoshop 5.

Figure 14-19: Francisco Rivera modeled the alien in Lightwave 3D and snapped the photo of the two women with a Kodak digital camera using the built-in flash. Notice how he was able to position the alien's hand so that it wraps around one woman's shoulder.

If you don't have a lot of experience with 3D modeling, you'll want to start with simple shapes and relatively inexpensive programs. Programs such as TrueSpace 4 (Windows only, $595) and RayDream Studio (Mac and Windows, $300) can do incredible things for a fraction of the price of professional modeling tools.

If you have a corporate budget and an engineering or illustration staff that's already familiar with high-end 3D programs, you can create anything, put it into a photograph, and manipulate it to look absolutely real by matching the color balance and film grain, and adding a little atmosphere and dirt—whatever you choose.

3D modeling programs are also extremely useful for creating "sets" for use as backgrounds in digital photographs. They are especially good at creating interior scenes. You might imagine that interiors would take considerable time to model and light in a realistic way. You'd be right, but libraries of interior scenes are available that you can simply "decorate" with additional furniture, atmosphere, and lighting. It's also pretty easy to change the fabrics on furniture or the color of walls. So one 3D "set" can serve as the background for many different photos.

Another use for some 3D modeling programs is creating atmospheric conditions such as smoke, fog, rain, and fire. Usually the best way to do this is to project your photos onto flat surfaces within the model and then create the atmosphere within the model. Then you simply render the finished result as a bitmapped file that you can edit further in any image-processing program.

Special-Purpose 3D Programs

Three programs made by MetaCreations are, so far, unique in their capabilities: Canoma, Poser, and Bryce. For all the modeling prowess these three programs have, their price is kept at an affordable level. Canoma sells for $499. Poser sells for $149. Bryce sells for $199.

Canoma

Canoma uses a new interface metaphor to make it easy to turn a digital photo into a three-dimensional model. You can even stitch images together in QuickStitch to get the wide-angle perspective needed to see all of a small room. The photograph is opened in Canoma and shapes are traced around the objects in the scene in such a way that the program understands the height, width, and depth of the traced items. It then becomes possible to move the "camera" around the objects in order to see them from all points of view. Canoma also features an Image palette that can be used to hold a series of photographs containing details of the scene to be modeled. These details can be used as surface textures for the objects in the scene. Thus, it becomes possible to create truly photographic models of three-dimensional objects from digital photographs. The resulting model can be placed on a Web site or in a CD-ROM presentation. A viewer can then take a stroll, for example, through a house that's for sale. The same technique could be used to show used refrigerators on a Web site.

You can also export Canoma models to other 3D software and use them as the basis for making whole new models as backgrounds (see "3D Programs"). Canoma exports to the following industry-standard formats: MTS, WRL, OBJ, PP2, SCN, and DXF. Bitmap images can be exported to image-processing software in BMP, JPG, PSD, PNG, and TIF formats.

Poser 4

Poser creates 3D models of human figures and, as of version 3, animals. You can use the program to create people for crowd scenes, to populate a static photograph, or to place an animal or two in a farm scene or backyard. As is the case with many 3D models, the program may generate models that are a little too smooth and perfect, but that shouldn't stop you from being able to take advantage of them. Just pick the sex, age, and body type of the model you want. Then use one of the preset poses and adjust it to suit your exact positioning requirements. Light it and place the camera at the desired point-of-view with a lens focal length that matches your target photo. Finally, you export the figure as a two-dimensional object against a solid background that contrasts with the figure and its clothing. That makes it easy to mask the figure so that it can be composited with a target photo. Place the figure on its own layer in your image-processing program and then adjust color, exposure, and grain to match the target image. If necessary, you can add real faces and hands or retouch details by hand.

Of course, you could also add figures to your digital photos by shooting real people under controlled conditions in a studio. However, if you need several types of people, you'll have to find them and arrange appointments. Depending on your use of the photo, you may also need model releases signed, which could cost you money. Finally, you might need poses that would be dangerous or impossible to achieve with a real person or animal.

Bryce 4

Bryce creates amazingly realistic 3D landscapes, complete with atmosphere and weather. Bryce can be used to create amazing backgrounds for photographed objects or to create custom skies for scenes that might otherwise be dull. I find the program's ability to create skies practically indispensable. You can create exactly the sun angle that you need to match that of your photo and you don't have to spend hours searching through stock photo libraries.

Bryce is nearly as useful for creating landscapes. It can, for instance, create the backgrounds for an entire outdoor clothing catalog.

The latest version of Bryce is even better at creating landscapes and skies in some important ways. First, there's a "sky lab" that makes it possible to interactively control the type of clouds, cloud layering, atmospheric conditions, sun position and angle, and many other factors. Second, you can import U.S. Geological Survey surface maps and create the actual terrain of nearly any place in the country.

You can also place masked photos into Bryce. This makes it really easy to match people, buildings, and other photographed objects with a background. Once the objects are placed in the scene, you can then move the camera to the angle that shows the desired perspective and point of view. Furthermore, the imported photos can be made to cast natural shadows.

Summary

This chapter characterizes software that performs peripherals jobs to enhance working with digital images, but that isn't specifically image-processing software—at least, that's not its primary job. You learned some criteria for choosing this accessory imaging software, the main purposes of the software, and the names and principle features of the primary players.

✦   ✦   ✦

Processing
Images Digitally

Setting Up the Digital Imaging Computer

Because computer display systems are built to be adjustable, you need to have a way to confirm that you've adjusted the picture on your computer to look pretty much like what you can expect from a specific printer. If you plan to send some of your output to the Web, some to your desktop inkjet, and some for four-color offset printing, you may need a different setting for each. This chapter tells you how to set up your system so that you at least see an image that's reasonably consistent with what your printer will produce.

Calibrating Your System

Printed material and your digital input and viewing devices (cameras, scanners, and monitors) use entirely different means of representing color. Printed materials represent color by mixing primary colors together to form darker, more saturated color. Because they can't produce a true black that way, they also have to add black pigment. Cameras, scanners, and monitors represent color by subtracting primary colors from pure white light. Black is simply the absence of light. Technically, there's no way to make a perfect match between what you see on a monitor by transmitted light and what you see on paper by light reflected off its surface. Thankfully, however, you can come "close enough."

Of course, how close is close enough is going to depend on the requirements of your business, your budget, and your personality (are you a perfectionist?). Accordingly, the means, effort involved, and cost of color calibration will vary widely. The best way I explain is to start with the simplest techniques and graduate to the costliest and most elaborate. Of course, the latter will come close to meeting even the most demanding prepress requirements.

Caution   Make sure you aren't running two color calibrators at the same time. They will conflict with each other and throw your color printing off. This happens most frequently when an application asks you to set up for color. If you are already using another calibrator, just say no.

The test-chart method

Regardless of which of the other methods you use, you should start with this one. The methods that follow concern themselves mostly with calibrating. Start with a test print that has a ten-step gray scale, a color chart, and a full-range photograph on it. You can buy these from print shops and professional photographer's stores. If you use Photoshop, you can also print out the file called Ole No Moire and use it in the same way (see Figure 15-1). It's a good idea to have several identical copies of the test print. Then you can have it handy for testing when you get a new camera or new film, when you compare a scan, or when you're calibrating your printer after a change of software or when testing new inks and papers.

Figure 15-1: The Photoshop Ole No Moire test image

Once you have the chart, take the following steps:

1. Start by calibrating your monitor using one of the methods listed below. You will have to judge the performance of your digital camera or scanner by what you see on your monitor.

2. Take pictures of the chart under controlled lighting conditions. You need to know the color temperature of the lighting and make sure that the print is evenly illuminated. Bracket your exposures. If you are going to be scanning your images, shoot with a film camera and use the type(s) of film you will be putting through any scanners you plan to use. If you have a digital camera, be sure to use that, too. Take all the pictures under identical lighting conditions, but bracket your exposures a full stop on either side of the indicated reading. Be sure to bracket in half-stop increments. Note the exposure for each frame. If possible, take your reading with an incident light meter held at the same plane as the test print. If you are stuck with your in-camera meter, aim it at a photographer's gray card. You can buy a Kodak gray card at any professional photographer's store.

3. Choose the slide, print, and/or digital photo that looks best without making any processing adjustments. Make a note of which film emulsion or digital camera was used and at what exposure. Also note how much, if at all, the exposure value of the chosen image differs from the exposure recommended by your meter. From now on, you will want to set your camera to compensate exposure by the same degree (at least as a starting point). You have now calibrated your camera.

4. Now you follow a similar procedure for your scanner, monitor, and printer — in that order. Scan the image you photographed on conventional film (and printed conventionally, if you're testing a flatbed) on your scanner. Every scanner's software is different, but almost all offer some way to balance red, blue, and green settings and to change brightness and contrast. Make the adjustments that it takes to make the scan look as much as possible like your test print. If possible, save the settings so that you can recall them any time you make a scan. You can see the settings screen for the Nikon Coolscan 2000 in Figure 15-2.

Note

Some people will tell you that you should scan in CMYK. This advice holds if you are scanning strictly for prepress final output and you have a very high end drum scanner, such as the Crossfield, which actually scans in CMYK. Almost all other scanners actually scan in RGB and then make their own CMYK conversion. You can do a better job in Photoshop. Furthermore, many of the commands in Photoshop (and most other image-processing programs) are disabled when you're working on a CMYK image. So what you really want to do is work in RGB and convert to CMYK only when you're actually ready to go to press. If you're still resistant to that idea, consider the fact that you will probably want to use your images in several different media, some of which (for example, the Web) are RGB media. If you start with CMYK, you won't have as rich an image when you convert back to RGB.

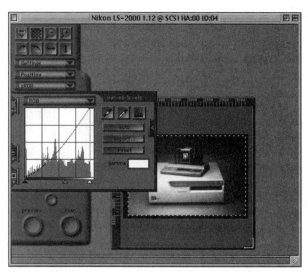

Figure 15-2: Coolscan lets you adjust levels or curves as well as brightness and contrast. You can adjust for primary colors or for composite color. Settings can be saved to a unique name for future use.

5. Scan and rescan the image until the adjustments you make open in Photoshop (or your other image-processing program) in a version that matches the colors in the test print. When you've got it perfected, save the settings so that you can use them any time you want. Scanners change with age, so you should perform this exercise at least once every six months.

6. Print the image on your color printer. Your color printer may have an ICC profile that can be read by Photoshop, but it won't matter unless you stick with the same inks and papers. Ask your printer manufacturer for as complete a list as possible of profiles for your printer and different ink and paper combinations. Some folks prefer not to work with ICC (International Color Consortium) profiles, in which case, you'll have to make a manual match. Whatever you do, don't use the image adjustments in your image-processing program. Make the adjustments using your printer software. You make these differently in the software for each brand (and, sometimes, model) of printer. You can see some of the basic adjustments for the Epson PhotoEX printer in Figure 15-3. When you've managed to get these adjustments perfect, just save the adjustments. Most printer software will let you save a settings file under a name that you find useful.

At this point, you should be pretty close to having a system that will produce more consistent results from shutter click to final print than if you just leave everything to chance.

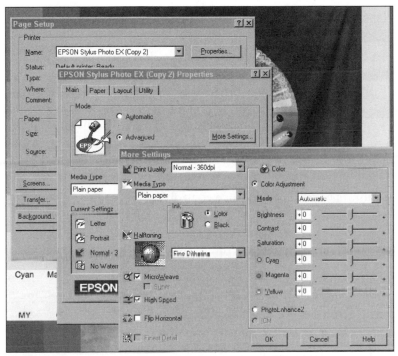

Figure 15-3: The Epson PhotoEX lets you adjust brightness, contrast, and the level of each color. You can also choose a paper type that is closest in characteristics to the actual paper you will be using. You can then save the settings to a unique filename that can be used again.

Calibrating your monitor

There's no doubt that in digital photography, as is the case with other digital graphics applications, calibrating your monitor is at the center of success in producing predictable results. In a sense, your monitor is your light table, where you examine the results of a shooting session. It's also the medium by which you judge any sort of interpretative changes in an image.

Any of the methods listed below are better than nothing. How much better (more accurate) you want your monitor calibration to be will depend largely on your budget. All of the methods listed here are much better than leaving it to chance. Having said that, I have to tell you that I have a neighbor, excellent at prepress work, who says that she trusts her eyeballs to calibrate a monitor more than she trusts any of the technologies she's seen. Few of us, however, have her experience. If you fall into that category, read on.

Before calibrating your monitor, there are a few preparatory steps you should take:

✦ Make sure your monitor has been turned on for at least half an hour before you start calibrating. Phosphors change color during the first 30 minutes and stay much steadier after that. By the way, this is a good reason to leave your monitor turned on during your working hours.

✦ Degauss the monitor, if that's possible. Some monitors don't have degauss buttons, which may be a good reason to buy another monitor.

✦ Clean your monitor's faceplate. If you use a glass cleaner (a good idea, unless your monitor has a plastic coating) be sure to spray it on the cleaning towel, not on the monitor. You could cause a short.

✦ Some monitors have a color balance control. If yours does, put your test picture on the screen and adjust the color balance until you find it pleasing. If you ever change this control, you will need to recalibrate your monitor.

✦ If your monitor has a color temperature switch, set the color temperature to 5,000K. If your calibration software asks for the color temperature of your monitor, just enter this figure.

Using Adobe Gamma

Many image-processing programs offer some method of letting you adjust your monitor's controls for the best possible settings. Adobe Gamma is a control panel applet that comes with Adobe Photoshop that is used for adjusting monitor gamma. In Windows NT and 95, it works only in conjunction with Photoshop. In Windows 98, it is a control panel for the entire system—as is the case for the Macintosh. The same is true of all software-based monitor calibration systems. That's one reason why the Macintosh still holds the lead among graphics professionals. Microsoft claims that Windows 2000 is compatible with system-wide calibration and with ICC profile matching. I wasn't able to test this claim before the book went to press.

To start Adobe Gamma, you must first install Adobe Photoshop. You then go to the operating system's menu for the control panel. On the Macintosh, you will find this on the Apple menu. In Windows, go to Start and choose Settings ➪ Control Panel. When the control panel menu or window opens, choose Adobe Gamma. From here on out, operations are pretty much the same for either platform. The first thing you see is the dialog box shown in Figure 15-4.

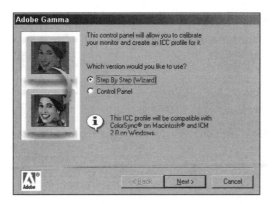

Figure 15-4: In Adobe Gamma, you can use the control panel or a wizard to perform this simple procedure.

You can choose either the wizard or the control panel. You can do a better job with the control panel because you can set your brightness and contrast controls properly and you can control the gamma of each electron gun. First, make sure that the lighting level is consistent with your usual working conditions. If you work at home, you'll probably want to create one profile for daytime and another for after dark. Also, it's a good idea to put a light baffle around your monitor (see the tip below). Then, perform the following steps:

1. After choosing Control Panel, the control panel will appear. At the top is a bar called Brightness and Contrast. Adjust your brightness and contrast controls so that the lower bar stays a bright white, while the upper bar turns a solid black.

2. Beneath that is a pull-down menu called Phosphors. If you know the phosphors code for your monitor (it may be stated in the specifications sheet for your monitor; if not, try checking the manufacturer's Web site or calling their technical support line), choose it. Trinitron phosphors are always listed. If you don't know, ignore this menu.

3. The next adjustment takes place in the gamma panel. Squint so that the screen blurs slightly. Drag the slider under the gamma box until the center square seems to match the lined outer square.

4. Uncheck the View Single Gamma Only box. You'll see three boxes — one each for Red, Green, and Blue. Use the same technique as for the single gamma box to adjust each primary color.

5. The white point of a monitor shifts over time, so it's best to make a manual adjustment. Click the Measure button in the White Point panel. Your screen will go to black and you will see three grayish squares on your screen. Click the square that is closest to a neutral gray. When that happens to be the center square, you have calibrated your monitor. You're almost done. Click OK.

6. You will be asked if you want to save your changes to the profile before closing. If you made your choices carefully, click Save.

Using Colorific

Colorific is another easy-to-use control panel calibrator. I'm not going to give you a step-by-step procedure here because you're not as likely to own the program. You should know what it's like to use it, however, if only to understand how easy it is to use. I find that it produces results that are somewhat more consistent when it comes to printing out something that matches what I see on my monitor than does Adobe Gamma (but make no mistake, using Adobe Gamma is much better than taking your chances).

Colorific is published by E-Color, Inc. (www.ecolor.com; 415-957-9940) and retails for $49.95. It also comes bundled with a good many products, including several monitors from Compaq, EyeQ, Hitachi, Iiyama, LaCie, LG Electronics, Acer, Artmedia, and Samsung.

Using the program is easy. You follow the steps as prompted by a calibration dialog box:

1. Adjust the brightness and contrast.

2. Adjust monitor gamma by choosing a square that is least visible when you're squinting (see Figure 15-5).

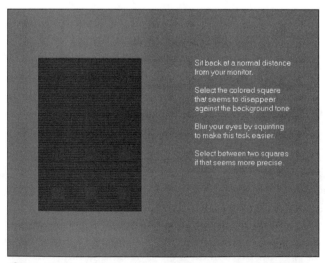

Figure 15-5: Calibrate in Colorific by choosing a square that comes closest to being invisible.

3. Measure the monitor's black point by a similar method.

4. Measure the monitor's white point by choosing a type of room lighting that prevails, attaching a "reference card" to the surface of your monitor, and adjusting your brightness and contrast controls until the color of the card matches the color of the monitor. This is the only tricky part, because the room must be brightly lit during this one stage.

5. If you're running Windows, you need to install a Colorific printer profile in your printer's preferences. Go to Settings and choose Printers. Right-click the printer(s) you are using to print in color and choose Properties from the In-Context menu. In the printer's Properties dialog box, choose the Color Management tab, and then click the Add button. An Add Profile Association browser appears. Choose the Colorific95 profile.

After this chapter was completed, a new product called Provelt! was introduced. It uses a hardware calibrator and costs less than $300 for both the hardware colorimeter and the software. It is given a full review in Chapter 19 in the section on making archival inkjet color prints. You can also find out more about Provelt! at www.color.com, or call 858-613-1300.

Using MonacoEZcolor

MonacoEZcolor (www.monacosys.com; 978-749-9944) works by prompting you through the steps necessary to calibrate your system. It creates custom ICC profiles for your scanner, monitor, and printer — so you get a complete workflow calibration system. Best of all, it provides a bridge between higher-end calibration systems, such as the Radius Pressview, and very inexpensive software-only solutions. You can buy the system with or without a hardware colorimeter. Called the MonacoSENSOR, the colorimeter sells for under $250 — thousands less than the more expensive systems.

You don't have to buy the MonacoSENSOR to use EZcolor. The software sells for just under $300, but it also calibrates your scanner. If you do a lot of scanning, the time you'll save in testing, calibrating, and Photoshop touch-up is well worth the price.

As you might suspect, running EZcolor is a bit more complex than using the two previous calibration methods. That doesn't mean that it's harder, just that there are more steps. The steps are all guided; and as long as you do as you're told, you definitely get more accurate results than if you just calibrate your monitor using one of the methods described above. One of the reasons for this is because Monaco uses a scanner target that's pre-prepared. A reflective target for flatbed scanners comes in the package. You can buy a Kodak 35mm slide target from Monaco for eighty bucks or buy the same target from Kodak for just under $30. You can also buy targets for larger-format film.

You can get an idea of Monaco's workflow sequence by checking out the screenshot shown in Figure 15-6.

Each of EZcolor's wizard's steps is pictured for you, so it's easy to understand what to do next. A good example is the screen you see after having scanned the reflective scanner target while calibrating your flatbed scanner.

Figure 15-6: This is the way MonacoEZcolor presents itself when it first opens. You can calibrate any of the devices independently or check all three to coordinate them.

You can see an example of the program's wizard by taking a look at Figure 15-7.

Figure 15-7: The MonacoEZcolor calibration wizard as it appears immediately after scanning the reflective target

The MonacoSENSOR makes the whole calibration process even more accurate because it attaches to your monitor screen and takes direct color measurements that are immediately specific to the individual monitor.

Mac owners should also take a look at Pictorgraphic's Candela ColorSynergy version 4.0. (www.candelacolor.com; 612-894-6247). ColorSynergy also does scanner/monitor/printer calibration. The software costs just under $500. It works with other manufacturers' color measurement hardware, such as X-Rite's Colortron II and DTP 22 — so you'd have to pay extra for the accuracy that hardware color measurement can provide. It lets you create ColorSync profiles for most any type of device in the color workflow chain: reflective and transparency scanners, monitors, inkjet printers, dye-sublimation or thermal-wax printers, film recorders, proofing systems, or printing presses.

The X-Rite Colortron II mentioned above comes with Mac-only color calibration software. The Colortron II is a spectrometer that can be used to measure color from any surface. That means you can also use it to match the color in a printed chart to the color on the monitor or to check the fading in a color print under certain conditions over a fixed period of time. The device sells for just under $1,000.

If you own an iMac, you might also want to check out Radius' iMac DISPLAY CALIBRATOR. (www.mirodisplays.com/home.asp; 650-988-7270). It sells for a mere $119 and uses technology borrowed from the $3,500 PressView XL (see below). It's a true colorimeter that automatically creates a ColorSync profile. Because I don't own an iMac, I haven't been able to test this product, but if I could get a colorimeter-based system for $119, I'd go for it in a big hurry.

Using high-end spectrometers and colorimeters

These are the most accurate of all calibration systems because all of the hardware is built specifically to produce predictable results (display card, monitor, and spectrometer or colorimeter). They're intended for anyone with a critical need (or perceived need) for accuracy — especially when it comes to collaborating. Two people at opposite corners of the planet will see exactly the same picture, provided they own the same system. All of these systems use large screens, and the screens are hooded to protect them from direct room light and glare. Several well-established companies make these systems for the prepress industry, as well as for designers, photographers, and corporations that do their own work in-house.

One of the most pervasive of these is Radius' PressView XL. For a bit less than $4,000, you get your own monitor bonnet, a huge monitor, and a highly reputable instrument-based color calibration system that includes the following:

✦ A giant monitor (21 inches, with a maximum true-color resolution of 1,800×1,350 pixels) that's been carefully tweaked to display maximum color

✦ A hardware colorimeter (color measuring device), software that lets you calibrate identically across both Windows and Mac platforms

✦ A monitor hood to cut out stray light and glare

✦ A set of Radius color profiles for scanners, monitors, and printers (including presses)

Carefully looking at the technology that makes up this system helps one to understand how carefully designed for the purpose such professional systems need to be. For instance, the entire case is made in a 50-percent, color-neutral gray. Faceplates are carefully treated so that they cut glare without diffusing the image. You can tune colors and focus in quadrants of the monitor, rather than having one adjustment apply to the entire surface. You can correct pincushion and keystone distortion (see below) in more than 20 different quadrants of the monitor. The result is absolutely distortion-free images. The screen has very high refresh rates, so there's no visible screen flicker at all. There's even automatic compensation for distortion caused by the magnetic fields specific to your geographical location.

The Radius PressView XL (www.mirodisplays.com; 650-988-7270) is mentioned here specifically because it has long been one of the most popular systems. However, there are other highly accurate systems worthy of your consideration. These include the Scitex (www.scitex.com; 781-275-5150) and the Barco (www.barco.com/display/index.htm).

How to Make a Monitor Hood

A good monitor hood will go a long way toward making your monitor's color more predictable. That's why you see them on so many high-end calibration systems. Another bonus is that they cut glare and, therefore, eyestrain. You can pay a fair amount of money for a pre-built monitor baffle or you can make your own for a few dollars and an hour or so of your time. If you have several monitors, you can make baffles for all of them at the same time. Then you cut your costs and time investment even more.

Go to an art supply store and buy some large pieces of foam-core mounting board. It should be coated black on both sides, but one side will do.

Measure the top and sides of your monitor(s) at their widest point. Cut three strips approximately 10 inches wide. One should be as long as the widest point of the top of the monitor case. The other two should be as long as the widest point of the sides of the monitor case. Use black tape to hinge the inside (black side) of the baffle. Fold the baffle in and tape the outside hinges.

An optional step is to cover both sides of the baffle with an even less-reflective surface. You might use adhesive spray to attach 50 percent gray paper to the outside of the baffle and a felt-flocked black paper to the inside.

Place the baffle on the top of the monitor and tape it down with black masking tape.

Setting Up Your Display Card

Because you are working with photographs, deciding which resolution and color mode to use is a relatively easy matter. You want to view your color photographs in a neutral setting, with as little glare as possible. Furthermore, you want to avoid arty backgrounds, screen savers, and all that other "cute stuff" — at least while you're editing your pictures. Then you can go back to your favorite wallpaper when all you're using is Quicken and e-mail.

Macintosh

For the most part, the Macintosh default settings are the best ones for working with photographs. To set up your card, use the following steps:

1. Go to Control Panels and choose Monitors & Sound.

2. When the Monitors & Sound Control Panel opens, make sure you've chosen the Monitor icon (see Figure 15-8).

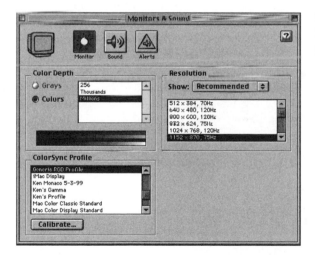

Figure 15-8: The Macintosh Monitors & Sound control panel

3. In the Color Depth panel, click the Colors radio button and choose Millions from the color palette. If you're on a budget and can't afford a high-performance display card that supports true color, you can limp along by choosing Thousands.

4. In the Resolution panel, choose Recommended from the Show pull-down menu. Choose the resolution for your monitor that gives you readable type at the highest resolution your card will support (see the monitor resolution note, below).

5. In the ColorSync Profile panel, choose the profile that you set with your color calibrator. (If you press the Calibrate button, you can perform a calibration with steps that are nearly identical to the Photoshop Gamma calibration described earlier in this chapter.)

6. Close the window.

Windows

The default Windows Monitors and Sound settings tend to be a bit more "colorful." Furthermore, Windows offers many opportunities to use wallpaper, screen savers, and truly garish color schemes. Therefore, it's even more important for Windows users to "think gray," so that they can be colorful accurately.

Take the following steps:

1. From the Start menu, choose Settings ➪ Control Panel.

2. In the Control Panel window, choose Display. You will see the Display control panel. Click the Background tab. In the Wallpaper panel, choose None.

3. Click the Appearance tab (see Figure 15-9). From the Item pull-down menu, choose 3D Objects. Use the Color pull-down menu to the right of Item and choose Other. A Color dialog box will appear.

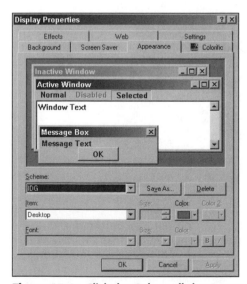

Figure 15-9: Click the Color pull-down menu and choose Other. In the Color dialog box that appears, enter 200 in the Red, Green, and Blue fields, and then click OK.

4. Go back to the Item pull-down menu and choose Active Title Bar. From the Item Color pull-down menus, choose Black as the left color and Medium Gray as the right color. Choose Arial as the font and enter 10 in the Size field. Choose White from the Font Color pull-down menu and then click the B button to make the font bold. If these settings are different from the settings that were in effect for the Active Title Bar, the Apply button will not be grayed. Click the Apply button.

5. From the Item pull-down menu, choose Active Window Border. Enter 1 in the Size field. From the Color pull-down menu, choose Other. When the Color dialog box appears, enter 200 in the Red, Green, and Blue fields. Click OK. In the Display Properties dialog box, click Apply.

6. From the Item pull-down menu, choose Application Background. From the Color pull-down menu, choose Other. When the Color dialog box appears, enter 120 for Red, Green, and Blue. Click OK, and then click Apply.

7. From the Item pull-down menu, choose Caption Buttons. Change the size to 18.

8. From the Item pull-down menu, choose Desktop. From the Color pull-down menu, choose Other. In the Color dialog box, enter 128 in the Red, Green, and Blue fields. Click OK, and then click Apply.

9. From the Item pull-down menu, choose Icon. Enter 32 in the Icon Size field. From the Font pull-down menu, choose MS Sans Serif. Enter 8 in the Font Size field. Click Apply.

10. From the Item pull-down menu, choose Icon Spacing (Horizontal). Enter 50 in the Size field and click Apply.

11. From the Item pull-down menu, choose Icon Spacing (Vertical). Enter 50 in the Size field and click Apply.

12. From the Item pull-down menu, choose Inactive Title Bar. Enter 18 in the Title Bar Size field. From the Color pull-down menu, choose Other. In the Color dialog box, enter 132 in the Red, Green, and Blue fields and click OK. Back in the Display Properties dialog box, choose Arial from the Font pull-down menu and enter 10 in the Font Size field. From the font Color pull-down menu, choose Other and enter 224 in the Red, Green, and Blue fields. Click OK. Back in the Display Properties dialog box, enter 10 in the Font Size field. Click Apply.

13. From the Item pull-down menu, choose Inactive Window Border. Enter 1 in the window border Size field. From the window border Color pull-down menu, choose Other; and enter 200 in the Red, Green, and Blue fields. Click OK. Click Apply in the Display Properties dialog box.

14. From the Item pull-down menu, choose Menu. From the Item Color pull-down menu, choose Other; and enter 200 in the Red, Green, and Blue fields. Click OK. From the Font pull-down menu, choose Arial. Enter 10 in the Font Size field. Click the B button. Click Apply in the Display Properties dialog box.

15. From the Item pull-down menu, choose Message Box. Choose Arial from the Font pull-down menu. Enter 10 in the Font Size field. From the Color pull-down menu, choose Black. Click the B button. Click Apply.

16. From the Item pull-down menu, choose Palette Title. Enter 18 in the palette title Size field. Choose Arial from the Font pull-down menu. Enter 10 in the Font Size field. Click the B button. Click Apply.

17. From the Item pull-down menu, choose Scrollbar. Enter 16 in the scrollbar Size field. Click Apply.

18. From the Item pull-down menu, choose Selected Items. Enter 16 in the selected items Size field. Choose Arial from the Font pull-down menu. Enter 10 in the Font Size field. From the Font Color pull-down menu, choose White. Click the B button. Click Apply.

19. From the Item pull-down menu, choose ToolTip. From the ToolTip Color pull-down menu, choose Other; and enter 200 in the Red, Green, and Blue fields. Click OK. Back in the Display Properties dialog box, Choose Arial from the Font pull-down menu. Enter 10 in the Font Size field. From the Font Color pull-down menu, choose Black. Click the B button. Click Apply.

20. From the Item pull-down menu, choose Window. From the Item Color pull-down menu, choose White. From the Font Color pull-down menu, choose Black. Click Apply.

21. Name the scheme you just created. This makes it really easy to switch back and forth between this seemingly dull-looking interface and the settings that the kids like. Click the Save As button. A Save Scheme dialog box will appear. Enter the name Digital Photography (or whatever best reminds you of the purpose of this scheme) and click OK.

Now that you've set up a color scheme you can work with, you want to make sure that you're working in true color (all 16.8 million colors and shades visible to the human eye) and at the highest resolution consistent with being able to read the type. Don't give up true color in favor of resolution, because all of your calibration efforts will have been in vain. Also, if you have enough memory, your display card may enable you to choose 32-bit depth for true-color. This is a good choice if you have a camera or scanner that captures 32-bit information. However, whether you can actually manipulate the digital image at that resolution depends on the software you use and on the settings you have made in that software.

Note I make this "highest resolution" recommendation strictly on the basis of editing photographs. In desktop publishing/graphic design applications, it's important that type be as close as possible to the same size as it will be on paper. If you constantly have to switch between desktop publishing applications and photo manipulation, you'll want to use the resolution that gets you closest to 72 dpi on your screen. The following table provides a good rule-of-thumb.

Screen Size	Resolution Closest to 72 dpi
12–14 inches	640×480
15–17 inches	800×600
19 inches	1,024×768
20–21 inches	1,280×1,024

Here are the steps you need to take to set screen resolution and the number of colors you can see:

1. If you don't still have the Display Properties dialog box in front of you, choose Settings ➪ Display from the Start menu. When the Display dialog box appears, click the Settings tab (see Figure 15-10).

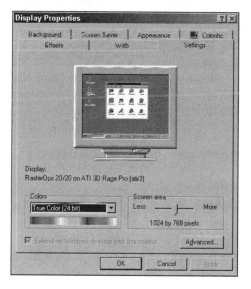

Figure 15-10: The Display Properties dialog box as it looks when the Settings tab is chosen

2. From the Colors pull-down menu, choose True-Color (32-bit if your card enables it).

3. Drag the Screen Area slider to the screen resolution you prefer (see the suggestions on resolution that preceded this tutorial).

4. Click the Advanced button. You will see the Properties dialog box for your display card.

Note The contents of these dialog boxes depend on the manufacturer of the display card you use, so it may vary somewhat from the ATI Rage Pro card used for all the Windows testing for this book. If your card doesn't support an option in this tutorial, ignore the step.

5. Click the General tab (see Figure 15-11). Choose Small Fonts. These are the fonts that appear in the interface and have nothing to do with the size of fonts in your applications. In the Compatibility panel, choose Ask Me Before Applying The New Color Settings. This enables you to restart the computer if you are using an application that won't apply the new settings automatically. If you find that you don't have any such applications, you can choose Apply The New Color Settings Without Restarting.

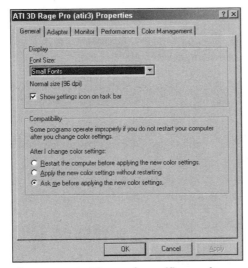

Figure 15-11: The card-specific monitor settings dialog box for ATI Rage Pro

6. Choose the Adapter tab. In addition to lots of information about your display card, you will see a Refresh Rate pull-down menu. Choose the highest rate your card supports at the currently chosen resolution. Some cards give you an Optimal choice that automatically sets the refresh rate as high as possible given your monitor and resolution settings.

7. Choose the Monitor tab. Make sure that the Reset display on the Suspend/ Resume tab is checked.

8. Click the Performance tab. Slide the Hardware Acceleration slider to Full. If your setup won't support this level of acceleration, you'll get a warning message. If that happens, keep sliding the slider slightly to the left until you see no further warning messages.

9. Click the Color Management tab. You will see a list of color management profiles that have been set for this card. Choose the setting you have calibrated for the workflow you are currently engaged in. In other words, you may have one profile for prepress and another for your inkjet printer.

You have now ensured that your display card is performing to your best advantage for working with digital photographs. These settings should work for most everything else you do (they certainly do for me), but if you need or want another set of settings for another purpose, be sure to repeat these steps before editing photographs.

Adjusting Your Monitor

This section will help you to adjust your monitor for the least distorted image possible, given your computer. If at all possible, choose a monitor with Trinitron technology. Many companies make such monitors. Some, such as Radius (Miro), sell excellent-quality Trinitrons at extremely reasonable prices. I'm not making this recommendation because other monitors don't have excellent qualities, but because Trinitrons (and their close cousins, the Mitsubishi DiamonTrons) have characteristics that make them especially well-suited to editing graphics and, particularly, photographs. First, the tubes are vertically flat, which results in fewer surface reflections and less linear distortion in the image. Second, these monitors use a single scanning gun to produce all three primary colors. As a result, it is much easier to judge colors because there is no chance of dot misregistration. Most important, all the color calibrators recognize Trinitron phosphor color.

Choosing a High-Performance Display Card

The performance of your computer when working with photos is greatly enhanced by a high-performance graphics card. These days, prices are quite low for graphics cards, so you should be able to improve the performance of most "generic" computer configurations for less than $200. If you're lucky, your computer has an AGP (Accelerated Graphics Processor) slot. If so, buy a card for it. If not, the next-fastest slot type (shared by both Macs and PCs) is a PCI slot. At least make sure your graphics card doesn't use one of the older types of slots. Look for a display card with at least 8MB of RAM so that you can display true-color at high resolutions on large monitors. Many cards these days have even more video RAM (don't pick a card that uses standard RAM, it's too slow). The extra RAM is used for advanced graphics processing and is especially worthwhile if you play or produce games, multimedia presentations, or do video editing. High-performance graphics accelerator chips are constantly evolving, but get the board that offers a late model of one of these. Because it's a moving target, you should refer to your favorite computer magazine or Internet site for reviews. Be sure to buy a board that supports the highest resolution your monitor is capable of.

Flat-screen monitors from Sony, Mitsubishi, NEC, and Radius were beginning to appear at very reasonable prices as this book went into production. Flat screens are even more distortion- and glare-free. They've been with us for a while in smaller sizes at higher prices, but the new models sell for nearly the same price as curved-screen monitors. Several of those monitors also have USB connections and USB ports at the front of the monitor. This can be very handy for viewing digital camera photos while they are still in the camera. That would be an excellent way to "proof" digital photos during a studio shoot.

Hardware adjustments

Your monitor may have either analog or digital controls. Some even have analog controls for brightness and contrast; and digital controls for horizontal and vertical size, horizontal and vertical position, and keystoning and pincushion distortion. The definition and purpose of each of these controls follows.

Brightness and contrast

You want to display a grayscale target on the screen when you adjust for brightness and contrast. If you don't have one, but do own Photoshop, use Adobe Gamma. You can also load the color and grayscale target found on the CD-ROM in this book. Turn contrast all the way up. Then adjust brightness until black is solid black and white is a bright, clean white. Now adjust the brightness so that you see exactly ten distinct shades of gray in the target.

If you are calibrating with Adobe Gamma or any other calibration software, don't readjust the brightness or contrast control. If you need to for some other reason, be sure to rerun your calibration.

Horizontal and vertical size

Use this adjustment to size the image so that it is as large as possible without being cut off by the monitor mask. Be careful not to cut off the edges; you may find yourself cutting off important information in menus and status lines that border your workspace. See Figure 15-12 for an idea of how properly adjusted vertical and horizontal size should look.

Horizontal and vertical position (shift)

This control moves the screen image from top to bottom and side to side so that you can center the image onscreen (see Figure 15-13).

Figure 15-12: This is a simulation of how properly adjusted vertical and horizontal size should look.

Figure 15-13: Here the image needs to be shifted both vertically and horizontally in order to be centered onscreen.

Keystoning

The keystone adjustments expand the top or bottom dimensions of the display equidistantly. Keystone and pincushion distortion are often combined. Figure 15-14 simulates keystone distortion in which the length of the bottom of the display is shorter than the length of the top of the display.

Figure 15-14: Exaggerated keystone distortion is simulated in this illustration.

Pincushion distortion

Pincushion distortion makes an image look as if it were projected onto a sphere—
which is how it was simulated to look in Figure 15-15. We had a little help from
Andromeda's 3D filter.

Figure 15-15: Pincushion distortion makes the display seem to bulge. The effect is usually more exaggerated on the sides of the display.

Corner pincushion distortion

Not all monitors give you control over this type of distortion, in which the corners of the display seem to shrink or blossom.

Managing Your System's Memory

Your computer system's memory is divided into RAM (Random Access Memory) and disk storage. Most of what you need to know about RAM requirements for digital photography can be found in the system requirements section of your image-processing software's user manual. That is to say, if you just want to get the job done and you're not hoping to create extremely high resolution images for advertising or fine art purposes, you can get by with the minimum requirements. There are a few things you should know about memory that are unique to the platform you'll be working on. There are also some ways to maximize the performance of RAM and hard-drive space.

The one thing you should never forget when you're considering serious digital imaging is that you can never have too much memory — either RAM or hard-drive space. Nor can you have RAM or disks that are too fast.

Windows

Windows doesn't require that you allocate a specific amount of memory to any application in advance of running it. If your image is too large to fit into RAM, Windows automatically uses virtual memory. How much virtual memory you have depends on the size of the swap disk that you allocate when you set up your system. You can reserve disk space so that you always have a minimum amount of virtual memory, but Windows will automatically use any additional disk space that's available.

Macintosh

Macintosh users need to allocate memory to each application. This becomes especially important for applications that handle photographs because the bitmapped files tend to be quite a bit larger than most of the other data created by other types of applications. Only video and animation are more demanding of memory. Your Macintosh applications' documentation will almost always tell you how much memory should be allocated. If you plan to run several applications simultaneously, make sure that the total amount of memory they require doesn't exceed the total amount of RAM. If you're using Photoshop (and many other imaging applications) it's best to turn off the Macintosh virtual memory. Otherwise, Photoshop's built-in virtual memory may conflict and cause your system to crash.

What you need to know about RAM

In addition to the requirements set by your application program and the amount of RAM used by your operating system, you will need about three times as much RAM as the largest image you plan to process. For Windows users, this is only true insofar as your limit for maximum performance is concerned. For Macintosh users, this rule of thumb comes closer to being the rule of law.

The more RAM you have, the faster your system will perform—even if it's not otherwise strictly required by the applications you are running. This is because RAM is very fast compared to hard disk access. The more the computer can do in RAM, the less it needs to rely on accessing instructions from the hard drive.

What you need to know about disk storage

You've already learned the most important thing you need to know about disk storage: You will never own a large enough hard disk. Images fill them up before you can say, "Jack Sprat could eat no fat." Fortunately, hard-drive prices have fallen to the point where you can buy several gigabytes for a couple of hundred dollars. SCSI drives (used by most Macintosh's) will cost half again to twice as much as IDE drives. If you plan to do digital video as well as digital still photography, you should invest in SCSI drives, because they are considerably faster.

Finally, a couple of types of disk storage are excellent investments for those who will be doing digital imaging: removable hard drives (such as the ubiquitous Iomega Zip and Jaz drives) and compact disk recorders.

The removable hard drives let you off-load projects by type or by client, enabling you to move images from one computer to another or transport images to service bureaus and clients. For this purpose, you will want to choose drives that are most likely to be owned by others, so I strongly recommend the Iomega products.

Compact disk recorders provide you with very inexpensive and universally portable means of storing large amounts of data. Images can be stored in ISO 9660 format, which can be read by virtually any computer. Recordable disks sell for as little as two dollars each and hold 640MB of data. Look for a recorder that records at four times the normal data rate because you will be able to record an entire disk in just over fifteen minutes. There are a few faster recorders, but they are priced at a hefty premium. Double-speed recorders don't cost much less than four-speed recorders.

A subspecies of CD recorders called *CD-RW* (for read-write) has also come down in price to the point where you almost might as well have the re-recordable capability they offer. Re-recordable CD media cost about ten times as much as write-once media, but it's cheap on a cost-per-megabyte basis when compared to other types of removable media.

Tweaking System Performance

Working with digital photography will quickly teach you the importance of having a fast computer. It's not just the old "time is money" saw — although that's certainly an important factor. It's just plain annoying to have to wait for the computer, even for a few seconds, when you're being bombarded by creative impulses that you want to experiment with. Aside from having a fast CPU (the very fastest CPUs generally sell for a price that's disproportionate to the added performance they provide), you want a CPU that supports high-speed data transfer and has the fastest possible graphics processor. It's also important to have a CPU that has a built-in graphics instruction processing set.

Transferring Photos from Camera to Computer

Professional digital cameras communicate to their host computer via very fast connections — either SCSI or FireWire. As a result, you can download images directly from the camera as quickly or more quickly than if you were to use an external card reader. In fact, professional studio cameras are usually hooked to the computer full-time because the computer is their only means of storing an image. If you take one of those cameras into the field, you simply take along a fast laptop with a large hard drive. Professional field cameras generally use PCMCIA cards for storage, many of which are internal hard drives. You can read the images from those cameras by putting them into the PCMCIA slot in a computer (usually a laptop) or download them directly via a FireWire or SCSI connection. Download times are comparable in either case.

Lower-priced cameras are a different story. All semi-professional digital cameras and all point-and-shoots (with the exception of the Sony Mavica series, which use floppy disks, and digital video cameras, which use FireWire) come with a cable that tethers the camera to a computer via a serial port. In most instances, the software that comes with the camera can be used to control the camera, to change its settings via menus, and to transfer the images from the camera's storage medium to the computer. The image transfer process typically takes half an hour. If you have high-capacity media, it can take what seems like a lifetime.

Devices for reading your images

If you own a digital camera under $2,000 and plan to make much use of it, invest in an external card reader. There are three types of these: floppy disk adapters, card readers, and PCMCIA adapters. Floppy disk adapters are an option only for cameras that use SmartMedia digital film. Those that use CompactFlash will have to use card readers or PCMCIA adapters. Card readers are available that fit into one of your computer's disk bays. These will be the fastest card readers, but they cost more and can't be moved from computer to computer.

Floppy disk adapters for SmartMedia

To use a floppy disk adapter, you must have your images stored on SmartMedia because CompactFlash is too thick to fit inside the form factor of a floppy disk. You push the SmartMedia card into a slot in the side of something that can easily be mistaken for an ordinary floppy disk. You must have driver software installed on the computer that uses the adapter, but you can put the driver software on a floppy disk. Then this device makes it possible to read your digital camera files much faster on any computer.

Floppy disk adapters are actually somewhat less portable than one might think, however. First, you need to check the list of incompatible devices to make sure that the host computer will be friendly. Second, you have to carry around different versions of the driver for Macs and PCs. Finally, they are battery-powered. If the batteries die, you can't read your files. Keep a spare set on hand. They use very thin watch batteries.

Floppy disk adapters operate at the transfer speed of a floppy disk and hold several megabytes of data (however many your SmartMedia card holds). So it can take a few minutes to transfer all the files to your hard drive. This is a fraction of the time it takes to transfer files from the camera via serial cable, but several times longer than it takes to transfer files from a USB-connected card reader.

The Toshiba FlashPath adapter is sold by several manufacturers, such as Olympus. Street prices have generally been in the $100–$120 range.

Card readers

Card readers are devices that enable you to insert the camera's memory media into a slot in a device that acts as a removable-media disk drive. They are available for SmartMedia, CompactFlash, or PCMCIA memory cards. Card readers come in versions that can be attached to the computer internally or externally via SCSI, parallel port, USB port, or PCMCIA card slot.

Other than price (most sell for between $60 and $120), the primary purchasing considerations for choosing a card adapter are transfer speed and portability.

Internal units that attach to your computer's hard disk controller are generally the fastest drives, but they can take up space and resources that you might prefer to devote to a CD recorder or removable-media drive (or both). Internal readers also cost significantly more. Of course, internal card readers aren't portable at all.

PCMCIA adapters

There are PCMCIA adapters for both SmartMedia and CompactFlash, although the latter are much more commonplace. If your computer has an internal PCMCIA slot (found on almost all portables), this is the fastest way to transfer your image files to a computer. However, keep in mind that unless you buy a PCMCIA internal slot for your desktop computer, you may have to spend extra time transferring the images from your laptop to a removable-media drive and then to your desktop computer. Or, you may have to transfer them via a LAN (Local Area Network).

Using the parallel port

You can find card readers for all the types of camera memory (including PCMCIA cards) that will attach to the parallel port of a Windows computer. These are not an option for Mac users. The good thing about parallel port connections is that they are as common to Wintel PCs as floppy disk drives. In other words, you can pretty much count on being able to find a computer that you can download to in any corner of the world. The bad thing is that they are slow and comparatively bulky (parallel connectors are a couple of inches wide and they use thick, stiff cables).

The cable connections for a parallel port drive also connect to a PS/2 keyboard port. Both cables have pass-through so that you can connect a printer and/or external removable-media drive to the parallel port, and an external keyboard, mouse, or digitizing tablet to the keyboard port.

Using a USB port

USB stands for Universal Serial Bus — a magical new invention from Intel that originally was meant as competition for Apple's FireWire. USB can transfer data at 12 megabytes per second (Mbps), and you can attach as many as 127 devices to a single port (most computers and adapters provide two ports). You can also plug in and unplug devices while the computer is running. Once you've installed the driver for a device, the computer will recognize automatically when it's plugged in and will know to deactivate the device when it's unplugged.

It didn't take long for Apple and Intel to figure out that these two new serial protocols — USB and FireWire — complemented, rather than competed with, each other. USB is very fast (only the most advanced SCSI versions are faster) and affordable. In fact, adding them to new motherboards does little to affect the price of the motherboard. FireWire (also known as IEEE 1394) is much faster and is most suitable for digital video applications. Nearly all current-generation computers are being supplied with USB ports, regardless of platform.

Even if you don't have the latest-generation computer, you can buy a USB card for any PCI bus machine for around $40. You can use the same card for Macs or PCs, so this is a piece of gear that you can hang onto if you want to switch platforms. If your computer runs Windows, you'll want to upgrade to Windows 98 for USB support. If you must stick to Windows 95 or NT, you will need a computer with the latest OEM (Original Equipment Manufacturer) extensions to the operating system. Check with the manufacturer of your computer to see if this is the case. USB cables and connectors aren't much bulkier than modular phone cables, so it's quite easy to pack one of these units into your camera bag.

Finally, adding USB ports to your computer can pay off in other ways. It's an ideal connection for all sorts of peripherals, such as spare floppy drives, mice, keyboards, monitors, and modems. Best of all, there's no worry about device or IRQ conflicts. Nor do you have to worry about having too many devices on your standard serial, parallel, or SCSI ports. The prevalent buzz is that USB ports will eventually replace all conventional serial and parallel ports.

Using a FireWire port

FireWire is very similar to USB. The most significant differences are as follows:

✦ It is much faster (up to 400Mbps).

✦ It costs a lot more (several hundred dollars).

✦ It is less common.

FireWire is only one of the names by which this interface protocol is known. Others are IEEE 1394, I-Link, and Lynx. FireWire is best-suited to digital video and other ultra-high-volume transfer operations. On the other hand, if you have it or can afford it, it's also by far the quickest way to transfer images from camera to computer. Many professional digital still cameras, particularly studio cameras, are counting on it because it can transfer very high resolution files virtually instantly. This greatly reduces the time needed between shots.

FireWire cables and connectors are nearly as small and convenient as their USB counterparts. But adding FireWire adds considerably to the cost of the system. If you're about to buy a new computer, you can add FireWire for a fairly nominal amount (about $100). You'll only find it on higher-end machines that have been specifically designed as graphics or video workstations. The new "blue" G3 towers from Apple are a case in point. The alternative is to buy a card from Pinnacle Systems (the $900 DV 300 and $600 DV 200), or the Adaptec Hot Connect Ultra 8945 Kit for just under $700. Other FireWire adapter manufacturers are Radius, Canopus, DPS, and FAST Multimedia.

FireWire, like USB, became officially supported in Windows as of Windows 98. All future versions of the operating system will support FireWire.

FireWire also acts a lot like USB. You can connect as many as 63 devices, and up to 17 of these can be daisy-chained. Hot-plugging (the ability to plug in and unplug devices while the computer is running with automatic device recognition) is also supported.

Windows or Mac?

Although this is the first decision you should weigh if you're just equipping yourself for digital photography, I've saved this discussion for last for a couple of reasons. First, most readers of this book will have already bought the computer they intend to use — at least for the time being. Second, religious wars have been fought over this topic. Both platforms have their advantages and disadvantages. I own and use both. When people ask me which one I prefer, I tell them it depends on which machine crashed last.

The first thing you should consider is which platform is most prevalent among your friends, colleagues, and clients. The answer will vary considerably from clan to clan, neighborhood to neighborhood, and corporation to corporation. Choose the computer with the following considerations in mind:

✦ It should give you the most choice in software tools pertinent to your interest in digital photography.

✦ It should make it easiest for you to transfer files between collaborators, clients, and service bureaus.

✦ It should make it easy to get support and advice from those most likely to provide it quickly and at no cost.

Ease of use and price and are often quoted as the reasons why you should decide on one computer over another. Neither is a very good reason. Ease-of-use is more dependent on the application you are working in than on the characteristics of the computer's operating system. Think about it: You spend at least twenty times as much time working within an application as starting up the computer and opening a file. Besides, ease of use is often a trade-off with power and flexibility. These days, both platforms use What-You-See-Is-What-You-Get operating environments that borrow heavily from each other. The "borrowing" isn't as one-sided as many Mac zealots would have you believe, either.

What about price? Well, it's not nearly as important as productivity. Time will always cost you much more money than hardware — unless you insist on staying on the very cutting edge. Remember that price depends on economies of scale. The latest generation of any technology is liable to cost you twice as much as the previous generation, while the performance boost is likely to be more like 20 or 30 percent. The smart buyer will be on the lookout for the "bang for the buck" factor. Having said all that, Windows computers will generally cost you significantly less. It's just a matter of competition and economies of scale.

On the other hand, you may want to use applications that are only available on one platform or another. Live Picture, for instance, is so far only available for the Macintosh. Conversely, Wright Design is only available on the PC. Finally, digital video-editing software and hardware are currently said to be more readily available for Wintel computers.

Summary

This chapter has covered all the things you should take into consideration when setting up the hardware for a computer system meant to specialize in digital photography applications: system calibration and calibrators; choosing, setting up and adjusting a display system; managing memory and other factors that affect system performance; hardware for transferring images from camera to computer; and how to decide which computing platform will best support your efforts.

✦   ✦   ✦

Saving and Uploading Digital Images

Saving images from your scanner or camera to your computer is almost as easy as the ads make it sound. However, if you want to download them with as little waste of time as possible, and save them in a way that will preserve their quality, you need to read this chapter.

A Few Simple Rules

There are a few things to keep in mind when you think about how and where to keep your digital photographs. Remember these "rules" and I promise that the digital picture-taking part of your life will be much more pleasant:

- ✦ Always add the file extension
- ✦ Never JPEG twice
- ✦ Always back up
- ✦ Use TIF as your cross-platform lossless format
- ✦ Save layered files in their native format
- ✦ Catalogue your images
- ✦ Keep a CD-ROM library

Always add the file extension

Make your image files readable by others, whether they own the same computer you do or not. The most important thing to remember is that non-Macintosh computers may not open files that don't have recognizable extensions. For most Windows users, adding the proper file extension will probably already be a matter of habit because most Windows software won't recognize files that don't have a file extension. This is the very reason why even Mac users should always remember to add one. To put it another way: Adding a file extension to all your files as soon as they're created will make them portable across platforms. If you add the extension as a matter of habit, you won't forget to add it when you're sending the file to a Web site, a service bureau, or a Windows-based client.

Macintosh users aren't required to use file extensions, as long as their files stay on a Mac. Some Windows users who are new to computers may not know what an extension is, either. That's because Windows lets you hide the file extension, even though almost all Windows programs automatically add one. For you folks, here's what a file extension is: a combination of three alphanumeric characters preceded by a dot that is placed after the name of a file. Here's an example:

```
myfile1.tif
```

The filename above is truly cross-platform. It can be read by programs running under Unix, DOS, all versions of Windows, the Mac, and any other recognized operating system on the planet. That is because it follows some very old, lowest-common-denominator rules:

✦ The filename (the part preceding the dot) must be less than eight characters in length.

✦ It must be written entirely in lowercase. Some operating systems are case-sensitive and will consider Myfile1.tif and myfile1.tif to be two entirely different filenames.

✦ There can be no illegal characters in any operating system's filenames. Such characters include spaces, slashes (\ or /), ampersands, asterisks, and many others. The only nonalphanumeric characters that are legal are the tilde and the underscore.

✦ There can be no spaces. It has been said before, but it's so easy for Mac and later-generation Windows users to forget it that it's worth saying again.

For those who don't want to take the time to stop now and carefully rename all their graphics files properly, you can download a utility called HTML Rename! (http://tucows.appollo.lv/adload/nt/dlrenament.html) that was written by my brilliant friend Terry Parker. He calls it HTML Rename! because "illegal" file-names can cause so many problems for Web site designers. Regardless of your purpose, the program will automatically "legalize" all the files in any directory. It also gives you the opportunity to change filenames that have been made obscure by the automatic renaming process. For instance, files that start with the same first five letters but are longer than eight characters (not including the dot and extension) will be named as follows: myfil~1.tif, myfil~2.tif, myfil~3.tif, and so on. The extra letter is reserved in case there are more than ten of these sequentially numbered files.

If you don't find these names descriptive enough, you can manually rename them much more quickly than if you had to do it in your operating system's file management program.

If you are a Windows user, it's a good idea to make your file extensions visible when you're using Explorer. To do this in Windows 98:

1. From the Start Menu, choose Programs ➪ Windows Explorer. The Explorer Window will open.

2. From the Menu bar, choose View ➪ Folder Options. A Folder Options dialog box will appear.

3. In the Folder Options dialog box, click the View tab (see Figure 16-1).

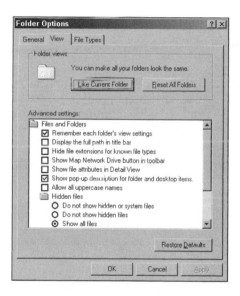

Figure 16-1: The Windows 98 Folder Options dialog box

4. Make sure the checkbox titled "Hide file extensions for known file types" is unchecked. Click OK.

The Macintosh OS poses a slightly different problem: You can name a file just about anything you like. There's no requirement for an extension. Instead, the programs place an invisible "header" in the file that lets the program know whether it's legal to open that file. This makes it hard for Mac users to acquire disciplined file-naming habits. Doing most of your image work in Photoshop can help. Here's how:

1. Open Photoshop. From the Menu bar, choose File ➪ Preferences ➪ Saving Files (see Figure 16-2).

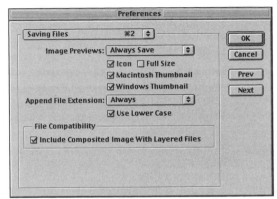

Figure 16-2: The Photoshop Saving Files Preferences
dialog box on the Macintosh

2. From the Append File Extension pull-down menu, choose Always.

3. Check the Use Lower Case checkbox.

4. It's also a good idea to have the program save thumbnails for both Windows
   and the Mac. That way, when Photoshop on the opposite program opens the
   file, a preview thumbnail will be seen in the File Browser dialog box.

Never JPEG twice

I've said this elsewhere in this book, but it can't be said often enough: Don't open a
JPEG file, make a change, and then save it again as a JPEG file unless you've made
all the changes you're ever going to need to make in that file. The same goes for
true-color PNG, which uses JPEG internally. Why? Because the file-save routine
recompresses the file each time it is saved and more data is lost in the process. The
worst of it is, you may be able to get away with this a few times before you notice a
significant difference. You will notice it more if you make an image adjustment, such
as changing brightness, contrast, or color balance. You're also more likely to notice
it if you use a filter that makes those adjustments in the process of doing its job.
You'll also notice it more in photographs that have large areas of smooth shading
or that have objects with hard edges against subtly shaded backgrounds.

Caution   Saving the same file to JPEG format multiple times will cause noticeable loss of
detail and definition. Save files to be archived in TIF format.

So what should you do? If you're doing your editing in a program that doesn't support layers, save the image as a TIF file (see below). If you're working in layers, you

have another reason for not wanting to save an image as a JPEG: You'll lose the layers. Instead, save it in your image-processing program's native format until you're ready to use the file.

There is one exception to the "never save it as JPEG twice" rule: if you digitally photographed something you plan to post on the Web and you want it to look photographic. In that case, you'll have to post a JPEG file to your server for Web publication. You'll probably have also made other changes to that photo in the interim, and you probably also reduced the size of the image. So you won't perceive much of a difference when you resave it to JPEG for the first time. Just be sure that you keep an uncompressed version of the file in case you need to alter and then republish the image.

Always back up

If you've been around computers for long, you know that it's always wise to back up any work you've done. It's doubly wise when you're dealing with photographs because the chances are slim-to-none that you can ever reproduce the same moment in time. Moreover, the opportunities for making creative changes to the original are so tempting and so infinite that you can really mess up the original. You'd better have a version you can go back to when that happens.

Note   Milburn's law of image backup: Only the images that you value most will be destroyed by overzealous editing, and these will always be the ones you forgot to back up.

Backing up is especially important when you have to send files to clients. They rarely get returned.

Use TIF as your cross-platform lossless format

When you want to send finished files to a client or store a flat (unlayered) file in the most efficient and portable lossless format, save it as a TIFF (Tagged Information File Format) file (the proper extension is .tif). It is a rare graphics program that can't read these files, regardless of the platform. The one danger is that there are several varieties of TIFF files and they are not all equally universal. If you come across a program that won't open a particular TIF file, try opening and saving it in another program. Chances are, the other program will save it in a more universal format.

It's also important to save your files to TIF format any time you're archiving them to CD-ROM. Years later, when you're working with who-knows-what computer and who-knows-which operating system, you'll still be able to open them.

Whatever you do, don't make PICT or BMP files your only copies or use them as CD-ROM archives. While Photoshop will open these formats on any platform, they are actually native to the Mac OS (PICT) or to Windows (BMP).

Save layered files in their native format

There is no "universal" format for layered files, although Photoshop's PSD comes close. The problem is, other programs that use layers may or may not be able to read Photoshop layered files. Even if they do, they may have specific layer commands or features that don't translate. On top of that, many other programs (such as MetaCreation's Painter) treat layers as objects, which can result in smaller files. So it's safer to save the file you're working on in the format of the program you're using to work on it.

If you need to shift between programs to get all the effects you have in mind, save a version in PSD format at the same time.

Always work on a copy of the original

If you're working on a copy of an image and really mess it up, you can always recover and start all over again. Programs such as Photoshop 5.5 and Painter 6 give you multiple undos, so you'll usually be able to recover anyway. There's no guarantee that this will be so, however. The only guarantee is to live by this rule.

Catalog your images

It won't be long before all your image filenames are close to useless. If you're like most of us, you'll tend to favor one subject type or theme over others. When you have 900 photos of daffodils, the filename pnkdaf014.tif isn't likely to identify exactly the pink daffodil you need.

The solution is *digital contact sheets*. You can probably make these simply by printing the thumbnails that your camera's download software provides (see Figure 16-3). There's always a Print command and the programs almost always put the name of the picture under the thumbnail.

Of course, if you also use CD-ROM stock photos, digital images from other sources, and scan images from film, your download software may not help. (Olympus' Camedia will make instant thumbnails of any directory, but not all bundled software is as cooperative.)

One of the most useful programs I've found is Cerious Software's Thumbs Plus. If you're on a budget, Thumbs Plus is less than $30. You can download it as shareware and try it out, too. Thumbs Plus provides some basic image-processing capabilities in addition to its prowess at visual file management. You'll find more about

Thumbs Plus in Chapter 15. A quick look at most shareware sites on the Web will provide you with a number of other programs that can make thumbnails as well.

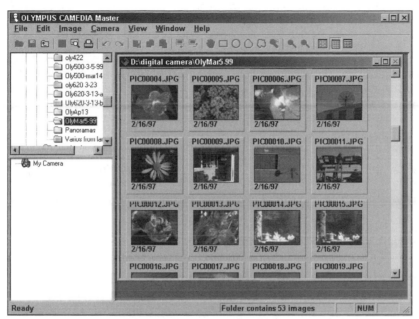

Figure 16-3: The easiest way to get a digital contact sheet is by downloading directly from a digital camera using its bundled software. Olympus' Camedia will instantly make a contact sheet of any directory of images, as long as they're in JPEG, TIFF, BMP, or PICT format.

If you need a corporate visual image manager that can also attach and correlate textual data to the image files, the best solution is to use a cross-platform program designed specifically for the purpose. Here's a list of information that you should record for each image you shoot:

✦ The date the picture was shot (there are both legal and practical reasons for this).

✦ The client's name, so you can quickly find all the images you shot for a particular client.

✦ A model release number, so you can quickly find it if there's a legal question or if a sale of the image requires proof of a model's release.

✦ A descriptive paragraph of the contents. This will help you recollect your feelings about a subject in case you want to publish the image later, annotate it on your Web site, or caption it for an exhibit.

✦ Category keywords. This can be anything you can think of that might help you find appropriate groups of subjects. For instance, a flower photo might have the following keywords attached: Flower, Garden, Daisy, Golden, Yellow, Potted Plants, Sunlight, and so on. This way, you can easily find all the photos of golden daisies in pots shot in direct sunlight.

✦ Technical information, including exposure, lighting type, film type (if applicable), camera used, and scanner settings. This is a great help in ensuring that you can duplicate the technical aspects of a photo. Clients often want you to shoot something that's similar to something they've seen in your portfolio. If you're shooting in a studio, notes about the type of lighting and reflectors used and their positions can be of great help later.

✦ Image-processing software used.

Be sure to keep a notebook with you at all times when you're shooting. By taking notes, you'll have the information you need in order to build your catalog later. Cameras that have a built-in voice recording capability are especially useful for keeping track of the aforementioned information. If your camera doesn't have such a feature, or if that's not how you want to use your camera's memory, micro cassette recorders are also very handy for making notes.

Making a catalog with Extensis' Portfolio

You were introduced to Extensis' Portfolio image-cataloguing program in Chapter 19. This section lets you try it out.

There's a demo version of the Portfolio program on the CD-ROM for this book. If you're not already locked in to a favorite system of image management, you'll have a better basis for judging these types of systems.

If you already think Extensis' Portfolio might be the system for you, here's a chance to work with the program a bit before you plop down hard-earned cash. If you're not familiar with this type of software, you'll also learn a lot about its value. If you're already using another system, you can still pick up some valuable tips. To make your catalog, follow these steps:

1. From the File menu, choose New.

2. A New Catalog browser opens (see Figure 16-4). Navigate to the folder you want to catalog and open it. Enter any name you prefer. It's a good idea to stick with eight-character names so that you can put the catalog on your CD-ROMs. Click Save.

3. A blank window bearing the title of your album will open. From the Catalog menu, choose Add Items. You can add items individually by simply choosing them in the browser window. However, when you're creating a brand-new catalog, it's much faster and easier to catalog an entire folder at once. That's what we're going to do here. Navigate to the folder you want to catalog (see Figure 16-5). Click Current Folder.

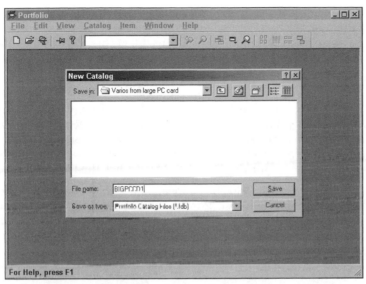

Figure 16-4: Portfolio's New Catalog dialog box is an ordinary file-browsing window.

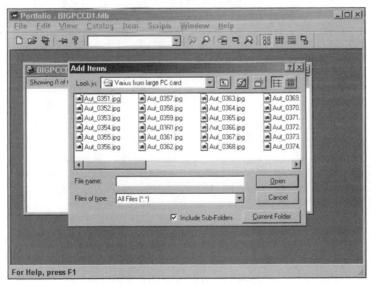

Figure 16-5: Portfolio's Add Items is another file browser dialog box. However, notice the Current Folder button on the lower right.

4. The Cataloging Options dialog box will open. If you click the various tabs, you'll see many options available to you. The ones I'm going to suggest are merely those that I find most generally useful at this stage. Remember, the purpose of this exercise isn't to teach you Portfolio, but to give you an idea of how useful it may be. Click the General tab.

5. The General Options dialog box presents itself. From the Modification Method pull-down-menu, choose Add. From the Path as Keywords pull-down menu, choose None. (If you want to put this catalog on a CD-ROM or Zip disk, which shouldn't be confused with a Zip file, it will have a different path anyway. Also, we're going to rename all the files in a moment.) Choose High for Thumbnail Quality and 112×112 for the Thumbnail Size. Click the File Types tab.

6. The File Types Options dialog box appears. Click the Catalog Only the Following Types radio button. Otherwise, Portfolio will catalog programs and document files. If you want to present a proof sheet to a client, you probably only want them to see what you shot. Uncheck all the other file types (see Figure 16-6).

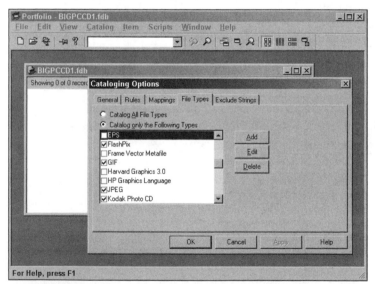

Figure 16-6: Portfolio will catalog just about every type of media file you can imagine, including presentation and text document files.

7. Thumbnails of all your files will appear. First, eliminate all the files that contain images you'll never have use for. They hog your hard drive and CD-ROM space and make you look bad to your clients and colleagues. Highlight all the files you want to eliminate (press Shift on the Mac or Control on the PC to select several nonsequential filenames). Choose Item ➪ Delete Original. This will delete both the thumbnails and the original files.

8. Next, there will be numerous images that were shot with the camera in a portrait (vertical) orientation. Unless you shot them with a Kodak or other camera that automatically rotates the file as it is stored, those thumbnails will be lying on their sides. Select all those you want to rotate to the left. Choose Item ➪ Rotate Thumbnail ➪ 90 Degrees Counterclockwise. All the selected thumbnails will almost instantly appear right side up. Repeat the process for any that need to be rotated to the right. Note that Portfolio doesn't actually rotate the files, only the thumbnails. The original files were never opened and then recompressed after rotation. As a result, no further data has been lost from the original.

9. If you've catalogued files from a digital film card, the files will probably all have sequential numbers. After all, the camera just can't second-guess what you'd like to call those files. The first thing you want to do is assign filenames that make sense (see Figure 16-7). Press Command/Control+Shift+N (or choose Item ➪ Rename Original).

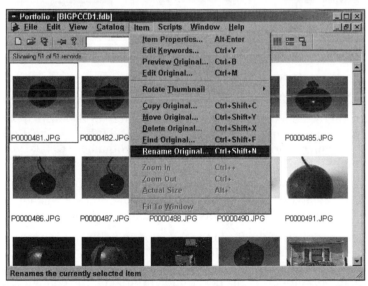

Figure 16-7: Notice that Portfolio has already made thumbnails of all the images in the current folder and captioned them with their current filenames.

10. A Rename File dialog box appears. Enter the name you'd like to use. You can use any number of letters and combinations, but if you're going to save the album on a CD-ROM, you'll want to use ISO 9660-legal names. Otherwise, the names you use will be truncated when you record to CD-ROM. Repeat this step as often as necessary to rename all the files in your album. In Figure 16-8, you can see that all the files have been named and correctly oriented.

Figure 16-8: This is the same thumbnail catalog shown in Figure 16-7. Here, we have substituted all our own filenames.

11. You may feel that the shortened filenames are a bit cryptic. No problem. You can give each thumbnail a real title, automatically have it displayed and printed on the contact sheet, and use it to search for files with a particular title. You can also enter all sorts of keywords and other information. If fact, there's so much more you can do, I only have room here to take you through a few more features.

12. Let's add a more descriptive name to each thumbnail. Highlight a thumbnail. Right-click (Win) or Ctrl+click (Mac) to get the In-Context menu for that item. Choose Properties. The Item Properties dialog box will appear (see Figure 16-9).

13. Type a description of the file in the Description field. You can type anything you like, but it's wise to keep the important information at the beginning of the description and to keep the description file as short as possible. Then you see the important part of the description printed on the contact sheet. You also ensure that you won't have superfluous words confusing any searching you do on the description text. When you've finished typing the description, click the Keywords tab. The Keywords dialog box appears.

14. In the Item Keywords field, type a keyword, and then press Return/Enter to add the word to the list of keywords that describe this item (see Figure 16-10). You can add as many keywords as you like.

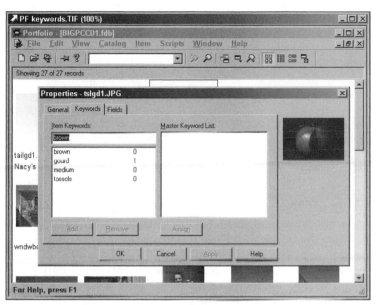

Figure 16-9: The Item Properties dialog box

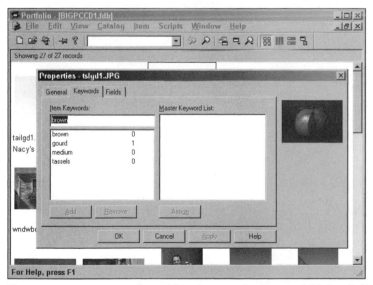

Figure 16-10: You can also add an item to the Keyword list by clicking the Add button, and clicking Remove deletes any highlighted keyword.

Making CD-ROM image archives

As your collection of digital photographs grows, you'll find that the best way to keep those massive amounts of information is on CD-ROM. As mentioned in the previous chapter, the disks are so inexpensive they are practically free, they take little space, and they can be easily reproduced for distribution.

As long as your CD-ROM's content is nothing but images, you can easily make a cross-platform disk on any commonly used computer system. If it can run a CD recorder, it can make a CD-ROM in ISO 9660 format. If you want to include programs that run slide shows or want to include viewers for thumbnail albums and still want your disks to be cross-platform, you'll have to make a *hybrid CD-ROM*. A hybrid CD-ROM is one that has several partitions, each of which has different compatibility characteristics. Typically, one wants a partition that is Windows-compatible (ISO 9660 format with the Rockridge extensions that support long filenames). This is for placing the slide-show program, presentation program, or image-management program viewer for those who are using the disk with a Windows computer. Another partition would contain similar programs for Mac users. Yet another partition holds files that are compatible with either system. This last is the partition where you place all your images or other content.

Caution   The problem with writing hybrid CD-ROMs is that you need a Macintosh — at least so far. No Windows-based CD recording software supports making hybrid CD-ROMs.

In order to make a CD-ROM, you need CD-ROM recording software. Some such program is almost always included in a CD-ROM recorder's retail package. Adaptec's is the software most commonly bundled, probably because of its popularity. Adaptec's two leading products are Easy CD Creator for Windows and Toast for the Macintosh. Both programs support copying CDs and making audio CDs.

Two other types of CD-ROMs sound synonymous with hybrid CD's: multi-session CDs and mixed-mode CDs. In fact, neither is at all synonymous.

Multi-session CDs are written in several different sessions at different times, and all the sessions are written in the same format. The disk can't be played on ordinary CD-ROM drives until the session is closed out. Then no more sessions can be written to that disk. Multi-session CDs are a good way to gradually collect images without crowding your hard drive. You can then copy all the files back to a single directory on a hard drive and record them to a single-session CD that could be more widely distributed.

Mixed-mode CDs are CDs that have data written in the first track and audio in CD-DA format occupying the balance of the disk. CD-DA is a format specifically reserved for digital audio.

If you have a late-model CD-ROM drive, you can buy software that can copy CDs. This is a very useful feature to look for because you may want to create image libraries that can be sent to several collaborators at once. However, you can also simply write the same collection of files (a session) to multiple CDs. If you have already erased that session from your hard drive, you could always copy the files back (provided you have the space) and then create a new session. Copying an existing CD simply requires fewer steps and less of your dedicated time.

Fine-tuning your system for CD-ROM recording

Following are a few things you should be prepared to do for your system before you invest in a CD-ROM recorder:

✦ Make sure you have at least 670MB of free space on your hard drive.

✦ Make sure your disk has at least 13-millisecond access time (read the data spec sheet for your hard drive or look it up on the manufacturer's Web site).

✦ Defragment your hard drive before recording the CD.

✦ Choose a CD-ROM recorder with a large data buffer and the ability to record at the speed you choose. If your hard drive isn't very fast and you have to write large data blocks, you may get more reliable results when writing at slow speeds. This is less likely to be true if you have a large data buffer.

Making a hybrid CD

Here's a checklist of items you'll need or things you'll need to do in order to make CD-ROMs that can contain both Mac and Windows software as well as a data segment that can be read from both platforms:

✦ A Macintosh (probably). It is a rare Windows CD-ROM recording package that can produce a Mac-compatible hybrid CD.

✦ Look for a program that supports the Rockridge extensions for ISO 9660. Some contemporary Windows software uses filenames that are longer than the eight-character filenames with a three-character extension enforced by the basic ISO 9660 standard. The Windows-compatible portion of a hybrid CD is written in ISO 9660 format.

✦ Name the data files according to ISO 9660 conventions.

✦ Place all the CD's images (and other data) in a single folder.

✦ Place Windows programs in a separate folder.

✦ Place Mac programs in the Mac partition.

Tip I like working with an external CD-ROM recorder that is SCSI-compatible (USB and FireWire might also become viable options, but I've not yet tested any of these). I can then easily move the recorder from one platform to the other. Of course, you will need separate CD-ROM recording software for both platforms.

Using Faster Connections

If you use a semi-professional camera that doesn't have a FireWire or SCSI interface to your computer, you will find that moving your images from camera to computer is intolerably slow. Chapter 19 introduced you to some faster hardware for transferring pictures. The following sections describe how you use those devices.

clik! disks

If you're thinking about taking a digital camera on a long trip and don't want to spend a fortune on digital film cards, or lug along a laptop, there's a very good solution. It's a very small (about the size of a fifty-cent coin) 40MB removable hard drive. You put your SmartMedia card in one end of a battery-powered unit that's about the size of a cigarette pack. You slip a click! disk into the other and transfer the pictures off the SmartMedia card onto the disk. The disks cost about $10 each and you can put about five 8MB SmartMedia cards worth of data on each one. When you do get back to a computer, just put the clik! drive into a docking station that's hooked to the serial port of your computer and transfer the pictures to your hard drive for processing. An alternative is to use the laptop unit, which attaches to a much faster PCMCIA slot. You can buy all the parts I've mentioned so far in a single kit for $300 or you can just buy the battery-powered drive and a docking station for fifty bucks less. Figure 16-11 shows all the components of the clik! drive system.

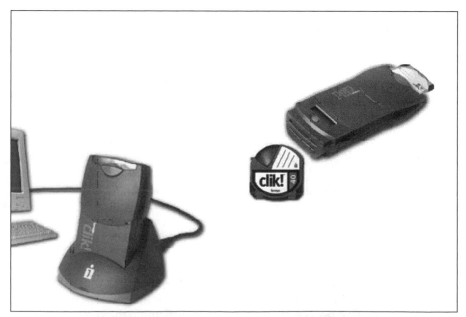

Figure 16-11: The clik! disk slips into the slot shown just above it; the SmartMedia card slips into the other end. After the transfer is made, the SmartMedia card is removed and the drive is placed into the docking station (lower left).

PCMCIA Cards

Flash memory cards that fit into the standard PCMCIA slot in a portable computer are often used in professional cameras for storing images because these larger cards can be made to hold more images. A Type III card can be made to hold a miniature hard disk with as much as 384 megabytes of data. Type I cards can host Flash Disks (solid-state disk drives) and the larger format allows for higher capacity than can be accommodated in the CompactFlash cards that use the same technology.

Using a PCMCIA card is no different than reading data from any external hard drive. This assumes that you're using a computer that already has a PCMCIA slot installed. If you don't have a PCMCIA card slot installed in (or to) your computer, you can purchase the necessary hardware. Dozens of companies make adapters for internal or external PCMCIA cards that will work with a wide variety of computers. You can find a current list of these on the Web at www.apresearch.com/cardrive.htm. One manufacturer, Microtech International, makes a wide variety of adapters, including SCSI adapters that can be moved from a Mac to a Wintel machine. You can see a list of their latest adapters at www.microtechint.com.

If you're looking for one device that can read digital camera media of all types on all platforms, a SCSI or USB PCMCIA card reader can do the job. That is because you can purchase adapters for PCMCIA cards for both CompactFlash (CF) and SmartMedia (SM) cards. You simply slide the smaller CF or SM card into the adapter, and then slide the adapter into the PCMCIA card reader (see Figure 16-12).

Card readers

There are card readers for all the popular types of digital film cards: PCMCIA, SmartMedia, CompactFlash and Sony Memory Stick. Using a card reader is at least 20 times faster than using the serial port hooked up to a camera. Exactly how much faster will depend on how your card reader is attached to your computer. In order of speed (fastest first), the alternative types of attachments are as follows:

✦ PCMCIA card slot

✦ SCSI

✦ USB

✦ Parallel

✦ Serial

It is awkward (if not impossible) to connect both a SmartMedia and a CompactFlash film reader to the same computer at the same time through the same type of port. For companies who have field staff carrying several varieties of cameras, and for service bureaus that may want to download images from a variety of cameras, it is very handy to have both types of readers attached to the same computer(s). Several companies make a single card reader that accepts both types of media. Some companies, such as Microtech, even have single readers that can accommodate PCMCIA, SmartMedia, and CompactFlash.

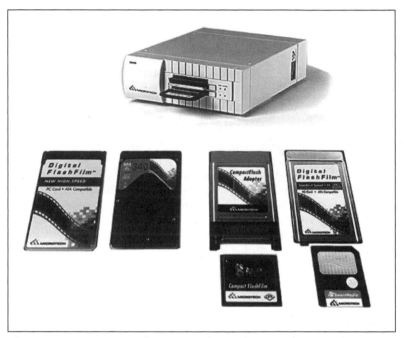

Figure 16-12: An external SCSI two-slot PCMCIA reader provides one solution for quickly reading nearly all types of digital film for the full range of 35mm and smaller camera bodies. Pictured from left to right: Flash disk, PC-card hard drive, adapter for CompactFlash card, adapter for SmartMedia card.

Caution　Don't try to use SmartMedia 5V cards in 3.3V readers or vice-versa. Also, be sure to use the right voltage cards as specified by your camera. Almost all cameras use 3.3V cards, but check your manual to make sure you're using the right media.

Card readers are not only faster than downloading directly from your camera (yes, even if your camera has a USB connection), they also save your camera's batteries. This is because the card reader takes its power from the computer. A card reader can format your media, so you don't have to waste camera battery power for that, either.

Card readers are seen by your computer operating system as external disk drives. This makes it impractical to use data switch boxes with card readers because flipping the switch to direct input from the port could cause a system conflict.

One company makes USB digital film readers for ATA (PCMCIA) Flash ($199), CompactFlash ($149), and a combination SmartMedia/CompactFlash reader ($129). This sounds like the reader to have if you think you may not always want to download images from the same camera. Microtech makes a combination CompactFlash and SmartMedia reader for half that price: $65.

The three leading manufacturers of digital film card readers (in alphabetical order) are as follows:

- ✦ **Lexar Media** (www.digitalfilm.com; 510-413-1200)
- ✦ **Microtech International, Inc.** (www.microtechint.com; 800-626-4276)
- ✦ **Sandisk** (www.sandisk.com; 408-542-0500)

Summary

This chapter provided additional facts, hints, and tips on transferring images from your camera to your computer. First you learned a few simple rules for saving image files. You also learned how to use the most essential parts of the leading image-management program, Extensis Portfolio. In the course of these lessons, you should have also learned some procedures that will prove valuable when using any image-management software. Finally, you learned the essentials of making CD-ROMs for the purpose of archiving and distributing images.

✦   ✦   ✦

Photoshop Image Processing Basics

After taking a look at what the "easy" entry-level programs can do, you may realize that they don't meet all your requirements — or don't meet them as efficiently as you'd like. As was the case with PhotoDeluxe and the other image-processing programs, what you find in this chapter is (or should be) applicable to most current-generation professional image-processing programs. That is to say, you should be able to

+ Work in an environment that's most likely to be familiar to your collaborators and outside resources

+ Access all commands in (almost) all stages of operations

+ Make image corrections with a high level of precision

+ Make precise selections quickly, including the ability to make vector path selections

+ Work on multiple layers and have complete freedom in deciding whether and how they are to be combined

+ Edit individual color channels and create new special-purpose ones (such as for masking or spot color)

+ Automate repetitive tasks

+ Take advantage of multiple levels of undo

+ Access desktop publishing–quality text entry and editing tools

Professional image-processing software is so powerful and versatile that users are always discovering new ways to combine their features to accomplish new tasks. That is why there will always be a never-ending stream of books written about them. It would be impossible to tell you everything you need to know in one chapter. You should, however, get a good idea of when and why you would choose a fully-featured, professional image-processing program over one that is more accessible. You should also get a good idea of how much greater an investment you will have to make to take advantage of software at this level.

The fundamental capabilities of professional image-processing software are discussed in this chapter in the order they are most likely to be employed. However, one of the important advantages of working with professional programs is that you can access any task directly, at the time you need it.

Cropping, Composition, and Enhancing Resolution

One of the reasons you might want to work in a professional image-processor is the degree of control you can exert over image quality. Because it's rare that either your shooting situation or equipment is perfectly tuned at the instant of shutter-click, you may well want all the after-the-fact advantages you can get.

There are several reasons you may want to start here with processing your images digitally:

✦ Disk space is precious and image files tend to be disproportionately large compared to other types of data (except analog sound and video). Therefore, you want to throw out data you definitely know you're not going to use.

✦ You may need more resolution than your camera or scanner can produce.

✦ Images are often slightly out of focus.

These problems are so common that if you fix them first, you'll generally have an easier time with the later steps. It's usually logical to take these steps in the order they were presented above.

Using the Cropping and Marquee tools

There are four reasons you will most often want to crop (trim) an image:

✦ To make it fit a prescribed layout (proportional space within a target document)

✦ To improve the composition

✦ To eliminate distracting elements

✦ To maximize file size for use in Web and multimedia projects

Photoshop provides you with two methods for cropping: (1) Use the Marquee tool in conjunction with the Image ➪ Crop command, or (2) Directly use the Cropping tool.

Using the Marquee tool

Using the Marquee tool is the most accurate way to crop if you need to crop portions of an image that are close to the border. The Cropping tool will automatically snap to the edge of the frame if it's within a few pixels of that edge. Also, you can set the Marquee to an exact size, thus ensuring that the image will be exactly the right size or proportion. To use the Marquee tool instead of the cropping tool:

1. Open your target image in Photoshop 5.0 (you can download a demo of the program from the Adobe site at www.adobe.com). The shot of the flower used in Figure 17-1, as is typical of many digital cameras, has the proportions of a 35mm film frame. Because we want the image to fit an 8×10-inch frame, we want the crop to fit a 1:1.25 proportion. You can get the proportion for any image by dividing the short side of the target frame into the long side of the target frame. In this instance, the picture has a "landscape" orientation (wider than tall), so we want the exact height. Choose Window ➪ Show Info. In the Info palette (see Figure 17-1), in the lower-right quadrant, you will see the (W)idth and (H)eight.

Figure 17-1: The Info palette can always be used to report the size of any rectangular selection. It's a good idea to keep your unit preferences set to pixels.

2. Open your computer's calculator and multiply the short dimension by the ratio of the longer dimension (in this case, 1.25). Because our image is 1,024 pixels high, we will want it to be 1,024 high × 1.25 wide or 1,024 × 1,280 pixels. Press Command/Control+D to Deselect All (which gets rid of the marquee).

3. Double-click the Marquee tool. The Marquee Options palette will open (see Figure 17-2). Choose Fixed Size from the Style pull-down menu and enter 1,024 for the height and 1,280 for the width. Click in the image and the marquee will instantly delineate the precise cropping frame. You can place the cursor on the marquee line and drag to change the placement of the marquee, but the size will stay the same.

Figure 17-2: The marquee's dots must be showing on all four sides.

4. Make sure that the marquee's dotted line is showing on all four sides. Otherwise, your cropped image won't have the correct proportions. Then choose Image ⇨ Crop. To save the cropped image to a new name (you should never obliterate the original by writing over it), choose File ⇨ Save As. In the Save As dialog box, choose a file format that is not lossy. Be sure to add the name of your file format's extension to the end of the file so that it can be read across platforms.

Using the Cropping tool

The Cropping tool is the best mechanism for quickly trimming when exact finished proportions are not a problem. For instance, suppose you need a picture to give to your significant other and you only have one, with your arms around your old flame. You just grab the Cropping tool from the toolbox and drag diagonally across the part of the picture you want to keep. You can fine-tune the exact area to be trimmed by dragging any of the bounding box handles. When everything is adjusted just the way you like it, double-click inside the bounding box. Photoshop instantly trims all layers of the picture.

Enhancing resolution

Actually, there is no such thing as enhancing resolution—only enhancing the apparent resolution. You can, however, resample the image to a different size. Instead of simply multiplying or subtracting pixels, the program tries to shade the duplicated pixels so that their color and intensity fall in-between those of their neighbors. Usually, the result is a smooth-shaded image with soft edges. In Figure 17-3, you see a segment of an image at its original size, and two versions that have been magnified by 400 percent. Notice that in the middle image, there is a pronounced "square pixel" effect that results from simply reproducing each pixel sixteen times. This is called *nearest neighbor resampling* because each additional pixel is a copy of its nearest neighbor. The image at the far right has been resampled using *bicubic interpolation* so that the new pixels form a subtle gradient between pixels that were formerly neighbors.

Figure 17-3: You can see how the image on the far right seems to have much higher resolution than the one in the middle. However, it doesn't actually contain more detail, so the edges look fuzzy.

Of course, you notice that the hard-edged lines still show some stair-stepping, even though it's less pronounced than in the middle image. That's because the contrast between the pixels that form the edges (lines) and those that form the background contrast so abruptly that the program can't enter enough pixels in between to form a smooth transition.

The other drawback is that the picture is softer. In other words, it appears to be slightly out of focus. We can fix that with an Unsharp Mask filter, but we will increase the jaggedness of the edges in the process. In Figure 17-4, the image on the left is the whole image, resampled using bicubic interpolation. The image on the right looks more detailed because some edges have been sharpened slightly with the Unsharp Mask filter.

Figure 17-4: You can see how the Unsharp Mask filter, if not overdone, can improve the illusion of enhanced resolution.

Using the Unsharp Mask filter

Entry-level image-processing programs generally make it possible to sharpen an image. However, it is rare for the user to be able to adjust the sharpening (except, of course, by repeating it). Photoshop 5, Corel Photo-Paint 9, and most other professional image processors feature an Unsharp Mask filter that lets you make wide-ranging adjustments over three parameters: Amount, Radius, and Threshold (see Figure 17-5). Amount refers to the increase in contrast between adjacent pixels. Radius controls the size of the area over which pixels will be controlled. Threshold controls the amount of contrast between pixels that must occur before sharpening will take place.

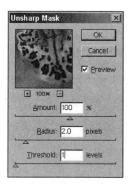

Figure 17-5: The Unsharp Mask dialog box in Photoshop 5

It is important to preview your image at 100-percent magnification while making these adjustments. Oversharpening results in sharply pixelated (jagged) edges, which creates the appearance of lower resolution.

To sharpen an image using the Unsharp Mask filter:

1. Choose Filter ⇨ Sharpen ⇨ Unsharp Mask. The Unsharp Mask dialog box will appear.

2. Drag the Amount slider (or enter a value). Adobe recommends 150 to 200 percent for images that will be printed at high resolution.

3. Drag the Radius slider (or enter a value). Adobe recommends a radius of one or two pixels for images that will be printed at high resolution. Lower values sharpen only the most predominant edges. Higher values can result in the appearance of graininess in smooth-toned areas of the image.

4. Drag the Threshold slider (or enter a value) to indicate the degree of contrast between pixels before they will be considered as edges to be sharpened. You probably don't want to leave the setting at the default of 0, because it sharpens all the pixels in the image. Again, this can result in sharper pixels, which looks grainier. Visible grain is the traditional indicator of low resolution in film.

5. When you're satisfied with the look of the preview, click OK.

Tip   It pays to set your Unsharp Mask settings as follows: Amount at 50 percent, Radius at 1 pixel, and Threshold at 1 or 2. Run the filter, and then press Command/Control+F to run the filter again. Continue to rerun the filter until the result seems overdone, and then press Command/Control+Z to undo the last step. This enables you to see the result over the entire image in small increments. If you really overdo it, you can use Photoshop's History palette to go back one step at a time until you like the result. Then delete the steps that follow.

There will be times when unsharp masking tends to make colors oversaturated. You can avoid that by choosing Image ➪ Mode ➪ Lab Color. Then choose Window ➪ Show Channels and select the Lightness channel. Now run the Unsharp Mask filter as prescribed above. The edge sharpening will take place without affecting the color components.

Smoothing jagged edges

As noted earlier, edges in the original that are jagged and contain a great deal of sharply contrasting detail (called *contrasty* in photographic lingo and usually implying an objectionable level of contrast) will appear even more so when you change resolution — especially when you make a large change. You can soften these edges by hand or by masking. Softening by hand usually works best because you soften each edge until the result is visually pleasing. Masking will save a lot of time and, unless you're good at softening by hand, is likely to produce superior results. This is because you can preview the amount of softening over the entire image.

To soften edges by hand, magnify your image to 100 percent (double-click the Magnifier tool). Choose the Blur tool (it looks like a water drop), pick a brush size that's just large enough to cover the edge you want to soften, and then just paint over the edges until they look right to you. Figure 17-6 shows an edge that has been resampled to 400 percent before and after the edge has been softened by hand.

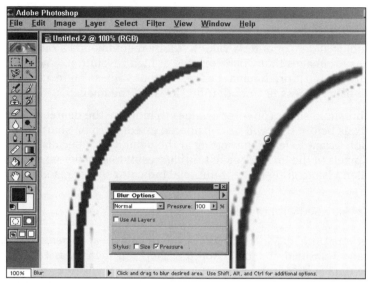

Figure 17-6: When pixelization (jaggies) is this severe, it usually takes several strokes to blur the edges sufficiently, even with the blur pressure set at 100 percent.

Caution   If you have a lot of jagged edges to repair and you want to be able to control the blending so that it is uniform throughout the image, you'll be better off masking the edges using the Quick Mask and Brush tools.

Here's how to mask the edges using the Quick Mask and Brush tools:

1. Choose the Brush tool. Choose Window ➪ Show Brushes. The Brushes dialog box will appear. Choose the brush size and softness that you will need in order to cover the edges you want to smooth. The brush should be slightly feathered, so that the strokes will have soft edges.

2. Press D to select the default colors. The foreground color will be black. Black will make your mask 100-percent transparent, so any effect you apply over it will be executed at full intensity. The graduated grays that form the smooth edges enable the effect to take place according to the gray level of the mask. Actually, you will be painting your mask in red. This is only to help you place the map accurately. If you save the resulting Quick Mask as a channel, you will see that the mask is grayscale.

3. Making the mask is really easy. Double-click the Quick Mask icon (it's on the right-hand side of the second row of icons from the bottom). The Quick Mask dialog box will appear. Activate the Color Indicates: Selected Area radio button. If you want, you can change the masking color to one that will really stand out from the predominant colors in your image. To do so, click the color square and the Color Picker will appear. Choose the color you'd like to use.

4. Display the image at 100 percent (or more, if you like) so that you can see the true resolution of the image. Carefully brush along any edges that need smoothing. Some bumpy edges probably belong, and smoothing them would only make the image look less realistic. Painting the mask by hand enables you to judge which edges should be smoothed and which should not.

5. When you have finished painting your lines, click the Edit in Standard Mode icon (to the immediate left of the Quick Mask icon). Freeform marquees will appear at scattered intervals. The area inside these marquees will be affected by the next step.

6. From the main menu bar, choose Filter ➪ Blur ➪ Gaussian Blur.

7. The Gaussian Blur dialog box will appear. Check the Preview box so that you can see the result of your slider adjustment in the original image. Drag the slider until the edges blur just enough. When you like what you see, click OK.

8. While the mask (selection) is still active, adjust the brightness and contrast so that you get a sharper smooth edge that blends with the original image. You are essentially done. Press Command/Control+D to drop the mask, save your image, and proceed with any other image editing you plan to do.

Tip   Change resolution by percentage in even increments. This makes it easier for the program to "guess" which pixel to duplicate for an increase in resolution or to dismiss for a decrease in resolution.

Correcting color and exposure

It's a rare "right-out-of-the-camera" image that can't be improved by making a few adjustments in color and tonal values. If you're coming to digital photography from a traditional photography background, this is the digital version of all the stuff you used to do in the darkroom: shooting and developing film for the maximum range of detail in the original, choosing the right enlarging paper contrast and development time, doing localized burning and dodging, and using filters during enlarging to balance color for natural tones.

The difference is that Photoshop gives you far more control over exposure, tonal range, overall contrast, and color balance than you could ever hope to achieve in the darkroom. I know that there are traditional photographers out there who are so accomplished that we can't imagine that they could do better by any other means. Many photographers who fall into that class (Jerry Uelsman, Milton Greene, and Graham Nash immediately come to mind) will also tell you that you can do still more and do it better — with a well-equipped computer, a professional image-processing program (such as Photoshop, Painter, or Photo-Paint), and access to a good printer.

In any case, it all starts with Photoshop (or one of the other aforementioned programs). The trick is to do the image-correcting processes in a sequence that's least likely to cost you image quality by throwing out data that you might need later.

Tip

I recommend working in 16-bits per channel mode as long as your system can afford the resources. You may have a camera or scanner that recorded the image in more than 8-bits-per-pixel color depth. If so, you want to retain all that information until you are sure that you have made all the adjustments you will need to make. Once you've made your adjustments, you can drop back to 8-bit mode.

As for sequencing your operations so that you lose as little data as possible at each stage, here's the order of operations. I think you'll also find that this is the most time-efficient sequence of operations:

1. Adjust the tonal levels.

2. Balance for natural or atmospheric color qualities.

3. Boost or reduce saturation for effect (when called for).

4. Do localized burning and dodging.

Making color balance look natural

If you want to build up your instincts for correct color balance, I can suggest a couple of routines that have worked for me. The first is to take head shots of the same person in a variety of typical lighting situations. They should all use the same brand and speed of film and be processed by the same lab (not a consideration if the images are captured by a digital camera — but be sure to use the same camera and computer display). The shots should include the following:

✦ **Outdoors:** sunrise, early morning, mid-morning, noon, mid-afternoon, sunset. At each of these times of day, shoot in full shade (some overhang is covering the direct light from the sky), open shade, and open sky. Also, shoot on days when the sky conditions are cloudless, cloudy, and overcast.

✦ **Indoors:** natural light from windows and skylights, tungsten light, fluorescent light, and a mixture of daylight and tungsten light.

If possible, have your model hold a Kodak gray card close to the head (but not so close that it's shaded or shades the head). You can buy a Kodak gray card direct from Kodak's Web site or from any professional photo dealer. These cards cost less than twenty dollars.

Cross-Reference

Be sure you have calibrated your monitor according to any of the instructions in Chapter 15.

1. In Photoshop, open the "open shade" photo and keep it open. Hold the gray card next to the monitor. Choose Image ➪ Adjust ➪ Color Balance. The Color Balance dialog box will open. Check the Preserve Luminosity and Preview checkboxes.

2. Drag the sliders for each color individually until you've adjusted the color balance so that the gray card is the same neutral gray both on the screen and off. You should never have to change the balance of more than two of the colors. If the gray card seems to be mostly too green, start with the middle slider and move it toward magenta. When you've come as close as possible with that slider, pick the slider that now shows the predominantly off color. The skin tone should now look quite natural.

3. Open each of the other images. One at a time, place them next to the first image you color balanced. For each of the images, drag the sliders until the gray card is neutral gray. The color balance of the face should now match the color balance of the original open shade photo. As you correct each photo, write down the color balance for each set of conditions.

From now on, you should be able to come very close to adjusting the color value for any picture just by knowing the conditions under which it was shot and adjusting the color balance according to your notations. This doesn't mean that I have given you a perfect recipe for balancing color. There will always be variances in the exact color of light, in light reflected from surroundings, in the color balance of different films and cameras, and on and on. What we're trying to do here is just hone your instinct for knowing where to start.

You'll probably notice that people find a slightly too-red color balance flattering in portraits — especially if your subjects are Caucasian.

Note Natural color balance isn't always the desired result (although it's generally a good place to start). A color imbalance can imply an atmosphere (a bit of extra yellow might imply a sunnier day, for instance). It can also imply a location or time of day. The best rule is to learn the other rules well enough to know when it's appropriate to break them.

Tip I find that Extensis' Intellihance does an excellent job of balancing color most of the time. It also does it very quickly. If you can afford the extra cost of the software and you have to process a volume of photos, you'll probably find that the program saves you considerable time.

Using the Levels and Curves commands

Any image-processing program, even the one that comes with your camera, will let you lighten or darken an image and change the overall contrast. These simple adjustments will usually make your picture more "readable." If you want to bowl people over with your ability to capture the richness of a full range of tonal values, you'll probably have to use the more sophisticated Levels and Curves commands.

The Levels controls, accessed through the Levels dialog box, represent the quickest and most efficient way to ensure that your image contains a full range of tones while the midtone values are adjusted to be as bright as you'd like them to be. To set Levels, choose Image ⇨ Adjust ⇨ Levels. The Levels dialog box appears (see Figure 17-7). It contains two sets of slider controls: Input Levels (represented by a histogram) and Output Levels (represented by a smooth gradient from absolute black to absolute white).

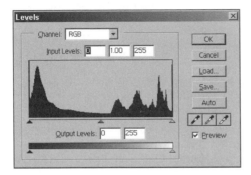

Figure 17-7: The Input Levels histogram (the shape that looks like the silhouette of a mountain range) shows the number of pixels assigned to each level of brightness.

Under the histogram, the black triangle lever on the left sets the darkest point in the image; the white triangle lever on the right sets the lightest point. The middle lever sets the brightness of the image's midtone. To increase the image's overall contrast, you move the two outer levers inward. To change the image's gamma (midtone brightness), you drag the middle lever. Take a look at the image shown in Figure 17-8. It is too dark and lacks pure white highlights and solid blacks. In photographer's parlance, the image is "too flat."

Figure 17-8: A photographer would describe this image as *flat* or *muddy*.

We can give this picture a full range of tones that would be the envy of Ansel Adams. To do so:

1. Open the image in Photoshop. Zoom in to at least 100 percent so that you can easily judge the brightness of very small areas. Choose the Eyedropper tool. Choose Window ⇨ Show Info to display the Info dialog box. Drag the eyedropper over what appears to you to be the brightest pixels in the image. Watch the RGB values change in the Info dialog box. When the eyedropper shows the highest number, you have found the lightest spot in the image. Make a mental note of exactly where that spot is.

2. Use the eyedropper and the method above to locate the darkest spot in the image.

Note   There will be times when you want the lightest and darkest spots in the final image to be different from those that are actually lightest and darkest. That is a perfectly legitimate subjective and artistic choice.

3. Choose Image ⇨ Adjust ⇨ Levels. The Levels dialog box appears. Be sure the Preview box is checked. Choose the White eyedropper, and then move the cursor (which now looks like an eyedropper) to the lightest spot in the image (or the one that you want to be the lightest) and click. The image will instantly brighten (see Figure 17-9).

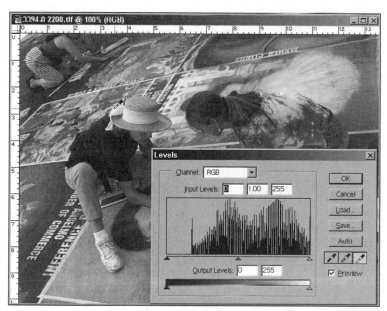

Figure 17-9: Clicking the brightest highlight on the hatband with the White eyedropper makes this the white point in the image. Any pixels that were actually brighter will now be white as well.

4. Choose the Black eyedropper. Move it to the darkest spot in the picture and click. Don't be afraid to drag the Levels dialog box out of the way so that you can reach your dark spot. When you click, the entire image will darken and you will see a full range of tones from black to white. If you are satisfied with the result at this point, your work is done. Most of the time, however, you'll find that the image can be considerably improved by changing the gamma (You want gamma? Boost the gamma).

5. In the example shown, I wanted to raise the gamma (brighten the value of the pixels that are currently 50 percent gray). When I do this, Photoshop (and most other professional image-processors) will raise the other tonal values in a smooth curve from the brightest point to the darkest point (see Figure 17-10).

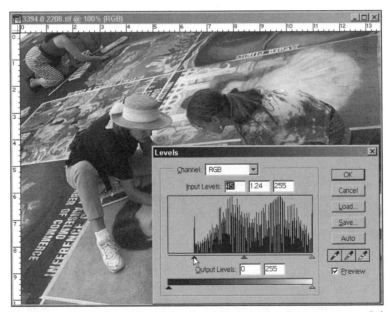

Figure 17-10: I wanted to make the skin tones brighter, so I moved the midtone pointer to the left until the preview showed me the result I liked.

Tip

You probably don't want to use the Gray (middle) eyedropper. It will change the color balance so that you get a neutral 50 percent gray from the point at which you click and after. This will evenly affect the overall color balance of the image. This is fine if you're shooting a series of photos for an illustration. Just place your Kodak gray card in the scene, shoot a frame, and then take it out. You can then digitize this frame, set the values for the image as described above, and then click the Gray eyedropper on the Kodak Gray card. Bingo! Perfectly accurate color (white) balance. You can now change the midtone value by dragging the gray slider, and color balance will not be affected.

Photoshop and most other professional image-processors have another, more powerful, command for changing overall tonal values: The Curves dialog box lets you control different brightness levels independently. When you first open the dialog box, it shows all the points of brightness as evenly distributed along a diagonal line that moves from black at the lower left to absolute white at the upper right (see Figure 17-11).

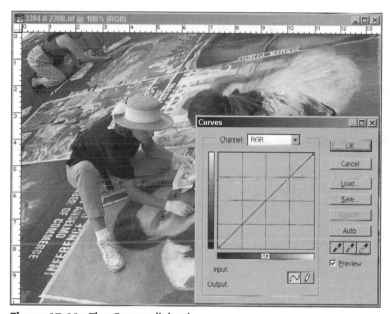

Figure 17-11: The Curves dialog box

You control the points of brightness by raising or lowering individual points on the curve. You can use the Curves dialog box in exactly the same way as the Levels dialog box: Pick the black and white points with the appropriate eyedroppers, and then drag the center of the curve up or down to change the overall image gamma.

You can also do much more with the Curves dialog box, including the following:

✦ Add detail over a specific range of tones.

✦ Create special effects.

✦ Balance color in specific channels.

To add detail over a specific range of tones:

1. Click at the spots along the curve that you don't want to modify. This will anchor them so that when you bend the curve in one segment, it won't affect the other spots. In this case, I wanted to bring out more shading in some of the darker areas of the sidewalk painting without changing the other tonal values (see Figure 17-12).

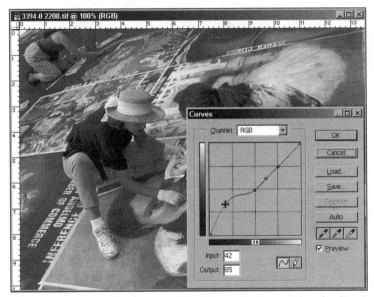

Figure 17-12: Use the curves dialog box to bring out the shading in the dark areas.

2. Click and drag in the area you want to change, dragging the point up to brighten or down to darken. In this instance, I wanted to see more shading in the artist's navy shirt, so I dragged the bottom third of the curve upwards. You can see the result and the curve change in Figure 17-13.

Click the Pencil button in the Curves dialog box. Now you can draw a freehand curve. This can be very useful for making subtle changes in specific areas of the curve without having to go through the "anchor and drag" procedure described in Step 1. If that's your purpose, you'll probably want to click the Smooth button after you've drawn the curve so that you get a clean transition between changes in specific areas of brightness. Suppose you have a picture in which you want to brighten the grass to give it more texture and make it look more inviting. You also want to darken the sky. Just draw a freehand hump in the lower third of the curve, and a dip in the upper third of the curve. This saves a lot of burning and dodging.

You can also create all manner of bizarre tonal effects by drawing the curve free-hand. I produced the psychedelic rendering of the sidewalk-painting scene by simply drawing a really erratic and squiggly curve (see Figure 17-14).

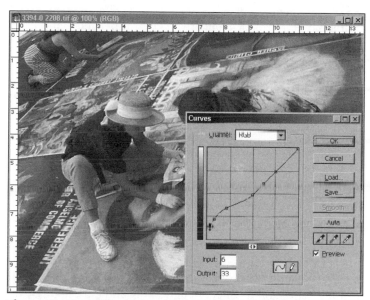

Figure 17-13: Adding more shading to the artist's shirt

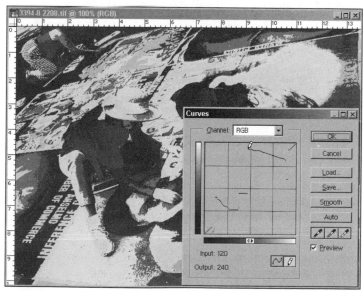

Figure 17-14: Tonal values have become highly stylized due to drawing the curves freehand.

Darkening and lightening small areas

In photo-speak, it's called *burning* and *dodging*. Traditionally, burning was done by punching a hole in cardboard and wiggling it in front of the enlarger lens so that only a small spot of the image could be exposed for a longer amount of time. Dodging was done by attaching a small circle of cardboard to a coat-hanger wire and using that to withhold light from a small area so that it became lighter.

Digital darkrooms such as Photoshop have carried on this tradition by providing Burning and Dodging tools. You can control the size and feathering of these tools by choosing a brush from the Brushes palette. Figure 17-15 shows Photoshop's Burn and Dodge tool icons and the Brushes palette.

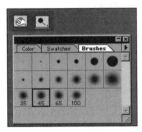

Figure 17-15: Photoshop's Burn (top left) and Dodge (top right) tools are shaped and feathered by your selections in the Brushes palette (bottom).

You can also control the degree of the effect of lightening and darkening by double-clicking the Burn or Dodge tool to open the tool's Options dialog box and then dragging the exposure slider. Setting exposure at a low percentage enables you to carefully blend the effect by applying a little at a time.

If you have a lot of burning and dodging to do on a given image, you might find it easier to do the following:

1. Select the areas you want to lighten with the Lasso (Freehand Marquee) tool.

2. Feather the selection (choose Select ➪ Feather in Photoshop).

3. Enter the number of pixels for feathering.

4. Use the program's Brightness/Contrast control to adjust the intensity.

This works very well if you have to lighten a number of areas to the same degree. If you have to make freehand lightness and darkness adjustments to a number of areas and each requires a different degree of help, you're better off sticking with the Burn and Dodge tools.

Using adjustment layers

Changes in color balance and image quality will take place only on the active layer. This can be a problem if you have to work on an image that is a composite of elements residing on multiple overlying layers. Photoshop 4 pioneered a feature that is just beginning to appear in competitive products. Photoshop calls this feature Adjustment layers. Adjustment layers have two advantages:

✦ They affect all the underlying layers equally.

✦ They don't actually affect the data in the underlying layers. This means that you can change or eliminate the adjustment at any time.

Photo-Paint has had this feature since version 7; Corel calls it *lenses*, not adjustment layers, but it's the same concept.

Selection and Masking Techniques

Masking is the act of isolating a specific portion of an image so that it will remain unaffected by the application of any of the program's tools or commands. Figure 17-16 shows a photograph of a flower that's unmasked on the left and masked on the right.

Figure 17-16: The left side of this flower is unmasked. The right side has been masked so that a white background layer shows through.

Masking enables you to do such things as isolate part of an image so that you can recolor it, add a special effect (such as those created by many filters), or cut out the image so that it can be composited with another. Photoshop lets you mask any area of the whole image or attach a mask to a specific layer. It also enables you to save masks, so that you can recall and modify them later. You can add and subtract masks from one another. When you save a mask, it is saved as a grayscale image channel (see Figure 17-17). If you feather the selection, the mask's edges graduate smoothly from black to white. The black portion of the channel is masked. The white portion is unmasked (100 percent transparent). Any gray forms a partial mask whose transparency is determined by its gray level. In other words, a 50 percent gray area of the mask enables 50 percent of the overlaid stroke or command to take place.

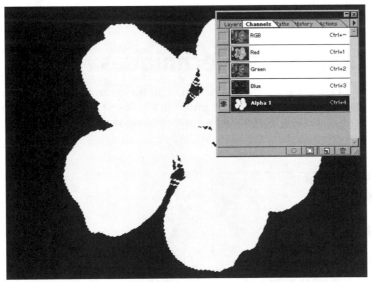

Figure 17-17: The grayscale mask and its alpha channel as seen in Photoshop's Channels palette

A mask's effect is applied only to the visible portions of the layers immediately below it.

One of the ways in which professional image-processing software distinguishes itself is in the variety and sophistication of masking techniques that it offers. Table 17-1 describes the types of edges that pose specific masking challenges, and the tools or techniques that are best-suited to masking them.

Table 17-1
Edge Challenges and the Tools That Best Correct Them

Edge Challenge	Best-Suited Tool
Jagged or irregular edges	Magic Wand Magnetic Lasso
Edges whose brightness is the same as the background's	Lasso, Pen
Objects with variable transparency	Hand paint Color select, if possible
Edges with highly complex detail and many shades	Hand Paint (such as hair or smoke) Color select if possible
Objects that are full of holes	Color select if possible
Textured and patterned objects	Pen, modified with Lasso
Geometric shapes	Pen
Objects clearly isolated against a solid-color background	Magic Wand
Objects blurred by movement	Feathered Lasso with hand painting

Substituting a background

One of the tricks that professional image-processing programs are really good at is placing objects in new surroundings. Whether you want to place a pair of beer-drinking women on a different planet or simply place an interesting background behind a subject, the secret to doing this well is in the masking. You have to be able to see through transparent and translucent objects. Tiny details at the edges of objects, such as stray human hairs or dandelion buds, should be visible in all their fine detail and should show the light normally reflected from their surroundings.

The Edge-Blending Trick

In order to look natural, the edges of the mask should be feathered very slightly. It is best to do this by making two copies of a hard-edged selection, and then feather or blur one very slightly. Make a selection of the hard-edged mask. While that marquee is still visible, make the hard-edged channel active and fill the selection marquee with solid white. You now have a hard-edged mask surrounded by a soft gradient from 50 percent gray to black. This simulates the way our binocular vision sees objects against their backgrounds.

Inserting a sky

There's a common misconception that the wonder of digital photography is its ability to create startling special effects and perform amazing trickery. To me, one of the greatest wonders of digital photography is that we no longer have to put up with vast expanses of burned out, flat, overcast skies—which is what we often get when we expose for the detail in the landscape. Next time you shoot outdoors, point your camera slightly higher than the landscape and expose for the sky, and then go ahead with the rest of the shoot. Repeat the sky shot after a long lapse of time, a sudden change in cloudiness, or when your shooting angle changes more than twenty or thirty degrees.

Once you're back at the computer and your images have been transferred over, you can just drop in the sky shots. Here's how:

1. Open the shot that's been exposed for the landscape. Then open the shot of the nearly matching sky (the one you filled with more of the sky and exposed for the sky, but that's shot at the same angle).

2. Make the landscape window the active window. Double-click the Magic Wand tool (or whatever tool your program uses to automatically select a range of colors). The Magic Wand Options dialog box appears. Enter 32 in the Range field (this is variable and depends on the contrast between the sky and the skyline—experiment to find the setting that captures as many pixels as possible without selecting areas that you don't want selected). Click in the darkest area of the sky (see Figure 17-18).

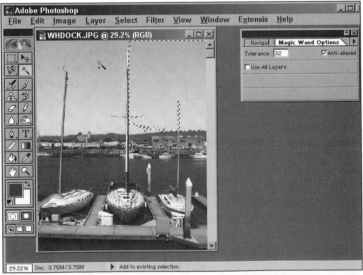

Figure 17-18: Notice that the marquee doesn't overlap the highlights in the masts. If it had, I would have clicked in an area that would have started the color selection range at a higher number.

3. Hold the Shift key down to add to the selection (some programs require that you select a different tool). Click several times more until you have selected all the sky.

> If clouds or streaks are left in the sky, add to the Magic Wand selection by clicking inside them where they touch the skyline. You can eliminate holes caused by clouds by choosing the Lasso (a freeform selection tool), pressing Shift to add to the selection, and loosely drawing a marquee around the clouds.

4. Press Command/Control+H to hide the marquee so you can see your results. Test your selection by choosing Image ➪ Adjust ➪ Brightness/Contrast. Slide the lever to either extreme. If there are gaps along the skyline, you will have to correct the selection mask.

5. To correct the selection mask, first save the selection (choose Select ➪ Save Selection, and then click OK when the Save Selection dialog box appears). This is so that you can easily return to the original selection should the next operation mess it up.

6. Expand the selection by the number of pixels that form the width of the gap. This is usually only one or two pixels. To expand the selection, choose Select ➪ Modify ➪ Expand. The Expand Selection dialog box will appear. Enter 1 or 2 in the Expand By Pixels field. Click OK.

7. To ensure that the new sky blends slightly with the skyline, choose Select ➪ Feather. In the Feather Selection dialog box, enter 1 in the Feather By Pixels field. Test the selection again with the Brightness/Contrast controls. If you're satisfied with the result, save the new selection in place of the original selection.

8. Now it's time to replace the existing sky with a more interesting sky. If you want to be true to the original and also maintain the direction of light accurately, use the sky shot that you shot before you shot this scene. Because you tilted the camera up, you should be able to slide the new skyline below the old skyline so that it is hidden. Activate the window that holds the original and choose Select ➪ Select All (or press Command/Control+A). Press Command/Control+C to copy the image to the clipboard. Place the cursor in the original window to activate it. Make sure that no selection is currently active by pressing Command/Control+D. Press Command/Control+V to paste the clipboard image over the current selection. Because both images are exactly the same size, the pasted image will be centered in the window and will form a new layer.

9. To see that you have a new layer, choose Window ➪ Show Layers (see Figure 17-19). The original landscape is on the background layer. Because you want to put the sky layer behind the Landscape layer, you will have to rename the Background layer. No problem. Double-click the Background layer name bar in the Layers palette. The Layer Options dialog box will appear. In the Name field, type a new name for your layer (I called mine Landscape). Click OK.

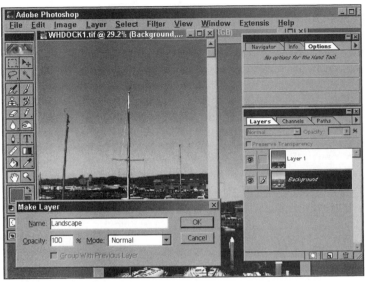

Figure 17-19: In the Layers palette, you can see that the sky photo has been pasted into a new layer. Double-clicking the Background layer name brings up this Layer Options dialog box.

10. In the Layers palette, drag the Layer 1 layer name bar below the Landscape layer name bar. You have changed the stacking order of the layers.

11. Now you are going to show your new sky. Retrieve your saved selection by choosing Select ➪ Load Selection. The Load Selection dialog box appears. From the Channel pull-down menu, choose Alpha 1. Click OK. Your selection (the sky mask) will appear as a marquee. Press Delete. The sky now shows through the background.

Note   You may still see a few telephone poles or other horizon details from the sky photo appearing in your new skyline. Activate the Sky layer and choose the Clone brush. Clone out the offending details.

Using paths

It's tough to draw smooth shapes and edges freehand, unless you've had lots of practice. If your image-processing program lets you draw Bézier-curve vector paths, you will have a much easier time selecting the edges of smooth, regular shapes. Once you've completed the path, you can treat the path as a selection. You can also convert selections to paths, and then save the paths. This will save you a considerable amount of disk storage space because paths are mathematical formulae stored as text, whereas selections are actually bitmapped grayscale Alpha

Channel images. Therefore, each saved selection can use as much disk space as one-third of the base RGB image.

Even if the edges are a little too irregular in some areas to be accurately or conveniently selected by a path, you can draw the path, turn it into a selection marquee, and then use the Lasso tool or Quick Mask mode to edit the result.

To make a selection with a path:

1. Choose the Pen tool. Click to place an anchor point, and then drag to indicate the direction of the path's curve. Click to anchor the next point, drag to indicate direction, and anchor the next point. If an anchor point needs to be a corner point (where the path takes a new direction at a sharp angle, rather than a gentle curve), press Opt/Alt before clicking to anchor the point. You can then drag in the new direction. Figure 17-20 shows the making of a path in progress.

Figure 17-20: The control points can be moved and the direction arrows stretched to edit the path so that it precisely follows the outline you intend.

2. Once you've completed the path, use the Paths palette to change the path to a selection. Choose Window ➪ Show Paths. The Paths palette will appear. Drag the workpath to the Path to Selection button (a dotted circle) at the bottom of the palette. The path becomes a marquee. You can now save the selection, edit it with Quick Mask, or edit it using any of the selection tools and key modifiers (Shift to add to a selection, Opt/Alt to subtract from a selection).

In Figure 17-21, the selection made with the path has been used to cut the flower from the background. It was then pasted to a new layer. The Background layer was then filled with a solid color. You can see how cleanly the path has selected the edges of the flower.

Figure 17-21: Using a path to make a selection creates a very clean-cut edge.

Eliminating the Unwanted

Entry-level image-processing programs are well-equipped to automatically clean up common defects, such as dust on a scanned image or red-eye. Some of them, such as PhotoDeluxe, even have a Clone tool, which is a great aid in spotting and fixing cracks and scratches without the oversoftening that tends to occur when a program automatically removes scratches.

If you own a professional image-processing program, chances are good you don't want to switch to an entry-level program just for quick cleanup (although I sometimes do when processing a few rolls of proof images). Following are some tricks to speed correcting common problems when using a high-end program.

Killing red-eye

When on-camera flash is close enough to the lens, it fires directly through the subject's eye's pupils and bounces off the back of the eyeball. It is most likely seen when subjects have been in dim surroundings and their pupils have dilated. Most modern cameras have a red-eye elimination feature that fires a preliminary flash that causes the subject's pupils to contract before the brighter flash that accompanies the actual exposure. If your camera doesn't have this feature, or if you forget to employ it, you'll get vampire photos (see Figure 17-22).

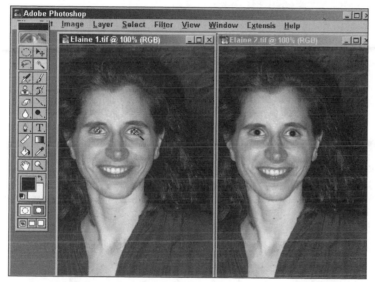

Figure 17-22: The red-eye is visible in the photo on the left. The marquee shows that the Magic Wand tool has already selected it. In the photo on the right, the selection has been filled with black.

Fortunately, red eye is easy to fix in Photoshop. Here's how:

1. Zoom in on the subject's eyes.

2. Choose the Magic Wand selection tool (the tool that selects all the colors within a given range of the pixel you click it on). Double-click it to bring up the Magic Wand options and set the range to about 50 shades.

3. Click in the red. A marquee should appear, which covers the entire red area, but doesn't expand beyond it. If this is not the case, press Command/Control+D to deselect (turn off the marquee). Raise or lower the range and then click again with the Magic Wand. An alternative is to choose Select ➪ Grow, which expands the selection by the current range.

4. Now you just fill the red pupil with black, as all pupils are black. Click the Default Colors icon just below and to the left of the foreground/background color swatches. Your foreground color is now black.

5. Choose Edit ➪ Fill. When the Fill dialog box appears (see Figure 17-23), choose Foreground Color from the Use pull-down menu. Make sure that Opacity is 100 percent and that the Blend mode is Normal. Click OK.

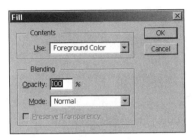

Figure 17-23: Photoshop's Fill dialog box

6. Your work isn't quite done. You should still have a specular white highlight near the center of the pupil that resulted from the reflection of the flash on the shiny surface of the eyeball. Double-click the Brush. In the resultant Brush Options dialog box, drag the Opacity slider to about 25 percent. Paint over the highlights to dull them just a bit. You're just cutting the glare in your subject's headlights.

Now you're done.

Spotting blemishes, dust, streaks, and cracks

You can add filters to Photoshop that eliminate dust and scratches automatically. As is the case with the entry-level programs, if you try to remove serious scratches automatically, you risk oversoftening the image. The best plan is to mask the scratches so that you can't accidentally soften or overpaint areas that aren't defective.

1. Double-click the Quick Mask icon. The Quick Mask Options dialog box will appear (see Figure 17-24). Click the Selected Areas radio button. You want the masking color to indicate the selected areas.

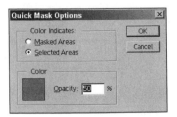

Figure 17-24: The Quick Mask Options dialog box

2. Choose the Brush, and then choose Window ➪ Show Brushes. Choose a brush that is just slightly wider than the widest scratch or crack. While you're in Quick Mask mode, quickly paint over the scratches and other defects. This will make it much faster to repair these defects because you won't have to worry as much about affecting the surrounding image.

3. When you've masked all the defects, click the Standard Mode icon. You'll see a marquee around all the scratches.

4. You'll repair the defects in two ways: by blurring and by cloning. If you blur first, you'll cut way down on the amount of cloning you need to do. Choose Filter ➪ Blur ➪ Gaussian Blur. The Gaussian Blur dialog box appears (see Figure 17-25). Drag the slider until the smaller defects disappear. Don't try to repair everything this way or you'll create another kind of defect. Click OK when you're satisfied with the preview. Make sure your selections stay active.

Figure 17-25: The Gaussian Blur dialog box lets you control the amount of blurring.

5. Choose the Clone (Rubber Stamp) tool. Choose a brush size that is just a bit wider than your selection marquees.

6. Place your cursor just outside one of the marquees and press Opt/Alt. Click to anchor the Clone tool. Anchoring sets the distance between the spot where the brush will pick up pixels and the spot where you indicate that they should be laid down. Keep your anchor point as close to the marquee as possible without having your brush radius overlap the marquee. Paint to clone in the area just outside the marquee. Paint only those areas that still need repair after you blurred. If the marquee changes direction, reanchor so that the anchor point stays parallel to the direction of the marquee.

Overlaying Text

This is a book about digital photography and not specifically about all the things you can do in Photoshop. Nor is it a book about page layout. Therefore, this isn't the place for a detailed discussion of how to use all the text-handling features of the program. In fact, you might even wonder why the subject comes up at all. The answer is because Photoshop actually makes text part of the photograph—something that the programs we traditionally use for typesetting can't even think about doing. Figure 17-26 shows you an array of ways that text can be made part of a photo.

Figure 17-26: Each of the letters that forms the words TEXT F/X has had one of Photoshop's effects applied to it. The last X has had multiple effects applied, including a third-party filter (from Kai's Power Tools).

Text created within an image-editing program becomes part of the image. In other words, it is bitmapped. This means that all of the capabilities and special effects of the host image-processing program can be brought to bear on it. Text can be a selection or a mask, can have layer effects applied to it (such as bevels, drop shadows, inner and outer glows, and inside shadows), and can be textured and treated by any of the program's special effects or plug-in filters.

Photoshop 5 does not enable text to conform to a circle or a path. You can, however, edit text after you've entered it. You can also control almost all aspects of typesetting, such as leading (interline spacing), kerning (spacing between individual characters), and tracking (spacing between characters). If you want to apply special effects, you must first "render" the type. At that point, it ceases to be editable, but you can still keep it on its own layer.

Extensis (at www.extensis.com) has a new Mac/Win Photoshop plug-in called Photographics 1.0 that enables a much broader range of text effects. You can create text on a path that can be edited at any time — even after the text effects have been rendered. You can also apply effects to basic vector shapes, which can be filled and stroked. Several other plug-ins will let you create text effects. Of course, once the text has been rasterized (converted from vector to bitmapped graphic), you can apply any effect from any filter that will work on any Photoshop image.

Placing a photo inside outlined text

One of the most common photographic uses for text is using it as a mask. This enables you to create the effect commonly used on World War II–era postcards in which photographs could be seen inside the text. You can do this in any image-processing program that enables layers and selections (see Figure 17-27).

Figure 17-27: In this image, text was used as the border for a mask. The unmasked text was then deleted, revealing the contents of the layer below.

Unlimited Undo and Use of the History Brush

Photoshop 5 finally caught up with the competition and now offers a uniquely powerful pair of features for implementing more or less unlimited undos. These give you the ability to go back to a specific stage in your image processing. Most of the time, you use this capability to correct a mistake; for example, if you suddenly painted outside your intended border, or needed to reverse the results of a combination of special effects that just didn't look as groovy as you expected.

Photoshop's History palette and History brush are much more powerful than that, however. The History palette is an excellent way to create frames for an animated movie; showing the process for a creative technique, for example, or as a control device to show each stage of creativity to a class. It is also an excellent way to show a client alternative treatments of a subject. You can click any of the name bars in the History palette and see your image as it appeared at that stage of production. If you want to fix something you've overdone, you can go back to the step at which the error first started to occur, highlight the name bar for that command, and then click the Trash icon at the bottom of the History palette. All subsequent steps are erased and you can either save your file or proceed in a new direction.

The History palette records as many steps as you specify in the History Options palette. You reach this palette from the History palette menu. The default is 20 steps, after which the topmost step is auto-deleted to make room for the latest step. If you are making several individual brush strokes, you may want to increase this number considerably. Just remember that the more levels of undo you permit, the larger your file will become and the more you will crowd your available memory. Figures 17-28 through 17-30 show some of the steps you may go through as you are working on your photo.

Figure 17-28: This step shows how the image was masked.

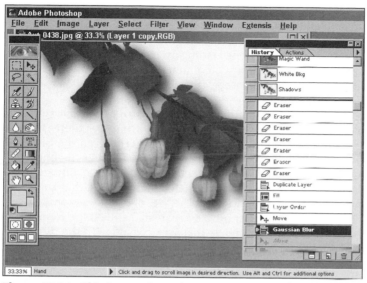

Figure 17-29: This image shows how the background was changed and a drop shadow introduced.

Figure 17-30: This image shows the final stage of completion.

One workaround to having recorded too few steps to get back to a wanted state is to add a *snapshot* to the History palette from time to time. Snapshots completely preserve the state of the image at the point that they were taken. So you can always return to a given state, even if the steps leading up to it have scrolled off the top of the palette — provided, of course, that you remembered to take the snapshot. Of course, a snapshot uses as much memory as the file itself.

The other feature related to "unlimited undo" is the History brush. It simply enables you to paint back in any portion of the image from any palette item, including snapshots. In Figure 17-31, I flattened the image, and then ran the Dry Brush filter. However, I didn't want the Dry Brush effect to actually cover the entire image, so I took a snapshot of the filtered image and clicked in the small square in the left column of the History palette. The History Brush icon indicates that this is the source image for a History brush. I can then activate any other snapshot or processing state in the History palette, choose a brush size and shape from the Brushes palette, and "brush on" the image that I processed with the filter. Thus, I have managed to keep the drop shadow and textured background that I created, but can make the flower bulbs look more "painterly."

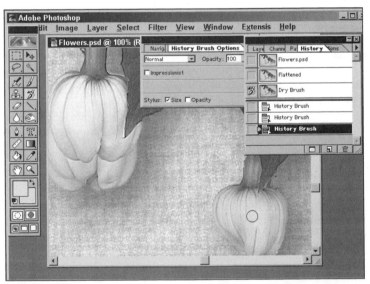

Figure 17-31: The bulb on the right has been painted with the History brush from a snapshot.

Automating Often Repeated Routines

If you do production image processing, I've saved the best part for last. Photoshop and most other professional-level image-processing programs let you automate almost any series of steps. You simply turn on the recorder, perform the steps, assign the recording to a keystroke combination or function key, and store the file. Next time you want to perform that same series of steps, whether on the same image file or another, you just press the hot key. The program does all the work for you.

Photoshop even lets you put in "stops" that interrupt the automatic procedure at predetermined steps. You can then perform operations (such as brush strokes) that are unique to that file. If you check the Allow Continue box in the Record Stop dialog box, you will be able to continue the Action after you've completed whatever you told yourself to do during the stop. When the stop occurs, a small Message dialog box appears. You do whatever the message you composed earlier tells you to do, and when you're ready to resume, you just click the Continue button in the Message dialog box and the automated sequence continues where it left off. You can insert as many of these interruptions as you need or want to.

Photoshop calls its script-recording feature *Actions*. All the commands for creating an Action are accomplished through the Actions palette, which is shown in Figure 17-32.

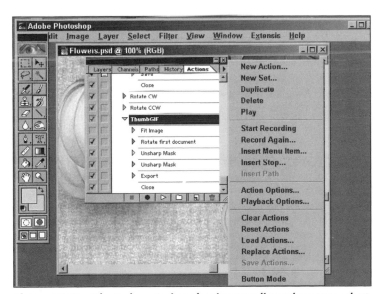

Figure 17-32: Photoshop Actions begin recording when you select the New Action command from the Actions palette. You can play back an Action by assigning a function key, switching the palette to a Button mode, and then clicking the appropriate button; or by pressing the Play button in the control buttons at the bottom of the palette.

Summary

This chapter covered the image-correction and manipulation tasks that you'll need most frequently. Cropping, composition, and resolution enhancement were the first topics of discussion. Then basic techniques for correcting color and exposure were explained, as were retouching and the use of text overlays. Finally, you learned about Photoshop's History palette (unlimited undo), History brush, and how to automate often repeated routines.

✦   ✦   ✦

Preparing Image Files for the Web

When you start thinking about preparing digital photos for publication online, the first thing you need to think about is download time. In other words, consider the following:

+ What image format will best show the type of image I want to publish?

+ What are the smallest dimensions that will show this file effectively?

+ Can I get away with using a very limited range of color?

This chapter explains what you can do to optimize the look and performance of graphics — especially photo-graphics — before placing them on a Web page. If you expect your photography to make a contribution to the professionalism and performance of an online presence, you have to know how to make graphics load as quickly as possible while preserving all the needed color and tonal range. These steps will usually be different for each and every image.

Unless you don't much care about the speed with which your Web pages load, you will most likely want to either purchase a Web-specific plug-in for exporting your images to GIF and JPEG or buy a program dedicated to that purpose.

 Software for processing Web images is the topic of
Cross-Reference Chapter 13, "Choosing Web Image-Processing Software."

Many sites require massive amounts of information to be posted to them every day. If you have volumes of images to process every day, get a copy of DeBabelizer. It can totally automate the process for you. Chapter 14, "Accessory Image-Processing Software," offers more specifics on what DeBabelizer can do for you.

This chapter isn't about software. It's about all the things you need to consider before deciding what size, format, and software you will need to accomplish the job at hand.

Why Your Web Pages Need Photographs

If you want your pages to hold viewers' attention while they're at your site, you must use pictures. There are several reasons why photographs are a good choice for those pictures:

✦ **Credibility.** If yours is a commerce or information site and you need to show viewers what your merchandise or a crime scene actually looks like, a photo is the most credible type of illustration. Even though it's totally untrue in this digital age, the public perception is that the camera never lies.

✦ **Speed.** Making pictures for the Web is one of the easiest ways to justify the purchase of a digital camera. Most of today's consumer and prosumer digital cameras produce four times as much resolution as you would want for a Web graphic and there's no time wasted waiting for the pictures to come back from the lab. Even if you digitize your photos from analog prints or film, you'll find it takes less time (especially if you don't have a competent artist on staff) to produce a professional-looking photo than it does to produce a professional-looking illustration.

✦ **Capturing the moment.** If news is your site's purpose (or part of it), using photographs is imperative. There is simply no better way to capture a fraction of a moment in history.

✦ **Showing all the detail.** If your site needs to show its audience detail that's critical to the understanding of the subject, there's simply no better medium than photography. This is particularly true of medical journals and other scientific reporting, such as a NASA report on Mars.

Note   People's attention spans are significantly shorter when they're looking at a monitor or TV set than when they're looking at a printed page. If they don't get the picture right way, they'll simply move on to a more captivating site.

Graphics can also lend color and texture to your backgrounds, give emphasis to important points, make logical divisions for page content, call attention to advertising on your site (which could make a big difference to a company's bottom line), and (as they say in the biz) much, much more. In short, adding graphics to your Web pages is the easiest way to make readers pay attention to you—at least as long as the graphics load quickly and look good.

I had a bit of an argument with myself concerning how much information to include here about nonphotographic elements. After all, this book is about digital photography, not about page layout and design. However, hardly a single reader of this book will deal strictly with photographs. At the very least, you should know enough to be aware of what some of the alternatives are, as well as of when you might want to use a photo in place of a more traditional type of graphic, such as a divider bar or navigation icon.

Knowing When Not to Use a Photo

Part of understanding how to effectively use photos on the Web is understanding when not to use them. There are many times when it would be more effective to use a bit of clip-art or to draw an image than to use a photo. Photos are always bitmaps and they are almost always true-color. The fact that they are always bitmaps may make it more effective and efficient to draw them. The fact that they are usually true-color (16.8 million colors) means that they must almost always be converted to JPEG format. Therefore, you should understand the difference between bitmaps and their alternative, vector graphics. You should also get a basic grounding in when it is appropriate to reduce an image to fewer colors than might look entirely natural so that you can save the image in GIF format.

About bitmaps

The GIF and JPEG files that are now the standard Web picture formats are *bitmapped graphics*. Bitmaps are so-called because the picture is made by coloring each pixel (picture element, or dot) individually. Imagine a mosaic tabletop. Each tile is in a particular place and is a particular color. Make the picture bigger and you still have the same number and size of tiles — they're just bigger and spread farther apart. This is why bitmapped images get rough looking (often called jaggy, blocky; or pixelated) when you zoom in on them. You can't make the picture dimensionally smaller without losing quality, either. Think about it: The only way to make the picture smaller is to throw away pixels (tiles, in our mosaic metaphor). The result is less definition in the image. Even worse, the computer doesn't know which pixels are most important to the shapes in the image. It throws out as many tiles in a pattern as necessary to achieve the target size.

The most important problem with bitmaps is file size. Because pictures are made up of individual pixels, it is necessary to store several bits of data (24 bits per pixel for 16 million colors) for each pixel in the picture. Therefore, to make file sizes small enough for pictures to load into a Web page within a reasonable amount of time, it becomes necessary to make as many compromises in image quality as possible. Then you can minimize both the number of pixels in the image (color palette reduction) and the amount of data used to describe each pixel (compression).

Tip If you need to change the size of a bitmapped image, you'll get the best results when you can multiply or divide the original size by an even number. The software can then guess more accurately when deciding which lines and edges to leave in and which to ignore.

About vector graphics

Vector graphics are *resolution-independent*. This technical term simply means that no matter how big or small you make the image — and no matter how many times you make it bigger or smaller — the image will always be reproduced at the maximum definition allowed by the device on which it is displayed. Furthermore, it is possible to create a highly detailed advertising illustration on a computer with marginal screen definition and very little memory, and then have that image reproduced with smooth lines and fills as a freeway billboard.

How is this possible? Vector images are stored as mathematical (more precisely, geometrical) formulae. Each shape in the image is a complete formula, known as an *object*. Because objects are self-contained entities, it is easy for the computer to specify changes to that object and to its relationship with other objects in the image. These changes will never affect the quality of other objects in the image. The other important quality of vector images that result from their being stored as formulae is small file size. Remember, it makes no difference whether a circle will represent something as small as a microbe or as big as the Earth. All the information it takes to describe the shape, color, line thicknesses, and other geometrical components can likely be stored in the same amount of space as a paragraph of text.

A short primer on Web graphics file formats

Choosing which graphics file format to use on a Web site used to be easier because there were half as many options as you have today. The GIF format was the only accepted format. The demand for photographic-quality color has since caused the JPEG format to be nearly as widely accepted. So now the question is, Which format is best under what circumstances?

There are four Web-compatible graphics file formats:

✦ **JPEG:** This format is visible to almost all Web browsers. It is a true-color format that uses variably lossy compression to reduce file size. It doesn't support transparency (alpha channels), and can't store images in a lossless format.

✦ **GIF87a and GIF89a:** These formats use lossless compression and are limited to 256 colors. They are best suited to hard-edged, flat-colored art such as symbols, text, and info-graphics. GIF89a enables the designation of one color as transparent and permits multiple images to be stacked in one file — to be seen as an animation. This has become known as *animated GIF*.

✦ **PNG:** A third bitmapped file format, designed especially for network graphics, is PNG (pronounced *ping)*. PNG (Portable Network Graphics) is a new format meant to be a patent-free replacement for GIF, but the format is just being incorporated into the most recent generations of browsers. Otherwise, you need a plug-in to see PNG.

✦ **SWF:** Macromedia Flash files. These are vector-based files (although they may include embedded bitmaps). They're not quite a universal format, but are the most widely supported multimedia format now on the Web.

Knowing which format to use in order to achieve a given goal is a matter of keeping a few "rules" in mind. The following sections explain how to match each of these formats with the job to be done.

GIF and GIF89a

GIF (Graphics Interchange Format) is the Web's most useful and most widely used graphics file format. It comes in two flavors: GIF87a and GIF89a. For static, rectangular pictures, both types are fully compatible with all graphical Web browsers. In fact, the specifications for a rectangular still image are the same for both formats. All GIF files are restricted to 256 or fewer colors. They are compressed at an average ratio of about 3:1 over a noncompressed image of the same size and number of colors. GIF is better for storing images that contain mainly flat tones because its compression technology works most efficiently when the image consists mainly of patterns made by adjacent areas of solid colors.

GIF is the file format to use when a graphic has the following characteristics:

✦ It is composed of geometric shapes filled with flat colors.

✦ The original contains 256 colors or less.

✦ It is small (fits within a 150-pixel square).

✦ It is irregularly shaped (think of a triangular traffic sign).

✦ It is intended as an animation not dependent on programming or special browser enhancements.

The original GIF format, 87a, was restricted to rectangular, static images. People also wanted a way to make images appear more quickly, to spare viewers from having to stare at empty placeholders. GIF89a, the more recent standard, overcomes these limitations by adding three enhancements:

✦ The capability to recognize a single designated color as transparent. Transparency makes it possible to create irregularly shaped graphics such as vignettes, buttons, and icons.

✦ The capability to store and display multiple discrete images in the same file. This makes it possible to create auto-playing "flipbook" animations and miniature slide shows.

✦ The capability to interlace images. Interlacing enables the image to load in several stages of resolution. It creates the illusion that graphics (and, therefore, whole pages) load more quickly, giving readers a chance to see a "fuzzy" but recognizable image quickly enough to know whether to wait or move on.

Saving files as GIF

Saving your file to GIF format is easy, provided it is already in a bitmapped (also known as "rasterized") form. If it is not, first convert it to Indexed Color mode. In Photoshop, that is done by choosing Image ➪ Mode ➪ Indexed Color. Once the file has been converted, open any image editor (such as Photoshop, Painter, Photo-Paint, or Windows Paint) and open the original file. From the main menu, choose File ➪ Save As. When the File Save dialog box appears, open the drop-down list of file types and choose GIF or CompuServe GIF.

If you own an image-processing program that is a couple of versions old, it may not be able to save to GIF89a, and almost certainly can't save animated GIFs. Most current image editors are capable of saving files in GIF89a format (but the list is growing daily), and most besides Photoshop are even capable of saving GIF89a animations. Photoshop 3.0.5 has an Export plug-in for GIF89a that enables you to preview color reductions, choose transparent colors by several methods, and activate interlacing.

On the other hand, you can almost always do a more efficient job of saving files to GIF format with a program dedicated to Web graphics, such as Adobe Image Ready or Macromedia Fireworks 2. If you don't want to make the investment in either of those programs (around $100), you can use a plug-in such as HVS GIF or Boxtop Software's PhotoGIF. These programs will do as good or better a job for half the price, but they aren't as versatile as the Web image-processing programs (which will save to GIF, animated GIF, JPEG, and PNG) and don't have as fancy a user interface. Conversely, the plug-ins enable you to keep working inside your favorite Photoshop plug-in-compatible image-processing program.

Tip   If your image-editing program has layers, they can be used for "onion-skinning" a GIF animation. That is, you can put each frame on a separate layer. Then you can temporarily set the exposure controls for each layer so that you can also see the objects on the layers above and below a given layer, enabling you to scale and position it relative to its neighbors. This technique is helpful in creating a smoother illusion of movement. When all the layers are positioned correctly, simply drag the contents of each into a frame in a GIF animation program. Photoshop 5.5's Image Ready can automatically interpret layers as animation frames.

There are also numerous utilities (mentioned in the appropriate sections of this chapter) that enable you to create GIF animations.

If you are planning to save to GIF format, it pays to understand the possibilities for, and ramifications of, color reduction. GIF files that have fewer than 256 colors can be stored at any bit depth from 1 to 8. The lower the bit depth, the smaller the file size and the faster it will load. Because the Web is a low-resolution medium when compared to print, you can often employ tricks to fool the human eye into seeing more colors than actually exist. The most important of these tricks are covered later in this chapter.

JPEG

JPEG is the file format in which to save your graphics if they are full-color, continuous-tone images (such as photographs) larger than approximately 150 pixels square. The JPEG graphics file format gets its name from the committee that originated it — the Joint Photographic Experts Group. JPEG is a 24-bit, true-color file format that uses a variable lossy-compression algorithm. Variable means that you can choose just how much data loss you want to incur in exchange for smaller file sizes.

When you save a file in JPEG format, you are given the choice of a range of compression levels. The higher the compression, the less faithful the image is to the original. Given the Web's resolution (typically 72 to 96 dpi), most images will look quite similar at the highest and lowest levels of compression. However, because the colors in photos vary so much from one to the next, you need to be able to preinspect the image before you save it to be sure of not getting any ugly surprises. At maximum compression, a JPEG file is typically 1/100th the size of the original.

A more recent variation on JPEG is *progressive JPEG*. Like interlaced GIF, progressive JPEG enables the image to load faster in stages of increasingly higher resolution. The difference between a progressive JPEG and an interlaced GIF is that the former permits a full range of color (24 bits per pixel versus 8 bits per pixel for GIF). However, it is only now that commonly found image editors enable you to save a progressive JPEG.

How do you save your files to JPEG? As is the case with GIF, most modern image editors or paint programs will handle the job. There are also several standalone utilities that will convert files from various bitmap formats to progressive JPEG.

The Macintosh PICT file format, possibly the most common Macintosh graphics format, enables you to use JPEG compression when saving a file without actually converting the PICT file to a JPEG file. However, neither the Web nor any program expecting a JPEG file will recognize this PICT file as a JPEG file. When choosing the file type, be sure to pick JPEG, *not* PICT. PNG format also enables you the option of using JPEG compression. However, as is the case with PICT files, a browser that doesn't recognize PNG files won't recognized JPEG-compressed PNG files as JPEGs.

PNG

Hopefully, the PNG format will become ubiquitous, because it supports both indexed and nonindexed color (see the following section for more information on color modes) and high (but lossless) compression and transparency. PNG's transparency is vastly better than GIF's because it is accomplished through an alpha channel, which makes it possible to have partial transparency. This means that PNG can provide a way to have drop shadows and vignettes for irregularly shaped graphics, without halos — even on patterned backgrounds. If your application is designed for an intranet whose readers use a single browser that supports the format, you should be using PNG already.

Caution   Your image-processing program can't be more than one generation old in order to save or export your files to PNG format. Most current versions of image-processing programs can open and save PNG files. Programs that save to PNG format vary a great deal as to which PNG attributes they support.

A Few Words About Color Modes

Three kinds of color "modes" are in popular use for Web graphics:

✦ Indexed-color

✦ High-color

✦ True-color

These modes are known by both their names and by their color depth, so if you hear one term or another, realize that they're synonymous. The *color depth* of an indexed color image can be anything from 1 to 8 bits per pixel. The number of colors possible in an indexed-color image is its color depth. In other words, a 256-color image is 8 bits per pixel, a 4-bit image contains 16 colors, a 5-bit image is 32 colors — and so forth.

The other two modes are high-color and true-color. High-color is also known as either 15-bit (32,000 colors) or 16-bit (64,000 colors). True-color is also known as 24-bit color, and consists of 16.8 million colors, which is quite a few more than most humans are capable of perceiving in any reproduced image.

Of the three color modes, only indexed-color relies on the use of a palette. Each color in a given image is indexed to a specific location in a palette attached to that image. Figure 18-1 shows the same image using three different palettes. In other words, a specific shade of green in a picture of a forest may be assigned to the third column of the fourth row in the palette. If you want to adapt an existing image to a palette other than the one that was used in creating it (usually invisibly assigned by the program that created it), you have to use a utility that changes the index position of each color in the image to match it to the index position of the closest color in the new palette. DeBabelizer is exceptionally good at converting the disparate palettes of individual graphics in a large collection to a single palette with all the colors in common.

Rules Governing Web Graphics

Web graphics have a number of unique qualities. Paying attention to these can make or break the success of your Web site. Do you want millions of viewers and lots of ad revenue? Here come the rules, but remember, there are exceptions to every rule!

Figure 18-1: The same image with three different palettes

Rule #1: File size is everything

People looking at a Web page have a much shorter attention span than people looking at a printed page. If your graphics take any significant amount of time to load,
you can bet your reader will quickly surf to another wave. The bigger the file's size,
the longer it takes to load. A 14.4 Kbps modem loads data from the Web at a typical
rate of about 0.8 Kbps. This means it takes about 28 seconds to load a 20KB file. A
typical 80×100 pixel graphic will compress to an average of about 20KB, provided
you judiciously use the tricks outlined in this chapter. You can also create illusions
to make it seem as though graphics are loading at several times the speed they
actually are.

Two such illusions are in common use: interlacing and alt imaging. Interlaced GIFs
and progressive JPEGs both fall into the first category. These images seem to load
faster because the image is progressively rendered. Each rendering uses more pixels
(dots) from the file to fill the image — so the picture appears quickly, but somewhat
"out of focus." Then it gets sharper until all the pixels have uploaded and the image is
fully revealed. The advantage is that one can usually get the information needed from
the image before it is fully rendered. So you know whether you want to wait for the
detail or move on. The second illusion, the LOWSRC (low-resolution source) image
tag, accomplishes the same end with a different technique. The LOWSRC image can
be a very small black-and-white or limited-color image. The LOWSRC image loads
first and stays onscreen only as long as it takes for the primary image to load.

It is possible to use code in an HTML tag to scale a graphic to a size different from
the actual file size. This is a good idea or a bad idea, depending on a few variables.

Tip
It's a good idea to scale down the file if the browser has already loaded it earlier
for use at a larger size. In that case, you've already stored the large file on the
server and spent the time uploading the first time. The second time the file is used,
it will appear almost instantaneously because all the browser has to do is scale it.
Be aware, however, that the file will be a bit "fuzzier" if it's automatically scaled
down. Test your file in a browser to make sure quality is acceptable. If not, scale
the file down conventionally, save it to a different name, and place the new, properly resized image on your page.

It's a bad idea to have the browser scale a file to a size larger than the original if that's the size at which you want the reader to view it — unless you're after a pixelated, jagged, artistic effect. Refer to Rule #7 for information about the use of *low sourcing* for another exception to this rule. It's also a bad idea to scale an image to a size smaller than the original because the browser will have to first load the whole file and then scale it down (which takes even longer), causing performance to suffer unnecessarily.

Rule #2: The Web is a low-resolution medium

Plan on your Web pages being viewed at a typical resolution of 72 dpi (dots per inch). Although 17-inch monitors set for 800 × 600-pixel resolution have become quite popular, a majority of viewers still use 12- to 15-inch monitors set at 640 × 480 pixels. A 640 × 480 × 13-inch viewing area is equivalent to 72 dpi on the Mac, or 96 dpi on the PC. This compares to a resolution of over 2,000 dpi in a typical corporate annual report.

Don't even think about placing page-size (or larger) detailed technical drawings, blueprints, or even organizational charts directly on your Web page. If you reduce them so they fit into a typical window at 72 dpi, there's not enough resolution to see detail clearly. Your diagrams will look like a bad case of acne. The solution is to scan the important parts of the drawing in a 1:1 ratio at 72 dpi, and then cut and paste small "close-up" sections of the drawing into separate files. These files can then be placed directly on your Web pages, in context with the appropriate descriptive text.

Tip   If you don't want to use vector drawing techniques for map details, you can use a Web image preparation program (such as Fireworks or Image Ready) to "slice" the image.

Cross-Reference   You can find out more about programs that do image slicing and linking in Chapter 13 on Web image preparation programs.

Better yet, if you have maps or technical drawings to display, scan them and then auto-trace them in a program such as Macromedia FreeHand, CorelDraw, or Adobe Streamline. Then import the vector tracing into Flash and export the image to SWF format. Most of today's browsers (about 78 percent at the time of this writing) can read this vector format without pausing to download and install a plug-in.

Meanwhile, there is another alternative that will work for some. If you're in an intranet environment in which you can control the viewer's platform, you can use Netscape plug-ins for inline viewing of numerous vector file formats. See the Netscape plug-ins page for a listing of these, at http://home.netscape.com/plugins/index.html.

Rule #3: The Web is color-sensitive

Make sure your graphics look okay in black and white (well, grayscale, actually). Although few people still use monochrome monitors, some will want to print out your pages on a monochrome printer. Also, if the picture looks good in grayscale, you're assured of enough contrast between important elements in the picture. Such image contrast is critical to the success of image maps and the legibility of text superimposed on graphics.

It's even more important that graphics look good in a mere 256 colors. This is because most viewers leave their monitors set at 256 colors and may not know that they're seeing the world through dust-covered glasses. Subjects that require photorealistic shading require display in millions of colors. Otherwise, they will appear to be "banded," or posterized. Artists whose work you display in this manner will definitely be unappreciative. Besides, someone once told them that their applications would run much faster with the monitor set at 256 colors. While this may be technically true, the real-world difference to most of us is imperceptible. By the way, these comments aren't meant to disparage people who are still using SVGA display cards and monitors that are not capable of more than 256 colors. This has ceased to be a limitation since the days of the 486 processor, but quite a few offices still use the older cards, as do many laptop color computers.

Caution Type and solid-color graphics really shouldn't use more than the 219 "Web-safe" colors — so called because browsers and Windows reserve the other 37 colors for their own use. Almost all current-generation image processing programs provide some means to let you convert images to this Web palette.

Having said all that, it's not strictly true that you have to reduce all images to less than 256 colors in order to be as efficient as possible. The JPEG file format accommodates only true-color (16.8 million colors) files, and most popular browsers, such as Netscape Navigator, will automatically adjust images (by dithering) to 256 colors on a 256-color display. However, experimentation will often prove that a file reduced to fewer colors will compress to significantly smaller sizes.

The exception to the 256-color rule is when you want to display high-quality images for photographs (browsers will do their own dithering). Even if you're showing photographs, they can often be successfully reduced to 256 colors through techniques explained later in this chapter.

Note If you decide to reduce a photograph to 256 colors, most image-processing programs will let you choose a palette and dithering method. Always choose an adaptive palette (one made up of the most prevalent colors in the image) and diffusion dithering. Otherwise, the colors will convert to solid, banded areas.

The photographs shown in Figures 18-2 through 18-4 show the differences between various methods of color reduction, with and without dithering.

Figure 18-2: A small photo reduced to 256 colors

Figure 18-3: A small photo reduced to 128 colors

Figure 18-4: A small photo reduced to 128 colors with dithering

Rule #4: There are only two workable graphics file formats for photographs — GIF and JPEG

Both file formats can be read equally well on any type of popular computer. In addition, all but text-only browsers now support both.

Rule #5: Never make a graphic's dimensions so large that the reader has to scroll

Most of your viewers will see your pages on a screen that measures 640 × 480 pixels. This is roughly the size of the image on 12- to 14-inch monitors, whether Mac or

PC. Although it's true that many viewers these days set their screens to higher resolutions (800 × 600 is quite popular) or have bigger monitors, you can't count on it. Besides, people who do that are still a small minority.

Unfortunately, you can't even make your images nearly as big as 640 × 480 because a lot of that space is taken up by your browser. In Netscape Navigator, if the window is set at maximum, the area of a viewable page is 610 × 280 pixels — and most people don't even maximize the window. The best rule of thumb is to limit width to about 450 pixels.

This means that the biggest graphic you should ever use should be about 600 pixels wide by 260 pixels high. If you plan to have anything in addition to the graphic on the page, the graphic will have to be appropriately smaller. Thus, your portrait (vertical) aspect images will have to be smaller than 260 pixels square.

The one exception to these size limitations is backgrounds. Single-image backgrounds should be as large as the largest screen likely to view them. Also, horizontal tiles should be as wide as the largest window in which they can be viewed (1,024 pixels wide is a safe bet). That way, people using large screens at a high resolution won't run out of background when these elements are used. Background elements repeat automatically if they are smaller than the viewing window. If you are making a tiled background, remember this: The smaller the tile, the faster it will load. For more information on backgrounds, see the section with that name later in this chapter.

There's another exception to this size limitation that many artists and photographers will insist on making. They feel that their images lose too much detail at such small sizes. The truth is, these images lose too much detail no matter how they are displayed on the Web.

Note   Poor image quality relative to the original image can be to your advantage in that it is one defense against the theft of your artwork.

Rule #6: Repeat the use of the same image file as often as possible

The browser only needs to load an image once, because it *caches*. Caching means that the information is held in memory on the local computer. Thus, any subsequent appearance of that image will load almost instantly. This excellent trick makes the performance of your site seem miraculously fast. Keep this rule in mind when you're tempted to make a different bullet for each subject list or to use nine different kinds of page dividers within the same site. Also, sticking to Rule #6 can save you considerable space on your Web server. Saving server space can save you money. Finally, it makes site maintenance easier because there are fewer links to track.

Rule #7: Don't depend entirely on automated converters

To put it another way, most converters can't do the refined steps in the Web-enhanced versions of GIF (GIF89a) or JPEG (progressive JPEG) and won't do anything to create a low-source image as a substitute. Each of these qualities can contribute to making your Web site faster to load, quicker to browse, and easier on the eye.

Transparency

Transparency refers to making one color in an image invisible, enabling the image to blend smoothly with any background. The same image can thus be used on a number of pages with varying background colors and textures. Transparency is a property currently unique to the GIF89a and PNG formats, so you can't make JPEG graphics transparent. Figure 18-5 shows a transparent GIF89a image.

Figure 18-5: A transparent GIF image. The transparent area was possible because the image was given a solid-color background. GIF89a enables you to specify any single color as transparent.

Some programs, such as Photoshop, enable you to specify that the transparent area of a layer or an alpha channel determine the border between opacity and transparency. Those programs actually substitute a single color for the masked area.

Interlacing and progressive JPEG

One way to speed the display of graphics-enhanced Web pages is to make GIFs *interlaced* and JPEGs *progressive*. Both interlaced GIFs and progressive JPEGs appear quickly because only some of the pixels in the image are loaded first. As a result, you see a rough (out-of-focus) approximation of the final image while the rest of the image loads. If you decide you're not interested in the detail (or you've seen it before), you can move on without waiting for the rest of the file transfer.

Never interlace a transparent background GIF. Interlacing in conjunction with transparency causes intermittent problems with some browsers (such as Netscape Navigator). The result is a "broken GIF" icon in place of the picture. Bad idea. All popular browsers that support graphics support interlaced GIFs.

Progressive JPEG quickly places a low-resolution version of the image in your browser, and then rescans the image several times, displaying it at higher resolutions each time. The last scan produces full resolution. This reduces viewer frustration because one gets a sense of what will be on the Web page much more quickly.

Built-in support for saving to progressive JPEG is somewhat rarer than support for saving to interlaced GIF at this point, but it's expanding rapidly. Progressive JPEGs, however, started being supported mostly in the second generation of graphical browsers such as Mosaic and Netscape Navigator. AOL's browser became fully compatible with progressive JPEGs in version 3.0. Microsoft Internet Explorer just incorporated fully progressive display in version 5.0.

Low-sourcing

Low-sourcing can be a substitute for progressive JPEGs (pJPEGs) or interlaced GIFs (iGIFs). Sometimes this method is more efficient than pJPEGs or iGIFs, but that depends on how you make the low-source images.

Low-sourcing gets its name from an HTML tag that substitutes an alternative file (usually of much lower resolution or monochrome) until the data for a higher-resolution file has been loaded.

You'll want two separate files to use in an image tag with a LOWSRC attribute, such as SRC= image or LOWSRC= image. The LOWSRC= image's file size should be much smaller than the original image (less than 25 percent). There are several techniques for making LOWSRC images. Which one you use depends on the size of the SRC image and the effect you want to achieve. The second file can be smaller, for the following reasons:

✦ It is a black-and-white version of the full-color, high-source image.

✦ You reduced colors.

✦ The image dimensions are much smaller. For instance, you could simply make a copy of a 200 × 300 image, scale it to 50 × 75 pixels, and then insert a size attribute in the image tag to force the display of both images at the same size.

✦ A combination of the above.

Tip

Using a grayscale image as your low-source image can be a very effective means of presenting photographs on the Web. Because a grayscale image is one-third the file size of a color image with the same dimensions, it loads quickly and you can still see all the detail in the image.

Rule #8: High bandwidth is no excuse for inefficiency

Even if your site is on a corporate intranet where every viewer has a high-speed connection, there are better things to do with bandwidth than waste it on unnecessarily large graphics (such as provide more viewers with more information and not create bottlenecks in the network).

Graphic Components Used on the Web

The kinds of graphics you're likely to need on your Web pages can be categorized. Understanding these categories, described in the following sections, will help you to create these types of graphical elements.

Text

If you want to design your pages for most browsers, using text converted to bitmap graphics controls the typeface displayed on your user's screen. Otherwise, the browser makes the choice. The browsers used by 95+ percent of Web surfers allow only two typefaces: monospaced Courier (typewriter) and a variable-spaced font (typically Times Roman). Furthermore, by using graphics, you can control much about the layout of text, headlines, pictures, and other content elements.

When you use graphical text, you can use any font in your computer at any size. You can also specify any typographical attributes, such as spacing, kerning, or leading. You can't do any of this with HTML text. Unlike HTML text, when you use graphics, the font style is not dependent on the destination system.

Other things you can do with graphical text are as follows:

✦ Freehand lettering

✦ Multi-colored letters

✦ Special effects, such as embossing, drop shadows, glow, gradient fills, or outlining

Illustrations

Illustrations are appropriate at some place in almost every kind of site, though they may be more important in digital magazines, catalogs, and children's sites than in heavily text-oriented sites. Illustrations differ from other types of graphics in that they are used primarily to tell a visual story alongside of (or to complement) the story you're telling in words. They are usually bigger than other types of graphics. Often they are full-color photos or gradually shaded artwork, so file sizes tend to be much larger than for other types of graphics. Illustrations can be decorative or instructional. Sometimes illustrations tell the whole story and there is little or no text on the page, as in Figure 18-6. Illustrations should never be so large that the viewer has to scroll to see the whole picture. When creating or placing illustrations, take care to keep their size slightly smaller than the typical user's browser window. (See Rule #5 under the section entitled "Rules Governing Web Graphics.")

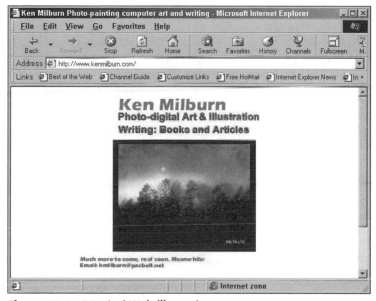

Figure 18-6: A typical Web illustration

Backgrounds

Backgrounds are the "paper" on which your Web content is printed. It is good to know how to control your backgrounds so that they can be designed to comple- ment your photos. Most browsers default to a medium gray or white background; however, you can specify any color for a background and any color for text. Any browser compliant with the HTML 3.2 specification, and most current versions of popular browsers, can properly interpret the instructions for colored backgrounds. Colored text is supported by Netscape Navigator 2+ and by Microsoft's Internet Explorer, but is not as widely supported as colored backgrounds. To be safe, keep your backgrounds light enough that black text is readable against them.

Suppose you want a photo or paper texture in the background. It is now possible for most browsers to read graphic backgrounds. Any image can be loaded into the background. This image will repeat itself from left to right and from top to bottom as many times as necessary to fill the entire frame. Remember, this repetition will occur more times for a full frame on a 20-inch monitor at 1,024 × 768 pixels than on a full frame on a 640 × 480 12-inch monitor.

Background images can be of any type, but need to be designed so that they don't interfere with the readability of text or unintentionally confuse the content of overlaying graphics. Also, because backgrounds are the largest element in a Web page, it is especially important to design photographic backgrounds so that they will upload as quickly as possible. Either use every trick in the book to make the file sizes for large images small, or use very small tiles. Actually, a background tile about 20 pixels square will load nearly as fast as a 1-pixel tile and will fill the screen about twenty times faster because there are twenty times fewer repeats.

You can expect to achieve several types of "effects" with background images. These are discussed in the following sections.

Semi-solid backgrounds

Semi-solid backgrounds are created by making a background image tile that is as wide as any viewing window is likely to be (1,024 pixels is a good number). We call them "semi-solid" because if the window happens to be larger, the background image will tile. The height can be as narrow as you like, as the tile simply repeats as often as necessary from top to bottom. Because this tile is so wide, its file size will be bigger unless it is very shallow. A height of one or two pixels will be the best compromise between loading time and screen-painting time. Figure 18-7 shows a good example of a semi-solid background.

Figure 18-7: This Web page has a solid background, which makes it very easy to read dense text. Solid backgrounds are also a clean environment for presenting photos.

Full-screen images

Full-screen images are those that provide users with all the needed information without requiring any HTML text. Usually such images contain graphic text. In addition, an image map is required for some sort of negotiation. A hybrid full-screen image could be a full-screen background image tile with minimal HTML text in links (such as a navigation bar) in the foreground. These images work best if they contain very few colors and large areas of solid color so that they compress to a small enough file size to enable them to load quickly. Figure 18-8 is an example of a full-screen image.

Figure 18-8: A full-screen image

Textured and patterned backgrounds

Textured and patterned backgrounds are variations on background tiles. Textured backgrounds are simply images with no definable subject, such as sand or burlap. Patterned backgrounds are repetitions of a shape, such as a drawing of an apple, flower, or company logo. Textured and patterned backgrounds are usually created as "seamless tiles" that repeat in contiguous left-to-right, top-to-bottom sequence. Figure 18-9 is an example of a patterned background.

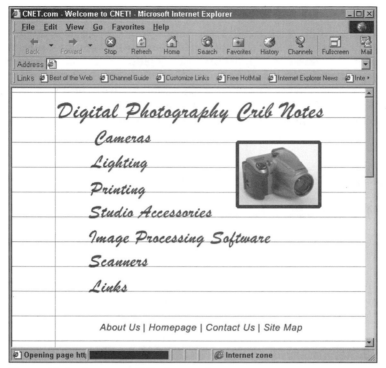

Figure 18-9: A patterned background

Multiple backgrounds

Multiple backgrounds are those that use images within an image to compose a full-screen background image that appears to be several backgrounds (see Figure 18-10).

Strictly speaking, what you see in Figure 18-10 isn't a background, but whole images inserted into table cells. The appearance of text over a background is "faked" by creating the text as part of the graphic image. The cell borders have been set at zero, so that they're invisible. The content has been placed within the cells so that it appears to float over the whole page. To make your design work, you'll have to spend some time experimenting with font sizes, colors, and object alignments.

Tip   The easiest way to create multiple backgrounds is to create one large graphic, place your text over it, and then slice the image in a program such as Image Ready or Fireworks. These programs will automatically create the HTML code needed to make the table and to place the graphic into the cells.

Figure 18-10: The multiple-background illusion

Irregularly shaped graphics

An irregularly shaped graphic appears to have a nonrectangular border, but is in fact rectangular. The graphic appears to be irregularly shaped because its solid-color background is either designated as clear in a GIF89a file or matches the page background's color. The name is a little misleading in another way: The shape can actually be regular (as in an oval, circle, or polygon) — it just can't be rectangular.

Irregularly shaped graphics have so many uses you will find them indispensable. For one thing, they are the only way to make graphics text appear to be a "typeset" element of the page layout. Navigation icons (illustrated in Figure 18-11) also integrate better into the layout when they don't appear to have a separate frame or background.

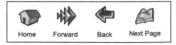

Figure 18-11: Typical navigation icons

Bullets

Bullets are simple-shaped graphics that call your attention to something. Usually, they look like tiny buttons without words and are used to set apart items in an unnumbered list. Several variations are illustrated in Figure 18-12.

Figure 18-12: All of these images can be used as bullets.

Icons

Icons are small, "high-concept" images meant to quickly give the reader a message that takes less time to read and is more universally understood than if the same message were spelled out in words. Some designers suffer from "icon mania" and use icons in places where a single word would have been more easily understood. The most universally understood icon is a circle with a diagonal line, meaning "negative, no, or not." Traffic signs make good icons for the Web. Figure 18-13 shows examples of icons.

Figure 18-13: The row of images at the very bottom of the page is meant to be used for navigation: Home, Back, Forward, Last page, Send us e-mail.

Rounded buttons

Rounded buttons give dimension to your page and can be used for navigation (with superimposed type) or as bullets to emphasize important text. See Figure 18-14 for examples of rounded buttons.

Making rounded buttons is easy if you have Kai's Power Tools (KPT) or an image editor such as Paint Shop Pro that has its own version of the KPT Glass Lens filter. Follow the steps in the next section to create rounded buttons.

Rounded button exercise

This exercise was written for Photoshop, but you can complete it with almost any image editor that supports Photoshop plug-ins.

1. Open a file that contains the color or texture you want to use for your button.

Figure 18-14: Here, the Hand icons shown in Figure 18-13 have been turned into round buttons.

2. Double-click the Rectangular Marquee tool and change it to Elliptical. Drag an ellipse around the area where you want a button. If the button has to be a particular size, make sure you have chosen Window ⇨ Palette ⇨ Show Info. If you want the button to be round rather than elliptical, press Shift as you drag.

3. Choose Edit ⇨ Copy to save your button to the clipboard. Choose File ⇨ New and click OK. Choose Edit ⇨ Paste. Save the selection. Choose Window ⇨ Palette ⇨ Show Layers. Double-click the Floating Layer bar and name the layer. You now have a floating layer and can fill the background with any color or texture you like. Your file is now cropped to exactly the size of your button. Keep the selection marquee active (or save the selection so you can bring it back).

4. Choose Selection ⇨ Load Selection and click OK. The selection reappears on the Button layer. Choose Filter ⇨ KPT Extensions ⇨ Glass Lens (Bright, Normal, or Soft for the effect you like). Presto! You've got a button! Choose the Options arrowhead at the upper-right corner of the Layers palette. A fly-out menu appears. Choose Flatten Image. This combines all the layers into one. Finally, save the file as CompuServe GIF.

You can also make rounded buttons in any 3D modeling program that does ray-traced, Gourard, or z-buffered rendering. Simply make a sphere, map your favorite texture to its surface, and render. Open the rendered file in your image editor, crop it, and save as GIF.

Banners

Banners are used to show and announce an advertisement. Banners often contain image maps to link to specific sites.

Standard advertising practices dictate two sizes of horizontal Web banners at 476 × 54 and 154 × 56, and a small vertical banner at 70 × 130.

Even if you don't have advertisers on your site, you may want to use banners to promote ideas, announce products your own company wants to sell, or point out features of your site.

Animations

There's lots of talk these days about the Web being "everyone's" vehicle for multimedia. Although there is some truth in that statement, don't think about putting conventional animated multimedia files on your Web site unless you are working within the context of an intranet with T1 or faster connections. As cable modems and other high-speed access becomes more widespread, multimedia will reach its full power over the Web. In the meantime, remember that most Web access is at 28.8 Kbps or slower. That means it takes a full minute or more to download a 60KB file, which is tiny for a motion file such as a QuickTime or Video for Windows movie. Surveys show that most Web surfers won't wait more than a minute for a page to load. You will really have to work to keep your animations as small as possible. Also, give viewers something to read or some other interesting graphics that will load first. If your viewer is busy looking or reading, pages will seem to load faster.

Animations can be anything from simple "flipbook" cartoons to live-action video footage. Simple cartoon-type animations that consist of only two to ten frames are best suited for use as inline attention-getters because their file sizes can be kept to a bare minimum for quick loading.

Animated GIFs

Animated GIFs are one of the most effective, lowest-overhead ways of using animation to attract attention. With a little time and practice, anyone can make an animated GIF.

Animated GIFs are simply multiple images saved within a single GIF89a file. When the file is placed on an HTML page (using the <IMG> tag and viewed with a supporting browser such as Netscape), animation will start almost as soon as the page is loaded. No special plug-ins or helper software is required.

Numerous software utilities for both the Mac and Windows will assist in saving the individual images or "frames" of your animation as a single GIF89a file. Some also provide drawing tools, and a few even provide "tracing paper" so that you can superimpose the drawing of a new frame over the drawing of the previous frame. This helpful feature enables you to check registration (the position of objects in one frame relative to the position of the same objects in the next frame) as you go.

For a list of GIF89a animation utilities, check Appendix B.

Content dividers (bars)

Content dividers are best known as horizontal and vertical rules. Horizontal rules are easily placed in HTML by using the <HR> tag, but HTML imposes the following limitations:

✦ There are no vertical rules.

✦ Horizontal bars are solid and act as visual barriers to proceeding further down the page.

Picture frames

Picture frames are actually not separate graphical elements, because in order for them to work, they must be merged into a single graphic with the picture they frame. Still, you can make one frame and then resize it to fit any number of pictures.

One of the best ways to make picture frames is to photograph real ones. Light them at a consistent key-light angle, so that if you mix frame styles they will all look like they're hanging on the same wall at the same time. Using an image-processing program that has layers, knock out the frame's background. In other words, it should float on a transparent layer. Copy the frame layer. On each layer, use the Polygon selection tool to draw a diagonal line from one corner of the frame to the other. Continue the selection around opposite sides of the frame on each layer. Delete the contents of the selection. Now you should have L-shaped frames. Place the photo you want to frame on yet another layer and drag that layer below the frame layers. Now use the Move tool to place the sides of the frame so that they just frame the photograph (see Figure 18-15). Finally, use the Polygon selection tool to trim the overlapping end of the frame so that the corners are mitered.

QuickTime panoramas and other virtual experiences

One of the most attention-getting things you can do with digitized photos is to use them to give the viewer the feeling of being inside an explorable environment. By far, the most popular way to do this is with a program that can "stitch" together a series of photographs so that they form a seamless 360-degree view. The result is then saved as a QuickTimeVR "movie." The QuickTime plug-in is now built-in to both the Netscape and Microsoft Web browsers, so most of your viewers will be able to use their mouse to pan the panoramic view and to zoom in on details within the scene.

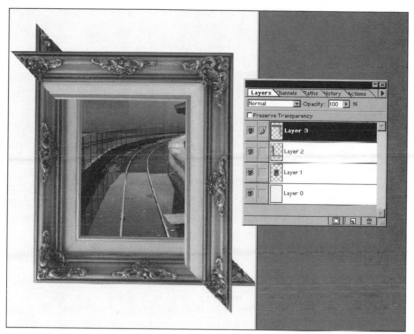

Figure 18-15: Overlapping the L-shaped frame sides and framing the picture

Numerous programs will stitch your images, including PhotoVista, QuickStitch 360, and Spin Panorama. Some image editors are also starting to include stitching capabilities. These include Corel PhotoPaint and ULead PhotoImpact 5.

Summary

This chapter has focused on why and how you should use photographs on Web sites. You learned when to use and when not to use photos (as opposed to other types of graphics) on a site. Also covered were Web file formats, a discussion of color modes as they apply to the limitations of the Web, and the characteristics of different types of graphics components used on the Web. Finally, you were introduced to the possibilities for QuickTime virtual experiences.

✦   ✦   ✦

Printing Digital Images

It's getting easier and cheaper to make prints that match (or come very close to) photographic prints that you'd expect from your local photographic processor. There are, however, a few things that you should be aware of. One of these is that the most popular printers to date produce prints that have a relatively short life span. This chapter concludes the book with a solution to that problem, one that will be valuable to those who want to make their prints collectible. In the meantime, printer manufacturers are recognizing their customers' desire for prints with photographic longevity.

Note Epson has announced (but had not shipped before our publication date) three new inkjet printers and companion materials capable of producing either matte or glossy six-color photographic prints whose life equals those made by traditional Type-C color printing methods. The models are the Epson Stylus 870 (a letter-sized printer at around $250), the Stylus 875 (which prints directly from digital film memory cards; price not yet announced), and the Stylus 1270 (which prints up to 13-inch-wide papers; just under $500).

Getting Ready to Make a Print

You can't hope to make a decent print unless your system is set up to show you what you want to see. The most important part of that equation is calibrating your monitor, which has already been covered in Chapter 15. If all you want to do is have a good idea of what you'll get from your desktop inkjet printer, those instructions are adequate. On the other hand, if you're the sort of person who won't be satisfied until you know that you can accurately predict what your printout is going to look like, you need to use hardware calibration. I suggest a new product called ColorBlind Prove it! (www.color.com; 858-613-1300).

The software-only version of the product is simply a more sophisticated approach to calibration. It is available for both Mac and Windows computers. Wizard-type hand-holding instructions (see Figure 19-1) take you right through the process, so it's hard to make a mistake.

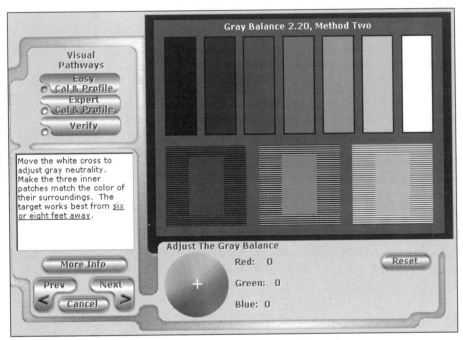

Figure 19-1: One of Prove it!'s visual calibration screens

The really good news is that you can also use Prove it! with a hardware colorimeter that attaches to the screen with suction cups. ColorBlind has its own device that it sells for $250, which makes the total cost of hardware color calibration less than $300. Just months ago, that cost would have been at least double. What's the advantage? The hardware measuring device takes the guesswork out of the equation.

There is no point in giving you a whole tutorial on using Prove it! The process is so easy it doesn't even require a manual. You install the software from a CD-ROM and then run the program. The program tells you exactly what to do at each step. Toward the end of the series of screens (which look like the ones shown in Figure 19-1), you are asked to attach the color meter to a target on the screen. You moisten the suction cups, press the device to the glass, and then click a button. Your screen flashes, makes automatic adjustments, and then the program tells you you're done. That's it.

Prove it! creates an ICC monitor profile in the course of calibrating. Then all the image-editing software needs to know is the ICC profile of the device to which it will be printing. I've tested this and found it to work very well with Photoshop 5.5. I haven't tested this combination with other software, but you can bet the other programs will work very hard to keep pace with Photoshop. In fact, many other image editors supported ICC profiles before Photoshop did.

Caution Make sure that you have (or will be interfacing with) accurate ICC profiles that take into account all of the characteristics of the output device being targeted: printer, printing method, inks, and papers. Often, these profiles are available through printer manufacturers—provided you use their brands of inks and papers.

If you are using custom combinations of devices, you'll need to make up custom profiles—or buy them. An alternative is to use software that makes printer profiles. Two examples are MonacoEZcolor (software $299, colorimeter $199; www.ezcolor.com) and Imaging Technologies Corporation's ColorBlind Matchbox ($995, including hardware; www.color.com). Then you print the printer target, making adjustments in your image editor until the printer target matches a printed target included in the EZcolor or Matchbox manual. The color-matching program then reads the TIFF file that was created by your image-editing program to make the match print and sets up a profile for the particular combination of printer, inks, and paper.

If you are calibrating your files for work that you are going to send out, you may be able to get a profile from your service bureau. Many print shops have made such profiles, know how to use them, and are happy to supply them to their customers. You just have to ask before you take your work there and be aware that some print shops are resistant to this new way of doing things.

Buying Premade Printer Profiles

If you want to make prints using your own printers and custom combinations of inks, you may be able to buy premade profiles. At present, I know of only one source for custom-made profiles, inkjetmall.com. A division of Cone Editions Press, inkjetmall.com (yes, their online address is www.inkjetmall.com) offers profiles for specific models of Epson printers and a wide variety of inks and papers. The printers supported are the Stylus Color 1520, the Stylus Color 3000, the Stylus Photo EX, the Stylus Photo 1200, and the Stylus Photo 750. Profiles for new printers seem to arrive very quickly after the printers are available in stores. Inks supported are Lyson (Lysonic E and Fotonic), Luminos Lumijet Platinum and Silver, MIS Archival Inks, and Epson standard inks. Numerous papers are supported from the following series: Legion Fine Art Paper, Lumijet Preservation Series, Ultra Stable Systems, Epson, Konica, Mitsubishi, Lysonic Fine Art Media, Hawk Mountain, Weber-Valentine, Pictorico, and Repeat-O-Type. The profiles are less than $50 for each specific combination of printer, ink, and paper. Print shops that may be called on to use a variety of inks and papers can buy them at a discount when they purchase entire collections from a single manufacturer.

The practical way to handle profile purchasing is to test sample papers with standard inks until you've narrowed your choice down to one or two papers. Then narrow your choice down to one brand of ink so that you don't have to keep cleaning your inkjets.

As you may have already guessed, Epson printers are the inkjets most widely chosen and supported for use in printing color digital photographs. This is because Epson took the lead in marketing to photographers and because they print at smaller dot sizes and with higher resolution than most of the competition. If you want a special paper or ink, your chances are much better of finding it in a version for an Epson.

What if you don't plan to use an Epson printer or, in fact, any kind of inkjet printer? You'll have to get your printer profiles from the manufacturer of the printer or buy software that can profile your printer.

Previewing to a Profile

I have warned elsewhere in this book against converting your files to CMYK until you are sure you are ready to send the file to the printing press or another CMYK device that will print it. That is because you *always* lose some (or a lot of) color when you convert from RGB to CMYK, after which *you can never get it back*. So what do you do if you want to see what final output would look like at an in-between stage of image manipulation and editing? To preview in CMYK, just select View ➪ Preview ➪ CMYK. Assuming you have correctly set your CMYK output profile in the Color Settings dialog box, you don't have to do anything else. You can also preview the uncompensated monitor gamut and have a gamut warning display.

In Photoshop 5.0 and later, you can also preview your output to a specific printer profile without actually converting the data in the file (which is what happens when you choose Image ➪ Mode ➪ CMYK). At the very bottom of the Mode menu is a command called Profile to Profile. Choose it and you get the dialog box shown in Figure 19-2.

When the dialog box appears, you simply choose the destination profile you want to preview from the Destination menu and click OK. You can also preview many other modes, but the one that will be most useful will be CMYK or the custom profile you have created for your printer or film recorder.

If you save the file, you will be saving it to its original ICC profile, not to the one you are previewing in. So it's a good idea to get in the habit of pressing Cmd/Ctrl + Z to undo the Preview command. You will return instantly to the mode you were in before you previewed. Of course, you could reselect Image ➪ Mode ➪ Preview to Preview and then choose CMYK to RGB, but this takes quite a bit longer.

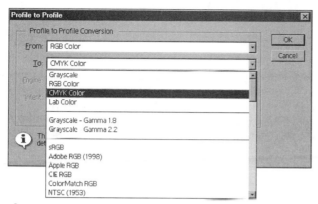

Figure 19-2: The Profile to Profile dialog box in Photoshop 5.5

There is an exception to the immediate undo suggestion I just made. You may want to perform an edit and make sure that it doesn't result in colors that will be out-of-gamut (unprintable) in CMYK. You can do this in Preview mode without actually affecting your original RGB data.

Choosing a Printer and Printing Method

You may not even be thinking about choosing a color printer to use for printing your digital photographs because you (or your company) already own a printer that you figure will be "good enough." If you work for a corporation, you may have options open to you (that you're not even aware of) that reside on other desks or in other departments. You'll find this section valuable because at some point you're likely to want something that's capable of producing the best that your digital images can be expected to show.

Of course, if you're a professional digital image maker, you have no choice. You simply have to buy the color printer that will best show off your work — even if you have to stretch your budget a bit. Not so long ago, that was a terrible penalty to pay for being a pro. Today, that situation (being a pro) has probably changed for you, but that will depend on your specific requirements.

Cost

Printers capable of making prints that look anywhere from "very" to "totally" photographic can be had for very little money. As part of system packages or when found on auction sites, they can be had for as little as $50. A more realistic range for affordable desktop inkjets capable of "totally" photographic quality would be from $250 to over $1,000.

If you need to either make prints as press-ready proofs or make "comps" (a close approximation of the finished printed product), you may want to consider other more expensive printers than inkjets.

Tip   Another alternative, though I haven't yet been able to test it, is using Adobe ImageReady to RIP the proof to an Epson 3000 — which happens to be the same printer I recommend as an affordable means of making gallery-sized archival prints later in this chapter. As I was proofing this chapter, copies of ImageReady arrived from Adobe. I must say that I'm mightily impressed with the accuracy of the results using the Mac and the Epson 3000.

Another reason you may want to move up in price is to make collectible (that is, archive-permanent) gallery-sized prints.

Proofing and comping capability

Printers used for this purpose are often dye-sublimation or high-end CMYK inkjet printers such as those made by Iris and ColorSpan. These printers are made for proofing and comping, and an experienced operator should be able to create a pre-press proof of astonishing accuracy. These printers generally start at around $40,000 and go way up from there. As a result, they are generally considered for in-house purchase only by sizeable corporations or by service bureaus that can count on taking in a steady stream of work from photographers, ad agencies, graphic designers, and people who need larger format output. If you are comping output for large posters, billboards, and other larger-than-tabloid applications, you'll pretty much have to stick to these printers or count on sending your work out to service bureaus.

Smaller firms that want to produce serious proofs in-house have, at least until recently, relied on higher-end inkjets or dye-sublimation printers. Tabloid-size (11 × 17 or thereabouts) is generally the upper size limit for these printers. Both require a RIP (Raster Image Processor), which generally sells for between $2,000 and $5,000. The printers sell for between $2,500 (for example, the Epson 5000 inkjet) to $12,000 (tabloid-size dye-sublimation printers).

More affordable options are just now becoming available to the rest of us. One of the most promising of these is Adobe's PressReady software RIP when used in conjunction with tabloid-size or larger inkjet printers. PressReady currently works with the following inkjet printers:

✦ Canon BJC 8500

✦ Epson Stylus Color 800/850/1200/1520/3000

✦ Hewlett Packard DeskJet 895C/1120C/2000C

✦ Hewlett Packard DesignJet ColorPro GA

PressReady also outputs to an Adobe PDF (Portable Document Format) file. Press-Ready can double as a way to convert your desktop publishing files or image files from an image editor (that doesn't already output to PDF) to create PDF files for distribution on CD-ROMs or across the Web. You can find out about late-breaking developments in PressReady by going to www.adobe.com/products/pressready.

If proofing and comping are your main objectives, and you have chosen to use an inkjet printer in-house, plan to dedicate the printer to that purpose. This is because the standard OEM inks and papers will give you the most accurate colors with the least hassle. However, these inks and papers cannot be easily mixed with third-party archival inks.

Size

If you need to comp posters, make large signs for trade shows, or make big prints for gallery exhibits, you need a big printer. The good news is that these are coming down in price to the point where printers such as the Encad Chroma 24 and the Epson 3000 can be considered for purchase by individual artists and photographers. The Encad Chroma 24 can make prints up to 24 inches wide and sells for right around $2,000 without a RIP. The Epson 3000 comes with a software RIP and can print images up to 21 inches wide. It currently sells for around $1,300.

Larger formats are available in very high resolution inkjets from a wide variety of manufacturers, but these get into price ranges ($9,000 to $250,000) that are in the province of service bureaus and large corporations.

Printing papers

If you are printing on a laser printer, photo printer, or dye-sub printer, your choice of papers will be somewhat limited. You had best stick with the options recommended by the manufacturer of your printer. In general, however, remember that glossy papers will usually reflect a wider range of tones. Matte and semi-matte papers are generally used for fine-art and gallery printing because their surfaces aren't as reflective and glare isn't as much of a problem when they're on display.

If you are using an inkjet printer, you have a huge range of options in papers, including linens, canvas, watercolor paper, and all the traditional photographic surfaces and weights. Nothing will make a bigger difference in the appearance of your prints than the paper on which you choose to print them.

You want to consider the effect you are trying to achieve. If your objective is to make your digital photos look as much as possible like traditional photos, choose a photo glossy paper. Some photo glossy papers work much better on some inkjet printers than on others. Kodak and Hewlett-Packard papers work well with non-Epson printers, for instance; but they tend to let ink puddle and can be very slow-drying when used with Epson printers. The best photographic paper for nonarchival Epson prints are Epson's Improved Epson Photo Paper (S041141) and Konica QP glossy papers. These papers are very good at showing deep blacks, minute details, and subtle tones such as skin tones.

Tip   The best resource I've found for reviews of printing papers is the Epson listserve. This e-mail list is created by an independent party and has a very large group of users. It is an invaluable resource for learning about color printing. You can find out all about this list and how to join at `www.leben.com/lists/epson-inkjet`.

Archival qualities

If your interest is in photography as collectible art (or what you can do with your photos), then you naturally want to make prints that will last as long as or longer than a standard photographic color print. Prints that meet or (often) exceed these criteria are generally considered *archival*.

The sad news is that prints made from the most popular and affordable printers — inkjets — tend to have a maximum display life of less than two years, although, as noted at the beginning of this chapter, that is starting to change. You'll find a more extensive discussion of archival qualities and expectations later in the chapter. For now, we can at least say that two years isn't nearly long enough. To be brutally honest, most inkjet prints won't even last more than about six months.

The good news is that archival inks and papers are now available for both four-color and six-color inkjet printers. However, four-color printers are a better choice for use with archival inks. A sizeable part of this chapter is devoted to making archival prints on inkjet printers. For now, it's enough to know that if you want to do this on an inkjet printer, you need to dedicate a printer to that purpose. You can work around that requirement, but it's not very practical — for reasons I'll explain later.

Also, if you're interested in making your own archival prints, you'll probably want the biggest printer you can afford. You will also want one for which archival inks are available. These include the Epson 3000 (about $1,250; a maximum of 17 inches wide), the Epson 9000 (less than $10,000, a maximum of 44 inches wide), and the IRIS and ColorSpan series of printers.

If you want archival prints that really look and feel like traditional photographs, consider going to a service bureau that owns a Cymbolic Sciences LightJet 2000. These printers actually print on photographic paper that is chemically processed. If tabloid or letter-size prints are big enough (the resolution of your camera may limit you anyway) the Fuji Pictography also produces prints that closely approximate an actual photographic print.

Tip   The most respected ratings for the longevity of paper and ink combinations are those produced by Wilhelm Research, Inc. As you can imagine, any testing for longevity takes some time, even though the labs have ways of simulating the effects of time over a much shorter period. So while you're not likely to find ratings appear at the same time a product is introduced, you can see the ratings for any paper and ink combination that has been tested by going to `www.wilhelm-research.com`.

Some Important Inkjet Printing Tips

Even if you're just printing with OEM (Original Equipment Manufacturer) supplies, there are a few things you should know about printing color on an inkjet printer that will help you to produce consistently satisfying prints. Here they are, in no particular order:

✦ Always specify the paper you are printing on in your application's Page Setup dialog box. Most printers have already profiled how their standard inks will behave on the papers that are standard for that printer. This is important because different paper surfaces and coatings can have a pronounced effect on the inks being used.

✦ Set your image resolution to match your printer resolution. This should be approximately one-third the resolution of your printer, because the printer's resolution is stated in terms of all the dots the printer produces. Yet it takes three dots (at least) to make up each color. Therefore, if you're printing on an Epson printer at 720 dpi, the maximum image resolution that will actually do you any good will be 240 dpi.

Making Archival Prints

If, as a digital photographer, you are interested in the fine arts market, you will need to make or have someone else make long-lasting prints of your work. Otherwise, neither collectors nor galleries will consider buying them.

On-site or off-site printing?

If you, like me, have an interest in making prints that are saleable in the fine arts market, you can't be limited to the printer or printers you own. You may want to look into service bureaus that have the equipment to make prints that are larger than your biggest printer can produce. Two of the best-established such service bureaus are John Cone's Conetech (www.cone-editions.com/conetech) on the East Coast and Nash Editions (www.nasheditions.com) in Southern California. There are hundreds of other highly qualified service bureaus — too many to mention here — and probably several in your own neighborhood. Prices for wide-format archival prints run from about $12 to $32 per square foot. Several factors are involved in these costs, including the type of printer used, the reputation of the service bureau, and satisfaction guaranteed (or not).

Tip When dealing with a service bureau, always ask about their policy regarding your satisfaction with what they produce. Insist, in advance of giving them the job, that they reprint your job if the result doesn't meet your expectations. Of course, it is only reasonable that they, in turn, insist on getting a print that is likely to correspond to your expectations. However, your expectations must be reasonable. A perfect match is nearly (if not totally) impossible. An acceptable match should always be possible.

Choosing a printer

When it comes to choosing a printer for desktop and in-house archival printing, the choices quickly narrow down to Epson printers (including the wide-format models made by Roland and C. Mutoh that use Epson heads). That is because these are the printers for which the widest range of options in inks and papers are available. In a given printer category, they are the most affordable.

You might consider the Epson 3000. Its maximum print size is just over 16×21 inches, so it's easy to make a 16×20 gallery print. This is a very popular size range for collectors, because the prints are large enough to occupy a feature space on a wall, yet not so large as to be overwhelming in the average room. Also, a print this size can be sold at an affordable price, but without being so low as to devalue the artwork.

There are also other reasons for choosing the 3000:

✦ **Affordability.** If you can split the cost with four friends, you can keep it in the $300 per person price range.

✦ **Real Estate.** Although it's about 50 percent larger than the Photo EX, it's still small enough to sit comfortably on a desktop. Moreover, you can move it from studio to studio if need be.

✦ **Four colors.** Prints made with four colors have at least twice the life span (all other factors being equal) of those made with six or eight colors. It's true that because this isn't a six-color printer, there are more visible half-tone dots; and colors don't transition as smoothly. However, if you print on watercolor-surfaced art papers, the difference is barely noticeable. Furthermore, when you view a 16×20 print at a distance that's normal for viewing such a print, there's virtually no noticeable difference.

Inks

Archival inks for inkjet printers come in two basic varieties:

✦ Extreme longevity "art inks"

✦ Photographic inks with more limited longevity

The extreme longevity inks, when used on the right papers, have very long life. The color in these inks is entirely pigment, rather than dye-based. They are rated by Wilhelm at between 60 and 125 years of constant display. In other words, with proper care, they will last even longer than most traditional types of paintings and artwork. If kept in museum conditions, they can last indefinitely. Unfortunately, their color range is somewhat muted. Blacks are usually a dull, brownish gray (think of the blacks you see in watercolor paintings) and colors aren't as bright as you expect from photographs. Watercolorists tend to love these inks because they look so much like watercolors. They can be useful for some photographs, if the mood is muted or if the photos have been used as the basis for "painterly" treatments that resemble watercolors. If your prints are going to be hung in bright light for extended periods, it may be worth compromising the color rendition for fade resistance by using one of the inks in this category. Some examples of pigmented inks are the Lysonic I (Iris) and E (Epson) inks; and their siblings, the Luminos Platinum series inks.

Most readers of this book will probably be much happier with the more photographic hybrid inks, typified by Luminos Silver and Lyson Fotonic. The longevity of these inks is currently "guesstimated" to be between 20 and 30 years. Although this is a much shorter life span than the pure pigment inks, it is nearly double the life span of most color photographic prints; and approximately the same as Ilfochrome inks.

Papers

Unfortunately, most of the companies that make archival inks and those that make archival papers have little to no relationship to one another. One exception is Lyson, which does make a series of papers specifically targeted for use with archival inks. Still, it is up to users and testing labs such as Wilhelm's to find the longest-lasting combinations of ink and paper.

To complicate matters even further, there are dozens of papers from which to choose. Of course, there isn't room to list them all here. Most of these papers come in rolls for wide-format printers, as well as sheets for printers such as the Epson 3000 and standard 17 × 22-, 13 × 19-, and 8.5 × 11-inch paper.

The type of paper or fabric (collectively called the *substrate*) will change the look of the image with respect to density range, smoothness of color changes, color saturation, surface texture, brightness, and ink drying.

The most popular surfaces for fine-art reproduction of digital artwork are those that imitate watercolor paper. The printing group I am a part of has settled on two Somerset papers, Concorde Rag and Photo Enhanced. Both papers have a very traditional watercolor texture and are heavy enough to feel like a fine-art paper, but are not so heavy that they won't feed through the printer. These papers (unlike many fine-art papers) are coated. Coated papers have a much wider color gamut than uncoated papers because the uncoated papers absorb so much ink and because their surface is also light absorbent. We also picked these papers for their reputation for longevity. Wilhelm has not completed testing on Photo Enhanced, but Concorde Rag has been tested and found to be exceptionally stable.

Archival qualities

Papers influence the longevity of the ink that's used to print on them. According to Henry Wilhelm, the acknowledged expert in print longevity, paper choice can influence longevity over a range of 20:1. That's quite a range, so carefully choose the paper you print on.

Wilhelm's lab has tested many ink and paper combinations for Iris printers, but the tests for desktop printers and inks are just now nearing completion and won't be out in time for inclusion in this book. However, you can see them if you go to Wilhelm's Web site (www.wilhelm-research.com).

Loading thick art papers

Some printers have trouble properly feeding thick papers because the paper's thickness doesn't permit it to catch in the feed mechanism. If you have this problem, you can try taping a half-inch strip of 20-pound paper (ordinary business paper weight) to the leading edge of your art paper. The leading edge of this strip must be perfectly parallel to the leading edge of your art paper. Use tape that can be removed without leaving a residue. The tape used to mount archival prints in their mats is perfect for this purpose. One tape you might try is 3M's one-half-inch-wide tape (product #924).

Tip

If you plan to use art papers and extra-heavy photo papers, use the manual feed on your printer and be sure that the printer has a setting for thicker paper. Otherwise, the printer may jam or you may get tracks embossed on your print from the printer's paper-feed mechanism.

The procedure

Here are the steps you need to take in order to set yourself up for printing archival images in a way that's most economical and efficient for your particular requirements:

✦ Choose your printer

✦ Choose your ink

✦ Choose your paper(s)

✦ Calibrating your monitor

✦ Profile the printer/ink/paper combination

✦ Be sure your printer settings are correct for manually loading fine-art papers

✦ Trim your print

✦ Mat your print

✦ Frame your print

Choosing your printer

When you choose your printer, plan your budgeting so that this printer will be dedicated to making archival prints. It is cheaper to buy a photo-glossy paper for making the occasional large comp than to pay $100 for cleaning cartridges that must be used if you plan to switch between archival and OEM inks.

Choosing your ink

Choose your ink carefully. We choose our inks by reading the user feedback on the Epson printer list (www.leben.com/lists), and then speaking to several dealers and getting a consensus of their opinions.

If you have the time, a better method is to have your supplier send you samples of prints made from the same image with different inks on the same paper. Then choose the look and feel that seems most suitable to the type of work you want to produce. It's expensive and time-consuming to change inks midstream. If you need to get a feel for different types of artwork, you're better off doing that with different types of papers.

Choosing your paper(s)

This is the tough part. We made our decision with the same method we chose for our inks, settling on Somerset Concorde Rag, which is slightly off-white and best suited to subjects with an antique or painterly quality; and Somerset Photo Enhanced, which is bright white and works well for photographs — especially those that get their impact from vibrant colors. However, you have several other options.

Read the user lists and visit the Wilhelm site for the latest numbers on longevity, as that should be your most important criteria. Be sure to remember that longevity can be greatly affected by the specific combination of ink and paper — so look for as much information as you can on how the paper you're considering reacts to the ink you've chosen.

Calibrating your monitor

Archival inks and papers are too expensive to leave monitor calibration to guess-work. You want your monitor to provide a good soft-proof. At the very least, spend the $300 it takes to buy Prove it! and the Sequel Imaging Chroma24 monitor colorimeter. It takes less than 15 minutes to plug in the USB version of the colorimeter and then run the Prove it! software. Every print we've made with these products, assuming the correct printer/paper profile was chosen, has been right on the money.

Tip

At a cost of approximately $10 for a 16 × 20 print, the $300 you spend on Prove it! and the colorimeter is a very small price to pay for not having to throw away mistakes.

Profiling the printer/ink/paper combination

If you know the paper and ink combinations you plan to use, you can simply buy the profiles from inkjetmall.com. The profile for a given printer/ink/paper is $50. If you think you may want to use a number of different papers, it would pay to buy MonacoEZcolor (which can also be used for monitor and scanner calibration) and use it to create scanner and printer profiles. EZcolor uses the scanner to read the printout, so it is important to properly calibrate the scanner first.

Tip   As much as we like Prove it!, if you think you may need to profile other devices and will be using several different types of papers, it would be more economical to simply start out with EZcolor and the colorimeter.

More sophisticated and accurate profilers, such as Color Blind Matchbox, require a hardware device for reading the printout. These devices are used by professional printers and typically sell for between $1,000 and $5,000.

Printer settings for manually loading fine-art papers

Now that you've done all your homework and bought all your supplies, you are ready to make your first archival print. Read your printer manual carefully. Because you are probably using heavy fine-art papers, you will have to feed them manually. Be sure you follow the proper instructions to set your printer for heavy-weight papers and for the proper paper type required to match your profile (your profiler should give you the instructions for doing this).

Using your image-editing program's settings

Be sure to set up the page so that your print matches the page size and will print at the correct resolution.

To do that in Photoshop:

1. Choose Image ⇨ Image Size. The Image Size dialog box appears (see Figure 19-3).

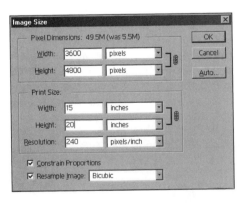

Figure 19-3: The Photoshop Image Size dialog box, showing the proper settings for a 15 × 20 image to be printed on the Epson 3000

2. Make sure that the Constrain Proportions and Resample Image checkboxes are selected (you click to toggle the check mark on and off). In the Resolution field, enter the optimum resolution for your printer. Then enter the desired height and width and click OK. The image will resize.

3. I find that Step 2 generally softens the image slightly, so I choose Filter ⇨ Sharpen ⇨ Unsharp Mask to run the Unsharp Mask filter at its default settings (Amount: 50 percent, Radius 1.0, Threshold 0).

4. Choose File ➪ Page Setup. When the Page Setup dialog box appears, choose your printer from the Name menu, and then click the Properties button. This will bring up the dialog box for your printer's properties.

5. Follow your printer's instructions for making and saving advanced custom settings. Also, make sure that the proper paper is chosen for your printer profile (instructions will come with the profile if it was purchased from inkjetmall.com, or can be found in your software documentation if you used software such as EZcolor to profile your printer). When you finish following the instructions for your printer and printer profile, click OK.

6. Place your cursor on the Photoshop status line where it shows the document's file size, and press and hold the mouse button. The window that appears will show how your image fits the page and is aligned to the paper (see Figure 19-4).

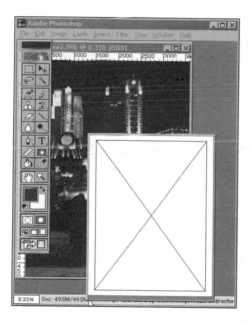

Figure 19-4: You should always preview the fit and positioning of your image before making an expensive archival print.

7. Place the paper in your printer's manual feed and make sure the paper thickness setting is for thick paper.

8. Choose File ➪ Print. When the Print dialog box appears, choose your printer profile from the Space menu (read your profiler's instructions about where to place the profile in your file directories).

After waiting for a lot less time than it would take to fix, wash, and dry a conventional photo print, your finished print will emerge. If you have done a conscientious job of calibrating your monitor and profiling your printer and ink combination, you will get exactly what you expected. Actually, what I got was better than what I expected because it truly had the look and feel of a collectible print.

A Warranty Warning

Epson does not support the use of inks made by other manufacturers in their printers and does not recommend it. This is understandable because the ink nozzles are microscopic in size and foreign matter could easily clog them. If you use third-party inks — whether archival or ordinary — you are risking damaging your printer and voiding your warranty. On the other hand, many reputable print shops have been using the inks and papers mentioned in this chapter for some time and with great success. Just remember that you're gambling (which is another reason why you want to start with a printer that is as affordable as possible). Also remember that you're well advised to buy your supplies from reputable and established manufacturers and suppliers.

Trimming your print

You may not see a need to trim your print if it is going to be matted, because the mat will cover the edges anyway. However, I find it easier to correctly position a print on the mat if the print is trimmed. Moreover, buyers prefer to do their own matting and framing — or you may just want to present your work in a box portfolio. Making a neat trim around the edges is a good habit to form.

If you are using large papers, you may need to trim your print with a straight edge and an X-Acto knife or single-edged razor blade. Be sure to use a fresh, sharp blade and a metal ruler. Place your print atop a virgin piece of backing board so that your cut won't be ragged.

Trim so that you can mat your print according to fine-art standards. This means that there should be approximately one-quarter-inch of border on the top and sides of the image and about one-half an inch at the bottom. For prints larger than 16×20, you may want to increase these sizes. If you are making limited-edition prints, use a pencil to sign the bottom of the print. Place the number of the print and the edition on the left (for example, 2/100 means print #2 of a limited edition of 100); and, optionally, the title of the piece in the center, with the artist's signature and date on the right.

If you plan to ship or distribute the print unmounted, place it in a protective sleeve and use corrugated board to keep it from being bent or folded.

Matting your print

Don't waste your time and money making archival digital prints and then use any old mat and mat board. Go to a dealer that sells acid-free, long-lasting backings and mat boards. I prefer foam-core as a backing board because it feels substantial but weighs considerably less, which keeps shipping costs down.

Your choice of mats can be critical. I generally use a very slightly off-white or eggshell mat because it works in any gallery. In addition, the collector has the option of cutting the mat opening a bit wider and placing a border mat inside it.

You can buy precut mats and make your prints to fit inside those mats. I have done this in the past, but now feel that an exhibit looks much more interesting if the mats have been cut to fit the actual composition of the image. If you do this, you will need a custom mat cutter. These can be purchased from most art supply stores.

Framing your print

Frame your print behind UV-coated glass or Plexiglas. I prefer the latter because it makes it possible to ship framed prints to shows and exhibits without worrying about them being broken in transit or by the people who are handling them when they are being hung. Figure 19-5 shows a properly matted, signed, and framed archival print.

Figure 19-5: Note the neutral color of the mat, the border between image and mat, and the manner in which the print is signed.

One hint about framing: The larger the frame and mat in relationship to the print, the more perceived value for the framed print. This is also true of matted prints.

Internet resources for digital color printing

As with any other topic, the Internet offers tremendous resources for digital color printing. Here are some of them:

✦ **The Digital Darkroom (**http://come.to/digitaldarkroom**):** This Hong Kong-based site reviews and tests printers and inks. Because it's located in Hong Kong, reviews about new products often precede the introduction of those products into the U.S. markets.

✦ **inkjetmall.com (**www.inkjetmall.com**):** This is the Web site for the retail division of Cone Editions Press. It is an excellent resource for information about making digital prints, and about supplies for both desktop and wide-format printers, including Iris printers.

✦ **Wilhelm Imaging Research, Inc.** (www.wilhelm-research.com)**:** As mentioned earlier, this is considered the ultimate authority on longevity testing.

✦ **Digital Fine Art Magazine** (www.giclees.com)**:** An interactive Web site in magazine format that's dedicated to the making of archival fine-art inkjet prints.

✦ **Epson Print Quality Comparison** (www.tssphoto.com/sp/dg/news/ dot_comp.html)**:** A direct comparison of the four different types of Epson printers at 8× or 17× magnification. It is very educational, and because the comparison is in color and the charts are very concise, you get an excellent idea of the actual differences between these printers.

✦ **IAFADP (International Association of Fine Art Digital Printmakers)** (www. iafadp.org)**:** This is a corporate membership site, so much of its content is closed to nonmembers. However, you can access some informative articles that define Giclee fine-art prints and the machines that make them. One very useful document is the California legal codes pertaining to the standards that define fine-art prints.

Summary

This chapter has covered the essentials of making digital prints. You first learned how to prepare for printmaking, including an accurate and affordable means of making instrumented color calibrations. You also learned how to choose a printer and printing method. Finally, and most important, this chapter has given you a blueprint for making gallery-quality archival prints that have a longer life span than most photographic color prints, on a commonly available and affordable inkjet printer, the Epson 3000.

✦   ✦   ✦

More Specialized Programs for Digital Imaging

Because digital photography is such a fast-developing field, I wanted to add a few useful accessory programs that came to my attention as we were about to go to press. It is obvious from the variety of these programs that digital photography is rapidly becoming more useful to more of us.

enotate

This program for Palm handhelds and compatibles from Informal Software (www.informal.com) enables you to use your palmtop as a digitizing pad in order to hand-draw notations on documents stored in your desktop computer. If you're a photographer who does business with clients who need to pass your work around for input, this is a quick and efficient way to personalize the comments that various people make about a photo. You can highlight areas of the image where you want changes to be made and write the nature of those changes in longhand.

enotate enables you to choose a color for the pen and lets you draw on a different layer than the image is on. You have a choice of seven colors for the pen. You can also choose from four different line thicknesses. This enables you to respond to a change by deleting the drawing layer and creating a new one of your own by saving and then reopening the image. The program also has multiple undo/redo. This enables you to back up a couple of steps, try something new, and then go back to the original if you don't like the result. Figure 20-1 shows the result of marking up an image on the Palm device, as it appears on the PC.

Figure 20-1: A notation made on the Palm device as seen when simultaneously recorded on the PC

enotate will work with just about any kind of document, whether it's a Microsoft Word document or an image in Photoshop. However, when you're "enotating" (making hand notations) on an image, you have to be sure to size the image so that it fits the enotate window. Images are always shown 1:1 (pixel for pixel) and you can't zoom out. This means that you may have to make a separate set of images to use for making notations. Although this may seem like a hassle, it keeps image sizes down to a practical size for e-mailing.

Speaking of e-mail, enotate also recognizes your PC's Internet connection and will let you instantly send the enotated photo to anyone via e-mail. If the person you are sending the e-mail to has a Palm-compatible handheld device, you can send the image in enotate format. The recipient can then modify the notations and send them back to you or on to another member of the creative team. If the recipient doesn't have a Palm device, you can simply send a layer-flattened version of the file in JPEG format. This could be a stupendous boon to photographers working away from the art director at satellite locations. After all, it's much better to spend another half day in Spain reshooting to comply with a client's request than it is to fly back to Spain after you've returned to your home base in Los Angeles.

Tip

I use enotate on a TRGpro (see Figure 20-2), which is a Palm handheld clone that can use CompactFlash Memory cards. The advantage is that this can be the same type of memory card used in CompactFlash-compatible cameras, so the cards can serve multiple purposes. The extra memory also makes it possible to use the Palm device as a miniature laptop in conjunction with a folding keyboard.

Figure 20-2: The TRGpro, running enotate software

Piccolo

Piccolo is an image management utility with a twist: It is especially useful for managing images before you download them from a digital film card. All you have to do is connect a camera or card reader in such a way that the computer sees the digital film as another hard drive. As soon as you open the folder with your images in it, you'll see a window that looks like the one shown in Figure 20-3.

The images are shown as slides right away. You can then rotate them, rename them, and do such basic image editing as changing gamma, brightness, and contrast. The rename and rotate capabilities are worth their weight in gold. First, you can rename and add a text description to any image, simply by clicking a toolbar button and typing in the clearly labeled fields. If you have a microphone attached to your computer, you can add a voice annotation by clicking the round button at the top right of the slide. Any time after that, if you want to hear what you've recorded, you click the button again (this time, it's the right-facing arrowhead indicating play — see the slide on the upper left). All of this information can be recorded right onto the digital film card. You can then e-mail the contents of the card back to your office, client, or publisher. Of course, all that information takes up space on the card. However, there's no reason you can't do the same thing for any file on your computer after you've transferred the files to a directory.

Figure 20-3: The Piccolo slide viewer screen

I also mentioned that the ability to rename before you download is worth its weight in gold. After all, who knows what a filename like PA060266.JPG means? If you can quickly rename the images while they are on the film card, you're always able to identify the subject — no matter where or how you transferred the files.

Tip You can also see any of the files at screen size by double-clicking the Slide view. Continuing to click zooms in, while right-clicking zooms out.

Piccolo isn't as sophisticated at image management as Canto Cumulus, Extensis Portfolio, or Thumbs Plus. Still, it's too handy to be without. Try it once and you'll be addicted. Unfortunately, there is currently no Mac version available. Check the Pixology site for any possible late-breaking news on that front. You can also download a copy of a 45-day trial version of the product. Piccolo retails for $40. You can find it at Ritz Camera online at www.ritzcamera.com.

Next-Generation Software for Turning Photos into Paintings

Once upon a time, MetaCreations' Painter had pretty much cornered the market of creating computer paintings and turning photos into paintings. Painter is still a magnificent program (and probably indispensable to most interpretative artists) — even more so in version 6. In the meantime, however, there have been some major developments. First, MetaCreations has put Painter and all its other professional graphics applications up for sale. By the time you read this, it will probably have found a new home. Second, Deep Paint blossomed out of Australia and made it possible to access a powerful "natural media" paint program from within any application compatible with Photoshop plug-ins (ironically, this includes Painter). Third, a small company in San Francisco, Synthetik Software, invented a program called Studio Artist that it bills as the world's first graphics synthesizer. If you run Windows, you can use Deep Paint. If you're a Mac user, you can try Studio Artist. Neither program is currently cross-platform, but I'm told you should keep an eye out. I'm lucky enough to run both platforms, so I can tell you what's special about each of these programs.

Deep Paint

Deep Paint was introduced in 1999 by an Australian software publisher called Right Hemisphere (www.us.righthemisphere.com). Right Hemisphere already had a heavyweight reputation for its software for hand-painting three-dimensional models, so when the company announced a natural-media paint program that would work as a plug-in for Adobe Photoshop, the press listened. The program quickly won awards from ZD-Net, the Washington Software Alliance, and several other prestigious publications.

To use Deep Paint, you simply install the software. It installs as both a standalone application and as a Photoshop plug-in. If you plan to simply work up a painting from a photo, the program will operate faster if it doesn't have to contend for memory with Photoshop. On the other hand, it's very convenient to be able to edit in Photoshop and then switch into Deep Paint whenever you want to create a brush stroke effect or do something such as paint a textured background.

To use Deep Paint as a plug-in, you just open the photo you want to work on in Photoshop. Then you do whatever Photoshop editing you want to do. For instance, it's often more effective to bump up the image's color saturation before creating a painting.

When you're ready to create the painting from the photo, you choose Filter ⇨ Right Hemisphere ⇨ Deep Paint. The Deep Paint Plug-in manager appears. You click a Send Mode button and Deep Paint opens, displaying your image.

The Deep Paint interface looks similar to Photoshop's, but the actual operations take a little getting used to. Once you figure it out, however, the process of creating a painting from a photo is pretty straightforward. You choose the Clone tool in the toolbox and then choose a cloning method from the Clone Options. (You can see this interface in Figure 20-4.) You then click the Layers tab in the Command Panel (which is usually on the right of the screen, but can be docked anywhere) and choose Clone Trace from the Layers menu. To access the Layers menu, click the right-facing arrowhead next to the Opacity field, and then click the command you want to choose.

Deep Paint automatically dims the original layer and creates a new layer on which the natural paint cloning will take place. Now all you have to do is choose from any of the gazillions of Deep Paint brush styles and start painting on the clone layer. You can control brush types and sizes, mixing them any way you want.

One of Deep Paint's features that I find especially valuable is the large number of impasto (dimensional thick paint) brush styles. You can easily use these without having to give the whole painting an impasto look — so you can vary your styles between thick and thin.

Figure 20-4 shows a Photoshop image partially cloned. Note how you can see the underlying photography, which was automatically dimmed when we chose the Clone Trace command in the Layers Panel. Deep Paint doesn't use the History palette, but it does have multiple levels of undo. If you don't like something you've done, you can back up and start over.

When you finish the painting, you can send both layers back to Photoshop by clicking the Photoshop (Eye) icon in the Deep Paint toolbar. (There are two other ways to do this, but clicking the button is easiest.)

Figure 20-4: Cloning a photo into a painting in Deep Paint

In this overview, I've covered only a very small part of what Deep Paint can do. First, there are the "brushes" — that is, the different effects that can be applied to an image or cloned with a brush stroke. There are nine categories of these: Standard Tools (52), Variations (39), Weird (10), Natural (59), Image Processing (12), Cloners (23), Metals (15), Fabric (15), and Tiles (16). This makes a total of 241 distinct premade brushes. Figure 20-5 gives you an idea of how varied these brushes can be. It doesn't stop there, though. You can also create your own brushes by changing the characteristics of the existing brushes, and then save the custom brush to a new name.

You'll notice that some of the brushstrokes are actually images — much like the Image Hose invented by Painter. Some of the brushstrokes can perform some image manipulation, such as burning, dodging, sharpening, and heightening contrast. However, Deep Paint is by no means an image-manipulation program. For that, you'll still need an image editor compatible with Photoshop plug-ins.

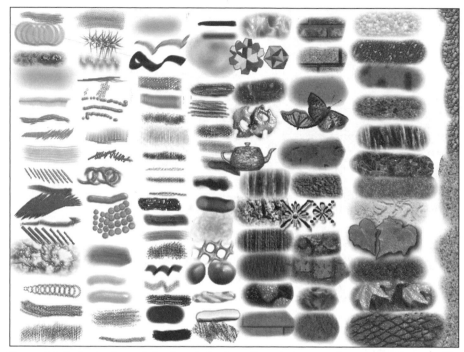

Figure 20-5: Just a few of the Brush Stroke effects in Deep Paint. Notice the 3D effect in some strokes.

Studio Artist

At $300, Synthetik Studio Artist (www.synthetik.com; 415-864-0433) is just sheer fun. It's not exactly a natural-media paint program, although the effects it creates can be very reminiscent of what you might expect from Painter or Deep Paint. However, Studio Artist works by painting scaled vectors. The program doesn't care what size the original is, and the only limitation on output size is the amount of RAM you have stuffed into your Mac and allocated to the program.

Working in Studio Artist is much faster than creating a painting from scratch in either Painter or Deep Paint. You can pretty much create strokes as fast as you can stroke — especially if you have a G4 Mac. However, what makes the program seem even faster is that you can create a painted image automatically. You can even paint automatically on a number of layers and then use Studio Artist's version of Blend modes to combine the layers in a nearly endless combination of effects.

Using Studio Artist is a whole new experience. The interface isn't much like anything you've likely seen before. That's OK, because the program is so much fun to play with, you can stay fascinated for hours. The interface, and a painting that took less than an hour to complete, is shown in Figure 20-6.

Figure 20-6: Studio Artist's interface and a painting created from the portrait seen at the upper left

To give you an idea of what it's like to use this program, here's the rundown on how I created the portrait: I opened the program and chose File ➪ New Original Image and Canvas. A dialog boxed opened and I entered a new size for the canvas (recall that the size of the original doesn't really matter). You want to size the canvas to be whatever your output will be. You just type in the size you want your canvas to be. If you want the canvas to have the same height-to-width ratio as the original image, just type in one dimension and be sure to select the Constrain Proportions checkbox. The program immediately opens the file. The original appears in the upper-left corner. The canvas appears in the space where you see the painted portrait in Figure 20-6.

I wanted to combine the original image with the effects created by the program, so I went to the Canvas ➪ Layer Window command, which brought up the Layers palette. I then made the source image the underlying layer and used a combination of automated styles on the other layer.

Note Whenever you click the Action button, Studio Artist paints for you in the style you have chosen in the Styles palette. Whenever you want to paint by hand, you just start stroking, and hand-painting automatically takes over.

After I'd played around this way for a while, I chose a blend mode that allowed the source image to show through, and adjusted the transparency of the painted layer so that I could control how much of the underlying layer showed. Finally, I experimented with different painting styles and hand-stroked over the image until it took on the look that I wanted.

Now, please keep in mind that I have shown you only the most basic and playful aspects of this program's capabilities. Even if you stayed at this level, you could come up with endless permutations. But there's lots more that you can do.

Studio Artist always uses a source image, but never modifies that image. It only uses it to let the brushes and assisted painting modes know what colors to use. The program also has some "intelligence" that claims to understand how the paint should flow and how the strokes should move according to what it sees in the original image.

If you want to paint in a completely freeform way and have the ability to choose your own colors, no problem. You just pick Source Color instead of Source Image from the Source pull-down menu. You can pick any color in the source image by pressing Opt and then clicking in the source image. You can also pick any color from the color picker that replaces the source image in the source area.

Another neat trick possible in Studio Artist is that you can change the source image any time you want. This way, you can paint in different foregrounds and backgrounds or combine images from two different pictures. You can also record any Studio Artist painting process as a QuickTime movie, so you can animate how your paintings evolved and put them on the Web.

You can create endless variations in Studio Artist. However, I've also discovered that it's even more powerful when I also pass images into Photoshop and Painter. Photoshop makes it very easy to lighten and darken specific areas of the image. Painter is simply more predictable and has incredible surface and texture modeling capabilities.

KPT 6

KPT 6 is the latest — and possibly most interesting — iteration of Kai's Power Tools, the most popular Photoshop-compatible filter set. There are an endless number of highly useful Photoshop-compatible plug-in filters. Almost all modern image-editing programs have been smart enough to make themselves compatible with these plug-ins. If you're curious to know about most or all of them, you should visit the Adobe Web site at www.adobe.com/products/plugins/photoshop/main.html. You should also check out the other filters in the KPT series (currently moving from MetaCreations to an as-yet-unnamed new publisher) and those made by Extensis (www.extensis.com).

Note KPT 6 does not come bundled with earlier versions of Kai's Power Tools, as did KPT 5. If you also buy KPT 5, you will get KPT 3 with it.

So why is KPT 6 being singled out here as something especially worthy of attention? Well, first, it's the latest thing. More important, it consists of ten programs that go beyond mere special effects, to the point where they can uniquely enhance digital photographs. These ten filters are as follows:

✦ Equalizer

✦ Gel

✦ Goo

✦ LensFlare

✦ Materializer

✦ Projector

✦ Reaction

✦ Scene Builder

✦ Sky Effects

✦ Turbulence

Equalizer

Despite its name, Equalizer isn't so much meant to change the overall contrast of the image as it is to sharpen, smooth, and blur in more powerful ways than using Photoshop's blur and sharpen filters. It is a godsend if you're using a camera with a low-contrast (soft) lens or got a bit of the jitters while you were shooting that low-light image. It's also capable of creating some very nice special effects, such as edges, glows, and washed-out images. Finally, it's very good at letting you remove small defects such as noise, dust, and scratches.

Equalizer's (see Figure 20-7) name comes from its use of a nine-band panel that's used for raising or lowering the crispness of specific tonal ranges in the image. Thus, it works in much the same way for an image as an audio equalizer. Actually, the nine-band equalizer is seen in only one of the program's three modes. In addition to the Equalizer filter, there's Bounded Sharpen and Contrast Sharpen.

At the lower left corner of the screen is a small circle with a grid of squares. Click it and you get a screen of preset settings. Trying a few is quite educational. You can quickly see the range of sharpness settings that you can get from Equalizer (see Figure 20-8). Picking one of these settings instantly makes the change.

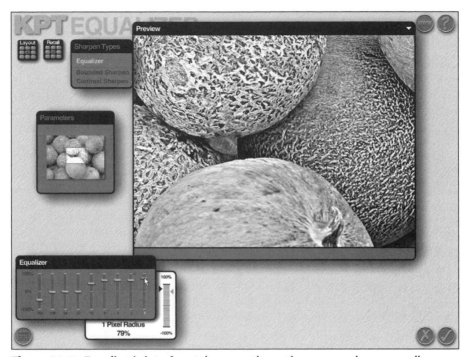

Figure 20-7: Equalizer's interface takes over the entire screen when you call up the filter from Photoshop.

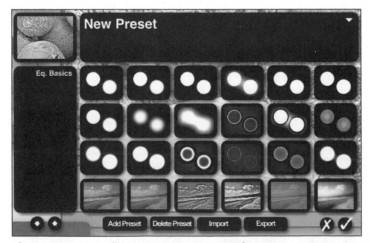

Figure 20-8: Equalizer's presets. You can also create your own presets.

To give you an idea of the range of effects you can get with equalizer, Figure 20-9 shows you the effects of creating the same flower at eight different settings.

Figure 20-9: The original, with no settings, is shown at the upper left.

Equalizer also has a Global Equalization slider that can be used to tweak your EQ settings. You access this slider from the Parameters panel. The default setting is 100 percent, meaning that your EQ settings will be applied full-strength. If you lower this setting, it will "fade," or lessen, the strength of the settings in the EQ sliders.

Then there are the Bounded Sharpen and Contrast Sharpen filters.

The Bounded Sharpen filter is meant to give you a "quick-and-dirty" way of correcting for edge softness that results from resampling (resizing) an image in your image editor. I've traditionally used the Unsharp Mask filter in Photoshop for this purpose, but Bounded Sharpen is a bit easier. While looking at the 100 percent preview, you drag one of two sliders, and then the other. Because you see the results instantly, it's easy to get maximum edge sharpening without overdoing it and without wasting a lot of time. The two sliders are Sharpen Percent and RGB Tolerance. Sharpen Percent controls the strength of sharpening, while RGB Tolerance defines how much difference there has to be between adjacent pixels before they will be considered an edge.

The Contrast Sharpen filter heightens the contrast of pixels within a designated residence. This is an excellent filter to use if you want to force highlights to bloom, as in high-key fashion pictures or dreamy, "foggy" landscapes.

Gel

Gel makes the surface of an image take on a three-dimensional look. It is as if you were painting in a gelatinous, semi-transparent material. As you can see from Figure 20-10, the effect can be startling. I used a photograph of a painting on the front of a motorcycle shop to dramatize how the flatness of the colors in the original takes on a 3D look after using Gel.

Figure 20-10: A two-dimensional drawing treated with KPT 6's Gel filter. The figure on the right has not been treated.

Gel gets its color and characteristics from a spherical environment map. If you have KPT 3 Spheroid Designer or a photo of a spherical object (colored Christmas tree balls would be perfect) you can create some great photos. There are also dozens of presets already available; you can choose from them just by clicking the Preset button.

Just as in Equalizer, you adjust most of the program's settings by dragging a slider in one of the panels. You can adjust the opacity of the gel, the degree that the gel refracts (bends) the underlying image, and the percentage that the environment map blends with the underlying image.

There are ten brush tools. You adjust their size with . . . guess what . . . a slider! You can also adjust the speed at which the gel flows from the brush, and the softness of the brush's edge. The sliders pop up any time you click a brush to pick it. The brush tools are as follows: Wide Brush, Thin Brush (for smaller, more precise strokes), Eraser (diminishes the gel until it disappears), Knife (carves away the gel), Smooth (blends gel strokes together), Splatter (lays down drops of gel that can be used to simulate water drops), Twirl (spins or twists gel you've already painted on), Pinch/Bulge (makes gel concave or more bulbous), Smear (lets you shove gel around to "finger paint" it), and Magnet (makes the gel bend to follow the brush).

If you've ever used Kai's Power Goo, you'll recognize all of these brush tools. They're identical to those in Goo—which is now a filter for Photoshop and is covered next.

Goo

Goo brings to Photoshop a capability it has long needed: the ability to bend and distort parts of an image in a freehand manner. This makes it possible to create photographic caricatures by stretching and exaggerating facial features. It can also be very handy in conceptual design work when you want to preview how you might like to alter the shape of an existing product. You can also make parts of an image match the size of the part of another image that you want to composite it to. For instance, you could put a man's legs on a cow—distorting the shape of the man's legs to suit the shape of the cow's. Another terrific benefit of Goo is its ability to record the permutation of a photograph as you distort it, and then output the result as a QuickTime movie or sequenced PICT (Mac only) or BMP (Windows only) files. In Windows, you also have the option of outputting to an AVI movie. If you want to create animated GIFs, you can convert the PICT or BMP files to GIF format and then use a GIF animation program (or something such as Fireworks or ImageReady 2.0) to create a GIF animation.

Goo's tools are used to distort parts of the image, to smooth the distortions, to erase the distortions, to let you pull parts of the image around (with the Magnet), or to gradually erase what you've done in case you overdo it. The filter is easy to use, but it takes a fair amount of practice to get it right (instead of making a mess). At least you'll have fun—it's kind of like playing with circus mirrors.

Tip   One very useful trick is removing from their backgrounds those parts of the image that you want to stretch and play with. In Figure 20-11, the person was knocked out of the background. Then the hands were selected and lifted to their own layer. After that, Goo was used in three stages: one for the face (on Layer 1, with the whole figure), one for the right hand (on Layer 2), and one for the left hand (on Layer 3). By breaking up the operation into these three layers, I was able to avoid unwanted distortion of the body and shirt. I also placed a texture filter created from the Texture Explorer filter in KPT 3 and blurred it with the Equalizer to create the new background.

Figure 20-11: The picture on the left is a straight shot, at right is post-Goo.

Note

If you need to do extensive warping and morphing of images, you may want to try Human Software's Squizz (another Photoshop plug-in) or one of the Valis Group's Flo series of programs.

LensFlare

The LensFlare filter in KPT 6 goes way beyond the lens flare filters native to Photoshop and most other image editors. Figure 20-12 shows a range of effects created with this filter and, believe me, these are just for starters. You can control the size and brightness of the flare, the size and color of the halo, and the number of radii in the sparkles. Actually, the filter is useful for creating many effects besides lens flares. You can put sparkles in people's eyes, put a halo behind an angel's head, or make supernovas explode in the heavens.

Despite its versatility, this filter is almost as easy to use as ordinary lens flare filters. Once again, you use sliders for everything: flare position and size, flare color, halo color, halo size, aspect ratio, and brightness. Creating glow and streak effects is a bit more complicated, but once again, plenty of presets come with the program.

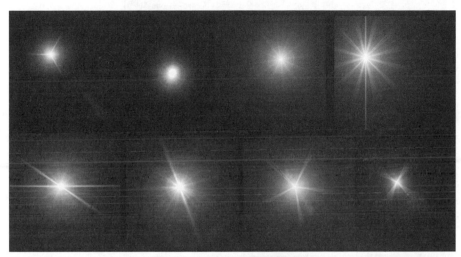

Figure 20-12: Eight very different lens flare effects

Materializer

Materializer lets you project three-dimensional surface materials onto your photograph. You can also use the filter to place controllable lighting from multiple "light sources" anywhere in the frame. These lighting controls perform a similar function to the Render ⇨ Lighting Effects filter in Photoshop. However, you'll discover that there are always differences in interpretation between the way one type of software accomplishes a task and another. Figure 20-13 shows the Material, Texture, 3-D Lighting, and Environment controls in Materializer.

As you can see just by looking at Figure 20-13, you are provided with an incredible amount of control over the appearance of your 3D effects, including how much the underlying image shows through; the direction, colors, and intensity of light; the depth of the texture; and so on.

You create the depth in the surface by using a surface map, which is nothing more than a photo. The program interprets white in the photo as higher elevation, and black as the lowest elevation. The darkness of the shades in between determines the apparent height of those areas. You can also use a photograph as an texture map, which makes it possible to tint and otherwise influence the appearance of areas you're "Materializing."

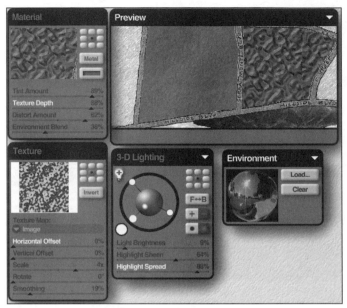

Figure 20-13: Consistent with the other KPT 6 filters, Materializer's controls are all sliders.

 Tip

If you want to make a texture map, just create a new image with a black background. Make your foreground color white and use your image editor's airbrush to create gradually lighter areas in the image. Then just click the image in the Texture panel and you'll get the usual dialog box. Use it to load the file you just created. You can create dozens of texture maps in just a few minutes.

The rolling landscape shown in Figure 20-14 resulted from applying Materializer twice to the same selection. The first time, one of the preset textures was used. In the second instance (Figure 20-15), I created hills and valleys by using the airbrush on a plain black background, and then saved the image as a TIF file.

In telling you about Materializer, I've emphasized its ability to give depth to an aerial landscape. However, it can also texture your image to look like canvas, marble, or an ancient cave carving.

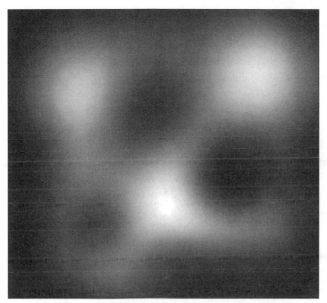

Figure 20-14: This texture map was used to create the rolling depth effect seen in Figure 20-15.

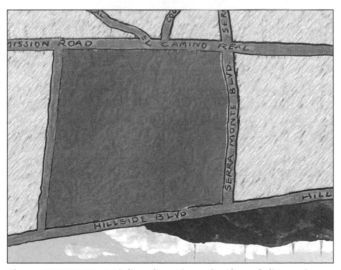

Figure 20-15: Materializer has given depth and dimension to this "landscape."

Projector

Projector lets you create perspective transformations in a previously unimaginable number of ways. Ordinarily it transforms the active layer, but (as with all the other KPT 6 tools) you can also apply it to the contents of a selection. The Projector interface is shown in Figure 20-16.

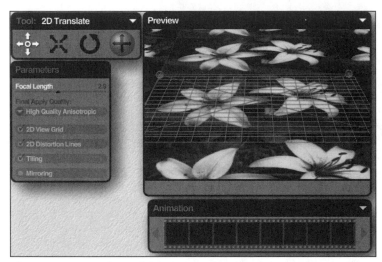

Figure 20-16: Projector lets you transform an image to any surface perspective.

You can tile an image, so that you get repeating themes going off into space. Of course, you don't have to tile the image. Suppose you just want to project a painting onto a wall so that it looks like a mural, a projected movie, or graffiti. You just select the area you want to project the image into, load the image you want to project onto another layer, and then use the Project filter to give the image the right perspective. Once the filter has run, you can use layer math (such as Photoshop's Blend modes) or layer transparency to make the projection blend with the original surface. You can also use Materializer to give a texture to the image you're going to project, run Projector, and then do your blending. You can see the result of this operation in Figure 20-17.

Reaction

If you're not a mathematician or scientist, you probably won't understand the principle on which Reaction is based. For laypeople, the bottom line is that you can create amazing natural-looking patterns such as zebra or leopard skin — not to mention zillions of patterns you never expected to see in nature.

Figure 20-17: Both Projector and Materializer were used to create this surreal landscape under the Oakland freeway.

You'll get a much crisper idea of what Reaction can produce by taking a look at Figure 20-18, which shows several different patterns that were created either from a source image or from the program's presets (and having nothing to do with a source image).

Figure 20-18: Three of Reaction's many possible patterns.

This is an incredibly useful filter. You can use it to make all sorts of seamless texture patterns and bump maps. You can make materials for Materializer and get some very sensuous results. You can color the patterns and mix them with layer blend modes to create attention-grabbing abstract art. You can use the patterns as bump maps in 3D image programs to apply realistic surfaces to models (See Figure 20-19). Given enough time and no deadlines, I could probably think of 30 other applications.

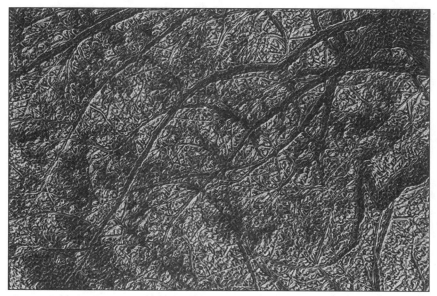

Figure 20-19: Here, a pattern created in Reaction is used as a surface map in Materializer.

Scene Builder

Scene Builder is a fairly full-featured 3D program that operates on a layer within Photoshop, rather than as an independent program. What this means in practical terms is a very flexible way to wrap photographs and other bitmapped graphics (such as a scan of a beer bottle label) onto the shape of a real-world object. You can then light that shape, give it surface characteristics (such as metal or plastic), and choose a point of view for that object. All of this makes it much easier to realistically composite the 3D surface onto your image.

You can't create the 3D objects themselves in Scene Builder. The CD-ROM has 135 expertly built Web objects. You can also import DXF files, which can be created by almost all 3D programs; and PICT files, which some Macintosh 3D programs can create.

You can see your current image in the program's preview window. This enables you to size and position your 3D object in relationship to the objects in your target photo.

Scene Builder (see Figure 20-20) is not easy to figure out. The documentation asks you to choose all sorts of things that simply don't appear in the interface.

Nevertheless, once you get it set up, you'll find this a very useful utility for making photographically textured Web buttons and for making realistic-looking composite images.

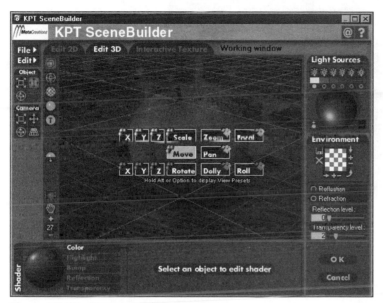

Figure 20-20: Scene Builder's interface

Sky Effects

KPT Sky Effects, like Scene Builder, was purchased from Rayflect and has a unique interface. However, this one is pretty easy to use. More important, the filter can save the life of pictures that suffer from blank or lifeless skies. Of course, you can always use skies shot on other days and in "interesting" weather.

Caution   Substituting photographic skies that weren't shot at the same time of day and in the same cloud cover as the photograph will cause the combination of sky and foreground to look phony.

The reason that Sky Effects can be a better alternative is that you can control almost everything: the amount and color of haze and fog, the angle of the sun or moon, and cloud color. You can even determine the tilt and angle of the camera and the angle-of-view of the camera's lens. So there's no reason you can't match up a realistic sky effect with your photo. You can see the Sky Effects interface in Figure 20-21.

Figure 20-21: The Sky Effects interface

Turbulence

Turbulence creates 3D "waves" wherever you drag your cursor. You can mix these waves with a gradient or have them react strictly on the image. Figure 20-22 shows the Turbulence interface.

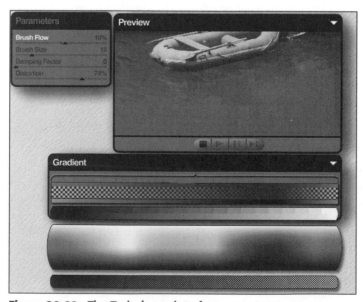

Figure 20-22: The Turbulence interface

In Figure 20-23, you see a photo of an inflatable boat that was shot in mirror-like water. First the water was selected, and then turbulence was created in the filter by rapidly dragging the cursor through the water. It takes a fair amount of trial and error to get the effect you want, but the tool is quite versatile.

Figure 20-23: The Turbulence filter created the waves in the water.

You could also use this tool to make a flag wave or to give artistic dimensionality to all sorts of images. Its too bad that this tool operates so quickly that you really don't have time to carefully study a result before you apply it to an image.

One very nice feature is that you can record the turbulence as a QuickTime movie, so you could put an animation of a rippling pond on your Web site.

Canoma

Canoma is a program that lets you build 3D models directly from your digital or digitized photographs. If you want to put package designs on the Web, you can easily create a 3D movie that shows the box from all sides. After that, it gets a bit more complicated as shapes become more complex. The next best application is architectural views in which the scene consists mainly of straight-edged buildings. Creating a model of a basket full of fruit or a crowd of people can probably be done, but it may take quite a bit of trial and error practice. On the other hand, using Canoma to create a three-dimensional scene is far easier (especially if you're not accomplished with 3D modeling programs) than working in a conventional 3D program.

Here are the basics of how it works: You start with an ordinary 2D photo—for instance, a box on a desktop (this is, in fact, the example used in the program's basic tutorial). You start by pinning the corners of a box shape to the box (see Figure 20-24).

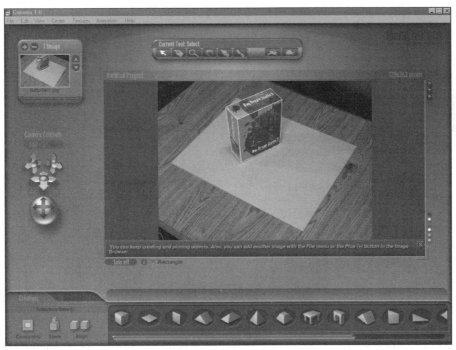

Figure 20-24: The Canoma interface. You can see the first box being pinned to the edges of the box in the photograph.

Because, in the photograph, we can see three sides of the box, three sides are mapped to the 3D object. You can then more or less instantly move and rotate the object so that you see the box from different perspectives. Of course, if you turn the box too far, you see that the back and right side are blank. Also, if you zoom in too much, and turn the box too far, the picture details can get pretty mushy unless your original picture was fairly high-resolution and shot from a straight-on angle. No problem, provided you take the time. You can shoot the sides of the box independently and at higher resolution, and then "pin" them onto the model in another series of steps. To build the rest of the scene, you keep adding primitives, pinning them to the shapes in the photograph, and then adding supplementary photos to the backs and sides of all the shapes. In Figure 20-25, you see the result of adding a photo of a gray card as a ground plane, rendering all the assigned textures (which is as quick as clicking a button), and then rotating the image. Note how quickly this 3D model was built from one still photograph.

Figure 20-25: A 3D model built from one photo. Additional photos can be added to fill in the blanks you see here.

The more photographs you have of a scene, the more realistic and complete your finished 3D model can be. Now, if your scene includes trees, people, and a lot of other organic shapes, you definitely have your work cut out for you. Canoma is a terrifically useful product, but consider its practicality for the projects that you have in mind before you jump into it.

Once you've made the model, you can make movies by clicking a few icons in the recording bar to designate keyframes, and then render a movie. You have a choice of having the movie rendered as either a QuickTime file or as individually sequenced PICT files. If you render to a sequence of still images, you can drop the still images into many other animation programs and GIF animators.

Canoma isn't exactly a casual purchase at $469 (suggested retail), but it can pay for itself pretty quickly if you have an application that demands fast 3D visualizations of physical sites, architectural models, or products.

Bryce

Bryce is a program that generates photographically realistic landscapes. You can even use U.S. Geological height maps to generate 3D landscapes of real places, such as the Yosemite Valley or the Grand Canyon. Take a look at the example shown in Figure 20-26. Not a single thing in it is actually real.

Bryce landscapes can be very useful for creating dreamy or glamorous backgrounds for objects that must be shot in ordinary settings. You can place the viewpoint for any Bryce landscape anywhere you want, so you can actually use a single model as the location for many different backgrounds. To better picture this, imagine the different backgrounds you could get for a fashion shoot by moving around inside Yosemite Valley.

Figure 20-26: This photographically realistic landscape was entirely generated on the computer.

The "gotchas" are the two Rs: resolution and rendering time. You can designate the output resolution to be anything you want, but if you want a scene that will fill a magazine page, you'd better have a very fast G4 or dual-processor computer, have *lots* of RAM, and be ready to go to the movies while you're waiting for your result.

Fortunately, you can do quick rendering while you're working, and you can interrupt that at any time if you decide you want to make a change. That means you don't have to wait for the long, high-resolution renderings until you're ready to commit yourself to the final (or near final) result.

Bryce 4 has even better sky rendering capabilities than earlier versions — and those were fantastic. As good as Sky Effects is in KPT 4, Bryce is that much more capable of drama (but Sky Effects is much faster — especially at publication-quality resolutions).

I mentioned that you could use Bryce landscapes as backgrounds (not to mention scenery on the other side of a window in an interior shot). There are a couple of other ways you can use photos in Bryce — either as cutouts that you can place in the scene or as textures for mapping onto any of Bryce's geometric primitive shapes. When you use a photo as a cutout, you can match the time of day, angle of the sun, and cloud conditions to those of the photograph, so the photo really looks like it belongs in the three-dimensional space. That is, it looks like it belongs as long as you turn it to face the camera. Because the photo is actually two-dimensional, placing it at an angle to the camera will make its flatness apparent.

Poser

Poser lets you create people and animals in any pose you want, after which you can dress them in any way you want, and then light them and "shoot" them from any angle you want. You can then place your photos into the application as backgrounds for the people and animals — or you can put the people and animals into your photos. Figure 20-27 shows you what the Poser interface looks like, as well as what a fully rendered figure looks like. Notice that I've made the background blue to make it easy to knock the figure out of the background for easy compositing into another image.

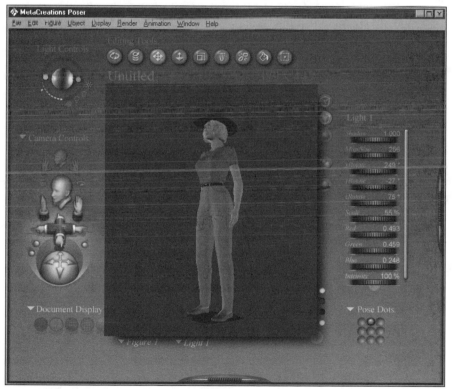

Figure 20-27: A fully rendered Poser figure

There's a caveat, though. Poser's people and animals don't look photographically realistic unless they're placed at a distance or "dirtied up" with some of the tools in your image editor after they've been composited into the image. They do work very well, however, when you have a beautiful scenic that needs a silhouetted figure gazing into the distance or standing on a far-away hilltop. Poser figures are also a good way to add people to crowds.

I've also found another use for Poser that helps a great deal in studio setups. You can model a studio and some flats, place a Poser model in front of the background, and then place various lights in the picture. You can then adjust the brightness and the type of the lights until you see exactly the effect you want in the rendered model. Then you know exactly how and where to place your lighting for the studio shot. You could even place 3D models of such props as tables, cars, or sofas on the set. Just use the stock model libraries that are created for such 3D modeling programs as Light Wave or 3D Studio.

 Tip   I've also found Poser enormously helpful in designing or "storyboarding" a real shot. You can place the figures where you want them and in attitudes that enhance the composition and story, lighting them to create the needed drama. Then, in order to get the models to understand what you're after, all you have to do is show them the finished scene.

If you're familiar with Poser, but haven't seen Poser 4, you're in for lots of pleasant surprises. You can change skin colors and other ethnic looks, facial expressions, hair, and clothing. You can morph parts of bodies to give them unusual proportions or special characteristics, such as a fat boy, a space alien, or a soon-to-be mom.

Summary

This chapter has provided a treasure trove of magical things you can do with a digital camera that you might never have thought possible. You've seen how you can use a Palm Pilot (or clone) to scribble handwritten notes on images. You've seen how to instantly create a library of thumbnails for any camera card or disk directory. You've seen the first art and sharpening synthesizers. You've also learned how to become a more or less instant painter (becoming an artist will be in the eye of the beholder). Finally, you've learned all sorts of amazing imagery trickery, from turning your 2D images into 3D models to creating whole new worlds. You can even play God and populate your worlds with people.

Just imagine what the next year will bring.

Digital Camera Makes and Models

This appendix lays out the makes, models, prices, and outstanding features of digital cameras. You'll find one table
per manufacturer. I have also included the Web sites where
you can find further information. Prices were gathered from a
variety of sources and may sometimes be lower than the manufacturer's suggested retail. Also, prices tend to go down over
time, so just use these prices as a guideline for relative value.

Table A-1
Agfa (www.agfa.com)

Model	Price	Resolution	Lens	Outstanding Features
ePhoto 1280		810K	3× Zoom	
ePhoto 1680	$549.95	1.3 Mp	1280960 3× Zoom f-2.8	B&W doc mode, swivel
EPhoto 780		XGA 350K	Fixed	
EPhoto 780c	$198.95	XGA 350K	1024 × 768 Fixed 50mm	Two seconds between shots
EPhoto CL 30	$329.95	1152× 864	Fixed 43mm	USB, 4MB CF
EPhoto CL 30 Clik!		1Mp	AF 2.8 43mm	Uses 40MB Clik! drive
Ephoto CL50	$499.95	1.3 Mp 1280 × 960	3×	10 picture burst, panoramas, voice, 8MB SM
Ephoto Smile	$99.95	VGA	40mm fixed	

Table A-2
Canon (www.canon.com; www.powershot.com; www.usa.canon.com)

Model	Price	Resolution	Lens	Outstanding Features
PowerShot S10	$670	2.1 MP	2×	USB, Supports 340MB IBM microdrive; fits in pocket; ISO 100 – 400
PowerShot A50	$399.95	1.3 Mp	2.5× 2.7 glass	2–1/750 sec. shutter
PowerShot Pro70	$1K	1536 × 1024	2.5× glass, 28–70mm	Swivel LCD, external flash, 2 CF card slots, 4 fps burst, ISO 100 – 400
EOS D2000	$9,000	1728 × 1152	All Canon EF	Same as Kodak DCS 520, 3.5 fps, FireWire

Table A-3
Casio (www.casio-usa.com)

Model	Price	Resolution	Lens	Outstanding Features
QV780		VGA	Fixed f-2 or f-8	Mini movie, panorama, burst
QV8000SX	$600	1.3Mp	8×	Wired remote, USB, swivel lens
QV770	$339	VGA	Fixed f-2 38mm	1/8 to 1/4000 sec.
QV7000SX	$510	1.3Mp	2× 2.8, 5.6, 11	Macro to 10cm, special program modes for sports and other uses
QV700	$399	VGA	fixed	
QV5500SX		1.3Mp	2×	Capture to HTML, AVI mini movies, panorama
QV5000SX	$499	1280 × 960	fixed	
QV2000UX	$599	2.1Mp	3×	USB, microdrive, 7 fps burst mode

Table A-4
Epson (www.epson.com)

Model	Price	Resolution	Lens	Outstanding Features
PhotoPC 650	$400	1152 × 864	AF 1× glass	USB, 8MB CF included
PhotoPC 750Z	$630	1.25 Mp	3×	ISO 90–360, panorama
PhotoPC 800	$700	2.1 Mp	AF 1× 2.8	Programs for sports, portraits, landscapes, microphone
PhotoPC 850Z	$800	2.1 Mp	3× 35–105mm	External flash

Table A-5
Fuji (www.fujifilm.com)

Model	Price	Resolution	Lens	Outstanding Features
DS-560	$5,509	1280 × 1000	All Nikon F SLR	SO 800 – 3200, 3 fps, external flash, Nikon body
DS-330	$1580	1.4 Mp 1280 × 1000	3× rangefinder	Auto or manual control, ISO 100– 400, external flash
DS-260Z	$1,000	1280 × 1024	3× 35–105	All weather
MX-2900	$799	2.3 Mp 1800 × 1200	3× 35–105 f-3.3	Auto or manual control, external flash
MX-2700	$700	2.3 Mp 1800 × 1200	35mm with 9mm macro	Smallest, lightest 2Mp camera, 8MB SM included
MX-1200		1.3 Mp	35mm with macro mode	
MX-1700		1.5 Mp	3× with macro	Fits shirt pocket
MX-500		1.5 Mp	Fixed f-3.2	PhotoDeluxe included
MX-600Z	$500	1280 × 1024	3× 35–105mm	PhotoDeluxe included
DX-10		SVGA	Fixed	

Table A-6
Hewlett-Packard

Model	Price	Resolution	Lens	Outstanding Features
PhotoSmart C200	$300	1152 × 872	f-2.8–11	8MB CF, macro, 2–1/500 sec.
PhotoSmart C500	$800	2Mp 1600 × 1200	3×	USB

Table A-7
Kodak (www.kodak.com)

Model	Price	Resolution	Lens	Outstanding Features
DC290 Zoom	$999	1792 × 1200 38–115mm	3× f-3.0–16	Programmable scripts, burst, audio, time lapse, USB, 16–1/400 sec., external flash
DC215 Metalics	$449	1152 × 864	2× 29–58mm	USB, 5 metallic colors
DC240i	$549	1.3 Mp 1280 × 960	3×	5 iMac-like colors
DC280	$849	2 Mp	3× 38–114mm	USB, comes with extra 16MB CF, case
DC265	$999		3× + tele and without adapters	
DC210	$349	1152 × 864	2×	
DC200	$250	1152 × 864	Fixed 39mm	
DC120	$440	1.2Mp	3×	
DCS 660	$20,000	3040 × 2008	Nikon F5 Interchange	1 fps burst, ISO 80–200 WYSIWYG View, 2 PCMCIA slots, FireWire
DCS 560	$19,999	3040 × 2008 12-bit	Canon Interchange	1 fps burst ISO 80–200 WYSIWYG View, FireWire
DCS 620	$9500	1728 × 1152	Nikon F5 Interchange	ISO 200 to 1600 3.5 fps
DCS 520	$8500	2 Mp12 bits 1728 × 1152	All Canon EF	ISO 200 to 1600 1 fps WYSIWYG View FireWire
DCS 420	$7,000– $8,000	1524 × 1012 36-bit	Nikon F5	Type III PCMCIA, ISO 100–400
DCS 330		3 Mp 30-bit 2008 × 1504	Nikon Pronea 6i Interchange	ISO 125–400 Internal mike, FireWire
DCS 315	$5,995	1.5Mp 1524 × 1012	Nikon Pronea 6i Interchange	FireWire, 2 fps, 2 PCMCIA slots

Table A-8
Konica

Model	Price	Resolution	Lens	Outstanding Features
QM200	$550	1600 × 1200	f-3.2–6.9	1/8–1/1000 shutter

Table A-9
Leica

Model	Price	Resolution	Lens	Outstanding Features
Digilux zoom		1.5 Mp	3× 38–114mm	25cm macro, can be used with accessory to digitize slides

Table A-10
Minolta (www.minoltausa.com)

Model	Price	Resolution	Lens	Outstanding Features
RD 3000 body only	$4,000	2.7 Mp 1,984 × 1,360	Any Maxxum AF lens	CF I and II, TTL focusing and metering, 1/2000 to 30 seconds, ISO 200–800, 3.5 fps, remote
3D 1500				Specially engineered to produce Web-ready 3D images
Dimage 1500 Dimage 1500 wide	$600	1.5 Mp 1344 × 1008	3× 38–115mm	7.5 fps, detachable and interchangeable lens, auto bracketing, time lapse

Table A-11
Nikon (www.nikonusa.com)

Model	Price	Resolution	Lens	Outstanding Features
Coolpix 950	$899	2.11 Mp	3× 38–115mm	4,746 step autofocus, swivel lens, 2 fps, matrix metering, optional add-on lenses, variable ISO, tone curve selection
Coolpix 800	$700	2.11 Mp	2× 38–76 mm	30 fps burst
Coolpix 700	$499	2.11 Mp	fixed	
E3		1.4 Mp 1,280 × 1,000	All Nikon F	WYSIWYG viewing, ISO 800–3200 SCSI
D1	$5,500	2.7 Mp 2,000 × 1,312	All Nikon F	FireWire, CF, 31 custom settings, ISO 200–6,400, RC via FireWire

Table A-12
Olympus (www.olympusamerica.com)

Model	Price	Resolution	Lens	Outstanding Features
C2500L	$1,499	2.5 Mp 1712 × 1368	3× SLR f-2.8 36–110mm	0.8 inches to infinity Fully manual exposure option, external flash, 0 wait between shots, 1/10,000–8 seconds, takes both SmartMedia and CF
D600L	$750	1.4 Mp 36–110mm	3× SLR	Takes accessory lenses
D620L	$850	1.4 Mp 36–110mm	3× SLR	Takes accessory lenses, external flash
C2020	$899	2.11 Mp	3× f-2.0	Like C2000 but can shoot 60-second QuickTime movie
C2000	$799	2.11 Mp	3× f-2.0	External flash (but not if flash can't control exposure), exposure control

Continued

Table A-12 (continued)

Model	Price	Resolution	Lens	Outstanding Features
D-340R	$300	1.3 Mp 1280 × 960	1× f-2.8	Macro to 4 inches, 1/2 to 1/500 shutter, can record uncompressed
D-450 Zoom	$500	1.3 Mp 1280 × 960	3×	2 fps burst, macro to 8 inches
D-400 Zoom	$500	1.3 Mp 1280 × 960	3×	

Table A-13
Panasonic (www.panasonic.com)

Model	Price	Resolution	Lens	Outstanding Features
SuperDisk Palmcam	TBA	1.3 Mp 1280 × 960	3× f-2.8	Uses 120MB Superdisk, USB, QuickTime movie mode, 2 fps
PV-DC 2590	$600	1.3 Mp 1280 × 960	3× f-2.8	Can transmit images directly to Web or fax, two CF slots, B/W capture
PV-DC 2090	$450	1.3 Mp 1280 × 960	3× f-2.8	Can transmit images directly to Web or fax, two CF slots, B/W capture

Table A-14
Polaroid (www.polaroid.com)

Model	Price	Resolution	Lens	Outstanding Features
PDC 300		320 × 240	52mm	Real cheap
PDC 640	$210	640 × 480	46mm, AF	Self timer
PDC 640 Floppy		640 × 480	46mm, AF	Self timer, floppy adapter
PDC 700	$240	1024 × 768	52mm	Tripod thread

Table A-15
Ricoh (www.ricohcpg.com)

Model	Price	Resolution	Lens	Outstanding Features
RDC 5300	$700	2.3 Mp 1792 × 1200	3× f-3.2 38–114mm	Internal 8MB + SmartMedia, optional IR remote
RDC 5000	$700	2.3 Mp 1792 × 1200	3× f-3.2 38–114mm	Includes remote, NiMH batteries and charger
RDC 4300	$500	1280 × 960	3×	Records sound notes, rotating lens
RDC 4200	$449	1280 × 960	3×	Rotating lens, time lapse
RDC 300Z	$349	640 × 480 45–135mm	3×	1-inch macro

Table A-16
Sanyo

Model	Price	Resolution	Lens	Outstanding Features
VPC-Z400	$540	1280 × 960 34–102mm	3×	Voice annotate

Table A-17
Sony (www.sony.com)

Model	Price	Resolution	Lens	Outstanding Features
DSC-F505	$1,100	2.1 Mp 1600 × 1200	5× Zeiss 28–140mm	Swivel lens, memory stick, USB, MPEG movies, auto macro to 4-in, no external flash
DSC-D770		1.5 Mp 1344 × 1024	5× SLR manual zoom, focus	Memory stick or PCMCIA memory, 4–1/2000 shutter, ISO 100–400, external flash
DSC-D700		1.5 Mp 1344 × 1024	5× SLR manual zoom, focus	Memory stick or PCMCIA memory, 4–1/2000 shutter, ISO 100–400, external flash, manual exposure mode

Continued

Table A-17 *(continued)*				
Model	*Price*	*Resolution*	*Lens*	*Outstanding Features*
DSC-F55		2.1 Mp 1600 × 1200	Fixed 37mm Zeiss	MPEG movie mode

Table A-18 **Toshiba**				
Model	*Price*	*Resolution*	*Lens*	*Outstanding Features*
PDR M5	$799	2.1 Mp 1200 × 1600	3× 38–115mm	USB, AVI movies, burst mode, no external flash, 16MB built-in memory
PDR M4	$499	1200 × 1600	35mm	USB
PDR M3	$399	1.5 Mp 1280 × 1024	3×	Outstanding resolution for price

✦   ✦   ✦

Other Digital Resources

3M

3M Center
St. Paul, MN 55144
www.3m.com
800-364-3577

3M has a broad range of interests in digital photography. If you work with an inkjet printer, for instance, you may have a 3M Microflex circuit in a printer cartridge. The company's circuits also are used for interconnections in hard disk drives. 3M Microflex circuits are being used for tiny electronic components commonly used in flash memory, and discrete semiconductors are used for cell phones, pagers, digital cameras, camcorders, or palmtop computers.

Abe's of Maine

www.abesofmaine.com
710-640-0402

This is a camera store that does considerable mail-order advertising in photography and digital photography magazines and also has an online presence. Its catalog features only the most popular cameras and accessories. This is not the place to look for esoteric stuff. Shopper's reviews have been mixed, but most comment on excellent prices.

ACTion Imaging Solutions

Kings Hall
St. Ives Business Park
St. Ives, Huntingdon, Cambridgeshire
PE17 4WY U.K.
www.action-imaging.com
+44 (0) 1480 464618

A British firm offering large-scale printing and scanning devices. Its products seem to be mostly used by engineering and large graphics firms, and architects. It manufactures the ANAtech, Colortrac, and Tangent lines of printers and scanners.

Adobe Systems Incorporated

345 Park Avenue
San Jose, CA 95110-2704
www.adobe.com
408-536-6000

Adobe is a leading manufacturer of design and graphics software and makes Photoshop, the king of photo-editing software. The site is valuable as a resource for breaking news, for downloading Adobe Acrobat Reader so you can read the many online documents and lessons given in that format, and for some of the industry's best professional graphics tips. Adobe manufactures the following software related to digital photography: Photoshop 5.5, Photoshop Limited Edition, PhotoDeluxe Business Edition and Home Edition, and PressReady (which can turn your inkjet printer into a proofing tool for prepress work). The Adobe site is also an excellent resource for finding third-party Photoshop-compatible plug-ins. Many valuable Photoshop tips and tricks also appear on the company's site.

Adorama

42 West 18th Street
New York, NY 10011
www.adoramacamera.com
800-803-0720

A brick-and-mortar full-spectrum camera store that advertises heavily in the mags and that has a comprehensive online presence. You can find most everything here from point-and-shoot cameras to camera bags to view cameras to studio equipment and accessories for professional photographers. Online reviews of this store and its policies are heavily mixed.

Agfa

200 Ballardvale Street
Wilmington, MA 01887
www.agfahome.com
800-685-4271

Agfa is a huge multinational company that specializes in imaging and prepress products. The company makes a line of digital cameras and is overdue for an announcement of a higher-resolution and more fully featured digital camera.

The company also makes an extensive line of desktop flatbed scanners (ten distinct models at last count), including the DuoScan series that is also capable of scanning film without pressing it against glass, thus eliminating the risk of reflections and

Newton rings. This series comes in a variety of sizes, capabilities, and prices to suite a range of buyers from the serious graphics hobbyist to the professional design shop.

Speaking of scanners, the DuoScan HiD is one of the most advanced flatbed scanners available, with an optical resolution of 1,000 × 2,000, a d-max of 3.7, and 42-bit color depth. The scanner also comes with color-matching software.

Finally, Agfa is a source for inkjet photo-quality papers. Navigate to this area of the site and you will find a wizard that shows you the proper settings for any of these papers when used with almost any of the popular printers. When I checked these settings for my two Epson printers, I found that the recommended settings would have worked well for most papers of similar quality from other manufacturers. For that reason, you may find this site useful whether you are actually printing on Agfa papers or not.

Akica Phototech Corp.

2F, 16, Sec 2, Chung Yang S. Road
Peitou, Taipei, Taiwan
www.akica.com
886-2-28915155

Akica offers an interesting thermal dye diffusion printer direct from a CompactFlash card or SmartMedia card. It has 300 × 300 dpi and uses 4 × 6-inch paper or label pages. You can print out an index of the images stored on your card and then choose one to print.

Altamira Group

www.altamira-group.com
818-556-6099

Genuine Fractals compression software that can create a virtually lossless compressed file much smaller than the original file. It can also create files much larger than the original without losing the sharpness of edges. This is an especially worthwhile product for making poster-size images from publication-quality photos.

Amherst Media Inc.

155 Rano Street, Suite 300
Buffalo, NY 14207
www.amherstmediainc.com
800-622-3278

A photographic book company with books on basic 35mm, black-and-white photography, techniques, portraiture, camera repair, and weddings. They only carry a couple of books specifically about digital photography, yet because many of the principles of photography are the same whether digital or film I feel a good book source may be important to you as a photographer.

Ansco

1801 Touhy Avenue
Elk Grove Village, IL 60007-5313
www.anscophoto.com
800-323-6697

A U.S. extension of an Oriental electronics manufacturer. It manufactures digital cameras, scanners, and printers. The Digipix Factory package the company offers is only $499 and you get a point and shoot camera and a color printer.

Antec

47900 Fremont Boulevard
Fremont, CA 94538
www.antec-inc.com
510-770-7200, 510-770-1200

Antec makes digital film card readers and an adapter so that PCMCIA cards can be used on a desktop computer — making it possible to exchange PCMCIA card devices and memory between laptops and desktops. One model ($99) of the digital film card readers will read from CompactFlash, SmartMedia, and PCMCIA cards — all in the same unit. However, you cannot read from both CF and SmartMedia at the same time so that the computer recognizes each card as a separate drive.

Apple Computer Inc.

www.apple.com
Digital Imaging Group (JPEG 2000):
www.digitalimaging.org
408-996-1010, 716-726-7984

This is the company that makes the computers that tend to be used by those most serious about digital photography. The company's Web site carries a wealth of constantly changing information about graphics hardware and applications, tips and tricks, and late-breaking developments.

APS Tech

6131 Deramus
Kansas City, MO 64120
www.apstech.com
816-483-1600

APS is a manufacturer of competitively priced hard drives, removable storage, and other computer peripherals. The company also distributes and has an online store for a good many third-party products related to digital photography.

Aztek, Inc.

23 Spectrum Pointe #209
Lake Forest, CA 92630
www.aztek.com
800-GRAPH-55 (472-7455)

Aztek is an industry supplier and consultant of digital software and hardware systems. Aztek claims to have sold more than 300 digital major production facilities/systems to a variety of Fortune 500 companies.

B&H Photo

420 Ninth Avenue
New York, NY 10001
www.bhphotovideo.com
800-947-5535

B&H Photo (no relation to Bell & Howell) offers an outstanding selection of professional format and digital photography supplies. This is also a brick-and-mortar superstore filled with hands-on demos. There are even downloadable PDFs listing used equipment. The company's print catalogs can be ordered online and are virtual encyclopedias of photo and video accessories.

Beseler Photo

1600 Lower Road
Linden, NJ 07036
www.beseler photo.com
908-862-7999

Known as a maker of photographic enlargers, Beseler also markets its own line of lighting equipment, chemistry, slide duplicators, copystands, camera and video carry bags, and various darkroom accessories.

Best Stop Digital

12 Warren Street
New York, NY 10007
www.beststopdigital.com
800-339-8357

Although this online store also carries 35mm film cameras, it also carries one of the widest ranges of digital cameras. As a result, it's a good place to look for current pricing. According to Best Stop, "Our prices are so low, you'll want to take a picture of them." (Or maybe a screenshot?) This store is also a comprehensive resource for digital video and photo printers.

Better Light, Inc.

1200 Industrial Road, Studio #17
San Carlos, CA 94070-4129
www.betterlight.com
650-631-3680

Better Light offers a line of digital backs for 4×5 cameras. The digital scanner type backs, software, and full setup start at below $9,000. The company also offers a digital back for the RB/RZ 67. You can find Better Light product for sale and rent at Calumet Photography locations and online at www.calumetdigital.com.

bitARTISTS

1550 McDaniel Drive
West Chester, PA 19380
www.bitartists.com
610-429-9294, 800-324-5450

Online stock photos that specialize in masked objects, frames, and backgrounds. You can view the catalogs online and then order the CD-ROMs at prices that range from $99 to $140. Images can then be used on a royalty-free basis. This is only one of many companies that offer similar types of images. A few of the others are Eyewire, PhotoDisc, and Corbis.

Bogen Photo Corp.

565 East Crescent Avenue
Ramsey, NJ 07446-0506
www.bogenphoto.com
201-818-9500

Exclusive U.S. distributor for a large number of photo and digital photo products and accessories. An especially good resource for light stands, tripods, strobes, and other studio accessories. Product lines are Manfrotto, Gitzo, Metz, LPA, Gossen, Bogen, Avenger, Aurasoft, Reflecta, Elinchrom, as well as a large number of smaller manufacturers of such items as camera and darkroom accessories.

Calumet Digital Solutions

890 Supreme Drive
Bensenville, IL 60106
www.calumetdigital.com
888-237-2022

CDS sells and leases a wide range of digital cameras, computer systems, lighting equipment, output devices, printers, proofers, and scanners, plus hundreds of other digital products. Some of its lines include MegaVision, Better Light, Kodak, Fuji, Nikon, Agfa, and Apple. It has locations in many major cities, and is a real source for digital equipment with a very helpful and knowledgeable staff.

Camera World of Oregon

700 NE 55th Avenue
Portland, OR 97213
www.cameraworld.com
800-226-3721

Yet another online and brick-and-mortar camera store that sells a fairly good
selection of digital cameras and camcorders. Camera World also sells a variety
of digital film cards, scanners, and printers.

Canon USA, Inc.

One Canon Plaza
New Hyde Park, NY 11042
www.usa.canon.com
800-OK-CANON (672-2666)
516-598-3350

Canon is an industry leader in professional and consumer imaging equipment and
information systems. Canon's extensive product line enables businesses and consumers worldwide to capture, store, and distribute visual information. The Web site
can be seen in Flash 4, and if you have a high bandwidth connection, the experience
is even better. Unfortunately, there's more show than go here. You can see animated
spinning movies of the products, but it's tough to get to the specifications.

Canon does feature some of the most advanced developments in digital cameras,
such as the three megapixel PowerShot S20 camera. The S20 is compatible with
both Type I and II CompactFlash memory cards and so can read and write to the
IBM 340MB Microdrive. Also, the ISO rating is selectable at 100, 200, or 400. The
camera also has a USB port.

Canon also manufactures a professional 35mm SLR digital camera that makes use
of the companies extensive line of EOS camera lenses and accessories, as well as
co-manufacturing several of the Kodak professional 35mm SLR cameras.

Canon is also a major manufacturer of scanners and has an extensive line of flatbed
scanners. Especially noteworthy is the under-$700 CanoScan FS2710 Film Scanner,
which features 36-bit input and output at 2,720 dpi (film resolution) and can scan
as fast as 13 seconds per frame (even faster than the Nikon scanners).

Casio, Inc.

570 Mt. Pleasant Avenue
Dover, NJ 07801
www.casio.com
201-361-5400

Large Japanese manufacturer of watches, digital cameras, digital color printers,
and handheld computers. Casio also makes many other products not related to
digital photography.

One of the most interesting new developments in digital photography is Casio's wrist camera. You can record name, address, and phone information along with the grayscale photo and transmit the photos directly to your PC wirelessly via an infrared port.

CES (Consumer Electronics Show)

www.cesweb.org
703-907-7600

The Consumer Electronics Show in Las Vegas has become one of the two leading trade shows for introductions relating to digital photography. The show takes place in Las Vegas in the week of January 6–9. This is the same timeframe as Macworld in San Francisco.

The Web site is an excellent source for learning about the latest announcements, contacting manufacturers, and reading keynote addresses. Great resource for finding contact information for companies in the electronics industry.

Club Photo Inc.

650 Saratoga Avenue
San Jose, CA 95129
http://clubphoto.com/
408-557-6845

Online image sharing.

Colex Imaging Inc.

347 Evelyn Street
Paramus, NJ 07652
www.colex.com
201-265-5670

A distributor, manufacturer and leasing agent of large photo processing equipment and digital processing equipment for image laboratories.

CompactFlash Association

P.O. Box 51537
Palo Alto, CA 94303
www.compactflash.org
650-843-1220

The industry association for CompactFlash. Here's where to find anything you want to know about the inner secrets of CompactFlash flash memory technology. You will also find a listing of the 99 digital cameras, 64 handheld computers, Palm devices, and 43 other electronic platforms that supported the CF+ specification at the start of the millennium.

Conexant Corporation

4311 Jamboree Road, P.O. Box C
Newport Beach, CA 92658-8902
www.conexant.com
800-854-8099

Conexant, a worldwide semiconductor engineering and manufacturing firm, was an early developer of the image sensors that use CMOS process technology in digital cameras, rather than the earlier charge-coupled device (CCD) approach.

Daylab-Pfaff Products

400 E. Main Street
Ontario, CA 917619
www.daylab.com
800-235-3233

Daylab manufactures and sells contained Polaroid transfer and emulsion transfer process machines. No digital applications or transfers at this time, yet the transfer process is an interesting alternative to normal film processing and printing.

Delkin Devices, Inc.

7950 Dunbrook Road
San Diego, CA 92126
www.delkin.com
858-586-0123

Makes a 244MB CF card and many other digital camera memory devices. They are also the manufacturer of the FlashPath SmartMedia floppy disk adapter. The company claims to manufacturer the highest-capacity flash memory cards in all types of any manufacturer.

Delkin also manufactures an external battery pack for digital cameras that connects through the AC adapter and offers as much power as 40,000 standard AA batteries.

SmartMedia, CompactFlash, FlashPath, and adapters are available.

Deneba Software

7400 SW 87 Avenue
Miami, FL 33173
www.deneba.com

Deneba manufactures Canvas 7, a program that does both vector illustration and bitmapped image editing. The program has matured to a high level of sophistication. It is available for both Mac and Windows. The latest features in the program enable it to run photographic plug-in effects on both vector illustration and photos, and these can be combined into a single image.

The Denny Manufacturing Company, Inc.

P.O. Box 7200
Mobile, AL 36670
www.dennymfg.com
800-844-5616

An innovative photography backdrop sales and manufacturing company with a sweet Web site. Denny also has an interesting retail Web site at www.dennyelectra. com for digital photography equipment. It seems they sell Fuji products mainly.

Desktop Darkroom

1944 Atlantic Boulevard, Suite 300
Jacksonville, FL 32207
www.desktopdarkroom.com
904-398-9934

Desktop Darkroom offers all you need in a digital store, from complete specific digital systems to the training and support needed to operate them. The company offers products ranging from cameras to printers for the amateur and professional.

Digi-Frame Inc.

181 Westchester Avenue
Port Chester, NY 10573
www.digi-frame.com
914-937-0318

A new way of displaying photographs . . . totally digitally. Digi-Frame offers different sizes of small table-top screens. You plug in a SmartMedia or CompactFlash card from your digital camera into the back. Your images appear instantly as a slide show.

Digital Camera Resource Page

www.dcresource.com/index.shtml

A whole site devoted to breaking developments and needed information on digital photography. Sections include breaking news, reviews and info, message boards, a buyer's guide, digicam FAQ, and a links page.

Digital Now Inc.

8401 Old Courthouse Road, Suite 130
Vienna, VA 22182-3820
www.digitalnow.com
800-329-9678

A supplier of packaged computer hardware and software systems for photo retailers to take images from roll film to digital to print or online. Digital Now also has the Digital Photo Factory Web site for viewing and downloading uploaded images.

Digital Output

13000 Sawgrass Village Center, Suite 18
Ponte Vedra Beach, FL 32082
www.digitalout.com
904-285-6020

Digital Output is a monthly digital industry publication distributed mostly to service bureaus, prepress and reprographic houses, designers, printers, and ad agencies.

D-store

www.d-store.com
888-313-1587

This online store specializes in digital photography solutions: digital cameras, CompactFlash, SmartMedia, card readers, printers, NiMH batteries. One of the solutions offered by this store is the Unity Pro power pack, which triples the length of time your camera can go without changing batteries.

Durst Dice America

16 Sterling Lake Road
Tuxedo, NY 10987
www.diceamerica.com
914-351-2677

Durst Dice manufactures equipment for recording images on many types of media. Products are used by both individuals and large companies. DDA products include Cheetah RIP/Servers, Durst Lambda and Epsilon imagers, LVT film recorders, and Vista lenticular materials.

Eastman Kodak Company

2/15/KO—Mailstop: 00539
343 State Street
Rochester, NY 14650
www.kodak.com
800-235-6325

Kodak manufactures both traditional and digital cameras, photographic plates and chemicals, processing and audiovisual equipment, as well as document management products, applications software, printers, and other business equipment. This was one of the first major companies to put its faith into digital photography and it still often leads the pack in new developments, innovation, and quality. The Kodak Web site is also full of helpful information and tips for photographers at all levels of expertise. The site also plays host to magnificent displays of professional photography, complete with stories of how the photography was done. This is also the place to learn about Kodak's Photo CD, Picture CD, and Picture Disk services, the company's full line of digital cameras and accessories, online photo print-making services, printers and printing supplies, and breaking news on new developments in conventional and digital photography. Kodak is also one of the leading manufacturers of digital image sensors for sale to other camera makers.

Energizer

800 Chouteau Avenue
St. Louis, MO 63164
www.energizer.com
800-383-7323

Eveready Battery Company is the world's largest manufacturer of dry cell batteries and flashlights and a global leader in the dynamic business of providing portable power. The Web site is a very rich resource for information on battery technologies and offers wizard-type guides to help you find the right battery. There's also a guide to finding stores that sell batteries. Did you know that you would have to buy $2,500 worth of alkaline batteries to take the same number of pictures as one $22 set of NiMH batteries?

Epson America, Inc.

3840 Kilroy Airport Way
Long Beach, CA 90806
562-276-1300
www.epson.com

Here you will find announcements of the latest developments in Epson cameras, printers, and papers. Excellent articles (that change from time to time) also cover such subjects as how to choose the right colors for use in a graphic design or how to share information between MS PowerPoint and other Office programs. Epson also has an extensive line of inkjet specialty papers and continues to make its photopapers more and more fade-resistant.

Epson Professional Graphics Division

www.prographics.epson.com
800-463-7766

This is the Epson division that specializes in wide-format printers and is the resource for checking up on the latest about proofing printers and printers for display and fine-art printing. You'll find an informative article on the workflow for digital proofing using an inkjet printer. There's also an article on how Nash Editions (one of the most highly regarded service bureaus for fine-arts printing) uses the Epson 5000 proof printer.

EZ Prints

www.ezprints.com
888-584-7040

EZ Prints offers archival prints from your digital files: 4 × 6s for $0.49, 8 × 10s for $2.95, and 11 × 14 for $5.25.

Ferrania USA, Inc.

1 Imation Place
Oakdale, MN 55128-3414
800-233-8579

Ferrania has acquired the photo-products division of Imation and manufactures
35mm color print and slide film, single-use cameras, and photo-quality inkjet paper
for the consumer photographic market.

Filmart

4111 Glenwood Road
Brooklyn, NY 11210
www.filmart.com
718-421 6517

An online photographic store that claims to have a large temperature-perfect
warehouse and offer excellent service to its customers. This is another in a long
line of New York retailers offering a full range of camera equipment cheaper than
you can get in your home-town store.

Filmguard Corporation

2110 Enterprise Street
Escondido, CA 92029
www.filmguard.com
800-777-7744

A commercial sleeving company, offering many styles and varieties of professional
roll and sheet sleeves for different film sizes and formats.

Focus Camera

www.focuscamera.com
888-221-0828, 718-436-6262

Large selection of digital cameras and some of the lowest prices I've seen.
The same online store also sells equipment and accessories for conventional
photography and a large selection of hobbyist underwater gear. Focus also has
a good assortment of accessory lenses and filters in sizes that will fit many of
the most popular digital cameras.

Font Shop

74 Tehama Street
San Francisco, CA 94105
www.fontshop.com
888-FF-FONTS (333-6687), 415-512-2093

An online font shop with an interesting collection of unique fonts. You can preview all these fonts online. You may wonder why this resource is listed in a book on digital photography, but many digital photographers use their photographs for greeting cards, signage, and business cards and need unique typefaces to go along with them. Individual fonts range in price from $49 to $100. There is no secure online order form, but you can phone in your orders or have them sent C.O.D.

Fotima USA

8620 Production Avenue, Suite B
San Diego, CA 92121
www.fotima-usa.com
619-549-6687

A wholesale distributor offering specialized throwaway cameras, photo albums, glass frames, photo batteries, and film.

FotoNation, Inc.

199 California Drive, Suite #207
Millbrae, CA 94030
www.fotonation.com
650-692-7434

FotoNation offers a continually growing family of software solutions for digital photography connectivity as part of the industry-wide FotoConnected initiative. FotoNation products include FotoNation-Explorer, an end-user application that enables the Windows operating system to view a digital camera as a standard folder on the desktop, FotoDeveloper, a multiplatform SDK to provide a unified interface to most popular digital cameras, and FotoSecure, a patented system of in-camera protection of original digital images from unauthorized duplication, distribution, and manipulation. FotoNation's technology is included in leading consumer-imaging products from Adobe Systems, Microsoft Corporation, and Nikon, Inc.

FotoWire Development

2420 Sand Hill Road, Suite #101
Menlo Park, CA 94025
www.fotowire.com
831-724-4700

Print online. More than 75 labs online in 15 countries. Make traditional prints from your digital images. A single 4×6 print costs $0.55. You can also get picture mugs, mouse pads, T-shirts, sweatshirts, aprons, and picture puzzles.

Foveon Inc.

3565 Monroe Street
Santa Clara, CA 95051
www.foveon.net
408-350-5100

Foveon is developing a new professional-quality in-studio digital camera and digital output package. The camera looks like a laptop with a lens attached to the bottom rear. The company is offering three sensor chips in its cameras, one for each RGB color, and is shooting for 4 × 5-like digital quality. The entire Foveon digital package with a Pentium processor moves an image from digital capture through to CD writing or print proofing on an Epson 900.

Fuji Hunt Photographic Chemicals Inc.

Paramus, New Jersey
www.fujihuntusa.com
201-967-7500

Fuji Hunt provides the high-quality photographic processing chemicals, paper, and services for the amateur and professional photo labs throughout the world.

Fuji Photo Film U.S.A., Inc.

555 Taxter Road
Elmsford, NY 10523
www.fujifilm.com
800-378-3854, 800-755-3854

Fuji is a large Japanese conglomerate with its fingers in many pies. The Fujifilm division deals with both digital and traditional photography products. Fuji is responsible for several of the most exciting upcoming developments in digital photography including the development of more affordable aspherical lenses for digital cameras and the Super CCD that uses octagonally shaped picture elements that measurably increase the detail and definition in a digital image of a given resolution. Fuji also sells the Pictography series of printers that make silver-halide prints from digital images.

Fusionworks Digital Corporation

www.fusionphoto.com

An online photo viewing and ordering site. Send in your film and view your photos here. It is soon to launch a community portal for its members.

Gagne, Inc.

41 Commercial Drive
Johnson City, NY 13790
www.gagneinc.com
607-729-3366

A manufacturer and distributor of lightboxes, frame boxes, projectors, light tables, and certain types of bellows.

Gamla Enterprises

16 West 36th Street
New York, NY 10018
www.gamlaphoto.com
800-442-6526

Distributor of 35mm, APS, digital and disposable cameras, lenses, flashes, batteries, cases, binoculars, telescopes, and transceivers.

Gammacolor Image Technologies

3496 N.W. 7th Street
Miami, FL 33125
www.gammacolor.com
800-330-3312

An exporter and retailer of new and used photo lab equipment and minilab supplies. Its products include photoprocessors, chemicals, and papers.

GEPE Inc./Geimuplast

Partenkirchner Strasse 50
D-82490 Farchant
Germany
www.geimuplast.de
+49 (0) 8821-685-0

Geimuplast is an experienced manufacturer of plastic slide mounts and mounters.

Global Imaging, Inc.

248 Centennial Parkway, Suite 160
Louisville, CO 80027
www.globalimaginginc.com
303-673-9773

Global Imaging, Inc. is a seller and leaser of high-end hardware for digital color graphics. Offers cameras, printers, RIP scanners, and monitors for the professional digital imager.

Graphic Intelligence Agency Inc.

4040 Embassy Parkway, Suite 370
Akron, OH 44333
www.graphintel.com
888-439-4403

The Graphic Intelligence Agency is attempting to make graphic output easier for the corporate world. The agency hosts seminars on everything from printing technology to Photoshop and scanning. It was founded to lessen the information gap for the graphic professional.

Graphx, Inc.

400 West Cummings Park
Woburn, MA 01801
www.graphx.com
781-932-0430

Graphx, Inc. designs computer software products to enhance the performance of color printers and film recorders. RasterPlus is software designed to meet the needs of a wide range of clients such as service bureaus, corporate imaging centers, desktop presenters, and the professional photo retouching industry. Some of its other products are designed to ease production flow including WinSlide/MacFilm and PackagePlus.

Greenfield Studios Ltd.

5-11 Taunton Road
Greeford, Middlesex
UB6 8UQ England
www.logistic-locations.com
011-44-181-575-6601

The Dubois Sun Position Compass will tell you the height and position of the sun at any time of the day and year anywhere in the entire world. So if you need to plan a location shot in accordance with the best sun angle, this little jewel can save you a lot of time and money. The cost in U.S. dollars is $39. Americans will also pay about $10 shipping and handling from the U.K.

Gretag Imaging Holding AG

2070 Westover Road
Chicopee, MA 01022
www.gretagimaging.com
413-593-6900

A Switzerland-based supplier to the global photofinishing and imaging technology markets. Gretag Imaging's products and services range from minilabs, central labs, and Internet applications to hardware and software for professional photography and the advertising industry. Gretag owns Rastergraphic supplies — products for inkjet printers.

Gross-Medick-Barrows (G-M-B)

1345 Export Place
El Paso, TX 79912
www.g-m-b.com
800-777-1565

Gross-Medick-Barrows is a long-time supplier for the professional photographer. Some of its product line includes folders, easels, folios, proof books, and wedding albums. G-M-B seems to go to some length to accommodate the changes in photographers' needs.

GTI Graphic Technology Inc.

211 Dupont Avenue
Newburgh, NY 12550
www.gtilite.com
888-562-7066

An industry supplier of overhead luminaries, transparency viewers, and large-format viewing stations.

Halo Data Devices, Inc.

1140 Ringwood Court
San Jose, CA 95131-1726
www.halodata.com
408-719-9600, 408-922-3400

This company makes a 265MB hard drive that fits into any CompactFlash Type 1 slot and that can be used in any camera that uses CF cards. No pricing was available on the site, as the device was not yet released.

Heidelberg

1000 Gutenberg Drive
Kennesaw, GA 30144
www.heidelbergusa.com
888-546-6265, 800-437-7388

Heidelberg is one of the largest and most influential companies in the digital printing industry. It makes both flatbed and drum scanners for serious users. These are the only drum scanners (according to Heidelberg) that natively work in CIE Lab color, which is also the native Photoshop color mode. Flatbed scanners are made by the company's Linocolor division at www.linocolor.com.

Hewlett-Packard Inc.

3000 Hanover Street
Palo Alto, CA 94304-1185
www.hp.com
650-857-1501

A well-known U.S. company that used to be known mainly for its handheld calcula-
tors, now has become a leader in the world computer market. Hewlett-Packard and
Kodak have announced the formation of a joint venture for retail photofinishing
solutions offering retail customers a wide range of digital-imaging capabilities for
both film and digital files. H-P also makes digital cameras and the best-established
range of desktop printers.

Hoodman

P.O. Box 816
Hermosa Beach, CA 90254
www.hoodmanusa.com
800-818-3946

Hoodman makes glare-reduction hoods for just about any kind of a screen you
might have to look at. You can get hoods to shade your computer or laptop monitor
to aid in more accurate color calibration. The company also makes hoods for digital
still and video camera LCD viewfinders in a variety of sizes, so it's a good bet that
you can find a hood that will fit your camera. All the Hoodman hoods attach by
means of Velcro strips, so you can easily and quickly remove them. The hoods fold
flat when not in use. LCD hoods mostly retail for a mere $19.95 and can be bought
directly from the company.

Hoya Corporation

7-5, Naka-Ochiai 2-chome
Shinjuku-ku, Tokyo
161-8525, Japan
www.hoya.co.jp
800-421-1141

Hoya is one of the most renowned optical lens and filter companies in the world,
boasting a 40-percent share of the world production of optical glasses.

Imagers Digital Production Center

Atlanta Technology Center
Building 400, Suite 490
1575 Northside Drive N.W.
Atlanta, GA 30318
www.imagers.com
404-351-5800, 800-398-5821

A service bureau for all sorts of digital imaging, including making film slides from your digital images. Other services include digital offset printing, Kodak Photo CD, digital color posters, color laser printing, digital photo prints, Web development, and video services.

The Imagers site is useful even if you don't use this company's services because it contains considerable online advice about how to prepare your files for the various processes.

For some services, such as digital offset printing, there's a price-calculating form that takes into account such variables as the number of colors, paper size, and so forth. You could use this site to give yourself a rough guide as to the competitive pricing for printing your image files.

Imation Enterprises Corp.

1 Imation Place
Oakdale, MN 55128-3414
www.imation.com
888-466-3456

An offshoot of 3M Corporation that specializes in data storage, digital imaging, and color correction.

Imation is the maker of the SuperDisk, a 120MB removable storage solution that is backward-compatible with the ubiquitous HD floppy disk. At least one manufacturer has already announced a digital camera that uses a SuperDisk as its storage medium: Panasonic PV-SD4090 digital camera features SuperDisk technology, which enables users to save images directly onto a 120MB SuperDisk disk or a 1.44MB floppy disk. SuperDisks have become popular with owners of iMacs because they provide a floppy drive as well as a higher capacity removable storage device.

Imation is also a source for CD-R and CD-RW disks.

Informal Software

2060 Walsh Avenue, Suite 192
Santa Clara, CA 95050
www.informal.com
408-845-9490

Enotate software enables a stylus-based device to be used as a direct PC input/output device alongside the traditional keyboard, mouse, and monitor. Unlike pen tablets, drawing/sketching software packages, or other pen-based computing solutions, Informal Software's unique "Informal Interface" enables stylus-based devices to interact naturally with a personal computer in a manner analogous to the comfortable "pen and paper" model. Enotate enables traditional pen-and-paper tasks to be completed digitally, including freehand sketching and real-time annotation of existing files, such as digital photographs.

Intergraph

Corporate Headquarters
Hunstville, AL 35894-0001
www.intergraph.com/ics
800-763-0242, 256-730-2000

A Windows-compatible computer maker that specializes in high-performance
workstations for visual production and publishing prepress applications. These
systems are tweaked to the max for speed and capacity and many have dual
processors. Some of the computers are capable of using up to 8MB of RAM. If
you are curious to see how much performance can be crammed into a Windows
machine, this is the site to visit.

International Paper / Gatorfoam

P.O. Box 1839
Statesville, NC 28687-1839
www.gatorfoam.com
800-438-1701

A subsidiary of International Paper, Gatorfoam is a supplier of formcore products
on which to mount photographs and other artwork. It is offering JetMount, a graphic
arts board designed to survive the rigors of digital imaging. The foam is reinforced
to resist dents and provide good durability.

IXLA USA, Inc.

17 Jansen Street
Danbury, CT 06810
www.ixla.com
203-730-8805

IXLA manufactures easy-to-use imaging software specifically for digital cameras.
Many of the company's products are bundled with digital cameras and scanners. If
you're a real beginner just wanting to try digital photography at the lowest possible
cost, you can buy IXLA's PhotoEasy Deluxe software for $99 and get a very simple
point-and-shoot VGA-resolution camera in the bargain (now available for both
Windows and Macintosh computers). IXLA also makes very powerful cataloging
software for a mere $29.95 that lets you batch-process image files, convert file
formats, e-mail photos, and create picture Web pages.

Jackson Digital Imaging Corporation

3595 S. Highland Drive, Suite 3
Las Vegas, NV 89103
www.jacksondigital.com
800-584-8181

Digital printing system packages, the hardware, software, and training for printing
on cups, T-shirts, and so on. The company sells these products online.

Kablink

www.kablink.com

Kablink is an online service that promises very fast image sharing. You can even add voice attachments to your images. The company provides software and a Web hosting service that enables you to upload your images directly from your digital camera to the Web, and then automatically mail the images to anyone you wish. Currently, support is available only for Windows, but the company promises that Mac support is on its way. Check the Web site; by the time you read this, Mac support could be a reality.

Kaidan, Inc.

703 East Pennsylvania Boulevard
Feasterville Business Campus
Feasterville, PA 19053
www.kaidan.com
215-364-1778

Kaidan makes products to help in making QuickTime VR stitched panoramas and object movies. For panoramas, the company makes numerous pan heads for tripods that center the optical axis of the camera over the control point and that are marked for specific degrees of rotation between shots. The resulting photos match very closely from edge to edge when rotated, making very smooth stitching possible. The company also makes rigs for QTVR object movies. Object movies enable the viewer to rotate a product photo to any angle.

Kenko-Tokina Company

Represented in the United States by:
THK Photo Products, Inc.
2360 Mira Mar Avenue
Long Beach, CA 90815
800-421-1141 (customer service)

Kenko makes an 8×32 monocular that can adapt to the lenses of many digital cameras — in particular the Nikon Coolpix 800, 900, and 950 series. It retails for about $140 U.S. (street price). One retail resource for this lens is www.ckcpower.com.

Kingston Technology Company

17600 Newhope Street
Fountain Valley, CA 92708
www.kingston.com
800-337-8470, 877-KINGSTON (546-4786), 714-435-2600

Kingston is a major resource for all kinds of memory upgrades, including flash memory for digital film cards.

Konica

500 Day Hill Road
Windsor, CT 06095
www.konica.com
800-456-6422

Konica is a digital and a photographic industry leader in providing digital solutions for document creation, production, and distribution: cameras, scanners, and more. At this time they seem to be highly involved in the race for a faster megapixel digital camera.

Kyocera

8611 Balboa Avenue
San Diego, CA 92123-1580
www.yashica.com
800-526-0266, 858-576-2600

This is the site for the Yashica camera division of Kyocera. Yashica's Samurai digital cameras include a 2.1Mp model with a 4:1 zoom lens. Too bad there's no provision for external flash synch. Yashica also makes bargain-priced 35mm SLR film cameras, either fully automatic or fully manual. Kyocera also manufactures Contax cameras and Carl Zeiss lenses.

LaCie Inc.

22985 NW Evergreen Parkway
Hillsboro, OR 97124
www.lacie.com
503-844-4500

FireWire and USB drives, calibrated monitors, CD-R/RW drives.

Largan Lmini

2432 W. Peoria Avenue
Building 9, Suites 1165 and 1166
Phoenix, AZ 85029
www.largan.com
1-877-4LARGAN (452-7426)

Largan is a Taiwanese manufacturer of entry-level digital cameras. The first two offerings in the line are VGA-resolution, fixed-lens cameras at $180. There are announcements on the site of higher resolution models to come (up to 1.5Mp), but no timeframe or pricing is given.

Leica

156 Ludlow Avenue
Northvale, NJ 07647
www.leica-camera.com
www.leica-camera.com/usa
201-767-7500

Leica makes high-end professional 35mm cameras and one digital camera, a pocketable 3:1 optical zoom 1.5Mp model called the Digilux Zoom. Leica also manufactures a professional scanning camera that comes in three resolutions (2570×2570, 5140×5140, and 4000×4000) that will take lenses made for most professional 35mm and medium-format cameras. Of course, Leica is also one of the oldest and most prestigious manufacturers of professional 35mm film cameras, binoculars, and lenses.

Lexar Media

47421 Bayside Parkway
Fremont, CA 94538
www.lexarmedia.com
510-440-3400

Lexar is the maker of some of the fastest digital film cards. The company offers both CompactFlash and SmartMedia digital film and connectivity solutions to the desktop. One of the company's latest developments is USB CompactFlash digital film. It is a CompactFlash card with USB integrated into its controller, optimized software drivers, and a special USB cable. Because the USB functionality resides in the CompactFlash card, the low-cost JumpShot USB cable and included software drivers are the only requirements for a CF-compatible digital camera to instantly gain USB capabilities.

Lexar also makes a USB connected "universal" digital film reader that can accept either SmartMedia, CompactFlash, or PCMCIA digital film.

Lexar also makes an imitation leather flash memory card case that doubles as a keychain for a mere $5.

Lexmark

740 West New Circle Road
Lexington, KY 40550
www.lexmark.com
606-232-2000

Makes laser, inkjet, and dot matrix printers and supplies for the office and home markets. Lexmark's inkjet printers offer the highest resolution in the industry (1200×1200 dpi) and at lower-than-usual prices. The company's Web site also contains information that helps you understand how to buy and use inkjet printers, though little of this advice is directly pertinent to printing digital photographs.

Linotype Library GmbH

Du-Pont-Strasse 1, D-61352
Bad Homburg, Germany
www.linotypelibrary.com

Linotype Library is one of the leading vendors of PostScript fonts. An automated search engine lets you preview fonts that are visually compatible and lets you find all the fonts that are of the same type (such as serif, sans-serif, decorative, hand). Prices for fonts average out at a reasonable $21 for a five-machine license.

LizardTech, Inc.

1008 Western Avenue
Seattle, WA 98104
www.lizardtech.com
206-652-5211

LizardTech has a new encoding technology for large digital image compression while maintaining the quality and integrity of an image. This new encoding technology is called MrSID Image Encoding, which has its own software and plug-ins for Photoshop, and is compatible with Macintosh and Windows.

Lowepro USA Inc.

3171 Guerneville Road
Santa Rosa, CA 95401
www.lowepro.com
707-575-4363

A successful and industry-recognized manufacturer and distributor of camera bags and carrying cases.

Macromedia, Incorporated

600 Townsend Street
San Francisco, CA 94103
www.macromedia.com
415-252-2000

Macromedia is the leading multimedia and Web software company, publishing such hits as Dreamweaver, Flash, Fireworks, Director, and FreeHand. The Web site is built using premier examples of the company's Web authoring product (particularly Flash and Fireworks) and offers lessons and hints covering many facets of using the company's software products.

Macworld Expo

www.macworldexpo.com

The largest Macintosh-oriented trade show. The Web site is an excellent resource for locating manufacturers of products related to digital photography and the Macintosh, though not all participating manufacturers link to their Web sites. This is also the place to look for upcoming show dates in San Francisco and New York. You can register online for upcoming shows and read descriptions of conferences and workshops. Although this is a Mac-centric event, you'll find a heavy focus on graphics and publication at this show. The great majority of products are cross-platform, so Windows users can find a great deal of information here, too.

Mamiya America Corporation

www.mamiya.com

A Japanese camera manufacturer specializing in medium-format cameras. Mamiya's cameras are among the most popular for adapting to professional digital camera backs.

Management Graphics Inc.

1401 E. 79th Street
Minneapolis, MN 55425
www.mgi.com
612-854-1220

A supplier of large-scale equipment for digital prepresses, such as document servers and image recorders.

Mediafour Productions

1854 Fuller Road, Suite 1
West Des Moines, IA 50265-5526
www.Media4.com/pub
515-225-7409

Mediafour makes software for Windows that makes it possible to open and read the content on Macintosh formatted disks. The program works on virtually all types of disk drives, including removable media. The software costs less than $60 and can be downloaded online.

Megapixel

www.megapixel.net

A monthly digital still camera Web magazine, published in both French and English. Another source of reviews of digital cameras and excellent articles on various aspects of digital still camera technology.

MegaVision, Inc.

P.O. Box 60158
Santa Barbara, CA 93160
http://acme.mega-vision.com
888-324-2580

MegaVision offers an award-winning list of high-quality digital camera backs for medium- and large-format cameras. The company also offers a battery-operated mobile hard disk pack to download images to and from a digital camera back. You can wear this pack on your belt for location shooting.

Microsoft Corporation

One Microsoft Way
Redmond, WA 98052-6399
www.microsoft.com
425-882-8080

Now here's a company that needs little introduction. It may surprise you, however, to discover that it publishes two image editing programs that are especially useful for "quick and dirty" manipulations for making digital photographs look professional: PhotoDraw 2000 and Picture It! 2000.

PhotoDraw 2000 is now in version 2.0 and features tools for optimizing Web graphics and for creating animated GIFs, image maps, and rollover events. Image editing includes such quick fixes as dust and scratch removal, one-click color balancing, and over 20,000 clip-art stock images. The program also includes templates for designing various types of documents. In addition to bitmap image editing, you can incorporate vector drawings (there's a healthy set of drawing tools) and do some natural media painting.

Picture It! is aimed at beginning and occasional users of digital cameras and is similar in functionality to Adobe PhotoDeluxe or other under-$100 digital camera editing software. Functions in this program also make it especially attractive to a wider range of users, including professionals. One of these is the ability to apply certain manipulations to make corrections to multiple images at the same time: crop, rotate, correct brightness, contrast, and tint. The program also includes image thumbnail cataloguing. Picture It! sells for under $55.

Microtech International, Inc.

Corporate Headquarters
242 Branford Road
North Branford, CT 06471-1303
www.microtechint.com
800-626-4276 (United States only), 203-483-9402

Microtech manufactures digital photography, middleware products, and memory solutions. These include CompactFlash, SmartMedia, and Type I/II/III PC Card media and PC Card readers for all systems.

The company makes the only digital film card reader that will read both CompactFlash and SmartMedia cards at the same time — seeing each as a separate drive. The CompactFlash slot is Type II–compatible and can read the new IBM 340MB Microdrive (which you can also order from Microtech).

Minolta Corporation

101 Williams Drive
Ramsey, NJ 07446
www.minoltausa.com
201-825-4000, 201-818-3512

Minolta makes one of the most affordable professional 35mm SLR digital cameras, the RD300, at under $4,000, and an extremely affordable line of high-quality film scanners, as well as consumer digital cameras with removable lens units that can be placed for photographing subjects at unusual angles or swapped with special-purpose lens units.

Minolta is also a large manufacturer of film-based 35mm SLR and point-and-shoot cameras and lenses as well as a manufacturer of office and prepress equipment. The company's Dimâge and QuickScan 35 film scanners are some of the best buys around. Unfortunately, you will have a very tough time getting replacements if you lose or misplace any of the parts, such as a film holder.

Mitsubishi Electronics America, Inc.

Display Products
5665 Plaza Drive
P.O. Box 6007
Cypress, CA 90630-0007
www.mitsubishi-display.com/default.html
800-843-2515

This branch of the huge Japanese conglomerate that also owns Nikon makes flat-screen and single-gun (like the Sony Trinitron) monitors in a variety of sizes. They also offer calibrated and LCD monitors.

Mitsubishi Imaging (MC) Inc.

555 Theodore Fremd Avenue
Rye, NY 10580
www.mitsubishiimaging.com
Graphic arts: 800-765-9384
Photographic materials and digital imaging: 800-233-7113

Mitsubishi Imaging markets photographic and digital printing paper. The company also manufactures and sells analog and digital platemaking equipment.

MGI Software

www.mgisoft.com

This company's focus is on imaging software for the mass market and for e-commerce Web sites. Most of its products are for Windows only. MGI recently purchased LivePicture, Inc. and sells the program for $149.95 on clearance. It once sold for several thousand dollars. If you're into compositing images for high-end use, this is the product to have. However, the company seems to have no plans to continue the program's publication into newer versions.

Most of MGI's applications are priced at under $100 and are intended for a novice audience—though some have quite powerful features. Products include Video Wave video editing, PhotoSuite image editing and Internet optimization, Digital Makeover Magic for checking out how you'd look in different hairstyles and clothing, Live Picture PhotoVista for 360-degree image panoramas, and Looney Tunes Photo Fun for helping kids to build party favors, greeting cards, and so forth.

NEC Computers Inc.

15 Business Park Way
Sacramento, CA 95828
www.nec-computers.com
888-863-2669

Company makes an extensive line of Windows-compatible PCs under both the NEC and Packard-Bell nameplates: laptops, handheld computers, and monitors. Some of the handheld computers can use CompactFlash memory, so you could use these cards for multiple purposes.

Nikon Corporation

1300 Walt Whitman Road
Melville, NY 11747-3064
www.nikonusa.com
800-526-4566, 631-547-4200

Cutting-edge products from a company that is famous for its traditional film cameras and (particularly) lenses. The company is one of those most heavily focused on digital photography.

The Nikon D1 digital camera made a significant price-performance breakthrough and the Coolpix 950 was the top-selling prosumer digital camera in 1999 and one of my personal favorites. This is also a company to look to for digital film scanners, which have recently undergone a price reduction.

The Nikon Coolscan III is a thoroughly professional 35mm/APS film scanner that sells for less than $800. Also, Nikon's Digital Ice technology is available on this scanner and can be a lifesaver in production scanning for removing surface dirt and scratches.

Norman Camera and Video

3602 S. Westnedge Avenue
Kalamazoo, MI 49008
www.normancamera.com
800-900-6676

Online photography store. This store carries an extensive array of both film and digital camera equipment, including scanners and printers. You'll also find a nice selection of tips and hints for beginning photographers.

Olympus Optical Co., Ltd.

Two Corporate Center Drive
Melville, NY 11747-3157
www.olympus.com
www.olympusamerica.com
800-347-4027, 631-844-5000

Olympus has consistently been among the most popular suppliers of digital cameras and has a particularly outstanding selection of prosumer digital cameras.

The company's breakthrough 3Mp 3030 Zoom and DL3500 single-lens reflex digital camera come as close as prosumer cameras currently get to breaking into more professional use and quality. Olympus also sells a healthy range of cases, straps, auxiliary lenses, and other accessories for its digital cameras.

PalmerDigital

650 Castro Street, Suite 140
Mountain View, CA 94041
www.palmerdigital.com
800-735-1950

This is John Palmer's site. Palmer is a photographer who specializes in digital photography and offers a variety of services to other digital photographers. Palmer offers Photo CD scanning services and there's a comprehensive description of Photo CD and its advantages on the site. He also offers advice on calibrating monitors for accurate output. Very reasonable prices for scans, drum scans, Photo CDs, and other services. You can download a PDF of Palmer's price list.

Panasonic

2 Research Way, Floor 3
Princeton, NJ 07094
www.panasonic.com
800-211-PANA (7262), 609-734-0800

Panasonic's latest digital camera development is a 1.3Mp digital camera with a
3× optical zoom that stores its images on an Imation SuperDisk and has a USB
connection to the computer. Because SuperDisks hold 120MB, you can store up to
1,500 images on a single disk. This is promising technology for those who would
like to take digital cameras on long trips away from home. The camera can be
used as an external SuperDisk drive and can also use and store images on ordinary
3.5-inch HD floppy disks. The built-in SuperDisk drive does mean that the camera
has to be as large as a Sony Mavica, but you do get a 2.5-inch LCD to do your
previewing on. This camera will also record QuickTime movies up to 100 frames
and will do burst recording of up to 16 images at half-second intervals.

Panasonic also makes a 1.3Mp 3× zoom camera that has dual CF card slots and that
comes with a modem in the CF card form factor. You can put the CF card into one of
the slots and directly e-mail images from the camera without having to rely on a
computer.

PanaVue

616 boul. René-Lévesque Ouest
Québec, Canada G1S 1S8
www.panavue.com
418-688-4720

PanaVue offers software for the digital stitching or assembling of two or more images
into a panorama. Windows only.

PC-Photo Review

Consumer Review, Inc.
701 Pennsylvania Avenue #106
San Francisco, CA 94107
www.pcphotoforum.com
800-306-3375

This site claims to be the most comprehensive resource for digital cameras on
the Web. It features consumer product reviews of more than 150 digital cameras,
has a classified section when you can advertise your outmoded equipment
(it all gets that way in very short order). There's also an online printing service,
a tips and tricks section, and announcements of breaking developments in
digital photography.

Pentax Corporation

35 Inverness Drive East
P. O. Box 6509
Englewood, CO 80155-6509
www.pentax.com
800-877-0155

Pentax has been a leader and prominent contributor to the world's 35mm SLR, its
lenses, and in the 35mm compact zoom market.

Phase One US Inc.

24 Woodbine Avenue
Northport, NY 11768
www.phaseone.com
888-PHASE ONE (742-7366)

Phase One offers digital backs for medium- and large-format cameras. Offering
quality one-shot digital high-resolution images.

Photoflex Inc.

333 Encinal Street
Santa Cruz, CA 95060
www.photoflex.com
800-486-2674

Photoflex offers a full array of flash strobe accessories from lightboxes to reflectors.
Photoflex also has a photography school that has classes in digital photography.

Photo Imaging Entrepreneur

www.photoprofits.com

An online magazine that seems to be an extension or offspring of "The List."
The magazine is for the digital printer who wants to make a living from his or her
photography and digital printing. PIE seems to have a nice layout and is a good
resource to find the newest photo-digital gadgetry and accessories.

PhotoLinks

www.photolinks.net

PhotoLinks is a free directory and portal service dedicated to providing easy
access to as many photographic resources as possible. You can search links by
category (there's one for nearly every facet of photography—digital or otherwise).
You can place your own site on PhotoLinks at no charge, simply by promising to
provide a link on your site back to PhotoLinks. When I visited this site, it was still
fairly new and most of the listings in the digital photography section were for

either digital photographers or online stores. I suspect that this will change over time as the site gains viewers.

Photo Marketing Association International

3000 Picture Place
Jackson, MI 49201
www.pmai.org
517-788-8100

This is the official organization of manufacturers, distributors, and retailers engaged in the marketing of photographic products. Its annual show in Las Vegas is the photography equivalent of Comdex as related to the computer industry. The Web site is a rich source of information on photography, especially on the digital level. The site includes breaking industry news, links to all the member associations (such as DIMA, the Digital Imaging Marketing Association), PMA Sections and Societies, Imaging Industry Links, and PMA publications (such as *Digital Imager*) — to name only a few.

PhotoPoint Corp.

200 W. Evelyn Avenue, Suite 200
Mountain View, CA 94043
www.photopoint.com

PhotoPoint is the largest and most critically acclaimed photographic community on the Internet, offering free online photo albums, news/reviews/how-tos, discussion boards, e-commerce, *Digital Camera Magazine* online, and access to shopping via State Street Direct.

Photosolve

www.photosolve.com

Photosolve makes solution-providing attachments for digital cameras, such as the Xtend-a-View detachable hood for LCD screens, extenders for attaching supplementary lenses and accessories to such retractable lens cameras as the Kodak DC-series of zoom cameras, and flash extension brackets. The company's prices are very reasonable.

PhotoTrust

1500 114th Avenue SE, Suite 130
Bellevue, WA 98004
www.phototrust.com
425-468-9041

PhotoTrust hosts and manages a password-protected Web site that archives photographs created in any film-based or digital format. It uses XML technology to give users a way to collect, protect, retrieve, record, share, and enhance photos online. The company says that other features will be added soon. You'll also find articles from publications dealing with digital photography and a section on tips and tricks.

Pixology Software & Systems

28 Frederick Sanger Road
Surrey Research Park
Guildford, Surrey GU2 5YD, U.K.
www.pixology.com
+44 (0) 1483 301970

This is a software development company that, so far, has one product: Piccolo. Piccolo is a very interesting utility for working with digital cameras and with media that has digital images stored on it. As soon as you log onto a drive (such as a card reader) that has images on it, the program finds and displays the images as thumbnails. A single click will transfer pictures into a document or album. From then on Piccolo provides total image management. You get a page of thumbnails and can name and rotate the images. You can do basic image editing — brightness, contrast, saturation, sharpness, and gamma correction — right in the program, and then drag and drop the image into a document or application. You can also program an Edit button to open the selected image in whatever image editor you've chosen.

Polaroid Corporation

784 Memorial Drive
Cambridge, MA 02139
www.polaroid.com
800-343-5000, 781-386-2000

Polaroid states that the professional photography industry will stick with silver halide for shooting the original. As a result, the company has chosen to focus its cameras on the casual Web user but builds an ultra-high-resolution 35mm slide scanner and also makes 35mm instant slide film and processors. One unusual product is a digital microscope camera. Polaroid also manufacturers inkjet media and color film recorders for converting digital images to conventional transparencies.

PosterPrints

11 Battleground Court
Greensboro, NC 27408
www.posterprints.com
888-676-7837, 336-274-0882

PosterPrints makes short-run photo-realistic large-format prints on paper, vinyl, cotton, canvas, and various films for backlit images. This company can print for many specialized advertising and exhibit purposes, including all those buses that you see covered entirely in advertising and floor graphics that you can walk on. They even make photo-digital wallpaper.

Pretec

40979 Encyclopedia Circle
Fremont, CA 94538
www.pretec.com
510-440-0535

This company makes a PDA (Personal Digital Appliance — think of a PalmPilot)
that combines a digital camera, USB PC camera, MP3 player, and voice recorder.
The camera is VGA (640 × 480) resolution and can record voice and play many
hours of downloaded MP3 music. The company also makes CompactFlash memory
cards with memory capacities from 2 to 320MB. The 128MB card is available in
iMac-like transparent colors. The company's other products are digital still cameras, PC cameras, video cameras, memory/solid-state disks, linear flash cards and
flash drives/modules, and communication, networking, and multimedia mobile
peripherals. Although most of the company's sales are to other manufacturers,
the site does maintain an online store that sells some cameras, memory cards,
and card readers at competitive prices.

Professional Photographers of America

229 Peachtree St. NE, Suite 2200
Atlanta, GA 30303
www.ppa.com
800-786-6277

A photography organization for the promotion of high standards in photography.
Includes magazines and marketing.

Q-Research

301 W. North Bend Way, Suite H
North Bend, WA 98045
www.q-res.com
425-888-6605

Q-Research has new image-enhancement software called PhotoGenetics. It works
by comparing images in side-by-side windows while you click to indicate your
approval/disapproval of the change in the right-hand window. The program cycles
through the changes until you approve a final version. The program can automatically apply the approved settings to multiple pictures, which is handy when you
have several shots from the same location and lighting conditions. You can get a
30-day free trial from the site or download the licensed version for $29.95.

QTL Imprint Supplies, Inc.

95 Morton Street
New York, NY 10014
www.qlt.com
212-691-1515

Extensive collection of inkjet transfer papers, wax thermal and sublimation ribbons and papers, mouse pads, buttons, key chains, mirrors, mugs, photo greeting card frames, posters, T-shirts, porcelain and ceramic heirlooms, aprons, bibs, and lucite snap-in novelties. You can add your digital images to all of these.

Quantum Instruments

1075 Stewart Avenue
Garden City, NY 71530
www.qm.com *(must be authorized to enter)*
516-222-6000

Supplementary battery for digicams.

Raster Graphics, Inc.

3025 Orchard Parkway
San Jose, CA 95134
www.rgi.com
408 232-4027

Raster graphics builds high-performance large-format color digital imaging systems and inks for professional printers.

Rexam Graphics

28 Gaylord Street
South Hadley, MA 01075
www.rexamgraphics.com
413-536-7800

Manufactures coated paper, films, and specialty substrates for imaging technologies. The site has an extensive list of links to related Web sites.

Ricoh

1996 Lundy Drive
San Jose, CA 95131
www.ricoh-usa.com
408-944-3310

Makers of the Ricoh ROC-5300 Digital Camera with 2.3 million pixel CCD and 3× optical zoom. Ricoh is a multifaceted Japanese electronics manufacturer that also makes copiers, CD-recordable and rewritable drives, handheld PCs, and numerous other office and prepress products. The company has an online store for its digital cameras and accessories on the site, as well.

Rochester Institute of Technology

www.rit.edu/~wwwism

Best known as the "Kodak" school. Founded by the maker of Kodak cameras, it is now and has been for many years a world leader in scholastic and scientific research into photographic technology. RIT offers both undergraduate and graduate studies in photography, digital photography and printing, and graphic arts.

Roland DGA Corporation

15271 Barranca Parkway
Irvine, CA 92618
www.rolanddga.com
800-542-2307

A manufacturer of computerized input and output devices used for engineering, architecture, signmaking, graphic arts, and 3D modeling. Roland is one of the few manufacturers of pen plotters.

Rollei

40 Seaview Drive
Secaucas, NJ 07094
www.rolleifoto.com
888-8ROLLIE (876 5543)

A maker of cameras. Rollei has entered the digital market but has not found a great deal of success to this point.

RPL Supplies Inc.

280 Midland Avenue
Saddle Brook, NJ 07663
www.rplsupplies.com
800-524-0914

An industry supplier of T-shirt, coffee cup, button, and plate printing devices. These presses use mirror-imaged prints on transparencies from an inkjet, laser, or dye sublimation printer to transfer to the different media. Dye sublimation printers are the most versatile for the different media and have the longest-lasting prints.

Sandisk Corporation

140 Caspian Court
Sunnyvale, CA 94089
www.sandisk.com
408-542-0500, 800-786-3475

One of the two largest manufacturers of digital film supplies and card readers. The company also manufacturers these products under the brand names of many major companies. You can find FAQs on all the products and download the latest drives from the company's Web site.

Sanyo USA

2055 Sanyo Avenue
San Diego, CA 92154
www.sanyodigital.com
619-661-1134, 619-661-6066

Sanyo, in conjunction with Olympus and Maxell, has developed a new digital film storage medium — a 50mm re-recordable optical disk called the iD Photo. The disk has a 730MB capacity. iD Photo's capacity makes it possible to store large amounts of image data on the camera for moving pictures, high-resolution still images, and still images with voices added. Sanyo says it expects that other exciting applications such as digital album disks with electronic photo album functions will also be possible. Sanyo expects the digital still camera market to reach more than ten million units by 2002.

Another extremely interesting product from Sanyo is a CD-R CD writer with built-in slots for SmartMedia and CompactFlash I and II cards (including the IBM Microdrive) so that you can record the contents of the cards directly to the CD-R without ever having to store them on your hard drive. The drive can also be used in conjunction with a computer for normal CD-R recording tasks as well. There are also video outputs (including S-VHS) so that the recorder can be connected to any TV set for previewing images, movies, and sound without having to connect the unit to a computer.

Scitex

Eight Oak Park Drive
Bedford, MA 01730
www.scitex.com
781-275-5150

Scitex specializes in manufacturing digital imaging solutions for graphics communication. It designs, develops, manufactures, markets, and supports products, systems, and devices for the digital preprint and digital printing markets. The product it is best known for in the digital imaging community is the Iris Printer series of large-format proofing printers. These printers are being used with high-longevity printing papers and archival inks to create collectible fine-art prints from digital files. The company's Graphic Arts Group includes Leaf digital cameras, smart scanners, data management solutions (including Ripro servers/archivers), Brisque digital front ends, Dolev imagesetters and platesetters, and Iris proofers.

The breakthrough news from Scitex is the development of the Leaf C-MOST 6.6 Megapixel CMOS image sensor. According to Scitex, this is the first full-size, 35mm CMOS sensor to be commercially developed. It is said to be thin enough to replace film in a standard 35mm camera. The result is that full-size, high-resolution images can be captured using standard 35mm lenses. Moreover, Scitex says that the sensors can be made price-competitive with standard CCD image sensors. No concrete announcement has yet been made as to when this sensor will appear in specific cameras or camera backs.

Sea & Sea Underwater Photography USA

1938 Kellogg Avenue
Carlsbad, CA 92008
www.seaandsea.com
760-929-1909

An industry leader in the manufacture of underwater cameras and underwater housing to contain both still and video photography. I saw nothing specific on its Web site about housing for digital cameras, but perhaps it's only a matter of time.

Seiko Instruments USA Inc.

San Jose Headquarters: Digital Imaging Division
1130 Ringwood Court
San Jose, CA 95131
www.did.seiko.com
800-888-0817

The Digital Imaging Division currently is recognized for its dye sublimation and thermal wax printing and color management technologies. The color printers are for medical, scientific, graphics, and prepress purposes. Seiko is also the parent company of Epson.

Seybold Seminars

303 Vintage Park Drive
Foster City, CA 94404-1138
www.seyboldseminars.com
800-472-3976, 650-578-6900

The Seybold Seminars are trade shows that occur principally in San Francisco and New York. The Web site is a valuable source of late-breaking news concerning many phases of the digital imaging industry — especially those developments that concern themselves with prepress and publishing.

shopnow.com

www.20-20consumer.com
602-992-6364

An online service that helps consumers find and compare the lowest prices online. According to the site, prices are updated daily. You'll also find ratings by consumers of the various sources that sell products online, so you can also choose according to the reliability and service of the vendor. You can also check consumer ratings of the online stores before you buy.

Shutterbug Magazine

5211 S. Washington Avenue
Titusville, FL 32780
www.shutterbug.net
407-269-3212

Photography's if-you're-looking-for-it, this-is-the-place-to-start magazine. This magazine has ads from virtually all the large camera makers and sellers in the United States. The magazine's ad prices are used as a benchmark for buying, selling, and trading cameras and camera equipment worldwide.

Sigma Corporation

Sigma Corporation of America
15 Fleetwood Court
Ronkonkoma, NY 11779
www.sigmaphoto.com
631-585-1144

A manufacturer of lenses for 35mm cameras. Now the company also has its own cameras. Sigma was one of the first manufacturers to successfully introduce interchangeable lenses.

Silicon Film Technologies, Inc.

16265 Laguna Canyon Road
Irvine, CA 92618
www.siliconfilm.com
949-417-2260

Silicon Film technologies has developed a digital camera insert for a few 35mm film cameras, mostly certain Nikons and Canons. This insert turns your SLR into a digital camera. Although the capacity for images is small, a downloader is also available.

Sima Products Corporation

140 Pennsylvania Avenue, Building #5
Oakmont, PA 15139
www.simacorp.com
800-345-7462

Sima produces unique products to meet the demands of different electronic interests. As for photography, the company produces a film shield to protect film from airport X-ray devices.

Sima also makes a portable 5.7-inch digital screen to view digital photographs. An additional hard drive enables storage of more than 10,000 pictures. Also in its line of products is a portable emergency power source and a power inverter that may be of interest to digital photographers.

Sony Electronics, Inc.

3300 Zanker Road
San Jose, CA 95134
www.sony.com
800-222-SONY, 408-432-1600

Sony's line of Digital Mavica cameras means no hassles with cables, interfaces, or drivers. The Digital Mavica uses standard 3.5-inch floppy disks, has an e-mail mode, and some models can even record video clips. The limitation is the amount of storage space available on a floppy disk and the slow speed at which a floppy disk writes. The amount of storage space limits these cameras to XGA resolution or less.

Sony's other line of digital cameras, the CyberShot series, uses the company's new Memory Stick as its digital film format. Sony's latest 2Mp digital camera, the CyberShot DSC F-505, was a breakthrough in zoom capability because it features a Carl Zeiss (super reputation for very high quality) 5× zoom lens (nearly twice the zoom range of other digital cameras). The other truly notable features are the camera's small size and swiveling lens (so you can shoot with the camera overhead or between your legs). Weaknesses are lack of standard external flash sync and use of the Sony Memory Stick for on-camera storage.

Sony also makes the DSC-D700 and DSC-D770. They are nearly identical true SLR digicams with 1.5Mp resolutions and 5× optical zooms. These cameras have a hot-shoe connection for external flash. One particularly notable feature of the D700 series is their ability to display a histogram of the brightness values in an image and then give the photographer the ability to adjust exposure to accommodate the displayed distribution of brightness values. Imagine being able to use the Photoshop Levels command *before* you take the picture. This feature has been adopted by the Nikon D1, and I'd love to see it appear on more affordable cameras. The DSC-D700 series cameras cost more than the 505, probably due to their SLR design. They'd seem to be ideal candidates for upgrading to 3Mp, but I haven't seen such an announcement yet.

Sony is pushing its own form factor for digital film, the Memory Stick. Memory Sticks are self-contained, like CompactFlash, but about half the size. Their maximum memory size in late 1999 was 64MB, but we are told to expect this to climb over the next several months. Sony is pushing the idea of using Memory Sticks across a wide range of personal electronics in everything from laptops to handheld computers, its upcoming line of Palm-compatible PDAs, MP3 players, and more. Another Sony development worthy of the attention of digital photographers — especially those who work in the field — are the VAIO series of super-slim notebook computers. These come with both FireWire (iLink or IEE1394) and USB connections for high-speed transfer of images from camera to portable. They are indeed super-slim and lightweight, but still sport Pentium III processors (fast image processing) and 6.4GB hard drives. Finally, you can get a 4× life lithium-ion battery, in case you have to work with a professional field camera. Sony also manufactures a digital camcorder that takes stills at 4× the resolution of a typical video frame.

SR Inc.

P.O. Box 166055
Irving, TX 75016
www.srelectronics.com
972-255-7490, 800-324-7745

This is the best resource for portable external flash units for any brand of digital camera because they work off internal slave cells that synchronize with the on-camera flash. Many digital cameras use a dual flash — a preliminary flash used for focusing and red-eye reduction and a second flash that actually makes the exposure. Most slave units won't work with the double-flash cameras because they fire on the first flash. SR makes DigiSlave digital slave flash units especially aimed at overcoming this problem, an excellent pistol grip, and a pistol grip with an external battery pack. Also, the PowerGrip Ultra also incorporates a NiMH rechargeable 3,750 maH power pack for digital cameras.

SR also makes a dual-mode slave trigger that works with either dual or single flash cameras that can be attached to the strobe units from other manufacturers, such as studio strobes.

Another very useful SR product is a camera bracket with a padded leather comfort grip including storage pockets for extra memory cards, and a neck strap. If all you want is a grip (without the battery pack), SR sells one for under $40.

State Street Direct

3613 Lafayette Road
Portsmouth, NH 08301
www.statestreetdirect.com
800-222-4070

State Street is an online consumer electronics superstore that has become noted for its selection of digital cameras. Cameras are listed by price range, making this a very quick way to see what features are generally available in a specific price range. State Street also carries SmartMedia, CompactFlash, and Memory Stick digital film, batteries, cases, and supplementary lenses for digital cameras.

Superior Specialties

2517 N. Casaloma Drive
P.O. Box 2397
Appleton, WI 54913-2397
www.superspec.com
920-830 5055

A supplier of seamless backgrounds and various seamless holders.

Synthetik Software, Inc.

30 Sheridan Street
San Francisco, CA 94103
www.synthetik.com
415-864-6582

Synthetik Studio Artist is a program that's the next new thing in programs that can turn your digital photographs into digital paintings. In some respects, this program takes over where MetaCreations' Painter 6 leaves off — with hundreds of brush-strokable effects at your disposal. In fact, the biggest problem with this program is figuring out what tools to choose and how they will interact with one another due to being presented with so many choices.

The program's amazing technology is based on music synthesis, cognitive neuroscience, and visual perception. More than 200 controls enable you to alter the appearance of a brush, so you can get either natural-media looks (similar to Painter's) or totally new and unique looks. The graphics engine is resolution-independent, combining the complexity and richness of bitmapped paint with the editability and scalability of vector paths. There's also artificial intelligence painting that will look at your image and then paint it automatically.

Tamron USA, Inc.

125 Schmitt Boulevard
Farmingdale, NY 11735
www.tamron.com
631-694-8700

Known for more than 50 years as a major lens manufacturer, Tamron also makes Bronica medium-format cameras.

TechniComp Software

www.technicompsoftware.com

These people make software that automatically creates picture Web pages. You just select the photos you want to put on the page. The program automatically makes the thumbnails, resizes all the images to Web size, and posts the page to your Web site at the appointed URL. A demo is available on the Web site. You can download a freeware version if you don't mind your Web pages having a bit of advertising attached to them. Pay for the program ($20 US) and register it, and the advertising disappears.

Tech Papers

P.O. Box 2099
Huntersville, NC 28078
www.tech-papers.com
800-948-7650, 800-948-1650

Tech Papers is a distributor of papers from a number of paper mills that focuses on products that are especially suited to digital imaging in a variety of applications. Its motto is, "If it's weird, call Tech Papers." They're not kidding.

The Big Picture Magazine

www.bigpicture.net

The Big Picture is an online magazine for the business and technology of large-format digital printing. It claims it is a learning center for the fast-changing technologies in digital imaging. It seems to be full of banner advertisements but may have some promise on upcoming technology.

The Tiffen Company

90 Oser Avenue
Hauppauge, NY 11788-3886
www.tiffen.com
516-273-2500

Since 1938 a major supplier and manufacturer of filters for still, video, and motion picture cameras. Tiffen now offers telephoto, wide angle, and close-up lens attachments for many digital cameras.

Toshiba Imaging Systems

9740 Irvine Boulevard
Irvine, CA 92618
www.toshiba.com/taisisd/dsc/index3.htm
800-288-1354, 949-583-3499

Three digital cameras are currently in the company's line, topped by a 3× optical zoom 2Mp model that sells for under $800. Reviewers have praised this camera for its ease of use and quick recycling between takes. Its digital film is SmartMedia and there is no external flash connection.

Ulead Systems, Inc.

970 West 190th Street, Suite 520
Torrance, CA 90502
www.ulead.com
310-523-9393

A large collection of affordable image editing, Web optimization, animation, and special-effects software: PhotoImpact (semi-pro and Web image editing), PhotoExpress (home image editing), COOL3D (3D extrusion), WebRazorPro (image optimization), JavaRazor (interactive Java Web graphics), GIF Animator, MediaStudio Pro (video editing), SmartSaver Pro (Web image optimization and interactivity), VideoStudio (easy video editing), Face Factory (3D photo faces from two 2D photos), and COOL 360 (panoramic photo stitching). Most products are available for trial downloads.

UMAX Technologies Inc.

3561 Gateway Boulevard
Fremont, CA 94538
www.umax.com
510-651-4000

UMAX has a strong position in the imaging market with a line of desktop scanners. UMAX is also making its way into the digital camera market with its new Astracam, a compact and inexpensive fixed-lens, fixed-memory digital camera. UMAX also makes high-performance computers that run Windows.

Unity Digital

105 North Pointe Drive
Lake Forest, CA 92630
www.unitydigital.com
949-580-1955

Unity Digital manufactures and distributes flash memory cards, card readers and adapters, and portable power solutions. The company maintains an online store at its Web site.

Vivitar Corporation

1280 Rancho Conejo Boulevard
Newbury Park, CA 91320
www.vivitar.com
805-498-7008

Originally known for its flashes and lenses, Vivitar has developed a comprehensive line of point-and-shoot digital cameras. The company has also developed a line of video monitoring and video conferencing products for both business and residential use.

VR Toolbox

P.O. Box 111419
Pittsburgh, PA 15238
www.vrtoolbox.com
877-878-6657, 412-767-4947

VR Worx is cross-platform (Mac and Windows) QuickTime VR software that will do object, scene, and panoramic stitching. Programs for objects, scenes, and panoramas are available individually as well, or you can buy the whole thing for $299, a savings of about $90. Works as a Photoshop plug-in. You can download a free demo version from the company's site. Differs from Apple's software in having more features and in being cross-platform.

Wein Products

www.saundersphoto.com/html/body_bat_free.htm

Wein produces the industry standard for off-camera flash slave triggers. Flash slave triggers are one way to synchronize studio strobes with prosumer and consumer digital cameras that lack a hot-shoe or PC connection for external flash.

Worldwide Direct — Digital Imaging Specialist

203 Route 22
Dunellen, NJ 08812
www.buydig.com
800-617-4686

Worldwide Direct will deliver to your home and business the latest technology of digital cameras, printers, scanners, memory, and accessories at the lowest legitimate price with excellent service.

ZBE Incorporated

7220 Hollister Avenue
Santa Barbara, CA 93117
www.zbe.com
805-685-2348

ZBE has developed a line of photographic laboratory enlargers and equipment controls. ZBE recently released its Satellite 3-D Digital Scanning System. The Satellite is the first auto focusing scanning system that can scan all types of images from small films to large three-dimensional objects. ZBE also has introduced a 30-inch wide high-quality digital printer.

Zing Network, Inc.

550 Fifteenth Street
San Francisco, CA 94103
www.zing.com

Zing is a online digital image community offering unlimited free storage, picture-upload and album-creation processes and ZingCard photo-greeting cards, The company seems to be marketing its site to the basic family consumer. From one-step digital camera-to-Web uploading to high-quality photo printing, Zing is building the infrastructure to advance and simplify digital photography.

ZoneZero

1333 Beverly Glen
Los Angeles, CA 90024
www.zonezero.com

An outstanding Web site for digital photography with excellent articles, provocative thoughts from leading digital photographers, and a definite Latin-American slant. The Webmaster is Pedro Mayer, an internationally recognized professional photographer.

Zoran Corporation

3112 Scott Boulevard
Santa Clara, CA 95054
www.zoran.com
408-919-4111

Zoran markets integrated circuits, embedded software, and IC intellectual property cores for digital video and audio applications. Zoran's products include JPEG codecs, digital audio processors, and MPEG and DVD decoders.

Z Reiss & Associates Inc.

www.zreiss.com
800-943-2000

Z Reiss, a film retailer, has an interesting new product called The Wallet. It is a CompactFlash card with a full-color pocket-size screen for presenting digital images right out of the camera or downloaded from your computer.

✦　　✦　　✦

What's on the CD-ROM?

In addition to featuring the exclusive sample figures in the color insert, this book's CD-ROM contains trial versions of most of the programs mentioned in this book. They are here so you can try them out. As you read about what they can do for digital imaging, you can use them to follow the book's exercises.

The demo programs included on the CD-ROM are as follows:

Adobe

✦ **Photoshop 5.5:** The most popular professional image-editing program. This latest version includes the ability to extract images with complex edges (such as flying hair) from their backgrounds and a complete application for optimizing and preparing images for the Web.

✦ **PhotoDeluxe Business Edition:** This is the more advanced version of the most widely distributed home/office image-editing application. This program also comes bundled with many digital cameras and scanners.

Macromedia

✦ **Fireworks 3:** One of the two most popular programs for preparing images for Web publication. It is also now the only one of those two that can be purchased separately and used with any other image editor.

JASC (Windows only)

✦ **Paintshop Pro 6:** The leading shareware program for image editing. This program has a full range of advanced features at a very reasonable price.

✦ **Media Center Plus 3:** Image management.

Ulead (Windows only)

✦ **PhotoImpact:** A full-featured image-editing program.

✦ **WebRazor Pro:** Excellent capabilities for preparing images for the Web.

✦ **Photo Express:** A great image-editing program for beginners.

MetaCreations

✦ **Painter 5:** The world's leading natural-media paint program.

✦ **KPT 3:** The best-selling collection of Photoshop-compatible special effects plug-ins.

✦ **Canoma:** A program for creating 3D models from 2D photos.

✦ **Poser:** A program for creating 3D animatable models of people and animals.

✦ **Bryce:** A program for automatically creating 3D landscapes.

Extensis

✦ **Intellihance:** A brilliantly executed program for automatically optimizing the color balance and brightness values in an image. Works as a Photoshop-compatible plug-in.

✦ **Phototools:** Another set of Photoshop-compatible plug-ins, designed mainly to enhance text with highly customizable beveled edges, variably shiny surfaces, and all sorts of textures. You'll also find tools for Web animation, seamless tile texture making, and text styling for fonts that don't have bold, italic, and other special styles.

✦ **Portfolio:** The leading program for managing digital images.

Installing and Using the Software

On a Macintosh, open the specific application's folder and double-click the installer icon for that application.

On a Windows computer, open the application's folder. You'll find two sorts of files: compressed Zip files and .exe files. If the application you want to install is zipped, unzip it (you may have to download WinZip from one of the online shareware libraries). If it's an .exe file, just double-click its name.

✦   ✦   ✦

Glossary

Many of the terms presented in this glossary have been adapted from or have an "equivalency" in conventional photography. Others are carry-overs from terms that computer users will find familiar.

35mm equivalent Most digicam makers state the focal length of their lenses as the equivalent focal length in a 35mm film camera. They do this because most of us know that a 38mm lens is a moderate wide-angle, but have no idea what to expect from a 6mm digital lens.

aberration Adverse or distorted affects on an image or film caused by various factors.

acquire In digital photography, *acquire* is the short form for image acquisition from a camera or scanner to a computer's storage media. Acquisition is generally accomplished through utility software that ships with the camera or scanner.

A–D converter Analog to digital. The image sensor in a digital camera is one type of A–D converter.

additive primary colors Scanners use a full combination of the additive primary colors of red, green, and blue (RGB), which can give the perception of white at 100-percent saturation. *See* RGB.

ambient light Refers to the prevailing general level of available light (as opposed to light from specific lighting such as a strobe or reflector) in a room or outdoor photography situation, usually referring to sunlight.

angle of view The maximum horizontal angle seen by the lens that can be recorded on the film from edge to edge. Small focal lengths have a wide angle of view (wide angle), and large focal lengths give a narrow angle of view (telephoto).

aperture Also known as the *diaphragm*, this is an opening that controls the amount of light allowed to pass through the lens. Usually, this "hole" is variable in size, which is expressed in f-stops (*see* f-stops). The aperture size (or f-stop) controls not only the length of time that the shutter must stay open, but the depth of field.

aperture priority An automatic camera mode where the user selects an aperture at which to shoot and the camera's computer selects a shutter speed when an exposure is taken. Aperture priority is a good setting when you want to control the depth of field but still want the camera to adjust automatically to changing situations. *See* shutter priority.

archivability Refers to a good-quality, long-lasting print, tape, or other media. How long will this last? Will it fade over time? Will it lose data or some sort of perceived value? Answers to all these questions determine the archivability of an object or image.

archival inks Inks used in fine-art reproduction that have been optimized for permanence.

archiving Images are saved, often on CD-ROM, for a specified period. Information necessary to reproduce the print is also archived, including ink, tables, sizes, and media used.

artifact Small spots of color in the picture that don't belong there. These usually occur as a result of too much JPEG compression. They can also occur because of raising the camera's ISO rating, cranking up the color saturation in a image, or overcompensating for loss of shadow detail while using an image-editing program.

artist proof Frequently, an edition will include a number of prints called artist proofs, or APs. These proofs are normally printed at the time of the initial printing of the edition and are outside of the numbered series. APs frequently sell for more than prints from an edition.

ASA American Standards Organization; the equivalent of the ISO (International Standards Organization) speed ratings for film, which have now been accepted as the global standard. Up until then, photographers had to sort out the meaning of ASA, DIN, and other standards organizations' ratings for film.

aspect ratio The ratio of width to height in media, usually referring to photographic prints or film.

aspherical surface These lenses are made to compensate for lens distortions that occur in the making of inexpensive lenses — especially wide-angle barrel distortion. One or more of the lenses' surfaces doesn't correspond to a section of a sphere (thus, aspherical), but the surface curve varies in radius from the inside to the outside of the lens.

autofocus The camera automatically focuses on the center of the image when the shutter button is depressed halfway (first stage). Autofocus usually works by adjusting the lens until edges appear sharp, but this method doesn't work well in dim light. Infrared autofocus can overcome this problem, but is usually found only on more expensive and advanced cameras.

background What is behind the object or main subject of an image and in a photographic situation. In other words, whatever is behind the object of interest in a photographic composition.

backlighting Backlighting refers to a light source illuminating the rear of the subject being photographed. Backlighting can eliminate dark edges or add a dramatic lighting effect to all or part of the subject.

balance In photography, balance refers to the ratio of intensity or EV (exposure value) between highlights and shadows.

bellows The folding, accordion-like part of some cameras. Usually a main part of a large-format camera.

bit The digital equivalent of an atomic subparticle: The smallest possible piece of digital information. One-eighth of a byte. There are only two possible stages of a bit: off or on — also expressed as 0 or 1.

bit depth The number of bits assigned to describing the color information in an image. The higher the bit depth of an image, the larger the file size at a given resolution. Also, higher bit depth equates to more colors. At a bit depth of 8 pixels, colors are limited to 256 and so must be indexed to a palette in which each color is assigned a specific position. At a bit depth of 24 bits-per-pixel, more colors appear than the eye can (theoretically) distinguish from one another, so there is no need for a color index. Higher bit depths simply give us more information to choose from before assigning tonal ranges to the final 24-bit file. This usually pays off in our ability to pull more detail from deep shadows and overbright highlights.

bits per pixel Another way of stating bit depth. Indicates the number of bits allocated to describing the color of each pixel. The more shades of color a pixel can represent, the larger the bit value.

blooming The result of adjacent image sensor cells reading light that was meant to be read by one of its neighbors. The result is an oversaturation of a particular color (usually reds and purples) and a diffusing of image detail.

bon á tirer *or* BAT The proof accepted by the artist that is used as the standard for comparing all subsequent prints (pronounced *bone-ah-tiray*). Some printers require a signed BAT before production printing can begin.

bounce light Refers to a flash aimed onto a reflecting surface. Often this produces a softening and diffused effect.

bracketing A method of making sure you get the best exposure by taking multiple pictures of the same image at different exposure setting intervals.

brightness A scanner and software measurement and control to lighten or darken the image.

buffer A temporary holding space for just-taken images in a digital camera so the camera can still shoot without waiting for the processing of each image after each exposure.

burning in A dark room term for making light areas darker, used to create more or less detail or to add effect. To *burn* or a *burning tool* are also terms used in some digital-imaging software.

candid pictures Usually referring to a picture of people who are not posing or don't know they are being photographed.

carriage The part of the scanner that houses the optical sensor and light source for scanning.

CCD Charge-coupled device. This is the term for the most popular type of image-sensing device for recording digital photographs. CCDs are made up of hundreds of light-sensitive cells, called *sensors*. The number of these sensors determines the resolution of the CCD.

CCD iris An automatic brightness level adjuster using a CCD sensor, built into certain types of cameras.

center-weighted metering When a camera's internal meter sensitivity is biased toward the center of the viewfinder.

coated lens A thin coating is applied to most lens surfaces reducing reflection; this can increase the amount of light transmission.

coating A coating provides protection from UV-induced fading and some protection from smudging and fingerprints. It does not materially improve the permanence of the print because most fading is due to visible light. On some material — as an example, canvas — coating can render the print water-resistant, enabling the print to be framed without glass.

CMOS Complimentary Metal Oxide Semiconductor. This is a term for a sensing device that records digital photographs in a digital camera. CMOS is less expensive and has lower power requirements than a CCD, but is just getting to the point where it's technically a viable choice for high-resolution digital still photography.

CMYK The primary colors for an image viewed by reflected, or subtractive, light: cyan, magenta, yellow, and black. *See* color separation.

color-compensating filter A color-compensating (CC) filter enables a photographer to make adjustments of color tone and density in color photography. They come in six basic colors: yellow (Y), magenta (M), cyan (C), blue (B), green (G), and red (R).

color correction A color managing method term for adjusting color image data with a particular type of device so that the production colors are as close as possible to the original or desired colors.

color management An advanced technology that uses profiles of the input and output devices to maximize color accuracy. Targets that include over 3,000 colors are printed and measured with a colorimeter to create profiles for the various ink/media combinations.

color separation A printing term to describe the process of separating or converting color images into a limited number of primary colors. Scanners use the RGB color separation method and the printing process uses CMYK color for separation. *See also* CMYK *and* RGB.

color temperature To help keep colors consistent, color temperature is measured in Kelvins (K). For example, the temperature of daylight on a sunny day is expressed as 5,500K; that of light from a tungsten lamp is expressed as 3,200K to 3,400K. Color temperature meters are available and widely used in professional photography.

color (temperature) conversion filter Color management at the end of your lens to adjust for color temperature. The B12 filter changes color temperature of light from 3,200K to 5,500K, for example, and is used for shooting under some photographic lamps with daylight color films to compensate for a red cast that would occur without the filter.

compact flash memory The most popular removable memory devices for use as digital film. A small card about ⅛-inch thick. Often called CF cards, they come in Type I (most common) and Type II thicknesses. Type II cards can hold small hard-drives, such as the IBM Microdrive.

compression Refers to the reduction of file sizes in computers and digital cameras. The two types of compression are *lossless* and *lossy*. JPEG compression, the most popular type for use in digital cameras, is lossy.

contrast-control filter These are yellow, orange, and red filters used with black-and-white film to emphasize contrast in a photograph.

copy work Refers generally to the process of copying original art work for purposes of reproduction. *See* transparency, museum quality.

darkroom A cold, wet, dark cave where our prehistoric ancestors developed and printed images using smelly chemicals and silver-halide paper.

deckled edges Fine watercolor papers have natural deckles on two or four sides. Frequently the look of a print is improved by tearing the paper rather then cutting it, creating *torn deckles*. After tearing, a bone knife is used to smooth the edge and create the deckled look.

dedicated flash Usually an external camera-mounted flash that is synchronized with a specific camera's settings and has the ability to measure the amount of flash needed for the chosen subject.

default An originally defined set of values used when no changes in settings have been made.

definition Refers to the clarity of detail in an image.

density Refers to the amount of permeability of light properties of a negative or positive. Density can also refer to the amount of darkness or contrast in a print.

depth of field The amount of "in focus" depth possible in a lens, film, or camera or evident in a digital image. Depth of field is affected by the speed of film or digital camera, aperture setting, shutter setting, subject distance, available light, and lens focal length (for example, a 28mm lens at f-11 has a greater depth of field than a 50mm lens at the same aperture).

depth-of-field preview function Some advanced cameras offer a control (usually a button) to preview a picture's depth of field. This closes the lens to the actual aperture setting, thus enabling a view of what is in focus for the lens at the current setting.

diaphragm A variable opening in a lens that controls the passing of light through the lens. Related closely to the terms *aperture* and *f-stop* (*see also*).

diffuse lighting A lighting situation where very little contrast exists.

digital fine-art print A fine-art print made by any digital process.

digital zoom This is a term for the cropping of an original digital image within a digital camera. This is only a simulation of zooming, and resolution is lost in this process.

dithering A process of simulating continuous tones with groups of dots by software or an output device.

dodging A darkroom term meaning to keep light from the image. Dodging or a dodge tool is used in some digital-imaging software.

double exposure Two images or one image twice combined to make one image on a print.

dpi Dots per inch. A measure of the detail of a print. *Apparent dpi* refers to the fact that the eye perceives a giclée (*see also*) as having greater detail than it does in physical reality.

DVD-RAM This is a recognized term for a rewritable DVD format. DVD-RAM can also read DVD-RAM, DVD-ROM, and CD-ROM-type discs.

DVD-RW A DVD RAM format that is rewritable. In other words, previously recorded information can be erased and new information recorded on the same disk.

dye sublimation A printing process that uses a heated print head to turn the dyes on the colored ribbons into gasses. Dye sublimation prints achieve the appearance of a continuous toned photograph by creating soft-edged spots that melt into one another.

emulsion The chemicals on film that are affected by light to produce an image. Usually one side of the film or negative is referred to as the emulsion side.

enlargement A print larger than the negative or positive from which it was enlarged.

EXIF Exchangeable Image File. Most digital cameras use EXIF to compress JPEG files.

existing light Refers to any and all of the light available in a photography situation before any light is changed or added. Can refer to natural or electrical or candle lighting.

exposure meter Also known as the light meter; senses all light available. Used to determine camera settings and contrast in a photography situation.

external flash synch A connection provided for the synchronization of an off-camera electronic flash. Enables a direct connection with large studio flash system for more complicated lighting use or for higher-powered units than are built in to the camera for photographing on-location events, such as news, sports, and weddings.

eyepoint The farthest point from the viewfinder where the entire image can be seen.

field of view The maximum area in an angular field that can be seen through the camera lens.

fill flash A technique that uses the flash to supplement ambient light. This can be used when photographing backlit subjects or subjects in shadows, or with very high-contrast lighting.

film The light-sensitive silver-halide or dye-coated transparent plastic traditionally used to record and store photographic images. Digital film usually refers to the removable storage media on which digital image data is temporarily stored (SmartMedia, CompactFlash, and so on).

film latitude A film's exposure level can be varied by a photographer; films with a wide latitude have a greater ability to accept over- and under-exposure. Negative films have a wider latitude than slide films.

film speed Refers to the ISO or ASA rating that indicates the light sensitivity of film or a digital-image sensor.

finder The viewing device, also known as the *viewfinder*, on a camera that shows the viewer the area that will be captured digitally or on film.

FireWire Also called IEEE1394 and iLink. A very fast computer peripheral data-transfer method that is especially suitable for transferring digital video. Connections are much smaller than SCSI or parallel connectors as are the connecting cables, so there is greater portability and less desktop clutter. Also, devices can be connected and disconnected while the computer is operating.

fixed focus A camera lens that cannot be made to change focus. This method relies on the use of depth of field to produce a good percentage of sharp images.

flash An intense amount of light for a brief period from an electronic light source or flash bulb. Flash also refers to the electronic light source itself.

flash path A floppy disk–sized shell into which a smart memory card is inserted to transfer digital camera images to a computer. A flash path is relatively slow and needs a battery, but can easily transfer images to almost all computers, iMacs excepted.

flash sync speed The speed of a shutter opening that exposes a frame of film to the full light of the flash; usually a shutter speed of $\frac{1}{60}$th second or slower. Cameras that offer higher flash sync speeds are better suited to using fill flash in outdoor situations.

flat Generally used to denote a lack of contrast, either in lighting or in the brightness values within an image.

focal length This is determined by the distance between the film and the optical center of the lens when the lens is focused on infinity. The focal length of the lens on adjustable cameras is indicated in millimeters on the inside of the end of the lens.

focal length equivalency The focal length of a digital camera's lens expressed as an equivalent of that focal length on a 35mm film frame.

focal plane shutter A shutter that moves a variable-width slot across the film plane. The shutter speed of a focal plane shutter is generally much faster than the time it takes the shutter to travel completely across the film plane. It indicates only the amount of time that the slot takes to travel its width — because that is all the time that the film it travels over is actually exposed.

fogging An effect caused when photosensitive materials are exposed to light before being fully developed, causing a change in apparent exposure and a definite loss of contrast.

foreground Refers to anything between the subject and the camera.

frame An individual negative on a roll of film or slides. Also refers to anything in an image that surrounds or frames an object or subject.

front lighting Lighting that illuminates the front of the subject or scene.

f-stop A number expressing the relative aperture of a lens for determining light allowance. This number is equal to the focal length and divided by the effective aperture of the lens opening. Each f-stop number is 1.4 times larger than the preceding one.

future ink test print From time to time, new inks are released to the marketplace that offer improved longevity, a larger color space, or both. A printer may switch production to new inks if the improvements are material and have been certified by an independent laboratory. Prints created from files that were imaged using older inks will look different when printed with new inks. The future ink test print gives you an opportunity to evaluate the effect of new inks on the print.

ghosting A doubled appearance in an image that results from using a flash in a bright light situation with a low shutter speed.

giclée Another term for fine-art inkjet prints (French for "a spraying of ink"). Originally applied to Iris prints, but now meant to apply to any inkjet using archival inks and substrates. Archival qualities notwithstanding, giclée prints should be protected from exposure to direct sunlight and moisture.

graininess When the pixels of an image are visible. Can refer to a characteristic of film or prints.

grayscale A photographic scale of the range difference of the different grays between black and white. In some software programs grayscale refers to a black-and-white image.

guide number This is a number that indicates the power of a flash in relation to film ISO speed. This is useful for choosing a flash and knowing its maximum range power for flash photography.

high contrast When you can see a noticeable (beyond normal) difference in image lines, colors, or in black versus white in an image or film.

highlight A bright or a light area of a subject or scene. Desired details can be washed out or overexposed in highlight areas.

high-resolution scan Professional scan at an output resolution of 150 dpi or 300 dpi using color tables optimized for archival inks on fine-art media. The 300 dpi file size for a 16" × 20" print is about 109 megabytes.

home position A scanner term for the at-rest or ready position of the scanning device.

hot shoe A mounting device, on top of a camera, that enables the addition of a flash unit or speedlight.

house papers Fine-art papers that are stocked by a printer.

inkjet A type of printing in which dots of ink are sprayed onto paper to create the image. Some inkjet printers can lay down 1,440 dots of ink per inch, resulting in photo-quality prints (provided that the image has adequate resolution in pixels to begin with). This is the most affordable (and therefore most popular) type of printer capable of producing truly photographic-quality color prints from digital images.

interpolation The process of adding or subtracting pixels to an image (usually in an imaging program) to increase or reduce its size while retaining a desired resolution. Also known as *resampling* or *upsampling* and *downsampling*.

iris lens A lens having a circular shutter opening that opens and closes to size depending on the amount of light or the f-stop setting of the camera and or photographer.

Iris paper Paper distributed by Iris for use on its inkjet printers. These include glossy, semimatte, and matte papers, which are used for commercial proofing. Also available are some fine-art papers such as Arches for Iris, a paper manufactured by Arches specifically for use on Iris printers.

Iris print Prints created on the Iris inkjet printer.

ISO equivalency Referring to a digital camera's light sensitivity relative to a film camera's film speed. Some of the new digital cameras have adjustable ISO equivalencies, giving them more latitude in different lighting situations.

jaggies The visual effect that results when pixels are enlarged so that you can see that they are solid squares of color. This is often called *stairstepping* because diagonal edges look jagged like the profile of a staircase. Jaggies can be minimized through interpolation and antialiasing.

JPEG Acronym for the Joint Photographic Experts Group. Usually stated to mean an image file that is highly compressed, causing varying degrees of data loss and image artifacts.

layouts Documents describing the precise layout of a print or prints on a sheet of paper. The layout indicates both the exact size of the prints and the amount of white space around each print. For example, a layout might describe the exact position of a 30" × 40" print on a full 35" × 46.75" sheet or the position of four different 16" × 20" prints on the same sheet, which allows for about 0.75" of white space.

LCD monitor Liquid Crystal Display. A type of flat-screen monitor used on digital cameras and laptop computers. As their prices drop, they are also winning some favor as desktop monitors.

lens One or more pieces of optical glass or plastic designed to collect and focus rays of light and form an image.

lens shade A hood at the front of a lens that keeps unwanted light from hitting the lens and possibly causing image flare.

line sequence A one-pass scanner operation to separate primary colors in color scanning.

lossy compression Some data is compromised in order to reach smaller file sizes. Most digital cameras use lossy compression and give the user a choice as to how lossy the compression will be. The smaller the file size, the lower the fidelity of the image.

macro The capability of a lens to focus at a very close distance.

manual focus The lens is focused by the person operating the camera, rather than by any automatic mechanism. This lets the photographer focus exactly on a chosen spot, rather than an area chosen by the camera. Also, manual focusing will stay focused at a specified distance until it is intentionally changed by the photographer.

matrix metering An advanced light-metering system using a multiple-segment sensor. Matrix metering is based on an algorithm that uses the configuration of different lighting situations. It works well in complex lighting situations such as outdoor sunlight and backlit subjects.

media The materials to be printed, such as watercolor papers, canvas, copper, wood veneer, cotton, or plastic.

megapixel One million pixels. Referring to the single-image resolutions of digital cameras. 1,500,000 pixels is equal to 1.5 megapixels.

minimum object distance (MOD) The closest focusing distance of a lens. This is measured from the front of the lens to the in-focus object.

monochrome Refers to black-and-white images.

multiple flash Refers to the use of more than one flash head at a time.

negative film A negative film shows a subject in reversed tones.

neutral density filter A filter designed to reduce the amount of light through a lens without cutting off any particular frequency range of the light.

NiMH Nickel Metal Hydride; a rechargeable battery geared toward longevity and strength, said to be environmentally safer. Also, NiMH batteries can be recharged at any time without shortening their lifespans.

noise Grain-like artifacts that tend to appear mostly when compensating for under-exposure in digital images or choosing too high an ISO rating. Similar to the graininess that appears in higher-speed conventional films that are used for photography in low-light situations.

OCR A term used in scanning, it stands for Optical Character Recognition. OCR is the technology that helps computers to recognize or interpret text from a scanned or photographic image.

optical viewfinder A rangefinder-like glass viewfinder that uses lenses to approximate the actual field of view of the lens. Optical viewfinders are essential on cameras with zoom lenses if one is to be able to preview the effect of zooming the lens.

optical zoom An adjustable camera lens that has continuously variable focal lengths for a continuously variable field of view. Also, this is an actual change of field of view, rather than a digital cropping and resizing of the image, so pictures at long focal lengths are of the same resolution and quality as those at short (wide-angle) focal lengths.

orthochromatic filter A green or yellow-green filter is used with black-and-white films. An orthochromatic filter compensates for the difference between film and the efficiency of the human eye for a more natural-appearing image.

overexposure A condition of a print where it is judged to be too light or having been exposed too long in processing. Also referring to a condition of a film where it was exposed to too much light and produces a too-light print with little detail.

panning Following a subject in the camera viewfinder and keeping it in the same position as it moves across the field of view. Panning can add a movement dimension to images.

panorama A photograph with an exceptionally wide aspect ratio.

parallax The parallax in photography refers to the difference in the image between a viewfinder and the image being recorded. This condition is solved with through-the-lens viewing found in single-lens reflex (SLR) cameras or a digital LCD display.

parallel port A computer port that sends and receives data 8 bits at a time over eight separate wires, and is one of the slowest data-transfer systems.

PC card reader An adapter for CompactFlash or SmartMedia memory cards that enables them to be read at very high speed through the PCMCIA (Personal Computer Card Memory Association) card slot found on most laptop computers.

Photo CD A Kodak process for scanning transparencies and storing them on CD-ROM in a format known as *Photo CD*. Acceptable results can be achieved from Photo CDs, but the professional version is required to create large enough files. The maximum file size is about 70MB, which limits high-quality reproduction to about 700 square inches.

pixel A measurement of resolution in a digital camera. A contraction of the words "picture element." The basic element of resolution. Digicam resolution is expressed in the total number of pixels recorded by the image sensor (not pixels per inch).

pixelization *See* jaggies.

polarizing filter A polarizing filter eliminates some reflected light from many subject surfaces and floating dust. A polarizing filter can be helpful in turning a washed-out sky to darker blue.

ppi Pixels per inch. One way to measure the resolution of a digital image. It is usually applied to the resolution of monitors and digicams.

processing Refers to the system of developing and printing film. Processing also refers to a computer program altering the appearance of image data.

preflash The first of two flashes that occur when the shutter button is depressed, one to measure white balance and to autofocus the camera and the second to expose for an image. Different than red-eye reduction, which uses weak multiple flashes to cause the subject's irises to stop down.

print A (generally positive) photographic image recorded on paper and meant to be viewed by reflective light.

print file The file used to produce a final proof that is archived for producing current and future printings of an edition.

print on demand The ability of the giclée process to reproduce prints over a long period of time with consistency. This facilitates orders of a small number of prints when needed — print on demand. While the process does offer a high degree of consistency over time, editions that require exact matching should be printed at one time. *See also* giclée.

proof A smaller print — often 8 × 10 inches — used to evaluate a file prior to final printing.

rangefinder A device on cameras to measure the distance between an object and the camera, automatically focusing the camera's lens at the same time.

reciprocity failure Reciprocity failure can occur when a film is exposed under conditions that are not within its designated range.

recycling time A term used for the time necessary for an electronic flash to recharge and be ready for another exposure. Recycling time has multiple variables; the time can depend on the type and condition of a battery or power pack and the power or guide number of the speedlight or flash head.

red-eye The reflection of a flash off the back of the subject's eye. Blood vessels in the eye cause the reflection to be bright red. The more dilated the pupil of the subject's eyes, the more pronounced the effect. Most digital cameras have an option to turn red-eye preflash on or off. If it's left on, it may fire an external slave unit at the wrong time. Because the external unit is usually a much brighter light that is not aimed directly into the iris, red-eye reduction is usually not needed anyway.

reflex mirror In most SLRs this is the mirror that reflects an image passing through the lens upward to the prism for viewing. This mirror face has a special coating and should never be touched. In some cameras, the reflex mirror can be locked in the up position.

reflex viewing A term for through-the-lens viewing by bouncing the image off a mirror and onto a prism or ground glass. Others are TTL (through the lens), SLR (single lens reflex), and TLR (twin lens reflex). The mirror swings out of the way at the instant the shutter button is depressed.

resize It is generally possible to resize files so prints can be made either smaller or larger. Significant upsizing is usually not successful, but an adjustment of up to 20 percent is acceptable. Determine in advance what sizes will be required on a print job.

resolution A measure of the amount of detail that can be recorded in an image. The higher the number of image sensors, the greater the resolution. Thus a two-megapixel camera has twice the resolution of a one-megapixel camera.

RGB Red, green, and blue; the primary colors for transmitted light. Slides, monitors, and other backlit media use transmitted light. *See* additive primary colors *and* color separation.

saturation A property of color, or the intensity of hue in a color. Colors considered saturated are called vivid, strong, or deep. Desaturated colors might be considered dull, weak, or washed out.

scanning The process of converting a transparency, negative, or print to a digital file. *See* high-resolution scan.

scanning area The size of the area of a scanner on which an image can be recorded.

SCSI Small Computer System Interface, a method of connecting computers and computer devices using cables.

SCSI chain A linear method of enabling several devices to be connected simultaneously to a single computer. Also known as a *daisy chain*.

SCSI ID The numbers that all devices in a SCSI chain use to identify each other.

seamless A wide roll of paper of various colors used as a background in a photograph. It is called a *seamless* because it curves as it meets the floor, making it difficult to discern where the ground ends and the background or wall begins.

self-timer Many cameras provide a delayed shutter of several seconds before an image is recorded, enabling the photography, for example, to get into the picture.

serial port A full-duplex channel that sends and receives data at the same time.

shadow A dark area, the opposite of a highlight in a subject or scene. Desired details can be lost in shadow areas.

sheets The sheet of paper or other material that will be printed. The largest Iris printers accommodate sheets up to 35" × 47". House papers for this are commonly 35" × 46.75".

shutter priority An automatic camera mode where the user selects a shutter speed at which to shoot and the camera's computer selects an aperture setting when an exposure is taken. Shutter-priority mode can be used to create or avoid blur in moving objects. *See* aperture priority.

shutter release button (*or* shutter release) That button you press to take a photograph. On many SLRs and more professional cameras the shutter can also be released by a shutter-release cable.

skylight filter A skylight filter removes some of the blue light. This can be helpful in taking photos in the shade on bright sunlight days — or when you simply want to "warm" the color balance of the image.

slave A light-sensitive module attached to a flash or flash unit to induce a flash when sensing another flash of light.

slide A 35mm transparency in a cardboard or plastic mount. The image is usually positive.

slow synch A camera flash mode used to bring out more detail in backgrounds. In slow-synch mode the shutter is opened for a longer period of time than required for firing the flash.

SmartMedia Smart media card; the second most popular type of removable memory for capturing and transfer images. It is smaller and cheaper than CompactFlash, but is more easily damaged. Also known as *SSFDC* (Solid State Floppy Disk Card).

soft focus Soft focus refers to an image that is slightly out of focus. A soft-focus effect can be achieved by a special lens or lens filter that spreads (blooms) the highlights into the shadow areas of the picture.

spot metering A metering setting used to find the best aperture setting from one designated spot or area in the viewing area.

stopping down This refers to changing the aperture setting to a smaller (higher number) aperture setting. An example of stopping down would be changing the aperture from f-2.2 to f-4.

street price The price you may expect to pay in a retail establishment for a camera and photo equipment in contrast to the suggested retail price given by a manufacturer.

substrate The material that underlies the image, such as canvas, watercolor paper, bond, or transparent plastic.

telephoto lens A lens that brings distant objects into closer view. This lens is usually a long lens type and is a separate and removable camera lens. A telephoto lens has a narrower field of view than a normal lens and a longer focal length. *See* angle of view.

terminator An excellent movie starring Arnold Schwartzenegger. Or an ending device that stops electronic signals, terminating them in order to keep signals from bouncing continuously between devices.

TFT Thin film transistor; a brighter and wider-angle-of-viewability digital monitor display than the standard LCD monitor. Also more costly.

thin negative A negative that wasn't exposed long enough. The density of the film doesn't have enough detail to produce a quality print.

through-the-lens focusing Used on most SLR cameras today. When you look through the view finder the camera enables you to see through the lens. You are able see what is in focus and what is not and can quickly adjust the lens's focusing ring to bring the image into sharp focus.

TIFF Tagged image file format; the most portable file format for lossless storage of true-color digital images. If a digicam offers the ability to save files as TIF or TIFF images, they can be saved at their highest quality. However, at this setting you will be able to store significantly fewer images in your camera's memory before you have to exchange memory cards.

time exposure A camera exposure lasting longer than one second.

tone The overall color tint of an image. For instance, slightly yellow printing papers tend to give an image a warm tone.

transparency, museum quality High-quality reproduction requires copy transparencies made by photographers experienced in art reproduction. Lighting is very important in terms of evenness, color, and lack of any specular highlights. Transparencies should either be 4 × 5 or 8 × 10 inches. The prepress process tries to create a print that looks like the transparency, not the original, so the transparency should reflect the original as accurately as possible.

tripod A camera or lens stabling device having three legs and a platform for mounting the camera so that it can be held rigidly during the exposure.

true color A term used to indicate that a digital device can store at least 16.8 million shades of color at a bit depth of 24 bits-per-pixel. So called because this represents as many (or more) shades of color as the human eye can discern.

tungsten film A color film balanced for use in 3,200K lighting situations.

tungsten light Tungsten lighting is the use of photo flood lamps (constant lamps); they have a color temperature of 3,200K to 3,400K. Tungsten film is recommended for use with tungsten light, or the images of regular daylight type film will take on a reddish tinge.

two-stage shutter release The most commonly employed type of shutter release on modern still and digital cameras. The two stages are focus and metering, and shutter release. The first stage is engaged when you push the shutter partway down; the second when the release is fully depressed.

ultraviolet photography Recording images of invisible ultraviolet rays with wavelengths shorter than 400nm. At the time of this writing, ultraviolet photography hasn't been developed by any digital imaging company or digital cameras.

underexposure Refers to not enough light on a film and creating a too-dark print image.

unipod A camera or lens stand with just one leg. Some unipods are built to double as walking sticks.

USB (universal serial bus) A relatively new computer peripheral connection designed to transfer data at faster rates than standard serial or parallel ports. The current transfer rate is 12 megabytes per second, but a new higher-speed standard is on the horizon. USB devices can be used with any computer platform without modification (as long as you have the supporting software appropriate to the target platform). Another advantage of USB is that you don't have to turn off a computer to change connections such as with SCSI (*see also*).

UV (ultraviolet) filter UV filters eliminate invisible ultraviolet light and enhance the contrast of a photograph. A UV filter can also be left on as a lens protector.

varifocal lens An adjustable focal length lens that is unlike a zoom lens because it requires refocusing when changing the focal length setting.

viewfinder The viewing device, also known as the *finder*, on a camera that shows the viewer the area that will be captured digitally or on film.

viewing area The area that is seen through the lens. Also called the *field of view* (*see also*).

vignetting The dark shadow-like edge sometimes found around an image. This shadowing is usually caused by a camera shade or can be inherent in some tele-photo lenses. This effect will be seen either with through-the-lens viewing or on the produced image. Normally, unless you desire the effect, vignetting is unwanted and should be corrected before an image is produced.

white balance The balance point at which color temperature is measured for best color representation. Used to correct for the color of a lighting source, such as daylight or tungsten. So called because white objects will appear to be white, rather than the color of the prevailing light.

wide-angle lens A lens that has a wider field of view and includes more subject area than a normal lens. *See* angle of view.

wide-flash adapter An external flash adapter to widen the span of a flash's illumination so that it will cover the field of view of a wide-angle lens.

zooming during exposure This creates interesting lines from the center of the frame. It is an effect that can give the feeling of movement.

zoom lens A lens in which you can adjust the focal length over a variety of ranges.

zoom ratio The ratio of the wide end to the telephoto end of a zoom lens. A lens with a 3× zoom ratio can magnify an image up to three times.

Index

Continued

Notes

Notes

Notes

Notes

Notes

Notes

Notes

Notes

Notes

Notes

IDG Books Worldwide, Inc.
End-User License Agreement

READ THIS. You should carefully read these terms and conditions before opening the software packet(s) included with this book ("Book"). This is a license agreement ("Agreement") between you and IDG Books Worldwide, Inc. ("IDGB"). By opening the accompanying software packet(s), you acknowledge that you have read and accept the following terms and conditions. If you do not agree and do not want to be bound by such terms and conditions, promptly return the Book and the unopened software packet(s) to the place you obtained them for a full refund.

1. **License Grant.** IDGB grants to you (either an individual or entity) a nonexclusive license to use one copy of the enclosed software program(s) (collectively, the "Software") solely for your own personal or business purposes on a single computer (whether a standard computer or a workstation component of a multiuser network). The Software is in use on a computer when it is loaded into temporary memory (RAM) or installed into permanent memory (hard disk, CD-ROM, or other storage device). IDGB reserves all rights not expressly granted herein.

2. **Ownership.** IDGB is the owner of all right, title, and interest, including copyright, in and to the compilation of the Software recorded on the disk(s) or CD-ROM ("Software Media"). Copyright to the individual programs recorded on the Software Media is owned by the author or other authorized copyright owner of each program. Ownership of the Software and all proprietary rights relating thereto remain with IDGB and its licensors.

3. **Restrictions On Use and Transfer.**

    (a) You may only (i) make one copy of the Software for backup or archival purposes, or (ii) transfer the Software to a single hard disk, provided that you keep the original for backup or archival purposes. You may not (i) rent or lease the Software, (ii) copy or reproduce the Software through a LAN or other network system or through any computer subscriber system or bulletin-board system, or (iii) modify, adapt, or create derivative works based on the Software.

    (b) You may not reverse engineer, decompile, or disassemble the Software. You may transfer the Software and user documentation on a permanent basis, provided that the transferee agrees to accept the terms and conditions of this Agreement and you retain no copies. If the Software is an update or has been updated, any transfer must include the most recent update and all prior versions.

4. Restrictions on Use of Individual Programs. You must follow the individual requirements and restrictions detailed for each individual program in Appendix C of this Book. These limitations are also contained in the individual license agreements recorded on the Software Media. These limitations may include a requirement that after using the program for a specified period of time, the user must pay a registration fee or discontinue use. By opening the Software packet(s), you will be agreeing to abide by the licenses and restrictions for these individual programs that are detailed in Appendix C and on the Software Media. None of the material on this Software Media or listed in this Book may ever be redistributed, in original or modified form, for commercial purposes.

5. Limited Warranty.

(a) IDGB warrants that the Software and Software Media are free from defects in materials and workmanship under normal use for a period of sixty (60) days from the date of purchase of this Book. If IDGB receives notification within the warranty period of defects in materials or workmanship, IDGB will replace the defective Software Media.

(b) **IDGB AND THE AUTHOR OF THE BOOK DISCLAIM ALL OTHER WARRANTIES, EXPRESS OR IMPLIED, INCLUDING WITHOUT LIMITATION IMPLIED WARRANTIES OF MERCHANTABILITY AND FITNESS FOR A PARTICULAR PURPOSE, WITH RESPECT TO THE SOFTWARE, THE PROGRAMS, THE SOURCE CODE CONTAINED THEREIN, AND/OR THE TECHNIQUES DESCRIBED IN THIS BOOK. IDGB DOES NOT WARRANT THAT THE FUNCTIONS CONTAINED IN THE SOFTWARE WILL MEET YOUR REQUIREMENTS OR THAT THE OPERATION OF THE SOFTWARE WILL BE ERROR FREE.**

(c) This limited warranty gives you specific legal rights, and you may have other rights that vary from jurisdiction to jurisdiction.

6. Remedies.

(a) IDGB's entire liability and your exclusive remedy for defects in materials and workmanship shall be limited to replacement of the Software Media, which may be returned to IDGB with a copy of your receipt at the following address: Software Media Fulfillment Department, Attn.: *Digital Photography Bible*, IDG Books Worldwide, Inc., 10475 Crosspoint Blvd., Indianapolis, IN 46256, or call 1-800-762-2974. Please allow three to four weeks for delivery. This Limited Warranty is void if failure of the Software Media has resulted from accident, abuse, or misapplication. Any replacement Software Media will be warranted for the remainder of the original warranty period or thirty (30) days, whichever is longer.

(b) In no event shall IDGB or the author be liable for any damages whatsoever (including without limitation damages for loss of business profits, business interruption, loss of business information, or any other pecuniary loss) arising from the use of or inability to use the Book or the Software, even if IDGB has been advised of the possibility of such damages.

(c) Because some jurisdictions do not allow the exclusion or limitation of liability for consequential or incidental damages, the above limitation or exclusion may not apply to you.

7. **U.S. Government Restricted Rights.** Use, duplication, or disclosure of the Software by the U.S. Government is subject to restrictions stated in paragraph (c)(1)(ii) of the Rights in Technical Data and Computer Software clause of DFARS 252.227-7013, and in subparagraphs (a) through (d) of the Commercial Computer   Restricted Rights clause at FAR 52.227-19, and in similar clauses in the NASA FAR supplement, when applicable.

8. **General.** This Agreement constitutes the entire understanding of the parties and revokes and supersedes all prior agreements, oral or written, between them and may not be modified or amended except in a writing signed by both parties hereto that specifically refers to this Agreement. This Agreement shall take precedence over any other documents that may be in conflict herewith. If any one or more provisions contained in this Agreement are held by any court or tribunal to be invalid, illegal, or otherwise unenforceable, each and every other provision shall remain in full force and effect.

Put a serious
dent
in your
workload with
Dreamweaver
and Fireworks.®

Introducing Dreamweaver 3 and Fireworks 3

The newest versions of Dreamweaver and Fireworks
work together to give you the power to create
Web sites faster. Design buttons, animations
and page comps in minutes with Fireworks 3.
Mold your graphics and code into completed
Web sites in record time with Dreamweaver 3.
Streamline development with support for the
content creation and Web application software
you use. Together, Dreamweaver and
Fireworks are one awesome team
for rapid Web development.

www.macromedia.com

macromedia®

my2cents.idgbooks.com

Register This Book — And Win!

Visit **http://my2cents.idgbooks.com** to register this book and we'll automatically enter you in our fantastic monthly prize giveaway. It's also your opportunity to give us feedback: let us know what you thought of this book and how you would like to see other topics covered.

Discover IDG Books Online!

The IDG Books Online Web site is your online resource for tackling technology — at home and at the office. Frequently updated, the IDG Books Online Web site features exclusive software, insider information, online books, and live events!

10 Productive & Career-Enhancing Things You Can Do at www.idgbooks.com

- Nab source code for your own programming projects.

- Download software.

- Read Web exclusives: special articles and book excerpts by IDG Books Worldwide authors.

- Take advantage of resources to help you advance your career as a Novell or Microsoft professional.

- Buy IDG Books Worldwide titles or find a convenient bookstore that carries them.

- Register your book and win a prize.

- Chat live online with authors.

- Sign up for regular e-mail updates about our latest books.

- Suggest a book you'd like to read or write.

- Give us your 2¢ about our books and about our Web site.

You say you're not on the Web yet? It's easy to get started with IDG Books' *Discover the Internet*, available at local retailers everywhere.

CD Installation Instructions

To install and use the software on a Macintosh, open the specific application's folder and double-click the installer icon for thatplication.

To install and use the software on a Windows computer, open the application's folder. You'll find two sorts of files: compressed Zip files and .exe files. If the application you want to install is zipped, unzip it (you may have to download WinZip from one of the online shareware libraries). If it's an .exe file, just double-click its name.